A trilogy of books based on articles from the *Journal of Economic Issues*, edited by Marc R. Tool and Warren J. Samuels and published by Transaction Publishers.

The Methodology of Economic Thought

The Economy as a System of Power

State, Society, and Corporate Power

THE METHODOLOGY OF ECONOMIC THOUGHT

Edited by
Marc R. Tool
and
Warren J. Samuels

Second Edition, Completely Revised

Transaction Publishers
New Brunswick (U.S.A.) and Oxford (U.K.)

Library of Congress Catalog Number: 88-20033
ISBN: 0-88738-757-8
Printed in the United States of America

Library of Congress Cataloging in Publication Data

The Methodology of economic thought / edited by Warren J. Samuels and Marc R. Tool.
p. cm. — (Institutional economics ; v. 1)
"Articles selected from the Journal of economic issues"—
Includes bibliographical references.
ISBN 0-88738-757-8
1. Institutional economics. I. Samuels, Warren J. 1933- . II. Tool, Marc R. III. Series.
HB99.5.M48 1988 88-20033
330—dc19 CIP

Contents

Preface

The continuing need to grapple with tough economic questions and obstinate economic problems has led many a thoughtful professor, active politician, anxious worker, and perplexed judge, to extensive head shaking and agonized soul searching. Economic problems have a powerful effect on individuals and on communities, large and small. Substantial jobs and income losses, increases in destitution, savaging of environments, erosion of access to health care, inflationary price increases, and the like all compete for our collective attention. Exploring economic questions often preempts conversations and seeking resolutions for such problems usually dominates legislative agendas.

The articles selected from the *Journal of Economic Issues* are being published as a trilogy of volumes intended to help inform and guide inquiry into these questions and problems, among others. They show how questions can be answered and problems reduced or resolved. Other volumes in the trilogy are *The Economy as a System of Power* and *State, Society, and Corporate Power*. The continuing formulation and critical assessment of ideas about the functioning of economies can help reduce the head shaking, instruct the soul searching, and turn frustrated and unproductive energies to serious scholarship and productive policy involvement. Such, at least, is one of the underlying purposes of these volumes.

With reflection, all would acknowledge that every major human community—advanced, intermediate, or underdeveloped—shares common and continuing tasks: the economic task of generating, distributing, and sustaining the flow of real income; and the political task of rewriting, as necessary, the agendas of economic institutions or organizations in quest of improved performance of major and continuing economic activities.

Many formal theories of political economy have been developed over the last two centuries or more to explain how real income is produced and distributed and how, through policy innovations, those tasks can be more effectually implemented. Indeed, the significance of economic theorizing has always been judged mainly on the adequacy of its contribution to understanding and resolving economic problems. Over this period, systematic inquiry has sought to displace problem assessments rooted in folk wisdom, religious dictums, coercive dictations, ideological dogmas, or utopian fancies, that, when put to the test by attempted application or introduction, have proved benignly useless or, regrettably, unintendedly destructive.

Economic inquiry matters! Inquiry that generates theory that really does explain what goes on is the most practical of contributions. The articles selected for the volumes in this series do indeed substantially expand and enhance one's collective grasp of the determinants of, and the impediments to, the flow of real income. And, because removing the impediments to that flow requires changing the institutional structures that prevail, problem solving requires institutional adjustment, a revamping of the structural fabric, in the areas where it has been found to be obstructive of the economic process. Economic inquiry, then, is addressed to the following questions: What is going on here? What ought to go on here? What can be done about it?

In the current period, there are three main foci of theoretical interest and writing in political economy, each of which claims explanatory relevance, and therefore significance, to the economic issues and concerns of our day. One, of course, is standard, orthodox, neoclassical economics, which is taught as the principles of economics throughout much of the English-speaking world and beyond. A second is Marxist theory, which has been the "orthodox" approach in China, the Soviet Union, and a few underdeveloped countries. The third is institutionalist theory, a mainly American contribution, which, though less often formally taught, remains a frequently used, pragmatic approach to real problems in most countries, but perhaps most obviously in Western Europe and North America.

The papers in these volumes are drawn from this institutionalist perspective on political economy. It is different from, and is sometimes critical of, both neoclassical orthodoxy and Marxist formulations. Since most readers will already have been exposed to one or both of these perspectives, often at some length, these volumes offer a unique opportunity for the concerned reader to initiate a running dialogue with, and join in a comparative assessment of, the third perspective.

The *Journal of Economic Issues*, well into its third publishing decade, has become one of the major international publishing outlets for scholars with an institutionalist bent or perspective. Although the selections composing these volumes were chosen for their incisive contributions to a particular subject area, the *Journal* itself publishes materials in all the major subfields of economics. One of the purposes of these volume, then, is to bring within individual volumes a number of articles addressed to a single topical issue or focus. In this form, an inquiring scholar can see not only something of the development of increasingly relevant and sophisticated institutionalist inquiry but observe the breadth of perspective that is represented among institutional economists, even when addressing a common subject area. The articles, then, are not cut of a single cloth. Divergent theories and interpretations are not uncommon. Even so, common threads permeate these selected contributions: As Jerry Petr has observed,[1] the institutionalist perspective may be characterized by the following distinguishing attributes: "values-driven, process-oriented, instrumental, evolutionary, activist, fact-based, technologically focused, holistic, non-dogmatic, and democratic."

In brief elaboration, institutionalists do not evade the social value question. Their inquiry is both normative and positive; it is concerned with economic well-being at all levels and times, hence "values-driven." It is, as well, "process-oriented"; it is an approach that addresses the social order as a process of becoming, not as a static given or an equilibrium-seeking order. "Instrumentalism" connotes the application in economic analysis of the growth of reliable knowledge and its application as technology in the broad sense—tool and idea combinations—to an understanding of causal determinants of social problems. Institutional analysis is processual analysis; it sees reality as a constantly changing phenomenon and has developed inquiry tools which themselves incorporate the processual trait.

Its "fact based" attribute refers to the endemic quest for evidential grounding of analysis and recommendations. Institutionalists see the growth of knowledge and technological innovation as a major source of problem initiation and concurrently as a vehicle with which problem solving can be facilitated. The "holistic" approach permits institutionalists to define the scope of their inquiries with reference to the problems addressed; they do not cut, shape, or redefine the problem so that a preconceived model can be used or a disciplinary boundary can be observed. The institutionalist perspective is "non-dogmatic" because it holds no given institutional model as inherently superior; neither is its inquiry mode frozen in time or place. Institutionalists seek "democratic" solutions involving participatory involvement of those affected by policy precisely to encourage the indentification, implementation, and acceptance, of the most pertinent and effectual change.

We hope you find all three volumes to be intellectually provocative, analytically persuasive, policy relevant, and, quite simply, a good, if thoughtful, read.

Marc R. Tool
Warren J. Samuels

Note

1. Jerry Petr, "Fundamentals of an Institutionalist Perspective," *Journal of Economic Issues* 18 (March 1984): 1-17.

Introduction

This volume of selected papers from the *Journal of Economic Issues*, on methodology in economic thought, is a second and heavily revised edition, with the same title, of an earlier publication by Transaction Books.[1]

In the recent past, in the United States and elsewhere, it has often seemed that there was something of a "Gresham's Law" operating in economic analysis: that is, that "poor" or inferior theory was driving "good" or problem-solving theory out of intellectual and academic circulation. Together with other volumes in this series, this anthology it is intended to help repeal that "Law," to contribute to the development and application of a comprehensive institutionalist perspective in political economy, and to find analytically sound ways to diminish the current deference to, and dominion of, standard neoclassical theory.

On the current scene, for example, one can observe: (a) the inferior performance of the economy under guidance of supply-side economists in their failed efforts to generate major increases in investment spending through significantly lower taxes on the rich; (b) the observable irrelevance of the rational expectation theorists' recommendation of a return, in effect, to laissez-faire in lieu of macromanagement of the economy; (c) the generation, by contestable market theorists, of a new apologia for monopoly control in which non-price competition is condoned; and (d) the "new institutional economists'" mistaken employment of neoclassical constructs in their analysis of internal behavior in large corporations. "Systems of orthodoxy are largely non reflective with regard to their own limits," as Warren J. Samuels observed.[2] The need for a fundamental recasting of economic theory appears to be increasingly urgent.

These current formulations of neoclassically based theories, as with all economic theories, are grounded in methodological assumptions and postulates. The dominion of orthodoxy then must rest finally on the presumed adequacy of these assumptions and postulates. No shift to a more adequate theoretical base is likely to succeed until the methodological foundations of orthodox neoclassical economic analysis generally are again put out on the inquiry table for serious examination, critique, revision, or even abandonment. It is to a renewed opening and consideration of the most basic modes and constructs of inquiry, then, that this volume is devoted. Herein, heterodox institutionalists address and assess methodological premises of orthodoxy and, in so doing, lay out an alternate methodological approach and perspective of their own.[3]

But as Samuels cautions in the Introduction to the first edition of this anthology:

> the study of . . . methodology and its status as knowledge (that is, the nature of the combination) is complex and capable of diverse factors and forces that govern general and specific attachments of psychic importance. Because something is "known" to be objectively correct does not mean that it will win out over ideological beliefs because it is comforting in the face of anxiety of one form or another. But the study of methodology can be a mode of self-reflection and can contribute to the elevation of the discipline to more sophisticated levels, although on those levels it may well be that ideology is only more subtly present.[4]

The efforts in this volume to raise the level of "self-reflection" and of "sophistication" of inquiry take the form of addressing such fundamental considerations as the philosophical underpinnings, methodological assumptions and procedures, and policy relevance of inquiry. The task here is to return to basic constructs on which particular theories rest in a spirited setting of vigorous claim and counterclaim to relevance and applicability. The primary function of the volume, then, is to reopen and sustain self-reflective and sophisticated inquiry. The method or mode of inquiry chosen shapes all subsequent areas to which it is applied. The adequacy and pertinence, for example, of a theory of wages, a theory of business firm behavior, or a theory of governmental involvement, depend on, or derive from, anterior philosophical and methodological premises.

Accordingly, this volume, "The Methodology of Economic Thought," presents a demonstration in some detail of how, in contrast to neoclassical orthodoxy, the mode of inquiry of institutionalists is conceived, how it guides their study of economic phenomena, and culminates in tentative, yet evidentially warranted, statements. The first section compares institutionalist views with those of neoclassical orthodoxy in a number of areas including cultural influences on inquiry, ideological biases, nature of causuality, meaning of rational action, and referents for social value. The second section addresses methodologies directly through considerations of inductive and deductive inference, the nature of truth, pragmatic dimensions of inquiry and the like. The third section continues these explorations through reference to inquiry concerns in the history of economic thought where matters of analytical bias in historical interpretation and linguistic influences are examined. A fourth section, in a wide-ranging series of articles, explores the relevance of methodological underpinnings of economic theory as they relate to the making of policy. Several papers address the questionable relevance of orthodoxy theory to policy making including its proclivity to employ utility-based criteria of judgments in choosing alternative institutional structures. Other papers make applications of institutionalist theory in the areas of welfare relief, macromanagement, foreign trade policy, and regulation of utilities. The volume concludes with three papers addressed to a more "meaningful political economy," where imaginative reflections on the relationship between the public and private sector are explored and new analytical techniques for problem solving are introduced. More extensive introductions to the individual papers will be found preceding each of the sections.

Given the variety of approaches to inquiry in this volume, readers must assume a special responsibility in this, or any, symposium: The task of synthesizing and integrating ideas from these papers must remain mainly that of the reader. Although this collection offers a refreshing breadth of views, a diversity of foci, significant insights, and excitement of intellectual stimulation, it does not offer a distilled, formal synthetic summary. And, of course, no claim to comprehensive or complete consideration of topics introduced can be made. Thus, at the end of the work, inquiry must remain open even as the volume sought to open inquiry at the outset. Sophistication of perception, we assume, is reflected in enhanced capacities for creation, analysis, and assessment of increasingly complex and significant theoretical contributions. If this volume contributes importantly to that outcome, all involved will be most pleased.

We intend this volume to contribute to the replacement of "poor" inferior theory with "good" problem-solving theory. Given the magnitude and significance of the economic problems awaiting resolution, any such contribution should be most welcome. Further scholarly contributions to the dialogues set in motion by these articles may be submitted to the *Journal of Economic Issues* for consideration.

Marc R. Tool
Warren J. Samuels

Notes

1. Warren J. Samuels, *The Methodology of Economic Thought,* (New Brunswick, NJ: Transaction Books, 1980).

2. Ibid., "Editor's Introduction," pp.xii.
3. For a recent and more definitive consideration of the institutionalists' perspective, see *The Journal of Economic Issues*, Volume 22, September and December, 1987. These special issues were republished by M. E. Sharpe, Inc., Publishers, in hard cover editions in 1988.
4. Samuels, "Editor's Introduction," p. xii.

PART I

HETERODOXY VIS-A-VIS ORTHODOXY

Introduction to Part I

The lead article by Hoyt S. Alverson provides an important anthropological underpinning for institutional analysis. Noting that the study of culture has been the central focus of anthropologists, he sees economics as one facet of culturally holistic inquiry. "Each empirically existing culture is seen as an 'adaptive' experiment, in which a distinct society or set of like societies adapts to a natural and human-made environment by means of distinct institutions, technology, and conditions of knowledge and belief."[1] In such inquiry, economics is perceived as a study of "institutional processes of production and reproduction." Alverson argues that, from an anthropological view, the classical economists' contribution is more consonant with cultural realities and regularities than is the more modern neoclassical marginalist analysis. He perceives a comparative study of economies as requiring consideration of an ecological dimension, an ideational or "ideological" dimension, and an institutional dimension. "The economy is an aspect of institutions, which are an aspect of culture." He concludes with an inquiry agenda of questions and issues that to a large degree is reflected in institutionalist papers comprising these volumes.

In the next selection, Clarence E. Ayres charges economists generally with the "ideological responsibility" of understanding "something of the nature and functioning of the ideology of our own society, and to convey this knowledge to the less advantaged community." Ayres is concerned, in particular, with the ideological and mythological bases in orthodoxy for productivity, for property rights, for earned income, and the like. "The doctrine which imputes creative potency to the factors of production . . . is of course a myth." For Ayres, in contrast, "what determines how well off any community may be is its science and industrial arts—the knowledge and skills possessed by that community; and the reason some elements of the community are better off, or worse off, than others is to be found in the institutions by which that community is structured." While he applauds the gains of the "Welfare State," he urges moving on to the "Creative Society."

Allan G. Gruchy addresses the "economics of dissent," with a broad view of challenges to orthodox economics that includes critics of current outcomes of economic institutions (consumer advocates), critics of the grounding and realism of orthodoxy, and critics of the fundamental tenets, structure, and relevance of standard theory. Gruchy sees the last of these as the most fundamental and identifies neoinstitutionalists not only as the most incisive academic analysts and critics of orthodoxy, but also as the only major group actively seeking to generate a comprehensive alternative to orthodoxy. In cataloging areas of dissent, Gruchy observes that "dissenting economists . . . do propose to explain to the people how their wants or goals come into being, how these wants are greatly influenced by the large corporations, how collective wants in the public sector are frequently unmet because there are no strong lobbying forces at work in the public sector promoting these collective wants, how obstacles are placed in the path of meeting wants not catered to by the private market place, how the failure of the private sector to take full account of all social costs not only lowers the quality of life but also indirectly lowers the productivity of labor, and how our archaic governmental system is unprepared . . . to take a comprehensive view of national needs or to take the necessary steps with the cooperation of the public to make sure that these national needs are assigned proper priority." Contributions to a neoinstitutionalist alternative approach to that of orthodoxy are found by Gruchy in the writings of Thorstein Veblen, John Kenneth Galbraith, Clarence Ayres, and Gunnar Myrdal among others. The quest of the neoinstitutionalists is not for new characterizations of moves to market efficiency, but to social goals and values of economic well-being generally.

With the paper by Kurt Dopfer, attention shifts to consideration of some central differences in the specific methodologies of orthodox neoclassicism and of institutionalism. It is Dopfer's purpose to demonstrate that the neoclassical concept of "linear causality" is logically and analytically inferior to the "sophisticated and realistic concept of circular and cumulative causation" of the institutionalists. Consideration of causality by orthodox economists is "redundant or methodologically impeding, and, where if it enters the scene at all, is given a deterministic interpretation which robs it of its original substance." Dopfer's basic contention is that the causality concept in orthodoxy was borrowed intact from classical physics. Neoclassicists sought to "free economic phenomena from accidental historical ties and to reveal their core of general validity, thus unfolding the 'laws of nature.'" They sought "axioms 'true beyond any doubt.'" "The validity of the linear causality concept of orthodoxy depends on "two considerations:

the validity of its transfer from physics to economics and its validity in physics itself." Dopfer demonstrates that neither of these claims to validity can be sustained. He concludes the paper with an extensive consideration of the institutionalist's concept of cumulative causation. This processual, evolutionary construct incorporates both the principles of mutation and retention. The significance of the differences between these two views of causality in formulating a theory of economic growth are explored briefly in the closing pages.

Geoff Hodgson continues the profound and fundamental critique of the methodology of orthodox neoclassicism through a critical examination of its "rationalist conception of action." In orthodoxy, "all action is regulated by rational calculation." All are assumed "to possess an individual mechanism for assigning values to policy outcomes." The "rational conception of action" constitutes a major part of the psyche of the calculating and maximizing "rational economic man." The argument advanced by Hodgson, "does not suggest that no actions are motivated or dominated by reason. It simply rejects the idea that all [relevant] action is dominated primarily by rational calculation." In contrast, "there is a large class of actions relevant to economics that arise in a different manner. The arguments are on methodological, psychological, sociological, and other grounds." Hodgson then, in development of his case, "confronts the idea that action can be dominated entirely by reason, . . . uses psychological, anthropological, and sociological materials to examine the cognitive basis of action, and to vindicate broadly the institutionalist challenge to the rationalist conception many years ago." His demonstration is that the rationalist conception of action is "methodologically unsound . . . psychologically crude . . . and . . . oblivious to important arguments from the other social sciences." "Veblen and other American Institutionalists drew our attention to the incompatibility of the modern scientific view of the human psyche with the basic assumptions of neoclassical economic theory. Modern psychology, as well as developments in sociology and anthropology, vindicates this claim."

This initial section concludes with a paper by one of the co-Editors, Marc R. Tool. Claims to significance of economic theorizing, argues Tool, have rested for over two centuries on the generation and relevance of economic policy for problem solving perceived as removing impairments in the flow of real income. In spite of claims to positivism by both nineteenth and twentieth century orthodox economists, their inquiry has required that they become normativists as well. "An inquirer cannot logically or empirically distinguish between what is and what ought to be without applying a criterion of judgment, a social value principle." Accordingly, "normative principles and standards which permit the identification and determination of what ought to be, which constitute criteria with which choices among institutional alternatives may be made, are regarded here as value principles in the philosophical sense and usage." Thus "criteria for social choice are principles of social value." Utility has been, and continues to be, the neoclassical principle of social value. Maximizing utility is the "ultimate and continuing purpose or goal of individuals" in the economy. The paper subjects this value referent to an extensive critque in which its unsuitability and inappropriateness is shown to derive from its tautological character, its relativistic content, and its demonstrated inapplicability. The assessment extends to include not only Marshallian-based cardinal utility but also the Paretian-based ordinal utility constructs. Extensions of orthodoxy into axiomatic analysis, though intended to evade the social value question, are shown to be vulnerable to the more general critique. The institutionalist's alternative instrumental value principle is developed elsewhere in Tool's writings.[2]

Notes

1. All quotations in these introductory comments throughout the volume are from the respective author's papers being discussed.
2. Marc R. Tool, *Essays in Social Value Theory: A Neoinstitutionalist Contribution*, (Armonk, New York: M. E. Sharpe, Inc., 1986).

1

Culture and Economy: Games That "Play People"

Hoyt Alverson

Discerning the boundary and linkages between the disciplines of economics and anthropology presupposes some agreement concerning the fundamental object the two disciplines claim respectively to study. In both the terms "culture" and "economy," there exists such a vexatious polysemy that we must first establish the meaning of these terms before addressing the question of disciplinary boundaries. The disciplinary boundary can only be drawn according to how one believes anthropologists and economists respectively conceive of human institutions, and what they respectively take to be the basis of validity of that conception.

Concerning the definition of economy, Leonard Silk aptly notes: "Some envision the economy as a set of flexible prices, wages, rents, interest rates moving up and down, bidding resources to their most profitable use as buyers and sellers assiduously pursue their self interest. But others see the economy as predominantly a set of powerful economic institutions—great corporations, highly concentrated industries, strong labor unions, big agribusiness, foreign cartels . . . and political blocs capable of turning policies to their own interests" [Silk 1980, p. D2]. To wit: is the economy "profitably," to be seen as a set of people each playing a game, or are powerful institutions—the "game"—in effect "playing" the set of people? These opposing conceptions are doubtless legacies of the schism that rent social science some hundred years ago when the authors of the marginalist revolution, William Stanley Jevons, Leon Walras, and Karl Menger, took their leave of political economy to found economics.

For purposes of this paper I will argue that neo-classical economics has resolved this debate by favoring a conception of the economy as a set of largely free, autonomous actors, each with a set of many tastes, goals, or wants, who seek to obtain from other like-motivated individuals satisfaction of those "utilities" by production and exchange at a *Pareto optimum.* Institutions, at least of the economy, are seen as an emergent property of the deals made by individuals using criteria of rational efficiency. Classical political economy, conversely, took as its essential object of study the totality of arrangements by which individuals were organized to undertake their tasks of production and reproduction necessary to provision themselves and the institutions that encapsulated them. The shift from political economy to economics is instantiated, as Christopher Gregory has noted, by the change of focus from commodity to goods, from use value to utility, from *histoire raisonee* to short-term prediction, from social formation or mode of production to the individual actor, from reproduction to scarcity/efficient allocation, and from labor value to factor prices/incomes and prices of supply-demand equilibrium [Gregory 1982, p. 12].

The essential object of study in anthropology is "culture." How this is conceived or defined will render the discipline of anthropology cognate to the way the conception of economy renders the discipline of economics. As I will try to show, the conception of culture most widely accepted in anthropology today is quite consonant with the classical conception of political economy and quite opposed to that predominating in modern economics. Since it is the marginalist analysis of moving equilibria that I take to be the central concern, not the analysis of economic culture, it is with the former that I shall seek to compare and contrast cultural analysis.

The Marginalist Conception of Economy

For purposes at hand I shall take Manuel Gottlieb's statement as a valid characterization:

> Established usage in Western economic thought . . . holds that economic behavior involves the administration of scarce and inadequate resources

> to minister to multiple ends . . . Resources have been called scarce because of the endless expansibility of human wants that underlie the uses for these resources. . . . This concept of economic behavior *almost precludes the notion of an economic system except one which institutionalizes this philosophy of choice itself, by rational individuals coming into juxtaposition in markets for exchange.* . . . For this reason modern economics tends to recognize only two kinds of economic systems: the rational kind . . . and the *abnormal kinds, which are [deemed] not very feasible except by the use of force or fraud* [Gottlieb 1984, p. 4] (emphasis added).

The only economies that are neither "rational" nor abnormal—that is, those in which the economic dimension or aspect of society is totally embedded in other, "non-economic" institutions and practices—are practically non-existent. Quoting Gottlieb once again for convenience and illustration: "it is necesary to exclude from our analysis those early economic systems most fully identified with their social context . . . [where] . . . any economic organization is submerged in social organization . . . it would hardly contribute to the analysis of economic systems of the more advanced societies if we included these early systems" [Gottlieb 1984, p. 19].

In the marginalist view, institutions arise from, follow in consequence of, individually motivated economizing behavior in production, distribution, and consumption. Thus, to explain the economizing behavior, which itself precedes institutional forms, one must invoke "human nature" as a direct, pre-cultural cause of such behavior. Societies that permit expression of the innate, economizing propensities of basic, sticker-priced homo sapiens are conceived as having "natural" or "normal" economies; those that prohibit or stifle these propensities are conceived, if complex, to be abnormal or fraudulent, and if simple, to be unevolved or undeveloped. What is excluded—that which all sciences ultimately come to be known for—is presumably retarded or pathological, but in any case is irrelevant to understanding "economy" and "economizing," properly defined.

Just as rational economizing is presumed to be a direct expression of human nature, so are tastes or utilities. People simply have them. Their origin is either inscrutable or irrelevant. So demand is simply the idiosyncratic expression of personal preferences, which can, of course, be aggregated and described, for example, as price elasticities.

Marginalist analysis of demand or any other quantity depends upon change or variation, for without such change there simply is no marginal—that is, instantaneous—difference to be analyzed, no marginal cost, price, demand, revenue, product, et cetera. Marginal analysis also requires continuous reliance on *ceteris paribus* claims: that *all other things being equal,* a small change in one variable can be mapped functionally onto a small change in another. Now, over time, the *ceteris paribus* conditions cannot possibly be met. So marginal analysis must presume an economy in equilibrium, where all equations are simultaneous and have solutions. Economics and economic history become two distinct and largely incommensurate undertakings.

Since all marginal analysis is aimed at prediction of behavior, the validity of its assumptions is secondary to its short-term (predictive) success. One seeks to know how the system seems to work at a moment in time rather than why it exists or where it is headed. Why it exists is simply deemed human nature set free; and where it is headed is nowhere, except perhaps bigger or smaller, unless interfered with by non-economic, therefore *theoretically* irrelevant, forces. Marginal analysis is, in short, functional analysis, an effort to describe how a set of behaviors leads to a set of effects, purposes, or consequences that in turn call forth the initial behaviors.

To be sure, there are many economists who doubt the truth, relevance, or efficacy of this conception of economy. But challenging the truth of a model or description is to pit one set of beliefs about "reality" against another set. Comparison of belief systems generally takes place within the perspective of one of them, thereby bestowing on a supposed reality the disguised prejudices of one of the belief systems itself. Criticisms of marginalist analysis coming from those of "institutionalist" and materialist persuasion have grown more numerous and persuasive in the past twenty years, as slowdown and stagnation have led economists to attend more to its anomalies. Robert Kuttner's recent jeremiad is certainly apt: "The world of perfect competition posited by neo-classical economics may be so far from the world in which we actually live that it is not a useful basis for theory, policy or advice" [Kuttner 1985, p. 76]. As suggested, these debates tend to be inconclusive because so much of what is at stake depends on the presuppositions and assumptions contained within the competing visions of what the economy is. The same problem arises in juxtaposing the anthropologist's conception of culture *cum* economy with that of the economist. Nonetheless there may be much to learn in such contrariety.

The Concept of Culture in Modern Anthropology

As economic analysis relies on continuous (correlative) variation in independent and dependent variables to ascertain functional relationships, anthropology relies on correlative difference among whole cultures. This comparative study of cultures spans the temporal and spatial extent of the human family, Hominoidea. That includes about four million years and most of the earth's land surface. In broad compass, each empirically existing culture is seen as an "adaptive" experiment, in which a distinct society or set of like societies adapts to a natural and human-made environment by means of distinct institutions, technology, and conditions of knowledge and belief. Ideally, comparison is carried out in terms of "controlled substitution and minimum variation." That is, one seeks to compare cultures where very few of the relevant features are different and where the vast majority are similar. Functional analysis consists in mapping variation in the independent variables onto variation in the dependent variables using familiar multiple correlation techniques.

The notion of culture in anthropology is of central importance in two distinct senses: (1) cultures are the fundamental, holistically conceived units of comparative analysis, and (2) the concept of culture serves as the analytic framework, or "meta-language" within which comparative analysis of distinct cultures is carried out. The first sense of culture provides the criteria for recognizing what the object of anthropology is to be. The second sense provides an apparatus for translating the various empirical cultures of study into a framework or "language," which ideally does not elevate the beliefs and prejudices of some one of the cultures that are the object of analysis, to the level of meta-language for comparison of all cultures.

While the concept of culture is conceived holistically, that is, as *not* reducible to a set of more fundamental underlying constituents, it is useful to begin a description by considering fundamental aspects.

Figure 1 below will help to depict the three fundamental aspects of culture and their interrelationships. As you see, it is a three-dimensional Cartesian coordinate with an origin and rays describing three quarter-planes. The three planes represent each one of the three fundamental aspects of culture: ecology, institutional organization, and the conditions of knowledge, or "ideology." Using a coordinate system suggests that all patterned human behavior takes place within the "cube," that any act so circumscribed has a value in *each* of the coordinates. Thus, all patterned human acts have an ecological value, cause, or effect, an institutional value, cause, or effect, and an ideological value, cause, or effect.

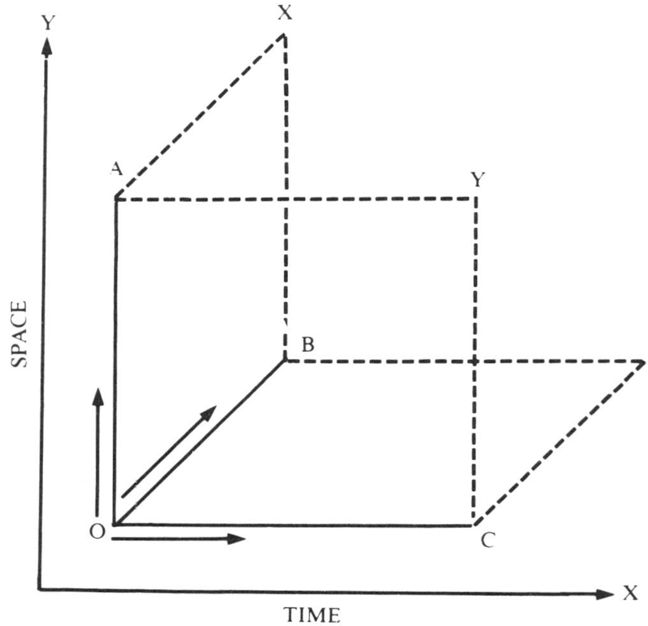

Figure 1. ***A Pictoral Metaphor: The Dimensions of Culture***

OBZC = The ecologic plane (or order) ≅ ecology
OAYC = The social/economic plane (or order) ≅ institutions
OAXB = The ideological/cosmogonic plane (or order) ≅ ideology

Each plane constitutes a *dimension* of culture. Therefore, all patterned events, acts, arrangements, institutions, et cetera are *defined* by their relations to all three of these planes or "orders." The entire "cube" of culture changes in space and over time. The boundaries of the culture are set by the analyst according to the level of abstraction in his/her project of study.

We avoid in this conception a vision of culture, once popular but now disputed, that culture is an ensemble or collection of traits that would be assigned to different domains on the basis of "function," for example, technology, religion, family, economy, or politics. Usually this taxonomic approach to culture argued for a stratification where material culture was the base, economy and politics were the structure, and ideas or beliefs were super-structure. Along with this layering went the conviction that the basic engine or determinant of culture was one or the other of these layers. Which one depended upon whether one was an ecological materialist, a Marxist, an idealist, or something else.

The view offered here insists that there is no such layering, but that all three dimensions are both necessary to culture and are necessarily an aspect of all patterned behavior. Further, this model emphasizes the fact that culture is organized. Among the ecological, institutional, and ideological dimensions of culture there are rather clear intercorrelations. Said differently, ecology, institutional organization, and ideology do not vary freely or widely. We would be shocked to find markets in a hunting and gathering society, hoe agriculture in a society with extensive urbanism, or doctrines of salvation in a society with no class structure.

This model of culture serves both senses of that word. We use it to conceive of each distinct social or communal manifestation of culture, and we use it as an abstract model or language for comparing disparate social manifestations of culture. As such, there is a time and space dimension that must be located within the "cube" and outside of it. Cultures, as empirically existing adaptive systems, change over time and move over space. So does human culture or our conception of it as a whole.

Before describing this model in detail, we must note certain commitments corollary to it. First, the vast majority of anthropologists would argue that there exist very few, if any, important or enduring correlations between human biological variability and human cultural variability. Human biological variability is rather slight to begin with, largely because culture, not phenotypic traits, is our primary means of adaptation. Second "human nature" is not some organically given disposition or propensity to do certain things or to act in certain ways. Rather human nature is a set of genetically endowed potentialities that are inchoate unless and until they are given expression in specific cultures. Culture is the completion and expression of human nature.

In light of this, human nature cannot be itself a direct cause of culture. Nor could any particular culture possibly be a privileged expression of human nature, precisely because all cultures are equally both expressions of human nature and crucibles within which that nature is made complete. In short, there are no known causes of cultural differences that reside in the genetic code. By implication, one could not judge any culture as normal, abnormal, deviant, retarded, or undeveloped by reference to genetic or other organic criteria. "Progress" in the sense just adduced is a concept foreign to biology and to organic evolution.

The Three Dimensions of Culture

Ecology, institutional organization, and systems of knowledge, or "ideology" have each been the object of close study within hundreds of cultures and in comparative study over the past several decades. A considerable fund of specialized scholarship has grown up devoted to each of the dimensions and to the typically anthropological project of striving continuously to integrate the specialized researches. For an audience interested principally in the interrelationships between anthropology and economics, it is probably most useful and interesting to emphasize the institutional dimension. In this way, the anthropologist's approach to those arrangements that come closest to what the economist would recognize as "economy" can be highlighted. But some mention of the ecologic and ideologic dimensions is important, if only to emphasize that no one of the dimensions in itself can constitute the basis for a cultural description.

The Ecological Dimension

Grossly stated, ecology is the study of interrelationships between populations of organisms and their effective environment. These interrelations are generally conceived in "systems-theoretic" terms, and are concerned with genetic, phenotypic, and behavioral adaptations of populations of organisms to their effective environments, which includes populations of other organisms. This entails study of population growth, dispersion, densities, and regulation; population-environment energy exchanges; physical alteration of environment due to adaptation; carrying capacities of eco-niches; and so forth. For our purposes we emphasize that all culture-bearing populations are energy-capturing and transforming systems. These transformations are carried out by human beings in a cultural context, which includes technology, institutional organization, and conditions of belief and knowledge.

The culture-bearing community and its environment are reciprocals; the nature of the cultural community defines the environment, actually and potentially, and the environment or niche defines the culture. There is no question of one being autonomous of the other. Environment does not cause culture to exist or to take certain forms, nor does it set strict limits on cultural manifestation. Rather, both are conceived as interaction effects within a complex system. All acts, artifacts, and beliefs have within a cultural community ecological implications and consequences—some direct, for example: raw materials, land, food sources, competent labor power, tools and machines, and transport, but also others less obvious, such as abstract precepts of ideology, kinship organization, dietary and sumptuary laws, and ritual celebrations, all of which affect environment-population interactions.

The most salient aspect of the ecologic dimension of culture, looked at over millenia of cultural evolution, is the general correspondence between the size and density of culture-bearing populations on the one hand and the amount of potential energy per capita that must be "captured" from the environment and transformed into materials and other energy forms on the other. Figure 2 below shows at a glance the "energy bill" associated with six ecologically defined stages of human cultural evolution. The implications of this model for future cultural change and for the "development" of Third-World nations is too obvious to belabor. It is somewhat amusing to see that Gottlieb, in an effort to describe as generally and as comprehensively as possible the "functions" of (advanced) economic systems, includes among them "conservation of the natural environment" [Gottlieb, 1984, pp. 424–26]. I dare say Andrew Carnegie, John D. Rockefeller, or Leonard Firestone would be surprised to learn that was a function of the economic system *they knew.*

One of the hoary myths of our own culture is the belief that material accumulation (economic growth) has been attained, or at least accompanied by, increasing "efficiency" of basic energy transformation systems. We tend to confuse the aggregate output of systems with their efficiency. Table 1 below shows the input-output efficiencies of five contemporary food production systems. Clearly, despite the effectiveness of Western agribusiness, it is not nearly as efficient in "energetics" terms as hoe agriculture or hunting and gathering.

Table 1. ***Energy input-output efficiency in five food systems***

culture	*technology*	*calories produced per calories expended*
Bushman	hunting/gathering	9.6
Tsembage (New Guinea)	shifting cultivation	18.0
	pig raising	2.1
	total	9.8
Genieri (Gambia)	hoe farming	11.2
China	irrigated wet rice	53.5
United States	factory farming	
	human labor	210.0
	nonhuman energy	0.13

SOURCES: Marvin Harris, *Culture, Man and Nature* (New York: Thomas Crowell Co., Inc., 1971); John H. Bodley, *Anthropology and Contemporary Human Problems* (Menlo Park: Cummings, 1976) p. 119.

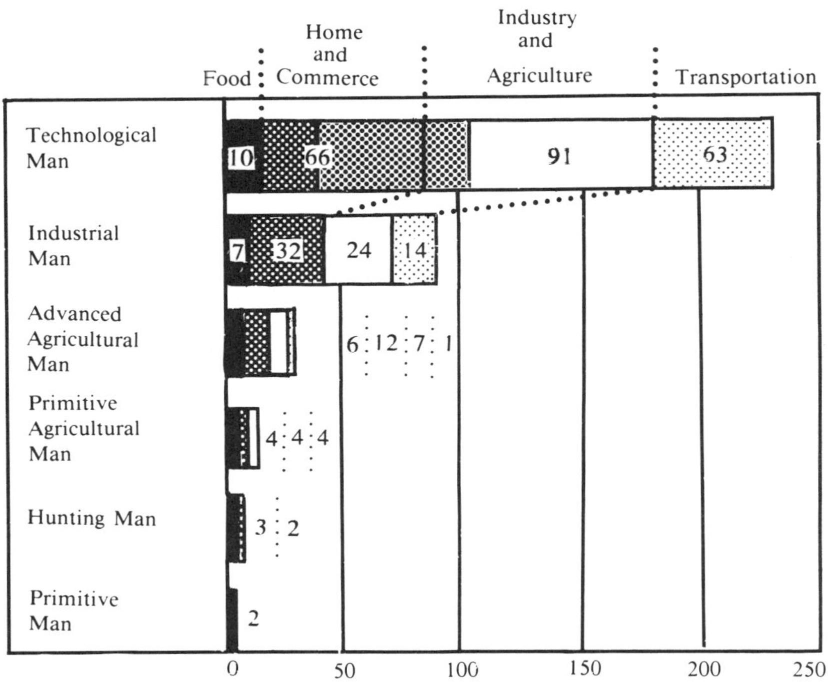

Figure 2. ***Daily Consumption of Energy per Capita for Six Stages in Human Development.***

Daily consumption of energy per capita is calculated for six stages in human development (and with an accuracy that decreases with antiquity). Primitive man (East Africa about 1,000,000 years ago) without the use of fire had only the energy of the food he ate. Hunting man (Europe about 100,000 years ago) had more food and also burned wood for heating and cooking. Primitive agricultural man (Fertile Crescent in 5,000 B.C.) was growing crops and animal energy. Advanced agricultural man (northwestern Europe in A.D. 1400) had some coal for heating, some water power and wind power and animal transport. Industrial man (in England in 1875) had the steam engine. In 1970 technological man (in the U.S.) consumed 230,000 kilocalories per day, much of it in the form of electricity (hatched area). Food is divided into plant foods (far left) and animal foods (or foods fed to animals).

SOURCE: Earl Cook, "The Flow of Energy in an Industrial Society," Scientific American 224 (January 1971): 136.

The Ideological Dimension

There is an ideational constituent that suffuses human behavior.

All objects, acts, experiences are both material entities and, at the same time, *symbols.* As the anthropologist Clifford Geertz has said, we live within "webs of significance," in a world of meanings. We perceive, think, and experience, not through brute sensation of things, but according to how we use language and other symbol-systems to represent all action, including thought itself. Humans are model builders. Many organisms build houses, but only humans can talk about them, or "play house." To experience subjunctively, conditionally, hypothetically, counter-factually is uniquely human. The water that poured over Helen Keller's hand as her teacher "touched" w-a-t-e-r was not just an event-turned-conditioned-association, it was an epiphany that lifted a mist and let her "see," who was both deaf and blind, a world of thought. And suddenly Helen realized, "everything has a name."

Names do not just exist in lists. They are organized in tales: theory, model, poetry, novel, recipe, law. These tales, which exist in all cultures, are not merely descriptions of experience; they have explanatory and mandatory force as well. Nor are they "just so" stories; we believe they are "true." The world is in accord with them. Or they are about what is just, beautiful, efficient, useful, and we ought heed their lessons. Simply to be conscious of the groups we live in requires that they be symbolic objects. We require a collective, or at least shared, symbolically coded consciousness of what group living ought to be if we are to maintain any communal order or solidarity.

Because culture is organized, we would expect that systems of belief and knowledge would show close correspondence with the ecological and institutional dimensions. Belief, knowledge, value, or morality exhibit the same cultural specificity as do ecologic interactions and institutional arrangements. They do not float around off the ground in propositional form, but are anchored to ecology and institutional arrangements just as surely as are the people who espouse them (generally as universal and obvious truths). Theories of "human nature" for example—a preoccupation of all cultures—are not conceived in innocence. Is it surprising that a culture "dedicated" as is ours to the ideal of meritocracy (however much a mystification that actually is) would work so ceaselessly, unflaggingly in its philosophy, social, and natural sciences to concoct a theory of "natural," human *inequality?* Is it surprising that the flowering of capitalism was accompanied by religious doctrines of spiritual individualism and belief that property is a sign of salvation? By the view that the Garden of Eden, that is, the natural world, was our human plaything to do with as we wish? That anthropology followed the colonial governments into Africa to help them "understand," and thereby administer, the peoples and territories? That economists see less-powerful societies who sit on things we want as "underdeveloped," or, if lacking things we value, to be simply "backward"?

The word, "idea" comes from the Greek, *eidos,* to see. Ideas are for seeing with. We "see" through ideas. The ineluctable reality that we "see" "out there," is born in the conditions of knowledge and belief within culture and in our heads. To be sure, we "succeed" in our projects because of what we see. We check our ideas against the evidence of our senses. But, ultimately, truth boils down to the basis of our certitude and how we justify beliefs to one another within a culture.

The Institutional Dimension

Human beings share with many animal species the characteristics of living in socially organized groups. The basis of this sociality is however cultural, not genetic. For this reason there is no species-wide form of sociality among human beings. Indeed, there is no reason to believe that the currently or historically existing sample of social forms exhausts the possibilities for social-economic organization. Hunting and gathering, including its institutional and ideological concomitants, ceased to exist in "pristine" form in this decade as more powerful societies have destroyed all the remaining niches and, in some cases, the people who subsisted by that means. This represents a real loss, as this mode of cultural existence is as old as our biologic species itself, and represents one of the fundamental cultural aspects of the natural selection that shaped our organic evolution.

There may be a universal core of institutional features among the social forms that homo sapiens has devised. But this thin skein is so profoundly overlaid, and its "functional" consequences so altered, by the culturally specific features of actual social forms that there is no basis for claiming that some particular kind of institutional life is "natural," "normal," or reflective of some vague natural propensity. The manufacture of theories about "human nature" to explain, or, more typically, to justify certain institutional arrangements in which the theories' authors have a deep vested interest is a lamentable pastime of the contemporary human sciences, in what amounts intellectually to little more than crack-pot reductionism. There just is no evidence to support, for example, Adam Smith's devout conviction that specific institutional arrangements, including "economy" are the "print-out" of some innate human disposition coded in the germ-plasm.

Included in culture's institutional dimension are kinship and family systems, class structure, legal systems, government, production and exchange systems, agencies of enculturation and education, and numerous types of formal organizations. In complex societies, each of these institutions will be functionally and formally distinct. In very simple societies, all these functions may all be carried out within the context of the family or band. Of concern to us here is how economists' conceptions, signified by the term, "economy," necessarily differ from those of the anthropologist, signified unfortunately by the same designation.

At the outset I suggested that while economists differ among themselves in how to conceive the extension of the term "economy," the majority view holds it to be coterminous with the principles of human behavior that maximize individual utilities (generally profit) by production and exchange in the so-called free, competitive, price-making market. The descriptive validity of the "laws" of economics depends, then, entirely on how closely in accord with the ideally conceived market actual production, distribution, and consumption arrangements are. Insofar as these arrangements are quite unlike those defining the market, it is not clear what economists would call them. I take Gottlieb's statement to be agnostic diagnosis: if there is no distinct market, then the economy is "embedded" in other institutions. How one then discerns the uniquely economic in such a cultural "bed" is not a question with which economists have in the main been concerned, but one that has preoccupied anthropology.

To define the "intension" (conceptual meaning) of analytic terms by their "extension" (denotation) or use in *our* society of culture simply transforms the institutions of other cultures into specious, but seemingly familiar, objects. Nowhere does this danger and confusion pose a greater threat to comparative study than in the case of "economy." Now, this raises the question implied by many economists' definition of economy: if "economy" as a technical term must have its intension (meaning) defined by its supposed extension in our society, then by definition societies whose production and exchange are not carried out principally in terms of a market, do not have an economy, *in senso strictu,* at all. Such a conception of economy or of any other important term in the analytic vocabulary of cross-cultural comparison forecloses genuine comparative study, and fosters cultural solipsism.

The inappropriateness of a concept for use in a language of comparison (the meta-language) does not necessarily mean it lacks local, that is, culturally specific, validity. The terms of the meta-language should permit translation among all terms in the several "object"—that is, culturally specific—languages. What cannot be admitted, however, is that the peculiar meaning and reference of a term in one of the object languages becomes mandatorially the only way to conceive of that term's meaning and reference in the meta-language. Conversely, if a term in the meta-language cannot accommodate a cognate term in a object language, then the meta-language or its term is inadequate.

Anthropologists have debated how best to conceive of economy for purposes of study in societies whose production and exchange is not dominated by market principles, while retaining sufficient cognizance of the workings of the market so that genuine comparison among all kinds of economies, including our own, can be undertaken. During the 1960s this debate came to a head in a three-way stand-off among: (a) formalists, (b) substantivists, and (c) Marxists.

Formalists argue that the theoretic apparatus of contemporary marginalist economics could serve as a framework for cross-cultural comparative study of disparate economies. Its assumptions and methods were sufficiently universal to make it a genuine language of comparison.

Substantivists (followers of Karl Polanyi and, belatedly, Alexander Chayanov) argue that institutional arrangements are a process that precedes human economizing decisions and actions. What people will or want or do is dependent upon the peculiar character of institutional arrangements for production and exchange. Hence, the rationality of the institutional processes of production and exchange is far more important than the economizing calculations that individuals make to "work the system."

Marxist analyses focus on the "labor-process," and technical or material transformations carried out by means of it. Value contained in any material object or activity is conceived as the labor requirement for reproduction of the competent labor power necessary to the production in question.

I think it fair to say that all three of these approaches to economy taken by anthropologists in the 1950s and 1960s were marked by a signal shortcoming that can rather easily be seen in hindsight. Anthropologists' thinking on economy was informed largely by the competing paradigms that had grown up in economics or in political economy for the study of industrial capitalism, or certain other complex systems. Said differently, the debates were carried out within an object language within a specific cultural milieu. Broad and systematic comparison of the full range of economies, even careful study of particular noncapitalist economies, is, even now, nascent. As suggested above, the ideas we hold affect profoundly the characteristics of objects we will see in our investigations, particularly when they are complex, ambiguous, or vague and therefore require "interpretation." Not surprisingly, earlier studies of economy tended to confirm one of the three paradigmatic "attitudes."

It would have been remarkable if any "language" or conception of economy developed for the analysis (critical or sympathetic) of a specific institutional form could have been pressed directly into service as a valid meta-language for systematic comparison of any and all "economies." To the degree that extant conceptions did serve the role of meta-language, they succeeded in elevating industrial capitalism's *particular* vaunted prejudices, or, conversely, the brilliant *critiques* of it, to the level of *universals.* (Of course, should one or another of the politically dominant economies succeed in its avowed mission of colonizing the rest of the world's cultures, what is particular and peculiar to one of them will become universal by default.)

A Framework For The Comparative Study of Economy

Consider some of the many points of contrast between the following two principles of exchange:

(a) sale transaction in a "market"

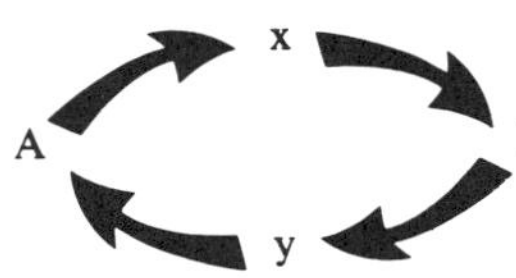

(b) gift transaction in a "ceremonial" exchange

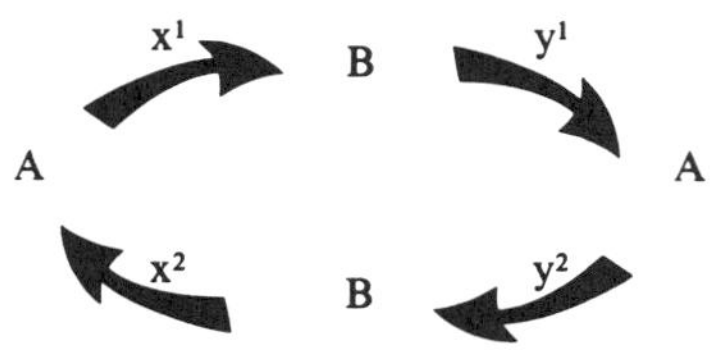

In (a), *A*'s conveyance of *x* to *B*, makes *A B*'s creditor. *B*'s conveyance of *y* to *A* cancels *B*'s debt, if *x* and *y* are equivalent in virtue of equality on a single dimension, for example, "price" or exchange value. The relationship between *A* and *B* is defined by their contractual obligations in this transaction. *x* and *y* appear to move between the transactors. Indeed it is this movement that defines the relationship between *A* and *B*, and that ceases when the cycle is complete.

In (b), *A* and *B* have a status-based relationship with each other as mutual givers/receivers of gifts. This may arise for any number of reasons; they might be kin of a certain type. When *A* conveys x^1 to *B*, *A* becomes *B*'s creditor. *B*'s conveyance of y^1 to *A*, makes *B* *A*'s creditor. *x* and *y* belong to two distinct classes or categories of gift-valuables and their exchange sets up two distinct creditor-debtor relations. When *A* conveys y^2 to *B*, *A* cancels his/her *y*-type debt to *B*. When *B* conveys x^2 to *A*, he/she cancels his/her *x*-type debt to *A* x^1 and x^2, (and likewise, *y*) are equivalent as valid members of the same category of gift-valuables. They often will not be equivalent in any other sense, for example, size, weight, scarcity, or reputation, although this is not necessarily so. *x* and *y* are totally incommensurate and no exchange among them is thinkable. Typically, neither *A* nor *B* would or could "own" their respective *x* and *y* as private property. The only valid disposition of *x* and *y* may well be to enter gift exchanges. There is no "comparative advantage" in the transaction because *A* and *B* wind up with precisely what they started with. The exchanges between *A* and *B* ratify and affirm their relationship, and may enhance their individual prestige as mutual givers/receivers of gifts. The completion of the exchange cycle, rather than ending the relation, bids it resume.

Now both of these kinds of exchange are equally and fundamentally "economic" transactions. But the two systems have very different rationality, very different "functional" consequences, and predominate in very different cultures.

Consider another example: the economizing decisions involved in what for us in our culture is a "public-goods" dilemma that pits the utility of acting to maximize immediate short-term personal gain against the utility of maximizing long-term collective gain. In many cultures this is no dilemma at all, but a clear case of each person "being a person in virtue of others." As the case of the "dilemma of the commons" described in Figure 3 below makes clear, there are two very different economic rationalities that can be applied to this economizing problem. But only one of them fits the neo-classical conception of how the system works. There are many cultures in the world in which the "defect" strategy would be purely hypothetical and a monstrosity to boot. This is particularly true when considerations of risk aversion are paramount.

Figure 3. ***Dilemma (Tragedy) of the Commons***

10 Shepherds
10 Sheep each, each sheep weighs 100 lbs.
For each sheep added to flock over 100
weight of every sheep is reduced by 2 lbs.
Cooperate: keep one's herd = 10
Defect: add a sheep

SELF \ OTHERS	C	D
C	90 sheep @ 100 lbs. = 1000 lbs. per person / 10 sheep @ 100 lbs. = 1000 lbs. for self	99 sheep @ 82 lbs. = 902 lbs. per person / 10 sheep @ 82 lbs. = 820 lbs. for self
D	90 sheep @ 98 lbs. = 980 lbs. each / 11 sheep @ 98 lbs. = 1078 lbs. for self	880 lbs. per person / 880 lbs. for self

Now, a conception of economy that is to serve as a basis for the understanding, comparison, and one hopes, explanation of economies as different as the two examples above instantiate will have to be robustly abstract. But equally, it cannot be so confined to the particular conditions of any one cultural setting that it forces all other specimens of economy onto the bed of Procrustes, to be lopped off, stretched, or parodied.

In an article of this scope I cannot, of course, begin to adduce even an outline of that in which such a comparative theory of economy should consist. Frankly, I have not thought the problem through to that extent. But I would like to suggest five fundamental questions or issues that may direct our thinking along profitable lines.

The first issue has already been prefigured in the tenor of my remarks as a whole: that the comparative study of economy entails the comparative study of culture and vice-versa. This bi-conditional implication follows from the observation that the three dimensions of culture are singly and jointly necessary aspects of it. To the extent that the study of institutions is itself partial, or ignores ecology and ideology, it is incomplete. Economists themselves acknowledge this whenever they seek to explain some "economic fact" by appeal to tastes, preferences, desires, concern for the environment, the scientific outlook, technological innovation, entrepreneurial spirit, business acumen, government responsibility, the yuppie generation, or a host of other "non-economic" factors. When one seeks to partition culture, one tears a seamless web. The economy is an aspect of institutions, which are an aspect of culture.

Second, by what criteria, principles, or processes is control over the use of material resources or forces of production allocated? Which individuals, groups, cohorts, gain rights or privileges to determine, or effectively to influence, how resources are used and by whom? What principles, that is, limitations or conditions, are placed on that control or use?

Third, how are individuals, families, communities, regions, nations, associated with specialized aspects or tasks of material production and transformation? How does this "division of labor" come about?

Fourth, by what principles are the material transformations of the production process controlled, used, or exchanged? Which individuals, groups, regions, social positions, gain rights to effect and affect the appropriation and exchange of the results of setting in motion specialized labor and other factors of production? What are the results of those "decisions" or processes? How in fact are the material transformations put to use, as for example in investment or trade?

Fifth, by what criteria and by what agents or agencies is the distribution of the products of labor for final consumption effected? I won't trespass on the indulgence of economists by suggesting how in the case of "free, competitive market capitalism" these questions might be answered. Nor will I importune and mystify the reader with answers that might be provided in the case of societies that lack commodity production. The point is, a comparative study of economy, *cum* culture, requires that data or findings for particular economies/cultures constitute answers to a *single* set of very basic questions *framed in the metalanguage.* The four or five suggested here are meant to be but prompts to further reflection and investigation.

Economists, anthropologists and others interested in cross cultural, or long-term historical study could very profitably cooperate in formulating an inventory of basic questions pointing to the fundamental aspect of institutions that in any context we could agree constitute *the* economy. Such a project might well be the harbinger of a general theory of economic change or evolution that returns to *structure* that aspect of economy currently realized only in relativistic terms as "history" or "cross cultural differences."

References

Geertz, Clifford. 1973. *The Interpretation of Cultures.* New York: Basic Books.

Gottlieb, Manual. 1984. *A Theory of Economic Systems.* Orlando: Academic Press.

Gregory, Christopher. 1982. *Gifts and Commodities.* New York: Cambridge University Press.

Kuttner, Robert. 1985. "The Poverty of Economics." *Atlantic Monthly* (February): 74–84.

Silk, Leonard. 1980. "Why Experts Don't Agree." *New York Times,* 26 March, p. D2.

2

Ideological Responsibility

Clarence E. Ayres

For a long time now I have been growing increasingly restive at the increasingly general use of the term "productivity." To be sure, it is most commonly used today in what is supposed to be a purely statistical sense. Increases in wages are commonly supposed to be "justified" by corresponding increases in "productivity." But what does "justified" mean? We may say that we use such words as "productivity" in a purely economic sense, meaning that we interpose the mechanisms of the market between our conclusions and the moral problems which gave rise to them. But moral considerations, being universal and omnipresent, have a way of leaking through the complexities of the market and coloring the results of even the most recondite analysis with a moral tint. This is true, and I think inescapably true, of the concept "productivity." This word suggests, whether intentionally or not, meanings which are not true and are exceedingly harmful; and all of us who know this to be the case have a public duty to repudiate these suggested meanings and to denounce the whole institutional structure they support. I propose to use this platform to try to do my public duty in this regard.

Not very long ago economists such as John Bates Clark were declaring that "Free competition tends to give to labor what labor creates, to capitalists what capital creates, and to entrepreneurs what the co-ordinating function creates." Today, only two generations later, few economists would advocate total reliance on this "tendency." But for most of them the reason for their hesitation is not skepticism with regard to the creativity of the "instruments of production." What they question is only whether competition is sufficiently brisk and sufficiently general to give effect to this salubrious tendency. The myth of "creativity" still passes virtually unquestioned.

Indeed, one of the most thoughtful, not to say philosophical, of living economists, Frank H. Knight, reaffirmed this only recently in the following language:

> The "communist" nations also must follow extensively the principle of productivity or "middle of the road," and even "marginalism," to achieve any efficiency or to make the economy function at all. And they lose much efficiency by pretending to the contrary, and especially by pretending not to recognize "capital" as productive. This is true [I assume he means that capital *is* productive] regardless of who has title to the property in which it is embodied or what the status of laborers or managers is.[1]

[1] Strangely enough, these sentences occur in a review-article which roundly condemns Henry Hazlitt's *The Foundations of Morality*, under the title "Abstract Economics and Absolute Ethics," in *Ethics*, LXVI, 3 (April, 1966). As the title suggests, Knight chides

Such a conception of capital as productive "regardless . . . of what the status of laborers and managers is" calls to mind a picture analogous to that of the sorcerer's apprentice: vast machines, cybernized by miniature computers, spewing forth continuous streams of steel ingots and finished automobiles. But that is not what was meant by Professors Knight and Clark and the whole succession of classical economists. What they have all meant is that capital is "productive" in the same sense that labor is productive, and therefore has a valid claim on the gross product regardless of who profits by that claim.

It is interesting to reflect that capital may be productive in a sense quite different from what the classical economists have had in mind. Capital, we say, is just as productive as labor and therefore no less entitled to remuneration. This is as much as to say that the claim of capital is indefeasible, for in our society no claim is more firmly established than that of honest toil. Whatever its amount, the workman is worthy of his hire. He has earned it.

It is interesting to reflect on the claim-justifying magic of the word "earn." The *Shorter Oxford* defines this word in terms that admit of no misunderstanding: "To render an equivalent in labour for; hence to obtain, or deserve, as the reward of labour." In short, the divine right of the worker to his wage is established by his sweat. But note how language drifts! The Random House *College Dictionary* is more up-to-date. After a succinct statement of the original meaning of the word "earn," "to gain by labor or service," it continues: "To gain as due return or profit: *Savings bonds earn interest.*" In effect, we are invited to picture the bonds in the locked steel drawer of some bank vault, sweating profusely as they heave and writhe in their efforts to perform the labor or service for which their owner is about to be rewarded. Am I indulging in absurdity? Should I declare that what the savings-bond buyer is being rewarded for is abstinence from frivolity in consequence of which some wheel of industry is being lubricated which otherwise would be stuck fast? Otherwise would a box of mortar shells be arriving at the front with an empty space containing only a sad little note to the effect that the citizens whose abstinence might have filled this space went to a football game instead?

But abstinence is not the only act of piety which is signalized today by use of the verb "to earn." In a strictly contemporary spirit the September 30, 1966, issue of *Time* referred to a distinguished American as having ". . . earned more than $1,000,000 by short-selling in 1929–30." In dedicating his hard-earned dollars to this cause this citizen was of course helping to turn the market, which indeed did eventually turn.

The point I am struggling to make is this. In all these matters, even including the wages of labor, we are dealing not with opaque matters of fact but with the luminosities of spiritual conjecture. This is not to say they are

Hazlitt for taking "the vastly simplified postulates that are legitimate and necessary for the first stage of economic analysis—but which should never be taken as describing reality, and still less as normative" and, as Hazlitt does, treating them "as universal ideals."

nonsense. The mores and *manas* of any culture make very good sense indeed to the people who are governed by them. John Locke was a notably practical man. His *Two Treatises Concerning Government* were written for the very practical purpose of justifying the "glorious revolution" of 1688; and when, in the course of those essays, he undertook to provide a solid ideological foundation for the propertied class which had now in effect supplanted the British monarchy, the most potent magic he could conjure up was that of the honest sweat of labor. If, as he argued, the rights of property were established when man mixed his perspiration with the soil, what could possibly be said against them?

The truth is, of course, that involuntary servitude has been the fate of mankind since the beginning of time. This does not mean that the yoke of cultural tradition has been a galling one. Generally speaking, men have endured the discomforts and inconveniences of their way of life because it has offered some measure of security and satisfaction and because no better way of life seemed to be open to them. For example, it would surely be a mistake to suppose that the lower orders of feudal society, the bulk of the population, endured the brass collar of involuntary servitude (so vividly described in *Ivanhoe*) for centuries in a state of smoldering and barely arrested mutiny. It was only when the early medieval towns provided a sanctuary to freedmen, that escape from involuntary servitude became the *beau idéal* of modern Western civilization.

This is the magic with which we conjure when we talk about the gains of speculators as being "earned," and about "capital" as being "productive" in the same sense that labor is. All such propositions are imputations of magic potency and would be instantly recognizable as such by all of us except for the fact that they are figments of the system of make-believe to which we all have been emotionally conditioned all our lives.

Since we know this, our situation is very different from that of John Locke and his contemporaries or even that of Adam Smith and his contemporaries. Although we know it quite well, it is easy to forget how great the difference is. We have lived all our lives in a world that takes absolutely for granted the evolutionary origin and zoological character of the human species: so much so that when Veblen declares that the classical principles of economics are "pre-Darwinian," we greet that aspersion with shocked incredulity. How can the concepts we still use be "pre-Darwinian" since we, who still use them, live far down the slope on the near side of the great evolutionary watershed? We know as well as anyone that *Homo sapiens* evolved from earlier species by the same process of mutation and natural selection that produced the whale and the elephant. But, we say, what has this to do with such concepts as "productivity"—or, for that matter, Locke's property itself? And the answer is: More than we ordinarily suppose, since it involves that whole universe of discourse in which we operate.

Except within the confines of the tribal belief, there is no such thing as "inalienable rights"—of capital, or labor, or any other component of society. In every society such "rights" derive from the mythology of agency, which is implicit in the system of beliefs to which the people of that society are emotionally conditioned, beginning in early childhood. As a matter of fact, whatever any society accomplishes—however it gets its living and otherwise maintains itself—is a causal consequence of the functioning of that society as a whole. This is what anthropologists mean by insisting that all cultures can be understood only as functioning wholes. But the beliefs, to which all peoples are addicted, deviate widely from matters of fact, even from facts of common observation. This is the anomaly to which Samuel Butler referred when he represented the Erewhonians as insisting that all transactions were brought about by the exchange of the currency of the "musical banks," even though everybody knew that the actual causal process was quite different. This, too, is what Veblen meant by insisting (in his double essay "On the Nature of Capital" and elsewhere) that the achievements of industrial society are due to the combined efforts of the entire community and its entire culture, and that any proposal to assign agency to any particular individuals or functions is nonsense.

It is not true that, as Proudhon said, "Property is theft!" but it is true that all property rights derive from the culture which defines and honors them. So do the rights of common labor, and so also do the rights of those who perform what John Bates Clark called "the co-ordinating function." This does not mean that culturally defined rights, privileges, and obligations are utterly nonsensical, in our society, or in any other. Whatever the mythology in terms of which rights and obligations are purportedly justified, neither the myths nor the social functions they define can be utterly irrational and obstructive: if they were, the community in question would disappear. They must be sufficiently permissive to allow the community to get its living by whatever profane means it has.

Such permissiveness may be of vital importance. Few historians would maintain that the rights of freedmen in medieval towns were devised to facilitate the growth of modern industry, or that the rights of transfer of title to hitherto entailed property were dreamed up by medieval geniuses for this same purpose. It just so happened that the freedmen were able to find juridical means to make good their escape from feudal serfdom. The ancient tradition of Roman citizenship may have helped, as Roman law may have contributed to the establishment of the rights of property. Whatever their sources these institutions did fit the requirements of emerging industry to a remarkable degree—to the very great advantage of the Western peoples and eventually perhaps the world.

I repeat: This does not mean that the institutions which have accompanied the rise of modern industry were designed for the purpose of facilitating that growth. Like all institutions, they sought to preserve ancient verities and time-honored traditions. By continuing to repeat the slogan, "A man's home is his castle," we remind ourselves that private property is an institution of medieval origin, and that its sanction derives from the past, not from the efficient operation of the industrial economy by which we now live.

In taking this line I do not mean to advocate immediate and wholesale revolution. The distribution of wealth and income is a matter too vast and complex to be encompassed by any economic planner, however wise and erudite, since it is coextensive with civilization itself, of which any economic plan can be no more than a minor and occasional manifestation. But it is the responsibility of scholars to know this. As scholars, we economists have a responsibility to understand something of the nature and functioning of the ideology of our own society, and to convey this knowledge to the intellectually less advantaged community.

This is our ideological responsibility. It is not true that free competition "tends to give" the various elements in organized society what they personally "create." Economists should know better than anyone else that no one creates anything except as a participant in the culture he shares with all the other members of the community, and that it is utterly impossible to determine how different the future of his society would have been if he had never been born. Better than anyone else economists should know that price theory is tautological: that we know what the various participants in our economy "create" only insofar as this is "revealed" by what they get. There is no independent gauge.

As every economist knows, the basic truth is that in our society, as in medieval and ancient societies, the upper classes get more than the lower classes. It is true also, and of vital importance, that the class structure of modern industrial society is very much more fluid than its forebears were. But it is also true that in our society, as in all others, the official ideology acts as a brake on social change and even on technological progress. It does so very simply by enshrining the past: by convincing the community, through the emotional conditioning of children as well as the intellectual bamboozling of the adult community, that the established ways are right and true and best.

This is a complex process. In all societies it involves the self-bamboozling of the intellectual elite. We have no knowledge of any society which has come into existence through a deliberate and conscious conspiracy of the intellectual elite to enslave simple and stupid masses. Always what the masses are taught to believe is already believed sincerely and devoutly by their mentors, and for the reasons given to all by the tribal traditions of which the elite are inheritors no less than the masses. This is the role of what Professor Galbraith has aptly called "the conventional wisdom." Adam Smith, by common consent the founder of our discipline, assumed a society in which the institution of property played a major role. That is, he assumed a class-stratified society, with ownership as the principal agent of stratification; and assuming this he undertook to show how buying and selling in the market would give effect to such a system, so that each participant, without giving any thought to the structure of society and the means of its preservation, would be "led by an invisible hand to promote an end which was not part of his intention."

In all fairness we must recognize that the preservation of the traditionally stratified order of society was no part of the conscious intention of Adam

Smith, nor of John Bates Clark, nor of Professor Knight. But such in fact is the result. Here we are, struggling to free ourselves from the shackles of the past, and we are still teaching our children that we owe all the triumphs of our advanced industrial economy to "free private enterprise," although even the children must see that the first thing we do when confronted with a major crisis, such as war or depression, is to abandon free enterprise and do our best to implement our (now clear) intentions.

What, then, should we do now? Professor Knight chides Henry Hazlitt for proposing to act on "the vastly simplified postulates that are legitimate and necessary for the first stage of economic analysis—but which should never be taken as describing reality, and still less as normative." One normative conclusion is that since economic analysis should never be taken as describing reality, and since presumably it is economic reality with which we wish to deal, we had better abandon this so-called analysis completely and forthwith. But this is a negative proposal, which therefore helps us not at all to clarify our intentions, let alone to realize them.

What are our intentions with regard to what reality? The whole theory of imputation—the imputation of causal efficacy (or ceremonial potency) to the so-called factors of production—is a distributive formula. The idea is that what people receive should be determined by what they produce, either by their own sweat or by some spiritual perspiration or other psychic output. Basically, this idea was a good one. Its intention was to stimulate production; and since production is the limiting factor, successful stimulation of production would increase the well-being of the community virtually by definition. The basic flaw in the whole theory lay in its misconception of the process of production.

What keeps the modern Western community alive and kicking is neither capital nor labor but advanced industrial technology. The physical apparatus of modern society, from which we derive food, clothing, shelter, communication, and physical mobility both local and worldwide, is not the product of sweat or abstinence or any combination of the two. It is the product of invention and discovery, science and technology. Universal, and therefore familiar, as this process is throughout the Western world, we have no single name for it. In one aspect it is a matter of physical tools, materials, and apparatus of all sorts. In another no less significant aspect it is a matter of knowledge, understanding of the materials, tools, and instruments, and generalization from the instruments to the physical universe itself. In still another, closely related to both of these, it is intellectual communication: the process by which the burgeoning material culture of the West spread like a lethal epidemic throughout the West, and now throughout the world.

This process, by which Western civilization was so quickly differentiated from all the rest of the world and from the whole of man's previous experience, began far back in our history. It may be that the situation and cultural posture of the Western peoples even as they emerged from the Roman Empire had already set them on a path no other people had as yet traversed. The journey along that path seems to have begun in what used to be called "the

Dark Ages," dark chiefly because, in the modern sense of the phrase, we "couldn't see" them. In fact, as scholars like Richard Lefebvre des Noëttes and Lynn White have established, a technological revolution had already begun in Western Europe something like a thousand years before Arnold Toynbee's "Industrial Revolution of the Eighteenth Century in England." Lynn White even declares that in terms of the discovery of basic principles the four centuries preceding Leonardo were more important than the four centuries that followed.

As everyone knows, this process is still going on, indeed faster and farther than ever. By common consent, the principal agent of change today is research and development. Or is it general, if not universal, education? Or is it the virtual disappearance from among the Western peoples of such cultural impediments as retarded the study of medicine, and indeed all the "life sciences" only a few generations ago: opposition to "vivi-section" and even to the dissection of human bodies?

In a sense "R & D" is going on everywhere today. There must be hundreds of thousands of young Americans now living who are electronics "hams," or "hot-rodders," or amateurs of some similar scientific or technological profession. Consider that if there is one in every two hundred of the population—an estimate which is by no means unlikely—there are a million altogether. Veblen insisted that economic development is the work of whole communities such as this.

If, then, we mean to distribute the benefits of industrial society in such a way as to further this process and thereby insure the continuance and growth of our society, agencies such as these should receive a generous share of the Gross National Product. Such was the intent of the classical theory. The "productivity" theory of distribution itself was a "creative" theory based on the presumption that the free market would assign or at least "tend" to assign to each "factor of production" what it "creates," thereby of course encouraging it to create more. That system of allocation has not been utterly disastrous. Obviously industrial revolution has flourished under this regime, far more, at least, than it did or could have done under feudalism or ancient despotism. But is this enough? Assuming that the market system is not utterly fallacious in theory or utterly intolerable in practice, is it sufficiently close to the truth in theory, or in actual practice sufficiently creative? Clearly the answer is negative on both accounts. We have never been satisfied to entrust our fate to the market unreservedly. For example, we realized long ago that universal (except for Negroes), free, compulsory education is a precondition of industrial progress. It is also, in the words of Sam Houston, "essential to the preservation of a free government," which is likewise a precondition of industrial progress. This is the precedent we should seek to follow.

To a degree we are already doing so. Certainly education is one of our chief concerns. The decades following World War II have been marked by a general quickening of concern for the quality and extent of education. For obvious reasons this concern has centered on scientific education. But it has spilled over in all directions. I am not one of those who worry about the fate of the humanities in a science-dominated culture. If the humanities really do make a significant contribution to civilization, civilized men will recognize it; and I think they do. For example, no part of our curriculum has received greater stimulus from recent events than language study.

Another significant development has been the progressive lowering of the barriers which have served to exclude substantial parts of the community from participation in the technological revolution. After all, half the population is female; and if we assume that woman's place is in the home, whereas our cultural frontier is the laboratory and the machine shop, we are perpetuating an institutional impediment which has come down to us from our primeval past. The same is true of racial barriers. It used to be assumed that only people with white (or rather, "flesh-colored") skins could build and operate machines. That is no longer arguable. The truth is that, within the limits of individual "talent," anybody can learn to play the piano; anybody can learn to operate a digital computer; and anybody can learn to operate an electron microscope. Hence any arbitrary exclusion is a cultural disaster.

These are not mere matters of humanitarianism. I mention them because although we have been doing the right things, we have quite generally done them for the wrong reasons. Humanitarianism is admirable, but stupid; and there is a real danger that we may be making a similar mistake with regard to "human resources" and "human capital." What is really significant in both areas is the removal of institutional barriers to the creativity of technological process. Human beings are not "resources," to be mined or otherwise harvested, and they are not "capital," to be owned and invested—even by themselves. It is the cultural process in which people are participants (or non-participants) which is relevant and significant. Understanding of that process and ideological candor with regard to it are important because what is at stake is nothing less than the life process of mankind.

Let me, by way of summary, try and state my thesis another way. In doing so may I recall again Edwin Cannan's two problems, which I have quoted so often as comprising the best definition of economics which I have ever found: why all of us taken together are as well off or as ill off as we are, and why some are better off and others worse off than the average. As we now stand, two-thirds of the way through the twentieth century, it seems clear that what determines how well off any community may be is its science and industrial arts—the knowledge and skills possessed by that community; and the reason some elements of the community are better off, or worse off, than others is to be found in the institutions by which that community is structured. These two conditions of course affect each other. A rigid and "time-honored" institutional structure will of course resist change and inhibit the growth of knowledge and skills; and a condition of chronic intellectual and technological revolution prevents institutional rigidity and induces institutional obsolescence.

As everyone knows, the latter condition has prevailed to a steadily increasing degree in Western civilization for several centuries. However, institutionalized superstitions die hard. In every society the prevailing degree of well-being is credited to the Defenders of the Faith and, in Veblen's phrase, "anointed keepers of the code." In the Middle Ages these were, of course, the feudal and ecclesiastical nobility. By the eighteenth century these gentry had largely disappeared from the scene and their place had been taken by a financial aristocracy. The doctrine which imputes creative potency to the factors of production (from which land has disappeared with the landed aristocracy while "the co-ordinating function" hails the arrival of corporate managers) is of course a myth appropriate to this condition.

As such it is already obsolete. Scarcely anybody believes it any more, since today everybody knows that all of us taken together are as well off as we are—and we are far better off than mankind has ever been before—not because of the anguished sweat of laborers or the abstinence or prudence of investors and not even because of the adroitness of managers in effecting tax-avoiding mergers, but because of the amazing discoveries which have become common knowledge and the almost incredible potency of instruments that are now in common use. We are all so well off that we are quite content to let the institutional system ride. After all it is not very ancient, and its ideology is not altogether archaic. How much easier it is to supplement the incomes of those who are worse off than to confiscate the fortunes of those who are better off than anybody has any business to be! Thus we are limning the Welfare State.

Now the Welfare State is a delightful creation. As a place to live it beats anything mankind has ever known. But as an idea it leaves something to be desired. All its emphasis is on distribution and consumption, and it is our ideological responsibility as students to recognize this defect. The defect may be only ideological. It may prove that a happy, healthy, and well-informed community is a superbly productive community: that when no one is very much worse off or better off than the common run, all will be more industrious and efficient than any previous community has even been. Nevertheless we must not rely on happenstance. Our ideal is—or should be—the Creative State, or the Creative Society. We favor the Welfare State because it tends to give the whole community what the whole community creates, and in doing so gives the community the greatest possible encouragement to create more, so that all of us taken together will be better off than anybody has ever been before. Thus the Welfare State is the working model of the Creative Society.

3

Neoinstitutionalism and the Economics of Dissent

Allan G. Gruchy

It is a pleasure to bring the honor of serving as President of the Association for Evolutionary Economics to a close with the opportunity to discuss some of the intellectual currents running through our Association. Since the Association is a very young organization, its future is quite naturally a matter of very great concern to all of us. I am not going to attempt to predict the future of our Association. However, I know that it was in the minds of its founders, when they came together in Washington, D. C., nine years ago, that this Association should have a unique function to perform—one not performed by old line economic associations. However otherwise this unique function may be described, it is clearly that of providing an outlet for economic dissent—dissent from what goes under the heading of conventional or standard economics.

If ever there was a fortunate coincidence, it was that the Association for Evolutionary Economics was organized at a time when dissent in many fields was running high. It is my conviction that this Association has a golden opportunity to provide a forum for economic dissenters at a time when old line economic associations and the economics profession in general are not providing the intellectual leadership called for by the times. Economic dissenters like Clarence E. Ayres, John K. Galbraith, Gunnar Myrdal, Adolph Lowe, Gerhard Colm, and others of a similar intellectual bent assert that conventional economics, as one sees it in standard economics textbooks and advanced economic writings, is hobbled with an excessively narrow view of the science of economics that concentrates on means and not ends; on inputs and not outputs; and on efficiency without asking the question of efficiency for what? The economics profession today directs its main energy to turning out technicians of knowledge who are experts in optimizing the decision-making process, but who do not display much concern for the purposes or goals of this decision-making. Our successful conventional economics textbook writers, following Lionel Robbins with his vintage 1925 definition of economic science, have given wide circulation to the idea that economics is concerned primarily with means and not with ends. It is not surprising then that in the current era of great crisis with respect to goals or values, conventional economics, having little to say about such ends, has become quite irrelevant to much of what concerns the man on the street or the student on the college campus. If ever there was a need to make economics a more relevant science, that need is now pressing for attention. Meeting this need is the aim of the economic dissent coming from Ayres, Galbraith, Myrdal, and other critics of conventional economics.

These dissenting economists, as scientists, do not propose to tell the people what goals they should seek to achieve. However, they do propose to explain to the people how their wants or goals come into being, how these wants are greatly influenced by the large industrial corporations, how collective wants in the public sector are frequently unmet because there are no strong lobbying forces at work in the public sector promoting these collective wants, how obstacles are placed in the path of meeting wants not catered to by the private market place, how the failure of the private sector to take full account of all social costs not only lowers the quality of life but also indirectly lowers the productivity of labor, and how our archaic governmental system is unprepared today to take a comprehensive view of national needs or to take the necessary steps with the cooperation of the public to make sure that these national needs are assigned proper priority.

Economic dissent falls into two categories. There are first those dissenters who criticize the way that the current economic system operates and who disapprove of many of the consequences of these operations. These dissenters usually operate outside the academic world and do not concern themselves with the inadequacies of standard or conventional economics. I am referring to such dissenters as Michael Harrington, Vance Packard, Ralph Nader, William H. Whyte, David Bazelon, and even Rachel Carson, who wondered if the day would come when our chemical companies would have achieved the miracle of a "silent spring." These dissenters have vividly and forcefully called attention to our noisy, dirty, and ugly cities, to the pollution of air and water, to the destruction of our heritage of buildings and urban areas of great historical significance, to the need to preserve the last landscape, and to the spread of what one critic has called the "materialistic Babbitism" of our affluent society.

The second group of economic dissenters is comprised of the academic world whose main concern is the inadequacies of conventional economics. Academic dissenters range from those at one end of the scale who simply want somehow to make standard economics more realistic to those at the other end of the scales who would reconstruct conventional economics into more social and less technical science. Those academic economic dissenters, who would be satisfied if conventional economics were made more realistic, argue that there should be more empirical feedback in the work of the conventional economic theorists so that conventional economic theory and economic practice would be more closely related. Dissent of this negative and unchallenging nature deplores the use of excessive abstraction and would like to see conventional economics shored up with the aid of more empirical studies.

Other economic dissenters in the academic world assert that conventional economics is too limited in scope, and that, since human problems are frequently more than economic in nature, an interdisciplinary approach is necessary if we are to tackle these problems successfully. The weaknesses or deficiencies of conventional economics are to be overcome not by reconstructing this economics, but by combining conventional economics with the other social sciences in the work of dealing with human problems. Those economic dissenters who merely want conventional economics to have more empirical feedback, or who would integrate conventional economics with the other social sciences in an interdisciplinary approach, present no basic challenge to conventional economics. This is so because the basics of conventional economics, as incorporated in its narrow definition of the nature and the scope of economic science, are left intact by the academic dissenters of the types just described.

There is a third and more fundamental type of academic economic dissent that is a distinct challenge to the view of economics held by standard or conventional economists. This type of dissent is positive and constructive in the sense that it challenges the view of economics cultivated by conventional economists and offers a different view of economics to replace that of the conventional economists. The economic dissenters who, I believe, present a constructive challenge to economic orthodoxy of both the Marshallian and Keynesian types include such well-known economists as Clarence E. Ayres, John K. Galbraith, Gunnar Myrdal, Gerhard Colm, and Adolph Lowe. Their economics I describe as neoinstitutional economics.

Perhaps some will think that I should apologize for calling attention to the institutionalist movement in economic thought. I know that in the minds of a majority of academic economists institutional economics is now regarded as something that has had its day and, as Professor Kenneth Boulding said a decade or so ago at one of these conventions, should now be placed among the museum exhibits. This attitude towards institutionalism was brought forcefully to my attention two years ago when I accidentally fell into the company of a young graduate student in economics from one of the most prestigious universities on the West Coast. Upon being introduced to me, this young student said that he was happy to shake my hand as he understood that I was the last of the institutionalists. I am sure that this young graduate was faithfully reproducing the views and opinions of the distinguished economics professors in that far western economics graduate school.

Whether or not this conventional view of institutional economics is wishful thinking—and I think it is—the fact remains that today we have a large body of economic thought that lies outside the boundaries of conventional economics. More than this it presents a significant challenge to conventional economics. My examination of the work of Ayres and others with a similar approach to economics leads me to the views that these critics of conventional economics are working in the institutionalist tradition, and that we can properly regard their work as basically an extension of the work of Veblen, Sombart, Hobson, Commons, Clark, Mitchell, and other heterodox economists of the first three decades of this century. However, the work of Galbraith, Colm, Lowe, and Myrdal is not the work of mere disciples. Thorstein Veblen has not cast his long shadow over these present-day institutionalists. None of these economists except for Ayres was influenced greatly in his formative years by Veblen and his work. For reasons to which I shall soon turn I prefer to call the work of current institutionalists "neoinstitutional economics" to distinguish it from the "old institutionalism" of Veblen.

The intellectual image that Veblen presented is significantly different from the image presented by the neoinstitutionalists. Veblen gave the impression that he would dispense with the inherited analytical or marginalist economics of his time, and that the mechanics or technics of economic decision-making would have no place in his technocratic regime of workmanship of the future. Also, Veblen did not clearly indicate what he thought were his own theoretical contributions with the result that both he and later institutionalists were criticized on the ground that they had not only dispensed with conventional economic theory, but had also put nothing in its place. Furthermore, Veblen's emphasis on the discipline of the machine process opened him to the criticism made by the conventional economists that his work was adversely affected by the acceptance of an untenable technological determinism.

The view that Veblen was an unsophisticated technocrat with little regard for the niceties of standard economic theory persists to this very day. As recently as 1968 Raymond Aron asserted that "Veblen made the mistake of thinking that the industrial order—the order of production—was sufficient unto itself," and was not subject "to the requirements of economic calculation."[1] Whether or not these views concerning the work of Veblen are well-founded—and I believe that they are not—they continue to find widespread acceptance among conventional economists. Such criticisms, however, cannot be made against the neoinstitutionalists, since they have been careful to avoid opening themselves to the criticisms to which Veblen has been subjected. The neoinstitutionalists cannot be described as anti-theoretical technocrats; they do not dispense with the basic building blocks of standard economic theory; and they avoid what is alleged to be Veblen's technological determinism. What the neoinstitutionalists do is to round out the standard or conventional economics of our time by making economics less of a technical and more of a social science. Of special importance in this connection is the neoinstitutionalists's theory of the modern industrial system with its central concept of the logic of the process of industrialization.

The neoinstitutionalists very clearly state that they have taken much

[1]Aron, Raymond, *Progress and Disillusion,* 1968, p. 187.

from the work of standard economists of the past and the present. Ayres, for example, explains in *The Industrial Society*: "This is not to say that all the inquiries of all the economists have been a complete waste of time. . . . The investigations of economists have given us a wealth of knowledge of price relationships the effect of which is to show how the various economic activities affect each other. All this is of great value."[2] Galbraith tells us in *The New Industrial State,* in referring to the work of standard economists, "I have drawn on their work, quantitative and qualitative, at every stage; I could not have written without their prior efforts."[3] Likewise François Perroux in his article on the domination effect of large industrial corporations informs us that his excursions beyond conventional economics involve no disavowal of standard economic theory.[4] Rather than dispense entirely with conventional economics, the neoinstitutionalists accept it for what it is worth, and then go beyond it to develop a broader economics which is concerned not only with decision-making in the market place, but also with the guidance of the larger evolving economic system. It is precisely at this point that the neoinstitutionalists part company with the conventional economists. The neoinstitutionalists have a larger view of economic reality which leads them to believe that their version of economics is much more relevant to the major problems of our time.

The contrast between the conventional economists and neoinstitutional economists is quite clearly indicated by inquiring into what these two types of economists think economics is all about. The conventional line, as presented in some of our most successful economics textbooks, is that, there is no consumer problem, since, as Professor Paul Samuelson puts it, "What things will be produced is determined by the votes of consumers . . . every day in their decisions to purchase this item or that."[5] In other words, student readers of these textbooks are informed that the market mechanism ordinarily satisfies consumer wants, but does not create them even though we annually spend 17 billion dollars on advertising. Furthermore, from the conventional point of view, deviations from a perfectly competitive economic system can be taken care of adequately by appropriate antitrust measures and various forms of the public regulation of industry. Since the allocation of resources in our mixed enterprise system is said to present no real problem, the only big issue is the rate of economic growth or the annual increase in real gross national product. According to conventional economists there is nothing like increases in gross national product to measure an economy's performance. Professor

[2]Ayres, Clarence E., *The Industrial Economy,* 1952, p. 36.

[3]Galbraith, John Kenneth, *The New Industrial State,* 1967, p. 402.

[4]Perroux, Francois, "The Domination Effect and Modern Economic Theory," *Social Research,* Vol. 17, No. 2, June 1950, p. 188.

[5]Samuelson, Paul A., *Economics, An Introductory Analysis,* Sixth Edition, 1964, p. 40.

Campbell McConnell tells us in his widey read textbook that national income accounting "allows us to keep tab on the economic health of society. . . . It is generally agreed . . . that the best available indicator of an economy's health is its annual total output of goods and services."[6]

According to the neoinstitutionalists this view of the measure of an economy's health does not stand up under close scrutiny. This is so because the national income accounting that is presented in our most widely used economics textbooks is an incomplete and biased form of accounting. It takes note of all the "goods" produced, but leaves out what Joan Robinson has called "negative goods," or what Ezra J. Mishan in his study of *The Costs of Economic Growth* calls the "bads." We know why conventional national income accounting accounts only for "goods," and ignores "bads" or the social costs of economic growth. The answer is that "goods" can be quantified and measured in the market place, but "bads" in the form of social disamenities frequently cannot be quantified, and so do not appear in the market place. This "goods-bads" problem is readily handled by conventional economists largely by ignoring it. One very well-known conventional economist, who felt constrained to make at least some mention of the vital difference between pecuniary and real social costs in his textbook, calls the attention of his student readers to this problem in a footnote in an appendix to a chapter.

It is all so very clear to the conventional economist: every extra billion dollars's worth of gross national product marks a step forward toward a healthier economy. As Professor Samuelson explains, "Although [economic] growth presents challenges, the subject is really a cheerful one."[7] Of course this is an unfortunate case of circular reasoning. Economic health is measured in terms of gross national product, and an increase in gross national product is regarded as an improvement in economic health. According to Colm, Galbraith, Myrdal, and other neoinstitutionalists, conventional national income accounting as it is currently used is a poor device for measuring economic health. Economic health is not something that can always be quantified. It is a condition that can be approached or improved by creating some things and by not creating other things—by creating "goods" and by not creating "bads," with the people, led by protest groups and aided by technical experts, deciding what is a "good" and what is a "bad." The neoinstitutionalists would say that an affluent society is healthy when its resources are allocated in such a way as to create not only an abundance of goods and services, but also cities free from excessive noise, pollution, and ugliness where citizens have adequate leisure, when they are fully informed about the social costs of economic growth, when nature's balance is preserved, and when industrial technology is adjusted to mankind and not mankind to technology.

[6]McConnell, Campbell R., *Economics: Principles, Problems, and Policies,* Second Edition, 1963, p. 166.

[7]Samuelson, Paul A., p. 792.

Gunnar Myrdal speaks for the neoinstitutionalists when he states that the ultimate purpose of economics is to "find out where we are heading."[8] Or, in other words, whose goals does the economic system serve, and whose goals does it fail to serve? In Myrdal's opinion, and also that of other neoinstitutionalists, the ultimate purpose of economics is to provide an interpretation of the way in which the industrial system operates with respect to the satisfaction of personal and collective wants or goals. To put the matter simply, the contrast between conventional and neoinstitutional economics is a contrast between "market economics" and "systems economics."

The main issue today in the field of economics, in the opinion of the neoinstitutionalists, is not "efficiency," but rather it is wants, goals, or values. In the past few decades standard economists have made great strides in developing the theory of optimizing or economizing. The theory of economic decision-making has been improved by important advances in both mathematical economics and econometrics. While economizing the use of scarce resources or inputs will always be a matter of great importance to all economists and to the general public, economizing or optimizing the use of scarce resources is not what is of major importance today to a large part of the population in an affluent society. The main concern today of an important section of the general population in Western Europe and the United States is not how to use scarce inputs more efficiently, but how to get the economic system to serve the people by producing what they want, or would want if they were free agents, free from dominating influence of the large industrial corporations which control much of the press, radio, and television, and so are able to impose their scheme of values on the general public. There is a growing concern today with the following three value problems which are of great interest to the neoinstitutionalist critics of conventional economics: (1) to what extent are wants or goals in the private sector of the nation's economic system created by producers and not by consumers, with the result that consumers are induced to purchase a never-ending flow of consumer gadgets and other goods of doubtful private and social utility; (2) what obstacles are placed in the path of collective want determination in the public sector by forces working from out of the private sector, and by the archaic and ineffective institutional arrangements found in our public sector; and (3) to what extent does conventional economics ignore the social costs of economic growth in the form of external diseconomies such as air and water pollution, the spoilation of the natural environment, and the destruction of the nation's historical heritage by the bulldozer and the speculating land developer—all of which lower the quality of life.

The neoinstitutionalists observe that the economic system is a goal- or want-directed system. Individuals, groups, and classes participate in the activities of the economic system with the aim of securing their wants or

[8]Myrdal, Gunnar, *An International Economy, Problems and Prospects,* 1956, p. 314.

goals. The economic system is not a monolithic system or metaphysical entity which gives expression to some vague national interest that is supposed to be common to all individuals and groups. The American economic system is not a monolithic capitalist system. On the contrary, there is in the American economy the state capitalism of the public sector, the large-scale capitalism of the big business sector, and the small-scale, laissez-faire capitalism of small business and the farmers. The economy moves to a great extent in the direction of the goals of those individuals and groups who have enough power to influence the economy and guide it towards the satisfaction of their wants.

The neoinstitutionalists define economics to be the study of the evolving pattern of human relationships which is concerned with the disposal of scarce resources for the satisfaction of personal and collective wants. What the neoinstitutionalists do is to place economizing or economic decision-making within the framework of the evolving economic system. Since the economic sytem's ulitmate concern is with human wants or goals and how they are achieved, economizing is tied up with wants or goals; and the main question confronting economists should be optimizing or economizing for what purposes or goals.

The conventional economist precludes any analysis of the existing and emerging goals of individuals and groups and the question as to whether or not these wants are being achieved, by defining economics so as to exclude the wants or goals problem. Professor Samuelson, in defining economics, states, "As a science, economics can concern itself only with the best means of attaining given ends."[9] Professor McConnell has expressed the same view much more succinctly with the observation that economics is "the science of efficiency."[10] Duplicating Samuelson and McConnell, conventional economists reduce economics to the technical subject of economic decision-making or decision theory in which, as one specialist in decision theory recently explained, "Rationality, as decision theorists think of it, has nothing to do with what you want, but only with how you go about implementing your wants."[11] The conventional economist asserts that economists have no business inquiring into the nature or origins of human wants or goals, because people are said to know what they want and to cast dollar votes for what they want. In effect, what the conventional economist says is that the market mechanism is a want-serving or want-satisfying mechanism. The neoinstitutionalists disagree with the conventional view of the nature of the market mechanism and assert that in the modern industrial society the market mechanism is in many cases a want-creating mechanism. Consumers do not always freely

[9]Samuelson, Paul A., *Economics, An Introductory Analysis,* First Edition, 1948, p. 314.

[10]McConnell, Campbell R., p. 25.

[11]Ward, Edwards, "Decision Making," *International Encyclopedia of the Social Sciences,* Vol. 4, 1968, p. 35.

express what they want through dollar votes. Instead, they buy what the large corporations induce them to buy with the aid of advertising and high-pressure or subtle salesmanship.

According to Galbraith, Myrdal, Ayres and other critics of conventional economics, the social system, including the economic system, is an institutional arrangement by means of which people seek to achieve their wants. To the social scientist people are goal-creating, goal-possessing, and goal-achieving individuals, and the social sciences, including economics, are properly concerned with the goals or wants of people. Economic goals are data which can be documented, analyzed with regard to their origins and what influences have shaped them, the conflicts among these goals, their impact on the nation's production and distribution systems, and what aids or militates against their being achieved. These goals can be treated objectively, and the scientific method can be applied to them in the sense that generalizations can be made about them. There is nothing normative about any such want or goal analysis. What is being done is to widen the scope of economic analysis to include studies of existing means and existing economic goals and their interrelationships. It is for this reason that Ayres states, "Economics is nothing if it is not a science of value."[12]

When the neoinstitutionalists, along with Ayres, state that economics is a science not of efficiency but of values, they are not raising any normative issues in the form of what "ought" to be. What they do say is that economics, viewed not as a technical but as a social science, deals with the material aspects of values or wants. The economist as a social scientist is concerned not with efficiency alone, but with efficiency in relation to the wants of the individuals and groups operating within the evolving economic system. These individuals and groups are interested in such wants as economic abundance, economic freedom, economic security, economic justice, and economic quality. The economist as a social scientist is interested in explaining how the evolving industrial system supplies these wants or does not provide them, how these wants may be achieved with the use of scarce resources, how individuals and groups are in conflict with regard to whose wants should be assigned a high priority, and how conflicts with regard to the satisfaction of wants may be reduced or eliminated.

In an affluent society consideration of people's wants or goals may take precedence over considerations of economic efficiency. A rich nation can afford at times to be somewhat inefficient if this inefficiency preserves wants or values that would be destroyed by asking for the utmost in efficiency. It may be more efficient to string power lines between poles rather than to place them underground, to put a transmission line through a Civil War battlefield rather than around it, to put a super highway through a wilderness area rather than around it, or to put former slum dwellers in unlivable 15-storied tenement buildings rather than in livable low-lying

[12]Ayres, Clarence E., *The Theory of Economic Progress,* 1944, p. 208.

garden apartments—but in an affluent society these efficiencies in the opinion of many protest groups are not worth the price in human disamenities.

The difference between the conventional view of economics as a narrow study of economic decision-making and the neoinstitutionalist view of economics as a broad study of the evolving goal-directed economic system is also the difference between a short-run view and a long-run view of the economic system. Gunnar Myrdal has severely criticized conventional economists on the ground that they are nearsighted and without a long-range view of the development of the industrial system. He tells us in the *Challenge to Affluence* that among "the things that have not changed in America and specifically in Washington during different administrations is . . . a general tendency to nearsightedness among both politicians and [economic] experts. . . . There are today an astonishing number of people in the United States who can offhand give a detailed and comprehensive analysis in quantitative terms of what is just now happening [in the business world], how all important economic indices have recently been moving, and how they are likely to move months ahead. Not only the President and Congress but also leaders in business are left without that intellectualized vision of what the future holds in store in regard to economic development in more general terms. But such a vision is needed for rational decision [-making]. . . . It is difficult to avoid the reflection that the neglect by government agencies as well as by American universities and other research institutions of the long range aspects of the American economy as a whole and the undue concentration on short-range issues . . . on timeless and by any standards less important terminological questions and unworldly [theoretical] constructs . . . all this is partly responsible for the failure of . . . economists to disseminate more economic understanding among the American people."[13]

When the economist takes a long view of the economy, he necessarily views the economy as an evolving system. The question then arises, can one develop a theory of the evolving economic system? The answer of Ayres, Galbraith and Myrdal to this question is that the evolving industrial system can be explained with the aid of the concept of the logic of the process of industrialization. The neoinstitutionalists would be the first to say that, while there are no universal economic laws governing the course of industrialization, the process of industrialization is not a haphazard, utterly random process which follows no discernible path. The neoinstitutionalists assert that there is a logic or pattern running through the process of industrialization. Clark Kerr has explained in *Industrialism and the Industrial Man* that there is a "pure logic of the industrial process" which reveals the inherent tendencies of this process. Kerr goes on to explain that: "Given the character of science and technology and the requirements inherent in modern methods of production and distribution," we may

[13]Myrdal, Gunnar, *Challenge to Affluence,* 1962, pp. 87-88.

deduce the likely characteristics and path of the evolving industrial system.[14] To the neoinstitutionalist, if not to the conventional economist, the general features of the process of industrialization are clear. These features constitute a pattern or logic through which all mature industrial nations have passed or are passing. The logic of the process of industrialization points in the direction of an urbanized society, a decline of the free competitive market, the rise of a large public sector, the separation of the managers and the managed, the emergence of conflicting economic power groups, the elevation of natural science over social science, and the development of the government as an agent mediating among conflicting economic power groups and providing guidance for the evolving economy.

The concept of the logic of the process of industrialization lies between the universal laws of pure economics and mere description. It is an explanatory device that finds a place for both quantitative and qualitative factors in explaining the nature and functioning of the modern industrial system. Conventional economists have no place in their analyses for the concept of the logic of industrialization, because by definition they exclude from economic analysis all consideration of the impact of technological change on the structure and functioning of the economy. They agree with Lionel Robbins who states that "Ends as such do not form part of this subject-matter [of economics]. Nor does the technical and social environment."[15]

The technological explosion works its way out very largely through the operations of the economic system; yet the conventional economists pay little attention to how this explosion is affecting both the economic decision-making process and the larger total economic process. The conventional economist can sit idly by without explaining how the technological revolution of the past few decades further urbanizes our society, clogs our roads and air lanes, pollutes our air and water, upsets the balance of nature, unites the nation with ribbons of concrete, dangerously raises the noise level of our environment, and fills our houses with a vast array of gadgets limited in number and variety only by the fertile and highly paid imagination of those in charge of the research and development departments of our large business corporations.

One of the major issues of today is who will harness the technological explosion, the large industrial corporation or the public as represented by the government? Who will plan the flow of technological change spurred on by scientific research, who will make certain that adequate account is taken of the social costs of technological progress, and how will the benefits of the technological revolution be shared? Will the contributions of scientific research be used largely to meet the commercial objectives of

[14]Kerr, Clark; Dunlop, John T.; Harbison, Frederick H.; and Myers, Charles A., *Industrialism and Industrial Man,* 1960, p. 33.

[15]Robbins, Lionel, *An Essay on the Nature and Significance of Economic Science,* Second Edition, 1935, p. 38.

industry or the welfare objectives of the general public? According to Galbraith, Ayres, Myrdal and other neoinstitutionalists modern industrial technology points in the direction of some form of national economic planning. Technology is a cultural imperative or "compulsion" that gives shape or pattern to the process of industrialization. As Galbraith puts it, "Technology, under all circumstances, leads to planning; in its higher manifestations it may put the problems of planning beyond the reach of the industrial firm."[16] In the opinion of the neoinstitutionalists it is no longer a question of planning or not planning, but what kind of planning and who will direct the planning. The neoinstitutionalists assert that it is up to economists to explain to the public the consequences of the alternatives of planning by private industry, or of planning by the government in cooperation with the nation's economic interest groups. Not much can be expected with regard to these issues from conventional economists, because their absorbing interest in the economics of decision-making prevents their viewing the economy as an evolving system, and also prevents their developing the long and comprehensive view necessary for analyzing the problems of a guided industrial society.

Simplistic conventional economics leads to simplistic economic policy proposals. When one looks at the superficiality of conventional economic analysis and all the important and complicating economic factors that it leaves out of account, it is not surprising that some conventional economists propose to solve our basic economic problems, as would Professor Milton Friedman and other monetarists, by simply making adjustments in the nation's supply of money relative to the changing size of the gross national product, while other simplists, the proponents of the so-called "new economics," propose to solve the same problems by simply altering tax rates in a countercyclical manner. The long, non-simplistic view of the economy held by the neoinstitutionalists suggests to them that complicated economic problems can probably be solved only in complicated ways. According to the neoinstitutionalists the "new economics" of the Kennedy and Johnson Administration can never successfully handle the long-term goals problem, because its main attention is on the employment and growth rates of tomorrow, not on the long-term national goals of the future. No one denies that full employment and rapid economic growth are important, short-run goals, but more important questions are full employment and rapid economic growth for what? It does not seem very rational to develop a finely-tuned economic engine without asking where it is going—without asking whether it is on the low road to commercialized affluence or on the high road to what Ayres calls a "reasonable society."

The industrialization process has not yet come to an end. We are now moving from an advanced industrial society to a post-industrial society. In the opinion of the neoinstitutionalists we are now entering a post-industrial era in which the economic power of the large industrial corporations

[16]Galbraith, John Kenneth, *Industrial State,* p. 20.

is being challenged by what George Kennan describes as "protest groups" which spearhead the development of public opinion and unite the weak economic interest groups. In the post-industrial society of the future the guidance of the economy will come less from the big business sector and more from the nation's educational, scientific, and artistic groups as well as from aroused citizens in general. The basic problem is, how will national priorities be determined in the post-industrial society? Before this problem can be met satisfactorily, new institutional arrangements will have to be made. We will have to substitute a new participatory democracy for our current outmoded ballot-box type of democracy which may have been adequate for the nineteenth century but which is obviously unable to cope with the problems raised by a technological society. It is now necessary to bring together representatives of all economic interest groups for the joint consideration of what should be the nation's economic and social priorities. Much progress along this line has been made in Western Europe where the United Kingdom has its National Economic Development Council, the Netherlands its Economic and Social Council, and Sweden, France, Belgium and other countries their similar joint councils.

There is no major nation so ill prepared as the United States to cope with the problem of determining national economic and social priorities. Although the Employment Act of 1946 opens the doors to the possibility of joint consultation by representatives from major economic interest groups, the Council of Economic Advisers under all administrations has consistently refused to provide for any such joint consultation, preferring to approach each interest group, if at all, on a separate basis. Consequently, national priority determination in the United States has become a running contest between the Office of the President with his troika or quadriad of governmental advisers and the Congress. The group that should provide a bridge between the President and the Congress, namely the presidential cabinet, is conspicuous for its docility and the infrequency of its meetings. The Congress has no adequate way of comparing and analyzing the nation's total resources and total needs, since, unlike most legislative bodies in Western Europe, it does not have presented to it for its consideration any annual and long-term national economic budgets of the kind recommended by Gerhard Colm, Gunnar Myrdal, Adolph Lowe, and François Perroux. In this connection the Congress does not lack the power to determine national priorities. What it does lack is an effective way of determining these priorities.

The New York *Times* recently reported that President-elect Nixon had said that national priorities are determined in the White House. This is a gross and misleading oversimplification of the national priorites problem. In fact national priorities are determined in part in the White House, but also in the Congress, in the large business enterprises, in the trade unions, increasingly in the ghettos, and elsewhere. Each economic interest group is out more or less on its own to advocate the acceptance of its own goals as something worthy of high priority consideration. But there are no well-established institutional arrangements for getting these various competing economic interest groups together for joint consultation with regard to the determination of national priorities. What we have in operation today in the United States is the outmoded advocacy concept of national priority determination which provides no adequate method of communication between the many economic interest groups at the bottom and the Congress at the top. This is an archaic way of determination national priorities that is more appropriate to the nineteenth than to the twentieth century. The neoinstitutionalists point out that the national priority determining process needs to be modernized, and related more effectively to the needs of our emerging participatory democracy. The lag between our political institutions and the rapidly changing industrial technology will have to be eliminated, before we can succeed in domesticating the technological revolution and in planning for the achievement of a life of high quality.

We can anticipate three criticisms levelled against neoinstitutional economies by conventional economists. The standard bearers of conventional economics will assert (1) that the neoinstitutionalists have made no theoretical contributions, (2) that, in assigning an imperative or compulsive character to industrial technology, the neoinstitutionalists are guilty of the sin of technological determinism, and (3) that the neoinstitutionalists, by raising the issue of wants, goals, or values, have become bogged down in normative considerations and so cannot qualify as scientists. These criticisms have been presented many times in the past, and will doubtlessly be dredged up again. If the conventional economists wish to continue to deny the validity of the concept of the logic of the process of industrialization, if they wish to deny that industrial technology is an imperative or compulsive force having much to do with the structure and functioning of our evolving industrial society, if they wish to deny that existing economic wants or goals of individuals and groups may be treated as scientific data, they are quite free to do so. But in the opinion of the neoinstitutionalists the conventional economists can do so only at the cost of keeping standard economics narrow and irrelevant with respect to much that is significant in the modern economic world.

I would like to conclude this discussion of neoinstitutionalism, the only significant academic economics of dissent in my opinion, by saying that we need both economic technicians or specialists and also what the Union for Radical Political Economists—an organization made up largely of disturbed graduate students in economics in our most prestigious universities of the northeast and far west—has described as "economic social scientists." I am fully aware of the important progress made in recent years in developing the theory and practice of economic decision-making. I am well aware of the contributions along the lines of econometric model building, linear programming, game theory, cost-benefit analysis, cost effectiveness studies, sampling theory and techniques, input-output analysis, and welfare economics with its emphasis on Paretian optimality. While this progress in the field of economic decision making has enabled us to manage ourselves more efficiently, it does not tell us whether we are moving toward Paradise or Purgatory.

While I would certainly not close the door on economic technicians, I would say that these specialists are not the best prepared to present economics as a social science in written form or on the lecture platform to the general public, or to young students who are coming for the first time to the study of economics. Also, it is my position that the general public and the political and other leaders of public opinion should see economics not through the eyes of the economic technician, but through the eyes of the economist as a social scientist.

What the neoinstitutionalists object to is not so much what is found in our widely used standard economics textbooks, but rather to what is left out of them. It was to meet these deficiencies in conventional economics that Galbraith wrote *The Affluent Society* and *The New Industrial State;* that Myrdal wrote the *Challenge to Affluence* and *Beyond the Welfare State;* and that Ayres wrote *The Theory of Economic Progress* and *Toward a Reasonable Society.* On a more popular level the Michael Harringtons, Vance Packards, William H. Whytes, David Bazelons, Bernard Nossiters, and Rachel Carsons have sought to offset the irrelevance of conventional economics by showing the public how the quality of economic life is being lowered in this age of affluence. Without these and many other economic dissenters whom I have not mentioned, economics would be still more of an irrelevant science than it now is—that is to say, irrelevant not to economic decision-making, but to issues relating to the creation and achievement of private and public economic wants, without a discussion of which economic decision-making becomes a routine without much social significance.

I would not like to close this discussion on a somewhat sour note. Neoinstitutionalists are by nature pessimistic optimists. While they are pessimistic about the immediate future, they are nevertheless sustained by a deep optimism with regard to the long-run possibility of making economics a social science that is highly relevant to the major issues not only of our time, but also of the emerging future. It is my conviction, and I believe the conviction of those unconventional economists whom I have called neoinstitutionalists, that economics will increasingly come to have more concern with what people think is the Good Society, and less concern with efficiently making decisions but never asking what the decisions are really about.

4

Causality and Consciousness in Economics: Concepts of Change in Orthodox and Heterodox Economics

Kurt Dopfer

Institutionalists have always considered causality a central concept of economics and have added weight to the theoretical orientation by contrasting the neo-classical concept of linear causality with the sophisticated and realistic concept of circular and cumulative causation pioneered by Thorstein Veblen [1898]. Neoclassical economists have not only failed to give further ontic and theoretical profile to their causality concept but have also tended to reject it altogether as a basis upon which an analysis of economic processes could be built. Bertrand Russel's insistence that the causality concept was "humbug" has left a deep impression on those economists who were prepared to derive from an axiomatic treatment the ultimate scientific status of economic theory. Thus, institutional economics, with its concept of circular and cumulative causation, is opposed to orthodox economics, where causality is considered redundant or methodologically impeding, and, where if it enters the scene at all, is given a deterministic interpretation which robs it of its original substance. The differences in the causality concepts of orthodox and heterodox economics are profound—and where there is smoke there must also be fire.

Given the mixed attitude of neo-classical economists toward causality, one is grateful for the linguistic help they provide when talking about "causal" models. In his *Foundations of Economic Analysis,* P.A. Samuelson defines a causal system as one "whose behavior is determined by initial conditions . . . in such a way that its behavior depends only upon the time which has elapsed since the establishment of such initial conditions. That is to say the specification of similar given initial conditions at a later period of time would result in a similar evolution of the system . . . at a . . . later time period" [Samuelson 1947, p. 317]. A "causal-deterministic" path has the solution

$$x = f(t - t^{\circ}; \bar{x}(t^{\circ}))$$

where $\bar{x}$ stands for the initial conditions at time t° and $\bar{x}$ and x for a finite or even infinite set of economic variables.

It is easy to recognize the classical world of Galileo and Newton in this formula. The self-justification with which the causality concept of classical physics is transferred to economics can be understood only if it is considered in the perspective of a century-old tradition starting with the so-called Marginal Revolution. Its founding fathers W.S. Jevons, L. Walras, H.H. Gossen, V. Pareto or J.B. Clark believed firmly in the laws of classical mechanics, and they frequently made analogies between mechanics and economics. Their idea was to free economic phenomena from accidental historical ties and to reveal their core of general validity, thus unfolding the "laws of nature." They aimed at axioms "true beyond any doubt" which would constitute the essence from which "pure theory" could be made. J.A. Schumpeter has considered it Pareto's merit that he lifted up "the logical core of the economic process above the ground of the institutional garb in which it is given to observation" [Schumpeter 1969, p. 125]. From an orthodox perspective, economics is thus simplified into a dualistic structure, with an endogenous core accomodating law-like relationships and an exogenous realm made up of historical factors. It may appear analytically useful to draw a demarcation line between economic and non-economic variables, and it seems equally sensible to declare the former as endogenous and the latter as exogenous to economic theory. However, the identification of the economic variables as nomothetical and of the non-economic variables as historical implies that only economics has the quality of being theoretical; other social sciences are thus discriminated against in this conferred status. It goes without saying that this claim does not provide a good starting point for interdisciplinary research.

The validity of the causality concept of orthodox economics depends on two considerations: the validity of its transfer from physics to economics and its validity in physics itself. In classical physics the principle of causality was stated unambiguously in Newton's law of gravitation. (See Section 1, Figure 1) The inclined plane and ball illustrated here are elements of a simple mechanical example. We may predict from common experience that the ball will roll downward if the external force indicated by the horizontal arrow is strong enough to bring it onto the slope. We know from classical physics that the ball will roll downward due to the gravitational force of the earth. According to

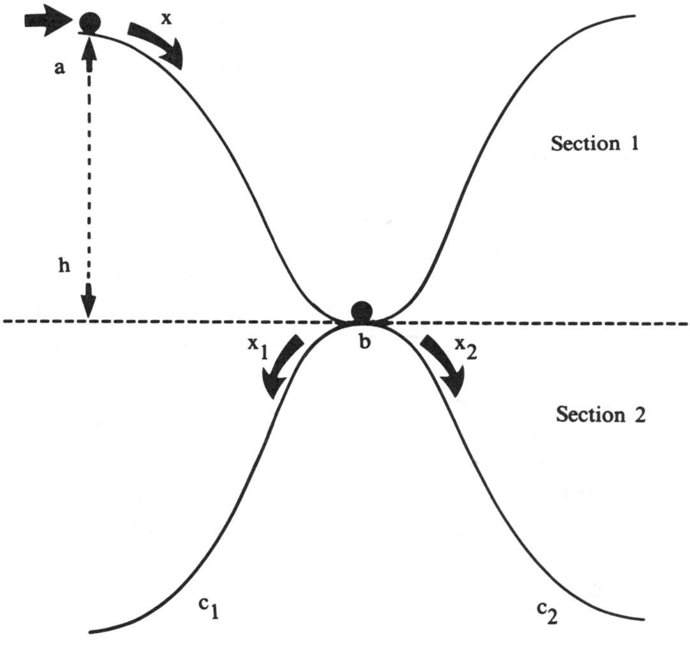

Figure 1: ***Initial conditions with deterministic and chaotic trajectories***

Newton's *universal* law of gravitation the gravitational force stands in a quadratic relationship to the distance of the two bodies. In our example the mass of the earth is incomparably greater than that of the ball, so that the gravitational force of the earth may be kept constant and the mass of the ball may be completely ignored. The behavior of the ball can thus be predicted on the basis of a *special* theory where the height h and Galileo's gravitational constant $\mathfrak{g}$ constitute the parameters. The inclined plane constitutes some kind of *environment* defined in terms of Euclidian geometry. Given all information about the environment's shape, a trajectory can be described deterministically. ***The type of environmental landscape can under no circumstances jeopardize the validity of the deterministic law; hence, it cannot erode the validity of the causality principle of classical physics.*** You may recall from the earlier definition of the "causal" system that *similar* given initial conditions will result in a *similar* evolution of the system. It must suffice at this point to state that the broadly defined range of validity discounts crucially the fact that the environment plays its part as a causal factor.

It is astonishing how well the neo-classical model fits the model of classical physics. Pareto accomplished a major methodological achievement for neo-classical theory by distinguishing between the *homo oeconomicus,* who behaves logically, and his non-economic *alter ego,* which, embedded in a historico-societal context, is inclined towards non-logical action [Pareto 1971, pp. 29-101]. He supplements the theoretical construct of the *homo oeconomicus,* with the distinction into "tastes" and "obstacles" [Pareto 1971, pp. 181-209, 211-50]. The mechanical nature of the analytical categories can be highlighted by reference to our example. We may conceive of the ball as a subject which is separate from the objective physical environment defined by the landscape of the plane. Both the properties of the subject and of its environment are assumed to be given and are consequently not explained by the theory. In the economic context the ball may be taken as analogous to the *homo oeconomicus,* whose preferences constitute equally invariant properties given by assumption. The physical environment of the plane corresponds, in turn, to the constraints of the economic environment imposed by technological and institutional obstacles. In classical physics the trajectory is predicted on the basis of the law of gravitation. In neo-classical economics the trajectory is predicted analogously on the basis of the maximization principle, which allows the pronouncement of a definitive statement about the differences between unsatisfied needs and satisfied needs. Given information about what is preferred and about what constraints are met in obtaining the preferred position, the economic outcome can be predicted with certainty on the basis of its deterministic trajectory law. The theoretical statement is made entirely in terms of a relative change in resources. In classical mechanics the trajectory may be stated as a relative change in the location of objects or as the time required to accomplish that change. There is an equivalence between space and time. The relative change in resource magnitudes corresponds to spatial change in mechanics, and hence economic processes can be explained without reference to time. Indeed, the differential equation $\dot{x} + x = 0$ can be written without reference to time. Time in the neo-classical model is always external time, imposed on the object from outside. It is not internal time that would allow for a change of the constituent elements themselves. Time is typically a parameter, not an operator (as in modern biophysics).

The economic trajectory discussed is conceived in *micro* terms, leaving open the question of how to arrive at *macro* economic relationships. In classical physics the various point trajectories can be expressed as canonical variables and represented simultaneously by a Hamilton function. There is an analogous tendency in the neo-classical research program, particularly in its neo-Walrasian extension, to conceive economic processes in the context of a universal space-time-continuum. The validity of this approach depends entirely upon the validity of reducing behavioral relationships to their physical correlates of resource relationships. If the macro relationships are composed of physical entities, they may be given a mechanistic representation. If economic actions are viewed in their original behavioral quality, a behavioral framework must be applied. It should be recognized that any orthodox approach operates on the basis of a *behavioral* assumption by its conventional reference to the principle of *competition*. The behavioral assumption may disappear from the surface of resource mechanics but it is in fact always present implicitly. Walras drew attention explicitly to the competition principle, though this behavioral premise is ultimately absorbed in the equilibrium state of the system. There is an apparent conceptual *inconsistency* in the orthodox research program caused by the stress upon the mechanical nature of the economic resources processes and by the concommitant reliance on a major behavioral assumption in the form of the evolutionary principle of competition.

The major threat to the theoretical validity of neo-classical theory stems from the recognized unpredictability of man. This is ruled out, however, by the maximization assumption, which serves as an invariant trajectory law not subject to further theoretical scrutiny. Given the acceptance of rational economic man, theoretical progress consists of the transformation of invariant behavioral relationships into pure resource relationships. Pareto suggested this view when saying that "science proceeds by replacing the relationships between human concepts . . . by relationships between things" [Pareto 1973, p. 150]. In a similar vein, E. Slutsky requested for economic theory that "we must make it completely independent of psychological assumptions and philosophical hypotheses" [Stigler 1965, p. 127]. The conceptual rationale behind these propositions is that the economic process should be reduced to its pure physical structure. In so doing the validity of the classical causality principle would be preserved. There has been much criticism of this assumption of rational economic man; but the counter objection has been that *homo oeconomicus* is only an abstraction which is not made invalid by reference to reality. The discussion has polarized into two extreme positions: one claims that the empirical voidness of economic man is itself proof of theoretical quality; the other stresses the irrelevance of the entire theoretical set up in view of the esoteric abstractions. The former extremists expect theoretical progress to come from further formalization; the latter expect progress from closing the apparent gap between theory and reality. While I strongly favor the latter position, there still remains a problem with regard to the concept of the environment.

The competing views may share equally the idea that the environment in which the agents operate can be constructed along the lines of classical mechanics. Hence, it would be assumed that the classical causality principle applies. This classical assumption, however, is challenged by recent results in modern physics which demonstrate that the *nature of the initial conditions* may be crucial for the specific path that a trajectory may take. Let us return to Figure 1, now to Section 2. The initial point is now a hump where the ball may be removed by using some mechanical equipment awaiting the gravitational force to pull it down. The crucial question is: in what direction will the ball roll? There is no way of determining theoretically whether the ball will follow trajectory x_1 or x_2. This is a most disturbing result for economists who rely on the deterministic laws of classical mechanics. We cannot argue anymore, as Samuelson did, that similar initial conditions will result in similar outcomes since a very small difference or change in the initial conditions may significantly influence the actual path of the trajectory. In our physical example it may not be possible to ascertain any mechanical bias in the bifurcation point, and hence the trajectory outcome would be perfectly uncertain. The trajectory would not be causal-deterministic but *chaotic.* We may consider the truth value of my own lecture in similar terms. One half of what I am telling you is correct, and the other half is wrong. Confronted with chaos, I do not know which half is correct. Referring to the neo-classical context, a consumer, for instance, is confronted with an indifference curve and, given his budgetary constraints, the consumption choice is uniquely determined on the basis of the postulated "axioms of choice." The individual may indeed be indifferent if the total consequences of his choice are predictable in the deterministic way he thinks they are. If he is confronted with a chaotic environment, a very small error in computation may have very large unexpected economic consequences. Theoretical considerations along this line are particularly important for macroscopic analysis. A very small cause (which may include the decision of an individual) may in the context of undetermined intitial conditions lead to significant macroscopic consequences which accumulate rapidly over time, leaving the system in hopeless chaos, for example, with large and unpredictable fluctuations.

The question then is how to resolve the theoretical problem posed by a chaotic environment. The first possibility consists of viewing the problem as an *informational* problem. In classical physics P.S. Laplace asserted that we may know all events of the past and the future if we possess sufficient information about a relevant segment of the space-time-continuum. The Laplacian demon makes predictions on the basis of a deterministic model. We may imagine that there also exists a Laplacian demon who is able to make predictions in a chaotic world. However, the demon of a higher order is a *contradictio in adjecto,* since by definition the chaos exists in not knowing *ex ante* the outcome, and since knowing it would make the system a non-chaotic one. If the initial conditions are perfectly unpredictable in their consequences, a probability of 0.5 applying to the trajectories x_1 and x_2, then the demon is powerless unless he does not have some information about a bias of the initial conditions. This bias makes the system exactly a deterministic one, because predicting it presumes also its existence.

Though the new demon is powerless in a truly chaotic system it is interesting to ask how he may try to predict the outcome even in a chaotic system. This chaos demon could look for information in two ways. He could investigate the ball to see whether it has a bias for one of the two trajectories or he could search for similar information about the environment. He would fail in this task for the reason stated, and he might then start reorienting his research questions and view as his new task, trying to predict exactly what is unpredictable. The demon of a higher order would start constructing a chaotic model where chaotic initial conditions are assumed and where the outcome of the trajectory is not determined by any bias of the environment or of the physical body that is subject to relative change. The original laws of gravitation would still apply. The demon would reconsider the properties of the ball, and would have to recognize that it has nothing like a mechanical personality. The ball as a physical entity has *no consciousness* of its own. The demon may try to take refuge in J.O. de Lamettrie's concept of an *homme de machine* but would realize that this construct depends in its decisions on the deterministic qualities of the system of which it constitutes part. The demon, having his intellectual ancestry in the 18th and 19th centuries, would not devote much further time looking for consciousness in a mechanical world.

This is exactly the state of the art in the neo-classical theory that tackles theoretically chaotic environments. The *homo oeconomicus* is still taken as an invarient constituent, analogous to the unbiased property of the physical object that faces chaotic initial conditions. Hence, the only possibility is to construct a mechanical chaotic system. The properties of such a system are straightforward, like the properties of a deterministic one. In the latter the outcome is perfectly certain; in the former the outcome is perfectly uncertain. The predictability is conserved in its deterministic status—only the content of the message has changed. The chaos theory can remind us of the fact that mechanical environments are not unproblematical, but may influence the dynamic properties of a mechanical actor. However, the new type of non-classical physics cannot contribute anything to the analysis of the consciousness of the actor. Analogously, the environment still has typical mechanical features. In a mechanical system the environment is ahistorical, that is the initial conditions are repeatable. In reality, the high degree of indeterminacy of a single trajectory may make it unique, meaning that the probability of its repeating itself approaches zero. However, the environment itself is still ahistorical in the sense that it cannot be determined by the actor.

The second way of coping in theory with chaotic phenomena was suggested by evolutionary economists. Their approach differs radically from the approach just outlined. Their systems have neither deterministic nor chaotic properties because they are not mechanical. The agents and the environment are not isolated but are rather conceived in the mutual *interactions.* Both are hence *ex hypothesi* not invariant, but are themselves subject to change. This change brought about by *reciprocal causation* which implies that *A* causes *B* and *B* causes *A.* The causality concept itself is not mechanistic, but *morphogenetic.* This means that *A* induces a change in *B* and *B* induces a change in *A.* The process is thus not conceived as a relative change of an object (defined in terms of time and space) under given conditions but as a mode of *causative interaction,* where the constituents themselves (the actor and the environment) are subject to *morphic change.*

In the context of genuine causation the concepts of *circular and cumulative causation* play a predominant role. This causality concept differs in its very substance from the mechanical concept applied by orthodox economists. The circularity idea has long been around in the economic discipline; but interpreted mechanistically constitutes merely an endlessly returning resource flow. Say's law states a circular "causation" of this type. It gains its causal momentum from an allegedly self-evident force immanent in the economic process itself and similar to the gravitational forces that make for the continous eliptic path of the celestial orbits. Keynes was one of the first economists to recognize that the traditional circular resource flow need not necessarily be given a mechanistic-hydraulic interpretation but may also be conceived in terms of expectations, uncertainty and time-asymmetry, all inherent in the behavior of economic agents and economic events. Evolutionary economists went one step further right at the start by not only assuming new models of man and new environments but by actually *analyzing* them and by so doing bringing in *uncertainty* as a constituent feature of the resulting process.

The causality concept applied by evolutionary economists to define theoretically the *dynamic* features of circular causation is *cumulative causation.* In the following pages I wish to outline an evolutionary model in which the cumulative causation plays a central role. Starting from the concept of circular causation, our imagination is not greatly challenged when it comes to conceiving figuratively the concept of circularity. We simply think of a circle with constituents, such as *A* and *B,* connected by arrows indicating circularity. We have to take a step further in our imagination, however, if a concept of genuine cumulative causation is involved. We may make the analysis easier by referring to a diagram. In Figure 2 the core figure is a *spiral.* The construct is assumed to have the common formal properties of a spiral. However, our spiral differs from any of the spirals analyzed in geometry in its point of origin. Generally the point of origin is indeed a point, while our point of origin is a *circle*. There is another feature in our spiral different from the

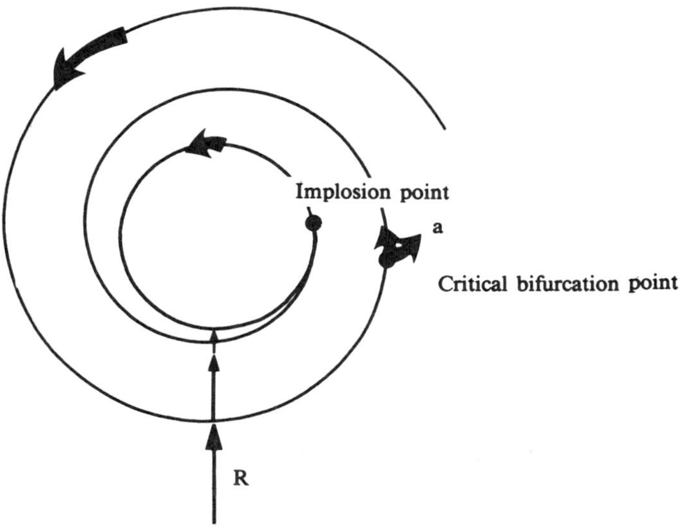

Figure 2: ***Involutionary spiral with stagnation circle***

standard type. The direction of the evolvant is inverse, indicated by the arrows pointing to the origin. This suggests that we should in fact speak of an *involution* rather than an evolution. In this model, the point of origin is some antecedent spiral, while the (ultimate) terminal point is defined by the circle.

There are two evolutionary principles which give the geometrical figure its theoretical meaning. The first principle is *mutation,* defined as the generation of novelties, that is, of traits that have not occurred previously in a class of which the mutant constitutes a member. The second principle is *retention,* defined as endogenous impetus impeding mutation and thus working towards retention of the *status quo.* In a socio-economic system a mutation may be defined as a *pool of vari-*

ations that provides new opportunities for the agents of that system. A crucial assumption in this model is that a given variation pool is an *exhaustible* entity. Any mutation thus constitutes an evolutionary potential that in itself is subject to decreasing returns in the intellectual and economic resources devoted to the variation of the mutant required to bring about the desired outcomes. The concept of mutation, though referring in principle to the individual behavior of a single element, has macroscopic consequences in the sense that it makes for a new environment for a large number of individuals. Given the principle of competition, the *selection* process may increase in its intensity as the exhaustion process proceeds. Both decreasing returns and increasing competitive selection justify the use of the term *involution* for the process that occurs within a single evolutionary regime as depicted by the spiral. In Figure 2, the *R*-line represents some indicator of the involutionary pressure. The question arises of how the agents involved will act on or respectively react to the changing environment. A first set of determinants has been said to constitute factors of *retention.* They are effective as established social norms and institutions. Institutionalists have long been pointing out that institutions may impede the socio-economic process by confining it to a suboptimal position on the involution spiral. However, they have equally pressed for the need to allow in theory for the forces of mutation bringing about the socio-economic change in our societies, and have actually advocated fostering such forces.

In interpreting *mutation,* two locations on the involutionary path may be distinguished. The first location is the circular flow reminiscent of the terminal point of the equilibrium position in classical mechanics (as defined in Section 1, Figure 1, by position *b*). The process is cumulative insofar as it cumulatively keeps down the mutation factors by reinforcing those of retention. The system is locked into an equilibrium position. Similar to a mechanical system that cannot initiate change by itself, the stationary nature of this position is difficult to overcome without exogenous stimuli. Clarence E. Ayres drew attention to this in *The Theory of Economic Process* [1944]. He stressed not only the impeding character of established institutions but also the necessity of conceiving economic and cultural progresses at large, on the basis of *open systems.* He explains, as Claude Levi-Strauss did later, the emergence of great civilizations, for instance, industrialization in early Europe, by the opportunities provided by the openness of those cultures.

There is another point concerning the endogenous part of the model that confirms the validity of Ayres' view. Let us consider the second hypothesis. It refers to the involutionary process up to a point before it collapses in the stagnation circle. The hypothesis seems plausible that the decline in the stock of opportunities provided by the potential of the mutant is associated with a simultaneous *increase in the energetic potential pressing for new mutations.* This hypothesis has two theoretical features. First, the environmental constraints and the agent's behavior are not given exogenously but emerge from and are explained by the process itself. The Pareto-obstacles stated earlier here challenge the creativity of man and release forces that increase the drive for novel combinations and for an increase of the forces opposing the institutional obstacles. It seems highly probable that, as a rule, the agents will try to break out from a given involutionary spiral evading further social and economic deterioration. We thus have a *critical bifurcation point* at some location on the involution spiral. Its actual location will depend concommitantly on the established forces of retention. Like the forces of mutation, those of retention must be explained by the process itself. My hypothesis is that they will probably increase at a rate similar to the increase in mutational forces, leaving the differential ratio of the two in a precarious dynamic balance where accidental historical factors may play an important role and where small disturbances may have a significant effect on the entire process. The theoretical considerations on chaos theory apply here. Further research along evolutionary lines should include in its agenda both the factors of retention and the factors of mutation, combined with an effort to highlight their casual interactions, thus further contributing to our understanding of economics as an evolutionary process. My feeling is that too much analytical emphasis on the factors of retention—Karl Marx devoted three volumes to *Das Kapital* but none to the future society—will unduly absorb the intellectual resources required to contemplate overdue mutations in our societies. We may conclude from the critical bifurcation point in Figure 2 that sustained evolutionary progress may be achieved only by the creation of *new* spirals, giving the overall evolutionary progress a sustained momentum.

Let me conclude with a Buddhist parable. A priest and a prostitute both face, after death, divine justice regarding their past lives. To their great surprise the verdict is that the prostitute should enjoy eternal bliss and the priest should go to hell. Most embarrassed, the priest asked whether this was a just reward for his upright life. He received the answer that throughout his life he had occupied his mind with the sins and misery of this world and that by so doing his mind had become dark and consequently incapable of seeing and enjoying the light of heaven.

This parable does not merely draw attention to the historically conditioned status of the observer in economic theory, but also to our potential to reinforce desirable mutations by participating appropriately in the evolutionary process itself.

References

Arthur, W.B., Yu, M. Ermolico, and Yu, M. Kaniouski. 1986 "Path-Dependent Processes and the Emergence of Macro-Structure." *European Journal of Operations Research,* forthcoming.

Ayres, C.E. 1944. *The Theory of Economic Progress.* Chapel Hill: University of North Carolina Press.

Backhaus, J. 1985. "Public Policy Toward Corporate Structures: Two Chicago Approaches." *Journal of Economic Issues* 19 (June):365–73.

Bergström, S. ed. 1984. *Economic Growth and the Role of Science.* Proceedings from a Symposium. Edsbruk: Holms Gards tryckeri.

Bharadwaj, K. 1980. "On Some Issues of Method in the Analysis of Social Change." Sri Krishnarajendra Silver Jubilee Lectures, Special Lecture, Series 78, University of Mysore: Mysore University Printing Press.

Bohm, D. 1980. *Wholeness and the Implicate Order.* London: Routledge & Kegan.

Boland, L. 1982. *The Foundations of Economic Method.* London: Allen & Unwin.

Caldwell, B.J. 1982. *Beyond Positivism: Economic Methodology in the Twentieth Century.* London: Allen & Unwin.

Capra, F. 1982. *The Turning Point.* New York: Simon & Schuster.

Commons, J.R. 1934. *Institutional Economics.* New York: The Macmillan Company.

Culbertson, J.M. 1984. "The New Potential of Evolutionary-Institutional Economics." *Journal of Economic Issues* 18 (June): 609–18.

Day, R. 1982. "Irregular Growth Cycles." *American Economic Review* 72 (June): 406–14.

Dopfer, K., ed. 1976. *Economics in the Future.* London and Basinstroke: Macmillan Press.

Dugger, W. 1979. "Methodological Differences Between Institutional and Neoclassical Economics." *Journal of Economic Issues* 13 (December): 899–909.,

__________. 1984. "Veblen and Kropotkin on Human Evolution." *Journal of Economic Issues* 18 (December): 971–85.

Eichner, A.S. 1983. "Why Economics is Not Yet a Science." *Journal of Economic Issues* 17 (June): 507–20.

Ford, J. 1983. "How Random is a Coin Toss?" *Physics Today* (April): 40–47.

Fusfeld, D.R. 1980. "The Conceptual Framework of Modern Economics." *Journal of Economic Issues* 15 (March): 1–52.

Gordon, W. 1984. "The Role of Institutional Economics." *Journal of Economic Issues* 18 (June): 369–82.

Hamilton, D. 1978. "Institutional Economics: Present Status and Future Prospects." *The Social Science Journal* 15 (January): 63–70.

Hayden, F.G. 1983. "Integration of Social Indicators Into Holistic Geobased Models." *Journal of Economic Issues* 17 (June): 325–34.
Heilbroner, R.L. 1984. "Economics and Political Economy: Marx, Keynes and Schumpeter." *Journal of Economic Issues* 18 (September): 681–95.
Heiner, R.A. 1983. "The Origin of Predictable Behavior." *American Economic Review* 73 (September): 560–95.
Hicks, J. 1979. *Causality in Economics.* New York: Basic Books.
Hirsch, A. 1980. "The Assumption Controversy in Historical Perspective." *Journal of Economic Issues* 14 (March): 99–118.
Hollis, M., and E.N. Nell. 1975. *Rational Economic Man.* Cambridge: Cambridge University Press.
Jarre, J., ed. 1985. *Die Zukunft der Oekonomie, Wirtschaftswissen-schaftliche Forschungsansätze im Vergleich,* Loccumer Protokolle 15/1984, Rehburg-Loccum.
Kapp, W.K. 1954. "Economics and the Behavioral Sciences." *Kyklos* 7, No. 3: 206–223.
Leibenstein, H. 1976. *Beyond Economic Man.* Cambridge, Mass.: Harvard University Press.
Leipert, C. 1982. "Gesellschaftliche Umwelt und Menschliche Bedürfnisse: zwei Notwendige Dimensionen Einer Humanwirt-schaftlich Fundierten Wirstschaftstheorie." *In Knzepte Einer Humanen Wirtschaftslehre, Beiträge Zur Institutionellen Oekonomie und zur Integration der Sozialwissenschaft.* Frankfurt: Haag & Herchen.
Lower, M.D. 1983. "Comments on R.S. Tompson's: 'The Spread of an Institutional Innovation'". *Journal of Economic Issues* 17 (June): 539–42.
Lutz, M.A. 1983. "Creative vs. Mechanical Evolution: A Commentary on Petr." *Journal of Economic Issues* 17 (December): 1113–8.
Marchetti, C. 1980. "Society as a Learning System: Discovery, Invention and Innovation Cycles Revisited." *Technological Forecasting and Social Change* 18: 267–82.
Mayhew, A. 1981. "Ayresian Technology, Technological Reasoning and Doomsday." *Journal of Economic Issues* (June):513-20.
Miller, J.G. 1978. *Living Systems.* New York: McGraw-Hill.
Mitchell, W.C. 1969. *Types of Economic Theory, From Mercantilism to Institutionalism,* ed. J. Dorfman. New York: A.M. Kelley.
Nelson, R. and Winter, S.G. 1982. *An Evolutionary Theory of Economic Change.* Cambridge Mass.: Cambridge University Press.
Pareto, V. 1971. *Manual of Political Economy.* New York: A.M. Kelley.
Pareto, V. 1973. "Sul Fenomeno Economico. Lettera a Benedetto Croce," *Giornale degli Economisti* 21 (August 1900); 139–62. Translated as "On the Economic Phenomenon," International Economic Paper 3 (1953):196; quoted "Vincent D. Tarascio, Wilfredo Pareto and Marginalism," in *The Marginal Revolution in Economics,* ed. R.D.C. Black, A.W. Coats and C.D.W. Goodwin. Durham, N.C.: Duke University Press, 1973, pp. 140–59.
Passet, R. 1983. *L'economique et le Vivant.* Paris: Payot.
Petr, J.L. 1983. "Creationism Versus Evolutionism in Economics: Societal Consequences of Economic Doctrine." *Journal of Economic Issues* 17 (June): 475–84.
Pichler, J.H. 1985. Ganzheitliches Verfahren und sein Anspruch in einzelwis-

senschaftlicher wie erkenntnistheoretisch überhöhender Sicht, In *Die Ganzheitlich Verstehende Betrachtung der Sozialen Leistungsordnung,* Festschrift Josef Kolbinger, ed. Buhler. et al., Wien: Springer.
Prigogine, I. and I. Stengers. 1979. *La Nouvelle Alliance.* Paris: Gallimard.
Samuels, W.J. 1970. "Thorstein Veblen, Heterodox Economist in Retrospect." *Social Science Quarterly* 60 (December): 454-59.
Samuelson, P.A. 1947. *The Foundations of Economic Analysis.* Cambridge: Harvard University Press.
Scumpeter, J.A. 1969. *Ten Great Economists, from Marx to Keynes.* Reprint. New York: Oxford University Press.
Semmler, W. 1986. "Financial Crisis as Bifurcation in a Limit Cycle Model: A Non-Linear Approach to Minsky Crisis." Mimeographed, New School for Social Research, New York.
Shackle, G.L.S. 1972. *Epistemics and Economics: A Critique of Economic Doctrines.* Cambridge: Cambridge University Press.
Steppacher, R. 1985. "Thesen zur Institutionellen Oekonomie." *Die Zunkunft der Oekonomie,* ed. Jan Jarre. Loccumer Protokolle, Rehburg-Loccum.
Steppacher, R. and B. Zogg-Walz. 1977. *Economics in Institutional Perspective, Memorial Essays in Honor of K. William Kapp,* ed. H. Hatzfeldt. Lexington: Lexington Books.
Stigler, G.J. 1965. *Essays in the History of Economics.* Chicago: University of Chicago Press.
Tool, M.R. 1979. *The Discretionary Economy, A Normative Theory of Political Economy.* Santa Monica, Calif.: Goodyear Publishing Company.
________. 1981. *Neoinstitutionalism: An Alternative Paradigm?* Presentation at the meeting of the Atlantic Economic Society, London School of Economics, London.
Veblen, T. 1898. "Why is Economics Not an Evolutionary Science?" *Quarterly Journal of Economics* (July): 373–97.
Weisskopf, W.A. 1979. "The Method is the Ideology, From a Newtonian to a Heisenbergian Paradigm in Economics." *Journal of Economic Issues* 13 (December): 868–84.
Wible, J.R. 1984. "The Instrumentalisms of Dewey and Friedman." *Journal of Economic Issues.* 18 (December): 1049–70.
Wilber, C.K. and R.S. Harrison. 1978. "The Methodological Basis of Institutional Economics: Pattern Model, Storytelling, and Holism." 12 (March): 61–89.

5

The Rationalist Conception of Action

Geoff Hodgson

In the social sciences we are suffering from a curious mental derangement. We have become aware that the orthodox doctrines of economics, politics, and law rest upon a tacit assumption that man's behavior is dominated by rational calculation. We have learned further that this is an assumption contrary to fact. But we find it hard to avoid the old mistake, not to speak of using the new knowledge.

Wesley Mitchell [1918, p. 161]

Dominant within mainstream economic theory is the idea that all action is regulated by rational calculation. Moreover, we are assumed to possess an individual mechanism for assigning values to policy outcomes. This is more or less what has been dubbed "the rationalist conception of action" by Barry Hindess [1977c] and the "analytic paradigm" by John Steinbruner [1974]. We shall use the former term here. The essential idea common to these definitions has been extensively criticized not only by Hindess and Steinbruner but also by a large number of other social theorists.

Note, however, that the term "the rationalist conception of action" is not identical to philosophical rationalism, nor to the propositions of "rational economic man" in neoclassical economics. (For a critique of the latter see [Hollis and Nell 1975].) However, "rational economic man" is clearly a calculator, with prominent and well-defined maximands. The rationalist conception of action purports to describe an essential component of his psyche.

The neoclassical system involves the maximization of a single value outcome (for example, utility or profits). In contrast, the behavioralist model (for example, [Simon 1975a]) incorporates a payoff vector rather than a single-value function as in the neoclassical case. Furthermore, each component of the behavioralist payoff vector is restricted to a limited number of outcomes (for example, satisfactory/unsatisfactory) rather than engaging in a continuous trade-off as in the neoclassical scheme.

However, the behavioralist model, like the neoclassical one, still assumes that agents are focussing on policy outcomes and subjecting them to some form of rational calculation. Rationality is "bounded," but it is still rationality, and it still dominates human action within the stated bounds. The work of the leading behavioralist Herbert Simon is thus an incomplete challenge to the rationalist conception, although it marks an important and positive step forward from the neoclassical theory.

Members of the Austrian School do not adopt a determinate model of human behavior. The process of assessment of policy outcomes is subjective, avowedly complex, and to some extent indeterminate, but it is assumed that action results from reason nevertheless. It is notable, therefore, that while challenging the neoclassical paradigm to different degrees, neither behavioralist nor Austrian theory abandon a rationalist conception of action generally.

Although the rationalist conception of action is certainly incompatible with the conception of human behavior in Marxist theory, it has largely been ignored, rather than directly confronted, by economists from this tradition. As we shall see below, the most direct and enduring challenge came from American Institutionalists such as Thorstein Veblen and Wesley Mitchell.

It should be emphasized that the critique embarked upon here does not suggest that no actions are motivated or dominated by reason. It simply rejects the idea that all (relevant) action is dominated primarily by rational calculation. It argues that there is a large class of actions relevant to economics that arise in a different manner. The arguments are on methodological, psychological, sociological, and other grounds. Part One of this essay confronts the idea that action can be dominated entirely by reason. Part Two uses psychological, anthropological, and sociological materials to examine the cognitive basis of action, and to vindicate broadly the institutionalist challenge to the rationalist conception many years ago. The arguments here against the rationalist conception of action are first that it is methodologically unsound, second that it is psychologically crude, and third that it is oblivious to important arguments from the other social sciences.

Reason and Action

Early Critiques

It is not popular to do so today, but there are precedents among economists for questioning the rationalist conception of action. Thorstein Veblen [1909] developed a critique of the view of human conduct "as a rational response to the exigencies of the situation in which mankind is placed." The view of his follower Wesley Mitchell has already been noted. It is striking that many decades ago the American Institutionalists were insisting that developments in psychological theory had completely undermined the neoclassical view of the economic agent (see, for example, [Veblen 1932, pp. 73, 157, 141]). Clearly, however, orthodoxy has survived. Neoclassical high theory has shelved its excessively hedonistic characterizations of human nature, and taken recourse in the Slutsky-Hicks-Allen indifference curves as a more rigorous and abstract version of its utility analysis [Coats 1976].

However, early rejections of the rationalist conception were not confined to the institutionalist school. Another precedent is found in the work of neoclassical economist and sociologist Vilfredo Pareto. He wrote an entire volume on what he called "Non-Logical Conduct," this being defined as behavior where means are not logically related to given ends [Pareto 1935, vol. 1, p. 77]. Pareto's notion of "logical" actions is more or less equivalent to what is called "means-ends rationality" in the modern literature. "Non-logical" conduct includes "the many human actions, even today among the most civilized peoples, [that] are performed instinctively, mechanically, in pursuance of habit" [p. 83]. Despite his belief that the "actions dealt with in political economy . . . belong in very great part to the class of logical actions" [p. 78], Pareto notes in his *Manual of Political Economy* that in real life non-logical and logical actions "are almost always mixed together" [Pareto 1971, p. 30].

Pareto's version of neoclassical theory, unlike the contemporary one, is thus not claimed to have near-universal applicability to social phenomena. His rationalist conception of action is applied to an important but limited class of conduct. In contrast, the tendency in modern neoclassical theory (particularly [Becker 1976]) is to accept fewer and fewer such limitations, and to claim that neoclassical theory (and by implication rationalist conceptions of action) can apply to an extremely wide variety of human acts.

The behavioralist position is more cautious. In one of his earlier works Simon took the view that the "assertion that human beings are always or generally rational . . . has been decisively refuted by modern developments in psychology and sociology" [Simon 1957b, pp. 61-62]. Simon is one of the very few contemporary economists who have tried to take such developments seriously, even if, despite this remark, his own solutions involve a limited challenge to the rationalist conception of action. It would be a great advance for economics if levels of skepticism about rationalist conceptions of action similar to those expressed by Simon, Pareto, Mitchell, or Veblen were to be found among the majority of the profession. Unfortunately, however, economics is currently moving in discernable annual increments in the opposite direction.

Reason and Discourse

According to the rationalist conception, action is primarily governed by reason. But rarely is it asked, What of the act of reason itself? If action is purposeful, what of the action of reasoning about purpose? Reasoning itself is action, as well as being intimately connected to other forms of practice. But how are we to account for actions in terms of reasons, if reasoning is an act? Reasons, stemming from the act of reasoning, will have to be given reasons in their turn. And these second order reasons have to be formed by reasons of a third order, and so on. To stop this potentially infinite regress we require a set of reasons themselves unformed by reasoning. Supporters of the rationalist conception of action are thus placed in a dilemma: either to admit the possibility of acts in general not governed by reason, or to suggest that reasoning in particular is non-rational in that it is not guided by reason. Both of these alternatives are strictly inconsistent with the rationalist conception of action.

B. Hindess [1977a, 1977c] raises the problem of inconsistencies or mistakes within the sphere of reason, and shows that the rationalist conception of action cannot admit the possibility of internal, logical contradiction within discourse. Such a contradiction would conflict with rationalist norms and presuppositions. The "rationalist conception of the production of discourse cannot be sustained without denying the very possibility of contradiction in discourse. . . . If contradiction is possible then discourse cannot be the product of *rationalist* mechanisms" [Hindess 1977c, pp. 218-19]. He shows, furthermore, that the attempt to deal with inconsistency or mistake by presupposing a higher-order decision rule "which specifies the conditions in which each rule may be called upon to take effect" [Hindess 1977a, p. 176] does not solve the problem. This super-rule has to exclude inconsistencies or mistakes within itself, or it has to fall outside the rational sphere.

We are thus forced to accept that some acts are not governed by reason. This judgment should not be confined to discursive acts alone. Indeed non-rationality would be expected to a greater extent with actions not necessarily and intimately connected with the reasoning process. But it is important to note that this problem for the rationalist conception of action arises when it is applied to the level of discourse: the same level as reasoning itself.

The rationalist conception divides social reality into two parts. It postulates "a realm of ideas (values, representations, meanings), a realm of nature and a mechanism of the realisation of ideas in the realm of nature, namely human action" [Hindess 1977a, p. 162]. To avoid self-contradiction the rationalist conception of action cannot itself be applied to the realm of ideas. Paradoxically, the rationalist conception does not apply to its own region of origin; it applies only to action in the natural or material world.

The rationalist conception of action is based on a "dualistic philosophy" involving a crude, clear, and Cartesian boundary between nature and the realm of human thought [von Mises 1957, p. 1]. But in doing so, however, it lapses into self-contradiction from which there is apparently no escape. Cartesian dualism permeates orthodox economic theory, from Adam Smith through John Stuart Mill to the modern neoclassicals and Austrians.

A Possible Rationalist Response

The rationalist response may be to accept that the rationalist conception of action cannot refer to reason, but to all other acts: "All action is rational, other than the act of reasoning. The latter is taken as a special case." This response overcomes one of the problems of logical inconsistency in the unqualified rationalist position, and apparently retains much of its conception of action intact.

However, this qualified rationalist conception of action is still open to severe criticism. The qualified version still cannot admit the possibility of logical inconsistency in the reasons that are assumed to relate to a set of acts. This is not a trivial matter. Action is sufficiently complex and varied that it would require a large number of inter-connected reasons if it were accounted for in rationalist terms. On reflection, from the known instances where we *do* act for conscious reasons, it is usually the case that our motives are complex and subject to a large number of related inferences or conditions. It is very rare that we simply do A to achieve B. It is more often that we do X and Y and Z to achieve P or Q, which may lead to I or J, or S or T, which may lead to other ends, and where there is a complex web of interrelations between many of the variables. It would be heroic to assume that the entire network of reasons is logically consistent and free of intransitivity and contradiction. For us to act in a rationalistic and logically consistent manner not only would we have to be fully aware of our ends and the relevant means, but also we would have to act as a mammoth logical computer, continually checking and monitoring the many and complex reasons for our acts.

As in any real-world organization, decisions to act have to be broken down and considered on a number of discrete levels. Major strategic decisions (jobs, residence, marriage, children) are taken on a higher level, but necessarily without full consideration of all the detailed implications. Given the complexity involved, it is not feasible to draw out all the logical consequences, even from the limited amount of available information. Lower-level decision making (what to have for lunch, whether to watch television or go to a restaurant) has a more "tactical" and non-strategic character. In a complex world, people, like organizations, have to incorporate a degree of hierarchy in their decision-making processes. Given any plausible amount of relevant information, it would be inconceivable that we could consider all the lower-level implications of any higher-level decision. Thus we cannot envisage or obtain a complete and consistent set of reasons to attach to all our acts.

As suggested by the lexicographic model of choice [Georgescu-Roegen 1954; Tversky 1969; Fishburn 1974; Earl 1983], even the choice of a single product is accomplished after consideration of a number of hierarchically ranked attributes. In purchasing a car we may first decide if it reaches certain minimal criteria of roominess. If so, we may then consider its petrol consumption. If it is satisfactory on that score we may then consider its potential reliability, and so on. This may appear to be a realistic choice procedure but it is not compatible with a complete and consistent preference ordering. In a lexicographic model people do continuously trade-off all the qualities of goods against each other, the gain of one thing compensating for the loss of another. At any given point in time, some qualities are considered and others ignored. If two goods have very different characteristics then a compensatory, trade-off relationship is ruled out.

If we move on from choices between attributes of goods to choices between goods and between different activities, then the necessity of some hierarchical ranking of the decision-making procedure becomes even more evident. Even if we do attach reasons to all of our acts it is unlikely that in their totality they will form a seamless and consistent whole. Such an outcome is ruled out by the sheer complexity of the decision-making process.

However, we could adopt a hierarchic decision-making model (such as a version of lexical choice) without breaking from a modified version of the rationalist conception of action. Even if our reasons are inconsistent when taken as a whole, at a given level of decision making we may still act for certain (consistent) reasons. Nevertheless, the adoption of a hierarchical model of decision making may open a Pandora's Box. To see this we must ask why a hierarchical approach should be considered in the first place. Initially, one of the most compelling arguments in its favor has to do with the computational limits of the human brain. In a highly complex world we are not able to engage in a complete and continuous trade-off of choices as in the neoclassical model. Even if we had the relevant information we could not carry out a full rational calculation of the likely payoffs from all the options. A hierarchical process of decision making is ostensibly a means of coping with this complexity by relating different types of decision and action to different levels of deliberation.

But if the problem of complexity is as severe as suggested here, then it is doubtful whether a multi-level hierarchy can overcome the computational limitations of the human mind within the framework of a rationalist conception of action. Even if we could break down decision making into some structured system, the rationalist conception would require that every tier of decision making were still at some full level of conscious deliberation. We would be liberated from the requirement to render all decisions into a coherent and consistent whole, but we would still be required to carry out and monitor decision making at all levels in the hierarchy. Even this is an awesome task.

Psychologists argue that mind and body can cope with this problem, but only through the use of unconscious and semi-conscious mental processes. The mental drives of human action are indeed structured in some sort of complex hierarchy, but they cannot all be subject to the fullest level of conscious deliberation. It is to this central and crucial point we now turn.

Unconscious Processes

Neoclassical economics does not make any distinction between actions that do and do not result from full conscious deliberation. All acts are programmed at the same level according to the given functions of preference or utility. The Austrian School makes an equivalent error by assuming that all (relevant) actions result from planning and deliberation at the same level of consciousness. Consequently both schools of thought in economics have an undifferentiated conception of the human psyche. This is apparently uninformed by Sigmund Freud and many of the varied developments in psychology since his death.

The behavioralist approach offers slight but significant improvements in this regard. For example, in his work Simon recognizes the existence and function of unconscious habit in human action [Simon 1957b, p. 88]. But it is difficult to see how habit, or unconscious actions in general, can play a prominent part in the formal behavioralist theory that is based on some type of ("bounded") rational decision making. By definition, habitual action does not imply the current articulation of *any* (maximizing or satisficing) goals. It could be argued that habitual action is simply the repetition of a previous action that was the subject of some (bounded) rational calculation. But to regard them merely as repeats of decisions that were fully rational is partially to degrade the importance and bearing of habits in themselves.

While the behavioralist approach has a great deal to offer, evidently there are some inconsistencies and inadequacies in this area. In one essay Simon makes the important point that we cannot "rule out the possibility that the unconscious is a better decision maker than the conscious" [Simon 1955, p. 104], but in another work he regards "the simplest movement—taking a step, focussing the eyes on an object—as purposive in nature" [1957b, p. 85]. It is strange to admit the possibility of "unconscious" habits in human behavior, but then to regard cognitive and other lower level acts as "purposive."

Despite frequent statements of the value and importance of psychology in behavioralist and Austrian theory, and to some extent in neoclassical economics as well, we find little reference to the possibility of unconscious, sub-rational processes. Of course, it was Freud who popularized the concept of the unconscious. But we do not have to tie ourselves to a Freudian theoretical framework to retain this idea. There is reason to be skeptical of much of Freudian theory. But it would be a blinkered mind that entirely dismissed the revolutionary change in the way we see ourselves that is offered by the Freudian analysis. The fundamental idea of there being processes at work in the human mind that are not fully conscious or deliberative has a following much wider than those of strictly Freudian persuasion. Indeed, if we exclude the behaviorist and "experimental" psychologists, who greet concepts like "consciousness" with extreme disapprobation, then the idea of unconscious or subconscious mental processes has wide allegiance. Outside economics the idea is commonplace.

One reason why economists have failed to embrace this twentieth-century innovation in psychology is not difficult to find. Freud and the post-Freudians suggest that our actions are not all determined by rational calculation or conscious deliberation. To put it bluntly, this flies in the face of the widespread assumption in economics that we are masters and mistresses of our fate. If we are not sovereign over all our mental processes and actions then how can such an idea as "consumer sovereignty" over the economy be entertained? How can an agreed contract between two agents be regarded as a fair expression of their needs if it results in part from motives or drives that are not fully conscious? The central idea of the inviolability of individual judgment is placed under threat. Post-Freudian theory undermines some of the main nineteenth-century liberal assumptions with which mainstream economics is often so keen to associate.

Cognitive Theory

The significance of the basic idea of unconscious mental processes is especially acute in the area of cognitive psychology. Consider in particular the visual perception of an object, say something moving through the sky. Without plan or intention our eyes pick up sensory data, and our mind becomes aware of something of a different color from its background, and which is moving and changing its apparent shape. We are at first unaware of what the object is, but we do not necessarily deliberate about its identity as we would with mental processes at a higher level.

Usually we recognize the object in a split second, without full conscious deliberation. In this time the brain manages to process the vast quantity of sensory data received by the eyes. Although this amount of data, measured in binary "bits" or whatever, is simply enormous, it is not sufficient to tell us what the object is and what it is doing. The brain has to carry out complicated mental operations to judge the speed, size, and form of the object. Without conscious rational calculation it attempts to identify the type of object it has perceived by searching its conceptual memory. Thus we recognize the object as a flying bird. We carry out this sort of mental operation almost continuously, accomplishing highly complicated and largely unconscious processing operations on vast quantities of data.

It is only in exceptional cases that our unconscious mind is unable to reach a firm decision and we have to deliberate about the identity of the object. Even when the sensory data is highly ambiguous, such as in the famous and contrived "optical illusions," our mind does not always consciously deliberate about whether, for example, the picture is of a single vase or of two human faces. As we stare at the image we may simply alternate our perception of it, from one interpretation to another.

Passages like the following are commonplace in cognitive theory:

> The incoming stimulus information confronts us with an infinitely complex universe. Limited to percepts, we would be hopelessly enslaved to the uniqueness of each object, event, or relation. But the chaotic jumble of sensory stimuli is reduced to manageable terms by the formation of *concepts*. By this process our knowledge is transformed to a limited number of informational units. We learn to pay attention to some features of an object and to ignore others. Some attributes are abstracted from the total percept and compared with those abstracted from other perceptions [Spradley 1972, pp. 9-10].

This echoes the definitive work of Ulric Neisser, *Cognitive Psychology,* and its "central assertion that seeing, hearing, and remembering are all acts of construction" [Neisser 1967, p. 10], and that of Jean Piaget, who argues that in the end "the relative adequacy of any perception to any object depends on a constructive process and not on an immediate contact" [Piaget 1969, p. 365].

Cognitive theory shows that the mind responds to the vast amount of sensory data it receives by working to reduce uncertainty at the conceptual level and by giving the "chaotic jumble" of stimuli some sense and meaning. *In general, and paradoxically, we simultaneously face the problem of having too little information and too much.*

It would not be possible to process all the given sensory data in a rational, conscious calculation. At least at the cognitive level we do not make the best use of all the available information; neither do we deliberate to any great extent upon it. The crucially relevant step is that we form concepts, based on our past experience, to categorize the sensory data and to endow it with meaning. Given these considerations, the orthodox economists' models of rational calculation cannot generally apply. As Steinbruner notes in his discussion of speech perception: "Here the performance far outstrips what can be done by conscious explicit calculation using even the largest and most sophisticated of computers, and, of course, the process proceeds without awareness or conscious direction" [Steinbruner 1974, p. 93]. Indeed, it is precisely the routinization of the cognitive processes and the lack of full awareness that makes such complex "calculations" possible.

Multiple Levels of Consciousness

One element common to all schools of "post-Freudian" psychology is the idea that human consciousness does not operate on a single, and in some sense rational, level. Basically, Freud divides the mind into the conscious and the unconscious. Arthur Koestler and others, however, have proposed a more complex demarcation:

> The Cartesian tradition to identify 'mind' with 'conscious thinking' is deeply engrained in our habits of thought, and makes us constantly forget the obvious, trivial fact that consciousness is not an all-or-nothing affair but a *matter of degrees.* There is a continuous scale of gradations which extends from the unconsciousness that results from being hit on the head, through the restricted forms of consciousness in dreamless sleep, dreaming, day-dreaming, drowsiness, epileptic automatisms, and so on, up to bright, wide-awake states of arousal [Koestler 1967, p. 238].

Koestler, like many others, has been influenced by systems theory, making use of its concept of a structured hierarchy of control mechanisms. It has been usefully applied to the human mind by a number of psychologists and systems theorists (for example [Angyal 1941, 1965; Ashby 1952; Sommerhoff 1974]). By whatever route, however, the argument for conceiving the mind and consciousness as multi-levelled and hierarchical is compelling. The argument about whether "economic man" is entirely rational or non-rational is a false dichotomy. Human agents are both rational and sub-rational at the same time.

At higher levels of consciousness and deliberation we do make a limited number of rational calculations upon which we base plans for future action. But it is a "common mistake," as John Searle points out, "to suppose that all intentional actions are the result of some sort of deliberation, that they are a product of a chain of practical reasoning." For example, deliberation is not always present in the act of everyday conversation. "In such cases, there is indeed an intention, but it is not an intention formed prior to the performance of the action." Searle calls this "intention in action" [Searle 1984, p. 65]. In general, Searle's work is distanced from behaviorist and mechanistic conceptions of the mind, and it does not make the error of assuming an undifferentiated level of consciousness and intentionality [Searle 1983, 1984].

The concept of "intention in action" is at a level similar to or slightly higher than "practical consciousness" as defined and used extensively by Anthony Giddens: "Practical consciousness consists of all the things which actors know tacitly about how to 'go on' in the contexts of social life without being able to give them direct discursive expression" [Giddens 1984, p. xxiii]. Notably, Giddens is aware of our intellectual debt to Freud but he rejects the psychic divisions of "id," "ego," and "super-ego," and the idea that "practical consciousness" is protected by a bar of psychological repression from reaching the full light of reason. The influence of

Freud on Giddens's adoption of a non-unitary concept of consciousness is, however, abundantly clear.

Somewhere below intentions in action lie habits. These are themselves of different kinds. There is the habitual twitch or nervous response. Other habits cover acts that are complex and were formerly planned, such as the daily habit of driving to work that becomes so deep-rooted that we switch, as it were, to "autopilot," and think consciously of other things, arriving at our destination unable to remember any incident on the journey. Below habits could be classified a variety of reflexes, and autonomic actions such as breathing.

There is also a category of act that suggests that the hierarchy may not be simple or one-dimensional. It is the case of "weakness of will" or "incontinence" in which persons act against their considered or "rational" judgment. We may act in a particular way while knowing that it is not in our best interests. An intemperate outburst in a meeting, or the one-drink-too-many before driving home, may be familiar examples. Weakness of the will provides a serious philosophical problem for the rationalist conception of action, resulting from the accepted inconsistency of intention and act. As Donald Davidson concludes after a meticulous discussion of this topic: "What is special in incontinence is that the actor cannot understand himself" [Davidson 1980, p. 42]. Habits or reflex actions may be consistent with higher-level intention, but incontinence, by definition, is not.

The structural complexity of the mind is further illustrated with the example of sleep. The varied phenomenon of dreaming shows that different levels of consciousness are possible within sleep itself, while full, wide-awake activity is curtailed. During sleep the majority of reflexes or autonomic actions remain functional. However, our senses may be unconsciously discriminatory in that we may hear a telephone ringing but not our own snoring.

Too Little Information and Too Much

Apart from difficulties with sleep and incontinence, and the above-discussed problem of inconsistency, rational choice theorists can always claim that each level of consciousness and action can be explained by a single, overall "rational" mechanism. Habits, for example, can be regarded as repeated acts that are perfectly "rational," given the lack of information in the hands of the actor that could lead to a change of behavior. Thus Anthony Downs [1957] suggests that habitual voting for one party, despite some ignorance of its policies, is "rational" because of the difficulty and "cost" of obtaining the appropriate information. Similarly, Gary Becker [1976] claims that there are stable underlying preferences that encompass not only simultaneous action at all levels but also that appear to be "changing" preferences through time. There are even highly sophisticated and avant-garde neoclassical models of human behavior that include decision-making processes at more than one level, but with overriding "rationality" [Thaler and Shefrin 1981; Winston 1980], in an attempt to incorporate some form of "habitual" action.

However, what is common to all these responses is the lack of an explicit differentiation between levels or degrees of consciousness in the decision-making model (even if there may be different levels of decision) and an assumption that there is an underlying, or long-run, stable preference function that governs behavior overall. As Barry Hindess argues, this type of response "misses the fundamental point. The objection here is not simply that the rational choice approach neglects important dynamic elements, but also that it treats actors, precisely because they are rational, as characterized by one form of assessment of their ends and conditions of action" [Hindess 1984, p. 270]. I would go further: an additional and equally fundamental argument is that the computational limitations of the human mind make full conscious deliberation at all levels of decision making impossible.

Faced with complex and multiple levels of consciousness, the neoclassical proponents of the rationalist conception of action are in some difficulty. It becomes highly implausible to assume that all action is equally rational, at all levels of consciousness and intentionality. With the assumption of global rationality and maximizing behavior the neoclassical economists do not distinguish between different acts in this way. In the neoclassical scheme all action is at the same level of consciousness—the level of a utility-maximizing machine.

The above argument against global rationality is very close to that of Simon [1955, 1959] in its emphasis on "bounded rationality," that is, on the limited computational capacity of the human mind. The behavioralist position is much superior in this regard to that of the neoclassicals. However, as pointed out above, there is no clear differentiation of substance in behavioralist works between conscious and unconscious processes. Furthermore, while there is a strong and necessary emphasis on the existence of imperfect information and its importance in decision making, there is insufficient recognition that information does not enter raw into the decision maker's mind. The perceptive, cognitive, and conceptual processes are often ignored. Thus in a highly stimulating and often persuasive behavioralist work on the firm, Neil Kay reduces almost every problem to one of information, for example producing the unacceptable statement that "the main distinguishing feature between types and grades of labor is *informational*. . . . Remove informational barriers and the main distinguishing feature or type of labor disappears" [Kay 1984, pp. 36-37]. It could be respectfully suggested that if this were the case then Kay's qualities as a teacher (which I have no reason to doubt) would be redundant, and supposedly could be replaced by a tape-recorder or some other device for pouring information into his students' heads. In reality, however, teaching, learning, and even training are largely cognitive and conceptual activities, which cannot be reduced simply to the transmission of information, and without which the information would be meaningless and devoid of value.

Turning to the Austrian School, James Buchanan has raised objections to the assumption of Ludwig von Mises and other Austrian economists that all action reflects "conscious, active, or creative choice" [Buchanan 1982, p. 15]. In an earlier article, Robert Nozick asks if conditioned behavior by humans is "action" in the Austrian sense, and if so would the same apply to rats and pigeons [Nozick 1977, p. 364]. The Austrian economist Karen Vaughn [1982] suggests that it would, citing the remarkable experimental work on rats by John Kagel [1981] and his colleagues who have "revealed" downward-sloping "demand curves" for food from their behavior. However, this response violates the rigid methodological dualism of the Austrian School, where the realm of choice and action applies specifically to the human and not to the natural world.

In one of the few passages of Austrian writing to confront some of these questions, von Mises writes:

> The vigorous man industrially striving for the improvement of his condition acts neither more nor less than the lethargic man who sluggishly takes things as they come. For to do nothing and to be idle are also action, they too determine the course of events. Wherever the conditions for human interference are present, man acts no matter whether he interferes or refrains from interfering. He who endures what he could change acts no less than he who interferes in order to attain another result. A man who abstains from influencing the operation of physiological and instinctive factors which he could influence also acts. Action is not only doing but no less omitting what possibly could be done [von Mises 1949, p. 13].

This argument is extremely weak. Action is here implicitly re-defined as that which "determines the course of events," in contrast to the spirited definition of action two pages earlier as "purposeful behavior." Admittedly (with the exception of incontinence) we can sometimes purposefully override habitual or autonomic actions. But it is not necessarily purposeful behavior to fail to attempt to override such acts. A purposeful act to buy (or not to buy) an expensive gift for a companion is not at the same level of purposefulness and rationality as the action of scratching (or even refraining from scratching) one's nose.

If the abstention from action is to be regarded as purposeful in the manner suggested by von Mises then it would imply that we continuously monitor not only our own physiology, but also our entire environment for opportunities to act. A person who is lethargic and fails to react when faced with a $100 bill lying in the street is not "acting" in the same way as one who thinks about it for a while and makes the conscious decision to leave it there. If all forms of real-world inaction are to be regarded as equivalent then this would imply some continuous and omniscient monitoring process governing all potential acts.

Ironically, the reason why this is not feasible derives from the very sort of consideration that the Austrians have quite rightly brought to the fore in a different context: the impossibility of dealing with and processing the vast quantity of information involved in the planning of a modern economy [Hayek 1935]. But a similar point applies to the human mind as well. Both our physiology and our environment are so complex that the mind cannot commit all the sensory data it receives to the same level of conscious deliberation. The process of concept-formation is indispensible precisely because it imposes some sort of order and meaning at some semi-conscious level, so that conscious deliberation can become possible to some higher and more abstract degree. Full conscious deliberation at all levels of mental activity is not possible.

Thus the Austrian standpoint has few advantages over the neoclassical one in this respect. In both cases it is assumed that all action is equally purposive and deliberative. This seems to contradict the Austrian emphasis on the information problem and the degree of complexity in human life. To use a phrase of Friedrich Hayek, just as a central planning agency cannot concentrate *all* the relevant information for national economic planning as if it were "in a single head," neither can the human mind fully and rationally process all the information relating to individual human action at the highest level of deliberation.

Once again there is considerable support for this type of argument from cognitive psychology. For instance Joachim Wohlwill [1962] argues that activity at the lower, perceptual level is characterized by the systematic rejection of excess information. In contrast, at higher, cognitive levels there is much less redundancy involved. In logic or mathematics, for example, few or none of the signs and symbols can be ignored. Thus we do not treat all information in the same manner at the same levels of thought.

At the perceptual level our minds have to simplify and be selective. We cannot monitor all our actions to equal extent, as von Mises and others imply.

With the argument cited above, von Mises [1949] has entered the Orwellian world of doublespeak. For him, inaction is action. After a dozen pages, the content of his *magnum opus* is emptied of the dramatic promise of its title.

The Rationalist Dilemma

In some respects Friedrich Hayek takes a more sophisticated stand. His critique of behaviorism in *The Sensory Order* deals directly with the question of the existence of purposefulness and consciousness in a psychological and neuro-physiological setting. Hayek views the human mind and nervous system as a complex and hierarchic structure, involving both conscious and unconscious mental processes.

However, in important ways Hayek's work in this area is a deviation from the mainstream Austrian position. The Cartesian, "methodological dualism" of von Mises is abandoned. In the process, however, key concepts such as purpose and action are degraded of the meaning invested in them elsewhere. For instance, Hayek suggests that machines can be produced to "show all the characteristics of purposive behavior." Although such machines "are comparatively primitive and restricted in their range of operations compared with the central nervous system," and for this reason "cannot yet be described as brains," Hayek believes that "with regard to purposiveness they differ from a brain merely in degree and not in kind" [Hayek 1952b, p. 126].

Strong arguments against this "computers can think" type of view are presented in Searle [1983, 1984] and they need not be repeated here. It is sufficient to note that in neoclassical, behavioral, and even Austrian theory the notion of purpose and choice ends up losing some of its essential content. Through its determinism, the neoclassical view of the mind excludes real choice. The behavioralists have been somewhat indiscriminate, seeing "purposive behavior sequences" [Simon 1956] in simple cybernetic models of adaptive behavior. Also, despite intentions, in at least two cases Austrian economists have ended up by degrading the notions of action or purpose. The Austrians draw a boundary between the social and the natural sciences, partly on the basis of the existence of purposeful action in the former and not the latter. When Hayek crosses this boundary from social science into psychology and neuro-physiology, he is thus forced to deny in the latter some of the propositions that elsewhere he lauds as axiomatic to his social science.

It may appear paradoxical, but only by denying that *all* mental processes are at the same level of rationality can we sustain the idea that *some* actions are purposeful and deliberative in character. Just as the solipsist, by asserting that life as a whole is a dream, degrades the concept of the dream itself, those that argue that all action is purposeful and rational end up by emptying those very concepts of much of their content. This, it turns out, is the rationalist dilemma.

Action and Institutions

Cognition, Culture, and Society

The significance of cognitive theory for the discussion at hand has been noted already, in that it shows that thought is not all at the same level of rationality or deliberation. In addition, cognitive theory relates to the argument in the present essay in an even more important sense. It introduces a social, cultural, and institutional dimension to human action that is prominent in the cognitive literature and difficult to avoid.

The attribution of meaning to the chaotic mass of sensory data requires the use of acquired concepts, symbols, rules, and signs. Perception is an act of categorization, and in general such categories are *learned*. The categorization process, as Jerome Bruner puts it,

> is the categorization of an object or sensory event in terms of more or less abundant or reliable cues. Representation consists in knowing how to utilize cues with reference to a system of categories. It also depends upon the creation of categories-in-relationship that fit the nature of the world in which the person must live. . . . Adequate perceptual representation involves the learning of appropriate categories, the learning of cues useful in placing objects appropriately in such systems of categories, and the learning of what objects are likely to occur in the environment [Bruner 1973, p. 12].

Noam Chomsky [1959] has proposed that the learning mechanism cannot fully account for the acquisition of language. He argues that the environment of a child is too complex and unstructured to convey the rules of grammar, and the capacity to do this must to some extent be genetically endowed. This controversial position cannot be assessed here. What is much more important for our purposes is the general, underlying consensus among cognitive theorists.

The significance of this issue for economics has to do with the process of acquisition of concepts and the conceptual nature of knowledge itself. The consequences are severe, whether we follow the behaviorists in the belief that our conceptual armory is acquired simply by a process of stimulus and response, or we follow alternative leads such as those of Chomsky or Piaget.

Furthermore, while cognitive theorists differ in the significance they attribute to the social dimension in the acquisition of concepts, it is rarely excluded. They are generally agreed that much of our conceptual apparatus is acquired through social interaction with others. There is a widespread acceptance, for example, that our education and socialization in early years helps us to develop our innate perceptual equipment and form a conceptual basis to understand and act in a complex and changing world. In fact, Bruner's work, quoted above, represents one of the more subjectivist theories of perception, contrasted with others, such as Neisser [1976], who give even greater emphasis to the function of anticipatory perceptual schemata through which new information is continuously processed.

At least for the socialized adult, most concepts and perceptual frames are expressed in a (social) language and they relate to the social world. For this reason cognition has cultural specificity. The acquired conceptual framework reflects our culture and the social norms and rules that have evolved over the centuries or much shorter periods of time. As Barbara Lloyd asserts: "Individuals growing up in different cultures may well learn different rules for processing information from the world around them" [Lloyd 1972, p. 16]. Just as our knowledge of the world does not spring out alive from the sensory data as it reaches the brain, only through the acquisition of a complex and culturally specific conceptual framework can sensory data be understood. This reality, outside our heads, is not simply there; the reality we "see" and "understand" is partially socially constructed [Berger and Luckmann 1967; Douglas 1973; McLeod and Chaffee 1972; Spradley 1972].

"The social construction of reality" is not an uncommon phrase in the wide and diverse literature in psychology, philosophy, linguistics, anthropology, and sociology that traverses this area. The differences in type of cognitive and cultural theory cannot be discussed here, and it is not necessary to do so. There is, to repeat, a wide consensus on the fundamental issue: Facts do not speak for themselves; the acquisition of knowledge about the world is not simply an individual but a social act. This passage is typical:

> Each of us likes to think of himself as being rational and autonomous. Our ideas seem to be peculiarly our own. It is hard for us to realize how little of our information comes from direct experience with the physical environment, and how much of it comes only indirectly, from other people . . . . One's prior beliefs, attitudes, and values form a frame of refer-

> ence—a kind of cognitive map for interpreting reality that precedes and controls the exchange of information and influence [McLeod and Chaffee 1972, pp. 50-51].

Despite economists' increasing interest in issues relating to information, knowledge, and uncertainty, the essential difference between sensory data and knowledge has not permeated orthodoxy at all. Apart from the Austrian School, there is rarely any suggestion that the presentation or availability of information does not mean that it will be equally or uniformly perceived. It is widely assumed that all agents learn in similar ways. The issue of cognition is excluded by default or by design.

Remarkably, however, cognitive divergence between economists themselves has become more and more prominent at the policy level. The polarization and controversy have increased to the extent that the common conceptual ground for the evaluation of policy has become quite narrow. Gone are the days when almost all economists were agreed on the criteria for the evaluation of policies. It is now possible for a group of economists to be presented with the same data concerning the performance of an economy, and to disagree diametrically as to whether the facts indicate a healthy condition. For example, there is wide disagreement in Britain today, even after six years of a New Right regime, as to whether their policies are working. It is a common error to ascribe these differences in evaluation simply to lack of full information or technical knowledge of the "true" workings of the economy. But in matters as complex as an economic system we have every reason to put cognitive differences to the fore. Disagreements about policy evaluation result partly from differences in conceptual framework, and the related value systems, and no amount of new information will *necessarily* reduce these over time.

Cognitive Theory and Subjectivism

One of the few economists to recognize the distinction between sensory data and knowledge is Hayek. He argues in some of his works that the empiricist idea of the direct acquisition of knowledge from the data of experience is flawed. Facts, he argues, are bound by concepts or theories, and agents in a sense "create" the reality in which they act [Hayek 1952a]. For this and other reasons there is a strong anti-empiricist element to Austrian theory, expressed by I. M. Kirzner when he writes of its "serious reservations about the general validity and importance of a great deal of the empirical work being carried on in the economics profession today" [Kirzner 1976, p. 40].

In fact, however, the accommodation to cognitive theory by the Austrian economists is partial and one-sided. It is used with positive and convincing effect to demolish empiricism and an over-emphasis on econometric testing. But the idea of agents "creating" reality is also used for the end of reinforcing the subjectivism of the Austrian paradigm. As Hayek puts it in an oft-quoted remark: "Every important advance in economic theory during the last hundred years was a further step in the consistent application of subjectivism" [Hayek 1952a, p. 31].

Undeniably, all human agents are unique in their cognitive abilities and in the body of concepts they have acquired. Consequently, cognitive theory *does* show that human knowledge has a subjective character. Beliefs and expectations are subjective in a sense that is incompatible with the crude empiricist idea of the direct appraisal of knowledge. But if the *subject-matter* of cognition is subjective, does that mean that the *process* of cognition is entirely subjective as well? As one commentator on Hayek has wittily observed: "If Social Science is subjective because its subject matter is, then by the same argument Ornithology would have to be considered a bird-like science and Archaeology an archaic one" [Rudner 1954, p. 165]. As Stephan Boehm [1982] shows, this ambiguity surrounding the very notion of subjectivism has damaging consequences for Austrian theory as a whole.

Emphatically, cognitive theory does not lead to the exclusion of the social dimension but to its reinforcement. We cannot hope to create a conceptual framework capable of handling vast quantities of information on our own. We have to rely on interaction with others to develop our cognitive skills, to form judgments about the world, and to acquire guidelines for action. This basic point is uncontroversial, even simplistic, at least for the social psychologist. Consequently, there are no clear boundaries between the sub-disciplines of cognitive and social psychology. Indeed the areas of study overlap and form the further sub-discipline of cognitive social psychology. In defiance of the extreme subjectivism of the Austrians, the social dimension to cognitive theory will not go away.

Consider the experiments in social psychology that reveal the influence of others on our formations of judgment and acts. For example, Solomon Asch [1952, chap. 16] showed that a single individual will very often alter his or her own explicit judgment when faced with an unanimous but erroneous majority. A group of subjects were asked to identify which of three lines of clearly different length was equal to a standard line. Unknown to the critical subject, it had been pre-arranged with the remainder of the subjects that they would call out the same wrong answer in some cases. It was found that the critical subject would make an incorrect judgment in order to conform to the majority in as many as one in three cases, despite the fact that the difference in length of the two lines was quite obvious to the observer.

Even more striking are the experiments of Stanley Milgram on obedience and authority. He found that a majority of ordinary, reasonable adults would administer to another person electric shocks that were apparently painful, dangerous, and even fatal, if ordered to do so as part of an ostensibly scientific experiment. In fact, the shocks were not real and the person receiving them was a trained actor, crying out in pain and eventually feigning unconsciousness or death. This challenging experiment indicates how much people will change their behavior according to the institutional setting. "*There is a propensity for people to accept definitions of action provided by legitimate authority*. That is, although the subject performs the action, he allows authority to define its meaning" [Milgram 1974, p. 145]. There are now a large number of experiments in social psychology that suggest, but not always in such a dramatic fashion, social and group influences on behavior and cognition.

These influences achieve even greater recognition when we approach or cross the boundaries with sociology or anthropology. An important illustration is found in anthropological work on the acquisitin of linguistic skills and the learning of signs and meanings. As Mary Douglas asserts: "Speech is a social phenomenon, and . . . social decisions mark off the boundaries between different provinces of meaning" [Douglas 1973, p. 13]. One of the few economists to take on this point is Ian Steedman [1980]. In a work tucked away in a relatively obscure journal, convenient for the orthodox to ignore, he writes of the "intrinsically non-autonomous" character of preferences and beliefs. From the moment we are born we begin to acquire a social language and a shared symbolic order. Individual knowledge is expressed in a social language and passed through a set of socially acquired cognitive filters. We perceive much of the world through language and symbols that have no meaning in an individual sense. Our express aims and purposes, whatever their individual qualities, are formulated in language that is in its essence not individual but social.

Action and Institutions

A point being stressed here is that most significant views on rationality and action outside orthodox economics are incompatible with the unsatisfactory notions that prevail in economics today. This is true for sociology as well as psychology and anthropology. Decades ago Talcott Parsons [1940] wrote a plea that economists should abandon their narrow and uncomplicated view of human motivation and rationality and pay heed to "work going on in other fields of the study of human behavior." Such a request is worthy of repetition and brief discussion here.

At the outset, Parsons emphasizes that economic activity takes place within an institutional framework. Institutions are not simply organizational structures: "They are *normative* patterns which define what are felt to be, in the given society, proper, legitimate, or expected modes of action or of social relationship" [Parsons 1940, p. 190]. While veering toward a questionable functionalism in an ensuing passage, with mention of "the requirements of institutional patterns," Parsons makes points that would be accepted by a wide range of social theorists. "Institutional patterns depend," he argues, "for their maintenance in force, on the support of the moral sentiments of the members of society" [p. 192]. Concerning the origin of these "moral sentiments," he writes:

> The prevailing evidence is that the deeper moral sentiments are inculcated in early childhood and are deeply built into the structure of personality itself. They are, in the deeper sense, beyond the range of conscious decision and control, except perhaps in certain critical situations, and even when consciously repudiated, still continue to exert their influence .... The fact that concretely economic activities take place in a framework of institutional patterns would imply that, typically, such disinterested elements of motivation play a role in the determination of their course [p. 193].

In discussing the idea of self-interested behavior, Parsons is keen to show that this too has social and institutional facets: "It can be seen that a very substantial component of the individual's own self-interest is directly dependent on his enjoying the favorable attitudes of others with whom he comes into contact." However, for Parsons "the most crucial point" is that the content, or objectives, of self interest are themselves socially formed: "For it is precisely around social institutions that, to a very large extent, the content of self-interest is organized." It is the organization of the diverse potentialities of human action into a coherent system that is "one of the most important functions of institutions" [p. 197].

The pleas of Parsons and other sociologists from a wide range of viewpoints have been ignored. Economists remain with their simplistic and untenable view of human rationality. One of the consequences of the argument in this essay is that neither the means nor the ends of "subjective" rationality can be taken for granted. Even at the level of fully deliberative decision making institutions and social culture make themselves felt, not merely as constraints, but also in molding the formation of preferences and the acquisition of knowledge upon which choices are made. Just as preferences are woven with a social thread, the bounds to "bounded rationality" must also bear the stamp of culture and institutions.

This theoretical approach may not lend itself to elegant formalization of the neoclassical kind, but it is not devoid of strong and relevant policy conclusions. If preferences are not immaculately conceived, and they are molded by social relations and institutions, then the very notion of *laissez faire* becomes a conceptual impossibility. In the tradition of institutionalist economics since its inception, a more favored place is found for interventionist economic policies and schemes of economic planning.[1]

Conclusion

Long ago, Veblen and other American Institutionalists drew our attention to the incompatibility of the modern scientific view of the human psyche with the basic assumptions of neoclassical economic theory. Modern psychology, as well as developments in sociology and anthropology, vindicates this claim.

At the philosophical level the rationalist conception of action involves a Cartesian division of the world into two, and it cannot explain the act of reason in its own terms without lapsing into self-contradiction. Modern psychological theory shows that consciousness is necessarily hierarchical, emphasizing the complexity of cognitive and thought processes and the large quantity of sensory data and information with which we have to deal. Cognitive theory suggests that for rational thought we are faced with the simultaneous and apparently paradoxical problem of having too little information and too much. Anthropologists and sociologists argue that the large quantity of sensory data is processed by means of concepts and norms that do not arise purely subjectively, but are acquired through social interaction with others and through social institutions.

Why has this weight of opinion elsewhere failed to shift neoclassical economics? Evidently, neoclassical economics has adopted a more and more instrumentalist attitude to its own theory and method. These are to be regarded as useful tools, to be tested according to their track record in prediction. Leaving aside the philosophical problems with this instrumentalism [Boland 1982; Caldwell 1982], it can be sustained only by a hermetic division between economics and the other human sciences.

Even beyond neoclassical theory there is a reluctance to bring to bear psychological developments on social and economic theory. But, as Paul Hirst and Penny Wooley [1982] demonstrate in their recent book, it is unjustifiable to regard social science as apsychological, just as psychology (and even human biology) cannot be constructed satisfactorily on an asocial basis. The breaking down of some of the barriers between the disciplines is long overdue. But this cannot be done if the hard core of orthodox economics is to remain intact. The ejection of the rationalist conception of action from economics is a preliminary and necessary step in rebuilding this hard core. Upon this can be built, with institutionalist materials, a radical and interventionist set of economic policy proposals.

Notes

1. Of course, one of the most important architects of economic interventionism was John Maynard Keynes. A case for rebuilding Keynes's theory on institutionalist foundations is outlined in G. Hodgson [1985]. For related comments see also A. Gruchy [1984]. For various recent institutionalist attempts to survey and develop the theory of planning see, for example, Gruchy [1982], Hodgson [1984], Troub [1982].

Bibliography

Angyal, A. 1941. *Foundations for a Science of Personality*. New York: Commonwealth Fund.

Angyal, A. 1965. *Neurosis and Treatment*. New York: Wiley.

Asch, S. E. 1952. *Social Psychology*. New York: Prentice-Hall.

Ashby, W. R. 1952. *Design for a Brain*. New York: Wiley.

Becker, G. S. 1976. *The Economic Approach to Human Behavior*. Chicago: University of Chicago Press.

Berger, P. L., and T. Luckmann. 1967. *The Social Construction of Reality*. Harmondsworth: Penguin.

Boehm, S. 1982. "The Ambiguous Notion of Subjectivism: Comment on Lachmann." In Kirzner [1982], pp. 41-52.

Boland, L. A. 1982. *The Foundations of Economic Method*. London: George Allen and Unwin.

Bruner, J. S. 1973. *Beyond the Information Given*. London: George Allen and Unwin.

Buchanan, J. M. 1982. "The Domain of Subjective Economics: Between Predictive Science and Moral Philosophy." In Kirzner [1982], pp. 7-20.

Caldwell, B. J. 1982. *Beyond Positivism: Economic Methodology in the Twentieth Century*. London: George Allen and Unwin.

Chomsky, N. 1959. "Review of B. F. Skinner's *Verbal Behavior*." *Language* 35 (January-March): 26-58.

Coats, A. W. 1976. "Economics and Psychology: Death and Resurrection of a Research Programme." In Latsis [1976], pp. 43-64.

Davidson, D. 1980. *Essays on Action and Events*. Oxford: Oxford University Press.

Douglas, M., ed. 1973. *Rules and Meanings*. Harmondsworth: Penguin.

Downs, A. 1957. *An Economic Theory of Democracy*. New York: Harper.
Earl, P. E. 1983. *The Economic Imagination*. Brighton: Wheatsheaf.
Fishburn, P. S. 1974. "Lexicographic Orders, Utilities, and Decision Rules: A Survey." *Management Science* 20 (July): 1442-71.
Georgescu-Roegen, N. 1954. "Choice, Expectations, and Measurability." *Quarterly Journal of Economics* 68 (November): 503-34.
Giddens, A. 1984. *The Constitution of Society: Outline of the Theory of Structuration*. Cambridge: Polity Press.
Gruchy, A. G. 1982. "Planning in Contemporary Institutional Thought." *Journal of Economic Issues* 16 (June): 371-80.
Gruchy, A. G. 1984. "Institutionalism, Post Keynesianism, and Neo-Marxism: An Evaluation." *Journal of Economic Issues* 18 (June): 547-56.
Hayek, F. A., ed. 1935. *Collectivist Economic Planning*. London: Routledge and Kegan Paul.
Hayek, F. A. 1952a. *The Counter-Revolution of Science*. Glencoe, Ill.: Free Press.
Hayek, F. A. 1952b. *The Sensory Order: An Inquiry into the Foundations of Theoretical Psychology*. London: Routledge and Kegan Paul.
Hindess, B. 1977a. "Humanism and Teleology in Sociological Theory." In Hindess [1977b].
Hindess, B., ed. 1977b. *Sociological Theories of the Economy*. London: Macmillan.
Hindess, B. 1977c. *Philosophy and Methodology in the Social Sciences*. Brighton: Harvester.
Hindess, B. 1984. "Rational Choice Theory and the Analysis of Political Action." *Economy and Society* 13 (August): 255-77.
Hirst, P. Q., and P. Woolley. 1982. *Social Relations and Human Attributes*. London: Tavistock.
Hodgson, G. 1984. *The Democratic Economy*. Harmondsworth: Pelican.
Hodgson, G. 1985. "Persuasion, Expectations, and the Limits to Keynes." In Lawson and Pesaran [1985], pp. 10-45.
Hollis, M., and E. Nell. 1975. *Rational Economic Man*. London: Cambridge University Press.
Kagel, J. H., et al. 1981. "Demand Curves for Animal Consumers." *Quarterly Journal of Economics* 96 (February: 1-16.
Kay, N. M. 1984. *The Emergent Firm: Knowledge, Ignorance, and Surprise in Economic Organisation*. London: Macmillan.
Kirzner, I. M., ed. 1982. *Method, Process, and Austrian Economics*. Lexington, Mass.: Heath.
Koestler, A. 1967. *The Ghost in the Machine*. London: Hutchinson.
Latsis, S. J., ed. 1976. *Method and Appraisal in Economics*. Cambridge: Cambridge University Press.
Lawson, A., and H. Pesaran, eds. 1985. *Keynes's Economics: Methodological Issues*. London: Croom Helm.
Lloyd, B. B. 1972. *Perception and Cognition*. Harmondsworth: Penguin.
McLeod, J. M., and S. R. Chaffee. 1972. "The Construction of Social Reality." In Tedeschi [1972], pp. 50-99.
Milgram, S. 1974. *Obedience to Authority*. London: Tavistock.

von Mises, L. 1949. *Human Action: A Treatise on Economics*. London: William Hodge.
von Mises, L. 1957. *Theory and History: An Interpretation of Social and Economic Evolution*. New Haven: Yale University Press.
Mitchell, W. C. 1918. "Bentham's Felicific Calculus." *Political Science Quarterly* 33 (June): 161-83. Reprinted in Mitchell [1937].
Mitchell, W. C. 1937. *The Backward Art of Spending Money and Other Essays*, edited by J. Dorfman. New York: McGraw-Hill.
Neisser, U. 1967. *Cognitive Psychology*. New York: Appleton-Century-Crofts.
Neisser, U. 1976. *Cognition and Reality*. San Francisco: Freeman.
Nozick, R. 1977. "On Austrian Methodology." *Synthese* 36 (December): 353-92.
Pareto, V. 1935. *The Mind and Society*. 4 vols. (translated from the Italian edition of 1923 by A. Bongiorno and A. Livingston and edited by A. Livingston). London: Jonathan Cape.
Pareto, V. 1971. *Manual of Political Economy* (translated from the French edition of 1927 by A. S. Schwier and edited by A. S. Schwier and A. N. Page). New York: Augustus Kelley.
Parsons, T. 1940. "The Motivation of Economic Activities." *Canadian Journal of Economics and Political Science* 6 (May): 187-203. Reprinted in Smelser [1965], pp. 53-66.
Piaget, J. 1969. *The Mechanisms of Perception*. New York: Basic Books.
Rudner, R. S. 1954. "Philosophy and Social Science." *Philosophy of Science* 21 (April): 164-68.
Searle, J. R. 1983. *Intentionality: An Essay in the Philosophy of Mind*. Cambridge: Cambridge University Press.
Searle, J. R. 1984. *Minds, Brains, and Science*. London: British Broadcasting Corporation.
Simon, H. A. 1955. "A Behavioral Model of Rational Choice." *Quarterly Journal of Economics* 69 (February): 99-118. Reprinted in Simon [1957a], pp. 241-60.
Simon, H. A. 1957a. *Models of Man: Social and Rational*. New York: Wiley.
Simon, H. A. 1957b. *Administrative Behavior: A Study of Decision-Making Processes in Administrative Organization*, 2d ed. New York: Macmillan.
Simon, H. A. 1959. "Theories of Decision-Making in Economic and Behavioral Sciences." *American Economic Review* 49 (June): 253-83.
Simon, H. A. 1965. "Rational Choice and the Structure of the Environment." *Psychological Review* 63 (March): 129-38. Reprinted in Simon [1957a], pp. 261-73.
Smelser, N. J., ed. 1965. *Readings in Economic Sociology*. Englewood Cliffs, N.J.: Prentice-Hall.
Sommerhoff, G. 1974. *Logic of the Living Brain*. London: Wiley.
Spradley, J. P., ed. 1972. *Culture and Cognition: Rules, Maps, and Plans*. San Francisco: Chandler.
Steedman, I. 1980. "Economic Theory and Intrinsically Non-Autonomous Preferences and Beliefs." *Quaderni Fondazione Feltrinelli*, no. 7/8.
Steinbruner, J. D. 1974. *The Cybernetic Theory of Decision*[*New Dimensions of Political Analysis*. Princeton, N.J.: Princeton University Press.

Tedeschi, J. T., ed. 1972. *The Social Influence Processes*. Chicago: Aldine Atherton.
Thaler, R. H., and H. M. Shefrin. 1981. "An Economic Theory of Self-Control." *Journal of Political Economy* 89 (April): 392-406.
Troub, R. M. 1982. "A General Theory of Planning: The Evolution of Planning and the Planning of Evolution." *Journal of Economic Issues* 16 (June): 381-90.
Tversky, A. 1969. "Intransitivity of Preferences." *Psychological Review* 76 (January): 31-48.
Vaughn, K. I. 1982. "Subjectivism, Predictability, and Creativity: Comment on Buchanan." In Kirzner [1982], pp. 21-29.
Veblen, T. 1909. "The Limitations of Marginal Utility." *Journal of Political Economy* 17: 235-45. Reprinted in Veblen [1936], pp. 151-75.
Veblen, T. 1919. *The Place of Science in Modern Civilisation and Other Essays*. New York: Huebsch.
Veblen, T. 1936. *What Veblen Taught*, edited by W. C. Mitchell. New York: Augustus Kelly.
Winston, G. 1980. "Addiction and Backsliding: A Theory of Compulsive Consumption." *Journal of Economic Behavior and Organization* 1 (March): 295-324.
Wohlwill, J. 1962. "From Perception to Inference: A Dimension of Cognitive Development." *Society for Research in Child Development Monograph 27(2)*, pp. 87-107.

6

The Social Value Theory of Orthodoxy: A Review and Critique

Marc R. Tool

The meaning and validity of economic theory has customarily been pursued and demonstrated in the context of its use in the identification, analysis, and intended resolution of economic problems. The creation of theory has routinely been prompted and warranted by its relevance (immediate or ultimate) to the formation of economic policy—policy intended to improve existing conditions.[1] St. Thomas Aquinas was concerned with the rise of commercialism and the dictum of just price. David Ricardo's strategic policy interest was the Corn Laws. Karl Marx disclosed the alienation and deprivation of industrial workers and sought a revolutionary end to exploitation. John Maynard Keynes diagnosed determinants of massive and continuing instability and urged public management of aggregate demand. Arthur Okun's inflation analysis generates recommendations for the use of tax powers to constrain administered pricing.[2] Accordingly, economic inquiry historically has been directed both to positive (what is) and to normative (what ought to be) concerns, even though from John Stuart Mill and Nassau Senior on, mainstream classical and neoclassical theorists have sought the posture and position of positivism solely.[3]

Normative principles and standards which permit the identification and determination of what ought to be, which constitute criteria with which choices among alternatives may be made, are regarded here as value principles in the philosophical sense and usage. In social (including economic) analysis, the choices must be made from among institutional structures, that is, prescriptive and proscriptive organizational arrangements for correlating behavior. Accordingly, the criteria for social choice are principles of social value. The identification of a problem and the choice of policies as institutional adjustments to resolve it require recourse to social value principles.

The essential point may be put categorically. An inquirer cannot logically or empirically distinguish between what is and what ought to be without applying a criterion of judgment, a social value principle. If there is general agreement with the foregoing that economic theory building is purposively addressed to problem solving, then such inquiry must implicitly or explicitly include normative as well as positive premises and constructs. The philosophical dilemma for traditional neoclassical economists has often appeared to be the simultaneous and contradictory claims to positivism and to problem solving relevance—the concern to eschew value judgments and yet to advise on economic policy which compels the use of value principles. The confusion generated by this dilemma as it appears in conventional texts and elsewhere is one reason for developing this review and critique of social value theory.[4]

A related and more important reason is the prevailing dominion of ethical relativism, which asserts that value principles and criteria are relative to individuals or cultures holding them. Values are noncognitive, subjective, and given.[5] Clarence Ayres characterized this dominion as "the pestilence of moral agnosticism."[6] Contemporary neoclassicism's affirmation of ethical relativism has been challenged, but it remains substantially intact.[7] This affirmation is manifested in the largely uncritical acceptance of "wants as given" in traditional demand analysis, the ambivalence of "better off" and "worse off" in the Paretian optimum, the uncertainty of meaning of "costs" and "benefits" in cost-benefit analysis, and the deference to ordered, but unexamined, preferences in indifference analysis. One of the consequences of such affirmation is to advocate or tolerate the removal from inquiry of any serious or credible concern with social value theory. This article is intended to help demonstrate that the views concerning social value of mainstream theorists are inadmissible on philosophical grounds and inapplicable on pragmatic grounds, and that a more warrantable social value theory is needed if headway is to be made in resolving major economic problems which are now producing agonizing, divisive, and destructive consequences.

From the perspective of neoinstitutionalism,[8] then, we offer a review and critique of the social value position of orthodoxy. *Orthodoxy* here refers to the contributions of, among others, the neoclassical Marshallian utilitarian theorists and their intellectual progeny, as well as the Paretian and Hicksian revisionists, including axiomatic theorists. The value positions of these constituents of orthodoxy are considered and appraised in the following sections.

Utilitarianism

In the classical and much of the neoclassical tradition in economics, the maximal satisfaction of wants, notably consumer wants, has been and remains the basic criterion of judgment, the standard of value, the basis on which to distinguish between good and bad, proper and improper, and desirable and undesirable. *Utility*, the ability or capacity of goods and services to satisfy human wants, has been and continues to be the value referent. Maximizing utility is the ultimate and continuing purpose or goal of individuals; this goal is thought to be most fully realized in a free enterprise economy.

Recall Jeremy Bentham's concern as a classicist to identify a scientific ethic. "Nature," he argued,

> has placed mankind under the governance of two sovereign masters, *pain* and *pleasure*. It is for them alone to point out what we ought to do as well as to determine what we shall do. . . . They govern us in all we do, in all we say, in all we think. . . . The *principle of utility* recognizes this subjection. . . . By the principle of utility is meant that principle which approves or disapproves of every action whatsoever, according to the tendency which it appears to have to augment or diminish the happiness of the party whose interest is in question. . . . By utility is meant that property in any object, whereby it tends to produce benefit, advantage, pleasure, good, or happiness . . . or . . . to prevent the happening of mischief, pain, evil, or unhappiness.[9]

Bentham's "hedonistic calculus" would compel the determination of worth or value from a quantitative balancing of pleasure and pain, of utility and disutility. Utility is embedded in the product or service. The utility derived varies with the intensity, duration, certainty, and propinquity of the pleasure experienced.[10] In such fashion, Bentham most extensively and conspicuously, if not persuasively, postulated a theory of human nature and gave explicit formulation to the utilitarian value principle as a basic premise of orthodox economics.

The utilitarian premise is also firmly embedded in mainstream neoclassicism, but with Alfred Marshall, utility becomes a subjective estimate of desire. Utility does not reside in the good or service itself; it is a derivative feeling state which price measures. Said Marshall: "Utility is taken to be correlative to Desire or Want . . . desires cannot be measured directly but only indirectly by the outward phenomena to which they give rise; and . . . in those cases with which economics is chiefly concerned the measure is found in the price which a person is willing to pay for the fulfillment or satisfaction of his desire."[11]

Dennis Robertson elaborated the theme: "We shall not go far wrong, so runs the [Marshall-Pigou] theory, if we assume that the normal consumer, in disposing of his income, seeks to *maximize* something which we can call indifferently his satisfaction, his utility, or his economic welfare. He does this in the light of his knowledge of a law of the diminishing increments of utility to be gained from successive increments of expenditure in any one direction—a knowledge which assists him so to distribute his expenditure that the *marginal* utility of the several goods he purchases is proportional to their market price."[12]

For the Marshallian utilitarians, utility is the referent for social value, and *price* is its measure. As the remarks of Marshall and Robertson quoted above affirm, prices people pay purport to record the fact of their efforts to satisfy desires, wants, and tastes and to measure the intensity of such wants and tastes by the character and extent of their purchases. Prices become the "objective" data with which to measure the depth and magnitude of "subjective" desires. Indeed, as most will acknowledge, so accepted is the foregoing, that "price" is frequently taken as a synonym for "value." A historian of economic thought could mark the shift from classical to neoclassical thought, not with a change from utility as the *meaning* of social value, but with a change from embodied labor to price as the *measure* of social value.

The identification of price with social value usually runs from value to price (not the reverse). Accordingly, price is held to represent real worth, which is utility. Thus price becomes a criterion of judgment in consumer and other economic choices. It serves as an evidential surrogate for a nonevidential feeling state. For this reason, among others, these orthodox theorists have long looked upon the analysis of price as their main object of inquiry. A general theory of price would, in fact, constitute a general theory of the economic process.[13] "Ah, sweet mystery of price," observed

Clarence Ayres; it is thought to be the central reality to be explained in economics.

The Inadequacy of Utility Theory

The effort to use utility as the criterion of judgment in economic and social analysis is fatally flawed for three interrelated reasons. It is inadmissible as a principle of social value because it is *tautological,* because it is *relativistic,* and because it is *inapplicable.* Tautology describes a circularity in reasoning; relativism imposes an ambivalence that renders the criterion inoperative; inapplicability arises from the conceptual sterility of a concept and its consequent inability to function in the role assigned, that is, as a criterion of judgment in choosing among institutional alternatives.

The *tautological* deficiency of utility was suggested some years ago by Joan Robinson: "Utility," she observed, "is a metaphysical concept of impregnable circularity; *utility* is the quality in commodities that makes individuals want to buy them, and the fact that individuals want to buy commodities shows that they have *utility.*"[14] The alleged subjective quest to satisfy wants is not demonstrated by the objective fact of market activity; it is a tautological affirmation and attribution for which demonstration is impossible. *Whatever* occurs as market involvement is assumed to reflect a utility maximizing judgment of the participant. On this small conjectural block is erected the edifice of utility value theory.

Consider this point further. If we assume that all economic behavior is intended either to maximize utility or minimize disutility, we appear to have a universal explanation for economic activity. Recall that in orthodox thinking there is no analytic interest in the character of wants, no discrimination between or among tastes and desires. They are whatever they are.[15] The purpose of the market is to satisfy such wants and tastes. There is no interest in the origin of wants and tastes; they derive from whatever source. The position is ahistorical and acultural.

But orthodoxy does not provide an explanation of economic behavior. To say that rational people maximize utility is to say nothing analytically informative. At most, it can only suggest that people are motivated in some way. The utility maximization principle is conjectural assertion; its referential content is illusive; it does not provide accounting or explanation. Explanation hinges on the ability to establish linkages or connections between or among items, the identities or meanings of which are knowable. Inquiry involves the quest for causal connections, for observable regularities of experience. Items become known when they are placed in the continuum of which they are determined to be a part, that is, when the ties, connections, or causal relations can be identified or evidentially inferred. But here, linkages can neither be discerned nor demonstrated. "Utils" are imaginary entities, of course. Subjective wants and objective behavior cannot be shown nor credibly or convincingly inferred to be causally related.

Accordingly, utility maximization does not distinguish, because it cannot, some actions from others. People are left in the position of saying that market behavior must reflect the quest for maximal satisfaction or satiated desires; otherwise, they would have acted differently. Thus, *whatever* the economic activity, it is assumed to be in quest of maximized satisfaction. Such conjectural affirmation tells us nothing about how market (and other economic) choices are made. Utility maximization provides no applicable standard for judging the propriety of actual market activity or of public economic goals.[16]

The matter does not end there. When neoclassical theorists take wants and tastes as given, they build into inquiry a related tautological and circular dilemma. "What is," say utilitarians, is an existing pattern of wants and tastes. Since the purpose of an enterprise economy is to facilitate the satisfaction of wants, orthodoxy effectively recommends that what is be used as a standard or criterion for judging what ought to be. But if what is becomes a criterion, what ought to be will, if possible, be made to look like what is. Thus, what is is elevated to the role of a value principle; the mores are raised to normative status. Existing wants and tastes are reenshrined and reinforced. The status quo is reaffirmed. The structural blend of capitalist institutions remains largely unquestioned. What is, is right. By so proceeding, utility theorists abandon credible efforts to identify a problem as institutional malfunctioning and do not sufficiently pursue inquiry into actual problem determinants (institutional, technological, ideational, ideological, motivational, political, and so forth). The conservatism of mainstream neoclassicism may now be understood to have roots in the tautological character of its value premises.

Consider next the *relativism* of utility as a value principle. As noted, utility theorists take wants and tastes as given in traditional price theory. The character of wants, their origin, and the consequences set in motion by their satisfaction are all, by deliberate exclusion, outside the purview of orthodox analysis. The claim to being ethically relative about wants and tastes permits the orthodox to sustain their posture of positivism. Whatever the mores and folkways of a culture set as goals (wants and tastes), those are the ones a capitalist economy should provide. The goals, note, are to be set outside the economic process. The posture of ethical relativism permits the utilitarian economists, qua economists, to profess their avoidance of the value problem. They allegedly take their goals and purposes from the community and continue to proclaim their positivism as economists. But in their roles as teachers, scholars, and advisors, they are practicing normativists.

Neither the positivist nor the ethical relativist position can be sustained. Every people at all times must and do discriminate between and among wants, tastes, and desires. They do so generally on the basis of their appraisal of the consequences expected or experienced. At the level of individual consumers, private and public bodies regulate or prohibit the sale of drugs and other products deemed harmful and displace, circumvent, or supplement "market allocation" of, for example, foods, medicines, housing, and transportation to various segments of the community. Illustratively, at the level of the community, private and public bodies directly and indirectly determine the priority use of resources in setting public budgets, in foreign trade policy, energy policy, overhead capital formation, and in manpower utilization. No political economy would survive if there were ambivalence concerning the character of wants and tastes actually experienced. Yet, the ethical relativism of utilitarians would compel the abstention of economists from applying their professional skills and knowledge in deliberations and recommendations regarding such concerns. The consequences of fulfilling some wants and tastes in lieu of others constitute a good part of the political dialogue in any government in which consent of the governed is a reality. Every political economy does, because it must, ignore professed ambivalence and indifference regarding wants and tastes; it must abandon positivistic pretenses. Every political economist who accepts the role of policy advisor, in person or in his writings, is compelled to abandon such ambivalence, claims to the contrary notwithstanding.

Finally, we argue that utility is *inapplicable* as a standard or principle of social value because it is conceptually sterile. It has, and can have, no conceptual progeny. It can neither generate nor be incorporated into creative hypotheses. It cannot be made an integral or operative part of a causal continuum. It cannot be linked or tied to other concepts; it is a conceptual *cul de sac*. Utility has no substantive or communicable content as a concept or value referent. It purports to stand for virtually anything; in consequence, it can stand for nothing analytically useful.

Assume for illustrative purposes that a community faces the problem of environmental pollution and is considering institutional options with which to respond to the problem. Proposals have been suggested concerning the offending polluted water-course. Option A would fine and punish polluting industries. Option B would use massive public funds to build more effective sewer systems. Option C would prohibit public use of polluted waters. Option D would publicly admonish polluters to abandon polluting activity. Option E would create a study commission to make recommendations two years hence. Option F would defer to presumed market forces for a solution and would involve no new public action. Do economists and communities address these options seeking to decide among or between them on the basis of what will maximize satisfaction? Here, the choice is not a trivial one between, say, whether to have baked beans or cauliflower for dinner, a decision to which, one supposes, some deference to acquired tastes might be shown. It is, rather, a matter of public policy and institutional adjustment. And the consequences of choosing one or more options over the others are predictable and substantial, and they are markedly different. But the appraisal of consequences cannot meaningfully proceed using utility (want maximization) as a criterion. "Want satisfaction" is not at issue. At issue is the functional role which cleaner water would demonstrably play in the health and well-being of those affected. Needed is a criterion for choosing among institutional options. For this purpose, utility is devoid of significance; utility is inapplicable. Accordingly, when problematic exigencies compel judgment, appeal to and use of some other criterion must occur.

Pareto Optimality, Indifference Demand, and Axiomatic Choice Theory

The conceptual embrace of the utilitarian philosophy of Bentham, Marshall, and others was allegedly broken by John R. Hicks, among others, in recent decades. As Hicks observed: "If one is a utilitarian in philosophy one has a perfect right to be a utilitarian in one's economics. But if one is not (and few people are utilitarians nowadays) one also has the right to an economics free from utilitarian assumptions."[17]

Pressure for the abandonment of utility, interpersonal comparisons of utility, and utility maximizing constructs was generated by the advent of logical positivism and the pursuit of a value-free economics, or at least the pursuit of economic inquiry without recourse to utility value.[18] Manifestations of the envisioned abandonment or avoidance are found conspicuously in the recourse to the Paretian optimum, indifference demand theory, and axiomatic analysis.

Ethical neutrality was sought with the Paretian optimum. As described by Kenneth Boulding, "the Paretian optimum . . . states in effect that condition A of a social system is economically superior to condition B, if nobody feels worse off in A than in B and at least one person feels better off. Better off or worse off are measured of course by preferences, so we could restate the condition by saying that state A is superior to state B if one or more persons prefer A and nobody prefers B."[19] The foregoing describes the situation of subjective or consumer optimality. In addition, a physical or productive optimum must concurrently be sought, whereby factors are allocated in a fashion such that no larger output can be achieved with the same factor input. An equilibrium for an economy would exist when these two optimums are simultaneously achieved.

Note that the Paretian optimum is by design a criterion of social value, even though it is perceived as a way of avoiding utility value judgments. It does offer *a* "meaning" of community well-being. It purports to distinguish between what is and what ought to be. Sidney Alexander recently characterized this social welfare criterion perceptively: "As a normative principle Pareto-optimality corresponds roughly to a cooperative egoistic hedonism plus the assumption that the individual is the best judge of what will make him happy, an alliance among monads. Whether Pareto-optimality is right or wrong, it is normative to the core."[20] He adds that this Paretian optimum is the only normative principle which traditional economists will admit to using.

The contribution of indifference demand theory, made by Hicks and others,[21] is characterized by the explicit abandonment of cardinally measured utility in favor of ordinally ranked utility. References to utility maximization are, for the most part, dropped in favor of optimization. The undergirding sensationalist psychology of the utilitarians is jettisoned in favor of the simple assertion that people have preferences which they are able to rank or order. The law of diminishing marginal utility is scrapped in favor of the marginal rate of substitution.

The heart of the matter appears to reside in two basic methodological shifts.[22] First, indifference theorists strip the term *utility* of any substantive meaning. As Paul Dale Bush has argued, with ordinal theorists, utility comes descriptively to mean an "index of preferences," simply and solely. It no longer connotes hedonism, pleasures, or happiness. Utility theorists presumed to explain behavior hedonistically, but, as we observed above, did not succeed. Indifference theorists, in contrast, do not presume to explain behavior psychologically.

Second, indifference theorists relieve utility of its maximizing connotations in favor of optimization. Optimizing becomes the general and governing principle; maximizing, as a subordinate principle, becomes one of several ways to optimize. Ordinal theorists do hold the view that consumers prefer to move to higher indifference curves and that such shifts generate more total satisfaction. But maximization of utility is neither a necessary assumption nor an explanation of behavior.

Preferences are assumed and given; a rational consumer orders his or her preferences. Preferences reflect that which will be found satisfying. The economy's purpose is to provide for exhibited preferences. Moving to higher indifference curves is presumed to be desired and desirable because preferences are more fully met, that is, a higher total "utility" (index of preferences) could be achieved.[23] Downward sloping demand curves are derived from indifference curves, and market behavior is described without recourse to utility maximization or interpersonal comparisons, according to ordinal theorists.

The recent development of axiomatic choice theory by Gerard Debreu and others appears in part as an effort to complete the exorcising of utility constructs begun and pursued by Hicks and others.[24] The formulation of choice theory involves the distillation of axioms which delineate the nature of choice as involving preference relations and indifference relations. These basic and inclusive axioms take the form of logical imperatives for the construction of judgments. Vivian Walsh's "pure science" version of these axioms includes:[25] comparability (options are comparable); transitivity (consistency of choices, that is, if A over B and B over C, then A over C); asymmetry (options A and B cannot each be preferred to the other); the most preferred if attainable will be chosen over the less preferred; "if something is attainable, *something* will be chosen";[26] therefore, one preferred choice exists; and unbounded or open attainable sets are ruled out.

When the foregoing inclusive choice theory is applied to consumer demand analysis, additional axioms are required. An example is the axiom of insatiability, an "unsatiability assumption on preferences," which posits the contention that one cannot be satiated with *all* commodities, although an individual may be satiated with some. "Ruled out is a world wherein one cannot improve his position by having more of anything."[27] And although improving one's position does not necessarily mean larger quantities of physical goods, it does connote increased satisfaction of, or fuller response to, preferences in some form.

In axiomatic theory, rationality is defined as observance of the axioms of choice theory. Preferences here are also given and are analytically unexamined as to origin and character. Criteria of choice, that in terms of which choices are made, do not enter the analysis. In the view of axiomatic theorists, optimization is sought in lieu of maximization of utility. Accordingly, the constructs of utilitarianism are allegedly evaded, and normative concerns are never raised. Formal scientific economic analysis can, it is believed, retain its positivistic posture.

The Inadequacy of Post-Marshallian Theories

In appraising the social value position of more recent contributors, it will be helpful and instructive to recognize the fact of a logical continuation of the assumptions of methodological individualism from cardinal utility theory to Paretian, ordinal utility, and axiomatic theory.[28] Of interest is the extent of the departure of the new from the old. As Figure 1 illustrates, there is similarity and commonality, not identity of positions.

Given the extent of this methodological commonality and connectedness of Marshallian and post-Marshallian orthodoxy, is there also some measure of normative commonality between these two traditions which

Cardinal Utility Theory	*Paretian/Ordinal/Axiomatic Theory*
1. Human nature is original and given; view is acultural and ahistorical.	1. Human nature is not explained; implicitly original and given; view is acultural and ahistorical.
2. People are isolated, discrete, definitive "globules of desire";* they are atomistic actor-agents.	2. People are isolated, discrete, definitive "globules of desire"; they are atomistic actor-agents.**
3. Individuals are egoistic; they seek to maximize utility; they are hedonistic.	3. Individuals are egoistic; they seek highest indifference curve, to gain satisfaction.
4. Wants and tastes are given; goods are selected on basis of amount of utility anticipated.	4. Preferences are given and ordered; goods are selected with reference to preference ordering.
5. Individuals are rational; they know their own wants and tastes and how to maximize in markets.	5. Individuals are rational; they know their own preferences and how to order them; they apply and follow axioms.
6. "Utility" is a function of quantity; more is better than less.	6. "Welfare" is a function of quantity; more is preferred to less.
7. Knowledge of economy is derived from individual wants, desires, and actions.	7. Knowledge of economy is derived from individual preferences, desires, and actions.

*Thorstein Veblen, *The Place of Science* (New York: Russell and Russell, 1961 [1919]), p. 73.

**Some axiomatic theorists do recognize the possibility of the "dependence of individual preferences on others' choices." See Peter Newman, *The Theory of Exchange* (Englewood Cliffs, N.J.: Prentice-Hall, 1965), p. 46, note B(6).

Figure 1

reflects this methodological similarity? The answer is affirmative. To anticipate, in the following discussion, on the one hand the Paretian optimum is found to be flawed as a normative principle in ways comparable to cardinal utility theory. Ordinal and axiomatic theorists, on the other hand, appear mistakenly to profess to abstain from offering value principles. An elaboration follows.

Recall that Alexander characterized Paretian optimality as an "alliance of monads." The social order is addressed, in Paretian optimality, as a collection of individuals with ordered preferences. Three basic limitations render the Paretian optimum of doubtful acceptability and relevance as a normative principle.

First, it is not ethically neutral, as presumed. Its intended application tends to perpetuate the status quo. What is becomes a criterion of what ought to be. As A. Allan Schmid has observed, "the Pareto-criterion does not escape the need for a moral choice among the conflicting interests of people. It implements the choice already implicit in status-quo property rights. To limit oneself to Pareto-better change only is to express preference for the current distribution of rights and income."[29] To put the matter even more generally, the Paretian optimum does not address or guide analysis of the institutional fabric and the character of its performance. In an institutional setting, in leaving the structure inviolate, it supports the existing prescriptive rules and power centers. Since it is actually addressed to imagined feeling states of being better or worse off, or of personal preferences, Pareto optimality, as is its cardinal utility forerunner, is also tautological in reaffirming that with which inquiry began, that is, unexamined ordered preferences and/or existing institutional forms.

Second, Paretian optimality displays ethical relativism in most respects comparable to Marshallian-based cardinal utility theory. "Preferences" are givens, even as wants and tastes were givens. No discriminatory index is provided which separates better off from worse off, or good preferences from bad ones. Said Peter Newman: "Primitive notions [are] not definable by means of other terms in the system. The main primitive notion in our theory of preference structures is the idea of preference itself. The idea that an individual *prefers* one commodity bundle in the set X to another such bundle is one that we assume has immediate intuitive meaning, and so one which will receive no further discussion."[30] Any preference is ethically relative to its holder or sponsor. Ethical ambivalence dominates. A discerning alternative view has been contributed by Alexander: "That wants are generated by the social process, not in the trivial sense that they are affected by advertising, but in the profound sense of their dependence on the whole cultural matrix, certainly threatens the entire ethical basis of economics, striking in particular at Pareto-optimality. It challenges the principle that more is better, and opens up the question of what sort of wants we should generate, what sort of men we should make."[31]

More *what* is better? More goods and services, more want satisfaction, location on a higher indifference curve? "What sort of wants should we generate?" The Paretian theorists stand mute; they have no counsel. The Paretian optimum exhibits circularity and relativistic ambivalence comparable to cardinal utility theory.

In addition, ironically, the Paretian optimum retains the atomistic individualistic bias of orthodoxy in inquiry. Kenneth Boulding has observed this attribute: "The Paretian optimum . . . assumes selfishness, that is, the independence of individual preference function [sic], such that it makes no difference to me whether I perceive you as better off or worse off. Anything less descriptive of the human condition could hardly be imagined. The plain fact is that our lives are dominated by the very interdependence of utility functions which the Paretian optimum denies. Selfishness, or indifference to the welfare of others, is a knife-edge between benevolence on the one side and malevolence on the other."[32] Whether or not the interdependence is one of "utility functions" is, in this context, very much to be questioned, but the *fact* of interdependence is not. No significant interdependence among individuals is allowed for; no pervasive interactive connections between individuals and the culture are accommodated. For the most part, the creed of atomistic individualism remains substantially intact.

Third, and finally, the Paretian optimum is inapplicable in its proffered role of a social value principle. The ethically relativistic ambivalence of meaning of such terms as "preferences," "better off," or "worse off" deprives Pareto optimality of applicability. Creation of and choice among options logically and experientially requires the application of a discriminating value criterion. And Kenneth Arrow demonstrated that a social value criterion cannot be derived from an aggregation of individual preferences.[33]

Can we achieve application of Paretian optimality through recourse to cost-benefit analyses? Will Pareto-better serve as a standard of judgment? For us, the answer is negative. Marc Roberts provided a useful commentary which supports this appraisal. He described the effort to make "given preferences" serve a normative role as shallow and of doubtful relevance.

Assume, with Roberts, that the question of improving water quality is before the community. Cost-benefit analysis suggests that "we compare the cost of making the improvement with what people would be willing to pay for the benefits it would bring, in order to decide whether or not to undertake the project."[34] If the question were put to the citizens, could they be expected to make a judgment in these terms when the "benefits" are yet to be experienced? "How accurately," asked Roberts, "can a man know how much he prizes an experience or opportunity he has not had? If we asked someone to put a price on the value of a river after it had been cleaned up and he had enjoyed its purified waters, would it differ from the value he assigned when the river was running dirty? Probably. The evidence is that experiencing an opportunity changes the degree of people's preferences for that opportunity. Almost all studies of the adoption of new goods have shown that familiarity breeds attachment."[35]

Living is a learning experience. So also is the evolving interest in goods and services. Neatly calculated cost-benefit equations in Paretian optimum terms are essentially static; the question of the development and character of these learned preferences is begged. Preferences are not given, they are acquired; and in learning about and acquiring them we do, because we must, discriminate among and between those that we ought to want and those we ought not to want. The experience continuum is the source of insight on the basis of which such distinctions are made. The cultural origin of preferences cannot be ignored, and the need for making value judgments about them cannot be denied. Continued Roberts: "The fact is that an individual's preferences and the sort of choice he is inclined to make in a given situation are affected by any number of unaccountable pushes and pulls, not the least of which are governmental and corporate policies. Ignoring the fact that choices are affected by such policies is not a neutral error. It has the conservative effect of giving ethical significance to existing preferences."[36] The what is is made to serve as an indicator of what ought to be. No problem of social import was ever resolved in this manner.

The applicability of the Paretian optimum is hardly plausible in the pragmatic sense, as well. Could the situation arise in which, as a result of social action, at least one person is made better off and no one is made worse off? Even if a referent for better off is imported from outside Paretian optimality (for example, greater equality of income distribution; nondiscrimination in employment) and used, could there be social and economic change that did not make someone worse off? It is not likely. Indeed, the presumption of an ability to make an empirical determination of such an outcome is seriously to be questioned. Operationally, the Paretian optimum does not constitute nor can it serve as a relevant and applicable criterion of judgment. And again, where problematic exigencies compel the making of institutional choices, some other criterion will have to be used in forming and choosing among alternative economic policies.

Many of the same reservations apply to ordinal utility analysis. The self-conscious abstention from the use of premises of human nature, social change, and even social value converts ordinal theory into an allegedly descriptive account of a universe of economic choice that does not exist. The meaning of choice is reduced to the arid, narrow, nonexperiential preference of good A over good B. Choices are not presumed to occur in a context that has antecedents or consequences in the educative sense for individuals. Account is not taken of time lapse or circumstances. Choices are substantially trivialized.

What is the net gain in insight of ordinal utility over cardinal utility? Preferences, like wants and tastes, are given and relative. Their origin and character remain unexamined. Herbert Marcuse's one-dimensional economic man prefers more to less. But the more *what*? The character of the "more" is of no analytic interest. The recasting of demand theory via indifference maps and derived demand curves offers at most an alternative route to the same resultant—a presumptive description of market pricing mainly under competitive conditions or of public decisions that mimic market pricing and competitive results under controlled conditions of, for example, socialist planning.

Axiomatic theory carries the departure from reality and relevance even farther. In a world of indifference and preference relations postulated for individuals, axiomatic theorists reduce inquiry methodology to a cogent set of logically coherent axioms. The "individuals" postulated are analytically and experientially sealed off from affective reflection, cognitive learning, environmental conditioning, human interdependence, enhancement of skills, revision of habitual responses, maturation of judgment, and the like. Axiomatic choice theory emerges as a reductionistic concern with matters of the perception and logical consistency of preference ordering. Rationality is stripped of any possible qualitative or consequential meaning or dimension. An "alliance of monads" is presumed to describe the human economic *community!*

The flaw relates not to matters of coherence, logical rigor, or mathematical elegance. It relates to the relevance of a model which purports to describe the nature of human economic choice but which places most of the elements that constitute, shape, and govern such choice outside the universe of inquiry. We are, in effect, offered a theory of economic choice which, by design, takes virtually no account of emergent human nature. But the paramount irony is that axiomatic choice theory is devoid of a criterion of social value with which to make economic choices! Axiomatic theorists have severed their own analytical legs in order to fit into the Procrustean bed of logical positivism, ethical relativism, and mathematical rigor. Fortunately, not all theorists and advisors are compelled to join them.

Conclusion

Orthodoxy, in its Marshallian cardinal utility form and its Paretian, ordinal utility, or axiomatic forms, is unable to offer an analytically defensible or experientially applicable principle or standard of social value with which to identify and seek resolution of major economic problems. Yet, at the outset we observed that that which gives warrant and significance to economic inquiry generally is its actual or probable relevance and applicability to such problem analysis. Since the incidence of problems cannot be evaded, the community will expect that the character and determinants of problems will remain concerns of high priority to scholars. The response to that concern must involve both normative and positive dimensions. Overt, value-laden judgments have decided past policy; overt value-laden judgments must and will determine what ought to be in the future. Relevant and defensible social value theory which may help the community formulate such judgments awaits further elaboration, clarification, and experiential assessment.

Notes

1. Leo Rogin, *The Meaning and Validity of Economic Theory* (New York: Harper and Brothers, 1956), chapter 1.
2. Arthur M. Okun, "An Efficient Strategy to Combat Inflation," *Brookings Bulletin* 15 (Spring 1979): 1–6.
3. T. W. Hutchison, *'Positive' Economics and Policy Objectives* (London: George Allen & Unwin, 1964), chapter 1.
4. For example, see Paul A. Samuelson, *Economics,* 10th ed. (New York: McGraw-Hill, 1976), pp. 7–8.
5. Marc R. Tool, *The Discretionary Economy: A Normative Theory of Political Economy* (Santa Monica: Goodyear Publishing Co., 1979), pp. 285–91.
6. Clarence E. Ayres, *Toward a Reasonable Society* (Austin: University of Texas Press, 1961), p. 42.
7. A recent and vigorous challenge is that of E. K. Hunt, *History of Economic Thought* (Belmont, Calif.: Wadsworth Publishing Co., 1979), chapter 15, and *passim.*
8. A perspective on neoinstitutionalism is set forth in my *Discretionary Economy.* Chapter 15 contains a preliminary formulation of an instrumental social value theory which is offered as an alternative to the social value position of orthodoxy.
9. Jeremy Bentham, "Of the Principle of Utility," in *Source Readings in*

Economic Thought, edited by P. C. Newman, A. D. Gayer, and M. H. Spencer (New York: W. W. Norton, 1954), p. 116 (emphasis in original).

10. Elie Halevy, *The Growth of Philosophic Radicalism* (Boston: Beacon Press, 1955), p. 30.
11. Alfred Marshall, *Principles of Economics*, 8th ed. (London: Macmillan, 1920), p. 92.
12. Dennis Robertson, *Utility and All That* (New York: Macmillan, 1952), p. 15 (emphasis in original).
13. J. Fagg Foster, "The Relation between Value Theory and Economic Analysis," unpublished monograph, mimeographed, University of Denver, 1950, pp. 6–10.
14. Joan Robinson, *Economic Philosophy* (Chicago: Aldine, 1962), p. 47.
15. "So far as we are concerned our economic subjects can be pure egoists, pure altruists, pure ascetics, pure sensualists. . . . Our deductions do not provide any justification for saying that caviar is an economic good and carrion a disutility. . . . Individual valuations . . . are outside the sphere of economic uniformity . . . from the point of view of economic analysis these things constitute the irrational elements in our universe of discourse." Lionel Robbins, *An Essay on the Nature and Significance of Economic Science*, 2nd ed. (London: Macmillan, 1952), p. 106. For an alternative view see my *Discretionary Economy*, especially chapters 3 and 15.
16. Recall, in this connection, John Kenneth Galbraith's insistence that *producers* are engaged in creating the wants their products and services are intended to satisfy. This "revised sequence" is discussed in his *Economics and the Public Purpose* (Boston: Houghton Mifflin, 1973), chapter 14.
17. John R. Hicks, *Value and Capital*, 2nd ed. (Oxford: Clarendon Press, 1941), p. 18.
18. I. H. Rima, *Development of Economic Analysis*, rev. ed (Homewood, Ill.: Richard D. Irwin, 1972), pp. 332ff.
19. Kenneth Boulding, *Economics as a Science* (New York: McGraw-Hill, 1970), pp. 125–26.
20. Sidney S. Alexander, "Human Values and Economists' Values," in *Human Values and Economic Policy*, edited by Sidney Hook (New York: New York University Press, 1967), p. 108.
21. Hicks, *Value and Capital*, chapter 1.
22. Paul Dale Bush contributed to the analysis of this section in personal correspondence.
23. Hicks, *Value and Capital*, pp. 13, 17.
24. Gerard Debreu, *Theory of Value, An Axiomatic Analysis of Economic Equilibrium* (New York: John Wiley, 1959); also see Peter Newman, *The Theory of Exchange* (Englewood Cliffs, N.J.: Prentice-Hall, 1965).
25. Vivian Charles Walsh, *Introduction to Contemporary Microeconomics* (New York: McGraw-Hill, 1970), chapter 9.
26. Ibid., p. 85 (emphasis in original).
27. Ibid., p. 139.
28. Paul Dale Bush also contributed significantly to this section. On metho-

dological individualism, see Bush's paper, "The Normative Implications of Positive Analysis," presented at the meetings of the Western Economic Association, Corvallis, Oregon, August 1968.

29. A. Allan Schmid, *Property, Power, and Public Choice* (New York: Praeger, 1979), p. 234.
30. Newman, *Theory of Exchange*, p. 9.
31. Alexander, "Human Values," p. 110.
32. Boulding, *Economics as a Science*, p. 126.
33. Kenneth Arrow, *Social Choice and Individual Values*, 2nd ed. (New York: John Wiley, 1963).
34. Marc J. Roberts, "An Unsimple Matter of Choice," *Saturday Review*, 22 January 1972, p. 46.
35. Ibid.
36. Ibid.

PART II

METHODOLOGY

Introduction to Part II

In the opening section, conceptions of the context of inquiry and basic constructs of causality, rationality, and value, as perceived by institutionalists and neoclassicists, were considered. The articles in this section take up attributes of economic methodology directly.

Eugene Rotwein in the first paper confronts one of the most controversial methodological questions: From a scientific point of view, on what must belief rest? His response, not unexpectedly, is that belief must be grounded on empirical evidence. While beliefs may be and are grounded on nonevidential feelings or visions, they cannot lay claim to scientific standing. Validity of belief in science hinges on empirical demonstration. As Rotwein puts it: "Science seeks general relations between matters of fact, or those general empirical relations that can be couched in the hypothetical form "if A then B," where A is the event denoted by the assumption (or antecedent) of the hypothesis, and B is the prediction (or consequent). When we speak of establishing belief in the context of science, we are then speaking of the method of validating or gaining acceptance of such propositions . . . the empiricist concerns himself with the probable and argues that, for purposes of ascertaining this, there is ample evidence to be drawn from experience." With this approach, Rotwein challenges Milton Friedman's contention that the empirical validity of assumptions in economic analysis does not matter, and he disputes the claim that successful prediction is sufficient. Rotwein insists that economics must take full account of "the central implication of empiricism, that is, the need for repeated testing of all empirical generalizations by reference to experience and the progressive modification of the theoretical apparatus of the discipline in light of such tests." Rotwein continues this methodological exploration through consideration of the views of Martin Bronfenbrenner, Fritz Machlup, and C. V. T. Bear and Daniel Orr.

In exploring "the relationship between value judgments and the methodology of economics," Melville J. Ulmer also enters an area of profound debate. Orthodox neoclassicism purports to be "value free," to eschew value judgments. It is Ulmer's purpose to demonstrate how that view cannot be sustained methodologically. Milton Friedman's claim that value judgments are emotive reactions, regarding which "men can ultimately only fight," and are therefore beyond the realm of reason and impervious to fact or logic, is refuted. Since economics requires the construction of judgments, and since judgments must involve reasoned deliberation over what ought to be desired, value judgments are a necessary and inherent part of economic analysis. Ulmer develops his position by reference to the familiar neoclassical assumption of given tastes and preferences. Insisting that "a measuring rod must be independent of the things to be measured," he argues in effect that given tastes cannot be used as a standard or criterion to judge given tastes. Judgment must enter to appraise or evaluate taste fulfillment in light of the consequences experienced. Although Ulmer does not presume to develop an institutionalist theory of social value, it is clear that he favors, on demonstrable grounds, policies that are derived democratically, that enhance opportunities for individual development, and that ensure an "equal right to life, as well as liberty and the pursuit of happiness." But perhaps, most importantly, Ulmer argues for the placing of value judgments, their character and consequences, back on the inquiry agenda of economists. We must, he contends, "bring to bear the most powerful tools of scientific method . . . to analyze them, to explore their meaning and repercussions, and to make known the full range" and merits of alternative policies. Economics cannot presume to be value free.

The opening question posed by Ken Dennis is this: "Does perfect competition tend to lead to equilibrium? If so, what kind of evidence, logical or empirical, do we require to establish the truth of such a claim?" Dennis then argues that "the theory of perfect competition is lacking genuine scientific support." He develops his case through the defense of two contentions: First, "the theory cannot be proved true by logical means because it is composed of inferences running from cause to effect, and causal inferences cannot be proved true by logical means." Second, "even if the theory is open, in principle, to empirical test as a set of refutable hypotheses, the fact remains that the theory has not been tested and therefore has not been corroborated empirically, notwithstanding vague assertions made about its cogency on the strength of 'casual empiricism'." "If this issue, the scientific status of the theory of perfect competition," he continues, "is to be addressed properly, it is most essential to recognize from the outset that the two alternative characterizations, 'provable theorems' and 'refutable hypotheses,' are indeed mutually exclusive, that is, one and the same truth claim cannot be both provable (by logical demonstration) and refutable (by empirical test) within a consistent definitional framework." Accordingly, another purpose of the article "is to clarify the distinct nature and roles of analytical theorems and refutable hypotheses in scientific inquiry." Dennis develops his position through extensive recourse to major historical contributions both in philosophy and economics, beginning with David Hume, and considers "the rationalist case," "the empiricist case," and the "role of mathematics" in disputing "truth claims" for the "theory of perfect competition."

J. Steven Winrich continues the erosion of confidence in the methodology of orthodoxy by challenging the "persistent belief among neoclassical economists that the mathematical and logical foundations on which their theories rest are secure." Recent contributions of mathematicians have revealed "the incomplete structure of the deductive method" on which orthodoxy remains, evidently, uncritically dependent. Winrich's main purpose is "to illustrate the mathematical and logical development of the principle of self-reference, and to show how this principle exemplifies the incomplete structure of neoclassical economics." Of special interest is his demonstration that "this supposition can be applied to the core of economics, that is, to the value question and the theory of choice." He concludes that "neoclassicism constitutes an incomplete theory of value, an incompleteness that cannot be overcome without a radical paradigmatic shift" to an evolutionary institutional analytical approach. Winrich's inquiry route encompasses the inescapability of self reference ("Human beings not only think but are conscious of their thoughts. . . . All thinking about thinking implies self reference.), the resulting lingual and mathematical paradoxers, the demonstration that formal, closed systems are incomplete because of self-reference, the demonstration that neoclassical economics as a formal system is incomplete and not the "exact and rigorous science" it purports to be, and the derivation that "the utility theory of value is an incomplete and closed system of analysis that maintains its consistency by misconstruing the essential nature of the valuation process. . . . A completely closed and formalized system leads not to truth, but to incompleteness. The flaw in neoclasssical thought is the failure to realize that science does not advance solely by more rigor but also by more imagination."

The paper contributed by James A. Swaney and Robert Premus begins with the contention that "the economic methodology literature [unfortunately] has been preoccupied with theoretical discussion of the appropriateness of methodological models, with insufficient discussion of the actual processes used by economists to construct theories." "Economics," they argue, "places excessive emphasis on the development of fully formulated theoretical systems without sufficient empirical grounding of behavioral assumptions and antecedent conditions." Further, "most of the problems encountered in identifying empirical relationships, which later become necessary in the process of theory testing and policy formation, are ignored." The mode of demonstration of Swaney and Premus involves a review of the nature and progress of the natural sciences in contrast to that in the social sciences, especially economics. In the former, the interactive juxtaposing of theory and fact occurs throughout inquiry. In the latter, orthodox economists develop "fully formulated theoretical structures based on casual empiricism, hunches, and unrealistic assumptions." Only after exhibiting "nonscientific behavior to develop their theories," do they "begin to employ modern empiricist scientific" procedures in an "attempt to link the theory's logical consequences to real phenomena by a process of model verification." The corrective is for economists "to place more emphasis, at the initial stage of theory development, on the use of inductive methods to analyze the institutional, cultural, social, and technological interactions of the phenomena. With this incessant give and take between data and concepts, redefinition and new concept introduction would occur *during* theory building." The needed "structurally inherent bridging devices necessary for empirical verification" would be provided as an integral part of the inquiry process. Swaney and Premus illustrate the significance of their recommendations with brief discussions of migration economics and monetary economics.

Turning now from critical assessments of neoclassicism, this section concludes with Yngve Ramstad's consideration of a general attribute of institutionalist methodology, its holistic character. Ramstad's specific concern is to clarify the analytical approach of one of the founders of institutional thought, John R. Commons, by demonstrating that Common's methodology is holistic and is much more intelligible when cast against that view of inquiry. Indeed, Ramstad considers Commons to be the "prototypical holist." Drawing on the work of Paul Diesing, Ramstad summarizes the holist view as follows: "Holists employ a part-whole mode of apprehending reality. Reality is conceptualized as an integrated whole, a unity, not as a set of logically separable structures and processes ... as perceived by formalists. ... Furthermore, there is no sharp distinction ... between the empirical and logical nature of things. Meaning, therefore, is linked to the context; entities or activities are assumed to be truly comprehensible only in their interrelations with other entities or activities. ... The whole is seen in the main to *determine* the part." [Emphasis in original.] The elements of this "pattern model" of inquiry include comparative analysis of fact-theory relationships, the emergence of observed themes that become hypotheses, the testing of these hypotheses against all available data, and the demonstration of causal linkages and complex interdependencies. If it lacks "rigor," it offers "varying degrees of plausibility" in lieu thereof. "For the holist, understanding of a *system* comes with the comprehension of the unique interrelations between the whole and the parts." In this view, the pattern model approach "is primarily an aid in achieving understanding, not an instrument for making predictions." The bulk of the paper then provides a demonstration of the considerable extent to which Common's pragmatic methodology may be characterized as holistic. This paper serves as a prime example of the modes of inquiry institutional economists employ in lieu of the formalistic, deductivist models of orthodoxy.

7

Empiricism and Economic Method: Several Views Considered

Eugene Rotwein

In the present period with its unparalleled emphasis on the empirical testing of hypotheses, the demands that the standards of science impose on economics are of obvious moment. Accordingly, it might be expected that writings on the methodology of economics generally would reflect these standards. This, however, is not the case. Insofar as economics is regarded as a "science," no one, of course, is flatly opposed to empiricism. Yet, the constructions of empiricism or of its applications to economics vary considerably and in ways which significantly affect both general perspectives and the treatment of important controversial questions within the field.

Some time ago, procedures employed in the empirical testing of economic hypotheses were attacked severely by Milton Friedman in his essay "The Methodology of Positive Economics."[1] Friedman's position, which branded much such empirical testing as a misguided use of scientific method, has been criticized in some detail by myself and others.[2] It is the principal purpose of this article to examine several more recent writings which deal with questions of a general methodological character within the context of economics. Either explicitly or otherwise these raise the same issue considered by Friedman, and, as I shall seek to show, they contribute in various ways to a perpetuation of error regarding the application of empirical principles to the area of economics.

Empiricism and the Background Controversy in Economics

Before considering these writings it will be helpful if brief attention is given two questions: What are the foundations of empiricism and, in light of this, the shortcomings of Friedman's position? What is the nature of the general methodological background, historically speaking, in which the issue raised by Friedman is to be viewed?

To turn to the first question, empiricism rests on an analysis of the manner in which human "belief" is formed. Since this is fundamental, it is ultimately on the acceptability of this analysis that the empirical method stands or falls. There is, of course, no single ground on which belief rests. Man has been transported to a state of belief on the basis of pure emotion, astrology, palmistry, and messages from crystal balls. He confuses dreams with reality, and he hallucinates. Were there nothing beyond such diversity, however, "science" would be impossible; for it is the hallmark of science that its methods of verification can *compel* general agreement. It is the kind of thinking that underlies science—but which in everyday affairs is far more common—that the empiricist takes as the basis for his position on the requirements for establishing belief. Needless to say, although it may have uncomfortable consequences, one may persistently reject even the most compelling empirical evidence. But insofar as the procedures employed in testing any view depart from the testing procedures of science, that view must be acknowledged to remain (more or less) private. It manifestly cannot be argued on scientific grounds that the view should be accepted as valid.

Science seeks general relations between matters of fact, or those general empirical relations that can be couched in the hypothetical form "if A then B," where A is the event denoted by the assumption (or antecedent) of the hypothesis, and B is the prediction (or consequent). When we speak of establishing belief in the context of science, we are then speaking of the method of validating or gaining acceptance of such propositions. In dealing with the question of validation, a basic premise of the empirical position is that it is not permissible to assert that, in the nature of things, relations conflicting with those observed *cannot* occur. If we could make such an assertion, this would imply that relations between matters of fact were logical, which is to say that the opposite of any such relation would violate the principle of noncontradiction (that is, the principle that nothing can be in and out of existence at the same time) and for this reason would be inconceivable or impossible. The opposite of any statement concerning matter-of-fact relations, however, is always conceivable simply because the entities or events related are conceptually separable and therefore can be imagined to assume any form we may choose. This, and only this, is the reason why—as distinct from propositions that are logically related—no proposition concerning empirical relations can be treated as "certain."

Rejecting certainty within the world of empirical relations, the empiricist concerns himself with the probable and argues that, for purposes of ascertaining this, there is ample evidence to be drawn from experience. Here the empiricist accepts the view (which must be treated as a faith) that it is through an understanding of the past that the future may be foreseen. If empirical predictions cannot be made with certainty, what is most likely to occur, in a word, is a repetition of the regularities between events already observed. In other words, our confidence in the occurrence of any prediction B is contingent on the occurrence of another event A, where evidence indicates that the two are invariably related. Our ability to foresee the future—or the transformation of the chaos of "possibility" into the more orderly stuff of "probability"—thus rests on a continuing refinement and improvement in the procedures for ascertaining such regularities.

To consider Friedman's central thesis, this arose out of criticism of certain doctrines fundamental to orthodox economic analysis, specifically, the theory of perfect competition and, more broadly, the principle of marginalism. The criticism centered on the realism of the assumptions underlying these doctrines. Seeking to rebut this attack, Friedman argued that the concern with assumptions represented a total misdirection of effort since, properly construing scientific method, the validity of a theory depended solely on the accuracy of its predictions and not on the realism of its assumptions. For example, the validity of the theory of perfect competition, Friedman contended, did not depend at all on the nature of the markets in which the theory was used for predictive purposes.[3]

As is clear, this argument totally brushes aside the rationale for empirical modes of testing in science. On probability grounds, the belief that any prediction will occur depends on the occurrence of another event (denoted by the assumption) which evidence indicates is invariably related to the prediction. Validity is an index of the confidence we may repose in the belief, and its test involves assertions with respect to the "realism" of both the assumption and the prediction.

Friedman thus ignored the essential condition in science for establishing the validity of a probability statement; he was asserting that confidence in a theory for predictive purposes was unaffected by an *observed absence* of association between the conditions specified by its assumptions and the event predicted.[4] The point may be stated in terms of the requirements for scientific explanation. Although there may be substantial variation in the explanatory content of accepted hypotheses, evidence of a constancy of association between the events related in the hypothesis is likewise essential (as it is for prediction) to the explanation of one of the events by the other.[5] It manifestly cannot be said that the conditions unique to a perfectly competitive market "explain" some given price or output phenomenon in cases where the market is monopolistic. Although Friedman applied the term *explanation* to cases of this latter nature, in arguing that the realism of the assumptions of a theory was irrelevant to its validity his analysis disregarded the requirements for *explanation* as this term is used in science and, commonly, outside the context of science as well.[6]

It should be noted that nothing in the foregoing implies that a prediction drawn from assumptions that are erroneous may not prove accurate. In the realm of relations between matters of fact anything is conceivable; it might turn out that the predicted phenomenon, to use Friedman's phrase, behaved "as if" the assumptions were true when they were, in fact, false. What is implied, rather, is that, to the degree that the prediction depends on the use of erroneous assumptions (which is, of course, what necessitates the employment of the "as if" formulation), it loses plausibility. Accordingly, the evidence concerning the prediction which is required to gain acceptance of its own probability will grow, which is but another way of saying that falsity in any assumption (even if it should, by chance, lead to a true prediction) is an "invalid" element in the hypothesis.[7]

We have been dealing with the foundations of empiricism. But this leads directly to our second question, which concerns the general background of contemporary methodological discussion. For since the principles considered are of general applicability, they are fundamental to the empirical tradition in economics and also go far toward setting the scene for current debate over economic methodology. This is not to say, of course, that in the past the practices of economists typically have been thoroughly empirical. Nor is it to say that formal methodological theory in economics traditionally has taken full account of the central implication of empiricism, that is, the need for repeated testing of all empirical generalizations by reference to experience and the progressive modification of the theoretical apparatus of the discipline in the light of such tests. However, in one basic sense which is of special relevance here—the recognition in principle that realistic assumptions are essential to the validity of theory—the empirical tradition in economics has a venerable lineage. The major classical economists, for example, relied heavily on deduction and argued that this was indispensable to the development of economics as a science. With an eye toward this, it has indeed been asserted—and approvingly—that various nineteenth-century classical economists believed, as does Friedman, that the realism of their premises was irrelevant to the validity of their theories.[8] The evidence is entirely to the contrary. Representing the more general view of the period, not a single classical economist who dealt extensively with methodological theory (for example, Nassau Senior, or J. S. Mill, or J. E. Cairnes) ever doubted that unrealistic assumptions would impair the validity of their theoretical analysis.[9]

This empirical standard, however, has been a constant source of difficulty. For the failure to meet the standard has been one of the most important general grounds on which both the classical and neoclassical economists have been criticized. And owing to its importance, both schools of economists have themselves given much attention to this issue. Considering all views, however, the positions taken have differed. Some of the classical economists, among others, acknowledged the lack of realism in the basic premises and the subsidiary assumptions they employed for deductive purposes and, in conformity with their methodological theory, stressed the need to keep these departures from realism in mind when applying the conclusions of their deductive analysis to experience.[10] Although similarly recognizing the pervasive importance of realism, others stressing the importance of deduction in economics have slighted or rejected the need for repeated and careful testing of the basic premises of their analysis on the ground that experience already had established their universal and immutable truth.[11] A third and quite different position—stated in its most extreme form by Ludwig von Mises and representing an outgrowth of the Austrian approach—has posited a separate deductive world of "pure theory" in which the basic assumptions of economics, although regarded as fundamental to an understanding of the real world, are held to be apprehended *a priori* and are hence alleged to be true independently of any empirical tests.[12]

The requirement that assumptions be "realistic" has indeed long been a heavy cross for the economic theorist to bear. And in propounding his new version of empiricism (a form of "demi-empiricism" which acknowledges the empirical nature of theoretical assumptions but denies the relevance of tests of their realism for "validity") Friedman was seeking to cast off this burden once and for all. In doing so, Friedman was concerned to defend his own brand of theory. Nonetheless, his position has had a broader appeal. It stressed tests of predictions. But pending such tests, it afforded *carte blanche* for the disregard of any and all varieties of "unrealism" in theoretical model-building and so appeared to provide a new and sweeping warrant for a practice which theoretical economists of many persuasions have not found uncongenial to their inclinations. To many (although clearly not all) it seemed that Friedman had made the breakthrough: In boldly proclaiming the "irrelevance" of the long gnawing criticisms of traditional empiricists, he had at one stroke gained for unrealistic economic theorizing a measure of scientific respectability that it previously had not enjoyed. It is scarcely surprising then that others dealing with economic methodology subsequently should have used his analysis, in one fashion or another, to defend the extensive use of "theory" in empirical inquiry.

An Eclectic View

To turn to these post-Friedman writings, let us consider first an essay by Martin Bronfenbrenner which, among other things, is pointedly concerned with the "Friedman controversy," or "the battle of the assumptions."[13] Notwithstanding his own deep interest in economic theory, Bronfenbrenner is an eclectic—in practice as well as in principle. Much of his essay reflects this open-mindedness and his unwillingness to bind himself to any orthodoxy. But in his treatment of the controversy it is largely this eclecticism that leads him astray.

Specifically, Bronfenbrenner contends that in their selection of hypotheses theorists are willing to sacrifice predictive efficiency and explanatory power for simplicity, whereas institutionalists are willing to sacrifice these same objectives for realistic assumptions. In his view both these approaches are legitimate. The particular approach which one adopts, he argues, is wholly a matter of personal preference. The Friedman controversy is thus to be regarded essentially as one concerning personal tastes, and it is misleading to suppose that the issues raised can properly be treated in terms of general methodological standards.[14] This position may appear to afford an inviting way out of the controversy touched off by Friedman's view since it offers something to everyone. But it should be apparent that this overextends eclecticism.

For the hallmark of science lies precisely in its employment of procedures which are based on general methodological principles.

The objectives of these procedures consist in nothing other than the discovery of propositions with predictive efficiency and explanatory power. Once attained, these are never sacrificed for anything else. As noted, it is likewise a characteristic of science that the evidence which its procedures yield (that is, evidence indicating a constancy of association between events) is capable of compelling general agreement. Were this not the case, science typically would have yielded little beyond the cacophony of interminable squabbles between rival personalities. Properly altered, there is manifest truth in Bronfenbrenner's view. Purely personal preference (depending on the character and background of the investigator) certainly will influence the choice among alternative hypotheses when the evidence for any one of the alternatives is not considered satisfactory. However, in treating predictive efficiency and explanatory power as matters subordinate to the indulgence of personal preferences, Bronfenbrenner not only misstates the ultimate objectives of scientific inquiry but also, through this misstatement, neglects the basic issue in the controversy. That issue is the evidentiary requirements for achieving predictive efficiency and explanatory power themselves. In substance this central question is not discussed.[15]

In his general statement Bronfenbrenner also misrepresents the essential methodological difference between the approaches of the theorists and the institutionalists. This flows from a misidentification of the issue of "simplicity versus realism" as it arises in Friedman's analysis with the issue as it arises in the context of disagreement between theorists and institutionalists. In the latter context the distinction between *simplicity* and *realism* refers to the degree and pattern of abstraction involved in the statement of a hypothesis. Theorists differ from institutionalists in the sense that, when treating the same problem area, they generally are disposed to "simplify" by rejecting as irrelevant various "realistic" considerations concerning institutions which the institutionalists regard as crucial. Nonetheless, they both agree insofar as they accept as essential the process of abstraction itself—or the omission from the assumptions of a hypothesis of factors considered irrelevant to the problem under analysis. Were this not recognized, one would be obliged, in treating any problem, to deal with everything in the universe at once (something which no institutionalist, however comprehensive and scrupulous his eye for detail, has yet undertaken or ever deemed necessary). Although differing in the character of their abstractions, both institutionalists and theorists can likewise agree—and as scientists are indeed constrained to agree—that the resolution of their differences regarding these assumptions depends ultimately on evidence concerning the extent to which the conditions specified in the rival assumptions do *in reality* form parts of regularly recurring relationships within the problem area under study. In this sense there is no methodological controversy between the two at all.

When considered in the context of Friedman's central argument, the distinction between simplicity and realism has a very different meaning. Although he was speaking of theory, Friedman's main point did not involve the question of abstraction or the legitimacy of confining theoretical assumptions to a relatively small number of facts surrounding a problem while *excluding* large numbers of others. As Bronfenbrenner recognizes, Friedman was arguing that it was legitimate (or did not affect validity) to *include* specifications in theoretical assumptions which contradicted or falsified the circumstances surrounding a problem.[16] The assumption (for the sake of "simplicity") that a given case was perfectly competitive when it was, in fact, monopolistic would, in his view, have no bearing on its validity either for purposes of prediction or explanation. This is a quite special view. In its disregard of the nature and test of a probability statement it sets Friedman methodologically in opposition to theorists and institutionalists alike insofar as both the latter pursue the objectives of science.

Science as Preeminently "Pure Theory"

A second view which warrants attention is the position taken by Fritz Machlup. Although Machlup has long been a defender of theoretical economic analysis, the nature of his defense has undergone change. In his well-known debate with R. A. Lester concerning the validity of the principle of marginalism, Machlup recognized that the realism of theoretical assumptions was a matter of central significance in evaluating economic theory.[17] But since that time, and specifically since the appearance of Friedman's essay on methodology, he has drawn away from his earlier concession to catholicity. In the treatment of the routes to the understanding of economic experience, Machlup's more recent methodological tracts (more fully reflecting the Austrian influence) increasingly have emphasized the difference between the world of "exact laws" or "pure theory" and the world of empirical generalization—to the advantage of the former and the disadvantage of the latter. His methodological theory, however, is not entirely in the Austrian mold but represents an attempt to amalgamate aspects of the Austrian position with the position taken by Friedman. Through portions of his treatment, moreover, there runs an empirical element that Machlup never attempts, much less manages, to harness to the rest of his analysis. His latest general methodological essay, in which his position appears in its fullest form, is of special interest because it well serves to highlight the difficulties inevitably encountered by anyone seeking to preserve a place of superiority for pure theory in the world of science.[18]

In Machlup's view, *theory* consists of the pure constructs of human reason; and, while such constructs bear a relationship to reality, the distinguishing characteristic of pure theory is said to lie in its reliance on "idealization, hypothecation and heuristic fictions" which are introduced for purposes of "analytical convenience." This is contrasted with "inductive generalizations," which are based on operational (empirical) constructs. If theoretical generalizations are regarded as "fictitious" or "ideal," Machlup has recognized that they are drawn from experience. Nonetheless, like von Mises, he sees pure theory as something basically different from inductive generalization. Despite any similarities, they differ "in kind." As such, the superiority of theoretical over inductive generalization is to be found in the logical relations within theoretical systems. For these enable us, through deduction from broad generalizations, to explain and interpret wide ranges of empirical phenomena. Theoretical systems make it possible for us to move from "causes to consequences" so that theoretical conclusions are "logically necessary." Inductive generalizations, on the other hand, are only "correlation statements." As such they are usually "narrow" and yield only "some more or less definite probability value."[19]

In its treatment of the relation between theoretical (or logical) systems and inductive generalizations, this statement is internally inconsistent and misleading. On the one hand, theoretical systems yield cause and effect relations, which means that they yield statements concerning matters of fact. On the other hand, theoretical generalizations—the basis of the logical systems—are sharply distinguished from "correlation statements." This implies that the theoretical generalizations do not themselves take the form of matter-of-fact statements, which leads us to wonder how these generalizations can form part of, or explain, any causal relation. Manifestly, if the material of logical sequences is to form part of a causal relation, the major premises of these sequences must contain the basis for establishing the relationship; and these premises (as in the theoretical proposition: "Entrepreneurs maximize profit") reduce to nothing other than "correlation statements" or statements of association between events or entities. A related difficulty is found in Machlup's treatment of the conclusions of logical systems. If these conclusions are statements of causal relations, they are probability statements, as are the matter-of-fact propositions that comprise the premises. No amount of deductive reasoning can alter this (although the showing that an empirical statement is deducible from more general and true premises enhances its own probability value). Yet, contrasting these conclusions with the probabilistic nature of inductive statements, Machlup treats the former as "logically necessary."

Also indefensible is Machlup's contention that empirical propositions are generally "narrow" and therefore cannot be employed as the major premises of logical systems. An empirical proposition, in Machlup's definition, is one that does not contain fictitious or ideal elements, but this has no bearing on the breadth or the degree of generality of the proposition. Is the empirical proposition: "All living things are mortal" narrower than the theoretical proposition: "All entrepreneurs maximize profit"? Propositions may be narrow and fictitious or broad and realistic and vice versa; and it is precisely the breadth of the empirical generalizations and the extent of their logical interrelations with lower order propositions that constitute the distinguishing characteristic of the most advanced sciences. Machlup argues that, owing to errors of observation and measurement alone, empirical propositions generally cannot, in fact, be logically interrelated. "The impurities and inaccuracies inherent in most or all practicable operations with sensory observations and recorded data," he states, "destroy the logical links between different concepts."[20]

The implication is that the "laws" of science, taken as statements which do not include error terms, contain fiction and presumably, therefore, must be classified as theories. Even allowing for the many relatively unrefined empirical generalizations (where there are no errors of observation), this would indeed entail an extensive reclassification. However, the errors in question are designated "errors of observation and measurement" precisely because the evidence (including evidence concerning the nature of measuring instruments, and so forth) creates a strong presumption that they spring from imperfections in experimental techniques. In other words, it may be presumed that, were it not for such imperfections, the laws would be seen to operate as stated, or that for purposes of the general analysis of experience they confidently can be used as they stand. This is quite different from Machlup's theories which contain "real fiction," or misrepresentations of experience which, for the sake of analytical convenience, are introduced deliberately. It may be added that when the laws are corrected to allow for observational errors the magnitude of the errors is small enough to permit for reliable predictions covering wide ranges of events, including events involving relatively precise measurement.

It has been observed that Machlup's analysis raises serious questions concerning the place of his theoretical systems in the (empirical) area of science because he treats the premises and conclusions of these systems as statements which differ from probability statements. Machlup's essay, however, throws further light on the issue, for it also deals explicitly with the test of theoretical propositions within the context of science. Since theory is said to contain fiction, here one encounters the crucial question: How can a proposition that is fictitious (and we are speaking of "real fiction") be regarded as valid either for purposes of prediction or explanation in the world of real experience? It is possible to argue—and indeed often has been argued—that fictitious theory, although invalid, is useful as a first approximation to experience because it simplifies complex phenomena and thus renders them more tractable to analytical treatment. A progressive rectification of the fictions and the conclusions drawn from them may then provide a fruitful basis for developing more satisfactory hypotheses. So viewed, the value of the first approximation would vary with the extent of its falsifications and with the difficulty, accordingly, in progressing through successive approximations to the real dimensions of the problem without substantially sacrificing the analytical advantages of the initial theoretical framework.[21]

Machlup, however, does not consider pure theory in its role as a first approximation; his statements imply that, as it stands, it has considerable scientific value.[22] But his treatment of the text by which its value is established is curious. Speaking generally, he points out that the constructs of a theory cannot be too fictitious because this would impair their value in explaining real phenomena.[23] This appears to be a recognition that theoretical generalizations *are* matter-of-fact statements and are so to be judged. The implication then, clearly, is that in appraising the validity of a theory it is appropriate to consider whether and to what extent its assumptions are fictitious, or to treat the realism of its assumptions as essential in evaluating both its predictive reliability and explanatory value.[24] In pointedly considering the test of a theory, Machlup, however, retreats from this implication. He contends, rather, that in testing a theory attention need only be given the realism of the initiating change in the problem under study (such as the imposition of an excise tax on an industry) and the accuracy of the consequences (with respect, say, to commodity price) which flow from the theoretical apparatus employed to analyze the effects of the change.[25]

An examination then of the realism of the theoretical assumptions themselves (in the above case those regarding the structure of the industry in question) is not, in fact, to form part of the test by which we judge the validity of a theory.[26] This turns out to be the same as Friedman's test of a theory, although the approach to it is somewhat different. Seeking to establish the validity of theory despite the falsity of its assumptions, Friedman spoke as though the fictions of theory did not at all impair its explanatory value. In contrast, Machlup acknowledges the functional relationship between the realism of theoretical assumptions and their value in explaining experience. But—persuaded nonetheless that theoretical generalizations somehow differ "in kind" from correlation statements and that a substantial measure of self-sufficiency can be claimed for theoretical systems solely on the basis of their "logic"—he then proceeds as though tests of theoretical hypotheses can disregard this critical relationship between "realism" and "explanation."[27] A final accent on this note of self-sufficiency appears in Machlup's concluding comments on the test of a theory. Disregarding the role of "repetition" in the testing process, he here contends that only "occasional" verification of its hypotheses suffices to establish confidence in the whole theoretical system.[28]

Accepting Questionable Assumptions as "Expedients"

A methodological position which differs from those already considered is that of D. V. T. Bear and Daniel Orr; for in this case it is argued unqualifiedly that tests of assumptions are relevant in testing hypotheses.[29] The analysis here, however, is also concerned with a special problem, namely, the testing of hypotheses when the realism of assumptions is difficult to ascertain; and it is this portion of their treatment that is open to criticism.

The authors argue that this problem is generally a vexing one because the testing of assumptions is always "hard" and typically far more difficult than the testing of predictions. However, where the assumptions "do not flatly contradict anything observable," it is legitimate, they point out, to treat their specifications as correct and proceed directly to a test of the predictions. In their view, on grounds of "expediency" there is a "powerful justification" for employing this method in economics, as elsewhere, because it enables us to "get on with the generation of testable prediction statements." Adducing the model of perfect competition as an illustrative case, the authors contend that "it is wrong categorically to disregard predictions from a perfectly competitive model on the ground that any of the four to five inadequately rationalized intermediate theory textbook conditions of perfect competition do not hold. Such a rejection is erroneous because of the difficulty in establishing how widely or how significantly the actual situation varies from perfect competition."[30] Although the rationale for the approach is basically different from Friedman's, and the scope and pattern of its application likewise would differ, Bear and Orr thus advocate a testing procedure which, presumably over a large range of cases in economics, is the same as that supported by Friedman. In these cases (where it is difficult to test certain assumptions relevant to particular hypotheses) our choice among existing hypotheses should depend wholly on the predictive findings; and (until the assumptions are tested) the theory with the greatest predictive success is to be given preference over the rest.

Setting aside the issue of its applicability to economics and considering the question on general methodological grounds, there is nothing objectionable in this mode of testing hypotheses when assumptions are unobservable. While the test is not as complete as one which also covers the assumptions, favorable findings on the observable implications of the assumptions support a presumption that these assumptions are correct and thus enhance our confidence in them.[31] Employed commonly on the frontiers of natural science (where it is especially likely that the hypotheses will contain unobservable assumptions), this method of testing may provide a basis for assessing rival theories (for example, different theories of light) and for the selection of a single theory as preeminent in explaining the class of phenomena involved.

In the natural sciences the procedure has indeed proved powerful. But is it likely to prove generally powerful in economics? To begin with, when certain assumptions of a hypothesis are unobservable the acceptance of the hypothesis on the basis of observable predictions requires highly imposing evidence of success in prediction simply because the experimental evidence must be drawn *wholly* from such findings. The importance of this consideration in a nonlaboratory field such as economics—where serious problems often are encountered in performing crucial experiments on predictions—should be apparent.

The authors' case for concentrating attention on predictions, moreover, is scarcely strengthened by their arguments concerning assumptions. There is no foundation for their view that assumptions (the specifications of the "if" clause of hypotheses) are generally more difficult to test than predictions (the specifications of the "then" clause). The nature of the assumption and the prediction (and hence the relative difficulty of testing each) varies with the particular analysis;

moreover, the assumption of one hypothesis may serve as the prediction of another.

Similarly, Bear and Orr present no substantial argument to support their view that economic assumptions in particular are commonly unobservable. The case drawn from the nature of market structure assumptions in the area of price theory, if anything, constitutes evidence of a contrary nature. On the basis of such considerations as the number of firms in the industry, the importance of product differentiation, and the conditions of entry into the industry (as affected by product differentiation and other factors), there are numerous departures from the assumption of perfect competition that—given the whole spectrum of theoretical departures—would be regarded as "wide" by virtually everybody.[32] There are also numerous cases where the nature of the market is difficult to ascertain in the sense that the question evokes disagreement. But here, contrary to the view of the authors, the relevant circumstances cannot simply be treated as "unobservable," since many observers believe that the cases in fact reveal a considerable measure of noncompetition.

There also is reason to believe that this kind of case is not at all atypical in economics. In a large proportion of the instances, statements appearing as assumptions in economic hypotheses are at least partially observable, or are commonly believed to be so. Included would be assumptions of a "subjective" character (for example, the profit maximization assumption) since these are to some degree testable by introspection and communication. Under these circumstances an evaluation of the plausibility of predictive findings on the basis of the "realism" of the assumptions is frequently unavoidable. In the area specifically of industrial organization (where there is abundant ground for doubting that any *one* existing model, or therefore its predictions, can be applied to all cases), the task of gaining acceptance of the general applicability of the perfectly competitive predictions would indeed require successful predictive evidence of monumental proportions. When consideration, furthermore, is given the difficulty in economics of conducting controlled experiments on predictions which are free of ambiguous results, the procedure urged by Bear and Orr is seen in a very different light. Economics is not physics, much less physics on the frontiers; and while evidence on predictions is basic to progress in any area of science, there is little reason to expect that in economics broad-scale progress can be made without a continued and concomitant examination of the assumptions which are germane to the predictions.

Concluding Comments

Among the deficiencies in formal treatments of economic methodology, the most general and significant (as revealed over a considerable time span) has been the uncritical acceptance of procedures that do not meet the stringent empirical standards of science. This shortcoming may be attributed to a tendency to view methodology within the context of the difficulties encountered in the area of economics, a pattern clearly apparent in the writings discussed. All deal with the role of deductive process in economics which, typically based on "analytically convenient" oversimplifications of reality, has been the principal mode of accommodation to the methodological difficulties of the discipline. Although this procedure has been of value within limits (and the limitations have not gone unrecognized), in practice the extensive dependence on the method has engendered a disposition to treat economic theory as though its validity could be established without full and repeated reference to experience. Again, as on occasions in the past, this perspective has prompted an attempt at justification through the use of formal methodological theory. On the contemporary scene the principal new attempt of this nature—Friedman's—has taken the form of a claim that the deductive process need only be opened to empirical test at the "prediction" end, but in one fashion or another the influence of his position is evident in the other writings considered.

Observing the difficulty in resolving controversy in economics, Bronfenbrenner accepts as correct methodology the unrestrained indulgence of personal proclivities in the choice of assumptions and hypotheses. (One wonders whether this is not an archly disguised statement of resignation to an unpalatable and presumably unalterable reality, or a wry way of saying that, given the nature of the field, an interminable clash between subjectively inspired views *is for economics* "scientific method.") Machlup—arguing for the superiority of unrealistic theoretical analysis while seeking to make allowance for empirical considerations—is led into a maze of insupportable and internally conflicting views (including the Friedman position) only to withdraw eventually into a substantially self-justifying deductive world of "pure theory." Bear and Orr explore the requirements of empiricism more thoroughly, but, similarly confronting the issue of conflict concerning "assumptions," they transform this into a demi-blessing by consigning the realism of a wide range of economic assumptions to the domain of the "unknown" and by supposing that, as such, they can be handled as science handles "unobservables." For an extensive variety of cases the way is thus to be opened for shifting emphasis to the process of deducing predictions at the expense of a concern with the realism of the assumptions employed.

The formal methodological analysis developed within a discipline affords one kind of overview of the discipline itself. Such an overview may be misleading, since methodological prescriptions may be honored in the breach—and often by their own authors. But it also may be significantly illuminating since (as one among several forces) persuasions of a methodological nature may lend momentum to intellectual movements by endowing them with a highly general rationale. The heavy reliance on deductive analysis in economics was the outgrowth of many influences, not the least of which were the vexing investigatory problems encountered in the field, but the sanction provided by methodological argument has helped perpetuate this type of approach. The more recent concern with the empirical testing of hypotheses, whatever its variants, is likewise the product of many forces, but it owes some of its momentum to persistent methodological criticism of the weight traditionally given deduction.

No science progresses in an "ever onward and upward" fashion. In the social sciences, where the subject matter is highly complex and the discipline of the laboratory is wanting, movements both backward and downward are particularly likely to occur, and perhaps especially so in the area of formal methodology. The standards of science in social fields are so difficult to meet that in these realms there is an ever-present susceptibility to more permissive versions of "science." Formal views on methodology thus generally are vulnerable to the winds of controversy over substantive doctrine, the prevailing climate of opinion, and the professional fashions of the period, all of which shape the special permissiveness that is legitimized. It is not at all paradoxical, then, that contemporary methodological tracts should contain errors that writers of a much earlier period—including the classical economists—would not have made.

Methodological theorizing that loses an eye for the full demands of empiricism may succeed in affording some sort of sanction for virtually any practice. Even inadequately justified lines of analysis and inquiry may not prove entirely sterile. But, in affording them sanction, methodological theory abets the perpetuation of practices whose costs are not small. These entail the continuing diversion of intellectual effort into channels that produce little of importance for new knowledge and the impairment of perspective and judgment in making use of knowledge we already possess.

Notes

1. See Friedman's *Essays in Positive Economics* (Chicago: University of Chicago Press, 1953), pp. 3 ff.
2. My criticism is contained in my article "On 'The Methodology of Positive Economics,'" *Quarterly Journal of Economics* 73 (November 1959):552–75. For other criticisms of Friedman's position, see Ernest Nagel, "Assumptions in Economic Theory," and Paul Samuelson, "Problems of Methodology—Discussion," *American Economic Review* 53 (May 1963):211-19 and 231-36, respectively; and Jack Melitz, "Friedman and Machlup on the Significance of Testing Economic Assumptions," *Journal of Political Economy* 82 (February 1965):37-60.
3. See Friedman, *Essays*, pp. 8-9, 14, 16-18.
4. Friedman argues that it is not the realism of all but only of "theoretical" assumptions that is irrelevant in testing hypotheses. He states, in fact, that in testing the predictions of a theory it is essential to observe and specify the conditions under which these predictions occur (see ibid., p. 19). Indeed, the predictions of science, as conditional general statements, always contain "assumptions," so that realistic assumptions are essential to valid scientific predictions themselves. A recognition of all this, however, is inconsistent with Friedman's position regarding the test of a theory. In stressing the necessity for observing and specifying the conditions under which a prediction occurs, Friedman is implicitly recognizing that in the future we will look for the reoccurrence of these latter *real* conditions to tell us when the event predicted will reoccur, which is to say that, insofar as they are unrealistic, the assumptions of the theory *lack* validity for purposes of prediction. To argue that it is the unrealistic assumptions of the theory that are valid whenever its predictions are accurate while stressing the importance of ascertaining the actual conditions under which the predictions occur is much akin to asserting that "in curing disease it is but necessary to rub a rabbit's foot, provided one takes the proper drugs." Cf. Rotwein, "On 'The Methodology,'" pp. 560-61.
5. Although typically there would be agreement on whether a particular association of events had explanatory content, the explanation afforded is a matter of degree; for it depends on the degree to which the conditions contained in the assumption can be related to other experience. The prediction: "Aspirin will alleviate headaches" would gain explanatory content if it were related to a broader condition which specified the manner in which the chemical properties of aspirin affected the brain. In turn this would become more explanatory if the chemical properties of aspirin were shown to have similar effects on other parts of the body, or if aspirin were shown to be a subgroup of chemicals having such effects, and so forth. For a discussion of the relationship between prediction and explanation and the range of variation between the two see Carl G. Hempel, *Aspects of Scientific Explanation* (New York: Free Press, 1965), especially pp. 364-74.
6. Cf. Friedman, *Essays*, pp. 8, 12-15, 20, 41.
7. Sometimes in support of the Friedman view that the realism of theoretical assumptions does not matter, cases are cited in which there is already

abundant evidence for belief in the prediction itself. This plainly begs the question since, for purposes of drawing the prediction or establishing belief in it, there is no dependence on the assumption whose falsity is said to be of no significance. For example, one can introduce any one of an indefinite number of false assumptions into an hypothesis whose prediction is that man is mortal without affecting our belief in the latter. Needless to say, however, as soon as we wish to explain man's mortality in terms of broader considerations, the realism of the assumption employed becomes crucial. Moreover, although we may believe that man is mortal independently of any explanation, such explanation—in principle—enhances the probability value of the belief.

8. Cf. below pp. 371-72 and n. 26. It should perhaps be pointed out that nothing in our argument implies that deduction is not important in the process of empirical inquiry. The question at issue concerns the significance of the realism of any proposition employed—whether deductively or otherwise—in exploring experience.

9. In the detailed attention given the realism of economic assumptions, the writers mentioned make unequivocally clear their belief that unrealistic assumptions would adversely affect the accuracy of their predictions. To cite but one of many of Mill's comments (which appear in his treatment of the "Logic of the Moral Sciences"):

> All the general propositions which can be framed by the deductive science, are therefore, in the strictest sense of the word, hypothetical.
>
> They are grounded on some suppositious set of circumstances, and declare how some given cause would operate in those circumstances, supposing that no others were combined with them. If the set of circumstances supposed have been copied from those of any existing society, the conclusions will be true of that society, provided, and in as far as, the effect of those circumstances shall not be modified by others which have not been taken into the account. If we desire a nearer approach to concrete truth, we can only aim at it by taking, or endeavoring to take, a greater number of individualizing circumstances into the computation.

System of Logic (London: Longmans, 1865), pp. 489-90. See also chap. 5 in Mill's *Essays on Some Unsettled Questions of Political Economy* (London: London School of Economics and Political Science, 1948); and J. E. Cairnes, *The Character and Logical Method of Political Economy* (London: Macmillan, 1878), especially pp. 45-57. In his treatment Senior raises objections to the use of unrealistic assumptions which are worth repeating on the present scene. He points out that such assumptions are objectionable because (1) their use renders a science "unattractive" since it renders it irrelevant to "what is actually taking place"; (2) anyone starting from arbitrarily assumed premises is "in danger of forgetting, from time to time, their unsubstantiated foundation, and of arguing as if they were true"; and (3) reasoning on the basis of unreal assumptions is especially susceptible to logical error since anyone dealing with an imaginary world is less likely to be startled by strange conclusions which might have alerted him to his mistakes. See N. W. Senior, *Four Introductory Lectures in Political Economy* (London: Longmans, 1852), pp. 63-65.

For a general treatment of the economic methodology of the period, see J. N. Keynes, *The Scope and Method of Political Economy* (London: Macmillan, 1917), especially pp. 11-20, 211-20.

10. Among the classical economists Mill and Cairnes best represent this point of view. It is for this reason that both—anticipating the later position taken by Alfred Marshall and others—emphasized that the conclusions of economic reasoning constituted only statements of "tendencies" subject to correction for errors of omission and commission in the treatment of reality in the reasoning process. Cf. Mill, *System of Logic*, pp. 487 ff.; and Cairnes, *Character and Logical Method*, pp. 48 ff. This view is an early statement of the position that the deductive analysis of economic theory represents but the first stage in a process of successive approximations. See below p. 371.
11. Senior's comments on the basic premises of economics are of this character. See his *Political Economy* (London: Griffin, 1873), p. 3. Among neo-orthodox economists, several statements of Lionel Robbins are of a similiar nature. See his *An Essay on the Nature and Significance of Economic Science* (London: Macmillan, 1932), especially pp. 78-92 and 83-86.
12. See Ludwig von Mises, *Human Action, A Treatise on Economics* (New Haven: Yale University Press, 1963), pp. 7-8, 32-41, 64, 351, 868.
13. See his "A 'Middlebrow' Introduction to Economic Methodology" in *The Structure of Economic Science*, ed. Sherman R. Krupp (Englewood Cliffs, N.J.: Prentice-Hall, 1966), pp. 5-24.
14. See Bronfenbrenner, "A 'Middlebrow' Introduction," pp. 17-18.
15. Although he does not amplify or seek to support his statement, Bronfenbrenner asserts that he does not agree with the view that a preference for realistic assumptions is "inherent in normal human nature" or that such realism is essential either to prediction or explanation (ibid., p. 18). With respect to human nature, as has been noted there is no single basis on which human belief is formed. The main issue here, however, concerns the procedures for validating propositions *within the context of science.* The "realism" which is essential to establishing the regularity of association between events on which scientific belief is based is, of course, also found to a substantial degree in "normal" human behavior. Otherwise, science itself would have little or no place in human affairs.
16. Notwithstanding the basic difference between these two positions, Friedman draws on the argument for the necessity of abstraction in support of his main thesis concerning the irrelevance of falsity in assumptions. Cf. Rotwein, "On 'The Methodology,'" pp. 564-65.
17. See his "Marginal Analysis and Empirical Research," reprinted from *American Economic Review* 36 (September 1946), in *Essays on Economic Semantics* (Englewood Cliffs, N.J.: Prentice-Hall, 1963), pp. 147-90. The acceptance of the importance of the realism of assumptions is evident throughout the article. Speaking of all aspects of theory, Machlup concludes that "the correctness, applicability and relevance of economic theory constantly needs testing through empirical research" (p. 190).
18. See his article, "Operationalism and Pure Theory in Economics," in *Structure*, ed. Krupp, pp. 53-67.
19. Ibid., pp. 57-58, 67.

20. Ibid., p. 61.
21. What is sought in the first and simplified approximation is a determinate solution, and the more this approximation falsifies experience the more difficult is it to preserve the elements of determinacy as the unrealistic assumptions are modified in successive approximations. It can be argued that first approximations themselves may afford valuable insights into experience. Insights, however, are not validated hypotheses and are usually the subjects of considerable controversy. See Rotwein, "Mathematical Economics: The Empirical View and an Appeal for Pluralism," in *Structure,* ed. Krupp, pp. 111-12.
22. Machlup, "Operationalism and Pure Theory in Economics," in *Structure,* ed. Krupp, p. 66.
23. Ibid., pp. 57-58.
24. In addition to assumptions whose specifications are demonstrably false, Machlup (in opposing the position of those who insist on operational definitions of theoretical constructs) argues for the legitimacy of using theoretical assumptions whose specifications are either unobservable or very difficult to observe. In these latter cases, the degree of falsification involved, if any, cannot, of course, be ascertained, or, if so, only imperfectly at best. This raises special questions which are considered below. See pp. 372-73.
25. Ibid., p. 65.
26. In an earlier article Machlup asserts that this was the position of Mill, Senior, and Cairnes and credits Mill with its original formulation. "The point to emphasize is that Mill does not propose to put the *assumptions* of economic theory to empirical tests, but only *the predicted results that are deduced from them.*" See his "The Problem of Verification in Economics," *Southern Economic Journal* 22 (July 1955): 7 [italics his]. Cf. the treatment of this question above on pp. 364-65 and n. 9. In light of the full nature of the evidence on the issue (Machlup cites but one statement by Mill taken out of context), his interpretation must be regarded as one instance of the not uncommon practice of misreading the past out of a zealous desire to discover support for the views of the present.
27. In view of the central significance of this inconsistency in Machlup's argument, it is not surprising to find that it should lead to vagueness and ambiguity elsewhere in his analysis. For example, while Machlup's test of a theory makes no place for an examination of the realism of theoretical assumptions, he subsequently states that it is necessary that there be "links" between empirical data and "*some* of the crucial theoretical constructs." Ibid., p. 66 [italics mine]. This same difficulty appears in even more striking form in Machlup's Presidential Address before the American Economic Association. Here he states: "The model of the firm in traditional price theory is not, as so many writers believe, designed to serve to explain and predict changes in the behavior of real firms; instead, it is designed to explain and predict changes in observed prices (quoted, paid, received) as effects of particular changes in conditions (wage rates, interest rates, import duties, excise taxes, technology, etc.). In this causal connection the firm is only a theoretical link, a mental construct to explain how one gets from the cause to the effect. This

is altogether different from explaining the behavior of a firm." "Theories of the Firm: Marginalist, Behavioral, Managerial," *American Economic Review* 57 (March 1967): 9.

The inescapable difficulty which the question of "explanation" poses for the Machlup-Friedman approach is conspicuously apparent in this struggle with ambiguity. The theorist's reference to any fictitious constructs he may have used of course "explains" what *he* did—or his own mental processes—in relating the variables here described as "cause and effect." But Machlup's view that these mental processes, insofar as they deal with constructs that falsify what we know about firms, can serve to explain *actual relations involving firms* (that is, relations between cost and price) is something which itself defies explanation. It is precisely because this procedure is "altogether different from an explanation of the behavior of the firm" that it *cannot* explain such price-cost relationships. If the "false" is to be regarded as in any sense explanatory of reality, then plainly a new term is needed to denote what is usually meant by *explanation*.

It is noteworthy that Machlup himself considers the behavior of *real* firms in a competitive industry and argues that, with respect to its impact on the direction of market changes, it does not significantly depart from what would be expected of the fictitious firm, that is, one that single-mindedly pursued maximum profits. (Cf. Machlup, pp. 12 ff.) This of course is to descend from the level of pure theory to an attempt at genuine explanation. But then what purpose is served by treating industry behavior as the product of single-minded maximizing agents? One can simply replace this with the statement: "*Some* firms in a competitive industry maximize profit" (while others, of course, do not seek losses). Or, probably more realistically, one can abandon reference to profit maximization altogether. With respect to the prediction of the *mere direction* of market changes, there is no inference that can be drawn from the maximization assumption (whether applied to some or all firms) that cannot be drawn from the assumption that competitive firms simply seek to "make money"—meaning that they exploit advantages to increase their profit in degrees unspecified. Nonetheless, with respect to the prediction as stated, Machlup not only insists on the retention of the concept of the maximizing firm as "a postulate in a web of logical connections" but also seeks to preserve the notion that mental processes employing such fictitious constructs "explain" experience.

28. Machlup, "Operationalism and Pure Theory in Economics," in *Structure*, ed. Krupp, p. 66.
29. D. V. T. Bear and Daniel Orr, "Logic and Expediency in Economic Theorizing," *Journal of Political Economy* 75 (April 1967): 188-96. The argument considered below is found on pp. 194-96.
30. Ibid., p. 195.
31. I discussed this point in my article "On 'The Methodology,'" pp. 570-73. In the literature of the philosophy of science the term *theory* often is reserved exclusively for the hypothesis with unobservable assumptions. This contrasts with a *law*, where all elements of the hypothesis are observable.
32. Bear and Orr give no justification for their assertion that the conditions

of perfect competition are "inadequately rationalized" or, more precisely, for the view that the model is so inadequately rationalized that no standards are afforded for determining when significant departures from the model exist. This extraordinary view is indeed contradicted by their own phraseology, that is, their reference to "the predictions from a perfectly competitive model." .If the model were as inadequately rationalized as their treatment implied, there would be little or no basis for *drawing* predictions from the model.

8

Human Values and Economic Science

Melville J. Ulmer

A few years ago twelve leading economists were convened at New York University to discuss the relationship between "Human Values and Economic Policy," a title almost identical with that of the present article.[1] It might appear, therefore, that we are wasting our time in exploring a territory already well mapped and traveled, particularly since the group included two Nobel Prize winners, Paul Samuelson and Kenneth Arrow, together with Milton Friedman, Kenneth Boulding, and other very bright stars of our profession. But the curious fact is that the proceedings of that colloquium, despite its title, had almost no connection with the central problem that concerns me today, and that I believe is of primary interest to you: that is, the relationship between value judgments and the methodology of economics. The NYU discourse was confined almost entirely to the determination of market values, under ideally competitive conditions, with a brief side trip to Arrow's theorem concerning majority votes at the polls.[2] Mention of value judgments, in the usual sense of that term, was as carefully avoided as sex at a Sunday school spelling bee.

That outcome, except for the ever hopeful, should have been expected. For orthodox economists contend that value judgments have been, and should be, effectively excluded from their science. As though it had been liberated from the deadly embrace of invading barbarians, they proclaim that economics is "value free." The argument is familiar.[3] There are two general questions, they say, that we may ask about economic affairs and, I am sure, about a lot of other things, to wit: What is? and What ought to be? The first question is the proper subject of scientific investigation. The second question extends beyond the realm of our science. Thus economists are instructed to obtain their values, or goals, from other authorities, presumably from voters or their political representatives. So goes the reasoning that, today as well as yesteryear, can be reproduced verbatim by most college sophomores.

Although it might appear to be so, this position—this circumscription of what economists properly can and cannot do—is not a mere arbitrary or politically convenient rule. It is a deduction that follows logically from an underlying notion of what a value judgment is. The classic statement of the matter, in modern economic literature at least, is that of Friedman.[4] He views a *value judgment* as an emotive reaction about which, as he says, "men can ultimately only fight." He further supports his position by reciting that precious gem of ancient wisdom, *De gustibus non est disputandum.* Judgments of value therefore are asserted to be beyond the realm of reason, impervious to fact or logic, and on *that* ground must be excluded from the business of economists. It is this assertion about the fundamental nature of values that is arbitrary.

Certainly, Friedman's interpretation does violence to the meaning that most people, and some philosophers, attach to the word *judgment,* which to them conveys something more than an emotional seizure, more than an irrational prejudice, or an inchoate "gut reaction." Thus, one outstanding authority on the philosophy of science, Ernest Nagel, defines a *value judgment* as "a reasoned approval (or disapproval) of something by someone, in the light of deliberation concerning what is desirable."[5] I would wish to underline the words *reasoned* and *deliberation.* If a judgment has those characteristics it must necessarily take account of relevant facts and general principles. If the situation being evaluated is economic, then the relevant empirical and theoretical evidence must relate in considerable measure to economic matters. In such instances, on that ground alone, value judgments would seem to fall within the science of economics. Nevertheless, after all the evidence is in, and after it has been distilled and redistilled with the most painstaking professional care, a nagging question persists: How can a generally satisfying, verifiable *conclusion* be reached in problems of evaluation? How can an objective decision be secured that one situation is better than another? We shall have to return to that question. First, it will be useful to look further into the claim that neoclassical economics is value free. Is it actually so in practice?

Consider the neoclassical assumption that we must take the tastes of consumers, or the populace in general, as given constants. Few of us would object to that postulate as a tentative device—a convenient fiction—for achieving specific objectives, such as the derivation of a demand curve. But I have used the imperative advisedly. We *must* take the tastes as given in neoclassical economics, and not only as given data but also as the ultimate standard for analyzing and evaluating the operation of the economy. Tastes, too, are considered outside the purview of science, a sacrosanct enclave in the economic environment that one must observe and obey, but never question. Here we have the central, even though unacknowledged, value judgment of neoclassical economics. It rates that situation unequivocally better that more fully satisfies prevailing wants, whatever they may be. It bears with it a normative corollary concerning the output of industry and national consumption, of "the more, the better," indiscriminately, or what one writer has termed the "pig principle."[6] I think that it is easy to show that this value judgment is both illogical and empirically wrong.

In the first place, like some other propositions in orthodox doctrine, this one rests solidly on an assumption that is flatly contrary to fact, viz.: that tastes are a basically stable set of propensities determined by biological and other factors external to the economic system. Since this proposition is a keystone in the structure of the neoclassical edifice, the abundant facts that oppose it, as you might expect, have been overlooked with exceptional determination.

One uncomfortable fact, for the orthodox, relates to the obvious flexibility of tastes. A measuring rod must be independent of the things to be measured. If it expands or contracts each time it is applied, it can be of no service. Mere casual observation is sufficient to show that tastes represent that kind of perversely flexible measuring rod. What people want, and the intensity of their wants, are determined largely by the performance of the economic system; hence their wants cannot measure that performance. Shaped primarily by economic events and experience, tastes are, in other words, endogenous to the economic system, not exogenous.

Thus, the very act of consumption changes our tastes. Everyone outside our profession knows that. In the words of an old song, "how're you gonna keep them down on the farm, after they've seen Paree." The experience of one way of life, as even Tin Pan Alley recognized, quickly alters our attitude toward another. We may live, contentedly, with frankfurters, radio, and dishcloths for a time, and later, with a change in income and prices, move up to beef, TV, and electric dishwashers. But can we then move back, if required, to the old regime—frankfurters and the rest—and *regain the old contented preference level?* If presented once again with the same prices and incomes that had prevailed in the first or earlier situation, would not people borrow, or take two jobs, to maintain the second, more expensive level of living? Since in comparable situations they frequently do, it follows from the facts that tastes change when consumption changes. And since, therefore, the scale itself has been altered, how can it be used to measure relative well-being over time?

The fact that tastes are dependent variables, economically determined, becomes even more evident when we take into account that they are individually interrelated. I do not mean simply in the superficial sense of "keeping up with the Joneses," but more fundamentally, more inexorably, more commonly. In multitudinous ways each of us is influenced by what others do. Let me cite some of my own observations of this matter since by chance they occurred at intervals that were particularly significant. In the medium-sized town of Leiden, Holland, about a decade and a half ago, most people rode to work on bicycles and appeared to like it. It provided daily exercise and a breath of the outdoors for old and young alike. Even Princess Beatrix rode to her classes at the university on a bike. Visiting there at seven-year intervals later, I noticed the following: As incomes rose, about half the people shifted over to automobiles. Then most of the other half, as the streets became more dangerous, were forced to do the same, or if they could not afford that, shifted to motorbikes. With nearly everyone using autos, inner city transportation became slower than ever, noisier, more congested, more nerve-racking, and of course more expensive. At present, now, can any individual in Leiden shift back to the bike and regain his old, simpler, and very likely more satisfying preference level? Clearly he cannot, and would not try, because his tastes—by which I mean of course his utility function or indifference map—have been changed by his own prior acts of consumption and even more by the acts of others. Since the measuring rod has altered its dimensions, can we accept without question the neoclassicist's appraisal that the people of Leiden are better off now, with respect to transportation, than they were fifteen years ago? For the orthodox economist that quaint conclusion is unavoidable. He reasons that the men, women, and youth of Leiden now have *more*—expensive automobiles, that is—and, as always, the more, the better.

I would not want anyone to suppose, from my two examples, that I oppose either automobiles or dishwashers. I favor them both, along with electricity and indoor plumbing. All I am saying is that material things cannot properly be abstracted from their social context—from the way they are used, and the way others use them, and from our changing attitudes and expectations. That means that we cannot, with accuracy, relate particular goods and services to specific levels of satisfaction that are comparable for people at different points in time, any more than we can do that for people living in different places. Comparing levels of welfare in that way, by merely counting up the value of goods purchased, may be an advertising man's dream and an orthodox economist's hang-up, but it cannot yield meaningful, verifiable conclusions.

I have saved for the last the most familiar reason for holding that our tastes are economically determined, that is, the argument presented so prominently by John Kenneth Galbraith. He conceives of big business as the driving force in our entire economy, influencing, in ways that serve its own interests, both consumers and government. It is the concern of big business, he says, to induce people to want more and more endlessly, particularly of the things that the "technostructure," from time to time, finds it profitable, secure, and convenient to produce. The technostructure—meaning the technicians who actually run the great corporations—is mainly concerned with perpetual growth. That preoccupation requires, above all, that they must continuously excite the hunger of the population for an ever expanding flow of output. If that implies planned obsolescence, limited durability, and appeals to purely artificial, fictitious, or even harmful needs, as they say on Madison Avenue, so be it. In a nutshell, Galbraith's point is that the tastes of consumers are in part deliberately shaped, not to their own needs, but to the needs of big business. Maximizing the output of goods and services under these terms, in accord with the orthodox value criterion, would in this view maximize business welfare instead of human welfare.

Up to this point I have concentrated on the neoclassical attitude toward tastes because of its central importance. In his most recent book, Galbraith has called attention to a variety of other value judgments that have somehow insidiously penetrated into the body of orthodox economics.[7] In *What's Wrong With Economics?* Benjamin Ward has mentioned still others.[8] Elsewhere I have described additional examples,[9] but I do not think it would serve a useful purpose to review them. I wish to remark only on two general aspects of these findings.

First, it is not the presence of value judgments in standard economics that is reprehensible, but the fact that they are unacknowledged, hidden, the fifty-third card in the casino deck, the medium's helper behind the arras, the sacred unmentionable that never can be exposed in the forum of public opinion. Such value judgments have a capacity only for harm, for distortion, for retarding or obscuring knowledge rather than advancing it. Second, the presence of value judgments—preferably openly proclaimed as testable hypotheses—is virtually inherent in the nature of our subject. I say "virtually" because I am reluctant to waive the possibility that a crudely empirical approach to economic activity could accumulate facts, figures, and even functional relationships in a formless jumble that conceivably could be called economics. It would be value free, but it also would be substance free. It would not be a science because it would lack order and objective, while its practitioners were drowned in a sea of meaningless trivia. No science can be created by exposing the blank sheet of an undirected human mind to the infinite stimuli of reality, each element of the universe of inquiry accorded an exactly equal chance of making its impression. One or more particular views of the economic system are required in order to bring intellectual order from chaos, and behind every view, as Gunnar Myrdal has said, there must be a viewpoint, a frame of reference that enables us purposefully to select, analyze, and appraise. In economics, and in any other social science, such viewpoints must be shaped and energized by values.

The reasons, it seems to me, are obvious. In the social sciences we deal with the behavior of human beings. Their activities in society are mutually interacting, mutually influential, and derive from causes or enabling circumstances, as perceived by men and women. Social decisions, necessarily, exercise an impact on people. It is of the essence of these activities, particularly in the economic sphere, that they enrich or impoverish, degrade or uplift, alienate or unite, persuade, abuse, exploit, befriend, and so on. A full, objective analysis of society requires that such interactions be recognized. Merely to describe them, meaningfully, implies at least an elementary process of evaluation. If a certain method of production serves to rob workers of their creativity, dignity, and intelligence, if it reduces them to routinized robots, alienated, surly, perhaps brutalized, it is a relationship at least as worthy of note as the estimated lag between a change in the quantity of money and a change in the GNP. It is also an observation that is clearly and necessarily motivated by a value judgment. It is ignored in standard economics not because value judgments are abjured—for we have seen that in practice they are present although unacknowledged—but because human values are buried and embodied in commodities, in the simple proposition that the more goods and services the market turns up, the better. Human values are equated with market values, the beneficiary being, of course, the status quo.

How can we distinguish what is good from what is bad? Is it, as Friedman has suggested, merely a question of taste, in the noneconomic sense of that word, like a preference for apples over oranges? Must we then, as he would have it, simply accept the majority vote on what is better or worse? If that were true we would indeed have little cause for complaint against the majority vote of the Germans in 1932. The selection of Hitler would have to be accepted as a standard of goodness provided by the highest source—the voice of the people. We would have no complaint at all, I suppose, so long as Arrow's conditions for consistency in voting were satisfied. Or, as an alternative to Friedman, are there certain *ultimate* values to which we can appeal, that will guide us always and unerringly to the right decisions? If so, what are their sources? What are the operations by which we can achieve such ultimates as "the ideal society," when will we get there, and whose version shall we accept? By their very nature, it would seem, ultimate values must be taken on authority, a great convenience in totalitarian countries, but surely the opposite of scientific procedure.

Value judgments become operative and part of science when they are formulated in more humble terms, when they are penultimate rather than ultimate, when they are specific and relate to particular problems, not to vague and distant goals; when they can be *tested by ongoing experience.* One situation or policy can be adjudged better than another on the basis of its scientifically determined consequences.[10] Let me cite an example.

Census Bureau figures show that family expenditures per person for medical care increase enormously with income, a relationship that is modified but by no means broken by Medicare and Medicaid. This result obviously does not stem from an inherent tendency for the rich to sicken. In fact, analysis by age group suggests that, in considerable measure, the medical care received varies inversely with need.[11] The upshot is that the lives of poorer people are much less adequately protected than others. In this respect the situation of the working, lower middle class seems to be even worse than that of the very poor. Their children have a much smaller chance for survival than do those of others. If we agree with the value judgment that all have an equal right to life, as well as liberty and the pursuit of happiness, we must agree also that the market system in the medical field has miserably failed. We have a basis then for concluding that something else would be better. We in the United States are now trying to shore up the market system with insurance schemes, in belated recognition of that failure. It may well be that economic science can show, particularly if it deigns to refer to foreign experience, that socialized medicine can achieve the stated objective most fully, and at the least cost of all available alternatives. If such is the case, economics has an obligation to bring its conclusions to the forum of public opinion. In the final analysis, to be sure, only the electorate can make an *effective* decision on what is better, but for accuracy the electorate must be fully informed, empathic, and unprejudiced, particularly in this instance, by the machinations of the AMA.

Note that astronomers do not ask the populace to vote on whether the universe is expanding, contracting, or remaining the same. As much as the astronomers, we have an obligation to seek the truth independently concerning the effect of economic institutions on people, regardless of what some majority may believe, and to make the truth known. Transforming the finding into public policy requires education, not simply nose counting; it requires controversy in a truly open forum, unbiased by vested interests, and *then* the critical vote.

The market, including especially its pecuniary calculations, is now the touchstone of standard economics. In the temple of the Pareto optimum, human values are sacrificed the way flies are swatted in a candy shop—quite dispassionately, of course—on the altar of profits. Once human reactions and needs are brought to the foreground, the structure of economics necessarily will change. Let me cite another example.

The replacement of an obsolescent machine or tool by a more efficient model is a frequent occurence in business and is commonly judged to be one sign of progress. It is considered even more progressive if the new equipment renders some human beings obsolescent. Indeed, one calculation that enters critically into the decision to purchase an improved model is nearly always the saving in labor costs gained from the dismissal of workers. The full wages of the discharged men and women enter into the accounts of the firm as a saving. The reckoning is only fair by conventional standards, quite impartial, since it also counts the full cost of maintaining a machine as a saving when *it* is scrapped. But a little thought shows that the calculation is neither fair nor accurate from the economy's point of view. Unlike the machine, human beings cannot be scrapped, and their costs of maintenance go on even after they are unemployed and are necessarily met in one way or another by society—through welfare payments perhaps, through unemployment insurance benefits as long as they last, through private charity, or, in some instances, through crime. Add to this the cost of retraining, where that is feasible, the cost of moving the family, when and if new jobs are found, and the psychic blow to the individual who is suddenly classified as obsolete.

The point is that technological unemployment is typically expensive in a variety of ways that do not enter business calculations. Were they taken into account, it would no doubt turn out that much of the world's so-called technological progress had in fact been regress; that, in other words, new laborsaving devices had in general been introduced too abruptly and too fast and that the net gains to society were in the aggregate much smaller than generally supposed and in some instances were probably negative. It also shows, as I have argued elsewhere, that there is a better case than is commonly assumed for a policy of guaranteed jobs backed by a strong program of public employment.[12] The case rests also on another value judgment with significant repercussions for economics as well as for education: Society has an obligation to offer each individual an opportunity to utilize his capacities fully, or more broadly, in the words of one social philosopher, to find and follow his "vocation."[13]

The latter point has to do with the nature and content of human labor. Work in standard economics is counted fully as a cost, but that rests on its own unacknowledged value judgment associated with the maximization of profits. Labor in that format becomes strictly a means to an end, and human values are once again, in this instance, submerged. Of course, it is true that man-hours enter as an input in the output of goods and services, as the orthodox view it. But that is only *part* of the truth. If we are concerned with human welfare, and not simply commodities, then work must be reckoned as an output as well as an input. The output is measured by the satisfaction the human being obtains from his work activity, from his creativity, from the utilization of whatever capacities he may have. If the satisfaction is negative in one productive process and positive in another, this would represent a powerful count in favor of the second. In practice workers do not have such choices, and in a society in which concentrated control over the means of production rests in private hands, no business firm is motivated to enter the quality of work experience into its accounts. But this is a lesser sin than that of orthodox economics, which does not permit such calculations to enter its thinking. In the imaginary world of the standard practitioners, there are innumerable firms in every industry offering innumerably different types of work experience, and the attitude of labor toward these alternatives is reflected in its supply curves. We have here another familiar legend that solves a problem by assuming it away.

We have in the legend, also, another illustration of the way in which neoclassical economics subordinates individuals to the needs of production, instead of the other way around. That perverse subordination is inherent in its narrow definition of efficiency, and in its tautological equation of maximum efficiency with maximum welfare. The more we pursue the consequences of that position, the more conflicts we uncover between its tenets and generally accepted human values. Thus, efficiency in the food industry in the United States, free competition has determined, lies in highly concentrated facilities for production and distribution. This centralization in turn requires considerable long-distance transportation and in general a lengthy time period for output and marketing. Food additives of various kinds, including preservatives and artificial coloring, become imperative. The ingestion of some of the additives, recent experience has shown, is toxic, and about some of the others it can only be said that we do not yet know—engaging the population, willy nilly, in a kind of chemical Russian roulette. The view of orthodox economics on this matter is characteristically hard-nosed; we have a trade-off here, say its proponents, between the quantity of poison on the one hand and the cost of food on the other. Greater purity *could* be obtained, but only at a price. The present situation reflects, simply, the decision provided by free competition. The people have spoken with their dollar votes, the market has functioned in response, and efficiency has been maximized. But does the housewife shopping in the supermarket, or any of us, have the range of choices this view supposes, even if she takes the trouble to read the fine print and has the knowledge to interpret it? Is not the entire food industry, barring the off-beat health foods, organized so that all brands of canned goods, all meat cuts and sausages, and all other produce have more or less the same doses of sodium nitrite, tartazine, cyclamates, and the rest?

Consider the decisions that business firms now make, as a matter of course, to reduce or expand their output, or to change the locale of their operations. The decisions are fateful in numerous ways for the workers who may be fired or hired, as well as for the communities that serve them. But the decisions on such matters, as well as on the organization of the food industry, are made by corporate bureaucracies on the basis of *their* version of efficiency. Their version also happens to be that of their faithful rationalizer, orthodox economics. I am not implying in these examples that cutbacks in output are never justified, or that costs of production are unimportant. I am leading to the proposition that the lack of democracy in economic decisions levies a tremendous, uncalculated cost on all of society. The value judgment I am implying is that a greater participation of workers and consumers in business decisions, either directly or through representatives, would make for a better economic world. At a minimum it would expand the range of data on which a broader and more accurate calculation of efficiency could be based.

I earlier mentioned the sacred position occupied in orthodox economics by prevailing tastes. In rejecting that role, I do not suggest that tastes can or should be ignored. Following them slavishly and uncritically is no more irresponsible, scientifically, than ignoring them completely. The remaining alternative to those extremes is to treat the community's tastes as an object of active scientific attention. This means that economic research must be directed, in important part, toward seeing to it that the community's tastes are informed, undistorted by the propaganda of business or other vested interests, unprejudiced by the irrational, self-serving appeals to which they so frequently fall victim. Thus, when individual wants are mutually self-defeating, that fact must be discovered and disclosed, even if it does mean lower sales and profits for some, and even if it violates, as I am sure it does, the hallowed Pareto criteria for an optimum. We cannot wait until the rising number of cars and people ring the globe with highways swirling above the underground cities of the human race, in which people live on tiny but nutritious, and only slightly carcinogenic, patticakes produced exclusively by DuPont. All of the foregoing implies that economics must not flee from values, but must bring to bear the most powerful tools of scientific method it can muster to analyze them, to explore their meaning and repercussions, to make known the full range of possible alternatives in policy, to distill through unrestricted controversy the relative merits of those alternatives, and, above all, to disclose the consequences for human beings of the choices they may make.

Notes

1. Sidney Hook, ed., *Human Values and Economic Policy: A Symposium* (New York: New York University Press, 1967).
2. The major papers of the conference were given by the twelve leading economists. Nine philosophers participated as discussants, and nearly all, particularly the chairman, Sidney Hook, indicated their disappointment with the direction of the discussion.
3. It also has an extensive history in economics and, of course, a longer

one in philosophy. See Robert B. Ekelund, Jr., and Emilie S. Olsen, "Comte, Mill, and Cairnes: The Positivist-Empiricist Interlude in Late Classical Economics," *Journal of Economic Issues* 7 (September 1973): 383–416.

4. "The Methodology of Positive Economics," in his *Essays in Positive Economics* (Chicago: Chicago University Press, 1953).
5. "Preference, Evaluation, and Reflective Choice," in *Human Values and Economic Policy*, Sidney Hook, ed., p. 76.
6. Sidney S. Alexander, "Human Values and Economists' Values," in *Human Values and Economic Policy*, Sidney Hook, ed., p. 110. Alone among the conference economists, Alexander recognized what the problem was.
7. *Economics and the Public Purpose* (Boston: Houghton Mifflin Co., 1973).
8. (New York: Basic Books, 1972).
9. "Toward Public Employment and Economic Stability," *Journal of Economic Issues* 6 (December 1972): 149–70.
10. John Dewey, *Theory of Valuation* (Chicago: University of Chicago Press, 1939). See also the excellent discussion in Sidney Hook, *John Dewey: An Intellectual Portrait* (New York: John Day, 1939), chap. 7, to which the present analysis is indebted.
11. Average family income, by age of head of household, reaches a peak in the age group 45–54 years and then declines markedly. Health expenditures per person in the family follow the same pattern, even though other evidence suggests that the need for medical care increases after the age of 54.
12. Ulmer, "Toward Public Employment."
13. Sidney Hook, *Education for Modern Man*, 2d ed. (New York: Dial, 1963).
14. I pass over here an additional theoretical alternative, which in the present context I do not consider it useful to mention. Instead of ignoring tastes, or, as I would propose, attempting to inform them in an open educational forum to enlighten and uplift them, some writers would *suppose* that a group of individuals could be found whose tastes were fully informed, unbiased, and otherwise ideal. The standards of this select group would serve to determine the relative value of alternative situations. Since such a device is obviously nonoperational, I have relegated it to this note. See John Rawls, *A Theory of Justice* (Cambridge, Mass.: Harvard University Press, 1971).

9

Provable Theorems and Refutable Hypotheses: The Case of Competitive Theory

Ken Dennis

Does perfect competition tend to lead to equilibrium? If so, what kind of evidence, logical or empirical, do we require to establish the truth of such a claim? I shall argue that the theory of perfect competition is lacking genuine scientific support. The argument consists of two parts. First, the theory cannot be proved true by logical means because it is composed of inferences running from cause to effect, and causal inferences cannot be proved true by logical means. (Throughout, *proof* will be used exclusively in the sense of demonstration by logical means.) Second, even if the theory is open, in principle, to empirical test as a set of refutable hypotheses, the fact remains that the theory has not been tested and therefore has not been corroborated empirically, notwithstanding vague assertions made about its cogency on the strength of "casual empiricism."

If this issue, the scientific status of the theory of perfect competition, is to be addressed properly, it is most essential to recognize from the outset that the two alternative characterizations, "provable theorems" and "refutable hypotheses," are indeed mutually exclusive, that is, one and the same truth-claim cannot be both provable (by logical demonstration) and refutable (by empirical test) within a consistent definitional framework. So, another purpose of this article is to clarify the distinct nature and roles of analytical theorems and refutable hypotheses in scientific inquiry.

Hume's Thesis

For a long time, philosophers and scientists uncritically assumed that inferences drawn from cause to effect could be proved true by logical demonstration. These so-called rationalists believed that "whatever was true could in principle be proved true by self-evident beginnings by self-evident steps" [Quine and Ullian 1969, p. 42]. But in 1739, David Hume ushered in the empiricist conception of science: " 'Tis impossible to demonstrate the necessity of a cause," for to do so would be tantamount to showing that the negation (or denial) of an allegedly logically true conditional about a causal connection would yield a logically self-contradictory statement. Yet, as Hume pointed out, the formal denials of causal conditionals yield no such thing, and therefore he concluded that causal conditions are "utterly incapable of demonstrative proof" [Hume 1969, p. 127].

Even though Hume's broader portrayal of the nature of causality is still subject to much controversy, his specific thesis about the nondemonstrability of causal inferences has become firmly established as one of the hallmarks of empirical science. It is accepted even by those who take an otherwise dim view of Hume's thoroughgoing skepticism (see, for example [Harré 1970, pp. 99–100]). In *The Structure of Science*, Ernest Nagel lucidly summarizes the empiricists' dismissal of the earlier tradition. On the one hand, he writes, "none of the statements generally labelled as laws in the various positive sciences are in point of fact logically necessary, since their formal denials are demonstrably not self-contradictory," reaffirming Hume's thesis; on the other hand, "if the laws of nature are logically necessary, the positive sciences are engaged in an incongruous performance whenever they seek experimental and observational evidence for a supposed law" [Nagel 1961, pp. 52–53].

Nagel's second objection refers to the incongruity of confirming or even testing by empirical means what is already alleged to be true on the basis of logical evidence. A gross paradox would ensue: To maintain that a scientific hypothesis is both provable and refutable is to court the outrageous suggestion that what is logically (and, hence, necessarily) true is also possibly false. The actuality, practicality, or even the outcome of an empirical test is of no concern to the paradox. The mere possibility of producing a negative test result would be paradoxical. I shall refer to this as the *rationalist* or *pre-Humean paradox*.

The relevance of Hume's thesis to the realm of economics has been amply acknowledged. Robert Dorfman agrees that "scientific theories are not proved ever" [Dorfman 1954, p. 375], while R. G. D. Allen warned his readers that mathematics does not serve to "prove theories" since the latter are to be "tested against facts" [Allen 1964, p. xvii]. And Paul Samuelson refers quite explicitly to Hume and his thesis in arriving at the conclusion that "nothing can prove anything about an empirical regularity" [Samuelson 1965, p. 103].

Yet, even though economists generally seem aware of the basic empiricist tenet that science admits among its hypotheses only those that are, in principle, open to empirical refutation, contemporary presentations of the theory of perfect competition illustrate the very real danger of confusion over the proper scope and role of logical demonstration in scientific inquiry. Scientists do, after all, make use of formal deductive proofs to support various theorems, but such theorems, if indeed provable, should assert nothing about causal connections, that is, nothing that is open to empirical test. Instead, such theorems serve a vital but distinct role of establishing the *logical*, not the *causal*, implications of any given set of statements.

In economics, however, one stream of thought appears to have tacitly revived the spirit of pre-Humean rationalism: the attempt to demonstrate that a perfectly competitive economy is "stable" or tends automatically to lead to a state of equilibrium. Very broadly speaking, the theory of perfect competition holds that *if* a market or economy is perfectly competitive, *then* it will tend to approach a certain kind of equilibrium state of affairs. Allowance is made for various exogenous disturbances that might upset the process of adjustment to equilibrium, and various stability-inducing restrictions imposed upon the supply and demand functions are added to the conditions defining perfect competition to ensure the stability or tendency to equilibrium of the models used.

Now, does the truth-claim that perfect competition tends to equilibrium rest upon empirical or logical foundations? To all outward appearances, the theory asserts a causal connection to hold between perfect competition and its asserted equilibrium tendency. In other words, a market or economy being perfectly competitive is what is thought to "cause" or "lead to" or "bring about" its particular kind of equilibrium, and the alleged sequence of events comprising the equilibrating process appears to be nothing less than a causally related sequence of events.

Symptoms of causal proof are to be found both in older and in contemporary accounts of this theory. For example, Léon Walras's many allusions to the process of "tâtonnement" bristle with clear indications of causal proof (see [Walras 1954, pp. 106, 146, 157, 162, 170, and so forth]), and the spirit of his inquiry is captured in such passages as "the proof of the theory must be given mathematically" (p. 43) and "up to this point we have reasoned from cause to effect" (p. 83). In short, Walras's aim was ostensibly that of "establishing proofs" for the "nature, causes and consequences of free competition" (pp. 255–56). A reading of Walras's *Elements* makes it very difficult to escape the conclusion that the author was trying to prove causal connections.

Similar indications are visible in the more recent treatise by Kenneth J. Arrow and F. H. Hahn, *General Competitive Analysis* [1971]. They state that their work is intended as "an analysis of an idealized decentralized economy . . . for which it is supposed in the main that . . . there is perfect competition" (p. v), their chief purpose being "the description of situations . . . for which we can *prove* that for the various economies discussed, there exists a set of prices that will *cause* agents to make mutually compatible decisions" (p. 16, emphasis added).

The suspicion of causal proof is especially warranted by a study of their chapters 11, 12, and 13, wherein they explore the concept of stability or "tendencies to equilibrium," which are also described as the "forces" that "tend to drive an economy toward an equilibrium if it is not in equilibrium already" (p. 263). In chapter 13, they write: "We shall show that in the pure-exchange economy with trade permitted at all times, relatively modest assumptions will allow us to deduce that the economy converges to equilibrium" (p. 325). Even though they carefully qualify their main conclusions, these qualifications do not modify their apparent aim of establishing causal connections by deductive means.

I shall return to the work of Arrow and Hahn and shall suggest an alternative construal of "stability theorems." But given these initial indications, there is good reason first to inquire into the manner in which empirical science meshes the two notions of refutability and demonstrability without invoking the pre-Humean paradox. What we need is a systematic framework for interpreting the structure of refutable hypotheses and for appraising their truth values, while at the same time differentiating these from provable analytical theorems.

Provable Theorems and Refutable Hypotheses

There are many varieties of empiricism, even within the discipline of economics, and it is not my purpose to articulate, defend, or justify any particular one of them here, but to present a brief account of the fundamental distinction between theorems and hypotheses within a broadly defined empiricist setting.

Most theorems and hypotheses take the *conditional* or "if . . . then" form. With the publication of Bertrand Russell and Alfred North Whitehead's *Principia Mathematica* (1910–1913), logicians, philosophers, and scientists have had a systematic method for interpreting theorems and hypotheses as so-called material conditionals, the sign '$\supset$' being commonly employed to symbolize the relation of material conditionality. (Readers unfamiliar with his now standard method might wish to refer to [Carnap 1966; Caws 1965; Hempel 1965; Quine 1974; Scheffler 1963; or Suppe 1974] for brief introductions and applications of the method.)

Material conditionals can be classified into those that are either logically true (tautologies being a principal subclass) or logically false (self-contradictions), and those that are neither logically true nor logically false but that are said to be "materially contingent" in the sense that their truth or falsity rests not upon logical considerations but upon material fact or empirical evidence. Tautological conditionals are said to be logically true in that their consequent or "then" clauses can be deduced validly from their antecedent or "if" clauses according to accepted principles of logical inference. By contrast, materially contingent conditionals are such that their consequent clauses cannot be deduced validly from their antecedent clauses. Scientific hypotheses belong to this latter class of conditionals, although to be refutable they must consist of antecedent and consequent clauses that are open to *independent empirical check.* Indeed, it is precisely *because they rule out on material* (not logical) *grounds something that is logically possible*, that is, something that empirical evidence conceivably could support, *that scientific hypotheses are deemed* to be "*refutable.*"

Some examples might be useful. 'If the price of coffee rises, then the quantity of coffee demanded falls,' or, in symbols, '$Pc \supset Qc$,' is a good candidate for an economic hypothesis.[1] 'Pc' does not logically entail 'Qc,' and both 'Pc' and 'Qc' are in principle open to independent empirical check. Thus, if empirical testing should show that 'Pc' is true and that 'Qc' is false, then the hypothesis '$Pc \supset Qc$' would stand refuted by that evidence. Of course, the quantity of coffee demanded depends upon more than just the price of coffee, and a major difficulty in the testing of most economic hypotheses is the familiar "other things are never equal" problem. However, that practical difficulty should not be allowed to obscure the basic *meaning* of refutability.

The hypothesis '$PC \supset Qc$' is about a single commodity, coffee, but it can be *generalized* to all commodities, for example, as '$(x)(Px \supset Qx)$,' where the letter 'x' serves as a *variable* replacing the *constant* 'c' for coffee. The *hypothetico-deductive method* involves generating *singular test-predictions* from *general hypotheses* and *singular initial conditions*, as in '$(x)(Px \supset Qx) \supset (Pc \supset Qc)$' or '$(x)(Px \supset Qx) \cdot Pc \supset Qc$.' The hypothetico-deductive method does *not* amount to proving hypotheses by logical means; it runs from the general to the particular, treating hypotheses as refutable propositions.

For contrast, consider this sentence: 'If the demand for coffee is elastic, and if the price of coffee rises, then total expenditures on coffee decline,' or, in symbols, '$Ec \cdot Rc \supset Dc$.' As it stands, this conditional is *not* strictly an analytical theorem *by itself*, but it becomes part of one when a definitional bi-conditional for elastic demand is adjoined to it, such as: '$(x)[Ex \equiv (Rx \supset Dx) \cdot (Fx \supset Ix)]$,' which might be read: 'For all commodities x, the demand for x is elastic if and only if: if the price of x rises, then total expenditures on x decline, and if the price of x falls, then total expenditures on x increase.' A general theorem about all commodities ensues: '$(x)[Ex \equiv (Rx \supset Dx) \cdot (Fx \supset Ix)] \supset (x)(Ex \cdot Rx \supset Dx)$,' as does a particular theorem about coffee: '$(x)[Ex \equiv (Rx \supset Dx) \cdot (Fx \supset Ix)] \supset (Ec \cdot Rc \supset Dc)$.'

In the first example, a causal connection is hypothesized: Quantity demanded rises as a causal consequence of a fall in price. But in the second example, we have a logical consequence, 'Dc,' which could not possibly be false if all the antecedent conditions were true. Thus, if empirical evidence showed that 'Rc' were true and 'Dc' false, this would not refute the theorem, but merely establish that the demand for coffee was inelastic, that is, that 'Ec' was false.

In other words, theorems are empirically *irrefutable* precisely because they claim nothing that is causally or materially significant, and in this sense they are said to be logically "trivial," although this does not mean that they are uninteresting or unimportant.

If, in practice, it is not always easy to distinguish clearly between theorems and hypotheses, this is not because the distinction is vague or ambiguous. It is because economic theory, when stripped of its mathematical substructure, is still woefully imprecise and informal in many of its verbal articulations. The glamour that has been attached to *mathematical* clarity and rigor has had the effect of drawing attention away from *semantic* clarity and rigor, a theme to which I shall return. But let us now reconsider the status of perfect competition.

The Stability of Perfect Competition

The theoretical statement, 'if an economy is perfectly competitive, then it tends to equilibrium,' can be symbolized as a generalized material conditional, '$(x)(Cx \supset Ex)$,' that is, 'for all x, if x is perfectly competitive, then x tends to equilibrium.' Should we view this as a provable theorem or as a refutable hypothesis? Does it assert a causal or a logical connection between competition and equilibrium?

To answer these questions, we must look to the semantics of the key terms employed. In appraising the possible meanings of, or definitions for, the two predicate descriptions, '*C*' (or 'is perfectly competitive') and '*E*' (or 'tends to equilibrium'), we are not searching for the "true" meanings or "correct" definitions of these expressions. Definitions are created arbitrarily to serve as convenient abbreviations of much longer strings of words or symbols. The most that any analysis can accomplish is to explore the differing logical implications flowing from alternative sets of definitions.

In the technically more advanced literature, perfect competition has acquired a somewhat elusive meaning which centers around the notion of infinitely elastic demand facing each individual seller, a meaning which tends to put the cart before the horse. Historically, it has been defined in terms (or has been understood to mean) a fairly fixed and recognizable set of *market structural and behavioral conditions*. Typically included are the following: *B* (an *institutional background* of free enterprise, private property, and market exchange between firms and households); *G* (certain *maximizing goals sought* by all economic agents, for example, profit by firms and utility by households); *L* (*large numbers* of buyers and sellers in each market); *M* (*perfect mobility* of resources moving from one market or use to another); *K* (*perfect knowledge* or complete information possessed by all market participants concerning current market conditions); and a few others, such as product homogeneity (absence of product differentiation within each market), trader anonymity, and individual trader independence or lack of collusion, to mention a few, but we need not bother detailing all of these. The general idea is that '*Cx*' abbreviates a long list of market structural and behavioral conditions, such that by definition we have the following bi-conditional: '$(x)\,(Cx \equiv Bx \cdot Gx \cdot Lx \cdot Mx \cdot Kx)$.'

Full definitions of equilibrium (and hence of tendencies toward equilibrium) are technically quite elaborate, but several standard features can be identified readily by means of brief suggestive labels: *Z* (*zero excess demand*, that is, the equality of supply and demand or the clearing of all markets); *S* (the *attainment of maximizing goals* by all economic agents); *U* (*uniformity of all prices* for all goods and services of the same class); *A* (*allocative efficiency* or marginal cost pricing of all outputs); *D* (*distributive efficiency* or marginal productivity pricing of all inputs as well as "normal" cost pricing of all outputs); and *T* (*technical efficiency* or long-run cost minimization at optimal choice of scale). In short, the expression 'Ex' abbreviates a long list of equilibrium tendencies such that by definition we have the following bi-conditional: '$(x)(Ex \equiv Zx \cdot Sx \cdot Ux \cdot Ax \cdot Dx \cdot Tx)$.'

Thus, the initial generalization, '$(x)(Cx \supset Ex)$,' can be viewed as a convenient abbreviation for the more elaborate and informative conditional, '$(x)(Bx \cdot Gx \cdot Lx \cdot Mx \cdot Kx \supset Zx \cdot Sx \cdot Ux \cdot Ax \cdot Dx \cdot Tx)$,' wherein the antecedent clauses spell out the market structural and behavioral conditions defining perfect competition and the consequent clauses detail the various tendencies to equilibrium associated with perfect competition. So interpreted, is the stability of competition provable or refutable?

Two basic schools of thought may be discerned. Following the trail blazed by Walras in the nineteenth century, a growing number of theorists in this century have taken up the rationalist exercise of treating the stability of perfect competition (suitably reinforced by a panoply of qualifications) as something that is both causal in nature (and hence something of material significance) and yet capable of proof by formal deductive methods as an analytical theorem. In the meantime, another group of economists, mainly researchers in the field of industrial organization, has treated the theory of perfect competition and allied theories of market structure, behavior, and performance as empirically contingent sets of hypotheses, maintaining that there is a statistical association between measurements of monopoly power and market performance such as would confirm the causal connection alleged to hold between competition and its predicted equilibrium tendencies. Let us consider these two schools of thought.

The Rationalist Case

Some brief indications were given earlier as to how Arrow and Hahn, in *General Competitive Analysis,* portray their theoretical investigations in a rationalist manner, conceiving their stability theorems as being both causal in significance and yet quite demonstrable. True, they do not claim outright that perfect competition by itself logically entails equilibrium. Their stability theorems require that perfect competition be reinforced in the antecedents of their proofs by additional stability-inducing restrictions and provisos. However, this does not prevent them from interpreting their stability theorems as causal conditionals of material significance.

In other words, Arrow and Hahn write as if they could provide substantive knowledge about the world, knowledge that is gained from armchair deduction, as if their proven theorems were not merely logically "trivial" but instead provided materially significant insights about the workings of causal relationships. In their preliminary summary, they write: "We have thus been able to establish that for the economy here described there exists a set of 'signals'—market prices—that *will lead agents to make decisions* that are mutually compatible. This is by no means a trivial result" (p. 29, emphasis added). Later, they assert that the "*causes*" of instability can be shown to emanate from the "production" side (p. 325), a claim about causal connections which they proceed to undertake to establish in the deductivist format of theorem and proof throughout chapter 13. And when they conclude that "we may claim to have learned something" (p. 346), the fact that they construe their theorems as possessing substantive import about economic causality is amply attested to not only by their own text but also by commentaries on it. For example, Roy Weintraub interprets their findings in this way: "Such a theorem, proved for the model economic system, might then provide a basis for trust-busting in practice" [Weintraub 1974, p. 105].

What Arrow and Hahn do *not* attempt to do is to frame testable hypotheses as the basis for economic theory. Oddly enough, they remark *en passant* that "sufficient degrees of freedom have been left for empirical information to make a difference to prediction; it is not a totally a priori construction" (p. viii). This curiously obscure statement underlines the need for Arrow and Hahn to clarify the role, if any, that they accord to empirical testing in the scientific appraisal of their theories.

How, then, do Arrow and Hahn justify their particular method? Perhaps they do so unwittingly in this *obiter dictum*: "while it is *possible to invent a world* in which the claims made on behalf of the 'invisible hand' are true" (p. vii, emphasis added). One might say that novelists and other writers of fiction metaphorically invent worlds of the imagination, but science deals with the one and only real world. Truths may be discovered, but they cannot be created arbitrarily by invention. The fantasy of "another" world misconstrues the scientific purpose as well as the quite legitimate use of abstraction in the framing of hypotheses. Even in its most abstruse theoretical constructions, science purports to deal with the real world. Granted, some hypotheses are devised for rather unusual sets of circumstances, seldom, if ever, met in the real world, but as scientific propositions these counterfactuals are nevertheless framed with reality in mind. This proviso applies as much to Albert Einstein's famous "thought experiments" as to Galileo's equally celebrated hypothesis of "free fall" through "perfect vacuums." Scientific abstraction does not entail otherworldliness.

Arrow and Hahn wish to invent a fictionalized world that accommodates their theorems and then to apply their results to the real world. What ensues is only a confusion of fantasy with reality. The error lies in the belief that any association between competition (albeit reinforced by stability-inducing restrictions) and equilibrium has been established by application of the mathematical method. All that has been proved formally is a series of abstract mathematical propositions mainly about numerical sequences approaching finite limits, mathematical propositions possessing in and of themselves no economic (or extramathematical) significance, even though some economic meaning has been attributed to, or "read into," those mathematical theorems through the habitual practice of naive translation, a subject to which I shall return.

Before leaving the rationalist case, I should add that adopting the Robinsonian definition of perfect competition as "a state of affairs in which the demand for the output of an individual is perfectly elastic" (see [Robinson 1934, p. 104]), a definition now generally favored in the mathematical literature on perfect competition, does nothing to strengthen the rationalist case but instead weakens it. The interpretation of '$(x)(Cx \supset Ex)$' is rendered all the more trivial, while the definition itself leaves unanswered the materially significant question: Will the market structural and behavioral conditions *B, G, L, M, K,* and so forth, lead to uniform prices and infinitely elastic demand curves facing each seller?

The Empiricist Case

Submitting the claims of the theory of perfect competition to empirical test is the desirable course. Two salient questions arise: Does the accumulated evidence actually test and confirm the theory? Is it even possible to subject the theory to an adequate and effective empirical test?

Since the 1940s, a not inconsiderable literature on empirical testing of market structure/performance relations has been amassed, and some interesting, if rather weak, positive correlations have been reported. (For extensive surveys, see [Collins and Preston 1968; and Scherer 1970].) Rates of profitability and price-cost margins for cross-sectional industry samples do appear to be fairly consistently, although weakly, associated with several measures of market power, notably seller concentration. Superficially, at least, these results seem to tally with the broad thrust of orthodox theories of market price, which place competition and monopoly at opposite extremes of the spectrum of market structure. But on closer inspection, the reported findings are by themselves far too imprecise to be of real consequence in testing the theory of perfect competition. Indeed, crude as they are, these findings are no less consistent with alternative theories, such as the Schumpeterian argument that profitability reflects not inefficiency and the abuse of market power, but the attainment of greater dynamic efficiency through technological progress. And without a satisfactory definition of (or criterion for recognizing) "normal" profits, we cannot properly assess deviations of actual profits from "normal" levels. Low profits could just as easily reflect subnormal as approximately normal rates of return.

The crux of the matter is this. The theory of perfect competition advances very precise claims about the relationships (in equilibrium) between prices and costs: marginal cost pricing and long-run minimum average cost pricing. But the only empirical information entering into tests has been for average *realized* costs alone, not the static-marginal and static-minimum costs of theory. Thus, rates of profit and price-cost margins alone tell us nothing about technical, allocative, and distributive efficiency. What is lacking and urgently required is a systematic, comprehensive, and reliable method of estimating static-marginal cost (with zero X-inefficiency, to boot) before anything relevant can be discerned in relation to perfect competition. In the absence of that information, some researchers have resorted to the dubious procedure of *assuming* that average realized costs always equal long-run minimum average cost, in order to estimate the misallocative effects of monopoly (see, for example [Harberger 1954]). This ploy, far from constituting an effective estimate, merely begs the very question at issue: Do firms in perfect competition tend to set price equal to marginal (and, in the long run, minimum average) cost? Unfortunately, a few isolated estimates of static cost curves have been too sporadic to be of any assistance.

Can the theory be tested at all, even in principle, quite apart from practical considerations? Not likely, although this is a moot point. Numerous semantic hurdles stand in the way. In addition to such vague terms as "normal" cost and "normal" profit, the theory presents us with a formidable array of baffling expressions: "perfect" knowledge, "perfect" (or costless) mobility of resources, "sufficiently" large numbers of buyers and sellers, and so on. Scientific observation is predicated upon semantic clarity as a prerequisite to any measurement, and the outlook for perfect competition in this regard is not very promising.

Other Defenses

A theory that cannot be proved logically, that has not been tested effectively, and that probably cannot be tested at all scarcely merits scientific approval, let alone acceptance. Yet, the continuing commitment to perfect competition throughout the scientific community of economics is still a very strong one, to judge by its solidly entrenched position in the textbooks of our discipline. To round out this survey, then, some brief comments on other defenses are in order.

First, the longstanding criticism that the theory is unrealistic in its assumptions is unquestionably correct, but it misses the crux of the matter (the internal cogency of the theory) and plays right into the hands of the theory's defenders. For they will readily grant this criticism, deplore the absence of perfect competition in the real world, and maintain that the theory is valid nonetheless, even if the world is not actually characterized by perfect competition. If the theory is to be challenged and overthrown once and for all, we must go beyond the question of immediate applicability to reality. The fundamental scientific question is whether or not the theory's predictions would hold true if perfect competition were actually to prevail.

Two secondary lines of defense remain: the appeal to intuitive causal plausibility and to casual empiricism. During the nineteenth century, perfect competition may have appeared quite intuitively plausible, but this is no longer the case. The precarious status of the price uniformity condition will illustrate. When W. S. Jevons enunciated his law of indifference in 1871, he did so as if it were self-evidently true that product homogeneity and perfect knowledge would guarantee uniformity of price [Jevons 1871, pp. 87, 91–92]. His informal statement of this "law" was a logical *non sequitur.* Only through force of habit did Jevons's law acquire its reputation for logical cogency, much as did Euclid's Parallel Postulate, and to this day it still carries an air of logicality in the minds of some theorists (see, for example [Henderson and Quandt 1971, p. 105]). Arrow and Hahn acknowledge that price uniformity is not automatically forthcoming from perfect competition, as Jevons once thought, and that without price uniformity stability analysis is grievously undermined [Arrow and Hahn 1971, p. 322]. A regime of perfect competition, lending itself to simple patterns and direct solutions, is an immensely complicated affair, as modern studies have shown, and we have long since passed the day when Adam Smith's "invisible hand" can be assumed to lead to "order" rather than "chaos" (for which see [Arrow and Hahn 1971, p. vii]).

There are also those who would maintain that, even though the theory has eluded formal proof and rigorous testing, it nevertheless merits our approval on the strength of casual observation of the efficacy of markets in general, perfect competition being only an extreme expression of that efficacy. But this "casual empiricism" merely invites counterclaims that only a more systematic scientific approach can adjudicate. For all we know, on the basis of casual empiricism, the efficacy of markets might be due as much to their imperfections as to their relative proximity to the norm or ideal of perfect competition. In short, casual empiricism hardly constitutes a worthy defense of what has been, after all, one of the most prominent of economic theories.

Finally, the Edgeworthian argument that equilibrium analysis is impossible without perfect competition seems to prejudge the question at issue. An alternative construal of equilibrium analysis, one that does away with specific institutional frameworks such as perfect competition, will be intimated in the next section.

History aside, any further presumption in favor of the theory of perfect competition is unwarranted, and the onus is with the theory's defenders to establish their case.

The Role of Mathematics

In a misguided endeavor to associate competition with equilibrium through logical demonstration, some economic theorists have placed great emphasis on the rigor of their logical demonstrations, but that appeal to logical rigor has been essentially *mathematical* in nature and hence has been partly misplaced.

The growth of mathematical economics during the nineteenth century gave rise to a semiarticulate and semiofficial *doctrine of translation*: the belief that the concepts and propositions of economics could be translated into the symbols and formulas of mathematics. (This doctrine is discussed extensively in [Dennis 1977, chapters 5–7].) The doctrine is only partially true. Mathematical symbols, formulas, and methods do enter into economic theorizing, but not in such a way as to formulate or prove *behavioral* propositions about human beings and their economic actions. Mathematics, in its traditional sense, is simply the logic of numbers and numerical relations; it is not a logic about *events* and the *conditionality of the occurrence of events*. (More modern definitions of mathematics, broader in conception, do not affect the force of the argument to follow.) Even though number systems and measurement systems have been shown to be homomorphic relational structures (see [Krantz *et al.* 1971]), numerical functional formulas do not express behavioral propositions about events and the contingency of their occurrence. Moreover, not all theoretical statements in economics are numerical or mathematical in nature.

Numerical functions, however they may be interpreted informally, are nothing more than sets of ordered pairs of numbers. Consider A. A.

Cournot's symbolic expression for simple demand, '$D = F(p)$.' By itself, this expression does not constitute a statement of the demand hypothesis; it merely states that both 'D' and '$F(\mathrm{p})$' act as variables ranging over the same set of numbers, the "range" of the function 'F,' while 'p' ranges over the "domain" of that function. The informal association of 'p' with price (or the pricing behavior of sellers) and 'D' with quantity demanded (or buyers' market actions) has no formal significance, *yet*. So far, the logical machinery for that association is lacking.

There does exist a method, however, for showing how mathematical logic can be integrated with a logic of events. This *method of numerics* (as I shall call it) demonstrates that the mathematical and behavioral components of economic theory are quite distinguishable but interrelatable. The method, using the demand hypothesis as an example, works as follows.

Initially, we can express the numerical functional relation, let us say '$y = f(x)$,' by means of a predicate logic as 'Fxy.' (To stipulate that 'F' describes a *single-valued function,* not a *multivalued relation,* we can write: '$(x)(\exists y)[Fxy \bullet (z)(Fxy \supset y = z)]$.') The behavioral content of the hypothesis is captured by two other predicates, 'P' and 'Q.' 'Pxt' is read: 'Sellers ask a price of x units of currency for their product during time-period t.' 'Qyt' is read: 'Buyers demand y units of product during time-period t.' The three expressions, 'Fxy,' 'Pxt,' and 'Qyt' can be combined to form a very simple version of the simple demand hypothesis: '$(x)(y)(t)(Pxt \bullet Fxy \supset Qyt)$.' More elaborate versions can be formulated. (For example, to stipulate price uniformity among sellers, we would write: '$(x)(v)(t)(Pxt \bullet Pvt \supset x = v)$.') However, these elaborations need not detain us here. What emerges from this very primitive sketch can be summarized in two parts.

First, the mathematical and behavioral aspects of the demand hypothesis can be integrated into a unified logical scheme by virtue of the fact that numerical symbols are employed in two different ways: to relate to one another for mathematical purposes and to act as "*numerics*" or *numbers assigned to measurements* in the description of economic actions. Thus, the letters 'x' and 'y' are variables over sets of pure numbers when occurring in 'Fxy,' but they are variables over numbers assigned to measurements when occurring in 'Pxt' and 'Qyt.'

Second, by the same token, the analysis shows that the mathematical and behavioral aspects of the hypothesis are quite distinct. The mathematical formula, '$y = f(x)$,' is translated into symbols centering on the expression 'Fxy,' but *not* into the behavioral conditional, '$Pxt \supset Qyt$.' Thus, by itself, the mathematical logic of economic theory provides a *numerical substructure* for the behavioral propositions but proves nothing of a behavioral nature. The rise of mathematical economics was inevitable, necessary, and none too soon, but one of the unfortunate outcomes of the doctrine of translation accompanying the use of mathematics has been a *double standard,* namely, mathematical rigor has been sought at the relative neglect of semantic precision, while mathematical proofs, through naïve translation, have been confused for behavioral proofs.

What, then, have Arrow, Hahn, and others proved by their stability theorems? To answer this question, I shall compare economic dynamics with dynamics in the physical sciences. The market dynamics of economic theory can be appreciated better by contrasting a theorem with an hypothesis from classical dynamics. Whereas *kinetics* is the branch of science dealing with the motions of physical objects with reference to the various forces (such as gravity and inertia) that are thought to *cause* their motion, *kinematics* is the branch of science that merely describes motion by its numerical properties without any reference to its causes. Thus it was that, in his *Discorsi* of 1638, Galileo gave both a *provable kinematic theorem* and a *testable kinetic hypothesis,* two very distinct propositions that have often been confused for each other under the common formula, '$s = \frac{1}{2} gt^2$.'

On the one hand, Galileo posited as a testable hypothesis the claim that bodies in free fall through perfect vacuums accelerate uniformly, an hypothesis which asserts a causal connection between the two materially distinct conditions of falling through vacuums and accelerating uniformly. Galileo believed this hypothesis to be true on the strength of a "highly probable guess" [Galileo 1974, p. 76]. Far from treating it as provable, he described a method for testing it. Modern science has done so and has found Galileo's hypothesis to be almost, but not quite, true, that is, *false* ("free fall is not uniformly accelerated" [Arons 1965, p. 54]). Just as Isaac Newton's inverse-square law corrected and superseded Galileo's inspired guess, so, too, was Newton's theory of gravitation corrected and superseded by Einstein's. Even though extremely precise gravimeter readings show that Galileo's hypothesis was not very far from the "truth," the point is that it *was tested* and was found wanting *on empirical grounds,* although admittedly long after Newton's own theory had appeared on the scene.

On the other hand, Galileo also advanced a provable theorem: "Proposition II, Theorem II. If a moveable descends from rest in uniformly accelerated motion, the spaces run through in any times whatever are to each other . . . as the squares of those times" [Galileo 1974, p. 166]. Nowhere in the discussion of this theorem did Galileo allude to the cause(s) of uniform acceleration. Bodies need not be falling through perfect vacuums to be accelerating uniformly. Galileo did not make the mistake of confusing theorem for hypothesis. The two are quite distinct, although the theorem aids in the testing of the hypothesis by providing an "empirical footprint" for uniform acceleration; we can measure acceleration by measuring distances traveled and elapsed times of motion and thereby determine whether or not acceleration is uniform. While the theorem is logically true, it asserts nothing causal in nature. While the hypothesis is not logically demonstrable, it can be submitted to empirical test for the causal assertion it makes.

The fact that these two very different propositions have been mistaken for each other, with some rather startling consequences, can be illustrated by Milton Friedman's essay, "The Methodology of Positive Economics." Even though Friedman professes a "positivist" philosophy of science, he somehow manages to misconstrue Galileo's refutable (and refuted) hypothesis as a provable analytical theorem: "The formula $s = \frac{1}{2}gt^2$ is valid for bodies falling in a vacuum and can be derived by analyzing the behavior of such bodies" [Friedman 1953, p. 18].

The parallel between the examples from physical science and market dynamics is this. Just as Galileo proved a kinematic theorem about motion without proving any causal link to perfect vacuums, so, too, economic theorists can prove certain *abstract numerical properties about patterns of economic adjustment* (such as whether or not they converge to some limit) *without thereby proving any causal link between those patterns of adjustment and such things as market structures or institutional frameworks.*

Thus, the economic dynamics of stability analysis, understood as a kind of "economic kinematics," explores the numerical properties of adjustment patterns or "paths to equilibrium," but the numerical properties of those paths describe only the abstracted quantities of such things as inputs and outputs, prices and utilities, and so forth. The latter are *dissociated from any institutional context*, just as '$s = \frac{1}{2}gt^2$' describes the numerical property of uniformly accelerated motion quite apart from any causal circumstances. Whatever association there may be between those stable paths and such behavioral/institutional settings as perfect competition is a matter for empirical methods to determine.

Note

1. In accordance with W. V. Quine [1951, pp. 23–26], when referring to expressions (be they single terms or sentences, in symbols or in prose), I enclose them within single quotation marks.

References

Allen, R. G. D. 1964. *Mathematical Economics*, 2d ed. London: Macmillan [1956].

Arons, A. B. 1965. *The Development of the Concepts of Physics*. Reading, Mass.: Addison-Wesley.

Arrow, Kenneth J., and F. H. Hahn. 1971. *Gneral Competitive Analysis*. Edinburgh: Oliver and Boyd; San Francisco: Holden Day.

Carnap, Rudolf. 1966. *Philosophical Foundations of Physics: An Introduction to the Philosophy of Science*. New York and London: Basic Books.

Caws, Peter. 1965. *The Philosophy of Science*. Princeton: Van Nostrand.

Collins, Norman R., and Lee E. Preston. 1968. *Concentration and Price-Cost Margins in Manufacturing Industries*. Berkeley and Los Angeles: University of California Press.

Dennis, Kenneth. 1977. *Competition in the History of Economic Thought*. New York: Arno Press.

Dorfman, Robert. 1954. "A Catechism: Mathematics in Social Science." *Review of Economics and Statistics* 36 (November): 374–77.

Friedman, Milton. 1953. "The Methodology of Positive Economics." In *Essays in Positive Economics*. Chicago and London: University of Chicago Press.

Galileo. 1974. *Two New Sciences* [*Discorsi*, 1638], trans. Stillman Drake. Madison: University of Wisconsin Press.

Harberger, A. C. 1954. "Monopoly and Resource Allocation." *American Economic Review* 44 (December): 77–87.

Harré, Rom. 1970. *The Principles of Scientific Thinking*. London and Basingstoke: Macmillan; Chicago: University of Chicago Press.

Henderson, James M., and Richard E. Quandt. 1971. *Microeconomic Theory: A Mathematical Approach*, 2d ed. Tokyo: McGraw-Hill Kogakusha [1958].

Hempel, Carl G. 1965. *Aspects of Scientific Explanation*. New York: Free Press.

Hume, David. 1969. *A Treatise of Human Nature*, edited by E. C. Mossner. London: Pelican [1st ed. in 3 vols., 1739–1740].

Jevons, W. Stanley. 1871. *The Theory of Political Economy*. London: Macmillan.

Krantz, David H.; R. Duncan Luce; Patrick Suppes; and Amos Tversky. 1971. *Foundations of Measurement*, vol. 1. New York: Academic Press.

Nagel, Ernest. 1961. *The Structure of Science*. New York: Harcourt, Brace and World.

Quine, W. V. 1974. *Methods of Logic*, 3d ed. London: Routledge and Kegan Paul [1953].

———. 1951. *Mathematical Logic*, 2d ed. New York: Harper and Row [1940].

——— and J. S. Ullian. 1970. *The Web of Belief*. New York: Random House.

Robinson, Joan. 1934. "What Is Perfect Competition?" *Quarterly Journal of Economics* 49 (November): 104–20.

Samuelson, Paul A. 1965. "Some Notions on Causality and Teleology in Eco-

nomics." In *Cause and Effect*, edited by David Lerner. New York: Free Press.
Scheffler, Israel. 1963. *The Anatomy of Inquiry*. New York: Alfred A. Knopf.
Scherer, F. M. 1974. *Industrial Market Structure and Economic Performance*. Chicago: Rand McNally.
Suppe, Frederick, ed. 1974. "Critical Introduction" to *The Structure of Scientific Theories*. Urbana, Chicago, and London: University of Illinois Press.
Walras, Léon. 1954. *Elements of Pure Economics*, trans. and edited by William Jaffé. London: George Allen and Unwin [1874–1877].
Weintraub, E. Roy. 1974. "Arrow and Hahn's General Competitive Analysis: A Perspective." *Economic Inquiry* 12 (March): 105–13.

10

Self-Reference and the Incomplete Structure of Neoclassical Economics

J. Steven Winrich

There is a persistent belief among neoclassical economists that the mathematical and logical foundations on which their theories rest are secure. But these foundations are not the rock of truth that some perceive them to be. The mathematicians were the ones who revealed the incomplete structure of the deductive method. Many economists of the 1980s are shockingly unaware of the "loss of certainty" in the developments of mathematics since the 1930s.

Recent developments in mathematics undermine the foundation of neoclassical economics and substantiate the findings of instrumentalism. The purpose of this article is to illustrate the mathematical and logical development of the principle of self-reference, and to show how this principle exemplifies the incomplete structure of neoclassical economics. In particular, this supposition can be applied to the core of economics, that is, to the value question and the theory of choice. It is argued that neoclassicism constitutes an incomplete theory of value, an incompleteness that cannot be overcome without a radical paradigmatic shift. Only an evolutionary economics can successfully overcome the incomplete structure of orthodoxy.

The first and second sections illustrate the self-referential nature of language and mathematics. The third section explains how self-reference leads to the development of the "incompleteness theorem" and explains the significance of this finding for economists. Finally, the fourth and fifth sections use these results to clarify the incomplete structure of neoclassical choice theory.

The Nature of Paradox

Human beings not only think but are conscious of their thoughts. They are for the first time "life aware of itself." Self-awareness arises from the fact that humans are not only users of symbols but also the object of the symbolism. People use symbols to refer to their own thought processes. Symbols refer not only to things "out there" but also to symbols themselves; thus, the symbolic process is a self-referral system.

The self-referential aspect of symbolism has given rise to a number of linguistic paradoxes. One must appreciate the paradoxical nature of self-reference in order to understand its epistemological significance. Of these, the most widely known is called *the Liar.* Eubulides version was, "The statement I am making is false"; a later version, discussed by Aristotle, was, "This sentence is false." Clearly, both of these statements leave us in a dilemma as to their truth. If the statements quoted above are true, then what they say must be true, so the statements must be false. On the other hand, if the statements above are false, that is exactly what they state, so they must be true.

Both of the previous paradoxes refer to themselves and deny themselves at the same time. Similar paradoxes not as direct but equally self-referential could also be produced. Statements may not be directly self-referential but are paradoxical at a higher level of generalization. Consider the following discussion:

SOCRATES: What Plato is about to say it false.
PLATO: Socrates has just spoken truly.[1]

Similarly, in 1913 the mathematician P. E. B. Jourdain introduced the following:

> On one side of a blank card print: The statement on the other side of this card is true.
> On the opposite side of the card print: The statement on the other side of this card is false.[2]

One may believe that both of these cases are examples of paradoxes without the existence of self-reference.[3] But Patrick Hughes and George Brecht have clarified their self-referential nature:

> It would be true to say that what Socrates says or what Plato says or what is said on either side of Jourdain's card is not *self-referential*, but it would also be true to say that what Socrates says or what Plato says or what is said on either side of Jourdain's card are *paradoxical*, and the paradox of Socrates' and Plato's remarks and the paradox of both sides of Jourdain's card are self-referential.[4]

As soon as we make statements about statements we are thrown into a universe of self-reference. Alfred Tarski illustrated the epistemological significance of self-reference.[5] In essence he showed that as soon as one says, "This statement is," one is no longer using language to describe things "out there"; one is referring to the symbols in the language itself. One is caught in a world of self-reference, and as soon as one adds "is true" or "is false" one opens the system to paradox. All thinking about thinking implies self-reference. Jacob Bronowski has made the self-referential nature of truth a fundamental premise of his entire philosophy: "The point is that these paradoxes enter into the language of science because we not only want to write sentences in science, we want to say about them that they are true or false. And at once we are back in the universe in which we are using language in which we *refer to ourselves*" (emphasis added).[6]

Mathematical Paradoxes

Mathematics has been persistently plagued with the problem of self-reference. Mathematicians asked themselves: Is it possible that mathematics and logic could be subject to the same paradoxes as language?[7]

One of the most significant illustrations of self-reference in mathematics was discovered by Bertrand Russell. What Russell noticed is that some sets contain themselves as members and some do not. For instance, consider the set of all cats. The set of all cats is not itself a cat, hence does not contain itself as a member. It appears that most sets are of this type, so they are called normal. Abnormal sets or self-engulfing sets, however, are not impossible. Consider the set of all sets, or the set of all things that are not cats, and so on. Now, divide all sets into the categories of normal or abnormal. Is the set of all normal sets normal? If it is normal, it does not have itself as a member. But, it contains all normal sets and it must contain itself. This is a contradiction: it must be abnormal. But, if it is abnormal, it has itself as one of its members. This is also a contradiction. If the set of all normal sets is neither normal or abnormal, what is it?[8]

There is a common culprit in both the paradoxes of set theory and of language—namely, self-reference. If mathematics (economics) is to be consistent, all traces of self-reference must go.

In *Principia Mathematica*, Bertrand Russell and Alfred North Whitehead undertook the monumental task of axiomatizing mathematics in an attempt to eliminate the paradoxes. To carry out this objective they introduced the theory of types, and within it established a hierarchy. In set theory, objects (but not sets) would be of type 0. Sets whose members were from type 0 would be of type 1. Type 2 would consist of sets of sets, and so forth. Logically, no statement of a lower type would refer to any statement of an equivalent or higher type. For analysis, a function would be of a higher type than that of its variables. On the basis of this system, Russell and Whitehead were able to exorcise contradictions from logic, set theory, and number theory.

Russell and Whitehead made a dramatic discovery when they applied the theory of types to mathematics. They found that as soon as they removed self-reference, mathematics became unworkable. The price of consistency was infecundity. Such notions as equality, least upper bound, maximization, and the real number system, among others, became unworkable. Since neoclassical economics depends greatly upon the calculus, it may be useful to mention the problem of maximization or minimization. The maximum must be of a higher type than the real numbers and could not itself be a real number. However, it must be a real number by the definition of a maximum. This is a contradiction. The calculus must be abandoned since the notion of a maximum is nonsensical.

To restore the power of mathematics, Russell and Whitehead introduced the axiom of reducibility. But the act of reducing the strong demarcation of types reintroduces the demon that the theory of types was designed to remove.

Many others attempted to axiomatize mathematics and prove completeness and consistency. The most noteworthy were the formalists, led by David Hilbert, and the set-theorists, led by Ernst Zermelo and Abraham Fraenkel. However, this dream would be crushed forever by the German mathematician Kurt Gödel.

Gödel and the End of Closed Systems

The formal systems that mathematicians construct belong to the world of mathematics; the descriptions and theories about these formal systems belong to a world of higher generalization called metamathematics. Recognition of the distinction between statements in mathematics and statements about mathematics led Hilbert to believe that he could "banish from the world all the foundational problems." Metamathematics would be the method of establishing the completeness and consistency of any formal system.

In his article "On Formally Undecidable Propositions of Principia Mathematica and Related Systems," Kurt Gödel proved that this goal is unobtainable.[9] Gödel illustrated that any system powerful enough to encompass the whole numbers as well as being complete would be inconsistent, and if consistent must be incomplete. He attained these results by showing that metamathematics could be mapped into mathematics itself, eliminating the sharp demarcation of the two and subjecting the system to paradox.

This mapping (or Gödel Numbering) is based upon the theorem that any natural number greater than 1 is either a prime or a unique product of primes. The process of mapping an axiomatic system into arithmetic is quite involved but the overall mechanism can be outlined as follows: First, assign a number to each symbol in the system. Second, convert every formula in the system to a unique number; for instance, assign 1 to ε, 3 to a, and 5 to P, then for the formula $a \varepsilon P$ we would have the sequence of numbers 3,1,5. Now assign to this formula a unique natural number by using the theorem of primes. Gödel's method would produce the number $2^3 * 3^1 * 5^5 = 75{,}000$ by using the first three primes. Whenever we run across the number 75,000 it can be converted into a product of primes in only one way, that is, $2^3 * 3^1 * 5^5$, which gives us the sequence of numbers 3,1,5, which is the formula $a \varepsilon P$. In a similar manner, a proof could be converted into a unique product of primes. So, from the number of a proof, we could reconstruct the formulas of the proof. Gödel then converted metamathematical statements into arithmetic. By converting statements *about* arithmetic *into* arithmetic the self-referential nature of formulation becomes clear: It is like a snake swallowing its own tail.

Gödel then showed how to construct a statement G that says that the statement with the Gödel number k is not provable. But, G has the Gödel number k, so G says of itself that it is not provable. Like Eubulides's *Liar*, Gödel produced a "mathematical liar" that asserts: "This statement is unprovable." If the statement is true it is not provable, and if it is not provable it is true. Hence, the statement is true if and only if it is provable. The formal system to which this assertion belongs is consistent only if it is incomplete.

After establishing his "mathematical liar," Gödel then showed that these results apply to *any* system that can under some scheme be mapped into arithmetic. Closed systems maintain their consistency at the price of completeness.

These findings are stark and dramatic, and they have given rise to other implications that must be noted. These results will be referred to as nonexcludability and noncategoricalness.

Since some statements are neither provable nor disprovable this is, in essence, a denial of the law of the excluded middle. Such a rejection produces a nondualistic interpretation of the world. Institutionalists, especially John Dewey and Clarence Ayres, have continually criticized dualistic conceptions of reality, and with this rejection the findings of Gödel clearly concur.[10]

A final, and equally significant, result that must be mentioned is known as the Lowenheim-Skolem theory. It implies that an axiomatic system permits essentially different interpretations than the one intended. For instance, suppose we were to write down a list of characteristics to describe a cat and only a cat. It might be possible to find an animal that satisfied all the characteristics mentioned but was not a cat. You might say, well, let's expand the list, but for any finite list this possibility can always crop up. Each axiomatic system contains undefined terms; it was believed that the axioms defined these terms implicitly, but the axioms are insufficient.

The principles of incompleteness, nonexcludability, and noncategoricalness form an intricate nexus of implications that question the traditional meaning of truth in economics. It follows from these principles that it is not completely possible to distinguish between "utility" and "disutility," or "efficiency" and "inefficiency," or "scarcity" and "abundance." Neoclassical economists must understand that theirs is a closed system. Notions such as utility, efficiency, scarcity, and so forth are not well defined, and extending the axiomatic framework will not lead to absolute precision. The neoclassicist belief that one can "measure" these variables is a myth—"the exactness is a fake."

In remarking upon Gödel's findings, Bronowski explains:

> One has, at this stage, simply to admit that mechanism is not a solution to the problem of the universe but a strategy, just as induction and all previous methods of doing science were.
>
> We have to realize that the total connectivity of nature is something that cannot be imagined in axiomatic systems. To that extent, no proposition that we put, no axiomatic system, no formal language, is ever final. (That is the Incompleteness Theorem.) What is far more important, none of these can possibly be proved to be consistent within the system itself.[11]

The goal of neoclassical economics has been to produce an exact and rigorous science by applying the axiomatic method to economic variables.

However, this goal is unobtainable because of the incomplete structure of formalization itself. All language is necessarily imprecise or dialectical, even the most abstract formalistic theories in mathematics. But what is surprising is that it is the paradoxical nature of language that provides its richness. If symbolism were completely exact it would be sterile—it would be impossible to discover anything new.

Attempts to eliminate possible contradictions in mathematics, the social sciences, and the natural sciences have failed. Theories that aspire to such precision become tautological, reductionistic, and static. A completely closed and formalized system leads not to truth, but to incompleteness. The flaw in neoclassical thought is the failure to realize that science does not advance solely by more rigor but also by more imagination. A new idea becomes formalized and axiomatized *only* after it is discovered.

Now we are face to face with the crucial question: If truth is necessarily self-referential, how are we to separate scienc from dogma? The answer lies not only in the findings of science but in the process of science. When faced with an anachronism we can either change the system to incorporate it, or we can attempt to *force* the outside element inside so as to agree with the pre-established circular structure. The acid test of a science is its adaptability. The paradox of self-reference is that in human discourse self-reference is always evident but there is the closed and the processual (open) aspect of self-reference. The former refers to the circular structure, the second to the processual structuring.

The closed system of economic analysis implies that the whole world has now been taken in under the roof of assumption and preconception and essentially described, and all else is only a "trivial embroidery" on the main picture. Neoclassicists claim that the closed system is theory and that other paradigms are ideologies, or unimportant. Another implication is that future economic analysis will blaze no new trails (neoclassicists expect no Einsteinian revolution in economics), that future discoveries will be simply slight variations on the main theme.

Why have developments in mathematics remained essentially neglected in orthodox economics for some fifty years? Perhaps because of an inherent belief in the myth of the infallability of logical and mathematical reasoning. Or have neoclassical economists been mesmerized by their own tools, as Morris Kline has said of the eighteenth-century mathematician?

> Having grasped the essence of a physical problem in some mathematical formulation, the eighteenth century mathematicians in particular were seduced by formulas. Apparently, formulas were so attractive to them that the mere derivation of one formula from another by a formal oper-

ation such as differentiation or integration was enough to justify it. The fascination of symbols overpowered and consumed their reason.[12]

Many have commented upon the fact that the neoclassical economist is wedded to the paradigmatic vision of Newtonian mechanics. Perhaps the neoclassicist might argue that science can develop only by specialization, and that economists should leave mathematical foundations to the mathematicians; only the results or tools are needed by the economist. But the questions remain: For example, should economics be based upon the intuitionalist school of mathematics? The intuitionalists reject the existence of infinite collections, the real number system, the calculus, the law of the excluded middle, the modern theory of real functions, and other topics. Good heavens, what would be left of neoclassical economics if such a mathematics were espoused?

The Incompleteness of the Implicit Structure of Neoclassical Value Theory

At the heart of the economic problem is the question of value. The effect of the theory of choice upon the value question deeply divides the neoclassical and institutionalist schools. It is therefore of fundamental importance that the previous methodological abstractions be given concrete expression in evaluating the efficacy of the utility theory of value. It is my contention that the utility theory of value is an incomplete and closed system of analysis that maintains its consistency by misconstruing the essential nature of the valuation process.

A theory consists of a collection of both implicit and explicit assumptions that define the system. The implicit assumptions form the paradigmatic vision that the explicit axiomatic structure should formalize. The formalistic structure is always built from the underlying system of implicit assumptions. All of the implicit assumptions must comport, forming a unified topological structure that defines the essence and richness of the system.

Four essential characteristics of neoclassicism should be noted. It is epistemologically absolute, methodologically deductive, ethically relativistic, and behaviorally individualistic. In *Human Behavior: An Economic Approach*, Robert Crouch makes the ideological position of neoclassicism quite clear: it perceives the utility theory to be an unchanging truth independent of time and culture.[13] In the preface he notes: "The purpose of this book is, in a nutshell, to propose a general theory of human behavior based on choice theory." Later in the prologue he states:

> So let us clarify here what we mean by a *general* theory. A general theory whose explanatory power is not restricted in time or space. The timeless characteristic of a general theory means that its predictive capacity would be as powerful in the past as it is now and will be in the future.
>
> A theory is geographically general (i.e., unrestricted in space) if its explanatory is as good for other cultures as it is for our own. Thus we say that a general theory of human behavior must be transculturally relevant.[14]

The method of deriving such a theory is deductive: "The theory of human behavior we will develop is an overtly deductive system. Certain assumptions will be made . . . and these assumptions will be supplemented by various definitions. From this set of assumptions and definitions, certain inferences, or implications, and predictions concerning human behavior will be derived."[15] While there may be some rebuttal, the ethical position of neoclassicism is not a neutral one, as is most often claimed. Again Robert Crouch illustrates this point with precision.

> Different individuals have different psyches, tastes, makeups, needs, and desires (call them what you will)that give them different scales of preferences. That, after all, is what makes them individuals. We accept this fact of life and state that preferences are individual, personal, and subjective. Preferences are not, therefore, objective.
>
> This means that it is not possible to devise one ranking of preferences over a field of choice that is in any sense *better* than all other conceivable rankings. It would be a different ranking, not a better one. (Unwillingness to accept this conclusion has been and still is a source of much mischief in the world.)[16]

And how lucky we are that such mischief abounds; complete relativism justifies all choices no matter how distorted, perverse, or destructive. It is worth noting that on the very next page, after stating this value position, he argues: "The positive analysis of human behavior—what people do and why they do it—is the domain of the behavior sciences, and it is on this subject that we will concentrate our attention. Our analysis will then be what is called value-neutral (or ethically neutral)."[17] I think the point is clear.

Finally, the preconception of human psychology is the ultimate core of the theory: "We assume that an individual faced with a field of choice and an attainable set of choices will choose that alternative that ranks highest in her scale of preferences. This is equivalent to postulating (claiming) that a human being is a *purposeful* animal and the purpose is to maximize enjoyment of life."[18] Furthermore, "we may now define what we mean by a rational individual. A *rational individual* is a person who can, given a field of choice, rank his preferences and then choose that alternative from his attainable set of choices that ranks highest on his scale of preferences, thereby maximizing his enjoyment of life."[19] Last, but not least:

> To explain human behavior, attention must be focused on the individual. It is always an individual who makes choices and takes action.
>
> The group's choice of an action is based on the choices of the individuals comprising the group. And an individual who dissents from the collective choice can always withdraw from the group if he or she chooses. Thus individual choices are the foundation of group decisions.[20]

Of course, this implies that changing cultures is like changing a pair of socks.

Elaborating the details of the spurious nature of these assumptions is unnecessary; the radical and institutionalist literature is replete with such repudiations. All challengers of the system have, however, met similar fates: either they have been ignored because of their "fuzzy" thinking, or their "fuzzy" ideas have been irreparably distorted and insipidly incorporated within the system. Orthodox progress is defined not as revolutionary but as a patchwork. The ability of an individual practitioner to patch a breakage in the seams is directly related to his or her intellectual esteem. In this regard, the fundamental purpose of research within the system is maintenance, not discovery—making sure that obscure foreign ideas do not distort the obvious clarity and purity of the system.[21] All maintenance systems are closed, tautological, and non-expansionary structures. The purpose of such a system is to maintain its own credibility and nothing more.

I am not saying that neoclassical economics is static; however, I am saying that it is teleological (directed toward an ultimate end), and all teleological systems are nondiscovery systems. Orthodoxy "expands" by applying the closed system to new ideas of inquiry. For instance, the demand-supply apparatus has been "expanded" to explain non-market phenomena (externalities) as well as market phenomena. As another example, consider the attempts to "expand" utility theory to explain cooperation, human capital, discrimination, marriage, divorce, and (most incredibly) suicide. Rather than adjust the system to take into account non-market behavior, all behavior becomes market behavior, and all motivation is reduced to hedonism. While orthodoxy can disparage heterodox attacks, it can not expand beyond its own inner circularity. The orthodox believe that all past attacks have been, and all future attacks will be, incorporated within the theory. The foundation, it claims, is secure and unchangeable; that foundation is the formalistic analysis of rational subjectivity.

The Incompleteness of the Explicit Structure of Neoclassical Value Theory

The implicit structure governs the derivation of the explicit axiomatic structure. However, as long as the explicit structure remains intact, the neoclassical practitioner will certainly argue that the foundations are secure. Perhaps this explains why the critics of utility theory have been unable to destroy the structure itself. Fortunately, we need not list the entire axiomatic system—the structure falls apart long before that. Nor have neoclassical economists attempted to build a complete axiomatic system. If they had, they might have seen the significance of the "incompleteness theorem." In this regard, axiomatic choice theory is said to be "naive." For instance, it takes logic and set theory for granted, and assumes that any problems that arise have already been solved by mathematicians. According to Patric Suppes,

> for most axiomatic work in mathematics the standard development of logic and general set theory is assumed without comment. If such an assumption is not made, then the complete apparatus must be built from the ground up; that is, the theory must be constructed with a completely and explicity formalized language. In axiomatic work in the empirical sciences, such as physics, psychology, and economics, it is customary to assume not only logic and general set theory, but the standard portions of mathematics as well.[22]

Indeed, one can argue that if everything had to be built "from the ground up" every time we wished to do something, we would never have time to do anything. A tentative presumption of a secure foundation is quite reasonable; however, someone should make sure that the foundation is secure. This is like piloting an aircraft without checking the fuel level: you need not do it yourself but you had better make sure someone has.

There may be another way out: perhaps it is possible to build a solid theory on a shaky foundation. If set theory is not consistent, remove that part causing the trouble.

> There is, however, another argument that can be used to justify the adoption of set theory in axiomatizing a science. For choice theory, the argument may be stated simply thus: The largest set with which we shall be

> concerned—our universal set—is the set of all conceivable choices or actions. Since we shall never be concerned with such notions as the 'set of all sets,' we need not explicitly consider the axiomatizations of set theory that have been aimed at avoiding certain paradoxes into which set theory is led if it has to consider the 'set of all sets.'[23]

Now this is a very strong statement. By avoiding the "set of all sets" we can avoid some paradoxes. However, the claim of completeness is clear because of the incorporation of a set of "*all* conceivable choices or actions." What about Russell's paradox? Is the set of "all conceivable choices" itself a conceivable choice? That is, is the choice set abnormal or self-engulfing? But, no matter, Gödel cannot be avoided. We cannot avoid the incompleteness of axiomatization itself.[24]

Equally significant is the fact that this failure is not just a failure of mathematics and logic but of economics as well. In this regard, let us *pretend* that the mathematical and logical foundations are secure. What I want to show is that even if economics should somehow avoid the mathematical and logical paradoxes, it would produce paradoxes of its own.

The minimal requirement for a preference function or preference ordering to exist is that it satisfy three fundamental axioms. (This is true for cardinally measurable, ordinally measurable, as well as "revealed" preferences.)[25] These are the requirements of reflexivity, completeness, and transitivity. That is, there exists a relation R such that for all x, y, z εC (C—choice set)

(1) xRx (reflexivity)
(2) xRy or yRx (completeness)
(3) If xRy and yRz then xRz (transitivity).

R can be interpreted as "is not preferred to."

All of the previous philosophical and mathematical questions that we have been pursuing are now reduced to this fundamental question: Does the relation R exist? As long as R exists, institutional and radical assaults upon the system will be impotent. But, of R does not exist, then atomic individualism cannot be used as a buttress, and the whole of neoclassical economics becomes amorphic.[26]

One can see the incompleteness of neoclassical choice theory as soon as one undestands that statements *about* preferences can be mapped *into* the choice set itself, just as Gödel mapped statements about number theory into statements in number theory. Preferences do not refer only to objects or states of affairs "out there" but also to preferences themselves. Consumers can not only choose but they can give reasons for their choices. Consumers have discretion over preferences themselves. This should not appear strange once the relation between language (culture) and preferences is realized.

In order for preferences to be complete the choice set must include preferences themselves! But, as soon as you allow preferences within the choice set you have preferences "talking" to preferences. In a world of preference self-reference we can, if you will, produce a neoclassical liar. As an example let our liar be a smoker. In such a situation it is not uncommon to hear a smoker say, "I dislike my desire to smoke." What are we to make of such a statement? In the static framework of neoclassical choice theory this is a contradiction. But at the same time, it cannot be prevented. Not only is the "act of smoking" an element in the choice set, but the "desire to smoke" is itself an element in the choice set and also subject to discretion.

Continuously expanding the choice set by including not only commodities but also social conditions in an attempt to explain invidious distinctions, other individuals in an attempt to explain altruism, and so forth, neoclassicism has been able to "absorb" heterodox attacks within the atomic individualistic perspective. However, the inclusion of choice itself is devastating to its own premise of consistency.

Let me make the point clear. Preference functions, preference orderings, or preference rankings do not exist. In order for a preference function to exist, R must be both complete and consistent (transitive), but this is an impossibility. The only way to claim consistency is to argue that preferences cannot be included within the choice set. However, to deny their entry is to deny their existence. This defeats the very principle that neoclassicals are trying to establish. In such a case, economists must deny the possibility of choice theory itself. This they cannot do—the very act of writing axioms of choice theory is blatant proof of the existence of self-reference. Lo and behold, there is no way out.[27]

The incompleteness of the neoclassical paradigm results from the implicit incorporation of Cartesian dualism. It is presumed that preferences refer to objective things but are themselves solely subjective. Whenever we think of preferences as "inside" and objects or states of affairs as "outside," we have "cut the world in two." We have produced an incomplete theory by ignoring the connectivity of the knowledge process. (Preferences are equally objective and their referents equally subjective.) What connects utility to its object of reference if one is exclusively subjective and the other exclusively objective? Only by realizing the dialectical nature (nonexcludability) of subject and object can the two be connected. This is the crucial analytic cut in which the individual becomes atomic and completely isolated from the universe.

With this cut the neoclassical theory has built an *artificial* barrier between statements about preferences and statements of preference. It can allow consumers choices but not awareness of their choices. However, human beings are not *preprogrammed* hedonistic calculating machines, and it is the process of self-reference that denies this conception. They can "change their minds," and I mean this literally.[28]

Self-reference is prodigiously human and must be incorporated into any theory attempting to explain preferences. To hold to a theory that ignores self-reference is to reduce human beings to machines. Furthermore, a theory that denies self-awareness cannot incorporate such notions as time, change, culture, emergent knowledge, development, etcetera. It strips life of its developmental and evolutionary aspects, making it passive and static; it strips human beings of evaluation and judgment, making them mechanistic and habitual.

Consider again the neoclassical liar. In the context of utility theory, his statement is nonsensical. But is it? It is not only possible to state a desire, but also to reflect upon its desirability. Self-reference permits an examination of the character of preferences themselves. It is not the case that an ex-smoker liked smoking one day, became indifferent the next, and disliked smoking after that. Between liking and disliking there is not indifference but conflict, the contradiction of actions being governed by passion, impulse, and habit, or by reason—the contradiction between desire and desirability. This point is crucial in evaluating the incompleteness of utility theory. As John Dewey states:

> Every person in the degree in which he is capable of learning from experience draws a distinction between what is desired and what is desirable whenever he engages in information and choice of competing desires and interests. There is nothing far-fetched or "moralistic" in this statement. The contrast referred to is simply that between the object of a desire as it first presents itself (because of the existing mechanism of impulses and habits) and the object of desire which emerges as a revision of the first-appearing impulse, after the latter is critically judged in reference to the conditions which will decide the actual result.[29]

One may ask: If people are not utility maximizers, what are they? What is their nature? Such a question misses the fundamental point. If R is not both complete and consistent, than a preference ranking does not exist. Hence, human beings cannot be said to be single-purposed or in possession of a *given* nature. Human beings are a living contradiction. The origin of their paradoxical nature is the self-referential nature of the symbolic (cultural) process. Human life is not a thing but a process. Human beings continually reconstruct themselves in the process of living. This is the significance of the "incompleteness theorem" when applied to humans themselves. On this point no one surpasses Eric Fromm.

> The difficulty in finding a satisfactory definition for the nature of man lies in the following dilemma: If one assumes a certain substance as constituting the essence of man, one is forced into a nonevolutionary, unhistorical position which implies that there has been no basic change in man since the very beginning of his emergence. Such a view is difficult to square with the fact that there is a tremendous difference to be found between our most undeveloped ancestors and civilized man as he appears in the last four to six thousand years of history. On the other hand, if one accepts an evolutionary concept and thus believes that man is constantly changing, what is left as a content for an alleged 'nature' or 'essence' of man?
>
> I believe that the dilemma can be solved by defining the essence of man not as a given quality or substance, but as a *contradiction inherent in human existence.*
>
> Man transcends all life because he is, for the first time, *life aware of itself.* Man is *in* nature, subject to its dictates and accidents, yet he *transcends* nature. . . .
>
> It is necessary to go beyond this description and to recognize that the very conflict in man *demands a solution.*
>
> If the essence of man is neither the good nor the evil, neither love nor hate, but a contradiction which demands the search for new solutions which, in turn, creates new contradictions, then indeed man can answer his dilemma, either in a regressive or in a progressive way.
>
> Man can choose *only* between two possibilities: to regress or to move forward. He can either return to an archaic, pathogenic solution, or he can progress toward, and develop, his humanity.[30]

This is why neoinstitutionalists have called the instrumental process the life process of mankind, and why the instrumental-ceremonial distinction is a fundamental tool for social analysis.

In summary, the incomplete structure of axiomatization and the deductive method originates from self-reference. Furthermore, self-reference is more problematic in the axiomatization of economics than of mathematics since the fundamental object of economic analysis is human rather than physical phenomena; self-reference is built into the very structure of economic analysis. Hence attempts by neoclassical economists to produce an "exact" science by the axiomatization of economic variables are doomed to failure. In particular, neoclassicism has maintained consistency by producing an incomplete system that ignores the self-referential structure of axiomatization *and* valuation. Finally, and perhaps even more startling to the neoclassicist, is the fact that the findings of mathematics and logic comport with the findings of neoinstitutionalism and not with neoclassicism; neoclassical economics has compartmentalized itself into theoretical obscurity. It has isolated itself not only from the other social sciences, but from the natural and mathematical sciences as well.

Notes

1. See Hughes and Brecht [1978, p. 10].
2. Ibid.
3. This was claimed by Martin Gardner [Gardner 1963, p. 174].
4. See Hughes and Brecht [1978, pp. 10-11].
5. See Tarski [1951].
6. See Bronowski [1977, p. 33]. Self-reference follows from the principle of connectivity. If all things are "totally connected" (nonexcludable), then it is impossible to remove the "self" from the the objects of analysis. Reference to oneself is an inseparable part of science.
7. For an excellent description of the developments in mathematics see Kline [1980]. See also Kline [1978] and Davis and Hersh [1981]. A more detailed treatment of mathematical paradoxes is in Bunch [1982].
8. A variation of Russell's paradox, called "Grelling's paradox," can be made using adjectives instead of sets. Adjectives either describe themselves or do not describe themselves. Call all adjectives that do not describe themselves heterological, and all adjectives that describe themselves autological. Is "heterological" heterological?
9. See Gödel [1931, pp. 173-198]. For an explanation of Gödel's proof see Nagel and Newman [1958].
10. For an excellent description of the methodological significance of dialectics see Georgescu-Roegen [1976].
11. See Bronowski [1979, pp. 85-86].
12. See Kline [1980, p. 168].
13. See Crouch [1979].
14. Ibid., p. xv.
15. Ibid., p. 19.
16. Ibid., p. 4.
17. Ibid., p. 5.
18. Ibid., p. 2.
19. Ibid.
20. Ibid., p. 25.
21. This is equivalent to what K. Popper refers to as "immunizing strategies," or what J. Kuhn would include under "normal" science, as distinct from "revolutionary" science [Popper 1959; Kuhn 1962].
22. See Suppes [1957, pp. 247-48].
23. See Walsh [1970, p. 72].
24. For an illuminating discussion of the relevance of mathematical consistency to human behavior and freedom see Barrett [1978, especially chapter 6].
25. See Henderson and Quandt [1971, pp. 16-17].

26. The requirement that preferences be complete and consistent (transitive) is equivalent to the requirement that consumers be "single purposed," and that the various qualitative properties of good can be reduced to a single property. For an explanation of this relationship and a significant critique of the existence of *R* see Sensat and Constantine [1975].
27. While I have been concentrating upon consumption, these implications are equally valid for production as well. As with consumption, production is a product of human judgment and experience. "Technique" is not given but is a product of the process itself. The self-referential nature of production and the incomplete structure of neoclassical production theory become clear when one realizes that statements about a production process can be mapped into the production process (resource set) itself. For a discussion of the significance of the incomplete structure of neoclassical economics with regard to scarcity see Winrich [1982].
28. On the philosophical significance of the paradoxical nature of change see Melhuish [1973]. In Hughes and Brecht [1978, pp. 69-70], Melhuish states:

> In order to define the innate flux of things, it is necessary to state a fundamental paradox and to say that what is the same as itself is in self-modification, whereby it is not the same as itself, for any less paradoxical operation will commit us to the acceptance of a merely static identity and this will change in order not to be the same. If we say dogmatically that something involved in change really amounts to different things, then these things will have independent and simple existence, and will not be actually involved in change. Certainly, by ordinary logical standards to say that the thing which is the same as itself is actually in self-modification whereby it is not the same as itself will appear unacceptably contradictory: but this does not imply an impossibility.
>
> It is necessary to see that logic is developed adequately only by a contradictory complementarity implying paradoxical coalescence. The total abrogation of identity would deprive us of our whole system of identification; yet to hold dogmatically to the principle of identity will be to maintain a merely static order where flux remains unexpressed and undefined. Only by the affirmation of the orthodox conceptual scheme and its abrogation, by a really antithetical conceptual scheme, will change be defined.

29. See Dewey [1966, pp. 31-33].
30. See Fromm [1964, pp. 115-18].

References

Ayres, C. E. 1961. *Toward a Reasonable Society*. Austin, Texas: University of Texas Press.

Ayres, C. E. 1978. *The Theory of Economic Progress*. Kalamazoo, Mich.: New Issues Press (Western Michigan University).

Barrett, William. 1978. *The Illusion of Technique*. New York: Anchor Press/Doubleday.

Bronowski, Jacob. 1965. *Science and Human Values.* New York: Harper & Row.
Bronowski, Jacob. 1977. *A Sense of the Future.* Cambridge, Mass.: MIT Press.
Bronowski, Jacob. 1979. *The Origins of Knowledge and Imagination.* New Haven: Yale University Press.
Bunch, Bryan H. 1982. *Mathematical Fallacies and Paradoxes.* New York: Van Nostrand Reinhold.
Crouch, Robert L. 1979. *Human Behavior: An Economic Approach.* North Scituate, Mass.: Duxbury Press.
Davis, Philip J., and Reuben Hersh. 1981. *The Mathematical Experience.* Boston: Houghton Miffin.
Dewey, John. 1966. "Theory of Valuation." *International Encyclopedia of Unified Science*, vol. 11.
Fromm, Erich. 1964. *The Heart of Man: Its Genius for Good and Evil.* New York: Harper Colophon.
Fromm, Erich. 1955. *The Sane Society.* New York: Holt, Rinehart & Winston.
Gardner, Martin. 1963. "Logical Paradoxes." *The Antioch Review* (Summer): 172-78.
Georgescu-Roegen, Nicholas. 1968. "Utility." *International Encyclopedia of Social Science*, vol. 16, pp. 236-67.
Georgescu-Roegen, Nicholas. 1973. "Utility and Value in Economic Thought." *Dictionary of the History of Ideas*, vol. 4, pp. 450-58.
Georgescu-Roegen, Nicholas. 1976. *The Entropy Law and the Economic Process.* Cambridge, Mass.: Harvard University Press.
Gödel, Kurt. 1931. "Über formal unentscheidbare Sätze der Principia Mathematica und verwandter Systeme I." *Monatschefte für Mathematik und Physik*, vol. 38, pp. 173-98.
Henderson, James M., and Richard E. Quandt. 1971. *Microeconomic Theory: A Mathematical Approach.* New York: McGraw-Hill.
Hofstadter, Douglas R. 1980. *Gödel, Escher, Bach: Eternal Golden Braid.* New York: Vintage Books.
Hughes, Patrick, and George Brecht. 1978. *Vicious Circles and Infinity: An Anthology of Paradoxes.* New York: Penguin.
Kline, Morris. 1978. *Mathematics in Western Culture.* New York: Oxford University Press.
Kline, Morris. 1980. *Mathematics: The Loss of Certainty.* New York: Oxford University Press.
Popper, K. R. 1959. *The Logic of Scientific Discovery.* New York: Basic Books.
Martin, R. L. 1970. *The Paradox of the Liar.* New Haven, Conn.: Yale University Press.
Melhuish, George. 1973. *Paradoxical Nature of Reality.* Bristol, England: St Vincent's Press.
Nagel, Ernest, and James R. Newman. 1958. *Gödel's Proof.* New York: New York University.
Quine, W. V. O. 1962. "Paradox." *Scientific American* 206 (May): 84-95.
Sen, Amartya K. 1977. "Rational Fools: A Critique of the Behavioral Foun-

dations of Economic Theory." *Philosophy and Public Affairs* 6 (Summer): 317-44.

Sensat, Julius, Jr., and George Constantine. 1975. "A Critique of the Foundations of Utility Theory." *Science and Society* 2 (Summer): 157-79.

Suppes, Patrick. 1957. *Introduction to Logic*. Princeton, N.J.: D. Van Nostrand.

Tarski, Alfred. 1951. *Logic, Semantics, and Metamathematics*. Oxford: Clarendon Press.

Tarski, Alfred. 1969. "Truth and Proof, the Antinomy of the Liar . . ." *Scientific American* 220 (June): 63-77.

Tool, Marc R. 1979. *The Discretionary Economy: A Normative Theory of Political Economy*. Santa Monica: Goodyear.

Walsh, Vivian C. 1970. *Introduction to Contemporary Microeconomics*. New York: McGraw-Hill.

Ward, Benjamin. 1972. *What's Wrong with Economics?* New York: Basic Books.

Winrich, J. Steven. 1982. "A Pragmatic Approach to Scarcity." *Economic Forum* 13 (Winter): 105-13.

11

Modern Empiricism and Quantum Leap Theorizing in Economics

James A. Swaney
and
Robert Premus

The literature on economic methodology has revolved around logical positivism, addressing its application to economic inquiry, its policy relevance, its implicit functions and goals, and its weaknesses. The literature has focused primarily on the logical structure of theory and the ideal approach to economic inquiry, with orthodoxy emphasizing logical positivism and heterodoxy emphasizing inductive development of theory.[1] These foci on how economists ought to behave, while important, have been to the neglect of how economists actually behave.[2] In other words, the economic methodology literature has been preoccupied with theoretical discussion of the appropriateness of methodological models, with insufficient discussion of the actual processes used by economists to construct theories.

This preoccupation has been partially remedied by Benjamin Ward's *What's Wrong with Economics* [35] and Charles Wilber and Robert Harrison's "The Methodological Basis of Institutional Economics: Pattern Model, Storytelling, and Holism" [36]. Ward argues that the primary activity in all social science is storytelling, that formalism has failed, and that open recognition of these facts would facilitate progress in economic science. Wilber and Harrison argue that both institutionalists and orthodox economists engage primarily in storytelling, respectively using the "pattern model form" and what might descriptively be termed the "incognito form." They agree with Ward that formalism has failed, yet they conclude: "The formal models of standard economics have their use, even by institutionalists, for certain types of problems" [36, p. 85]. Formalism is more appropriate than the pattern model "when one or two factors or laws determine what is to be explained and when these factors or laws are better known and understood than the specific instance" [36, p. 85]. Apparently, formalism's general failure in economics (as a science, but not as a storyteller) is the result of attempts to apply logical positivism where it cannot work.

While social and natural sciences differ in important respects, and while these differences severely limit the appropriateness of natural science methodology for the social sciences, there is more to the story.[3] We argue that logical positivism's failure is also due to economists' failure to actually follow the methodology of logical positivism where it *is* appropriate.[4]

Economic theories often resemble, in their logical structure, theories in the natural sciences, but the process economists use to construct their theories is peculiar to the discipline. While the underlying causes of this peculiarity are many,[5] the primary outcome is ineffective or counterproductive policy.[6] Unlike other sciences, economics—primarily but not exclusively neoclassical economics—places excessive emphasis on the development of fully formulated theoretical systems without sufficient empirical grounding of behavioral assumptions and antecedent conditions: economists "are virtually the only would-be scientists who are content to use stale, second-hand data collected chiefly by government agencies for other purposes" [32, p. 241]. Thus, most of the problems encountered in identifying empirical relationships, which later become necessary in the process of theory testing and policy formation, are ignored. Often developed with only a judicious use of mathematics, economic theory consequently lacks empirical import and policy usefulness in comparison to theory in the natural sciences.

We begin our analysis with a brief discussion of progress in natural sciences, employing Thomas S. Kuhn's model of scientific progress, followed by discussion of the process of theory construction in natural sciences. This process involves conscious interaction between realism and abstraction when systematically progressing from lower to higher order theoretical formulations within normal sciences. In the next to last section, we discuss the application of methodological principles in economics. Two representative case studies suggest that the process of abstracting in economics can best be described as a "quantum leap" from the factual domain to the theoretical domain rather than as a systematic departure from reality as frequently occurs in the natural sciences. A major conclusion of the paper—presented in the last section—is that the efficiency of the logical positivistic methodology, in terms of generating valid abstract models with substantive policy content, would be greatly enhanced if economists would place more initial emphasis on establishing empirical relationships among variables within a framework that incorporated institutional barriers, changes in technology, and individual and social norms and goals.

Progress in the Natural Sciences

The methodology of the natural sciences is diverse, and philosophers of science disagree over how scientific progress occurs.[7] The processes of scientific progress will continue to be debated, but for the purposes of this paper Thomas Kuhn's distinction between normal and abnormal science will suffice.[8] Normal science, where most science is conducted, consists of progress by accretion. Inquiry is directed toward finding the missing pieces of the paradigm-defined puzzle. In the terminology of logical positivism as enunciated by Carl Hempel and Paul Oppenheim [13], the "General Laws" of the science, when applied logically to the "Antecedent Conditions," allow one to deduce accurate descriptions (as *ex post* explanations or *ex ante* predictions) of relevant empirical phenomena. The paradigm, then, consists of the General Laws, which, in combination with alternative antecedent conditions, define the realm of inquiry.

When logical deduction yields a prediction repeatedly refuted by empirical testing, a seed that may eventually produce scientific revolution has sprouted. If this violation of paradigm—induced expectation, or anomaly, inhibits important practical applications or clearly calls into question explicit and fundamental generalizations of the paradigm [17, p. 82], a crisis, or abnormal science, will ensue. Alternative paradigm-aspirants will compete. If one of these world views eventually supplants the paradigm from which the anomaly arose, scientific revolution has occurred.

In preparadigm, or immature science, there is no generally accepted paradigm and therefore no potential for revolution. But there is also nothing to direct inquiry. "Early fact-gathering is a far more nearly random activity than the one that subsequent scientific development makes familiar [and] is usually restricted to the wealth of data that lie ready to hand" [17, p. 15]. Hence, immature science is characterized by an absence, if not of

General Laws themselves, then of the links that connect and organize these General Laws into a coherent view of the subset of reality under scrutiny. Logical positivism, then, does not apply to an immature science because the embryonic condition of the Explanans (General Laws in combination with Antecedent Conditions) renders logical deduction of Explanandum (hypothesis) impossible. Thus, normal science is assumed in the following discussion because logical positivism does not apply to preparadigm or abnormal science.

The Process of Theory Construction in Natural Sciences

Theoretical systems are developed in an attempt to understand and explain for the purposes of predicting and controlling the environment. In normal science, theory construction usually proceeds in stages from lower order (descriptive) concepts to higher order (theoretical) concepts, within the boundaries of perception, problem definition, and unquestioned general laws given by the discipline's extant paradigm. Potentially available data is prescreened by the view of reality implicit in the paradigm, but the remaining quantity of conceivably relevant data is nevertheless immense due to the complexity of reality. Even the normal scientist is confronted with a paradoxical demand for simplicity and realism. His or her first challenge is to organize the relevant but raw descriptive (or protocol) data, which is the complexity of observations of reality organized only by the world view of the paradigm, into the "common and crucial elements" relevant to the problem at hand. Thus, certain facts associated with the phenomenon being analyzed will be discarded in the abstracting process used to organize the protocol data.

The abstracting process proceeds in an orderly manner if the scientist is cognizant of the facts he or she is eliminating. In particular, it is an orderly and systematic process when the interactive effects between the common and crucial elements and those considered peripheral to the problem at hand are known. The retention of certain elements and rejection of others involves judgments necessarily shaped by the basic tenets of the ruling paradigm. By defining and redefining the realm of common and crucial elements, the scientist eventually reaches a level of theory development wherein protocol data is organized. From this delimited, organized protocol data the scientist develops (abstracts) the constructs upon which higher level theory is based.

Empirical terms and relationships constructed during the first step of theory development serve as a foundation for higher level theory development. As this development proceeds, the scientist tests the theory on a related set of protocol data where the hypotheses are expected to apply. Hence, tentative identification of common and crucial elements both *allows* and *commands* inclusion of additional protocol data. If those elements that were previously cast aside are in fact insignificant, the inclusion of a broader range of phenomena will not sacrifice theoretical accuracy, and the theory will be shown to be more general and inclusive. However, if a mistake has been made—if significant elements have been cast aside—attempts to apply the theory to a broader range of phenomena will fail, and the scientist will retreat to a lower theoretical level to reexamine the set of common and crucial elements. If this reexamination is successful, theoretical development can once again progress to a higher level and encompass previously peripheral phenomena. Hence the generality of high theory is achieved by gradually building from new data on a specific phenomenon toward an increasingly general and inclusive set of hypotheses.

Furthermore, the "incessant give and take" [30, p. 45] between fact and theory involved in this process produces higher level theory that is simpler as well as more inclusive, because peripheral elements have been discarded. While simpler, the constructs of higher level theory will in one sense be less "realistic." That is, in the process of developing theoretical terms and hypotheses that are more inclusive (explain more of reality), the detail of empirical reality is sacrificed. Thus, higher level theoretical concepts begin to take on the appearance of purely mental constructs. However, so long as the "incessant give and take" continues, the pitfall of losing contact with reality by overgeneralizing will be avoided.

The link between theoretical constructs and realism is found in the organization of the original protocol data, which initiates the process of identification of the common and crucial elements of the phenomenon under investigation. It is from the original protocol data that the "bridge principles" [12, pp. 74–5], or rules of measurement necessary for applying the theoretical constructs, are derived. Of course, the more *a posteriori* knowledge that the theoretician possesses about the phenomenon that he or she is attempting to explain (that is, the more delimited the original protocol data or the broader the historical experience of the researcher),[9] the less difficulty he or she will have in establishing bridging devices between the logical consequences of higher level theory and actual circumstances. Such knowledge generally increases over time since remaining problems become narrower and more precisely defined as the paradigm matures.

Normally, not all of the theoretical constructs are capable of being applied directly. Some are merely verbalizations of the original cognitive act or "vision" [30, p. 41] while others represent linkages with the extant paradigm. However, according to the philosophy of modern empiricism, this presents no problem in science as long as the constructs' meanings within the context of the theory are antecedently understood. This distinguishes modern empiricism from the ultra-empiricist position, which maintains that all concepts in science must be "operationally defined."[10]

Economic Methodology in Process

The methodology of logical positivism is capable of contributing to effective public policy formation. As pointed out in the introduction, this should not be construed to mean that logical positivism is the sole appropriate approach to economic problems. Our point is that the apparent failure of logical positivism in economics is not *solely* the fault of the methodology; it is *also* the fault of economists who label their work "Produced by the process of logical positivism," when they in fact subvert the process by shortcutting.

Were it not for the fact that a good economic theory does not improve with age, an analogy with wine making would be appropriate. While the good winegrower will spend years learning the skills of cultivation and wine making, the "do-it-yourselfer" will purchase everything needed to make wine in the kitchen in a matter of weeks. Similar shortcutting in economics we call quantum leap theorizing. Much as the "do-it-yourself" wine maker puts trust in the local grocer, the economist puts trust in whatever data lies ready to hand. While the kitchen wine maker may or may not recognize as unhealthy the yeast energizer used to speed fermentation, the economist, often knowingly, overlooks poisonous data inaccuracies [24]. In short, both the kitchen wine maker and the kitchen logical positivist sacrifice quality for expedient production.

While not in the school of logical positivism, John Dewey's methodological approach more nearly approximates natural science logical positivism than does the kitchen variety. Dewey argued that to be appropriate, ends are never given but are subject to modification as analysis proceeds; hence, "ends-in-view" [34, p. 283]. "The only situation in which knowing is fully stimulated is one in which the end is developed in the process of inquiry and testing" [6, p. 146]. Modern empiricism confirms this position during the initial stages of theory development with its insistence on empirical selection of the common and crucial elements and the recurrent building of bridges of correspondence between raw protocol data and the conceptual systematization thereof. Dewey's correct contention was that scientific analysis required a "conjugate correspondence" between "factual and conceptual subject matter" [5, p. 491]. In the language of modern empiricism, bridges must be built between empirical elements and theoretical concepts in the scientific process. In Dewey's language,

> if there is one lesson more than any other taught by the methods of the physical sciences, it is the strict correlativity of fact and ideas. Until social inquiry succeeds in establishing methods of observing, discriminating, and arranging data that evoke and test correlated ideas, and until, on the other side, ideas formed and used are (1) employed as *hypotheses*, and are (2) of a form to direct and prescribe operations of analytic-synthetic determination of facts, social inquiry has no chance of satisfying the logical conditions for attainment of scientific status [5, p. 491].

Scientific status had not yet been achieved by the social sciences in the 1930s. Dewey argued that in matters of policy formation, "it is commonly assumed that the problems which exist are already definite in their main features . . . . The consequence of this assumption is that the work of analytic discrimination, which is necessary to convert a problematic situation into a set of conditions forming a definite problem, is largely foregone" [5, p. 493].

In other words, policy formation was based on theories insufficiently rooted in empirical reality. This was seen as evidence of the immaturity of social science: "The immature state of social inquiry may thus be measured by the extent to which these two operations of fact-finding and of setting up theoretical ends are carried on independently of each other, with the consequence that factual propositions on the one side and conceptual or theoretical structures on the other are regarded each as final and complete in itself by one or another school" [5, p. 507]. Having progressed beyond this stage of development, economics as a science continues to fall short of a methodology that consistently produces scientific progress.

When a logical positivistic approach is called for in economics, the scientific process, following Joseph Schumpeter, should consist of a vision, a verbalization or conceptualization of that vision that facilitates organization of raw (protocol) data, collection of further facts (common and crucial elements) along with abandonment of irrelevant facts, and, *pari passu*, via bridging devices, the addition of further relations and concepts (higher level theoretical constructs) and elimination of irrelevant and inaccurate hypotheses.

> Factual work and 'theoretical' work, in an endless relation of give and take, naturally testing one another and setting new tasks for each other, will eventually produce scientific *models*, the provisional joint products of their interaction with the surviving elements of the original vision, to which increasingly more rigorous standards of consistency and adequacy

> will be applied. This is indeed a primitive but not, I think, misleading statement of the process by which we grind out what we call scientific propositions [30, p. 42].

In normal science, visions are at least framed in the context of the extant paradigm and, as Schumpeter argued, visions tend to be imbued if not distorted by ideology [30, p. 42]. The "crushing out" of ideologies is a time-consuming and never ending task [30, p. 44], and "we shall not be able to live up to the program" of how economists should proceed [30, p. 14]. Yet Schumpeter was sharply critical of economists' performance [30, pp. 18–19], arguing that insufficient "historical experience" and inadequate statistical knowledge were common among economists. Regarding historical experience, which is composed of both "an adequate command of historical *facts* and an adequate amount of historical *sense*" [30, p. 13], Schumpeter argued that "most of the fundamental errors currently committed in economic analysis are due to lack of historical experience more often than to any other shortcoming of the economist's equipment" [30, p. 13]. Regarding statistical methods, he writes, "It is impossible to understand statistical figures without understanding how they have been compiled. It is equally impossible to extract information from them or to understand the information that specialists extract for the rest of us without understanding the methods by which this is done—and the epistemological backgrounds of these methods" [30, p. 14].

It is during the initial stages of the scientific process that both of these weaknesses are most glaring in contemporary economics. The painstaking effort necessary to systematically analyze interactions within the protocol data, thereby providing the basis for establishing bridge principles at a later stage of theory development, is largely bypassed. Instead, a common practice in economics is essentially to invert the scientific process by developing fully formulated theoretical structures based on casual empiricism, hunches, and unrealistic assumptions. The "applications" of theory that follow ignore or misrepresent important aspects of reality, resulting in irrelevant if not destructive policy prescriptions.

The first stage of theory development in normal economic science, then, is typically a quantum leap from reality to theory. Economists typically engage in nonscientific behavior to develop their theories, and only then do they begin to employ the modern empiricist scientific process described by Carl Hempel and other logical positivists. *After* the fully formulated theoretical systems have been unscientifically developed, economists *then* attempt to link the theory's logical consequences to real phenomena by a process of model verification. The result is that model verification in economics is frequently a highly subjective trial-and-error process involving numerous applications of econometric methods. It is trial-and-error because the econometric models are not based on reality, but rather contain the nonscientific biases of the theoreticians. A voluminous and often controversial empirical literature on the subject consequently emerges. This process may eventually result in a sorting out of the common and crucial elements and a forging of a qualified consensus of opinion, but it is a far cry from logical positivism as practiced within normal natural science.

In applying theoretical concepts developed through quantum leap methods, continued redefinition and new concept introduction occurs *after* theoretical systems are highly developed. In this manner theories do evolve and take on new forms as new facts are discovered. However, a more straight-forward procedure—consistent with the application of scientific methods in the natural sciences—would be to place more emphasis at the initial stage of theory development on the use of inductive methods to analyze the institutional, cultural, social, and technological interactions of the phenomena. With this incessant give and take between data and concepts, redefinition and new concept introduction would occur *during* theory building and would therefore be part of the process. Hence, theory developed beyond the initial stage would have structurally inherent bridging devices necessary for empirical verification. As human behavior changes over time, the theory would continually require vision, but realism would not have to be sacrificed for simplicity.

Furthermore, with a "sub-quantum leap" process of theory development, the final product would be substantially different from the higher level theory developed by the quantum leap method. In general, the sub-quantum leap method would yield, in comparison to quantum leap theorizing, superior policy recommendations.

The thesis that economics, as a rule, relies upon the excessive use of deductive methods at the initial stages of theory development, and that such a method is a relatively inefficient and imprecise process, can be evaluated by an analysis of the "state of the art." To do this, we restrict our discussion to the application of methodological principles in migration and monetary economics. These subdisciplines are characterized by extensive theoretical and empirical work that we take to be indicative of the nature of the scientific process in other subdisciplines of economics.

Migration Economics

In attempting to understand human migration behavior, economists have applied utility theory within a human investment framework. Migrants are assumed to respond to economic opportunity differentials among aerial units. And when the frictions of space, political institutions, imperfect knowledge, and differential amenity variables (for example, climatic conditions) are assumed away—by a quantum leap abstraction process—the resulting geographical population distribution is optimal in the sense that national product is maximized. Thus, population mobility displays desirable normative properties because it facilitates the efficient allocation of resources over space.

Testing the pure (deductive) theory of migration for relevance produces bridge principles identifying migration flows, and measures of economic opportunities such as wages and unemployment. This process relaxes (identifies) basic assumptions relating to the costs of migration, information flows, public sector variables, and amenities to make the model realistic. Empirical knowledge of the interrelationships among explanatory variables and the interdependence of migrants' "utility functions" are at best vaguely perceived. Nevertheless, through a process of successive testing and model respecification (introducing new concepts, postulating alternative functional forms and refined measurements) the relevant facts concerning the common and crucial elements, and hence the irrelevant facts, begin to become empirically discernable.

However, after surveying the massive post-1970 empirical literature on migration behavior, Michael Greenwood's concluding remarks strongly suggest that the common and crucial elements are only vaguely discernable in the migration literature [10]. The magnitude of effects, the direction of causality among explanatory variables, definitions, and functional forms vary among the numerous tests. Thus, on the determinants of migration Greenwood concluded:

> One of the most perplexing problems confronting migration scholars is the lack of significance of local unemployment rates in explaining migration. . . . Migration does occur from low to high income regions, but some debate remains regarding the relative importance of origin and destination characteristics in explaining migration. Appreciable differences have been uncovered in the magnitudes in which income and other factors influence various population or labor force subgroups in their decisions regarding whether and where to migrate. . . . A number of studies suggest significant differences in the migratory behavior of whites and nonwhites. However, the conclusions of many of these studies may be misleading because of a failure to control for age and education, and in some instances for employment status. . . . To attribute the observed behavioral differences to race or to discrimination has frequently been inappropriate. . . . Crucial questions that remain to be analyzed . . . involve the importance of welfare and of the quantity and quality of public services in general on

the decision to migrate, particularly on the decisions of low-income persons [10, pp. 411, 412].

Also, controversy over single equation versus simultaneous equation models remains unresolved. Greenwood illustrates the potential gravity of this problem: "An assumption that underlies the many single-equation, multiple regression approaches to migration is that while the various explanatory factors influence migration, migration does not in turn influence these factors. If this assumption does not in fact hold, the parameter estimates of the various models possess a simultaneous-equations bias that may be great enough to vitiate the findings" [10, p. 412]. Finally, lacking empirical import, migration models have little relevance in the policy arena. This is consistent with Greenwood's observation that "what is perhaps most striking about the massive literature on the determinants of interregional migration is the lack of direct policy implications" [10, p. 412].

Monetary Economics

Empirical models in monetary economics provide a second case in point for the basic thesis of this paper, namely, that deductive systems developed by quantum leap abstraction procedures, as a "first approximation" of reality, are likely to be both extremely difficult to validate in the presence of actual circumstances and, concurrently, void of policy direction.

Central to the efficacy of monetary policy (defined in terms of efficiency of control over monetary aggregates) is a stable demand function for money, or at least a predictable demand function for money under a wide variety of circumstances. Being a crucial link in the transmission process, econometric research in monetary economics has developed an extensive empirical literature on the determinants of the demand function for money. Thus, analysis of the process of developing a demand function for money serves to indicate the normal process of theory development in other areas of monetary economics.

J. T. Boorman and Thomas Havrilesky [2, p. 285], after surveying numerous empirical works in applied monetary theory, concluded that the *consensus* of monetary economists is that "the interest rate plays a significant role in the determination of the public's demand for money," but this conclusion depends upon a particular definition of money and interest rates as well as on the time period of analysis. Likewise, income was found to affect the demand for money in numerous tests, but this conclusion is contingent upon the definition of income (permanent or current) and upon the time period involved. Moreover, there appears to be little agreement concerning appropriate functional relationships, and the controversy over single equation versus simultaneous equation systems has not been resolved. Thus, probably the most definitive empirical proposition derived from the vast monetary theory literature is that "there is no empirical basis for the liquidity trap hypothesis: the proposition that the demand for money function becomes infinitely elastic at some low level of interest rates" [2, pp. 285–286]. Of course, economic conditions may not have presented the circumstances to adequately test the liquidity preference hypothesis. However, this suggests that whether it exists under certain nonexistent conditions is trivial.

Because of the present "state of the art" in monetary economics, a greater emphasis on measurement, concept definition, and establishing empirical laws might be expected. This may be occurring to some extent, but it is not indicative of recent theoretical developments in monetary economics. For example, the traditional view of money as a "consumer good" that facilitates the exchange process is being replaced by a view of money as a "producer's good" that enters as a factor of production into the aggregate production function. However, since economists lack significant empirical knowledge of aggregate production functions and are unsure which definition of money is relevant, it is not surprising that the rigorously deduced consequences of theoretical models representative of this approach are of questionable relevance for empirical research.

A more efficient approach and one far more consistent with the methodology of modern empiricism would be to spend considerably more time in the empirical domain analyzing the actual behavior of the phenomena under investigation. For example, economists have been unable to understand the behavior of banking institutions and monetary authorities because they spend a great majority of their time studying actions and inferring purposive behavior. Thus, when the money supply is increased they might interpret it as a deliberate attempt to change monetary policies, but in fact money supply growth may be linked to growth in the economy. The usual assumption of exogeneity of the money supply may be unrealistic. We contend that study of the institutional framework in which money is created would lead to more fruitful empirical formulations of money supply behavior.

In summary, disagreements over relevant variables, the functional relations of these variables, and estimation procedures and interpretations of empirical works are combined with a general vagueness of concepts in both the migration and monetary literature. We interpret this generally poor state of empirical knowledge as reflecting a peculiar and inefficient application of the scientific process; namely, the repetitive econometric applications of models in an attempt to "discover" facts that are relevant (irrelevant) to the common and crucial elements of theories insufficiently grounded in empirical reality.[11]

Summary and Conclusions

We began our analysis with a discussion of the process of theory construction in natural sciences. There we argued that during normal science, abstraction is an orderly and systematic *process* which requires eliminating facts within the domain of inquiry that are irrelevant to the problem at hand. Normal science views the common and crucial elements of a theory as an empirical question that must be resolved at each stage of abstraction. In general, theoretical models, logical consequences of those models, and rules of correspondence are developed by a process of "systematic abstraction." Thus, as a general rule, hypotheses are postulated with considerable *a posteriori* knowledge of processes and interactions within the empirical domain—a process we have described as subquantum leap theorizing.

Our analysis of the scientific process as applied to migration and monetary economics suggests that in economics quantum-leap theorizing provides the theory, which is then refined by a process of successive testing and adjustment through a gradual discovery of factual circumstances. Interactive elements that are either (1) irrelevant to the theory, (2) possibly relevant to the theory but not initially incorporated into the theory's set of primitive terms, or (3) relevant and consistent with the theory's logical consequences, are discovered during this process of refinement. Thus, factors that are endogenous to the common and crucial elements are gradually identified and systematized by a repeated application of econometric and other statistical methods.

The trial-and-error approach to theory development and policy formulation is by no means limited to the migration and monetary economics literature. Wassily Leontief, in recent testimony before the Joint Economic Committee of the U.S. Congress, echoed these same sentiments when he commented on the current status of the various macroeconomic theories underlying policy making in Washington. According to Leontief, "The factual validation and implementation of these theories is based on what is often referred to as 'casual empiricism' or on construction of more and more intricate econometric models. In these models, increasingly ingenious but still utterly unreliable methods of indirect statistical inference are employed in vain to compensate for the lack of hard, systematically organized factual information" [19, p. 2]. Continuing, he adds: "At the present time it is the inability—or occasionally the reluctance of official statistical organizations—to collect and systematize large masses of readily available specialized information, not the lack of analytical tools, that seems to hinder effective practical implementation of the planning as contrasted with the traditional trial-and-error approach to policy formation in the economic field" [19, p. 7]. Finally, according to Leontief, the "creation and maintenance of a comprehensive data base would permit a drastic reduction in the amount of guesswork, and one might add, of idle theorizing that is involved in our policymaking process now" [19, pp. 8–9].

In principle, the economists' method of quantum leap theorizing could lead to empirically relevant theories through successive testing, but apparently this procedure has not been successful in establishing theories with significant empirical import. We suggest that these severe inefficiencies in theory development in economics will continue to exist if economists insist on a continued inversion of the application of scientific principles. Thus, the continued proliferation of theories, rather than indicating economics is preparadigmatic science, suggests that the dominant neoclassical paradigm is such a complete and dominating world view that it inhibits inductive development of theories that reflect economic reality. In short, economists all too frequently leap from their oversimplified view of the nature of man and their naive view of the institutional framework as a God-given constant to elegant and sophisticated theories void of constructive policy content. It is through this quantum leap process that overgeneralization occurs and "realism" in the sense of policy relevance is lost. The "conjugate correspondence" and "incessant give and take" between the empirical and conceptual realm, between fact and theory, should be part of the theory development process, not just an *ex post* appendage thereto.

In conclusion, current economic methodology is within the mainstream of modern empiricism in the sense that hypotheses are evaluated in terms of the canons of science; however, this paper questions the efficiency of the actual process of theory development in economics and argues for a more systematic evaluation of the role of social and economic institutions within the context of economic theory.

The methodology suggested herein argues against both the excessive reliance on government documents for data and the direct application of formal economic theory to these data to test hypotheses about human and institutional behavior. This is the principal method used by many economists to find empirical support for their previously developed models. The failure to obtain first-hand knowledge of human behavior in the institutional context in which hypotheses about human behavior are being tested is an inverted form of empiricism. For example, a considerable body of literature has been developed to examine the role of welfare assistance on the location decisions of the poor. Welfare is generally defined as AFDC payments and the poor are generally defined as the black migrant population. The AFDC payments are presumed to reflect the diverse bundle of welfare benefits available to the poor and the poor migrant population is presumed to be reflected in the black migrant population. These are both heroic assumptions that we consider a quantum leap from the factual domain to the theoretical domain.

We argue that a far more fruitful approach to hypothesis formulation and testing would be to place far greater emphasis on examining the historical and institutional environment confronting poor migrants. This approach suggests that the historical method, interviews, case studies, experiential learning, and questionnaire studies have a far more important role to play in economic science than they have been afforded. The counter-arguments that these methods are too cumbersome and that data requirements are too large are untenable in light of recent advances in computer technology and information processing. Such arguments are based not on net benefit determinations, but rather, as Leontief makes clear, on ingrained habits of behavior:

> [The] lack of necessary factual information [is due to the] continuous unwillingness of academic economists to give up their traditional reliance on abstract mathematical formulas—linked to reality only by a very fragile bridge of indirect statistical inference . . . . [20]

The methodology suggested in this paper has important implications for graduate training in economics. Universities can do much to improve the educational process and place economics more in line with modern empirical methods. Students in economics cannot conduct controlled experiments to the extent that they are conducted in the natural sciences, but they can be given an opportunity to acquire experience by working as an intern in a business or public environment. Greater familiarity with primary data and with habits of human behavior relevant to the problem at hand would lead to more fruitful hypotheses and more rapid advances in economics as a science.

Finally, the peculiar application of methodological procedures in economics has contributed to the excessive trichotomization of economics into pure theory, applied theory, and institutional analysis. This trichotomization has unnecessarily inhibited the development of both applied theory, by removing institutions from the domain of pure theory, and institutional analysis, through the healthy distrust of orthodoxy's version of empiricism. Applied theory has been unnecessarily juxtaposed against institutional analysis, thereby hindering communication and knowledge development.

Our analysis suggests that it is quite appropriate to object to purely deductive theory whenever such theory is offered as science. Such objections have been voiced previously, primarily on the grounds that these approaches tend to be biased, self-serving, or apologetic. The objection raised here is that any purely deductive approach to theory formulation, while it may tell a convincing story, will be scientifically weak and will lead to misguided policy. If quantum leap theorizing within normal economic science is increasingly replaced by sub-quantum leap theorizing, both the efficiency of the scientific process and the level of effective communication between applied theory and institutional analysis will be enhanced.

Notes

1. For the long running debate on how economists should pursue knowledge, see Boland [1], Friedman [8], Rotwein [27], Machlup [21], Hill [14], Margenau [23], and Northrup [25].
2. The "positive-normative" connotation is borrowed from Ward [35, p. 190].
3. In addition to previously referenced works, the reader is referred to the cogent review of many authors and the original presentation of differences between natural and social science contained in T. W. Hutchison's *Knowledge and Ignorance in Economics* [15], particularly chapters two and three.
4. We intentionally skirt, in addition to discussion of the differences between natural science and social science, the issue of how, other than through trial and error, the areas appropriate for logical positivism are to be identified. By focusing on the problem of how logical positivist methodology is (not) applied in economics, we also intentionally avoid discussion of the appropriate (and inappropriate) uses of various forms of storytelling. Our purpose is only to address the process of (would-be) logical positivism in economics.
5. See the discussion of these causes in the section of this article sub-titled "The Process of Theory Construction . . ."
6. Implicit in this statement is the assumption that logical positivism's appropriate (but not necessarily exclusive) role in economics is in developing theory for policy purposes.
7. For the literature in this debate, see Lakatos [18], Popper [26], and Kuhn [17].
8. The choice of Kuhn [17] for a typology of scientific progress is for two reasons: First, Kuhn's conception is familiar to most economists; second, we believe Kuhn's original schema as employed in the following discus-

sion could be replaced with his more recent concept of disciplinary matrices or with the schema of Popper or Lakatos without altering our analysis.

9. This term, taken from Schumpeter, is explained in the following section.
10. See Rudner [28], Hempel [12], and Scheffler [29] for cogent discussions of the modern empiricists' justification of the use of nonoperational concepts in scientific analysis and for discussions of the ultra-empirical position on this matter.
11. The references cited provided only a very general overview of the migration and monetary literature. Although they hardly do justice to the important technical developments in the field, they are indicative of the application of methodological principles in economics.

References

[1] Boland, Lawrence A. "A Critique of Friedman's Critics," *Journal of Economic Literature* 17 (1979): 503–522.

[2] Boorman, J. T., and Thomas M. Havrilesky. *Money Supply, Money Demand and Macroeconomic Models*. Boston: Allyn and Bacon, 1972.

[3] Brody, Baruch, ed. *Readings in the Philosophy of Science*. Englewood Cliffs, N.J.: Prentice-Hall, 1970.

[4] Caldwell, Bruce. "Positivist Philosophy of Science and the Methodology of Economics," *Journal of Economic Issues* 14 (1980): 53–76.

[5] Dewey, John. *Logic: The Theory of Inquiry*. New York: Holt, Rinehart and Winston, 1938.

[6] Dewey, John. *Reconstruction in Philosophy*. New York: Henry Holt and Company, 1920.

[7] Feyerabend, Paul K. "How to Be a Good Empiricist—A Plea for Tolerance in Matters Epistemological." In [3].

[8] Friedman, Milton. *Essays in Positive Economics*. Chicago: University of Chicago Press, 1954.

[9] Goodman, Nelson. *Fact, Fiction, and Forecast*. New York: Bobbs-Merril, 1965.

[10] Greenwood, Michael J. "Research on Internal Migration in the United States: A Survey," *Journal of Economic Literature* 13 (1975): 397–433.

[11] Gurwich, Aron. "Social Science and Natural Science." In *Economic Means and Social Ends*, edited by Robert L. Heilbroner. Englewood Cliffs, N.J.: Prentice-Hall, 1969. Pp. 37–55.

[12] Hempel, Carl G. *Philosophy of Natural Science*. Englewood Cliffs, N.J.: Prentice-Hall, 1966.

[13] Hempel, Carl G., and Paul Oppenheim. "Studies in the Logic of Explanation." In [3]. Pp. 8–27.

[14] Hill, Lewis. "A Critique of Positive Economics," *American Journal of Economics and Sociology* 27 (1968): 259–266.

[15] Hutchison, T. W. *Knowledge and Ignorance in Economics*. Chicago: University of Chicago Press, 1977.

[16] Kuhn, Thomas S. "Second Thoughts on Paradigms." In *The Structure of*

Scientific Theories, edited by Frederick Suppe. Chicago: University of Illinois Press, 1974.

[17] Kuhn, Thomas S. *The Structure of Scientific Revolutions*. Chicago: University of Chicago Press, 1970.

[18] Lakatos, Imre, and Alan Musgrave. *Criticism and the Growth of Knowledge*. Cambridge and New York: Cambridge University Press, 1970.

[19] Leontief, Wassily. "The American Economy and Its Prospects." Statement submitted to the Joint Economic Committee of the United States Congress, January 19, 1982.

[20] Leontief, Wassily. "If Mr. Reagan's Policies Flop, Then What?" *The New York Times*, February 22, 1981.

[21] Machlup, F. "Operational Concepts and Mental Constructs in Model and Theory Formation." *Giornali Degli Economisti E Annali De Economia* (September-October 1960): 553–582.

[22] Mannheim, Karl. *Ideology and Utopia*. New York: Harcourt, Brace, and World, 1936.

[23] Margenau, Henry. "What Is a Theory." In *The Structure of Economic Science*, edited by S. R. Krupp. Englewood Cliffs, N.J.: Prentice-Hall, 1966. Pp. 23–28.

[24] Morgenstern, Oskar. *On the Accuracy of Economic Observations*. Princeton, N.J.: Princeton University Press, 1963.

[25] Northrup, F. S. C. *The Logic of the Sciences and the Humanities*. New York: The World Publishing Company, 1947.

[26] Popper, Karl. *The Logic of Scientific Discovery*. New York: Basic Books, 1959.

[27] Rotwein, Eugene. "Empiricism and Economic Method: Several Views Considered." *Journal of Economic Issues* 7 (1973): 361–382.

[28] Rudner, Richard S. *Philosophy of Social Science*. Englewood Cliffs, N.J.: Prentice-Hall, 1966.

[29] Scheffler, Ismael. "Prospects of a Modest Empiricism, I and II." *Review of Metaphysics* 10 (1956–57): 383–400, 602–625.

[30] Schumpeter, Joseph A. *History of Economic Analysis*. New York: Oxford, 1954.

[31] Shubik, Martin. "A Curmudgeon's Guide to Microeconomics." *Journal of Economic Literature* 8 (1970): 405–434.

[32] Silk, Leonard. *The Economists*. New York: Avon, 1978 (originally published by Basic Books, 1976).

[33] Tarascio, Vincent T., and Bruce Caldwell. "Theory Choice in Economics: Philosophy and Practice." *Journal of Economic Issues* 13 (1979): 983–1006.

[34] Tool, Marc R. *The Discretionary Economy*. Santa Monica, California: Goodyear, 1979.

[35] Ward, Benjamin. *What's Wrong with Economics?* New York: Basic Books, 1972.

[36] Wilber, Charles K., with Robert S. Harrison. "The Methodological Basis of Institutional Economics: Pattern Model, Storytelling, and Holism." *Journal of Economic Issues* 12 (1978): 61–89.

12

A Pragmatist's Quest for Holistic Knowledge: The Scientific Methodology of John R. Commons

Yngve Ramstad

It has always been difficult for noninstitutionalists to describe and interpret the knowledge produced by institutional economists.[1] However, if the literature of institutionalism in general is perceived by the outsider to be obscure, the writings of John R. Commons must be regarded as practically unfathomable. Students of Commons's work have frequently commented upon the convoluted—if not outright unintelligible—route by which he typically "explained" his concepts, an approach that has generally been attributed by the noninstitutionalist to Commons's "confusion" regarding the nature of scientific explanation, or to his alleged failure to develop a discernable explanatory structure.[2] Significantly, even institutionalists have found it difficult to summarize the structure of Commons's thought or to explain *why* he organized his work as he did.[3] Indeed, there can be little question but that, within the institutional movement itself, Commons is the least understood of its major theoreticians.

The question is, why so? It is my purpose in this article to offer a partial answer: Commons's consistent adherence to the unfamiliar methodological precepts of "holism."

Economists, as a rule, evince little interest in, or self-consciousness about, the philosophical issues underlying scientific methodology [Bolan 1982, pp. xiii, 1–2]. As a result, explicit methodological instruction is seldom emphasized in the economics curriculum, and most students "learn" methodology as part of the "personal knowledge" they acquire through studying exemplars and by "doing" economics under the tutelage of an established practitioner.[4] To the extent that a methodology is "taught," it is likely, at least in "reputable" departments, to reflect the formalist perspective associated with mathematical model-building and econometrics. Seldom, if ever, is the aspiring practitioner presented with, or encouraged to explore, an explicit alternative. Hence, there are few within the economics profession today, as there have been few throughout the past half century, who would question the putative applicability of formal methods to all "scientific" activity within economics.[5]

Eight years ago in this journal, Charles K. Wilber, with Robert S. Harrison, in an article entitled "The Methodological Basis of Institutional Economics: Pattern Model, Storytelling, and Holism," argued that another *and fundamentally different* methodological orientation—holism—underlies the scientific endeavors of institutional economists [Wilber and Harrison 1978]. Despite its apparent wide-spread acceptance, there are, in my view, sound reasons for doubting the general validity of Wilber and Harrison's thesis that there is *an* ("the") institutional methodology [Blaug 1980, p. 126; Ramstad 1981, pp. 376–79].[6] Yet, despite the exaggerated nature of Wilber and Harrison's claim, it *is* plausible that many or most institutionalists have proceeded along the lines they outlined.

Unfortunately, Wilber and Harrison provided no real examples of how holist underpinnings manifest themselves in the form and structure of the actual research programs and writings of present or past institutional economists, and, regrettably, neither they nor anyone else has subsequently provided a case study that illustrates just how an institutionalist's writings and his/her commitment to holism are related. As a result, those interested in the institutional approach are no more informed about how to "do" holist work today than they were at the time Wilber and Harrison's article was published.

Having developed his version of "institutional economics" prior to the creation of the word "holism," Commons, of course, never used the term himself to describe his own methodological perspective. Moreover, whereas the connections between Commons's approach, the German Historical School, and the philosophical precepts of American Pragmatism are by now well-established, no one has yet linked the structure of Commons's conceptual framework to holism.[7] Nevertheless, in what follows, I attempt to demonstrate, primarily through textual analysis of Commons's major theoretical works—*Legal*

Foundations of Capitalism [Commons 1924], *Institutional Economics: Its Place in Political Economy* [Commons 1934a], and *The Economics of Collective Action* [Commons 1950]—that Commons *did* approach economic analysis exactly as if he were a holist; in fact, Commons appears to be the prototypical holist. In addition to showing that Commons was a holist, I further attempt to show that his convoluted explanatory style becomes a great deal more systematic if one keeps that fact in mind.

It will be recognized that far more than a short article would be required to fully demonstrate how Commons's methodological commitments are related to his writings. Commons's complex framework emerged only gradually in the at least forty-four articles and seventeen books he wrote (occasionally with his students) over a career spanning more than fifty years.[8] Furthermore, Commons's theories were themselves continually tested and revised through their applicability to the innumerable concrete problems he wrestled with as a member of both state and federal commissions and as the author of several pieces of innovative legislation.[9] In this article, I attempt to establish conclusively only that the term "holism" summarizes the methodological posture from which Commons pursued his lifelong quest to round out conventional economic theory.[10] It is my hope that, once his methodological precepts are clearly understood, this knowledge can be used to render the structure of Commons's "institutional economics" more intelligible, to the benefit of noninstitutionalist and institutionalist alike. It should be emphasized that, to the extent the analysis is successful, it will not only illuminate Commons's writings, but will also constitute an explicit "exemplar" with which to support many of the generalizations forwarded by Wilber and Harrison.

What is Holism?

In order to show that Commons proceeded "as if" he were an holist, it is necessary first to spell out the essential features of the holistic approach. It is to this task that I now turn. To facilitate understanding, the holist's standpoint is frequently contrasted with the more conventional views of the "formalist."

The term "holism" first surfaced in Jan C. Smuts's *Holism and Evolution*, published in 1926, and its application to economics can be traced back at least to 1947, when Allan G. Gruchy published his *Modern Economic Thought* [Gruchy 1947]. The methodological precepts associated with the holistic approach as applied to economic questions were first examined by Henry W. Briefs in his *Three Views of Method*

In Economics [Briefs 1960]. A more detailed and comprehensive examination of the holistic approach, as well as a comparison of its tenets with the methodological beliefs underlying mainstream economics, was undertaken by Paul Diesing in his *Patterns of Discovery in the Social Sciences* [Diesing 1971]. The article by Wilber and Harrison was, in large part, a summary of Diesing's analysis.[11]

Given its integration into the literature concerning institutional economics, one can properly ask, what does the term "holism" connote?[12] As is so often the case, the exact meaning imputed to this widely used term is not always easy to discern. In practice, "holism" is used to convey three quite different (though interdependent) meanings. In one usage, holism refers to an ontological perspective (What is the nature of reality?). Gruchy is representative; he explained that he coined the term "holistic economics" to "call attention to what is most characteristic of the new economics [of Thorstein Veblen, Commons, Wesley Clair Mitchell, John Maurice Clark, Rexford Tugwell, and Gardiner Means]: its interest in studying the economic system as an evolving, unified whole, or synthesis, in the light of which the system's parts take on their full meaning" [Gruchy 1947, p. viii]. The "individualism versus holism" debate also revolves around this meaning of the term. In a second usage, holism connotes an epistemological posture (When do we "know" something?). Most methodological debates within economics—for example, verificationism versus falsificationism—involve this meaning of the term.[13] In its third usage, holism is assumed to be a perspective on method (How do we "do" social science?), that is, to indicate a commitment to a set of procedures that must be followed if one is to produce "knowledge."

As noted, the term holism—as, for that matter, "methodology" and its many variants—often, if not usually, is employed so as to simultaneously imply all three meanings.[14] It is important, however, that these three dimensions be kept distinct, and every effort will be made to do so in the following discussion.

The Holistic Standpoint

Paul Diesing has summarized the basic position of the holist as follows:

> The holist standpoint includes the belief that human systems tend to develop a characteristic wholeness or integrity . . . a unity that manifests itself in nearly every part. . . . The characteristics of a part are largely determined by the whole to which it belongs and by its particular location in the whole system. . . . The holist . . . believes not only that wholes exist, but that his account of them should somehow capture and express this holistic quality. . . . By "holistic quality" is meant, not only the manifold

interrelations among parts that appear in the original, but also some of the unique characteristics, the distinctive qualities and patterns that differentiates this system from others [Diesing 1971, pp. 137–39].[15]

In other words, holists employ a part-whole mode of apprehending reality. Reality is conceptualized as an integrated whole, a unity, not as a set of logically separable structures and processes (for example, "the price system") as perceived by formalists [Wilber and Harrison 1978, p. 80]. Furthermore, there is no sharp distinction perceived between the empirical and logical nature of things. *Meaning*, therefore, is linked to the context; entities or activities are assumed to be truly comprehensible only in their interrelations with other entities or activities. Additionally, the whole is seen in the main to *determine* the part. Obviously, if one is committed to this interpretation, one should study a whole living system rather than just one part (for example, the "labor market") taken out of context. Indeed, in principle, one should investigate nearly the whole culture in order to understand and explain one institution [Diesing 1971, p. 204].

The Production of Holistic "Knowledge"

Capturing the nature of a whole system is, to be sure, no easy task. Nonetheless, the process by which holists pursue this end has been isolated and described by Diesing. Diesing's characterization of that process can be summarized as follows:

Suppose there exists a whole system, say the one shown in Figure 1a, comprised of many interrelated parts.[16] Initially, the researcher focuses

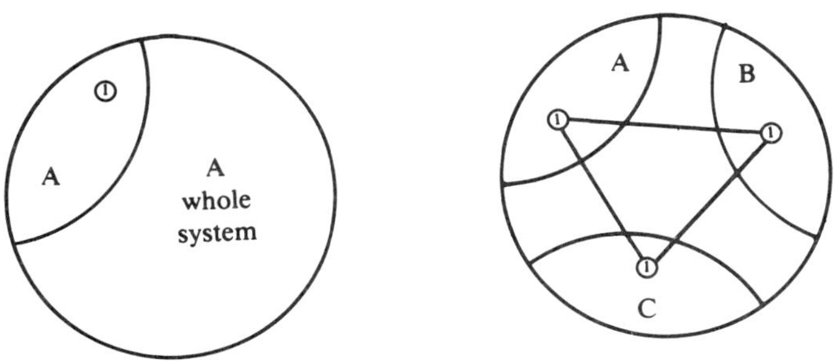

(a) (b)

Figure 1

on a small part of the entire system, say Part A. Through close observation of this limited domain, an analytical theme (generalization), Theme 1, emerges in the mind of the researcher. The researcher then shifts his focus to other parts of the whole system, Parts B, C, and so forth, in Figure 1b, as he attempts to determine whether this same theme (generalization) can also be isolated in other contexts. Thus *a reliance on the comparative method is one of the cornerstones of holism* [Diesing 1971, p. 149]. As the researcher proceeds to compare cases, he will become aware of differences as well as similarities. Over time, a typology will be developed that summarizes the systematic differences encountered. Note that, if the holistic method is faithfully pursued, those types summarize real cases; that is, they are real types.[17]

Once the researcher feels a given theme has a real existence, he tries to see what links it with other themes [Diesing 1971, p. 155], for example Themes 2 and 3. What the researcher now strives to accomplish is to capture the linkages, the interconnectedness, as depicted in Figure 2, that constitute the system's unity or wholeness. These *specific* linkages are what contribute to the system's uniqueness.

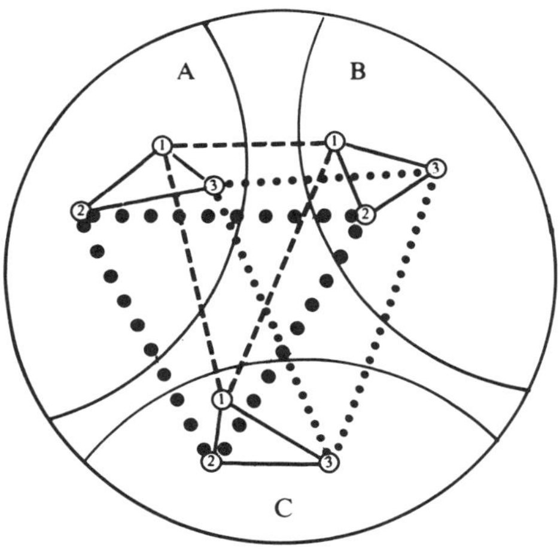

Figure 2

At some point a theme becomes a tentative hypothesis. The researcher then tests the hypothesis by consulting as wide a variety of data as possible—statistical data, survey data, participant observation data, case studies, anything he can get his hands on. No particular type of data is considered supreme; all are subjected to "contextual validation" [Diesing 1971, p. 147]. In other words, evidence is evaluated by comparing it with other *kinds* of evidence bearing on the same theme. In this way, a many-sided, complex picture of the subject matter gradually emerges. Quite obviously, the analysis possesses no "rigor," only varying degrees of plausibility.

After several themes have been "validated" (that is, found consistent with many types of data), they are linked into a network and interpreted to comprise a pattern [Diesing 1971, p. 158].[18] The resultant "pattern model" is the holist's "theory." It is here that the parts are unified into a whole. Accordingly, parts of the system are explained by showing via the pattern model how they are connected to the whole. The pattern model is similarly tested by observing how well new evidence can be incorporated into or explained within the pattern [Diesing 1971, p. 158]. It must be emphasized that a pattern model will never be complete, because the whole can never be comprehended in its entirety and, furthermore, is itself constantly changing [Diesing 1971, pp. 164–66]. Hence, there are always "loose ends." Despite this difficulty, the researcher continually looks to fit more and more detail into the pattern so as to obtain a finer and finer degree of coherence between his account and the real world [Diesing 1971, p. 159].

As the holist labors to improve the pattern model, he simultaneously strives to refine the associated typologies he is employing to interpret a specific system. In fact, the one task necessarily involves the other, as the characteristics of a specific system (a pattern) are explained by the holist when he shows how they reflect a unique blend of the characteristics associated with each of the "types" found mixed together in the whole under study. Further study of how the characteristics of specific types are reflected in widely varying wholes may lead to hypotheses about which features of a pattern are of primary importance in conditioning others. As the final step of the holistic method, the researcher will identify universals emerging from the comparison of widely varying types. Diesing refers to the identification of such universals as holistic "general theory" [Diesing 1971, pp. 225ff.].[19]

Sources of Confusion

It is obvious that those steeped in the ruling methodological principles of economic analysis are likely to find the work of holists to be perplexing.[20] First of all, since holists find *meaning* to be contextual in nature, they provide "definitions" of basic concepts that differ enormously from the precise terminology employed by formalists. As Diesing put it:

> Holistic definitions are likely to be long, complex and open-ended. The definitions of such concepts as institution, function, folk-society, or role will take a chapter or a long article and will really be essays in theory. Such concepts may have a vague core meaning, but the core shades off rapidly into a series of variants, circumstances, aspects, standpoints, and relations or contrasts with other concepts. And no such "definitions" will pretend to be complete; there is always more to be said and discovered [Diesing 1971, p. 211].

Walton Hamilton's discussion of an "institution" in the *Encyclopaedia of the Social Sciences* is a perfect example of the approach used by holists to define fundamental concepts [Hamilton 1932].[21]

A second source of confusion is likely to inhere in the holist's understanding of the term "explanation." For holists, an event or system is explained by identifying its place in the whole or in a pattern [Diesing 1971, p. 158]. It must be remembered that each segment of the holist's theory (the discrete typologies) is developed, interpreted, and tested independently of the other segments of the pattern. Therefore, except in those cases where a "general theory" has been developed, explanation proceeds by showing how the unique pattern of a specific system manifests, one by one, the features associated with the types of which that specific whole is comprised. The structure of explanation, accordingly, is concatenated rather than hierarchical. Nowhere are there to be found "covering laws" to render the underlying conceptual structure intelligible and thereby to explain how "data" are converted into outcomes. As a result, "explanation" based on the pattern model looks to the formalist to be nothing more than "description."

This last point leads directly to yet another source of confusion—the holist's casual attitude toward prediction. For the holist, understanding of a *system* comes with comprehension of the unique interrelations between the whole and the parts. An incomplete pattern model, therefore, does not determine the nature of unobserved parts; in fact, study of unobserved parts will undoubtedly alter the researcher's understanding of those parts of the system previously investigated. Prediction of unobserved parts (events), thus, is not regarded as an important factor in assessing the truth or falsity of a pattern model [Diesing 1971, p. 164]. As long as the pattern model can be modified to accomodate the new discovery (part), there is no basis for its rejection. For the holist, in short, theory (the pattern model) is primarily an aid in achieving understanding, not an instrument for making predictions. This orientation, though, provides the formalist with another reason for concluding that "explanations" based on the pattern model are "unscientific," that is, merely "descriptions."

A final source of confusion is to be found in the attention accorded by the holist to the individual case. This is because, for the holist, the primary locus of validity is not the general law or even the typology, but one's understanding of the individual case: "[The holist's] ultimate interest always returns to individual cases, and if he makes long ventures into theory it is for the eventual purpose of understanding cases better" [Diesing 1971, pp. 179, 195]. As a consequence, one needs a theory capable of saying a great deal about a few cases, rather than very little about all cases. This reflects the overriding aim of the holist to develop "practitioner's knowledge"—that is, knowledge directed to the understanding and control of the specific case. This is in sharp contrast to the formalist's preoccupation with the development of knowledge applicable to aggregates even if it is of limited applicability to individual cases.[22]

Commons's Methodology

It would be impossible to comprehend the logic underlying Commons's approach to the pursuit of knowledge without first grasping what it was that he wanted to know and why. As emphasized above, it is beyond the scope of this article to provide a systematic statement of Commons's theory of economic life, but a cursory overview of his interpretation of the economic process may be helpful.

Commons saw the "transaction"—the actual exchange of ownership rights, that is, the rights to control use—as the fundamental unit of economic life. Each transaction, in turn, was interpreted as taking place within the domain of a "going concern," whether it be the family, the enterprise, or the nation. To ensure that transactions do not disrupt order within the concern, "working rules" are adopted. Working rules specify the rights, duties, et cetera, that individuals have in their transactions with other "citizens" of the going concern, and their primacy over behavior was seen by Commons as absolutely necessary for maintaining order within the concern. Thus Commons rejected the orthodox view that economic order emerges spontaneously through truly voluntary activity channeled by the price mechanism ("free will"); instead, institutions—defined as "collective action in control of individual action"—were declared to be responsible for orderly economic life. Because the transaction was seen by Commons to be the fundamental unit of activity lying behind allocational and distributional outcomes (including exchange values), he made it the focal point of his analysis. In Commons's mind, the transaction had to be explained if one was to explain actual outcomes.

Commons was of course as much reformer as scientist.[23] All his life he was preoccupied with the task of attaining more equitable outcomes ("Reasonable Value") through collective action.[24] Since outcomes were interpreted to be foreshadowed by transactions, and the content of transactions, in turn, to be the consequence (in part) of the underlying working rules, more "reasonable" outcomes necessarily presumed the existence of more "reasonable" working rules. Thus if he were to promote more equitable economic outcomes (viewed broadly), Commons had to know or to understand the relationship between working rules and outcomes. As a result, Commons's scientific activities were directed primarily to the task of obtaining knowledge about transactions and their determinants for the purpose of altering specific working rules in such a manner that outcomes would become more "reasonable." As will be shown, there can be no doubt that Commons's methodology was perceived to facilitate the development of such knowledge.

Unfortunately, Commons never set down his methodological views in one place. What he did have to say about methodological issues is scattered here and there throughout his writings. The following analysis, therefore, represents an attempt to synthesize Commons's pronouncements in such fashion that a coherent methodological stand-point is revealed. It should be kept in mind that the end-in-view here is to determine whether *what Commons himself wrote* can be so organized and interpreted as to permit classification of his methodological approach as holist; hence the many, and sometimes lengthy, passages incorporated into the analysis.

Commons and Pragmatism

The subject matter of economics, in Commons's view, is "collective action in control of individual action according to the evolving working rules of the various customs and concerns" [Commons 1934a, p. 655]. And those rules, Commons averred, can "be investigated by the pragmatic method of science" [Commons 1934a, p. 655]. But what did Commons mean by "the pragmatic method of science"?

As noted earlier, Commons had no realistic opportunity to label himself a holist since the term was coined only late in his life. Nevertheless, Commons did learn of Smuts's new term and, in at least one passage, seemed to imply that his own thory embodied the economic meaning of the "modern term, 'holism'" [Commons 1950, p. 135]. What Commons did consider himself to be was a Pragmatist: "We endeavor to follow [C. S. Peirce] and to accept the term Pragmatism as the name of the method of investigation which we apply to economics" [Commons 1934a, p. 150]. Commons emphasized that by Pragmatism, Peirce, and thus he, "meant merely the *method* of scientific investigation" [Commons 1934a, p. 150].[25] Hence the reference to "the pragmatic method of science." According to Commons's student and disciple, Kenneth H. Parsons, Peirce's essay on "How to Make Our Ideas Clear" was most influential in shaping Commons's point of view regarding the nature of scientific thought [Parsons 1950, p. 343].[26] Commons's one extended discussion of Pragmatism, a section in *Institutional Economics*, draws heavily on this essay [Commons 1934a, pp. 150–56]. Although Commons does not tell us much here about the *method* he uses—instead he focuses on epistemological issues—this is Commons's only substantive discussion of his interpretation of Pragmatism, and it consequently merits close examination.

Commons begins by addressing the question of what an idea or thought "is." He finds its meaning to lie, as Peirce asserted, in the feeling of "belief." Commons then quotes Peirce:

> "The essence of belief is the establishment of a habit. . . . The whole function of thought is to produce habits of action. . . . To develop [the meaning of a thought], we have, therefore, simply to determine what habits it produces, for what a thing means is simply what habits it involves. . . . What the habit is depends on *when* and *how* it causes us to act. As for *when*, every stimulus to action is derived from perception; as for the *how*, every purpose of action is to produce some sensible result. Thus we come down to what is tangible and practical," for which reason Peirce gave it the name Pragmatism, "as the root of every real distinction of thought. . . . Our idea of anything *is* our idea of its sensible effects" [Commons 1934a, p. 152].

Commons next cites Peirce's cardinal rule "for obtaining scientific clearness" in our ideas: "Consider what effects, which might conceivably have practical bearing, we conceive the object of our conception to have. Then our conception of these effects is the whole of our conception of the object" [Commons 1934a, p. 152]. Commons's dictum that "Public programs [themselves initially 'ideas'] . . . must be judged by the practical consequences of their operation" would appear to reflect this perspective [Commons 1950, p. 137].

It is evident from the foregoing discussion that in Commons's mind, ideas have no necessary correspondence with "reality." They are simply mental aids for channeling action. Thus, for example, Commons's most fundamental concept, the transaction, was explicitly, as "defined" by him (more on this shortly), "not a copy of nature or reality—it is merely a mental configuration of the least unit of economic theory—a unit of investigation by means of which reality may be understood," that is, by which the effects of action can be identified or anticipated [Commons 1934a, p. 59].

Having established that ideas are beliefs regarding effects of action, Commons discusses how an idea/belief (which ultimately is combined with other ideas into a "formula" or a theory) can be judged "scientific" rather than simply the product of individual bias. In other words, how do we know when a belief is "true?" Peirce is again the authority: "The opinion which is fated to be ultimately agreed to by all who investigate is what we mean by truth. The object represented in this opinion is the real" [Commons 1934a, p. 152]. Commons thus grounds the "truth" of an idea (and thus, presumably, of a "theory"), not in the accuracy with which it copies "reality" or isolates its logical structure, but in social consensus—"the existing state of knowledge which changes with further truth" [Commons 1934a, p. 152, n. 38]. In short, scientific "truth"—that is, knowledge—is nothing more in Commons's mind than an ever-evolving consensus of opinion as to the effects of action [Commons 1934a, p. 153].

Commons next turns to the problem of locating the *source* of ideas, which leads him to Peirce's concept of the mind as "an active, continuing organizer and reorganizer of impressions": "The mind does not wait for impressions, it is continually looking for them, breaking them up into parts, and reconstructing them into new feelings [concepts, or ideas, or theories]" [Commons 1934a, p. 153]. Even if it pertains to no one else, this passage certainly captures the activity taking place in Commons's mind—recall his aforementioned passion for "classification, subclassification, reclassification, and overclassification." For Commons, such activity was no doubt perceived to be the very essence of scientific creativity. In any case, significantly, Commons at this point adds: "[I]mpressions themselves are seized upon [by the mind] in their external relations of parts related to the whole activity, past and future, instead of coming into the mind as separate impressions associated only by resemblance, contiguity, and succession" [Commons 1934a, p. 153]. The mind, in other words, grasps things in the same part-whole relationship that characterizes the external world, that is, reality. *Commons here has revealed himself to share the ontological perspective of holists.*

Commons neglects throughout this entire discussion to inform us what he means by the word "theory" (and it is best that explanation of its meaning in Commons's mind be deferred). He nonetheless concludes his discussion of Peirce's Pragmatism by expressing his own pragmatic interpretation of a theory's adequacy, that is, of its "validity": "[I]f a *theory* 'works' when tested by experiments and verified by others, then the *theory* is true and right, so far as present knowledge is concerned and all the known facts are included" [Commons 1934a, p.

156]. This passage is crucial to Commons's approach throughout his career of conducting experiments based on his theories—that is, applying them to actual cases and adjusting them when they provided an inadequate explanation of observed effects, in short, when they were "invalid."

Peirce's discussion pertained exclusively to our knowledge of nature, whereas Commons was interested in social activity. Therefore, he appended to his discussion of Peirce a short section titled "From Nature to Going Concerns," in which we are told what it is Commons himself is attempting to "know":

> Something similar is the test in economic science, as Peirce found in physical science. But the essential difference is that physical science deals with knowledge of the activities within the body of the cosmos, including human beings as nature's objects; while economics deals with the individual as a citizen endowed with rights, duties, liberties, and exposures, in varying degrees imposed by various concerns. . . . Peirce's pragmatism, applied to institutional economics, is the scientific investigation of these economic relations of citizens to citizens. Its subject-matter is the whole concern of which the individuals are members, and the activities investigated are their transactions governed by an entirely different law, not a law of nature but a working rule, for the time being, of collective action [Commons 1934a, pp. 156–57].

Commons's Conception of Economic Theory

Commons perceived scientific activity to involve three distinct elements: facts (information regarding the current status of objects or activities), purpose (on the part of the investigator), and theory [Commons 1950, p. 120]. Commons was quite explicit regarding the scientific role of theory: "The task of theory [is that] of arriving at an understanding of the part-whole relation to be obtained in economics"; it represents "a statement of what we now expect [effects of action to be] from our present knowledge of the factors and our present understanding of their interrelations" [Commons 1934a, pp. 734–35]. It should be noted that in the first passage we get our first hint that Commons also shared the holist's belief that explanation must capture the nature of part-whole relationships.

The word "theory" has two distinct connotations. It can signify an *outcome* produced by thinking, a specific complex of ideas about the relationship between facts or events. It can also convey the mental activity itself, the way one thinks about concrete problems. One concept leads to a conception of theory as specific content, the other as process. Commons usually, though not exclusively, employed the word "theory" to connote process [cf. Commons 1934a, p. 98].

The nature of theory as an activity was summarized by Commons in the following manner: "[A Pragmatic theory] is a complex activity of Analysis, Genesis and Insight" (and here his concept of the mind surfaces) "actively constructed by the mind in order to understand, predict, and control the future" [Commons 1934a, p. 102]. The constituent parts of the activity—Analysis, Genesis and Insight—are further delineated: Analysis is "the process of classification by which we compare similarities and distinguish differences" (cf. p. 1070); Genesis is "the analysis of the changes that are continually going on in all of the factors"; and Insight involves the synthesis or "the union of Analysis and Genesis into a formula [this term will be explained shortly] of the changing relations of the parts to the whole." Through synthesis, then, the investigator is able to "unite the changing parts into a changing whole" [Commons 1934a, p. 99]. It hardly need be noted that this is a radically different interpretation of the word "theory" than that accepted by modern-day economists. At the same time, it is fully consistent with the holistic standpoint adumbrated in the preceding section.

Reflecting his commitment to the Pragmatic perspective, Commons averred that ideas are what permit the scientist to "do" theory, that is, to think his/her way through a concrete problem. Thus ideas can be seen as the basic components of theory. Commons isolated five types of ideas necessary for investigation and understanding. These "inseparable and interdependent mental tools"—Percepts, Concepts, Principles, Formulae, and Social Philosophies (the parts)—together constitute Theory (the whole), and serve as the source of any meaning attributed to the subject matter being investigated—that is, the meaning of facts [Commons 1934a, pp. 98, 735].

Comprehension of this typology is absolutely fundamental to an understanding of Commons's method of investigation and to his circuitous style of explaining the phenomena and activities he investigated. Commons defined a percept as an idea that attributes inside feeling (sensation) to something happening outside the person experiencing the feeling; percepts are roughly equivalent to "non-reflective awareness of objects and relations" [Commons 1934a, pp. 94, 735]. A concept was defined as an idea that captures similarity of *attributes* among some of those objects and relations (for example, "Man" or "Use-Value") [Commons 1934a, p. 94]. A principle, in like manner, is an idea capturing similarity of *actions* (such as the principle of scarcity). Because a principle involves the sequence of time, *it embodies cause, effect, and purpose* [Commons 1934a, p. 94]. The term "formula" was used by Commons to represent a mental picture or idea of a relation between the parts and the whole. It "is a . . . mental tool constructed for research and action, and it is a formulation of the relation of the parts to each other and to the whole" [Commons 1934a, p. 736]. Finally, a social philosophy is an idea capturing similarity of *purpose*. Its role is subtle yet fundamental: "If a man starts out to prove a thing, it is wonderful how he can select the facts that prove it. It is our social philosophies that unconsciously select for us our facts [ultimately percepts] and our definitions [percepts, concepts, and principles]" [Commons 1934a, p. 98].

According to Commons, "Methodology is the logical structure of the concepts and principles in which each science formulates its own knowledge" [Commons 1934a, p. 739]. In a discussion nominally directed to the significance of Max Weber's "ideal types," Commons traces through the logical structure of the knowledge produced by political economy [Commons 1934a, pp. 736–38].

The interrelations between the five components of economic theory are shown by Commons to be quite subtle. Some percepts (objects or relations assigned meaning by the mind) yield concepts (percepts with similarity of attributes). However, a percept is not a part of which a concept is the whole; a percept is only a special attribute of something that is unknown as a whole [Commons 1934a, p. 735]. Other percepts yield principles (similarity of action or motion). This also is not a part-whole relationship; a percept is not a part action of which the principle is the whole action [Commons 1934a, p. 735]. Thus the need for a formula, the mental process uniting parts and wholes. But is it a formula of concepts or a formula of principles? Ultimately, Commons argues, this depends on the researcher's *specific* problem of research and action. Commons also shows how easy it is to transform a concept into a parallel principle [Commons 1934a, p. 735]. Another complication comes from the reality that a concept or principle can be either part or whole, again depending on the task at hand. The concept of a transaction in one case is a part of the whole, "going concern" [Commons 1934a, p. 97]. In another case, that same transaction, now transformed by Commons into the underlying state of mind, willingness, may itself be conceived as the whole comprised of its own parts [Commons 1934a, p. 738]. The general case, then, is that "The parts are themselves wholes, requiring each its own formula, and so on down to the parts which we consider ultimate" [Commons 1934a, p. 736].

Commons also outlined his interpretation of the formula's place in the "logical structure" of economics [Commons 1934a, p. 734]. Its role is to furnish an "elastic outline . . . of the interdependence of *all* factors [concepts and principles], which must then be investigated both separately as part-whole relations in their own rights and as interdependents" [Commons 1934a, p. 738]. A formula, furthermore, is constantly subject to revision:

> An hypothesis is a statement of what we now expect from our present knowledge of the factors [Concepts and Principles] and our present understanding of their interrelations. . . . But when, on investigation and experiment, we "try out" the hypothesis—our formula—and find that it does not exactly fit, then . . . we change the formula to get a better fit. . . . [Thus] we have a changing hypothesis, taking in new factors or retiring older ones. [Commons 1934a, p. 734]

Commons's perspective regarding the nature of theory—both as activity and as structure—is summarized in Figure 3. It should be noted that "facts" plus "[economic] theory" (as a product of thought) are what we know about the economic realm, that is, it is the content of political economy.

Figure 3 *Scientific Activity*

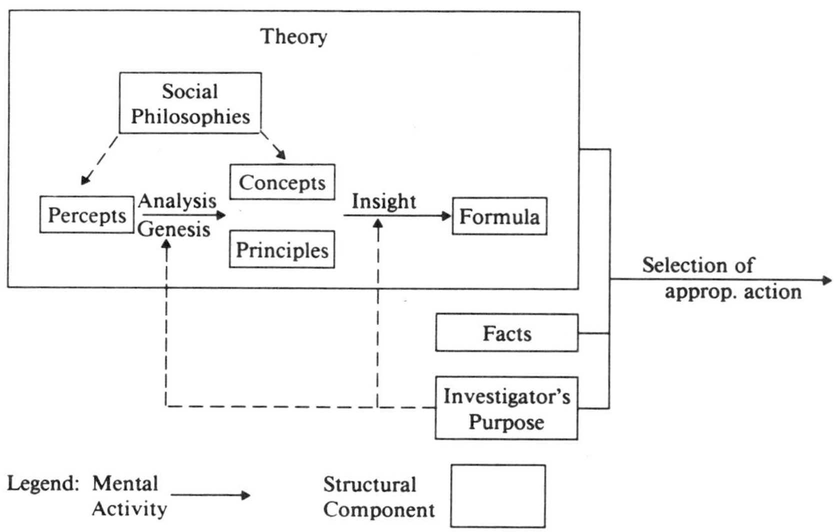

The significance (in the present context) of the preceding discussion can now be summarized. What Commons has done in his attempt to delineate the structure of economic theory is to lay out a framework remarkably like that summarized by Figures 1 and 2, above. The emergence in the researcher's mind of a percept is equivalent to Theme 1 being discovered in Part A of the total system portrayed in Figure 1a. The emergence in the researcher's mind of a concept or principle is equivalent to that same theme being identified in Parts B and C of the system as portrayed in Figure 1b. Themes 2 and 3 also become concepts or principles, as an awareness of their existence in other parts of the system enters the investigator's mind. Finally, the creation in the researcher's mind of a formula is equivalent to the researcher specifying the linkages and interconnections among themes through which they become a "whole" (p. 1073 above). As confidence in the formula grows, it becomes equivalent to the "pattern explanation." At the same time, the formula—the pattern model—is always in the process of further refinement as new information is incorporated into the pattern (cf. page above). *It is quite apparent that Commons has articulated exactly what Diesing described to be holistic theory.*

On the Meaning of Theoretical Terms

Commons was disposed to use the word "understanding" (versus "prediction" or "explanation") when describing the objective of scientific activity. For example:

> The subject-matter with which the economist deals is not a mechanism or organism whose motions the investigator cannot *understand* [versus "classify, measure, or mechanize"]—it is human beings whose activities he can fairly well understand by putting himself "in their place" and thus construct the "reasons" in the sense of motives or purposes, or values, of their activity. . . . [What we really want is] . . . to understand the reasons *why* people act as they do under the particular circumstances selected. [Commons 1934a, pp. 723, 725]

But what did Commons believe to be the appropriate way for the economist to communicate his understanding of an activity (or the outcomes produced by the activity)? An example will be instructive.

In a chapter of *Institutional Economics* devoted to outlining his "method" (Chap. 2), Commons introduces his "smallest unit of institutional economics," the transaction [Commons 1934a, p. 58; also cf. p. 55]. Commons states that transactions "are the alienation and acquisition, between individuals, of the *rights* of future ownership of physical things. . . . [They] are *transfers of these rights*" [Commons 1934a, p. 58]. This approximates a "definition" as the term is conceived by formalists. But in Commons's view, apparently, this does not convey information sufficient for the economist, conditioned as he is to the traditional way of interpreting economic life as a series of *exchanges*, to understand the meaning of a *transaction* [cf. Commons 1934a, pp. 56–57;

60–61]. First of all, one must recognize that transactions are embodiments of the three "social relations" of conflict (conflicting interests in ownership rights), dependence, and order (security of expectations) [Commons 1934a, pp. 58, 92]. One must also appreciate that the transaction is a unit of activity having simultaneous meaning in law, economics, and ethics (which are thereby interpreted as an inseparable whole); for example, the legal relation of "no duty" (versus right, no right, and duty), the economic status of "liberty" (versus the corresponding security, exposure, and conformity), and the working rules of "may" (versus can, cannot, and must/must not) are "correlated" in the transaction [Commons 1934a, p. 59; cf. the chart on p. 78].

Then there is the part-whole problem. From one angle, transactions are the parts of which the going concern is the whole; thus we must grasp the nature of a going concern to understand the meaning of a transaction [Commons 1934a, p. 59; cf. pp. 58, 69]. From another angle, a transaction is the whole (as an outcome) of which the parts (its "causes") are the five principles of scarcity (similar, but not identical, to the conventional idea of supply and demand), efficiency (productivity), working rules and custom (this is what links Commons to other institutionalists), sovereignty ("the changing process of authorizing, prohibiting and regulating the use of physical force in human affairs" [Commons 1934a, p. 684]), and futurity (anticipation of the future); therefore we need to have a grasp of the interrelated operation of these principles to understand the meaning of a transaction [cf. Commons 1934a, pp. 69–74 and 77–83 (Working Rules and Custom), 74–77 (Scarcity), and 83–84 (Futurity)].

But this is not the end! There are actually three quite different types of transactions: Bargaining, Managerial, and Rationing [p. 58]. In fact, it should be kept in mind that Communism, Fascism, Nazism, and Capitalism are, as alternative economic systems, nothing more than "wholes" comprised of different mixtures of bargaining, managerial, and rationing transactions [cf. Commons 1934a, p. 93]. However, one cannot "add up" the different types of transactions; the five principles interact differently as "parts" within the three types of transactions, each exhibiting its own "legal, economic, and ethical correlation," that is, each requiring its own formula [Commons 1934a, pp. 59, 64]. We therefore need to know something about those formulas in order to understand what a specific transaction means [cf. Commons 1934a, pp. 59–69]. Furthermore, behind value lies a transactional—or negotiational—psychology (versus the earlier "individualistic psychology"), that must also be understood; "[A] scientific understanding of negotiational psychology" therefore necessitates an understanding of *its* principles so that they may be sifted and weighed [Commons 1934a, pp. 90–92]. The investigator, if he is to understand a transaction, must pinpoint the personalities of the participants in a transaction, as well as their relative power, the circumstances in which each personality is placed—and so on. What is required to understand a transaction, in other words, is an understanding of "willingness" [Commons 1934a, p. 94]. In addition, the principles of performance, avoidance and forbearance are crucial to the meaning of a bargaining transaction [Commons 1934a, pp. 87–89].

On a somewhat different tack, Commons indicates that the meaning of a transaction also cannot be fully understood unless it is grasped that the principle of an Institution—"collective action controlling, liberating, and expanding individual action"—is reflected in every transaction [Commons 1934a, pp. 70, 92]. Concomitantly, transactions, and hence institutions, foreshadow ("cause") Value [Commons 1934a, pp. 86–87]. Therefore, if things are viewed from the social action perspective (reflecting a desire on the part of the investigator to see values—and thus transactions—altered), the strategic transaction must be distinguished from the routine; but of course, which of the observed transactions is the strategic one depends in part on the objective(s) of the investigator [cf. Commons 1934a, pp. 89–90]. *And there is much more.*

As Commons moves through this discussion, each time a new consideration is raised, the transaction is rediscussed with the new shading added to its meaning. By the time he has discussed everything that must be kept in mind if one is to *understand* what a concrete transaction is, that is, to discern its *meaning,* Commons has provided a synopsis of his entire conceptual framework. In other words, he has described one part of his analytical structure by attempting to explain how it is interconnected with other concepts into a whole (his conceptual framework). It must be emphasized that this approach has not been accidental: "Even for strictly logical purposes a term cannot be defined except with reference to the context of other terms with which it is associated. Its meaning depends upon the meaning of the other terms defined along with it. It shades off into different meanings in order to fit itself to their meanings. . . . Then it operates with different degrees of power according to its part in the total of complementary qualities and faculties." [Commons 1924, p. 347] According to *Webster's Collegiate Dictionary,* a definition is "an explanation of the meaning or meanings of a word." One can perhaps legitimately question whether the content of the thirty-eight pages Commons has taken to outline his understanding of the word "transaction" [Commons 1934a, pp. 55–93] constitutes a true definition. There is no doubt, however, that if it does, *it is a "holistic definition"* (cf. pp. 1073–74 above).

The Evolution of Commons's Theory

It should be apparent by now that Commons can appropriately be classified a holist. It is beyond the scope of this article to show in detail the evolution of his pattern model as articulated in the three theoretical works in which he "summarized" his point of view. A brief overview would appear appropriate, however, since it will provide further confirmation of his holistic orientation. It will also be helpful to briefly discuss the holistic perspective underlying the organization of Commons's three theoretical works.

Commons first hit upon "collective action" as his central concern when he and his brother, as college students, worked in competing print shops. Commons's shop was unionized; that of his brother was not. By comparing their situations, both in earnings and working conditions (note that he is already relying on the comparative method), Commons learned first-hand the meaning of "collective action in control of individual action" (he did not yet call this an "institution"), *and* how the rights and liberties of typesetters were *created* by collective action [cf. Commons 1934b, pp. 17–20; Commons 1950, pp. 25–28]. This was the original theme (p.1071 above) produced by Commons's active mind, one that he later extended "as a part of economic science, to all corporations, trade associations, banks, and every occupation" [Commons 1934b, p. 19].[27]

Commons's first significant publication was *The Distribution of Wealth,* an attempt to grasp the "practical outcomes" of the theories of distribution developed by leading economists—that is, marginal productivity analysis [Commons 1893]. Commons was always suspicious of what he termed the "single-track mind" [1934b, p. 28] and consequently habitually "looked for the omitted factors, or the ones taken for granted and therefore omitted" [Commons 1934b, p. 28]. Thus, after first outlining the (single track) marginal productivity theory, Commons awkwardly spelled out what he considered to be "omitted factors," with special emphasis placed on the "rights" created by contract or custom [cf. Commons 1893, Chap. 2]. "Years later, in *Institutional Economics,*" the omitted "natural order" (created "rights") had become the Principle of Custom [Commons 1934b, p. 49]. In his effort in this early work to specify the omitted factors—already by employing analysis (classification of similarities and differences)—and to show how they were linked to the included factors (marginal productivity theory), Commons developed an extensive typology of the factors that must be kept in mind in constructing a formula capable of yielding an explanation of distributional outcomes (see Commons [1893], chart preceding p. 1). In the concluding third of the book, Commons used that framework to develop a crude formula (pattern model) capable of approximately explaining actual distributional outcomes.

The pattern model provided in *The Distribution of Wealth* is not, to be sure, the one Commons ultimately incorporated into his "institutional economics." Indeed, the constituents of his theory emerged only gradually over the course of his career. First came the principle of sovereignty, as developed in a seven-part essay published during 1899 and 1900, "A Sociological View of Sovereignty."[28] Significantly, Commons later concluded that "'A Sociological View of Sovereignty' . . . became for me eventually Institutional Economics"[Commons 1934b, p. 44].[29] In 1901 came the Working Rule: "[I read] . . . Webb's [sic] new book on *Industrial Democracy* with its remarkable analysis of the 'common rule', which afterwards I generalized as the 'working rule' of all collective action, including the state" [Commons 1934b, p. 71].

By 1907, Commons had concluded that the concept of an exchange of objects and activities should be replaced by a "unit of analysis" capturing the more fundamental exchange of the rights of ownership to the object or activity [Commons 1934b, p. 27]. This was not an easy task for Commons: "it took me more than twenty-five years . . . to work out persistently, by numerous mistakes, the transition to the concept of a 'transaction'" [Commons 1934b, p. 27]. When finally "worked out," the transaction had become the fundamental unit of activity underlying a full-blown Theory of Reasonable Value.

The path to this theory was not a direct one. As he was developing his explanatory principles (pattern model) during the 1890–1909 period, Commons also articulated, in a series of remarkable essays, his "social philosophy"—one he at that time summed up with the term "utilitarian idealism" [Commons 1913, Chap. 1].[30] At this early stage of his career, Commons also settled upon three principles that would guide his research activities: one regarding the type of knowledge he sought; the two others, the method by which he would seek it. With respect to the first principle, Commons discerned three distinct types of research, each motivated by a different purpose. The first type, "academic research," was asserted by Commons to be directed to the end of "truth for its own sake" [Commons 1913, p. 7]. The second type was "constructive research," that is, the pursuit of "truth for the sake of utility" [Commons 1913, p. 7]. The third type, "journalistic research," had as its objective "to awaken the public" by "exposing [a] disease" and thereby showing "that something must be done" [Commons 1913, p.

8]. Commons's overriding motivation throughout his academic career was to "save Capitalism by making it good", by which he meant to bring about outcomes more favorable to the laboring masses [Commons 1934b, p. 143; cf. Commons 1894, Chaps. 1 & 2; Commons 1913, Chap. 6]. Regulation of economic life was seen by Commons to be the mechanism for bringing into effect that "good" type of capitalism [cf. Commons 1934b, p. 118]. Constructive research, accordingly, is investigation, first, that facilitates the drafting of legislation that promises to *actually* advance the public purpose it was enacted to promote, and, second, that facilitates the administration of that legislation [Commons 1913, pp. 7, 10; also cf. Commons 1950, pp. 124–25]. Commons clearly intended that his research be of the "constructive" type.

The second and third considerations underlying Commons's research activity related to the method by which one can develop "constructive" knowledge. It was Commons's view that a theory capable of providing guidance for administration must be structured so as to facilitate the comparative method of reasoning (cf. p. 1071), that is, one that allows for the isolation of strategic similarities and differences between the specific problem or case awaiting resolution and others with which an agency has had to grapple [Commons 1950, p. 124]. Furthermore, an adequate theory must induce the administrator to consider *all* the factors of the part-whole relationships that determine the content of a specific transaction [Commons 1950, pp. 136–38; also cf. Commons 1919, p. 63].[31] In other words, constructive research has as its ultimate locus of validity its utility in determining what to do in a specific case or context[32] (p.1075 above). Commons believed it is only through the development of a theory based on the comparison of individual cases that this type of "practitioner's knowledge" can be acquired. In studying individual cases, however, Commons believed it mandatory that the investigator "look and see" for himself, an approach first advocated by his teacher and mentor, Richard T. Ely [cf. Ely 1938, pp. 154, 161].[33]

Attempting to proceed in compliance with these precepts, Commons studied individual cases with a voracious appetite, first in the area of public utilities and then in labor. For him, this was definitely not a short-cut to knowledge. Commons reported in his autobiography that whereas "The genius can see through to the bottom of things without digging, . . . I must dig and re-dig" [Commons 1934b, p. 3]. His voluminous publications prior to 1924 attest to the magnitude of his effort to "dig and re-dig." To supplement his fieldwork, Commons structured his classes in such a fashion that they were little more than an attempt to sift through the implications of his latest findings and to incorporate them into an ever-changing set of theories (principles and formulae) so as to give them greater and greater empirical content [cf. Commons 1934b, pp. 47–48].[34] Moreover, Commons's students were made active partners in this process, being instructed to "test their own and all economic theories by experience" before they graduated—and upon doing so, said Commons, "They came back and corrected my errors" [Commons 1934b, p. 4].[35] In addition to being tested in the classroom, Commons's ideas were also subjected to the Pragmatist's criterion—did they work when incorporated into legislation or regulatory decisions? Whenever his ideas were shown, through practical application, to be lacking—that is, to be inapplicable to actual problems or to bring about unanticipated consequences, as invariably happened, he at once set to work to modify them.[36]

On the Structure of Commons's Theoretical Trilogy

Given that his overriding purpose was to "make capitalism good" through the exercise of explicit social control over the wage bargain (labor contract) and the pricing of essential commodities and services, what Commons sought throughout his thirty years of "constructive research" was knowledge that would permit him to understand how the complex of working rules that define "property rights" could be altered so as to bring into effect "reasonable"—that is, fair and just—economic outcomes.[37] Specifically, he sought a theory that would provide him with the insight needed in actual situations to identify legislative language and administrative structures capable of actually bringing about such outcomes.[38]

Legal Foundations of Capitalism is Commons's first attempt to articulate the theory he had developed in the pursuit of that end. In this remarkable book, Commons first attempts to define the concepts—foremost among them are property, transactions, and going concerns—and principles that constitute his theory [Commons 1924, chaps. 1–5]. Developing and then using typology after typology to facilitate a comparison of similarities and differences as they are found in concrete applications to real cases (analysis), while simultaneously proceeding in genetic fashion so as to convey as full an understanding as possible of their evolving meaning (genesis) [cf. Commons 1924, p. vii], Commons attempts to transmit a part-whole understanding of all the constituents of his theory, each conceived as both its own whole and as an interrelated part of the larger theory.[39] Specific examples illustrate each point, thus ensuring that the meaning of all ideas is related to actual cases. Commons next shows how the various elements of his theory (pattern model) are reflected in the whole that is each transaction [Commons 1924, chaps. 6–8]. Here he also demonstrates that the ever-changing parts incorporated into his theory (pattern model) can be converted into verbal formulae capable of explaining—that is, yielding an understanding of—the ever-changing content of actual transactions as reflected in the typical rent bargain, price bargain, and wage bargain (each conceived to be a related, yet unique, type of whole). As in the earlier chapters, specific cases, the true locus of validity, illustrate all points. Having thus shown that his theory is valid, Commons concludes the book by arguing that his "Theory of Reasonable Value," as he labeled it, provides the insight required to ensure progress, by means of strategic legislative alteration of the working rules controlling property, towards a world characterized by "reasonable" values [Commons 1924, p. viii].[40] *Legal Foundations* was consequently a personal triumph for Commons. Without yet having a name for it, reasonable value was the normative end that he had embraced so many years earlier during his stint as a union typesetter. *Legal Foundations* announced to the world that he had developed at last, through years of "constructive research," the scientific foundation—or in his terminology, the "evolutionary and behavioristic, or rather volitional, theory of value"—required to ensure its realization [Commons 1924, p. vii].

Surprisingly, *Legal Foundations* is devoid of examples illustrating how Commons applied the Theory of Reasonable Value to actual problems.[41] Also missing is any substantive attempt to explain how that theory was related to or affected the more familiar economic theories. Commons explained that the omitted material was to be incorporated into "another volume in contemplation" [Commons 1924, p. vii]. Nonetheless, these omissions only exacerbated the difficulties that economists experienced in attempting to grasp the essential logic, not to mention the significance, of Commons's highly original conceptualization of economic life.[42]

Commons soon came to recognize that he had failed to successfully communicate the "whole" that was his theory, a reality that he subsequently acknowledged: "Readers and students of . . . *Legal Foundations* . . . could not understand my theories nor what I was driving at" [Commons 1934a, p. 1]. So, *Institutional Economics*, published ten years later, contains a full restatement of Commons's theory (pattern model), although by this time the model had been "corrected" to include two additional principles ("efficiency" and "futurity"). However, remaining true to the agenda he had established a decade earlier, Commons's main objective in this volume was to render the theory intelligible to economists by showing how it was related to economic theory as it existed at that time. Thus he begins the preface by proclaiming:

> This book is modeled upon textbooks in the Natural Sciences. Each idea here incorporated is traced back to its origin, and then the successive modifications of that idea are developed and the earlier double or triple meanings of the idea [either relative to different considerations or as interpreted from different vantage points] are separated, until each, as a single meaning, is combined with the other in what I conceive to be the Science of Political Economy, as it is developing since [World War I] [Commons 1934a, p. v].

Practically indecipherable to the unprepared reader, this passage can now be seen as Commons's direct way of stating he is going to use genesis and analysis to synthesize the "magnificent insights" of earlier economists— all "parts"— with his own insight of "collective action in control of individual action"—another "part"—into the "whole" that is Political Economy [cf. Commons 1934a, pp. 7–8]. The task, in other words, "as I shall endeavor to show throughout, [is to give] collective action its due place in economic theorizing .... What I have tried to do is to work out a system of thought that shall give due weight to all economic theories, modified by my own experience" [Commons 1934a, p. 8]. Only in this way could Commons, as a holist, achieve the aim of this work, as expressed in its full title, *Institutional Economics: Its Place in Political Economy.*

The structure of the maze that is *Institutional Economics* becomes comprehensible if one keeps in mind Commons's methodological presuppositions *and* his objectives. Of particular significance is the extremely ambitious nature of his aims. One task is to impart his (part-whole) understanding of the theoretical constructs (concepts and principles) that he employs, each conceived of as its own whole (cf. p. 1081). A second task is to impart his (part-whole) understanding of the interconnections of those constructs as they unite into the whole of the theory that has by now been relabeled "Institutional Economics." But this is not all. As a third task, Commons also seeks to impart his (part-whole) understanding of how that theory—now itself a part—interconnects with the other theories to form the even greater whole that is political economy. In other words, each of Commons's constructs has a (part-whole) meaning dependent upon which whole is the frame of reference. Complicating the task of communicating these (part-whole) meanings is Commons's evident belief that no one of them can be fully comprehended without grasping their interconnections with the others. Given that he sought to impart as full an understanding of his theory as possible, he consequently found it necessary to pursue all three of his aims *simultaneously.*

Institutional Economics is organized to impart this type of holistic understanding. Commons begins by providing an overview of his theory in consecutive chapters titled "The Point of View" and "Method." Although these chapters run to a total exceeding one hundred pages, there is no real attempt made here to communicate a complete understanding of either parts or whole. Rather, the concepts and principles central to Commons's theory are simply introduced and (holistically) defined—yet even here, in holistic fashion, the discussion is replete with references to the ideas of other economists. Following this introduction, Commons provides more than six hundred pages of discussion devoted to the ideas of earlier "Pioneers of New Insight, each of [whom] has contributed something [to the concepts and principles Commons employs] which, in the wind-up [the formula], must be given due weight along with the conflicting or contradictory opinions of all the others" [Commons 1934a, p. 121]. As he proceeds, Commons demonstrates that many of his ideas were implicitly contained in earlier theories and that others were "omitted factors." Throughout, Commons uses his own concepts as the reference point, and by the classification and comparison of similarities and differences (analysis), attempts to develop a deeper understanding, both of his own constructs (each as its own whole) and of the extent to which preceding theories are and are not reflected in his theory (the intermediate whole) and in his conception of political economy (the largest whole). As he proceeds to review the theories of one economist (broadly defined) after another, Commons shows how preceding insights had to be modified and ultimately transformed into his own constructs, due in part to their own incompleteness and in part to the evolving landscape with which economic theory must deal.[43] Thereby, through genesis, Commons gradually develops a deepening understanding of his own constructs, both as evolving separate wholes and as parts of the successively larger evolving wholes. Significantly, nowhere does Commons attempt to describe the whole. Presumably it is only through an ever-deepening grasp of the parts and their interconnections that comprehension of the whole *as a whole* is to be slowly obtained by the reader.

In a section titled "Accidents and Unemployment—Insurance and Prevention," Commons provides examples that demonstrate how his theory served to guide him in drafting actual legislation. Again, it is in the application to concrete cases that the validity of the theory is demonstrated and its pragmatic meaning revealed. In the final chapter, titled "Communism, Fascism, Capitalism," Commons attempts to survey then-contemporary developments from the vantage point provided by his part-whole understanding of political economy. In this chapter, he exposes to the reader's view, once more, the social philosophy underlying his own scientific activity.

Even sympathetic reviewers like A. B. Wolfe conceded that *Institutional Economics* did not effectively lay bare the structure of Commons's "system of pragmatic philosophy" [Wolfe 1936, p. 206]. A third and final attempt was, therefore, made by Commons to articulate the essential logic of his conceptual system as it bears on public policy, this time, according to Kenneth H. Parsons, in "simple terms" [Parsons 1950, p. v]. *The Economics of Collective Action*, published posthumously, is the product of that effort. In the main, no attempt is made in this work to convey the whole that is political economy. Nor is there as complete an account of his own system, in part-whole terms, as that forwarded in *Institutional Economics*. Instead, Commons merely summarizes his framework (Parts 1 and 2), as well as his method of investigation and the principles he believes control effective implementation of his concept of Reasonable Value (Part 3). Then, through extended actual examples, he shows how his ideas are linked to the structure of working rules actually imposed on going concerns as a result of federal legislation and regulatory action—again, the specific case (a law or agency) constitutes the ultimate test of the theory's validity.[44] *The Economics of Collective Action*, in effect, is the practitioner's version of Commons's theory, whereas *Legal Foundations* and *Institutional Economics* were contributions to economic theory and hence directed to scholars and theorists. For the economist, the latter work represents the best expression of Commons's framework *as a whole*.

Summary

Over the many preceding pages it has been shown: that Commons's conception of reality was holist; that his beliefs regarding scientific explanation were holist; that the procedures he used to develop and test his theories were holist; that the concepts he developed to communicate his understanding of scientific method can be easily translated so as to correspond with the language used by Paul Diesing to describe the holist's precepts; and that if one keeps in mind those holist presuppositions, it is apparent that Commons's three attempts to outline his theory were not "organized by means of the random walk" but rather were organized in accordance with those same holist presuppositions. In other words, it has been shown beyond any reasonable doubt that if Diesing has accurately described the general contours of the holist standpoint, Commons must be classified as a holist.

Concluding Observations

John R. Commons was that rare scholar who somehow manages to reinterpret familiar events in such fashion that they take on an entirely new meaning. Commons's own contribution was to reveal how *collective control of individual transactions* is the "general and dominant feature of [economic] life," an insight that led him to advocate explicit social control over the process of institutional adjustment [Commons 1950, p. 21]. The Theory of Reasonable Value was the instrument he crafted to guide the search for progressive adjustments to existing institutional arrangements.

Commons's ideas are of fundamental import to the economist concerned with the problem of instituting progressive institutional change, and they deserve to be taken seriously. But, in the main, they have not been.[45] It is the premise underlying this article that Commons's ideas have been neglected in part because they have not been well understood. Indeed, in the first paragraph of this article it was asserted that economists generally have found Commons's writings to be "practically unfathomable." While no attempt was made to establish this as a fact, there surely can be little question that most professional economists have found it virtually impossible to isolate and articulate the structure of Commons's framework. The foregoing analysis suggests that this state of affairs can be traced in some measure to Commons's consistent adherence to holist precepts.

For example, Commons's writings are replete with two tendencies for which he has been roundly criticized—repetition and overclassification. Yet both are necessary characteristics of holistic explanation. Regarding the former, Commons offered the following justification in the preface to *Institutional Economics*:

> I confess that this book is burdened by much repetition. But this I could not help, partly on account of unfamiliarity of students and readers with the novelty of the subject and partly because, in a theory that gives due weight to the many sources of multiple causation, a single concept or principle recurs at every point where one or the other many changeable causes infringes. If a preceding cause . . . is omitted or forgotten at this different angle of vision of the same thing . . . I am compelled to repeat it. [Commons 1934a, pp. 8–9]

In short, Commons found holistic definitions rendered in part-whole terms to be indispensable for true understanding. Yet Commons routinely created new terms or appropriated unfamiliar ones from other disciplines, and, without precise definitions of these terms, the unprepared reader no doubt feels both restive and confused.

Commons's undeniable penchant for classification and (sometimes multiple) *re*classification was also part of his "scientific method." As noted earlier, it is only through the process of systematically classifying similarities and differences that the holist is able to construct the typologies so fundamental to his partitioning of the world. Thus, the more complex the whole, the more "types" that one must incorporate into a pattern explanation of any one of its parts. Moreover, the key to effective action is to "discover the similarities [and] recognize real differences" [Commons 1950, p. 121]. This is the comparative case method of reasoning that is so fundamental to recognizing the extent to which previous actions (cases) serve as models for the present problem. And as noted, this is the method Commons deemed fundamental to the production of knowledge that is applicable to the individual case [cf. Commons 1950, p. 121–24]. Since Commons dealt with extremely complex problems, involving at the same time legal, ethical, and economic dimensions, it is not surprising that he developed an extensive set of typologies to guide him in his application of the comparative case method. It is evident, therefore, that Commons's extensive reliance on classification schemes, while admittedly overdone, is but the systematic application of holistic procedures. But the unprepared reader, searching in vain for explicit structural relationships, is left perplexed by the stream of unfamiliar typologies that Commons forwards, each with its terms only partially defined—again in accordance with holistic procedure—when first presented.

Serious as the roadblocks presented by these deficiencies may be, there is yet a greater complication facing the student of Commons's thought. As indicated earlier, Commons was cognizant of the fact that readers had difficulty understanding his theories, leading him at one point to wonder whether "my theories were so personal to myself that perhaps nobody could understand them" [Commons 1934a, p. 1]. This was not idle musing. To truly understand the meaning in part-whole terms of any component of Commons's thought, *one must first grasp his entire framework.* How else can one grasp *his* part-whole relationships? This reality, however, complicates enormously the task of understanding Commons, for his "whole" was exceptionally comprehensive. Through a lifetime of study, Commons had managed, by the time he completed *Institutional Economics* at seventy-two years of age, to acquire a truly staggering knowledge of intellectual history, legal history, and economic history (including an exceptionally keen appreciation of U.S. economic history), all of which he synthesized into his conception of "political economy"—and, moreover, which he felt compelled to communicate in part-whole terms.[46] Given the ambitious task Commons set for himself, the comprehensiveness of the "whole" he sought to delineate and the unfamiliar language he used to clarify its "parts," the reader of *Institutional Economics* is faced with a truly formidable challenge.

In fact, that challenge is in many ways similar to the undertaking of an anthropologist who is set down in the midst of a primitive social group and instructed to discover the meaning of activities and objects as understood by the members of this alien culture themselves. Only slowly, as the participant-observer gradually becomes familiar with the activities of the new culture and the *contextual* nuances of the language in which its members express their thoughts, do accurate meanings, and thereby genuine understanding, emerge. In like fashion, one simply cannot grasp what Commons is driving at on an initial reading. Indeed, even approximately to grasp fully his framework in part-whole terms, as Commons attempted to articulate it in *Institutional Economics*, it may be necessary first to read and *re*read *all* of Commons's major works. In short, Commons is not a "quick read"; one *must* persist long enough to acquire a sense of the whole before the parts themselves can be understood.

These complications—all traceable to the holistic method itself—do much to explain why *Institutional Economics*, in particular, and the other theoretical works, to a lesser degree, are so difficult to comprehend upon a first reading. All too often, though understandably, the reaction is to throw up one's hands in frustration, declare Commons's thoughts to be something approximating "muddled," and move on to another, and perhaps more lucid, writer.[47]

In spite of these obstacles to rapid comprehension, one nonetheless can anticipate that occasional scholars will continue to take up the task of rearranging the various elements of Commons's thought into "the clearly integrated system of pragmatic social philosophy which, in all but form, it actually is."[48] It is a well-established truism that a writer must be interpreted *on his own ground* if his meaning is to be understood. The foregoing analysis shows clearly that, over the course of his long career, Commons developed and communicated his theories in strict adherence to the requirements of the holistic method.[49] It is to be hoped, therefore, that explicit consideration of his holist standpoint will permit future scholars to follow more easily the twists and turns of Commons's multi-level, part-whole mode of explanation, and thereby to render at last this neglected intellectual giant's complex system intelligible—*as an interconnected whole*—to all.

Beyond any light it may shed on Commons's writings, the analysis additionally gives rise to some important questions for all who seek to develop a more humanistic and comprehensive type of economic theory to structure the ongoing process of implementing, on a case-by-case basis, progressive institutional adjustment—a search that appears to be the motivation for further development of the domain described by the term "neoinstitutional economics."[50] A major thrust of this effort has been to move toward agreement regarding the nature of the evaluative principle that is to be used to distinguish "better" from "worse" states of the world. As Commons emphasized, however, an economic theory—and thus neoinstitutional theory—will be meaningful (instrumental) only if it permits one to *act* correctly, that is, to show how institutions can be altered *in a specific context* so as to actually effect the intended consequences.

To effect such changes, however, one *must first* possess a mental image of the structure that comprises a given context. Recent contributions by Paul D. Bush and F. Gregory Hayden can be cited as two highly creative and promising efforts to conceptualize that structure [Bush 1983; Hayden 1982, 1983]. It should, therefore, not be overlooked that Bush's characterization of reality is formalist in nature, whereas Hayden's is holist. In other words, the ontological question regarding the formal versus the holistic structure of reality *must* be addressed if the effort to craft *a* neoinstitutional theory or perspective is to move forward. Should the holist conception be deemed more appropriate, several questions must next be addressed.[51] For example: How can the conceptual components of Hayden's "social fabric matrix" be transformed into the most appropriate set of concrete components? How are the components to be defined? How is a "correct" understanding of the interconnections between those components to be developed? How can such an understanding be most effectively communicated? How is the *evolving* nature of their relationships to be accomodated and communicated? And so on. As the effort moves forward to transform the promising idea of a social fabric matrix into an effective shared instrument for the guidance and implementation of institutional adjustment, the vexing nature of these problems will quickly become apparent.

Thus it is extremely important to recognize that these were the very methodological problems with which Commons grappled. As his career progressed, Commons slowly constructed in his mind the equivalent of Hayden's social fabric matrix. At the very least, Commons's theoretical writings provide us with an exemplar of the difficulties that must be surmounted if the effort to construct a holistic neoinstitutional theory, and then to successfully communicate it to others, is to bear fruit. For this reason alone, John R. Commons's lengthy, and ultimately unsuccessful, struggle to articulate his holistic theory of Reasonable Value would appear to be of particular relevance for all who seek to contribute to that effort.

Notes

1. For example, David Seckler has observed that "The chapters on 'institutionalism' are uniformly the weakest chapter in any standard text in the history of economic thought" [Seckler 1975, p. 4].
2. Seckler has been quite explicit about this aspect of Commons's work, asserting his "resentment over having been forced to read [in the preparation of his own manuscript] . . . several thousand pages of Commons's writings (which seems to be organized by means of the random walk) in order to obtain what would constitute a good small book" [Seckler 1975, p. 154, n. 22]. Similarly, according to Kenneth Boulding, "[Commons's] theoretical writing is obscure and cumbersome" [Boulding 1957, p. 7]. Or, as Neil Chamberlain has put it, "There have been few economists who have been so given to classification, subclassification, reclassification, and overclassification as Commons" [Chamberlain 1964, p. 80]. Benjamin Ward was surely thinking of Commons when he opined: "The institutionalists seem to have suffered from a methodological confusion regarding the nature of theory. They thought a description was a theory; or alternatively, they thought that a good theory should explain everything" [Ward 1966, p. 187]. To provide another example: "Theory was never Commons's metier. When he calls his 'theories' are almost exclusively poorly wrought and somewhat lackadaisical classifications and sub-classifications of phenomena as they appear to him from the dimly held and mainly intuitive conception impossible to define" [Seckler 1975, p. 124].
3. Harter provides the most comprehensive treatment of Commons and is an indispensable source for anyone seeking to comprehend the enormity of Commons's endeavors [Harter 1962]. Gruchy is more limited in scope but also provides a sweeping overview of Commons's ideas [Gruchy 1947]. Neither of these authors, however, shows how Commons's conceptions combine into an analytical *system*, nor do they explain clearly why Commons presented his theories in the seemingly clumsy manner that he did. (For a partial exception to this generalization, see Harter [1962, pp. 210–12]). For shorter, yet insightful discussions of Commons's framework, or a specific aspect thereof, see, among others, Chamberlain [1964], Chasse [1985], Dugger [1979], Gonce [1976], Parsons [1950], Reed [1986], Rutherford [1983] and Wolfe [1936]. These contributions to the literature on Commons similarly fail to shed much light on the question of *why* Commons was unable to communicate the essential logic of his theories in a more effective manner.
4. See Polanyi [1958] for the argument that such is necessarily the procedure in *all* sciences.
5. It is not being asserted that all but institutionalists share a single methodological perspective. Certainly the modern Austrian economists should also be classified as "outside the fold." Perhaps also the Neo-marxists. It is nonetheless true that the overwhelming majority of economists today accept the formalist standpoint. On this point, see Ward [1972, p. 43].

6. See, for example, Caldwell [1982, pp. 200–205].
7. Commons's familiarity with, and high regard for, the approach of the German Historical School is discussed by Harter [1962, pp. 32, 177]. The relationship between Commons's approach and Pragmatism is outlined by Gruchy [1947, pp. 155ff.].
8. Commons's published writings are listed in their entirety in an appendix to his *Economics of Collective Action* [1950].
9. See Commons's autobiography, *Myself*, for an overview of Commons's involvement in the world of public affairs [Commons 1934b]. Harter also details the particulars of Commons's participation in the formulation of public policy [Harter 1962, Part 2].
10. Commons's avowed aim was to "round out" existing economic theory, not to create a different paradigm divorced from orthodoxy. See Commons [1934a, p. 5; 1950, p. 117]. See Ramstad for the argument that, whatever Commons's intent may have been, he in fact created a framework that is incompatible with the vision underlying orthodox (neoclassical) economics [Ramstad 1986].
11. Wilbur and Harrison subtitled their article "Pattern Model, Storytelling, and Holism." Diesing, however, argues that the "pattern model," a concept originated by Abraham Kaplan, rather than *an addition to* holism (thus "and") is instead a characteristic *feature of* holism [Diesing 1971, p. 158; Kaplan 1964].
12. It should be noted that not all institutionalists have embraced holism as a defining characteristic of institutional economics. Two recent major works by prominent institutionalists, Marc R. Tool and Wendell Gordon, fail to mention the term [Tool 1979; Gordon 1980]. See Bush [1983] for a presentation of institutional theory along formalist lines.
13. On this point, see Dray [1967] and Agassi [1975].
14. Cf. Wilber and Harrison [1978].
15. The present analysis is taken in its entirety from Diesing's *Patterns of Discovery in the Social Sciences* [Diesing 1971].
16. Holists apparently have varying concepts of how "whole" the system has to be [Diesing 1971, p. 141].
17. A real type is a generalization that has emerged from an observation of actual behavior. The concept of economic man, in contrast, is not based on generalizations from observed behavior. For an extended discussion of the difference between real types and "ideal types" such as economic man, see Diesing [1971, pp. 197–99].
18. Blaug [1980] labels this approach "verificationism." It should be noted that Blaug charges that not only institutionalists, but also the overwhelming majority of neoclassical economists, actually practice verificationism rather than the espoused doctrine of "falsificationism" [Blaug 1980, p. 256].
19. Veblen [1899; 1904, 1918], Ayres [1962], Brady [1943], Kerr et. al. [1960], Myrdal [1968], and perhaps Galbraith [1973] should be included, perhaps, among the institutionalists who have tried their hand at "general theory."
20. This is quite aside from any judgment rendered as to the scientific adequacy of the holistic approach *once it is understood.*
21. It should be noted that Veblen's work is replete with such "definitions."
22. Thus Albert Rees has written: "The purpose of science is to achieve understanding either for its own sake . . . or as a basis for prediction and control. Although both elements are present in economics, the latter is particularly

evident. The predictions sought generally refer to the aggregate behavior of sizeable groups of people and not to the behavior of individuals. . . .The focus on aggregates makes it possible to summarize the accumulation of economic knowledge in statements of observed regularities, or 'laws,' that do not apply to individuals [or, presumably, cases] considered singly" [Rees 1968, p. 473].

23. Dugger [1979] provides an excellent summary of Commons's reform orientation.
24. See Ramstad [1986] for a detailed examination of Commons's Theory of Reasonable Value.
25. Commons emphasized that he was a follower of Peirce only with respect to scientific method. Regarding social philosophy, Commons made it clear he regarded his perspective to be derived from John Dewey's brand of pragmatism [Commons 1934a, p. 150].
26. To the reader who has been left befuddled by Commons's narratives: No, this is not a bad joke.
27. For Commons's argument that collective action is the "dominant principle" of modern economic life, see [Commons 1950, Chap. 1].
28. Commons's holism came through clearly in these essays. In his autobiography, Commons observed that a critic had renamed the series "An *Economic* View of Sovereignty" due to the emphasis Commons placed on the changing nature of property as an explanatory factor underlying the changing nature of the state [Commons 1934b, p. 44, emphasis added]. Commons responded to this "criticism" in direct (and "holistic") fashion: "I always thought that both political science and sociology were branches of political economy" [Commons 1934b, p. 44]. Commons expanded on this theme in his final work: "As I have studied practical problems it has always seemed to me that the life-and-death struggle of making a living and trying to get rich was at the bottom of all other problems. . . .Consequently I have never been able to think of the various social sciences as separate fields of history, political science, law, economics, ethics, and administration. What we need is some way of working through the whole complex of problems that grow out of this fundamental struggle" [Commons 1950, p. 118].
29. Somewhat puzzling is the fact that Commons did not elevate "sovereignty" to the status of a full-fledged "principle"—thus, in part, explaining the content of a transaction—until after the publication of *Legal Foundations of Capitalism.*
30. These essays were collected and republished as *Social Reform and the Church* and *Labor and Administration* [Commons 1894; 1913].
31. See Commons [1919, p. 110] for a simple but fascinating example.
32. The fundamental difference between "academic" and "constructive" research may be the source of John Dunlop's complaint that he was unaware of even one piece of economic research performed by an academic that provided him with policy-relevant conclusions applicable to a specific problem he encountered as Secretary of Labor (see Dunlop [1977]).
33. Dugger emphasizes that even Commons's conception of specific ends—"good" capitalism—emerged from this "look and see" approach [Dugger 1979, pp. 370–71].

34. Commons did not see specific cases and theory as separate entities. He reported in his autobiography, with evident pride, how an associate had remarked on his ability to "stick to details and make generalizations at the same time" [Commons 1934b, p. 130].
35. In interviews with Commons's students, Harter learned that many of them apparently had great difficulty obtaining an understanding of their mentor's theories. Indeed, some confessed to having no understanding of them at all! See Harter [1962, pp. 79, 206]. This suggests that Commons probably overstated to a considerable extent the active contribution of his students to the development of his theoretical framework.
36. "The full consequences [of public programs and policies] can never be anticipated before programs are put into effect" [Commons 1950, p. 137].
37. "Property-rights . . . we define as the working rules enforced by the community upon individuals in their transactions respecting that which is or is expected to be scarce" [Commons 1934a, p. 75]. See Ramstad [1986] for the argument that by the term "Reasonable Value," Commons meant outcomes that represent the maximum degree of "fairness" (as he interpreted the meaning of "fair") attainable at any given historical moment without undermining social order.
38. It was Commons's emphasis on the practical application of his ideas ("theory") to individual cases that led Edwin Witte to characterize the approach of Commons and his students as a "practical problems approach" [Witte 1954, p. 133; also cf. n. 28 above].
39. It will be recalled that, for the holist, it is actual cases that serve as the *source* of theoretical constructs; similarly, new cases provide the conceptual problems that precipitate modification of those constructs, and thereby of the theory (pattern model). Commons, therefore, cited cases to illustrate where his (or the courts') conceptions originated, not to illustrate a principle derived through deductive reasoning. Commons's evolutionary approach is another factor that links him to the institutional movement in general. On this point, see D. Hamilton [1970].
40. "I wanted to work on the strategic factors" [Commons 1934b, p. 129].
41. Numerous illustrations had earlier been provided, however, in *Labor and Administration* [Commons 1913, esp. Chap. 21], *Industrial Goodwill* [Commons 1919] and *Principles of Labor Legislation* [Commons 1920, written with John B. Andrews].
42. The reaction of Jacob Viner is representative: "The book is at times incomprehensible to me, and I therefore feel incapable of appraising its merits. Almost every page leaves me lost in a maze of novel terminology or of new, and therefore confusing, applications of established terms" [Viner 1925, p. 711]. See Mitchell [1924] for a review by an established economist who *did* believe himself to discern what Commons was driving at.
43. Thus Commons entitles sections in *Institutional Economics* with headings such as "From Nature to Going Concerns," "From Individuals to Institutions" and "From Natural Rights to Reasonable Value."
44. Commons did not attempt to conceal his awareness that his principal mechanism for bringing "Reasonable Values" into effect—regulatory agencies—were not working as of the early 1940s, to actually promote that end [Commons 1950, pp. 270–77]. He attributed this, not to a deficiency

in his "theory," but to the practice of allowing the appointing authority to select individals "who are favorable to its own economic or political point of view" rather than ensuring through the legislation itself that designated *organizations* be permitted to select their own representatives, as Commons had specified in *Institional Economics* [Commons 1950, p. 275].

45. To illustrate this point, the following history of economic thought texts contain *nothing* of substance regarding Commons's ideas: Blaug [1978], Gill [1963], Ekelund and Hebert [1975], Finkelstein and Thimm [1973], Hunt [1979], Pribham [1983], Rima [1972], and Roll [1974]. Except for Oser and Blanchfield [1975], no modern-day history of economic thought text has an extended discussion of Commons's framework.
46. Commons evidently had a prodigious appetite for work. He reported in his autobiography that he awakened each day at four or five in the morning because "In this way I could study and write three or four hours before breakfast while [the others in my family] were asleep." [Commons 1934b, p. 24]
47. Countless individuals have reported to me, "I once started to read Commons, but, unable to figure out what he was driving at, I moved on to something else." On Commons's behalf, it should be pointed out that his early works—see, in particular, [1894, 1899–1900, 1907, 1913 and 1919]—are models of clarity. The problem was not one of being unable to write clearly.
48. This was the evaluation of A. B. Wolfe, who provided what remains to this day the best summary of Commons's "message" in *Institutional Economics* [Wolfe 1936, p. 206].
49. It must be emphasized that it is *not* being argued that the analysis thereby establishes that Commons's ideas were "correct," or "science," or even "economics."
50. See, for example, Foster [1981], Gordon [1980], Munkirs [1985], and Tool [1979]. Stanfield [1979] uses the term "social economics," but his perspective is, in its general contours, quite similar to that of the "neoinstitutionalists."
51. It is my suspicion that Bush's ingenious effort to formalize such qualitative and evolving concepts as "social values," and then to combine them into concepts such as "ceremonial encapsulation" or into quantitative indexes such as the "index of ceremonial dominance," will ultimately prove sterile. But that would be another article.

References

Agassi, Joseph. 1975. "Institutional Individualism." *British Journal of Sociology* 26 (June): 144–55.

Ayres, Clarence E. 1962. *The Theory of Economic Progress,* 2d edition. New York: Schocken Books.

Blaug, Mark. 1978. *Economic Theory in Retrospect.* 3d edition. New York: Cambridge University Press.

______. 1980. *The Methodology of Economics.* New York: Cambridge University Press.

Bolan, Lawrence A. 1982. *The Foundation of Economic Method.* London: George Allen & Unwin.

Boulding, Kenneth E. 1957. "A New Look at Institutionalism." *American Economic Review* 47 (May): 1–12.

Brady, Robert A. 1943. *Business as a System of Power.* New York: Columbia University Press.

Briefs, Henry W. 1960. *Three Views of Method in Economics.* Washington, D.C.: Georgetown University Press.

Bush, Paul D. 1983. "The Structural Characteristics of a Veblen-Ayres-Foster Defined Institutional Domain." *Journal of Economic Issues* 17 (March): 35–66.

Caldwell, Bruce. 1982. *Beyond Positivism: Economic Methodology in the Twentieth Century.* London: George Allen & Unwin.

Chamberlain, Neil W. 1964. "The Institutional Economics of John R. Commons." In *Institutional Economics: Veblen, Commons and Mitchell Reconsidered,* pp. 63–94. Berkeley and Los Angeles: University of California Press.

Chasse, John D. 1985. "John R. Commons and the Democratic State." Paper delivered to the History of Economics Society, 21 May 1985. Fairfax, Virginia.

Commons, John R. 1893. *The Distribution of Wealth.* Reprints of Economic Classics. New York: Augustus M. Kelley, 1963.

______. 1894. *Social Reform & The Church.* Reprints of Economic Classics. New York: Augustus M. Kelley, 1967.

______. 1899–1900. *A Sociological View of Sovereignty.* Reprints of Economic Classics. Augustus M. Kelley, 1967.

______. 1907. *Proportional Representation.* 2d edition. Reprints of Economic Classics. New York: Augustus M. Kelley, 1967.

______. 1913. *Labor and Administration.* Reprints of Economic Classics. New York: Augustus M. Kelley, 1964.

______. 1919. *Industrial Goodwill.* Reprint edition. New York: Arno Press, Inc., 1969.

______. 1924. *Legal Foundations of Capitalism.* New York: Macmillan.

______. 1934a. *Institutional Economics,* 2 vols. Reprint edition. Madison: University of Wisconsin Press, 1961.

______. 1934b. *Myself.* New York: Macmillan.

______. 1950. *The Economics of Collective Action.* New York: Macmillan.

______ and John B. Andrews. 1920. *Principles of Labor Legislation.* New York: Harper & Brothers Publishers.

Diesing, Paul. 1971. *Patterns of Discovery in the Social Sciences.* Chicago: Aldine-Atherton.

Dray, W. H. 1967. "Holism and Individualism in History and Social Science." In *The Encyclopedia of Philosophy,* vol. 4, ed. Paul Edwards, pp. 53–58. New York: The Macmillan Company and The Free Press.

Dugger, William M. 1979. "The Reform Method of John R. Commons." *Journal of Economic Issues* 13 (June): 369–81.

Dunlop, John T. 1977. "Policy Decisions and Research in Economics and Industrial Relations." *Industrial and Labor Relations Review* 30 (April): 275–82.

Ekelund, Robert B., Jr., and Robert F. Egbert. 1975. *A History of Economic Theory and Method.* New York: McGraw-Hill.

Ely, Richard T. 1938. *Ground Under Our Feet.* New York: Macmillan.

Finkelstein, Joseph and Alfred L. Thimm. 1973. *Economists and Society: The Development of Economic Thought from Aquinas to Keynes.* New York: Harper & Row.

Foster, J. Fagg. 1981. "The Papers of J. Fagg Foster," edited, with introductory notes, by Baldwin Ransom. *Journal of Economic Issues* 15 (December): 857–1007.

Galbraith, John K. 1973. *Economics and the Public Purpose.* Boston: Houghton Mifflin.

Gill, Richard T. 1967. *Evolution of Modern Economics.* Englewood Cliffs, N.J.: Prentice-Hall.

Gonce, Richard O. 1976. "The New Property Rights Approach and Commons's *Legal Foundations of Capitalism.*" *Journal of Economic Issues* 10 (December): 765–97.

Gordon, Wendell. 1980. *Institutional Economics: The Changing System.* Austin: University of Texas Press.

Gruchy, Allan G. 1947. *Modern Economic Thought: The American Contribution.* New York: Prentice-Hall.

Hamilton, David. 1970. *Evolutionary Economics: A Study of Change in Economic Thought.* Albuquerque: University of New Mexico Press.

Hamilton, Walton. 1932. "Institution." In *Encyclopaedia of the Social Sciences,* vol. 3, ed. Edwin R.A. Seligman, pp. 84–89. New York: Macmillan.

Harter, Lafayette G. 1962. *John R. Commons: His Assault on Laissez-Faire.* Corvallis, Ore.: Oregon State University Press.

Hayden, F. Gregory. 1982. "Social Fabric Matrix: From Perspective to Analytical Tool." *Journal of Economic Issues* 16 (September): 637–62.

———. 1983. "Integration of Social Indicators into Holistic Geobased Models." *Journal of Economic Issues* 17 (June): 325–34.

Hunt, E. K. 1979. *History of Economic Thought: A Critical Perspective.* Belmont, Calif: Wadsworth.

Kaplan, Abraham. 1964. *The Conduct of Inquiry: Methodology for Behavioral Science.* San Francisco: Chandler Publishing Co.

Kerr, Clark, et. al. 1960. *Industrialism and Industrial Man.* Cambridge: Harvard University Press.

Mitchell, Wesley C. 1924. "Commons on the Legal Foundations of Capitalism." *American Economic Review* 14 (June): 240–253.

Munkirs, John R. 1985. *The Transformation of American Capitalism: From Competitive Market Structures to Centralized Private Sector Planning.* White Plains, N.Y.: M. E. Sharpe, Inc.

Myrdal, Gunnar. 1968. *Asian Drama.* New York: Pantheon.

Oser, Jacob, and William C. Blanchfield. 1975. *The Evolution of Economic Thought.* 3d edition. New York: Harcourt Brace Jovanovich.

Parsons, Kenneth H. 1950. "John R. Commons' Point of View." *In The Economics of Collective Action,* by John R. Commons, pp. 341–75 (Appendix).

Polanyi, Michael. 1958. *Personal Knowledge: Towards a Post-Critical Philosophy.* Chicago: University of Chicago Press.

Pribham, Karl. 1983. *A History of Economic Reasoning.* Baltimore: Johns Hopkins University Press.

Ramstad, Yngve. 1981. "The Analytical and Methodological Orientations of Institutional Economists: Inferences From the Case of Labor Economics." Ph.D. diss. University of California, Berkeley.

______. 1986. "Toward a Just Price: John R. Commons and Reasonable Value." Department of Economics Working Paper 86–08, University of Rhode Island.

Reed, Mike. 1986. "John R. Commons and Futurity." Paper delivered to the Association for Institutional Thought, 24 April 1986, Reno, Nevada.

Rees, Albert. 1968. "Economics." In *International Encyclopedia of the Social Sciences*, vol. 4, ed. David L. Sills, pp. 472–85. New York: The Macmillan Company and The Free Press.

Rima, I. H. 1972. *Development of Economic Analysis*. Revised edition. Homewood, Ill.: Richard D. Irwin, Inc.

Roll, Eric. 1974. *A History of Economic Thought*. Homewood, Ill.: Richard D. Irwin, Inc.

Rutherford, Malcolm. 1983. "J. R. Commons's Institutional Economics." *Journal of Economic Issues* 17 (September): 721–744.

Seckler, David. 1975. *Thorstein Veblen and the Institutionalists: A Study in the Social Philosophy of Economics*. Boulder, Colo.: Colorado Associated University Press.

Stanfield, J. Ron. 1979. *Economic Thought and Social Change*. Carbondale and Edwardsville, Ill.: Southern Illinois University Press.

Tool, Marc R. 1979. *The Discretionary Economy: A Normative Theory of Political Economy*. Santa Monica, Calif.: Goodyear Publishing Co.

Veblen, Thorstein. 1899. *The Theory of the Leisure Class*. New York: Macmillan.

______. 1904. *The Theory of Business Enterprise*. New York: Charles Scribner's Sons.

______. 1918. *The Instinct of Workmanship and The State of the Industrial Arts*. New York: B. W. Huebsch.

______. 1919. *The Place of Science in Modern Civilization and Other Essays*. New York: B. W. Huebsch.

Viner, Jacob. 1925. "John R. Commons, *Legal Foundations of Capitalism*." *Illinois Law Review* 19 (April): 710–12.

Ward, Benjamin. 1966. "Institutions and Economic Analysis." In *The Structure of Economic Science*, ed. Roy Krupp, pp. 184–200. Englewood Cliffs, N.J.: Prentice-Hall.

______. 1972. *What's Wrong With Economics?* New York: Basic Books.

Wilber, Charles K., with Robert S. Harrison. 1978. "The Methodological Basis of Institutional Economics: Pattern Model, Storytelling, and Holism." *Journal of Economic Issues* 12 (March): 61–90.

Witte, Edwin E. 1954. "Institutional Economics As Seen By An Institutional Economist." *Southern Economic Journal* 21 (October): 131–40.

Wolfe, A. B. 1936. "Institutional Reasonableness and Value." *Philosophical Review* 45 (March): 192–206.

PART III

THE DEVELOPMENT OF ECONOMIC THOUGHT

Introduction to Part III

Although, as Ben B. Seligman argues in this opening paper, economists have tried to separate themselves from philosophical inquiry in an effort to make economics more scientific, they have not been successful. "The most rigidly scientific system in economics still displays its views of how the world *should* function." No matter how the economist "might twist and turn, ethical and other philosophic questions keep intruding into the economist's ratiocinations, behaving like unwanted weekend guests." Economists who have contributed importantly to the historical development of the discipline have had to come to terms, though in widely differing ways, with the need for judging economic behavior. Accordingly, Seligman's basic concern is "to sketch philosophy's relationship to economics and to attempt to outline some of the intellectual questions that are bound to rise." His specific concern is to provide a basis for a less classical consideration of the role of the public sector. In this historical parade of economic paradigms, from Plato and Aristotle to the present day, economists have been compelled to consider matters of justice, to appraise the nature of economic conduct, to take account of policy as reflected in, in succession, Plato's elitism, Aristotle's prudence, Aquinas's teleological ends from natural law, Smith's unresolved tension between sympathy and self-interest, Marshall's utility maximization, Marx's class-based appropriation, and Spencer's natural law survivalist notions. Philosophical notions, embodied in economic paradigms, specified what was proper policy. That the emerging economy might require a viable public sector and normative judgments therein was little discussed. Seligman closes his paper with a call for a new paradigm that "will be achieved by relating a relevant and meaningful theory to practical policy," reflecting a concern "with *political* economics and *social* economics and with the public sector."

Warren S. Gramm opens his paper with a quote from A. L. Macfie: "But successors cannot continue on the level of genius. One aspect of the great man, *probably that which suits later conditions*, is chosen, much of the rest probably rejected" (emphasis added by Gramm). Of nearly 1500 pages in

Adam Smith's two major works, observes Gramm, "only a few lines from several pages of the *Wealth of Nations* are regularly mentioned in orthodox economics texts. These are the statements on division of labor, paradox of value, the invisible hand, and the functions of government. On these grounds, he is known primarily for rationalizing individual self-interest as the necessary strategic medium for promoting economic welfare." It is the burden of Gramm's argument to contend "that a correct understanding of Smith's perspective leads to the opposite conclusion." That is, "his political-economic perspective is seen to be social, not primarily individualistic, and his major contributions to economic analysis involve elucidation of economic growth." Gramm's demonstration of this "selective interpretation" is accomplished through the application of "a general epistemological thesis concerning the selective interpretation of major analytic systems over time." Four elements of this interpretive thesis are: "(1) major contributors and their analytic systems have interrelated normative and positive elements; (2) in its initial formulation, the positive analytic content of the new system is directly related to and supportive of its normative element; (3) there then occurs a rebalancing of the relative weight of the positive and normative elements; and (4) in this process the system undergoes a transformation in which ingredients most compatible with the existing power structure come to be regarded as the essence of the system. An "apologetic transformation" turns Smith's social orientation into a defense of the "hyper-individualism of contemporary orthodoxy," when, in fact, it could and should provide insights for a contemporary shift to a social or institutionalist economics perspective.

The contribution of Walter C. Neale to this anthology offers an argument that "derives from the histories of political philosophy and economic thought and from ideas garnered from linguistics." His basic proposition is that the chasm-wide distinction between an institutional economist and a standard, neoclassical economist "is fundamentally philosophical rather than ideological or methodological." Standard theorists "follow in the tradition of the philosophers of natural law;" the strain is observable "from Locke on through Smith and the classical economists (including Marx), the neoclassical economists, the Keynesians, and the monetarists." This natural law tradition "assumes that there is a set of rules governing all human action and interaction . . . that these rules are universal . . . that they are very limited in number," and that "the rules can be stated in a logically precise way." Given claims of universality and precision, they "happily derive a great many conclusions about policy, about welfare, and especially about what people are really doing." Locke even contributed a "natural ethic" derived from natural law. Institutionalists, as Neale explains in detail, wholly reject the natural law formulations and implications deduced therefrom, including the "natural ethics." But Neale's special contribution here is to demonstrate that, through an analysis of language structure and usage, one can expose "the elements of natural law implicit in standard economics." Contending, for example, that meaning depends upon context, Neale discusses cases "where economists have asked the wrong questions and tried to argue the impossible because they have violated some of language's rules for meaning." In sum, Neale demonstrates that "the absence of contexts restricting the meaning of words helps to explain why some primary concepts in economics—utility and choice, for instance . . . are incurably flawed by universalizing in violation of language's rules;" that "some explanations in standard economics are incurably flawed by confusing grammatical rules with what goes on 'out there' in the world of human action;" and that "these flaws have reinforced the tendency for elements of the philosophy of natural law to continue to permeate economic thought." Institutional economists, fortunately, have been, and are, relatively free of these flaws. They emphasize "verbing" in preference to "nouning," because their fundamental tenets of institutionalism are philosophically processual.

Building in part on Neale's contribution, Richard G. Fritz and Judy M. Fritz continue the analysis of the import of language systems on the development of economic thought, especially in this century. More pointedly, the purpose of their article is to explore "the impact of linguistic structure . . . on the theory and methods of economic science." "Linguistic studies have revealed the relation of language to perception, thought, and behavior. Incorporated into the structure of our unconscious, a language acts as a filter, conditioning not only what we are able to think or say but also what we are able to see." "When," they continue, "the language used in communicating social, political, and economic ideas changes" for example, from verbal to mathematical, the "theoretical structure of the discipline in question"—here, economics—can be affected. These differing language structures "may inhibit progress in the evolution of economic thought as a result of the reduction in phenomena to which the knowledge is applied." Moreover, the use of the symbolic linguistic structure of mathematics masks . . . the ideology of the author, as well as social meanings unconsciously marked in the structures of the text." In consequence, versions of standard economic theory may falsely be promoted as "value-free scientific inquiry." Moreover, in a historical context, the Fritzs show that "the natural language system of the classical economists represented a different set of meta-assumptions (or methodological priors), compared to the symbolic language system of the marginalist economists." Transforming "mental models" into "working models" of the disciple "led to differences in policy conclusions." They conclude with an analytic defense of the linguistic structure employed by institutionalists. This model is based on endogenous explanations and "parallels the refutationists' insistence on causal explanations." It provides "increasing objectivity through refutability. Institutionalists have a strict syntax and structure." The linguistic systems of institutionalists and system dynamics theorists are quite similar; a future synthesis is conceivable.

13

Philosophic Perspectives in Economic Thought

Ben B. Seligman

Seeking a purely scientific study of income and wealth, the economist became the first of the social scientists to abandon philosophy. Yet try as he might, he could never completely sever his intellectual roots in philosophic discourse, for even the most rigidly scientific system in ecomonics still displays its views of how the world *should* function. For the economist is always "absorbed in the behavior of [his] fellow man, first as he created worldly wealth, and then as he trod on the toes of his neighbor to gain a share of it"[1] However, he might twist and turn, ethical and other philosophic questions keep intruding into the economist's ratiocinations, behaving quite like unwanted week-end guests.

Ancient writers did not mind such intrusions: indeed, they were most welcome, for ethics supplied the major criteria for judging economic behavior. Economics could be understood only in the context of social, political, ritualistic, moral, and even aesthetic considerations.[2] Kinship relations and status governed exchange, and social norms determined the nature of lending and whatever investment may be said to have existed. Of course, I refer to pre-capitalist times when society was less complicated, less interdependent, and when markets — not yet *the* market — reflected direct personal relationships more than they now do.[3]

But as the economy became more complex, shifting from an agrarian base to an industrial one, a new model or paradigm was needed to grasp what was taking place. Here I borrow T. S. Kuhn's useful concept.[4] It may be recalled that Kuhn spoke of a paradigm as a shared set of rules and standards for the conduct of scientific research. Such rules made sense of the great mass of facts that an investigator had to confront and they gained acceptance because they were more successful than other rules in solving pressing and acute problems. Kuhn's classic example is the displacement of the Ptolemaic system of astronomy by Copernicus in the 16th century.

Employing a model like Kuhn's, it would not be difficult to demonstrate that pre-18th century economic doctrine gradually became "Ptolemaic" in its incapacity to deal with newly evolving fact. Adam Smith was so well received — even eagerly awaited — because he offered in place of earlier theory a new conception that seemed to exhibit a Copernican power to explain the wealth of nations. It was a new paradigm in economics that successfully incorporated new facts into its model and gave economists new rules for research. Though challenged later by Karl Marx and others, the classical paradigm appeared invulnerable, especially after it was buttressed by the Austrians and by such "analysts" as Cournot, Walras, Jevons, Pareto and Wicksell.[5] It seemed that their economic analyses most effectively and realistically described what occurred in the market and that their theories suggested an extraordinary capacity to predict the most likely outcome of any course of action. These theories were declared valid because they could ingest the universe of economic fact. Quite simply, the economic order functioned autonomously once the Prime Mover had acted. A kindly providence insured corroboration everlasting for the lucubrations of the economist.

But, as Adolph Lowe has recently demonstrated, Classicism and its near-cousins began to be discomfited by facts that failed to meet the standards of 19th century economic paradigms.[6] Competition underwent significant alteration; unemployment interfered with the circular flow of income; and the automaticity that the economist demanded was not always manifested. Disarray in the real world led to disarray in economic theory, reluctantly compelling the economist to concede that the world of fact did not "obey" the rules of those elegant and internally consistent models he was wont to construct.

The paradigm had to be altered. Increasing disarray meant that economic institutions and their behavior remained unexplained, an intolerable scientific situation for many, impelling them to voice a certain measure of dissent. Norms of action, purpose, and even prescription — decisive elements in pre-classical theory — once again began to merit attention. Sectors of the economy that had received relatively short shrift in classical doctrine — largely the public sector — assumed more weight, for it became increasingly clear that if theory was to be meaningful, it would have to explain their functioning. And the more one became concerned with these troublesome sectors, the greater the need for philosophy to define standards of economic behavior and social purpose.

Hence, it would seem most appropriate at this meeting to sketch philosophy's relationship to economics and to attempt to outline some of the intellectual questions that are bound to arise. This may be done either historically, that is, vertically, or in terms of problems, or horizontally. My own taste in the matter accords with the historical approach. However, whatever method is adopted, the exploration must be undertaken, else what we seek to accomplish in the public sector will remain largely ill-defined. We are confronted by a society in which scarcity as a goad to achievement need not be of as great moment as it once was; in which producers long ago decided to replace rivalry with gentlemanly co-operation; where consumers are mercilessly cuckoldized; where the welfare state can, if it only so desired, redistribute the blessings of affluence; where the Puritan ethic is now a quaint standard of behavior; and where growth, regardless of cost, is deemed to be a proper requirement for reaching a state of grace. Modern technology has reduced the fluidity of capital and labor to a mere trickle, and the inflexibility of the economy forces decision-makers, whether they like it or not, to peer into that famous glass through which one sees only darkly. All we really know is that we live in a new economy blessed, or cursed, (depending on when and where one has learned his economics) with an immense public sector. New facts are continuously generated and these can only be absorbed in a new paradigm in economics. One ingredient of that paradigm must be philosophy.

PLATO, ARISTOTLE AND SOCIETY

If I return to Plato and Aristotle for a moment, I do so for illustrative purposes and to bolster my case. The texture of their society — Ancient Greece — compressed an intricate web of social relationships in which exchange, risk-taking, and competition were but minor strands. Economic action was conditioned by higher social needs and requirements. Markets were primarily local (foreign trade was governed by state treaties) and price was often established by convention. It was expected that the rule of equivalency would prevail which in most cases satisfied the parties in a transaction.

By Plato's day, this archaic society was undergoing severe stress. Men paid less and less attention to social needs, as they crowded into cities seeking riches. For many the sole aim in life became an unceasing quest for wealth. The philosophers sought in vain for incorruptible standards of behavior.[7] It was not surprising that one of Plato's major concerns should focus on the decay of the Greek polis. The Athens of his own lifetime bore witness to an oppressive oligarchy, succeeded by a democracy that then destroyed his beloved Socrates. The descent into a raging individualism constituted for Plato retrogression and the destruction of social unity and order. He saw a corrupt society and was revolted.[8]

Plato concluded that mortal men could not prevent community collapse, a contingency in which the gods would simply leave mankind to its own stupidities. If there was to be a renascence, its fundamental elements would have to be situated in the community: the individual was hopeless. And inspiration would have to come from a recent past that had been peaceable and had been governed by moral standards that transcended the judgment of ordinary men.[9] As a consequence, Plato's social thought — and, by implication, his economic ideas — rejected the competitive struggle for gain and all that accompanied it.

None of this suggests that economics as we know it today can be discovered in Plato, or for that matter in any of the Greek philosophers (except for some hints in Aristotle). Economics was embedded in broad social and philosophical concerns emphasizing ethics and politics. Thus, insofar as one can detect any economic thinking at all in ancient Greece, it reflected certain relationships among men rather than things. Even Aristotle's model of exchange involved primarily transactions among parties of disparate skill, with the goods they offered being essentially vehicles of "justice".[10] But if justice was to be achieved, then private relationships were to be governed by the same ethical precepts that held for the community. The public and the private were virtually identical.[11]

As elements of his political philosophy, Plato's economic ideas were more than just guides to household management — they were intended to help in the proper functioning of the polis. If, as some would have us believe, the *Republic* and *Laws* described a planned society, such planning surely must have sought to enhance what was valuable in life.[12] It was meant to produce a good and virtuous existence, one that the polis could insure only by carefully balancing society's contending forces. Hedonism as a spring to action was rejected; if pains and pleasures were indeed expressions of human psychology, they would have to be manipulated and controlled by the guardians.[13]

Whatever else there may be in Plato, we must recognize his insistent demand for justice. And its attainment had to start in the individual soul, for only then would it be possible for the guardians to move toward the harmonious balance that a properly constituted society should reflect. And, as an essential element in the political viability of the polis, each member of society was expected to perform his specialized tasks in careful, authentic, and rational manner.[14]

A theory of exchange was a minor element in Greek thought. Exchange itself was but begrudgingly acknowledged by the philosophers and was to be rigidly controlled, for the market place could only lead to excess and corruption. Plato wanted a "good" human nature, unsullied by the hurly-burly of the agora. And the order of his perfect society was to stem from inherited tradition. Alas, like all utopias, of which his was perhaps the first, it was but a dream filled with the shadows of the past.

Aristotle was more practical-minded. Though disturbed as much as Plato was by the decaying moral fibre of civilization, he nevertheless recognized the constraints that institutions imposed on individual behavior: ethics had to consider the potentialities of men living in a setting of practical politics.[15] Virtue was not a natural acquisition, but had to be inculcated through education. A major facet of virtue was the exercise of prudence, which dictated the pursuit of a happy mean. For Aristotle this was the mean of the middle class, lending to the state the sort of stability necessary to the good society. Comprised of equals, the middle class could supply a requisite moderation; it was not overly ambitious; and its actions were molded by the prudence and rationality of household management.[16]

Attached to Aristotle's prudence and moderation was a glimmering recognition of the market. Why else would he have gone to such pains to explicate the nature of exchange, which it seemed was increasingly important in the determination of justice? Improper pricing could create an immoral situation, violating justice by its distortion of reciprocity. A just exchange, based on an equality of the ratios involved, was one way of relating natural forces to each other and maintaining social equilibrium. Such were some of the Aristolian dicta on economics; and they exerted an important influence on men's minds well into the 18th century. But they failed because they attempted to straddle two camps — the traditional concern with the time honored values of the polis and the emerging "rationality" of the market.[17]

Implicit in this philosophy was a concern with nature. Knowing nature made it conceivable that man might escape the pain engendered by human wants. With Stoics and precepts of nature dictated a turn to man's inner soul, and consequently, a rejection of the turbulence of the market place. It was argued that such rejection meant accomodating oneself to the laws of nature. Yet in later centuries the same laws of nature would be transformed to support the market and convert its activities into natural pursuits. History's irony would make virtue an ingredient of trade and business perfection a personal attribute to be assiduously cultivated, thus giving a quite different twist to the concept of natural law.

As we know, the complete identification of virtue with trade was not accomplished until the Reformation. In the meantime, it was necessary to transform the idea of natural law so that it might offer a suitable setting for the new paradigm that was to come. With Cicero, for example, the ethics of natural law was divorced from the ethics of economics, so that it was possible to preach high minded morality while doing whatever one wanted to in economic matters. He had no difficulty in making the distinction. In essence, Roman philosophy restricted the scope of ethical inquiry, refusing to examine behavior in the market because it was so undignified, thereby denying to economics a legitimate place in the spectrum of philosophical questions. It was a perverse act that was to be repeated two millennia later when economists decided that it was undignified to flirt with philosophy.

CANONISTS AND SCHOLASTICS

Yet the tradition of natural law persisted and in the Middle Ages was strengthened by Canonist and Scholastic writers. To scholars of the time the old paradigm, modified by the Christian faith, still seemed useful. The traditions of the ancient world were kept alive, as the Church became the primary, if not the only, transmitter of culture.[18] And while over the decades philosophy followed a line of development from the faith of St. Augustine to the formal doctrine of Peter Lombard to the divine reason of Aquinas, the underlying theme and reliance on natural law remained untouched. For example, Gratian's 12th century codification of court decisions, theological commentaries, and papal pronouncements relied on natural law as a unifying moral principle.

Ethical standards were derived from the law of nature and man naturally tended to know what was good. However, the meaning of these ideas was soon diffused, so that it became unclear whether the notion of the natural was meant to be applied to man's origin or to his destiny. One thing was evident: behavior had to be shaped by something more general than the practical needs of man. Its source lay in the demands of a Supreme Ruler whose will was to be obeyed once perceived. As the world consisted of things placed in it by the Supreme Ruler, one learned what to do simply by observing how things moved. Yet following nature did not always provide suitable guides to conduct, resulting in some philosophic confusion.

Seemingly the confusion was clarified by St. Thomas Aquinas. By fusing the principle of "following nature" with precepts derived from reason, he made natural law once again palatable. The teleological ends of existence, which were inherent in nature, could be accepted by all men, he argued. Hence, one could speak of certain social functions, or allude to higher levels of development as natural.[19] The implications of such thinking for economics were not exposed until many decades later when Thorstein Veblen cast a mordant eye on the concept of the natural. [20] The natural law approach, argued Veblen, merely issued in a set of logically consistent propositions what had little to do with what went on in the real world. It led to the use of conjectural history, a belief in an ideal state, and, eventually, to apologetics.

But we move too rapidly. May I once more emphasize that we are wrestling here with changing paradigms in social analysis. Even in philosophy the paradigms were shifting. The Thomistic system was seriously questioned by Duns Scotus who, in effect, separated theology from philosophy. Roger Bacon avoided appeals to authority, preferring rather to study phenomena directly. With William of Occam, theology could still rely on scripture, but science required a different order of inquiry. Concepts became perceptions or symbols of objects in the external world, making science a matter of ordering concepts. Here one observes the beginnings of the positivism of a later era. In any case, the medieval paradigm was no longer useful for a Europe eager to move on to new achievements. Scholasticism, which had sought to infuse a sense of ethics into the practices of the market, urged rules of conduct that were inappropriate for a rising capitalism. For example, the usury doctrine, though continually modified, could not survive. In the

16th century, merchants were sufficiently irritated to evade it with strategems; bu by the 18th century no one paid much attention to its proscriptions.[21]

Yet throughout these shifting emphases, the theme of natural law remained a hardy one. It told men that ethical goals could be reached through the faculty of reason, enabling men to apprehend what was good; and what was good now shifted from the social to the individual. The Scottish moral philosophers, borrowing from Hugo Grotius and Samuel Pufendorf, incorporated natural law in its new guise into their system of thought; later it became an integral element of Anglo-Saxon economics as founded by Adam Smith.[22]

Thus, by the 18th century natural law had been given a reverse twist, one that supported individualistic trends in moral philosophy and in economics. Individuals became the ultimate units of account in human relationships and all social action was explained as the sum of their actions. Whether the philosopher argued from benevolence or from self-interest, it was the individual who was the focus of attention. Economic discussion began with atomistic assumptions, making it possible for self-interest to become the fundamental moral principle

The connections between individuals, however established, were all part of nature, for the way in which one person accommodated himself to another had been set forth in the Great Design: they were part of the rational order of nature, timeless and immutable. Yet all this was a flexible enough philosophical system, employed to justify various and sundry political arrangements, even underpinning the revolutionary assertion of the rights of man.

Yet some questions were raised. Montesquieu, in his *Spirit of the Laws* thought that institutions were relative to the needs of those they presumably served. David Hume gravely doubted the efficacy of natural law rationalism[23] and such writers as the Earl of Shaftesbury and Frances Hutcheson preferred an appeal to benevolence rather than self-interest as a basis for human relationships. Indeed, Hume's "principle of communication", according to which human association sustained social unity, suggested the abandonment of individualism as an ethical precept.

ADAM SMITH: BENEVOLENCE OR SYMPATHY?

These developments reach their climax in Adam Smith. Yet with Smith there seems to appear an unresolved tension between benevolence or sympathy, and self-interest. The apparent clash was striking enough for some scholars to speak of the problem of Adam Smith.[24] *The Theory of Moral Sentiments* employed the idea of sympathy, defined as the capacity of a person to enter into another's situation and thus establish accord with him, an idea that crops up in modern phenomenology. The *Wealth of Nations,* however, is based on self-interest as the motive force in social behavior. In the *Moral Sentiments* one detects the influence of Shaftesbury and Hutcheson; in the *Wealth of Nations* it is the notorious Bernard de Mandeville who provides the inspiration. One is a vindication of certain spiritual values; the other, an assertion that social ends are attained only through the unintended consequences of self-interest.

But we must recall that Smith thought of spiritual value as a compound of prudence, justice, and benevolence. If prudence is a derivative of rational self-interest set within the constraints imposed by justice and benevolence, then the clash between the earlier and later Smith evaporates, for self-interest would be implied by man's primary sentiments.[25] Hence, it was not too much of a task for those who followed Smith to maintain that his system was consistent: they could discourse on an economic man governed by certain moral sentiments in which those defined by criteria of self-interest did not clash too seriously with a concern for the common weal.

And it all stemmed from nature. The social order was "admirably contrived to serve all needs of the individuals who compose it. . ."[26] Whenever individuals pursued their own aims they contributed to the social order. The theory revealed not only a sublime faith in the benign order of the universe, but it was as well a paradigm that suited quite satisfactorily the needs of a rising middle class and its political and economic demands. Natural law was thus commercialized, focussing on market transactions. Its substance was to specify the rules of behavior among men of means.

English economic success was thus vindicated by a system of natural law that was as inviolable as the laws of Newtonian physics. Hobbes might view society as a war of all against all, necessitating the imposition of a social compact, but Locke knew that men were social by nature, and that their individual rights were insured by natural law. There was no need, therefore, for a strong central government: the only proper function of the state was to secure middle class claims. And when the state failed to protect that most natural of all rights, property, then a revolution was permissable — provided it was a middle class revolution.

But the emphases of paradigms do change, especially when circumstances alter. By the end of the 18th century some shift could be detected. With Jeremy Bentham, for example, the discussion moved from natural law to utility. Bentham weighed institutions by a pragmatic test and was ready to discard those that failed. The mainspring of action was the pleasure-pain nexus, a criterion that led to the sum of individual happiness as the prime social good. Happiness for the greatest number became the touchstone of social ethics and the guiding principle of economic behavior. It is a concept that is still persuasive enough to move many people, though we now know that human motives are infinitely more complex than any "net" sum of pleasures and pains would indicate.

But the concept of happiness could be used to support general rights, lending a tone of humanitarianism to economic theory. A vague yearning for amelioration gradually began to manifest itself in classical writings: Alfred Marshall, you may recall, hoped that knowledge and progress would rid the world of poverty and ignorance.[27] Philosophers and economists began to praise the universality of toleration and it was anticipated that a gentle spirit of accommodation would soon transcend national boundaries. Progress became a natural phenomenon, inherent in society, always moving upward in ascending spirals, and totally self-sufficient. Writers were blissfully unaware that such luminous optimism represented little more than a class-centered doctrine rooted in the belief that middle class careers always rise higher and higher. They made history predictable and beneficient and men became happy subjects of a kindly fate.

However, such thinking did not diminish the stress on the individual, even though there might be a few occasions when it might be employed to support state action. The individual was still the best judge of his own interest. While Adam Smith might have rejected utility, preferring the sentiment of sympathy as a way of explaining social experience, his epigones had no difficulty in assimilating the new utilitarianism into their justification of the sort of economy they preferred. Free trade and the "spontaneous identification of interests" were all they required; even the infrequent action of government could now be discarded.[28]

In essence, post-Smithian writers stressed standards of usefulness as the basis of esteem. What a man did, rather than his inheritance, became the criterion of judgment. The stress on individual achievement was crystal clear. And as rewards were apportioned according to individual contributions, economic success became the wedge that the bourgeoisie could employ to gain a place in society, establish its identity, and eventually become the first order in the polity. As all citizens were deemed equal and endowed with the same natural rights, the privileges of older ruling groups could be challenged. Natural rights now emanated from the market. It was not enough that a man might express high ethical intentions: that only supplied him with the garb of a saint. It was economic results that counted, results that flowed from a rational evaluation of actions in the market. Natural law was thus wedded to individual performance.[29]

There was a reaction, of course, especially on the Continent. So mechanical an individualism seemed repugnant, for it missed the emotional side of man and ignored the true richness of the human personality. Everything that man felt and witnessed testified to the complexity of experience. Man had ideals and there had to be a way of expressing them. The sort of economics that had been developed in England, with its mechanistic precision, offended the sensibilities of Continental critics, especially in Germany. Such was the Romantic protest, one that was flexible enough to support religion, the soul of man, revolution—and political reaction.[30] While it had some value, this paradigm was unacceptable to most reasonable men. It was far too redolent of youthful *weltschmerz* to be useful for scientific analysis.

MARXISM AS A UNIFIED ORGANON

Yet there was a more useful approach to economic problems that had its origins on the Continent to which attention must be paid, much as Anglo-Saxon economists might not want to. I refer, of course, to the rough, grand system developed by Karl Marx.[31] As a unified organon Marxism, as we know, had its roots in German philosophy, French utopian socialism, and English economics. As such, it became not only an economic theory, but a philosophy of history, a sociology, and a prescription for politics. It was, above all, a *weltanschauung,* a world outlook, which recognized change, not as the progressive blandness of the Victorian era, but rather change through strife.

Only when standard economics began to acknowledge the growth of monopoly and the possibility of such disturbing phenomena as unemployment did the contempt for Marx begin to dissolve. More and more, social scientists began to acknowledge that his effort to look at the economic system in its totality was relevant to the problems at hand. They noted that Marx had tried to work out carefully and analytically the relationships between the various social and economic components. He even set up "models", so dear to the hearts of modern theorists, and dealt with technology, underconsumption, unemployment, and the concentration of capital. These were big questions and Marx sought to supply the big answer. That he was not always able to come up with the right one is beside the point. The fact is that he was a serious thinker who dealt with serious problems. That so many of his supposed intellectual descendants assert all the Marxian phrases as absolute truth is merely sad, for this reveals them to be precisely the sort of fools that Marx abhorred.

Whatever else we may wish to say about Marx's economics, I submit that the problems of circulation and accumulation as he explored them were perhaps the most spectacular parts of the doctrine, for they represented in a fundamental way a theory of economic development. The central theme of *Das Kapital* was precisely what the title implied — man-made means of production and the social relations that governed their use. Since the latter were rooted in the wage relationship, capital had to be defined by alienation from tools and ownership of property. Workers not only were legally free but also free from the means of production. And because of this, capital began to assume a monopolistic aspect, for it was the capitalist who, upon hiring the means of production, came into possession of the entire product which he then distributed to the factors of production. The Marxian schema, then, may be visualized as a flow analysis of income, one of the most analytically effective ones in the history of economics.

Accumulation and growth were central, for this was the locus of all fundamental contradictions of the capitalist order. Involved in this process was the fall in the rate of profit and the periodic eruption of economic crisis. And superimposed on all this was group conflict, class consciousness, and the whole sociology of revolution — the political elements in the story which have served, unfortunately, to obscure the economic analysis. Basically, the economic problem was to discover how the continuous reduction of labor requirements affected accumulation and the changing structure of capitalism. English history provided Marx with many striking illustrations of this inexorable process.

Marx's analysis of accumulation and growth was internal to the economic order and did not require any outside stimulus to get it going. This is the basic message of his theory, one that is frequently overlooked. Further, the values of Marx may be seen in his emphasis on technology and the central role of the capitalist. Stability could be attained only if economic growth was properly balanced between the producers' and consumers' sectors of the economy — an unlikely contingency by virtue of capitalism's essential nature. And the under scoring of political power was an element that other economists might have acknowledged a good deal sooner than they did.

We must agree with Schumpeter when he said that Marx's economic ideas could not be easily dismissed. Despite the enormous handicaps under which Marx worked, he was able to carve out a significant body of theory. The errors and false trails notwithstanding his ideas cannot be blithely ignored, as is all too often done, for their numerous indights can provide useful leads to an understanding of the real function of the economy.

A PARADIGM HARSHLY REJECTED

But such a paradigm was harshly rejected; there were errors in it, and perhaps more important, it threatened the status quo. It seemed that ideas of organic growth, as suggested by the theory of evolution, would be a more effective counter weight to the old mechanistic models. Applied to the world of man, growth, of course, implied the use of foresight to counteract social entropy.[32] But it also meant a continual climb to perfection. The blatant Hegelianism, the reach for political virtue displayed in such a concept was challenged by Darwin's theory of evolution which was later applied to economics with brutal precision by Veblen. For all evolution could investigate were the cumulative effects of increments of change. The idea of wholesome progress really had no place in it. Change might mean advance: it might mean retrogression.

Futher, by responding so enthusiastically, and so erroneously, to the theory of evolution, economists, and other social scientists, often manifested an invidious egocentricity. The later stages of the process were always preferable; that which came earlier was depreiated as "primitive". Yet to judge by present day experience, it is difficult to say for certain that one society, or one economic system, is superior to another.[33] To assert such superiority, and to base it on a movement toward perfection, simply provides new trappings for ancient natural law.

Evolution is continuity, a process of becoming, in which society is alway confronted by an assortment of alternatives. Often the direction of change is a matter of happenstance: often that direction leads into a blind alley. Who is to say that now with our technology, our politics, and our environment, we are not at the entrance to one of those blind alleys, leading to the same evolutionary impasse that long ago confronted the dinosaur and the saber-toothed tiger?

But let us leave these flights of morbid fancy and shift to a brief consideration of the social uses to which evolutionary theory has been put. It seemed inevitable that a victorious middle class would demand an ideology that would serve also as a paradigm for its conception of the good society. The philosophy — and the economics — of natural law, laissez faire, and individualism performed that function most satisfactorily. For example, the ideas of Herbert Spencer, adopted with great alacrity especially by the American middle class, rejected aid to certain groups in the polity as an outright desecration of the law of nature and of laissez faire. Spencer's views have been rightly described as anarchy plus the cop on the beat.[34]

Spencer's brand of Social Darwinism, published some years before Darwin's *Origin of the Species,* was a compound of the Puritan ethic and crude Malthusianism. It produced some rather odd notions of freedom and the precept that only the fittest will survive. The principles were divine in origin, reflecting little more than elementary justice. The government was not to be trusted: the only good legislature was the one not in session. The state had no business educating the young, carrying the mails, minting the currency, providing charity, regulating industry, operating a lighthouse, improving sanitation, or being concerned with outbreaks of the plague. (Curiously, there are some academic centers that still give voice to these quaint ideas.) If nature functioned unimpeded, it would expel those lacking merit. The state should not come between man and his suffering, Spencer seemed to say. His philosophy ignored man's role as a social being, concentrating only on his economic performance. It was a philosophy for those who knew no other.

So optimistic a people as Americans quite readily digested Spencerian perorations on unceasing progress and how to achieve it. The implied hint that Americans would eventually march to domination over others was most palatable. Individualism and self-interest became a positive good. Trade unionism was a foolish venture, for workers had merely to surrender to the predestination of natural law without a murmer. And economists, notably John Bates Clark, proved beyond doubt that the economy rewarded everybody justly.

The middle class grasped this philosophy to its bosom in all its vulgarity. It was quite comfortable with so self-serving a paradigm. It enjoyed the assurance that success was to be attributed to simple virtues and that the poor lacked its qualities of heart and mind. The idea that those who survived the economic jungle were indeed the fittest was an agreeable piece of self-congratulation sustained by the pieties of political economy. Indeed, for some members of the middle class economics was good because it "hardened men's hearts".

MARGINALISM AND THE SOCIAL CONTEXT

Thus economic science offered few genuinely new ideas to explain what was happening, nor was it able to predict the course of events. Most writers, particularly those in the academy, were retailing the same brand of natural law that had been advanced a hundred years before.[35] There were modifications and changes in economic theory, to be sure: marginalism, propounded by Jevons and the Austrian school of economists around 1870, was absorbed into the text books by the turn of the century;[36] Alfred Marshall stressed concepts of elasticity and time; and Leon Walras developed an elegant model that was attractive to those who wished to explain economic action with but a few principles. But I should contend that from a philosophic standpoint very little had been added. I shall pass over the utilitarianism still evident in many writers, the latter day positivism of Milton Friedman, the apodictic or apriorism of Ludwig von Mises, the moment-in-being of G. L. S. Shackle and the operationalism of Paul Samuelson. I regret that time does not allow a more detailed discussion of these writers, for their paradigms do imply, as much as they might deny it, prescriptive models. Let us rather focus on two other contemporary economists — Frank H. Knight and Friedrich A. Hayek.

I have chosen them, not only because they are important economists, but because they exhibit a greater awareness of philosophic foundations than most. Indeed, in Knight's case, a thorough grounding in philosophy and theology makes him a formidable adversary. Yet his approach to the relationship of philosophy to economics has been somewhat indecisive. Initially, he restricted economics to supposedly objective data; later, he thought that these data had to be related to a broader metasystem from which they derived their characteristic shape.

But, I should argue, there was not much advance in Knight's formulations over Adam Smith, for ultimately he was compelled to resort to some conception of natural law. Individualism was still a fundamental precept, making Knight's version of the economic process little more than a subtle restatement of 18th century philosophy. Indeed, he has argued that man is social because he pursues individual interests.[37] Human society is to be distinguished from an anthill he says, because it presents problems to man as an individual, making him a "motivated" person. Thus Knight has endeavored to carry on his analysis on two levels, but without success. For if there is purpose in action, as he has argued, then it must be recognized that individual purpose and social purpose are frequently at odds with each other. When this happens, as it so often does in our own time, then a paradigm that incorporates such a contrast should specify modes of reconciliation. Unfortunately, in Knight's paradigm the reconciliation moves easily toward the individual since his "social purpose" is little more than a mask for what the latter seeks. That hardly represents a gain over Adam Smith.

The consequence is indecision, an indecision that is self-defeating. In order to pass judgment on matters of economic policy, for example, such judgments must be based on "defensible" criteria of values, that is, on ideals. But these, according to Knight, are not economics, which is "science" and cannot be related to arguments on goals and ends.[38] Thus, consideration of what are matters of science and what are matters of philosophy are kept apart, although he had earlier conceded that the economic analysis of wants could proceed from the level of wants to an investigation of the ethical framework of wants.

Should economics, then, be pure analysis or should it be set within a broader framework of institutional description? Knight cannot decide: on the one hand individual economic behavior is a factitious notion because such behavior is part of the total cultural environment; on the other, scientific economics studies the behavior of abstract atomistic units.[39] Such a safe position may be a desirable one for those who wish to be traditionalists when arguing with institutionalists and at the same time rip-roaring institutionalists when confronting a traditionalists, but that it would enable us to know where we are headed is dubious.

If economic behavior is embedded in culture — a truism that needs frequent iteration — and if culture is shaped by those who comprise it, then social change is possible. Thus Knight's paradigm is inconsistent and Ptolemaic. Moreover, his violent attack on John Dewey's instrumentalism, which did stress the need for change, can be interpreted only as a preference for the purportedly scientific side of economics, that rooted in the philosophy of individualism.

While Knight recognizes that some limitations on the individual may be necessary, in reality he would go no further than Herbert Spencer.[40] Thus the instrumentalities of society are precluded from dealing with what are fundamental social problems. In the modern context this invites disaster. The social problems I have in mind are precisely those we have been discussing at these sessions — the city, its environment, its transportation, its people, and a host of others. To appeal to "law and order" — in the philosophic sense — is to appeal to archaic notions of what is natural, offering only a set of homilies that would do justice to Dr. Pangloss.

The alternative to this dilemma is to avoid any consideration of the social. This is the path taken by Hayek and it leads to odd destinations. As I have remarked elsewhere, Hayek's psychological studies offer a good starting point for an examination of his philosophical biases.[41] For Hayek, perception, located in the individual nervous system, is the basis of mental constructs, so that meaning and experience represent nothing more than ordered perception. Mind is but a sequence of events unrelated to external environment; thus, one can never really know objective reality. Social analysis is not possible, according to Hayek, for all that mind can do is to seek new relationships between mental constructs. But Hayek has evaded the problem of intersubjectivity, the connection of one mind to another, and thereby has converted economics into nothing more than a heterogeneous collection of disembodied spirits who float past each other like amoeba on the water's surface.

Investigations of what is real are dismissed by Hayek as forms of "scientism", an ostensibly fatal mode of thinking that employs materialism in a patently unsuccessful attempt to discover the nature of human action. Accordingly, such concepts as "society" or "capitalism" are presumably unamenable to analytic treatment. With mental constructs the only proper basis for analysis, Hayek thus reduces social science to sense perception, and nothing else, thereby evading the possibility that these mental constructs might establish connections between human beings. Quite simply, he avoids the now familiar idea of intersubjectivity.[42] If people classify experiences in the same ways — about as far as Hayek allows himself to go — how do they learn these common patterns? There is no answer.

Facts become mere opinions, argues Hayek, and knowledge

offers no guide to action, since what we know exists in incomplete form, dispersed among many minds. Yet for Hayek even such bits-and-pieces knowledge somehow produces order. Somehow social facts arise Phoenix-like out of scattered items of knowledge. Somehow Adam Smith's providential hand has sneaked in the back door. And all this has taken place without connectibility and without intersubjectivity. But surely, the latter require antecedent study if we are to grasp the nature of social and economic action.

Hayek's philosophy, so crucial to his economics, denies that ideas and consciousness are functions of social involvement, which is itself firmly planted in intersubjectivity. Only if this relationship is accepted, does it become possible to investigate ideas and their situations. These situations are not artificial; they are rather genuine settings for weighing, evaluating, accepting, or rejecting ideas. We communicate ideas and aspirations and fears because we function in a social context. These are important areas of exploration, if we are to learn why man behaves as he does.

THE SOCIAL DIMENSION OF MEANING

Economics is not exempt from this task of exploration. Economics is not merely a set of propositions tautologically derived from a priori concepts. Meaning has a social dimension that arises only in the context of human connectibility. Thus institutional abstractions such as capitalism can be analysed, permitting an understanding of division of labor, income, and other categories of analysis without always resorting to the putative psychology of individuals. Consequently, capitalism implies certain sociological and economic performances that together condition — and illumine — the behavior of individuals.

I should argue, therefore, that all the paradigms offered to date by received economics no longer serve our needs. Decisions once made by individuals have been transferred to groups, organizations, governments. The parameters of action, to employ a favorite term, have been altered. Moreover, the areas of performance are no longer strictly economic. To assume that groups, organizations, and governments will behave exactly as individuals do has been shown to be fallacious. Organizations have quasi-political objectives, and their motivation and direction shifts depending on the relative strength of contending internal forces. They have a logic of their own that is as distinct from that of neoclassical theory as a tropical forest is from a moonscape.

What then are the elements of the new paradigm that economics now demands? The basic element is the acknowledgement that those who built our economy and perform roles in it — craftsmen, merchants, manufacturers, farmers, financiers, legislators, rag-pickers, teachers, and toll-takers — are actors in a social system and that their acts are not only economic but political as well. Whatever decisions they affect take place in a social setting that conditions more mightily than we know the sort of behavior described as economic. Goods and services are not only commodities and performances with price tags attached to them but are directions and actions and are significantly related to human actors who control them.

Thus the paradigm of the pure market has little relevance to the problems we are discussing at these meetings. The city, the environment, medical care, welfare — the public sector — are in many ways not subject to the criteria of the market. Yet we lack adequate tools of analysis that would enable us to comprehend the turbulent political economy of the public sector. Someone once said that economists are blockheads who design fancy band-aids to cover the sores in the body politic: they do not seem to know that a nation can be sick. And what we fail to do is evidence of that sickness.

To be sure, refined economic theory offers numerous suggestions — Pareto optima, turnpike theorems, and dynamic stability. But propositions of this sort often turn out to be counsels of quiescence, suggesting that nothing be done about such problems as distorted income distribution, external diseconomies attendant to growth, or inflation mixed with unemployment. Economists do on occasion turn their attention to these latter questions, only when reminded that Emperors often dress in invisible garments.

CONSTRUCTING A NEW PARADIGM

Constructing a new paradigm in economics will be achieved by relating a relevant and meaningful theory to practical policy. This suggests a concern with *political* economics and *social* economics and with the public sector. In this context, meaning and goals must precede analytical elegance. If economics is to be a science of fact rooted in the human condition it will have to check its theory against political policy and social unrest. Relevance demands that the economist make his theory a meaningful way of perceiving reality. Unless this perception is available, theory cannot perform its primary function — that of guiding empirical inquiry.

A new paradigm must be constructed because pure competition

no longer describes the realities of the market; private capital accumulation has lost it religious imperative; resources and factors are less mobile; technology, a dominant element in change, is often malign; scarcity is no longer a prod to achievement, having been displaced for many by at least a modest affluence, the Puritan ethic does not convince anyone; natural law is now a matter of educated superstition; and primarily because the public sector now conditions much of our daily lives. We need a paradigm that embraces these new facts of human existence; one that will explain and hopefully predict the consequences of social action; that will provide understanding of motivation and aetiology and relate these to economic analysis; that views the market as an institution of significantly reduced importance; that acknowledges the role of corporate behavior; that recognizes the urgency of giving direction to science and technology; that specifies correctives for the failure of affluence to spill over into the public sector (exclusive of defense); that is, as Professor Heilbroner has said, holistic or global in its aim and above all, one that will be genuinely instrumental in its application of human intelligence.

It is against this background that one must establish the need for a fresh approach to the science of economics. Basic to such an approach would be the realization that there really are no *a priori* behavior statements: everything must be specified and always subjected to critical examination. Investigation must start with an aetiology or a statement of what exists initially. Then one can shift to a consideration of what would be desirable, employing propositions about moving the economy from the initial state to the desired one. There is a marked difference between so radical an approach and traditional methodology in that behavioral premises cannot be merely accepted, but must be subjected to continual test.[43]

The hypotheses involved would acquire fresh significance, for there would be an attempt to relate them to goal-seeking behavior. In a sense, one works regressively, as in solving a problem in plane geometry, by moving backwards to establish the instrumentalities that might be employed to reach an economic goal. To be sure, there are many unknowns in this approach. We need to know the behavior patterns of individuals and firms; we need to know the motivations that give rise to these patterns; we need to know the path that the system will take in reaching the specified goal; we need to know the character of the parameters that are embedded in the meta-economy.

Needless to say, the goal itself is not subject to empirical observation, and indeed if the economy fails to attain its objective, the goal may never be observed. Clearly this takes us into the judgmental area, but it is one that economists need not fear to explore. For, it is perfectly possible to specify the conditions for a social decision process based on some sort of collective rationality stemming from a social ordering of preferences.[44] There are problems, certainly. Questions may be asked as to who decides on the nature of the social ordering. Or what is the metaeconomic set by which the orderings may be confirmed or tested? And how do the institutions of the society exert their influences on choice?

Now, we do have some understanding of the technical means by which resources and facilities can be arranged to obtain optimum results. Thus the relation of goals to instrumentalities is mainly a "technological" matter. But our society is inhibited in clearly establishing these relationships by the exigencies of politics or by the ideology of some defunct economist. Assuming that our "technical" information is fairly advanced, then it ought to be sufficient to describe the paths available to a rational society. Embedded in this approach would be an appreciation of the motivations and psychology of the economic actors. These notions presuppose that economics is concerned not only with the confrontation of man and matter but also by the confrontation of man and man, for surely the latter relationships are also economic.

If the relationship of man to machine is fundamentally a question of technology and its impacts, then the confrontation of man and man is a matter of the behavior to which the confrontation gives rise. In a stationary economy it takes little more than following established rules of production to maintain equilibrium. The motivations for such routine behavior would stem from inelastic expectations based on a kind of stabilizing feedback mechanism. The behavior patterns and motivations can be rigorously defined in such a model.[45]

But in a complex world such a model is simple-minded. One needs rather information on motivations, social organization, rules of production, and above all where we want to head. With these data we can describe a path that brings us close to the target. One does not suggest that such an approach would display full predictability. It cannot be assumed that all the forces at play will move the economy along desirable paths unless specific action is taken to provide the necessary motivations and behavior patterns.

My argument essentially is an appeal for a social economics. More and more, the so-called free goods of our society demand a price tag. The scarcities today are pure water, clean air, privacy, mental health, space, cities that are liveable, highways that are not parking lots — everything that the population explosion, industrialism, and urbanism are undermining and threatening to destroy. These are not mere esthetic scarcities: their lack vitiates our ability to enjoy rising levels of material abundance. How much utility does the consumer obtain when he must crawl in and out of town each Sunday in search of green pastures?[46]

If one wishes to describe such concerns as *political* economics, that will be acceptable, for social goals must be pursued in a context of political decision-making. The fact is that so many services are required in the public sector that we have already made large parts of the market mechanism otiose. I repeat, the choices in the public sector are political rather than economic. If this means active intervention in economic affairs, so be it. Haven't we been doing just that in greater or lesser degree ever since Alexander Hamilton's Report on Manufacturers? What were tariffs, land grants, and government subsidies for canals and railroads, if not interventionism? The War on Poverty, despite its patent failures, represented a shift from the market to the political process.

What sorts of cost would be generated as the economy moves along these paths? Great sums of money would have to be allocated to clean the air, purify the water, wipe out the slums, improve traffic flows, provide urban transportation, and control population densities. There will be auxiliary costs as well: industry might have to be relocated and livelihoods disturbed. But set against these costs would be the immense and perhaps immeasurable value of more healthful living, both physical and mental, decent recreational space, and the mitigation of the festering sores that now plague the cities.

Constraints abound, of course: there are numerous elements in society that tend to cancel each other. Human behavior at times confounds the best-intentioned of social scientists. But surely the goals of the public sector would be sufficiently in harmony with individual aspirations so that conflict between the two levels of behavior would be minimized. In any case, as the external diseconomies of the private sector become more and more intolerable, is it not likely that public sector macro goals and individual micro goals will have to come together?

Let me close with an anecdote about John Dewey. At the age of 90 he returned to Columbia University, where he had taught for many years, to lecture to a group of post-graduate students. In his address, he developed sadly the theme that philosophers had retreated to purely technical matters, while the world was facing violence, irrationality, and dogmatism. It was a difficult time, he said, to be a philosopher. Then he sat down, but quickly rose to his feet to add that he was afraid he had been too discouraging to young scholars just starting out. Perhaps it was a good time to be a philosopher, he remarked, for the old formulas, the old paradigms were not working. The challenge was to create a bold, new analysis, to venture creatively in thought. All it required, said Dewey, as he turned to take his seat once more, were ideas, imagination, and, he added, guts.[47]

NOTES

1. R. L. Heilbroner, *The Worldly Philosophers*, New York, 1953, p. 6.
2. cf. J. Robinson, *Freedom and Necessity*, London, 1970, p. 24.
3. cf. M. Gluckman, *Politics, Law, and Ritual in Tribal Society*, Chicago, 1965 and R. Firth, ed., *Themes in Economic Anthropology*, London, 1967.
4. T. S. Kuhn, *The Structure of Scientific Revolutions*, Chicago, 1962.
5. cf. P. A. Samuelson, *Collected Scientific Papers*, V. 2, Cambridge, 1966, pp. 1499 ff.
6. A. A. Lowe, *On Economic Knowledge*, New York, 1965, pp. 165 ff.
7. cf. R. Firth and B. S. Yamey, eds., *Capital, Saving, and Credit in Peasant Societies*, London, 1964, pp. 20-23; M. Rostovtzeff, *A History of the Ancient World*, V. 1, London, 1925, pp. 197, 218, 316.
8. cf. E. Voegelin, *The World of the Polis*, Baton Rouge, 1957, p. 333.
9. Plato, *Laws*, 679.
10. Aristotle, *Nicomachean Ethics*, 1133.
11. Plato, *Statesman*, 259, 285.
12. cf. J. Wild, *Plato's Theory of Man*, Cambridge, 1948, pp. 101 ff.
13. *Laws*, 709 a-e, 732 e, 733 c; *Republic*, Bk. 9, 583 ff.
14. *Republic*, 443 c, d, 590 c; *Laws*, 918 b; *Philebus*, 55, 56.
15. cf. Voegelin, *Plato and Aristotle*, Baton Rouge, 1957, pp. 289 ff.
16. Aristotle, *Politics*, 1259 b ff, 1304b.
17. *N. Ethics*, 1131 a 30 ff, 1132 b 33; *Politics*, 1257 b 15, 1261 a 14, 1263 a ff, 1266 b 5, 1330 a.
18. cf. W. Jaeger, *Early Christianity and Greek Paideia*, Cambridge, 1961; H. O. Taylor, *The Medieval Mind*, V. 1, London, 1911, pp. 11 ff.
19. cf. H. Meyer, *The Philosophy of St. Thomas Aquinas*, London, 1944; D. J. O'Connor, *Aquinas and Natural Law*, London, 1967.
20. T. Veblen, *The Place of Science in Modern Civilization*, New York, 1919; cf. also D. Hamilton, *Evolutionary Economics*, Albuquerque, 1970.
21. J. Gilchrist, *The Church and Economic Activity in the Middle Ages*, New York, 1969.
22. R. de Roover, "Scholastic Economics: Its Survival and Lasting Influence", *Quarterly Journal of Economics*, March, 1955, pp. 188ff.
23. cf. P. Gay, *The Enlightenment*, V. 2, New York, 1969, p. 457.
24. cf. A. L. Macfie, *The Individual in Society*, London, 1957, pp. 71ff; J. Viner, "Adam Smith and Laissez-Faire", *Journal of Political Economy*, April, 1927, pp. 198ff.
25. G. R. Morrow, *The Ethical and Economic Theories of Adam Smith*, New York, 1923, p. 8.

26. *ibid,* p. 41.

27. A. Marshall, *Principles of Economics,* Variorum Edition, 1961, Bk. 1, ch. 1.

28. cf. E. Halevy, *The Growth of Philosophical Radicalism,* London, 1949, pp. 479ff.

29. A. W. Gouldner, *The Coming Crisis of Western Sociology,* New York, 1970, pp. 61ff.

30. cf. F. Stern, *The Politics of Cultural Despair,* Berkeley, 1961.

31. cf. R. L. Heilbroner, *Between Capitalism and Socialism,* New York, 1970, pp. 117ff.

32. cf. A. O. Hirschman, *Exit, Voice, and Loyalty,* Cambridge, 1970.

33. cf. C. Levi-Strauss, *Structural Anthropology,* New York, 1963.

34. R. Hofstadter, *Social Darwinism in American Thought,* Philadelphia, 1944, pp. 31ff.

35. cf. J. Dorfman, *The Economic Mind in American Civilization,* Vol. 3, New York, 1949, pp. 188ff.

36. E. Kauder, "The Retarded Acceptance of Marginal Utility Theory", *Quarterly Journal of Economics,* Nov. 1953, pp. 564ff.

37. F. H. Knight, *Freedom and Reform,* New York, 1947, pp. 231ff.

38. *idem, Ethics of Competition,* London, 1935, pp. 40, 42ff.

39. cf. *idem,* "Economics and Anthropology", *Journal of Political Economy,* June, 1941, pp. 247ff.

40. *idem, Intelligence and Democratic Action,* Cambridge, 1960, p. 124.

41. cf. F. A. Hayek, *The Sensory Order,* London, 1952.

42. cf. A. Schutz, *The Phenomenology of the Social World,* Evanston, 1967, pp. 97ff.

43. cf. A. A. Lowe, *On Economic Knowledge,* New York, 1965.

44. K. Arrow, *Social Choice and Individual Values,* New York, 1951.

45. Heilbroner, *Between Capitalism and Socialism,* pp. 165 ff.

46. cf. J. K. Galbraith, *The Affluent Society,* Boston, 2nd edition, 1969.

47. I. Edman, "America's Philosopher Attains an Alert 90", *New York Times Magazine,* October 16, 1949.

14

The Selective Interpretation of Adam Smith

Warren S. Gramm

"But successors cannot continue on the level of genius. One aspect of the great man, *probably that which suits later conditions,* is chosen, much of the rest probably rejected" (emphasis added) [28, p. 20]. Of the 1,438 pages written by Adam Smith in his two major published works [44 and 45], only a few lines from several pages of the *Wealth of Nations* are regularly mentioned in orthodox economics texts. These are the statements on division of labor, paradox of value, the invisible hand, and the functions of government.[1] On these grounds, he is known primarily for rationalizing individual self-interest as the necessary, strategic medium for promoting economic welfare. Yet it may be argued that a correct understanding of Smith's perspective leads to the opposite conclusion. That is, when his life's work is considered as a unit, his political-economic perspective is seen to be social, not primarily individualistic, and his major contributions to economic analysis involve elucidation of economic growth.

These relationships are elaborated in applying to Adam Smith's thought a general epistemological thesis concerning the selective interpretation of major analytic systems over time. The thesis consists of four major interrelated propositions: (1) Major contributors and their analytic systems have interrelated normative and positive elements; (2) in its initial formulation, the positive analytic content of the new system is directly related to and supportive of its normative element; (3) there then occurs a rebalancing of the relative weight of the positive and normative elements; and

(4) in this process the system undergoes a transformation in which ingredients most compatible with the existing power structure come to be regarded as the essence of the system.[2] In brief, despite wide recognition that Smith's "primary concern was evidently with the dynamic [positive] question of growth" [1, p. 25], William D. Grampp has observed that "what Smith is best known for, although he probably did not want to be, is the . . . [normative proposition] that self-interest is the principal motive of economic behavior" [17, p. xii].

The relevance of interaction between positive and normative elements of economic analysis is indicated in Joan Robinson's observation that "economics itself . . . has always been partly a vehicle for the ruling ideology of each period as well as partly a method of scientific investigation" [38, p. 1].[3] Application of the general thesis to major contributors to economic analysis may add quantitative, historical substance to her open-ended, "partly-partly" proposition.

This specific application of the general epistemological thesis is as follows. Adam Smith's theories of economic growth and value are regarded as his positive economics, while his statements concerning individual behavior, institutional aspects of market relationships, and the proper role of government are identified as his normative analysis. The supportive interrelationship of the positive and normative elements is seen in the stimulation of economic growth provided by individual self-interest and open markets. Major manifestations of the third and fourth elements are the interpretative imputations that Adam Smith placed *primary* emphasis on market (versus long-run, natural) price determination and the private market as guarantor of social harmony.[4]

A full treatment of this evaluative scheme would have to deal with all of Smith's major concepts in terms of their position and weight in his own work, supplemented by scholarly interpretations and the textual consensus of histories of economic doctrine. This short thematic essay presents a relatively brief elaboration of two major elements of the apologetic transformation: the isolation of the *Wealth of Nations* from the remainder of his thought and writing and analysis of the positive-normative transformation.[5] Primary emphasis is placed on two major interpretative responses to *Wealth of Nations*: (1) the submergence of major ingredients in Smith's value theory and (2) transformation of his usages of the invisible hand and behavioral competition into a new metaphor—the mechanistic, short-run, competitive equilibrium market model.[6]

Use of the terms, the relationships, *transformations, new system,* and *new metaphor* and assumption of a classical-neoclassical sequence in economic analysis reflects general acceptance of the Kuhnian (even Marxian) perspective of scientific revolutions. Essentially, this means only that the truism of historical continuity, "the inevitability of gradualness," is qualified by the parallel truism of accelerations that culminate in what may be designated *ex post* as "relatively fundamental turning points." Thus, the term *revolution* "can be, and has been, widely applied to the history of political economy and economics without any implications or commitments whatsoever regarding [other, related] Kuhnian ideas" [23, pp. viii–ix]. Major operational elements in the process of accelerated change which leads to analytical turning points—and scientific progress—are formulation and professional acceptance of a "new question," commonly accompanied by change in analytical method.[7]

It is a truism that *Wealth of Nations* is a masterly historical synthesis of a century or more of economic thought.[8] The genesis of this analysis was in the socio-historical setting of eighteenth-century, optimistic, humanistic rationalism. Its basic purpose was to show how economic progress will be promoted by allowing the fullest possible play of individual self-interest—in promoting frugality and division of labor.

A generalized belief in man's capacity for self-determination was based on the new ideas of progress and human perfectability. As a spokesman for this perspective, Adam Smith's philosophical statement in *Theory of Moral Sentiments* focused on the problem of socially responsible behavior of the individual. The concepts of "sympathy" and the "impartial spectator" were developed as surrogates for the individual's social conscience. The normative thesis of *Wealth of Nations*—that self-interest was dominant in individual economic behavior—was not meant to override or cancel out the role of sympathy, of self-restraint, in the overarching realm of social action. Thus, Smithian political economy is social economics in its analysis of the individual in a given social setting. (For major substantive "descriptive" elements of social economics, see below, pp. 133–34 and note 20.)

Despite the admixture of positive and normative elements in Smith's work, particularly in Books I and II of *Wealth of Nations,* it is argued that there is a significant element of sequence, of priority. That is, in this scholarly work of long gestation, one may hold on *a priori* grounds that Smith's opening emphasis on the strategic role of labor in economic growth was not accidental. His theories of growth and value build on the specific relationships that affect the quantity and quality of productive labor that can be put to effective use. His method was almost uniquely eclectic. Wary of "excessive abstraction" and "political arithmetic" (received statistics), he presented a pioneer effort in system building, in his blending of analytic generalizations and historically weighted facts [23, pp. 8–12].

The Paring and Compression of Adam Smith's Theories of Value

Adam Smith's analysis of value was inclusive—eclectic. A major element in the subsequent selective interpretation of his social economics is the successive deletion from orthodox value theory (and from recognition of their strategic position in Smith's own thought) of all but one major value relationship.

In the perspective of late eighteenth-century political economy, the value problem was broad and inclusive. It encompassed the two basic relationships of absolute and relative value which could be examined under three dimensions or questions of value: the source, determinants, and measure of value. Classical economists (especially Smith and David Ricardo) grappled, with limited success, with all five relationships [8, p. 325; 43, pp. 188–90, 308–309]. By 1900, and certainly by the 1930s, orthodox neoclassic value theory had reduced the problem to that of relative value, that is, the analysis of the measure of value in terms of market prices as exchange ratios of commodities. The eighteenth- and nineteenth-century *real value* orientation (both objective and subjective) became supplanted in the 1940s by the highly schematic *abstract value* base, whereby consumption, production, and welfare analysis is founded on indifference analysis.

Objective real value, oriented primarily to the supply side, to real cost elements in production, was an incidental casualty, a side effect, of eliminating human labor (the labor theory of value) from orthodox economic equilibrium analytics. The significance for value theory of exclusion of natural resources from orthodox economic analysis has been noted recently by Nicholas Georgescu-Roegen: "Since the economic process materially consists of a transformation of low entropy into high entropy, i.e., into waste, and since this transformation is irrevocable, natural resources must necessarily represent one part of the notion of economic value" [13, p. 18]. It seems clear that this value dimension must be regained for serious analysis of allocation of resource scarcity, for linking economics, ecology, and human welfare.

In the 1930s, under the parallel "positivistic" influences reflected in the arguments of Lionel Robbins, J. R. Hicks, and R. G. D. Allen, *subjective* real value (and the welfare content of absolute value) was effectively eliminated. For example, Robbins's proposition that "goods are just goods" served to dismiss the historical, truistic distinction between necessities and "luxuries." It set in motion the drift to acceptance of the principle of "revealed preference," whereby analysis of the *determinants* of consumer demand (such as income distribution and social bases for wants) is placed outside the economist's jurisdiction. The methodological-conceptual basis of indifference analysis was substitution of ordinal for cardinal utility to bypass the "subjectivity" of subjective values. (As Joan Robinson has noted, this did not expunge from human experience the relevance of the "good juice of *utility*" [38, p. 52], it merely removed it from abstract analytical economics and reinforced the new self-image of positive science.)

In this process, value theory became price theory; the humanistic, behavioral, social process elements in value theory have been removed. A mechanistic, logically rigorous, ostensibly positivistic value theory displaced the subjective and objective real value positions of classicism. It is important to note, however, that the necessity of an inclusive, classical, real value perspective has received powerful reaffirmation within the larger schema of Georgescu-Roegen: "We cannot arrive at a completely intelligible description of the economic process as long as we limit ourselves to purely physical concepts. Without the concepts of *purposive activity* and *enjoyment of life* we cannot be in the economic world [13, p. 282]. . . . Everything that supports life enjoyment directly or indirectly belongs to the category of economic value" [13, p. 287].[9]

The condensation of value theory is examined briefly as a major element in the excision of Adam Smith's thought. On the source of value question, Smith's position was essentially the same as that of most contemporary observers. This is the perhaps truistic position reflected in William Petty's observation that "Labor is the Father and active principle of Wealth as Lands are the Mother"; land and labor are the "natural" sources of surplus, of economic growth. The Physiocrats had argued that the relationship held only for land. Adam Smith extended the insight, in formal if general terms, to human labor. This is the strategic link between his positive analysis and his humanistic normative position which embodies empathy for productive workers in general. The strategic value of human labor and the "natural system of liberty" are the foundations of his social economics.

Was the world of Adam Smith industrial or "preindustrial"? One's position on this question is strategic in understanding and interpreting Smith's analytic system—his integration of value, distribution, and growth. The judgment here is that Smith was analyzing commercial capitalism, enriched by prescient insights concerning elements of industrial technology. "During the lifetime of Adam Smith, the modern industrial organization was not yet born . . . [and the issue] is not futile quibbling. The contributions of Adam Smith to modern thought cannot possibly be appreciated unless one realizes that he lived and labored in a pre-machine civilization" [14, p. 148]. The general issue has appeared in two related contexts: the hierarchy of production controversy (the relative preeminence of agriculture, commerce, and manufacture) and the relative or comparative importance of labor and physical nonhuman capital.

In *Wealth of Nations,* the productivity of land is taken as given; the most generally productive use of labor and capital is in application to agriculture [45, p. 360].[10] The output of land—as well as of manufactures—varies with the quantity and quality of productive labor. The quantity of labor is a function of the wages fund, the supply of savings, of money capital, and the social base of frugality. The quality of labor is based on the interaction of increased division of labor and the quantity and quality of tools and equipment (the social base of education and human capital being treated analytically as given). Unproductive labor does not yield a permanent "vendible commodity, which endures after that labour is past" [45, p. 315]. Its general association with services—honorific as well as menial—reflected Smith's emphasis on real, tangible (versus pecuniary and/or abstract) value.

Substantive elements in analysis of the two remaining value questions—the determinants and the measure of value—cannot be sharply distinguished. They have common, overlapping dimensions. The determinants of economic value include both real objective and subjective ingredients. Objective value involves the absolute scarcity of real resources—nonrenewable natural and human resources. Hence, its analytic and social relevance concerns the real cost of production for both political units (nations) and workers (for example, the real cost of a day's work for the worker includes the forgone opportunity for alternative activity, the using up of one day in a finite lifetime, and risks involving psychic or physical injury). The issues attending real subjective value are more readily recognized by economists, since they have recurred in the development of demand theory during the past century. However, a major point in understanding the value theory of Adam Smith and its contrast with both his predecessors and neoclassical price theory is that, for him, demand was a parameter, a given.

"He seems . . . to have rejected the [subjective] value theory which he inherited" [23, p. 15][11] and the related association of exchange value with relative scarcity. Prevalence of want for necessities—of "absolute scarcity"—meant that supply (production) was the relevant economic problem. In Smith's discussion of market adjustments of price and quantity for both short-run (market) and long-run (natural) price, supply (cost) factors are the variables. "The quantity of every commodity brought to market naturally suits itself to the effectual demand" [45, p. 57]. If the quantity supplied exceeds effectual demand, resources will be withdrawn from production, and vice versa.

Thus, the determinants of value, the variables in his analysis, are the prices of inputs, the cost or supply side. Here, we necessarily shade into the measure of value question. The most succinct statement of Smith's value theory is that it is a "naïve" long-run cost of production theory. It is such a theory because the long-run natural price of commodities (including factor inputs themselves) is determined by the sum of the prices of inputs. Smith identified three major elements in the cost-price of inputs (labor and stock): (1) the real objective and subjective value of labor, (2) resource scarcity, and (3) the working of the system of natural liberty. Concerning the first, Smith observed: "The real price of every thing, what every thing really costs to the man who wants to acquire it, is the toil and trouble of acquiring it" [45, p. 30].[12]

Smith's theory is considered naïve on several counts. The primary problem is lack of a satisfactory theory of factor price determination, of costs of production. Repeated reference to the metaphysical "system of natural liberty" was not satisfactory; explanation of long-run natural price required specific determination of short-run market values, of nominal market price. Finally, there was no direct contact with the capital value problem, for example, the determination of the interest rate as a market price [43, p. 333]. Application to capital of the subjective real value relationship—the disutility of saving—awaited the work of Nassau Senior.

Even with this highly abbreviated statement of Smith's discussion of value theory, it is clear that in *Wealth of Nations* many, perhaps all, strategic value relationships are considered. But it is generally accepted that none was resolved. Emphasis on embodied labor as the key source of value opened the question of accounting for capital as a cost and the problem of distributive allocation of the resulting social product.[13] Formulation of the command of labor as a measure of final product value posed, but did not solve, either the problem of "increasing" embodied real inputs (that is, labor and capital) or of exchange value.

For his major concern, explication of the "nature and causes of the wealth of nations," Smith did not need a rigorous theory of market price [8, pp. 325–26]. Commenting on the open-endedness of Smith's theory of long-run natural "equilibrium" price, Joan Robinson observes: "As a theory of prices this is rather simple-minded, but it is doubtful whether the doctrines taught nowadays, though so much more elaborate, are any more penetrating. However that may be, the point is not in the analysis. . . . This book is devoted not to moral sentiments but to expediency. The way lies ahead, through the increasing productivity that follows the division of labour. A sketchy theory of value will serve well enough, for the main point is to argue the advantages of free trade and accumulation of stock" [38, p. 30].[14]

Neoclassicism "changed the question" from the classical problem of the source and determinants of economic growth [8, p. 317] to determination of relative price.[15] Thus, the problem of exchange value, under the aegis of marginalism, is the only major economic value problem that has been solved. As indicated above, it was not of primary concern to Smith. A strategic epistemological element of this historical process was the redefinition of value theory as price theory [43, p. 311].

One of the most visible manifestations of the revision of the Smithian perspective on value theory is adherence by orthodox micro analytics to the position that price theory—short-run micro equilibrium analysis—has *solved* the paradox of value, something that Smith had been unable to do. Given the nature of paradox, this cannot be true.[16] A paradox is a tenet that is true in fact, although contrary to common sense. Hence, it presents a relationship to be explained, rather than a puzzle to be solved (like a mathematical proof or building a bridge). The two basic value questions embodied in the diamond-water paradox are indicated in Smith's distinction between value in use and value in exchange. Use value embodies the problem of real value in relation to human welfare, and the relevant variable is *total utility*.[17] Water has great value in terms of maintaining life. Since this is the fundamental purpose of economic activity, the use value of necessities is strategic for real welfare analysis. Diamonds have no value for subsistence. The explanation of the paradox, then, must incorporate the second value dimension of exchange value and relative scarcity.

Marginal analysis—*marginal utility*—provides a formal explication of the problem of exchange value, of the short-run market price of diamonds and water. But the paradox remains. A full and satisfactory explanation, one that encompasses the welfare problem, would have to incorporate as analytic variables important elements that price theory assumes away as givens: the distribution of income and the social values of a community which jointly influence or determine the structure of consumption and production in a given society. It would require renewed contact with the distinction between necessities and luxuries which is an element of real subjective value and real welfare analysis [13, p. 277; 45, pp. 821–22].

We will now consider the connections between these reinterpretations of Smith's value theory and normative positions and the transformation of his critique of mercantilist monopoly into a testament for industrial capitalism. Smith's long-run cost of production theory of natural price and his related vision of workably open markets has been displaced, essentially, by imputation of short-run market equilibrium connations to his metaphysical metaphor, the invisible hand.

From Invisible Hand to Pure Competition: Substitution of Metaphors or Transformation from Metaphysics to Science?

There is a second and largely unrecognized paradox that links Smith's two major works. It involves the presence in each individual of behavioral elements of selfishness and social consciousness. It is presented in the opening sentence of *Theory of Moral Sentiments*: "How selfish soever man may be supposed, there are evidently some principles in his nature, which interest him in the fortune of others, and render their happiness necessary to him, though he derives nothing from it, except the pleasure of seeing it" [44, p. 3].[18] The "altruism-egoism" controversy has been judged "the matrix of Smith's scholarly concerns" [8, p. 318]. Continental economists in the nineteenth century labeled the relationship "the Adam Smith problem."

This paradox, like the diamond-water paradox of value, presents, simultaneously, an unsurmountable barrier to a socially relevant equilibrium economics and an entry to a social economics based on history and process analysis. It presents the social reality that economic activity—production and consumption—involves the simultaneous play of cooperation and conflict. The actors on the economics stage need each other, at the same time that they often are in opposition. In general, production requires cooperation among diverse individuals, while distribution, or allocation of the social product, is a basis for conflict. These interdependencies were simultaneously heightened and altered in form in the transition from agrarian feudalism to industrial capitalism.[19]

Smith's usage of the term "invisible hand" was his conceptual and sociopolitical means for resolving this paradox. In contemporary micro equilibrium economics, this is the function of the concept of the purely competitive market. The transmutation of Smith's use of the metaphorical invisible hand into the logical fiction of perfect competition (and the substitute metaphor, the "free" market) is the strategic element in the ideologically based reinterpretation of Smith. It has been a key factor in movement from the initial humanistic social discipline of political economy to economics as a mechanistic intellectual defense of capitalism.

The "material" essence of the invisible hand of *Wealth of Nations* is Smith's recognition of the general necessity of social restraint on self-interest. It links the overt perspective of social conscience in *Theory of Moral Sentiments* with the later book's emphasis on individualistic self-interest. In sum, the two works as a unit are the basis for F. A. Hayek's characterization of the social individualism of Adam Smith as "individualism true."[20] This Smithian perspective of social individualism extends through the English pre-Cambridge classical tradition, particularly in the persons of David Hume and J. S. Mill. The emphasis on individualism and self-interest extended into ultrarationalism, to what Hayek has characterized as individualism false, which began with Jeremy Bentham and Nassau Senior. It became formalized in neoclassical analysis in the linking of marginalism, mathematics, and the principle of individual maximizing behavior as the behavioral pillars of micro equilibrium analysis. In the latter context, in the setting of monopolistic industrial capitalism of the late twentieth century, individual profit seeking has become the strategic ("ideologically" sufficient) means to the end of economic progress and, coincidently, has evolved—in institutional terms—into the *de facto* status of an end in itself.

What substance may be imputed to Smith's invisible hand? Its statement appears quite late in *Wealth of Nations*. In Book IV, "Of Systems of Political Economy" (the essentially normative section on "comparative systems"), the term appears in a discussion of mercantilism and the relative importance of domestic and foreign trade. Thus, in preferring domestic investment, the individual "intends only his own gain, and he is in this, as in many other cases, led by an invisible hand to promote an end which was no part of his intention. Nor is it always the worse for the society that it was no part of it. By pursuing his own interest he frequently promotes that of the society more effectually than when he really intends to promote it" [45, p. 423].

It is important to recognize that the invisible hand is a metaphysical relationship—a metaphor—and that it incorporates basic qualifications. A metaphor often appears as an "as if" statement; hence, it is not intended to have quantitative, "scientific," content. If it is useful, it clarifies reality, but it must not be mistaken for an hypothesis or theorem amenable to proof or disproof. For Smith, the metaphor of the invisible hand calls attention to the paradoxical simultaneity of diversity (conflict) and community in individual interests.[21] It seems reasonable to infer that if the concept, the relationship involved, were purely metaphysical, it would have had little continuing interest for either social science or ideology.

Appearing first in *Theory of Moral Sentiments* [44, p. 264], the metaphor reflected the social reality—the social and political necessity—of workers' retaining an appreciable share of the social product. In a setting of increasing agricultural production, the political security of the landlords is enhanced by allowing the producers (workers) to share in the larger product (such increase being limited by physical consumption capacity) while collecting the growing net surplus for their own use and sale.[22] In *Wealth of Nations*, the same principle applies concerning political security for the rising commercial and industrial interests. However, the social function and problems of administering long-run self-interest are different in the new commercial and politically liberal (compared with the transitional, quasi-feudal agricultural) setting. The muscle and sinew of the invisible hand are the operational elements of the system of natural liberty, which is a strategic element in Smith's analysis. These elements include those characterized by Warren J. Samuels as "the nonlegal, or nondeliberative, forces of social control, operating as morals, religion, custom, and education" [41, p. 22]. There is, then, no " 'Invisible Hand' analysis" [in answer to the question of how the system] . . . will work coherently if you let economic agents do as they please" [26, p. 91]. The satisfaction of "succeeding generations of economists" with the Smithian metaphysic has been more a function of "faith" (for example, C. E. Ferguson) and what is recognized as a strategic "willful suspension of disbelief" (as in the political "belief" in the existence of democracy, which in reality remains a goal rather than a fact).

The self-interest of the seller, for example, the butcher and baker, is to realize a pecuniary gain on exchange, to make a profit. This is reflected instrumentally in the market maxim "buy cheap and sell dear." But the early fears of Aristotle and Thomas Aquinas concerning the antisocial potential of monetary exchange and pecuniary gain are reflected in the prospect that maximization of individual self-interest presents the "natural prospect" of a shift from the "natural limit" of fair or necessary gain on exchange to the miser's drive for unlimited accumulation. Thus, a second market maxim, "let the buyer beware," illustrates the potential for self-interest to evolve into conflict between buyers and sellers.

How does the invisible hand work as a vehicle for conflict resolution, for resolving the paradox of cooperation and conflict? The answer, in general, is to be found in identifying the social constraints on self-interest present in Smith's England. There are three of major importance. The primary economic element in his system of natural liberty is the existence of open markets, the operational reality of those elements of smallness of productive units and free entry of firms and workers now associated with a perfectly competitive market. The second, an extension of the first into the larger society, is the social setting of small-scale community relationships; the butcher and his customer are friends or neighbors. It is a quite different matter to cheat or poison a stranger as compared with family, friends, or close associates. Finally, there existed the religious constraint on anti-social accumulation and expenditure, the Protestant ethic.

The importance of correct identification of Smith's "world"—the institutional setting to which he addressed his positive analysis of economic growth—was emphasized above. It is equally important in understanding ongoing interpretations and applications of his normative position, particularly in judging the continuing "workability" of the invisible hand, to recognize that Smith and conservative acolytes have taken the institutional setting as *given*. Thus, "this assumption of a stable social framework . . . permitted the development of classical, neoclassical and Keynesian economics in Britain. . . . But to the extent that [this] assumption . . . *may be* becoming significantly less valid" [23, p. 7] or, indeed, has not been valid for the past century, the need for a new metaphor (for example, the visible or invisible fist) and new analysis is clarified.

In the course of nineteenth-century development of industrial capitalism, the substance of the "Smithian" institutional governors underwent significant change. Elements of market monopoly impinged on open markets, community relationships gave way to "absentee ownership," and the religious ethic was supplanted by the scientific and other secular ethics. At the same time, the rise of neoclassical analysis culminated in acceptance by the 1930s of the twin concepts of pure competition and consumer sovereignty, the formal equilibrium analytic construct that became extended into the normative realm, into the ideological reinforcement of industrial capitalism as a "free market system." Thus, Fritz Redlich observed that "American businessmen adopted the idea of the invisible hand and derived therefrom the attitude of irresponsibility" [36, p. 316].

Adam Smith's statement that he had "never known much good done by those who affected to trade for the public good" [45, p. 423], which seems directed toward the hypocritical businessman, has been rhetorically reinterpreted as a judgment that *anyone* who professes sympathy for his fellow man is deluded or dishonest. Since the 1950s, this quotation has been repeatedly adduced in support of the proposition that everyone is basically governed by self-interest. In the process it has become a "philosophical" base for extreme *laissez-faire,* for opposing social action oriented to a social or public interest.[23] Smith's highly qualified optimism concerning the possibilities of a workable system of natural liberty, based on generally open markets, has become transformed into contemporary neoclassicism's acceptance of the analytical assumption of perfect markets as a relevant and realistic approximation to actual economic relationships. Milton Friedman's 1962 statement remains representative of this position:

"I have become increasingly impressed with how wide is the range of problems and industries for which it is appropriate to treat the economy as if it were competitive" [12, p. 120].[24]

It may be argued that in this transformation of Smith (and the classical political economists who immediately followed, such as J. B. Say and David Ricardo) twentieth-century neoclassicism joins, perhaps reinforces, the social detachment, the irresponsibility, of the businessman. Referring to the classical setting, Eduard Heiman has observed:

> It is important to realize that objective, autonomous economic theory, as a "value-free" intellectual effort, is a reflection of "harmony" thinking and would not have arisen in another intellectual climate. The objectivity of the Classical School did not repudiate the moral and political responsibility of the scholar; the classical economists presented to the world the one system that could live and prosper without intervention from man. They claimed that the organization of the capitalist system of production embodied an inherent wisdom; they did not disclaim wisdom but lifted Nature's wisdom—or that of Providence—above that of man. Once the belief in Nature's harmony and wisdom had been given up, however, the adoption of the same attitude of detachment connoted something else—indifference and irresponsibility [20, p. 111].

A current manifestation is in the attribution by many contemporary neoclassicists (for example, Henry C. Wallich) of a social conscience to the metaphysical-metaphorical "corporate person."[25]

The Selective Interpretation of Smith and the Problem of Social Economics

In the interpretative transformation of Adam Smith—the process of natural selection based on the ideological needs of the newly established power structure—Smith's positive economics of growth and eclectic value theory were first transmuted into the normative behavioral element of rational self-interest; the operation of the latter was then made conditional upon the private (assumed as free) market system. Two major aspects of the process have been the transformation of the meaning of market competition and loss of contact with Smith's essentially social-humanist perspective.[26] Concerning the former, it is necessary to recognize, with Milton Friedman, that "competition has two very different meanings. In ordinary discourse, competition means personal rivalry. . . . In the economic world, competition means almost the opposite" [12, p. 119]. Smith's usage emphasized the former, that is, behavioral competition. As Paul J. McNulty has observed, "the Smithian concept of competition was of a fundamentally different character than that which was later perfected by economic theorists" [29, p. 395]. In essentially aggregative and clearly long-run terms, Smith elevated "competition to the level of a general organizing principle of economic society" [29, p. 396]. We have already noted its role as a major component of the invisible hand. But his development of the concept of long-run natural price has little in common with the positivistic, mechanistic, short-run equilibrium of contemporary price theory. The latter is rhetorically associated with Adam Smith's system of natural liberty. However, there is increasing recognition that the short-run free market equilibrium model is more akin to storytelling than hard science [31, p. 109–17], perhaps a post-Smithian metaphor in pseudo-scientific wrappings. As such, it offers literally no insight concerning the industrial and financial structure and long-run performance of industrial capitalism. The real economic world that lies between pure competition and pure monopoly, for example, the world of oligopolistic multinational corporations and dual labor markets, involves the behavioral competition and sociological linkages of classical political economy.

Smith's social perspective is palpable when his works are viewed in their entirety and as a unit. Thus, Robert Heilbroner observes that "*The Wealth of Nations* is much more than a treatise on economics. It is the application to a given society of Smith's larger views of the processes of historic evolution, and these again, like the theories of Marx, represent the working-out in history of even more fundamental premises with respect to man and the universe. These latter views find their expression in between the lines of *The Theory of Moral Sentiments*" [19, p. 7]. As was Karl Marx's *Capital,* the *Wealth of Nations* was simply a fully rendered element of a much larger canvas [8, p. 317; 23, p. 5]. The essays that survived Smith's ordered destruction of some sixteen volumes of manuscripts just prior to his death reveal the breadth of his interests [27, pp. 29–223]. His projected, incomplete work on jurisprudence indicated his intent to return to, and elaborate upon, the broader themes introduced in *Theory of Moral Sentiments* once he had made his detailed detour into economics. The parallel with Marx invites speculation concerning the rounded system that might have been found in succeeding volumes assembled from Smith's "work in progress" by a sympathetic editor.

Smith's social, eclectic perspective—and the elements of social economics, past and future—are presented in his realistic behavioral and institutional qualification of his general analytic precepts. The strategic productive role of specialization is balanced by the later powerful statement on the stultifying effects of overspecialization [45, p. 734]; the characterization of services as "unproductive labor" is qualified by the realistic recognition that services include "some both of the gravest and most important, and some of the most frivolous professions" [45, p. 315]. His analytical support of private property, self-interest, profit, and accumulation—of capitalism as a system—is qualified by recognition of the working reality and dangers of economic power. Workers possess inferior bargaining power [45, p. 66]; "merchants and master manufacturers" are characterized as deceivers and oppressors of the public [45, p. 250]; and monopolistic businessmen are held to make the worst governors [45, p. 537].[27] His orientation to what came to be called Say's Law, for example, the proposition that savings tend to be spent (invested) in a liberal economy without significant lag or friction [45, p. 321], was tempered by recognition of the "safety-value" of foreign trade, of foreign investment of surplus capital stock [45, p. 354], and of the necessity of foreign sales to relieve domestic glut [45, p. 415].

Thus, Smith's simple system of natural liberty was actually a complex social mechanism which could produce too much of a good thing. Paradox—disequilibrium—is as palpable as consistency and equilibrium. The paradox of plenty, of plenitude alongside poverty, is reflected in the ongoing realities of idle capital and redundant goods, given a particular institutional or distributional set.

The social orientation of Adam Smith has been displaced by the hyperindividualism of contemporary orthodoxy. A new political economy, a social economics, will build on rediscovery of the social base of Smithian classicism and survivals in the "outerworld" of contemporary social science. Again, the interdependence of content and method appears. Quoting E. J. Mishan, David Riesman emphasizes that

> a "mass flight from reality into statistics" is not enough. . . . [Adam Smith's] humanism caused him to leave the paradise of positive science and dwell East of Eden with those who as Albion Small put it, saw the human process as "the tribunal of last resort for verdict upon the economic process. . . . The apostolic succession in social philosophy from Adam Smith is through the sociologists rather than the economists. The sociologists have kept alive the vital spark of Smith's moral philosophy. They have contended for a view of life in terms of persons rather than in terms of technology. That is, they have put *persons* in the center of their picture of life, and have assigned a subordinate place to the theory of those technical activities which deal with the material products of persons" [*Adam Smith and Modern Sociology*, 1907] [37, p. 19].

Concerned with the "Standards and Values in a Rich Society," Alvin Hansen pleaded, over twenty years ago, that economics must "concern itself with social priorities. In other words, it must, in a sense, become a branch of moral philosophy, as Adam Smith indeed had it." Perhaps, as Macfie has averred, "a Scottish revival is due" [28, p. 21]. He adds that "if there is a future for sociological economics and politics . . . then there is an opportunity for the resurgence of the Scottish tradition" [28, p. 41].

Contemporary indications of such a drift are seen in growing recognition of labor as a source of value in relation to analysis of X-efficiency, of human capital and education as strategic elements in economic growth. Cognizance of real subjective value has reappeared with increased critical analysis of real welfare content of the gross national product, alongside recognition of the emptiness of the abstract value box.

Notes

1. Smith's observations on these topics appear in [45, pp. 3–5, 28, 423, and 653–69 and 681, respectively].
2. The thesis is stated more fully in [16, pp. 2–7]. It has significant elements in common with Thomas Kuhn's analysis of paradigm change [24; and 26, p. 83, note 32], and particularly with Redlich's concept of the "heterogony of ideas" in relation to his observation that "the original ideas may become more or less twisted. In other cases it may be possible to turn a set of ideas upside down instead of developing it; one may think of what Karl Marx did to some of Hegel's epistemological ideas" [36, p. 317]. Thus, "it is important not to oversimplify the complexity and organic solidarity of Smith's writings into a neo-Benthamite utilitarian ideology which it most assuredly was not. Smith is a difficult author *whose name has often been invoked by men he would instantaneously have disliked to support causes he would have viewed with extreme suspicion*" (emphasis added) [37, p. 18].
3. This contrasts with the position of Milton Friedman and of the Chicago School, in general, that positive and normative economics are separable and independent. The Chicago position is a logical extension of positivist methodology, since important normative propositions are seldom amenable to rigorous quantification and disproof. See [31, pp. 127–28].
4. It is desirable to note, in this context, the contrast between an absolutist and relativist perspective in judging the present significance of earlier ideas. The absolutist tends to regard as relevant only those past ideas that are consonant with what existing orthodoxy accepts as "truth." Hence, what is important in Smith's work would be those ideas that are important, that are accepted, today. In this regard, Mark Blaug, as an absolutist, represents the most common current interpretation of Smith: "The central theme that inspires the *Wealth of Nations* is the workings of 'the invisible hand' " [5, p. 57]. This is in direct contrast to the relativistic position developed here, namely, that Smith's central concern is with the overall determinants of economic growth, the "invisible hand" being one of several means to that end. See [5, pp. 1–5] for a useful discussion of the absolutist-relativist relationship.

5. It may be true that the bicentennial literature on Smith presents a "kind of *renaissance*" among scholars, a revival of late nineteenth- and early twentieth-century perception [23, pp. 4–5; 32, p. 59] in "viewing Smith's work comprehensively, as an integrated *whole*" [35, p. 56]. However, until the scholarly perspectives of academic specialists are incorporated into both mainstream economic theory and social practice, the *de facto* apologetic use of *Wealth of Nations* will continue. As suggested in closing (see below, pp. 133–34), this application likely will await a fundamental reorientation of economic analysis.
6. Warren J. Samuels has presented interpretative perspectives that are similar to, and reinforcing of, those emphasized here: "Each generation has the task and the opportunity of reinterpreting Smith for itself" [42, p. 3]. It is in the substance of the given interpretation that we learn about both the interpreter and social setting out of which it develops. "One indicator of the historic importance of Smith's work has been that the interpretation of the *Wealth of Nations* has become a facet of the social control system of the Western economies" [42, p. 4].
7. Axel Leijonhufvud offers an excellent discussion of the problems for social sciences presented in the recent growth of knowledge literature, for judging "the applicability to economics of Growth and Knowledge theories [of Kuhn Lakatos, Hanson or Toulmin] developed to 'fit' physics or biology" [26, p. 67].
8. The element of originality in the book, in contrast, has been the subject of controversy. Representative of the negative judgment is Clyde E. Dankert: "There is little that is original in our author's discussion. It has been found that most of what he said had been said before" [7, p. 233]. But the affirmative position, which is that of the present author, seems predominant in the current generation. On the general nature of creativity (invention), see C. E. Ayres [2]; for its specific application to economists, including Smith, see George J. Stigler [48, pp. 4–5].
9. Georgescu-Roegen's work is perhaps the leading example of an expanding genre. "Only now, as the second centenary of Smith's book arrives, have the students of society and the students of nature once more begun to explore common problems. . . . [Thus, in addition to Georgescu-Roegen] Daly and Boulding have followed in the footsteps of Marshall and Spencer in suggesting that economists should take closer notice of the similarities which exist between the economic and biological processes" [11, p. 194]. Also see note 26.
10. This position is supported by Leo Rogin on the general interpretative ground that a major element of Smith's analysis was "his ultimate interest in repudiating the mercantilistic hierarchy of productivity [hence his subordination of] replacement and accumulation of fixed assets to the conception that the advance of capital constitutes [the basis for] increase in the number of productive laborers employed, which is the ultimate premise for increased investment in improved tools and processes" [39, pp. 69–70]. "While, as Smith emphasizes, exceptionally high profits seldom accrue to agricultural enterprise and large fortunes are rarely accumulated in agriculture, employment of capital in agriculture is most productive" [39, p. 74]. Samuel Hollander presents a detailed discussion of

the "hierarchy of production" issue concerning Smith, as well as a qualified rebuttal of the "agriculture first" position. For example, he states: "The significance to Smith of manufacturing is *implied particularly clearly* in the fact that it is . . . this sector, and not . . . agriculture, in which he envisaged the greatest prospects for technical improvements" (emphasis added) [22, p. 102].

11. In Smith's market analysis, "when it comes to the determination of natural price, demand is supposed to have no influence" [5, p. 41]. Analysts in Smith's time "saw no relationship between utility, in their sense of the term, and demand and, moreover, dismissed demand and supply explanations of relative price as superficial" [5, p. 42]. The neglect of demand by Adam Smith may be explained at several levels. In general historical terms, the scarcity of most necessary goods meant that demand as desire always would exceed supply. In his analysis of long-run natural price, "effectual demand" (desire plus purchasing power) determined that actual supply. Finally, it seems possible that his general "subordination of utility to the intellectual or aesthetic sentiments of *wonder, surprise,* and *admiration* . . . [his repudiation of] *utility* as the main object of scientific inquiry" [49, pp. 218–19] contributed to his essential disregard of consumer demand.

12. The interconnections between the value elements of labor as a measure of absolute value and the three input cost determinants of price are presented in Smith's statement: "The real value of all the different component parts of price, it must be observed, is measured by the quantity of labour which they can, each of them, purchase or command. Labour measures the value not only of that part of price which resolves itself into labor, but of that which resolves itself into rent, and of that which resolves itself into profit" [45, p. 50]. His position that labor is a source of surplus—the producer of net value—is seen in this statement: "The value which the workmen add to the materials, therefore, resolves itself in this case into two parts, of which the one pays their wages, and the other the profits of their employer upon the whole stock of materials and wages which he advanced" [45, p. 48]. These value and distribution relationships, supplemented by Ricardian rent, provided the foundation for Marx's theory of surplus value [30, pp. 5–8].

13. A recent manifestation of the long-run process of disassociating Smith, and other major classicists, from an emphasis on labor as a source of value is seen in the argument that capital (and capital analysis) is *the* strategic factor in Adam Smith's (and classical) analysis. Two leading examples are an article by Haim Barkai [3] and a recent book by Robert V. Eagly [9]. Barkai develops a highly refined, mathematical, and geometric "restatement of Smith's model [which purports to indicate] why it was capital which Smith identified as the strategic factor in the process of economic evolution" [3, p. 414]. Eagly is less assertive with respect to Smith. However, Smith is identified as a major contributor to classical economic theory [9, p. 34], wherein capital is judged to be "the dominant theoretical construct" [9, p. 60]. These positions contrast sharply with that of Joseph Schumpeter, who emphasizes the neglect of analysis of

capital by Adam Smith compared, for example, with A. R. J. Turgot [43, pp. 324, 333].

14. In a similar vein, Schumpeter observes that Smith wanted "a price theory by which to establish certain propositions [for example, regarding economic growth] that do not require going into the background of the value [that is, relative price] phenomenon at all" [43, p. 309].
15. The controversial nature of this position is indicated in Leijonhufvud's statement that "the history of economic doctrines has for the most part been written as a 'straight' historical narrative—as a chronological story of 'progress' by accumulating analytical improvements . . . with a largely fixed set of questions" [26, p. 67]. However, the economics profession's loss of contact with the classical-neoclassical distinction (and the underlying changes in question, content, and method) is most tangibly identified in its acceptance of J. M. Keynes's redefinition in a footnote to chapter 1 of the *General Theory*. He noted there that characterizing Alfred Marshall, F. Y. Edgeworth, and A. C. Pigou as classical economists was to "perhaps perpetuate a solecism," that is, speak incorrectly.
16. Thus, Richard Leftwich states that "the subjective value, or marginal utility economists of the late nineteenth century . . . [provided] the answer" to the diamond-water paradox [25, p. 125]. Through many editions of his widely used elementary economics text, Paul A. Samuelson has retained the statement that "today even a beginning student can give a correct answer to this problem [a solution to the paradox of value]." In direct contrast, Piero Mini rebuts the "claim that hyperclassicism [neoclassicism] resolved the Smithian paradox of the relative value of diamonds and water." Mini concludes that "the solution is a purely formal one which throws no light on the problems" [31, p. 117]. Contact with the fundamental methodological issue involved is presented in Hollander's statement that "the 'paradox of value' was not formulated as a *problem* requiring a *solution*" [22, p. 137]. Positivist methodology, which now dominates the economics profession (exemplified here by Leftwich and Samuelson), deals only with problems that are conceivably amenable to solution, with questions to which there are presumably unequivocal answers in either logic or fact. Thus, contemporary positivistic economics cannot deal with paradox. As it does with other complex individual and social realities attending human behavior, it deals with them by denying their existence or defining them away.
17. "Exchange value enabled the classicist to say whether the welfare of one socioeconomic class, the landlords for instance, increased or decreased relative to the welfare of another class, the workers or the capitalists; but it did not allow them to make statements respecting a change in total output and a change in total welfare" [47, p. 129].
18. Heilbroner characterizes this paradoxical relationship as a puzzle: "Moral sentiments, in Smith's time, was the phrase used to describe the puzzling ability of man—by instinct, it was supposed, a creature of self-interest—to conceive judgments in which his self-interest was held in abeyance" [19, pp. 7–8].
19. The broader base of this "political" or "social" paradox is detailed by

Henry Spiegel under the heading "Paradoxes of the Commercial Society" [46, pp. 234–37]. This section provides a catalogue of quotations from *Wealth of Nations* indicating Smith's awareness of the varied facets of social conflict in a market society. These defects in the natural order provide "sufficient ammunition, as Viner said, for several socialist orations" [5, p. 56].

20. Hayek characterizes individualism true as "primarily a *theory* of society, an attempt to understand the forces which determine the social life of man" [18, p. 6]. The contrasting "false individualism" is characterized by ultrarationalism and ethical pragmatism. The perspective of true individualism is closely associated with "The Scottish tradition in Economic Thought." Thus, Macfie observes "that there is a characteristic Scottish attitude and method [that] may be called the philosophical approach, though many of us may prefer to call it, equally aptly, the social approach" [28, p. 19]. This "classical line" runs from Francis Hutcheson and David Hume through Smith, the two Mills, and Marshall [28, p. 20]. See [41, pp. 77–78] for detailed references to this set of relationships, and see [15] for an application of them to the evolution of neoclassicism to the present.
21. It seems likely that understanding of the development of economic institutions, thought, and policy will be clarified by more systematic application of the paradigm of metaphor. Robert A. Nisbet has employed the development metaphor of "genesis and decay" as the basis for understanding the essentials of social change [33]. Such applications stem from recognition that there may be a sense in which "every perspective requires a metaphor to organize it. Metaphors lie at the base of inquiry and animate it" [10, p. 119].
22. Boulding employs the concept of "positive payoffs" in stating the need for a power center—the state—to share in the social product as a condition of maintaining its position. "An institution or an organization which is perceived as having positive payoffs both for its participants and for the people in its environment is more likely to achieve legitimacy, especially in the long run, than institutions with low or negative payoffs" [6, p. 300]. The strategic nature of power and conflict resolution has been emphasized by Samuels, both in the general setting of classical political economy [41] and the specific content of *Wealth of Nations* [40].
23. A formal philosophical base for this position is the "objectivism" of novelist Ayn Rand. An early example of this usage of Adam Smith in the coordinate support of capitalism and derogation of socialism, in particular, and the social-humanist perspective, in general, is Jack Hirshleifer's 1959 article, "Capitalist Ethics—Tough or Soft?" Apropos the "individualistic" interpretation of Smith, he states: "All the world is largely governed by self-interest and all the world knows it" [21, p. 116]. The acceptability of Hirshleifer's caricature of a social orientation (that is, that of nonsocialists such as Adam Smith and F. A. Hayek, as well as socialists, both Marxian and non-Marxian) to orthodox economics, in the setting of the Cold War, is indicated by its reproduction in the readings text coedited by Paul A. Samuelson, John R. Coleman, and Felicity Skidmore.

24. Thus, Jacob Oser and William Blanchfield state: "Smith assumed a society with perfect liberty, a society in which all were free to choose and change their occupations" [34, p. 76]. This is very difficult to accept in light of Smith's recurrent recognition of market and social imperfections (see, for example, notes 19 and 27, as well as his skepticism concerning abstract analysis, discussed on p. 125 above). Presented here is the political—the ideological—necessity of accepting the existence of competitive markets as a working reality (of the functional interrelationships of positive and normative analysis in the linking of the analytical assumption of perfect competition to socially acceptable performance of capitalism). Unconsciously, perhaps, the positivist Friedman employs the metaphorical "as if" form in his normative defense of capitalism "as if it were competitive."
25. It has been argued [15, pp. 754, 760–63] that contemporary neoclassicism embodies, in significant degree, the characteristics of false individualism (see note 20 above) in its application of nineteenth-century market logic to twentieth-century conditions. Neoclassical supererogation of individualism and rationalism is an extension of "the hyperclassical period insofar as [they] represent that culmination of the logical tendencies of the Cartesian ego" [31, p. 104]. Given the perspective of exaggerated, perverse individualism, one may account for the defense and support of repressive regimes (as in post-Allende Chile) by nineteenth-century liberals such as Milton Friedman and William Buckley. The pure "logic" of the competitive market metaphor is that "free" markets will "naturally" evolve in any "rational" polity, providing automatically thereby the socioeconomic benefits of the "invisible hand."
26. The fundamental change in analytical method that has been referred to in several contexts above constitutes a third major transformation that cannot be treated in detail here. "It is a paradox of history that [adoptions of] the analytics of Book I . . . have eclipsed the philosophical and historical methods in which [Smith] so revelled and which showed his Scots character" [28, p. 21]. It is the latter that are now being revived with widening recognition of the limits of equilibrium analysis and the necessity of *process* perspective for dealing with problems of environmental quality, resource limits, human welfare, and growth. Thus, Macfie continues, observing that "the positive analytic method is a mere strippling. An immense future stretches ahead; and the past certainly shows that each phase of social development produces its own philosophy and method in all the social disciplines" [28, p. 21]. See note 9 concerning the methodological perspectives of Georgescu-Roegen and others that reflect contact with such a future, and also see [26, p. 96] on the likely necessity of change in analytic method for basic change in understanding, in the "pattern of beliefs."
27. Smith's critical perspective concerning the overall social position of merchants (businessmen) is readily identified in the Index to *Wealth of Nations* under "Merchants":

    silent with regard to the pernicious effects of their own gains, 98; clamour and sophistry of, 128; their judgments more to be depended upon respecting the interests of their particular branches of trade, than with regard to the public interest, 249–250; . . . customs of, first established to supply the want of laws, and afterward admitted as laws, 293; . . . [not citizens of any particular country, 395;] . . . [derive greatest advantage from monopoly of the home market, 426;] are actuated by a narrow spirit of monopoly, [429;] . . . the government of a company of, the worst a country can be under, 537;" [45, p. 944].

References

[1] Irma Adelman. *Theories of Growth and Development.* Stanford: Stanford University Press, 1961.

[2] Clarence E. Ayres. *The Theory of Economic Progress.* Chapel Hill: University of North Carolina Press, 1944.

[3] Haim Barkai. "A Formal Outline of a Smithian Growth Model." *Quarterly Journal of Economics* 83 (August 1969): 396–414.

[4] R. D. Collison Black. "Smith's Contribution in Historical Perspective." In *The Market and the State: Essays in Honour of Adam Smith,* edited by Thomas Wilson and Andrew S. Skinner. Oxford: Clarendon Press, 1976. Pp. 42–63.

[5] Mark Blaug. *Economic Theory in Retrospect.* 3d ed. Homewood, Ill.: Richard D. Irwin, 1978.

[6] Kenneth E. Boulding. "The Legitimacy of Economics." *Western Economic Journal* 5 (September 1967): 299–307.

[7] Clyde E. Dankert. *Adam Smith Man of Letters and Economist.* Hicksville, N.Y.: Exposition Press, 1974.

[8] Peter L. Danner. "Sympathy and Exchangeable Value: Keys to Adam Smith's Social Philosophy." *Review of Social Economy* 34 (December 1976): 317–31. Special issue on "The Social Economics of Adam Smith."

[9] Robert V. Eagly. *The Structure of Classical Economic Theory.* New York: Oxford University Press, 1974.

[10] James Fernandez. "The Mission of Metaphor in Expressive Culture." *Current Anthropology* (June 1964): 119–45.

[11] Vernard Foley. *The Social Physics of Adam Smith.* West Lafayette, Ind.: Purdue University Press, 1976.

[12] Milton Friedman. *Capitalism and Freedom.* Chicago: University of Chicago Press, 1962.

[13] Nicholas Georgescu-Roegen. *The Entropy Law and the Economic Process.* Cambridge, Mass.: Harvard University Press, 1971.

[14] Eli Ginzberg. *The House of Adam Smith.* New York: Columbia University Press, 1934.

[15] Warren S. Gramm. "Chicago Economics: From Individualism True to Individualism False." *Journal of Economic Issues* 9 (December 1975): 753–75.

[16] Warren S. Gramm. "Natural Selection in Economic Thought: Ideology, Power, and the Keynesian Counterrevolution." *Journal of Economic Issues* 7 (March 1973): 1–27.

[17] William D. Grampp. *Economic Liberalism.* New York: Random House, 1965. Volume 1.
[18] F. A. Hayek. *Individualism and Economic Order.* Chicago: University of Chicago Press, 1948.
[19] Robert Heilbroner. "Homage to Adam Smith." *Challenge* 19 (March/April 1976): 6–11.
[20] Eduard Heimann. *History of Economic Doctrines.* New York: Oxford University Press, 1945.
[21] Jack Hirshleifer. "Capitalist Ethics—Tough or Soft?" *Journal of Law and Economics* 2 (October 1959): 114–19.
[22] Samuel Hollander. *The Economics of Adam Smith.* Toronto: University of Toronto Press, 1973.
[23] T. W. Hutchison. *On Revolutions and Progress in Economic Knowledge.* Cambridge: the University Press, 1978.
[24] Thomas S. Kuhn. *The Structure of Scientific Revolutions.* Chicago: University of Chicago Press, 1962.
[25] Richard H. Leftwich. *The Price System & Resource Allocation.* 6th ed. Hinsdale, Ill.: The Dryden Press, 1976.
[26] Axel Leijonhufvud. "Schools, 'revolutions' and research programmes in economic theory." In *Method and Appraisal in Economics,* edited by Spiro J. Latsis. Cambridge: the University Press, 1976.
[27] J. Ralph Lindgren, ed. "Essays on Philosophical Subjects." In *The Early Writings of Adam Smith.* New York: Augustus M. Kelley, 1967. Pp. 29–223.
[28] A. L. Macfie. "The Scottish Tradition in Economic Thought." Reprinted in *The Individual in Society: Papers on Adam Smith.* London: George Allen & Unwin, 1967. Pp. 19–41.
[29] Paul J. McNulty. "A Note of the History of Perfect Competition." *Journal of Political Economics* 75 (August 1967): 395–99.
[30] Ronald L. Meek. *Smith, Marx, & After.* London: Chapman & Hall, 1977.
[31] Piero V. Mini. *Philosophy and Economics.* Gainesville: University of Florida Press, 1974.
[32] Glenn R. Morrow. *The Ethical and Economic Theories of Adam Smith.* New York: Augustus M. Kelley, 1969 (1923).
[33] Robert A. Nisbet. *Social Change and History.* New York: Oxford University Press, 1969.
[34] Jacob Oser and William C. Blanchfield. *The Evolution of Economic Thought.* 3d ed. New York: Harcourt Brace Jovanovich, 1975.
[35] Horst Claus Recktenwald. "An Adam Smith Renaissance *anno* 1976? The Bicentenary Output—A Reappraisal of His Scholarship." *Journal of Economic Literature* 16 (March 1978): 56–83.
[36] Fritz Redlich. "Ideas Their Migration in Space and Transmittal Over Time." *Kyklos* 4 (1953): 301–20.
[37] Ravid A. Reisman. *Adam Smith's Sociological Economics.* New York: Barnes & Noble, 1976.
[38] Joan Robinson. *Economic Philosophy.* Chicago: Aldine, 1962.
[39] Leo Rogin. *The Meaning and Validity of Economic Theory.* New York: Harper & Brothers, 1956.

[40] Warren J. Samuels. "Adam Smith and the Economy as a System of Power." *Indian Economic Journal* 20 (January-March 1973): 363–81.
[41] Warren J. Samuels. *The Classical Theory of Economic Policy*. Cleveland, Ohio: World Publishing Co., 1966.
[42] Warren J. Samuels. "The Political Economy of Adam Smith." *Nebraska Journal of Economics and Business* 15 (Summer 1976): 3–24.
[43] Joseph A. Schumpeter. *History of Economic Analysis*. New York: Oxford University Press, 1954.
[44] Adam Smith. *Theory of Moral Sentiments*. London: George Bell & Sons, 1907.
[45] Adam Smith. *Wealth of Nations*. New York: Modern Library, 1937.
[46] Henry William Spiegel. *The Growth of Economic Thought*. Englewood Cliffs, N.J.: Prentice-Hall, 1971.
[47] Matthew A. Stephenson. "The Paradox of Value: A Suggested Interpretation." *History of Political Economy* 4 (Spring 1972): 127–39.
[48] George J. Stigler. "The Nature and Role of Originality in Scientific Progress." In *Essays in the History of Economics*. Chicago: University of Chicago Press, 1965. Pp. 1–15.
[49] Herbert F. Thompson. "Adam Smith's Philosophy of Science." *Quarterly Journal of Economics* 75 (May 1964): 212–33.

15

Language and Economics

Walter C. Neale

My argument derives from the histories of political philosophy and economic thought and from ideas garnered from linguistics. The basic proposition is that the deep difference—the chasm—between people whose cast of mind or intellectual position leads them to call themselves institutionalists, and those people whom I shall call standard economists, is fundamentally philosophical rather than ideological or methodological. One difference is that the standard side tends to follow in the tradition of the philosophers of natural law. While that school certainly dates back twenty-four centuries, I shall not push back before John Locke. I think it is clear that there has been a consistent strain of natural law philosophy running from Locke on through Smith and the classical economists (including Marx), the neoclassical economists, the Keynesians, and the monetarists. Although not all of them subscribe to a view that there is a universal, natural social order, few, I think, take a position which must necessarily be inconsistent with the philosophy of natural law.

It would, of course, simply be wrong to say that standard economists believe that there is a natural order and that institutional economists believe that there is a disorderly universe—and that this is the difference between the two. It is not. The natural law tradition believes or assumes that there is a set of rules governing all human action and interaction (behavior, whatever people do); that these rules are universal; and that they are very limited in number. As importantly, standard economists believe that rules can be stated in a logically precise way. The contrast here is not with illogical or sloppy. Rather, I am contrasting the sort of logical definition one gets in mathematics—perfecly discrete and unambiguously neat, like four and nine and thirty-six[1]—with the sort of descriptive definition (for example, for a horse) or the sort of operational definition (for a boiled potato, for example) that one uses to identify in the world one observes.

It is the logical precision—for instance, in propositions about maximization of profits or of welfare in terms of marginal rates of substitution—that allows standard economists to derive a lot of subsidiary propositions, whether they are the shutdown point of a firm in the intermediate run, the income and substitution effects of price changes on consumer demand, or whatever else. Given the universality and precision of their general premises, they happily derive a great many conclusions about policy, about welfare, and especially about what people are really doing. Much of standard thought has gone into spelling out the full implications of the limited number of general propositions.

In addition, standard economists appear, as do philosophers of natural law, to have a set of views about ethics and values and welfare that amounts to a natural law of ethics. Its modern form derives, to a large extent, from the behavior of some of our ancestors with respect to their rulers: in short, from beheading one Stuart king and chasing another out of England. When one had gone so far as to become Protestant and then to behead one's king, there was very little left of that older, semi-divine order that had justified holding property or enforcing civil and criminal law. So at this point our ancestors—I use the phrase in a manner analogous to that of the French administrators of the schools in their African colonies, who supplied basic readers beginning, "Our forefathers, the Gauls . . ."—at this point our ancestors needed some other way to justify civil government and the maintenance of existing institutions. A natural ethic could provide one. The economics tradition as well as the larger Anglo-American political tradition in this respect owes a great deal to John Locke, for providing a natural ethic presumably derived from the nature of man and therefore a natural law not unlike the Newtonian laws of the solar system. Locke could then derive not only rights to liberties and property, but also the powers of government to protect property and to force citizens to cooperate in the pursuit of public policy.

It is not that institutionalists disbelieve in an orderly universe; they too have universals, but their universals do not pretend to such logical precision. Nor do institutionalists agree that *a* revealable or discoverable natural law governs the behavior of people. They do not believe that the natural law of philosophical tradition (whether ethical or otherwise), or the orderly social universe as portrayed in standard economics, are correct versions of any actual social universe. One can, of course, have orderly universes that are not real. The flat earth universe of Ptolemy is a very orderly universe. The proposition that comes with Columbus is not that it is a disorderly universe; nor did Columbus say that he would sail around the earth because of a random probability that he would get home; he also believed—intensely, one imagines—in an orderly universe, but in a different one from Ptolemy's.

Institutionalists too have ideas about the shape of an orderly social universe. Not only are they sure that it is not flat—not logically neat and definitionally discrete—they also often find that the ethics implicit in standard theory rest upon philosophical foundations that are weak indeed. There seems no other basis for these "natural"—or intuitive, or self-evident—ethics than a personal preference that often coincides too closely with the maintenance of existing privilege.

Institutionalists have long criticized the philosophical foundations of standard economics, and I shall do the same here. However, I shall put the critical case in terms deriving from analysis of language—not because it is fun to restate the old in a new way (although it is fun)—but because putting the argument in these terms may expose elements of natural law implicit in standard economics to light from an independent line of analysis, and because it will emphasize the importance of *process* in institutionalist thought. Specifically, I have been strongly influenced by Benjamin Lee Whorf's *Language, Thought, and Reality*.[2] Ludwig Wittgenstein, whom I read later, reaches much the same position as does Whorf, but starts with the state of philosophical discourse as developed by Bertrand Russell and others during the first two decades of this century, rather than with a comparative analysis of languages, which was Whorf's starting point.[3] In this essay I follow Whorf, with some confidence that Wittgenstein would approve.

I am what a rude linguist might call an amateur polyglot in one language, so I shall stick to English for my examples, with a faith that much of what I shall say is true of many other languages as well. What I shall be saying about language and its effects upon our thought should not be taken to mean that language is to blame for errors in reasoning. Whether or not there could be a perfect language, a perfect language does not exist and we must live with one or another language that we have. Thus, while I shall be arguing against nouns, I shall be using many nouns. I could not talk to you if I did not. Neither should what I say be taken to mean that our language forces particular perceptions or reasonings upon us. Rather, its structure and content often allow and sometimes encourage errors in thought, and the point is to see how this happens and what it has done to economics.

A grammar structures our universe of discourse, and meaning derives from the contexts in which words are used. By grammar I do not mean Painini's Sanskritic grammar as it was applied to Latin and then borrowed to torture an English with a different grammatical structure—not *that* grammar, which we learned in school. I mean those rules of word order, word form, and selection that allow us to communicate in a language. We all recognize that *broad* has quite different meanings when spoken by a geographer describing the Mississippi, a travel agent suggesting a trip to East Anglia, and a sailor about to start his leave. When one speaks of a word having a meaning one refers both to its use in those places in speech (or writing) where the occurence of the word seems proper to a native speaker, *and* to the particular circumstances of its utterance that make the native listener feel that he understands a statement. "I furtive tense his on spit" does neither. "I spit on his furtive tense" fulfills the first requirement, but not the second. "Shoes his I on spit" does neither, but "I spit on his shoes" does both. But a word—a cluster of phonemes—is not necessarily restricted to one sort of grammatical place or to one kind of experiential referent. "His spit makes me tense"—an understandable English sentence —move *spit* from grammatical verb slot to grammatical noun slot, moves *tense* from grammatical noun slot to grammatical predicate adjective slot, *and* the phonemes constituting *tense* now have a very different referent in experience.

Let me take up the dependence of meaning upon context, discussing some cases where economists have asked the wrong questions and tried to argue the impossible because they have violated some of language's rules for meaning. To start with a simple, non-economic example: consider the English language question, "What happens when an *irresistible* force meets an *immovable* object?" This is a non-question or meaningless question. In normal discourse, each word has specific contexts. Thus *irresistible* means "in the circumstances, of which we engaged in this conversation are all aware, we do not know how that force can be resisted." And similarly, *immovable* means "in the circumstances, of which we engaged in this conversation are all aware, we do not know how that object can be moved." When the words are removed from their normal contexts and given an absolute or universal meaning in the question, it appears that one has a puzzle or paradox, but one does not. Instead of asking, "What happens when an irresistible force meets an immovable object?" one might as well ask, "What happens when a logarithm meets a stork?"

The same escape from context has happened in economics. Words with meaning in contexts are generalized and made universal. Of course, all disciplines take words—clusters of phonemes—from normal discourse and give them specific meanings that are different from the meanings they have had in normal discourse. In fact, the new use has its own new context. "Quarks have charm, spin, and color" is a meaningful statement; and, although they are not part of my normal discourse, physicists have given these words *such limited contexts and contrasts* that they have acquired new meanings. An example from economics with a like justification might be *rent*. When the classical economists began using it, *rent* meant payment by a tenant to a landlord for use of land. Adopted and redefined by economists over the years, economic *rent* acquired an additional use in somewhat different contexts. It came to mean "the differential productivity of a non-reproducible input." One can now speak of the licensing fees and royalties, and even of the corporate profits tax and much of the net profits from North Sea oil fields, as *rent*. One can speak of a large part of the income of talented athletes and actresses as *quasi-rents*. Statements one makes can be perfectly meaningful. *Rent* and *quasi-rent* have contexts and contrasts: receipts of money income flows, and identifiable uses of the inputs for which rents are paid. Rents contrast discretely with other money flows (a money flow cannot be both an economic profit and an economic rent). And all economists recognize the wide range of meanings of *investment* in different contexts with different contrasts: in macrotheory, in finance and accounting, and in "investing two dollars on the nose of a horse." But what is pleasantly true of some "words of the art" adopted and adapted from other realms of discourse is unpleasantly untrue of others.

Utility is a prime example. In its normal context of discourse *utility* means "mundanely useful." In economics it has come to embrace any aspect of an event or the perception of an event, real or imaginary, conscious or subconscious, correct or mistaken, that is desirable. It has escaped its normal contexts; and, like *irresistible* and *immovable*, no longer has a clear referent. It is no longer limited by contextual restrictions, and contrasts only with its absence. (I do not think that Edgeworth or Marshall can be accused of this error: Edgeworth said he was talking about "the lower order of wants" [mundane]; and Marshall about "everyday" [mundane] things.) Whatever the substitution of *preference* for *utility* may have done for the logical structure of postulates in the theory of demand, it has not cured the problem of referent. Again, unlimited expansion of range of meaning has resulted in meaninglessness. "I prefer chocolate to vanilla," or "I prefer to live close to campus" are perfectly sensible English statements. The usual classroom examples drawing upon fairly close substitutes to explain and justify indifference analysis may make sense—although the profession might have taken warning from the difficulty economists have had persuading non-economists that we *are* making sense. But our ability to say sensibly "I'd rather have X than Y" about a very large number of alternatives, perhaps running to eight or nine at a time, is more than exhausted when we assert that the same is true of ten to the zillion factorial alternatives in four dimensional space-time, with probabilities attached. Experience, gut feelings, and a dirty mind cannot be generalized into a preference function and retain meaning. That which explains all explains nothing.

A more curious example is *choice*. In this case the use of the word has not escaped limits, but rather the use shifts between and even combines meanings from quite different contexts. Unlike the different uses of *investment*, the different uses of *choice* are not clearly discrete. Some of us choose chocolate over vanilla, some choose this spouse over that possible spouse, and some choose the path to salvation. While there is a similarity in all uses of *choice*—this rather than something else—the connotations, the emotions, the consequences, and even the denotations of "Chocolate or vanilla?" "Your money or your life?" and "Will you choose Jesus?" are not the same. There are choices that can be modified at the margin (a cheaper rug *and* some drapes); there are choices that cannot (whom to marry; whether to be a loyal American). There are non-choice choices—the offers that cannot be refused.

Then there are choices with strong moral connotations. In one sort of context are the simple, mundane choices of the sort with which neoclassical economists first dealt. In another are the choices which come once to every man and nation: choices about salvation and spiritual commitment—although, some say, these choices are predestined. The referents for mundane choice are memory, mental pictures of self, advertising, mother's advice, and spouse's carping. The referents for choices about salvation are eternity, God's will, and faith. In Catholic thought one is morally responsible for choices with respect to one's faith, but Grace is infinite and one can pull oneself from the very jaws of hell. In Puritan thought, however—and Puritan thought is an important element in modern economic thought—choice is stark and error unforgivable. Puritan thought did not start quite this way, and it is not quite Puritan theology at its highest level, but as Puritan doctrine became Puritan feeling, the consequence of error was binding punishment: "You made your bed; now lie in it!" Or, as the actor playing the part of columnist James Kilpatrick in the film *Airplane* said about the passengers, "Shana, they bought their tickets. . . . I say, let them crash!"

What has happened in economics is historically understandable but semantically peculiar; the *mundane choice* which allowed individuals to pick what they would rather have and so be "better off" combined with the *Puritan choice* for which one is morally responsible—with the result, *mirabile dictu*, that if your choice does not make you happier, then you *deserve* to be miserable!

Now let me take up a matter of grammar. We do several things when we speak. We use lots of nouns. We also have a language that requires us to use a noun to begin a statement (allowing for pronouns, for inverting word order in questions, for poetic license, and so on). This has several results. It makes any word in initial position a noun; and (as one learned in school) a noun is a person, place, thing, or idea. Now, *idea* here is really a garbage bag. A word in initial position is a noun, so if it is not a person or a place or a thing, then, by elimination, it is an idea. Things like trees and people and places are concrete—you can spit on any of them. An *idea* does not fit such an operationally defined group. Ideas are mental processes, doings (verbings) of the brain; but, because of the way our language slots them into the same position as people and places and things, we tend to think of them as things "out there," with independent existences, and not as doings going on in our heads. Aided and abetted by metaphor, ideas become as solid as trees: for instance, one "grasps an idea" by "getting a handle on it." Second, nouning has a lot to do with our way of thinking because the first noun, this word that goes in the noun slot, does something: it verbs. Sometimes it just verbs: exists or acts. At other times it verbs another noun, and this influences our ideas about cause. In both cases the nouns exist separately from their being or doing.

Then there are other noun slots, such as "objects of prepositions," so that a preposition with a slotted noun can become an adverbial place. These too allow, and even induce, some peculiar arguments. Let me first illustrate with a philosophical issue, one certainly relevant to economics. The basic structure of the English language allows the sensible English question, "Do you come from Knoxville?"—a person and a place. This pattern makes it easy to generate another English question: "From where does justice come?" A perfectly good question from the standpoint of the English language, but, to an instrumentalist at least, a silly question. There is no *justice*—I do not mean that one cannot *behave justly* (I am coming to that)—but there isn't *a justice.* And from what place could justice come? Obviously, the answer cannot be, "From Cleveland, Ohio." We have here a false question, a non-question, a meaningless question, but a question that the language not only allows but actually encourages.

There is sense to talking about justice because one can certainly learn that some particular person, in a particular role of authority, is regarded as behaving justly; but the referent is not *a justice* "out there" or "up there" or "universally immanent," but people feeling and thinking about the actions of the person in authority. Thus what we need is a language world with only a few nouns but lots of verbs and adverbs. Instead, we live in a language world of nouns: not "authorities *acting* in a way that people *approve* or *accept,*" but a noun thing, *justice.*

The language does allow meaningful sorts of questions about justice. Why does this or that person—a judge—do something? There are various ways of going about answering. If you are asking about a particular judge in a proceeding that puzzles you, you might decide to consult a psychiatrist to find out what it was in that man's early background that caused him to take such a strange position on the bench. Or you may answer the question in terms of the circumstances and the rules of the group with whom that judge is dealing, and in terms of the consequences, as the judge perceives them, of the different decisions he might make. Then you can start to answer the question, "Why did he act like that?" Instead of asking—"From where does justice come?"—one should ask, "What has been happening that has led that group of people to hang this man or to recompense that man?" When one has answered such questions, one has answered the question of what that group thinks is just. If and only if—and here I shall be a logician—*if,* and only if, people in all cultures (or 99.6 percent of all cultures) take the same view in similar circumstances—circumstances with which they are all familiar—*and if,* and only if, they have experienced the consequences of similar trials of possibly just and possibly unjust actions, *only then* can we speak of a universal perception of just action.

Nouning has contributed to confusion about meaning, and to confusing word order with cause. It is important to distinguish between value as a noun (thing), which it is not, and *to value* as a verb. The former generates a bunch of non-questions, such as the classical economic question, "Why do diamonds have more value than bread?" Diamonds do not *have value.* They have mass, density, reflectivity, and chemical composition, but they *do not have value*. Instead of asking, "Why does a diamond have value?" one should be asking, "How do people value diamonds?" And answering by saying, "They value them by stealing them, buying them, insuring them, killing for them," and so on. Stealing, buying, insuring, killing are *how* people value diamonds.

In standard economics *nouns are explanations*: utility, preference, satisfaction, revealed preference, tastes. As English speakers have spoken in terms of *having values*, so economists have spoken about *having tastes*, as if the frontal lobes were filing cabinets full of electronic tapes of tastes ready for a program of opportunities. We do *not have tastes*. We enjoy, we dislike, we remember, we feel. The structure of our language encourages us to account for an event by a noun being or doing, or by a noun doing something to another noun. "Taste causes people to eat apples." I recognize "people" and "apples" as noun things. But *taste*? Unless the people have had some very bad damage done to their mouths and throats, a chemo-bio-neurological *process is going on*. When eating an apple, people taste the apple. They may repeat the process. As S. H. Frankel would say, "People like eating apples."[4] They like, if you will, to taste apples, but they do not get something other than tasting the apple. They will probably remember tasting an apple. But, they do not get *a* utility or satisfaction from tasting the apple. What happens is tasting, which is not a thing. What happens is that people who eat apples taste apples and some enjoy tasting apples—it's all *verb process*. I have always found rather appealing Gilbert Ryle's asking whether there would be any way of persuading an angler to have the satisfaction or utility of fishing when not allowed to go fishing.[5] It is quite clear that anglers enjoy fishing; but *an* enjoyment does not come from fishing or because of fishing—the pleasure *is* the process, which means *doing* (verbing, fishing).

One way to understand what institutional economists have been about is to see them as rejecting nouning and arguing for processual verbing. A major branch of the institutional tradition derives from the work of Clarence Ayres.[6] This tradition, borrowing from Veblen's language, has pointed to a conflict between values stemming from technology and those "ceremonial" values stemming from institutions. I subscribe to the thought behind the phrasing, but the way it is stated may cause problems. We are in danger of getting right back into nouns. Technology is not a thing. There are various ways of *doing*. The technological values are *processes*. You could say that the values are inherent in the processes, if you want to use nouns, but I would rather say that the values *are* the processes. *How* you *use* things—these *are* the values. There is a further stage as Ayres presented the argument: particularly effective ways for handling problems tend to be universal values. These are the technological values that, a bit more widely in philosophy, are called *instrumental*—so-called because they work. When our natural lawyers, the standard economists, assume values as tastes or as parametric psychological propensities, and then treat them as one treats propositions about Euclidean figures or differences between two quantities of output, and thereby derive logically valid conclusions—which aren't necessarily so—we then have, I think, one of the sorts of reasoning that Ayres called "ceremonial."

The basic propositions, I think, can now be fairly clearly stated: there are no *noun values*, we *verb value* things—we value apples by eating apples; we value, in a very Ayresian statement, "a wrench by twisting a bolt." One does not value a wrench independently of twisting something—except, of course, occasionally, when someone is in a terrible rage with his wife or neighbor, he may find another way of valuing the wrench. But one does *not* value a wrench independently of using it. One may, like Elizabeth Taylor, value diamonds by hoarding them. If one happens to hoard shoes, one is known as a fetishist. But one values the shoes by hoarding them in the closet or looking at them, and that is "the value" of the shoes. To refer to a *preference* for the wrench or the shoes does not explain: it slots in a noun as the cause.

Institutionalists have spoken and written in the English language, and perforce they have used nouns; *but*, in the terms in which I have been arguing, they have come as close as is perhaps possible to analyzing economies as *verb processes*. The institutionalist is an instrumentalist: that is, one who argues that values emerge from the experience of testing ways of handling problems that arise. When a problem arises—if people do not like the way things are going or find life frustrating—they set about changing the old system and the values implicit in it. They do this by experimenting with new ways and by discovering from their experiences with the new ways whether the new ways are better than the old ones in solving the problems and alleviating the frustrations. Learning-by-testing is the way people solve their problems: which is to say, the way their values evolve. Answering the question, "How do we act in this new situation?" is a problem. It is solved by trying out new ways until a way is developed that integrates activity in a new kind of situation with the other activities of the group. If a new rule about what people may or should do works in the new situation, then it has passed the test. If it does not work, then another new rule is tried.

This instrumental problem solving is not a matter of expressing individual preferences such as are portrayed on indifference maps. Rather, it is a matter of a *group* of people (a *going concern*, in John R. Commons's phrase) trying out a new program or policy or way of doing things (new *working rules*, again in Commons's phrase).[7] Any going concern—a family, a village, or a nation—has ways to modify the working rules guiding the actions of its members. There are parents, chiefs of Homeric *oikoi*, elders, priests, prophets, councils, commissions, legislatures, and courts. While some processes work within relatively narrow confines—within families, unions, or caste panchayats—other going concerns, such as legislatures or courts, follow their own working rules to examine and evaluate the working rules of lesser groups in the light of the *public purpose* of the larger group. The *collective will* or purpose of any going concern—I continue to use Commons's phrasings—guides this experimental process and shapes future collective action. Commons called this evolutionary process the *artificial selection* of working rules. In his autobiography Commons says, "In economic conflicts, reasonable values and reasonable practices were not the subjective opinions of anybody, but were the collective opinion, expressed in action, of those whose economic interests were conflicting. . . . This, I found afterwards was Peirce's 'pragmatism'. . . . I am now told by a colleague in philosophy that it is 'instrumental pragmatism,' which philosophers were beginning to formulate."[8]

The test of a new set of working rules is *not* reference to some idea of a natural law or a natural justice, nor is it some hypothetical history—whether of noble savages in Rousseau's world, hardworking middle-class savages in Locke's world, or, in what I understand to be John Rawls's world, of highly educated men with a first-class capacity for introspection and reasoning but without any effects of acculturation or personal life histories. Rather, the test is whether people continue to go on working with these new rules, approving them by generally abiding by them and by enforcing them on any recalcitrant minority. If people continue with the new working rules, they have found them *instrumental* in solving their problems. If they have not found them *instrumental*, people go on to try still newer working rules. Since circumstances change, and since any new set of working rules will inevitably cause new frustrations and conflicts, the instrumental process of making new rules must go on forever. Thus are the constantly changing values of a people, a culture, or any sub-group derived, whether we are examining a butcher's union, dairymen in Wisconsin, the nation of the United States, or Christendom.

The theory of instrumental valuing is a set of statements about how in fact people evaluate and re-evaluate a thing or a social relationship or a process. In this treatment of valuing there is no dependence upon an *a priori* or "given" set of values, but rather a taking of values as observed in the behavior of people. Tastes are not ultimate but products of experience and become known to others from what people do. In the same Charles Sanders Peirce and John Dewey tradition of "learning is doing" or "knowing is doing," "valuing is doing." Thus one values a wrench by twisting a bolt and values a hammer by hitting a nail. Similarly one values courts by pleading before them and abiding by the decisions of judges; one values a constitution by citing it to courts and interpreting it to others. The using of wrenches and courts is simultaneously a testing of wrenches and courts. The testing is a continuous questioning of whether people like the consequences of using the wrench or the courts. When the wrench starts slipping, they stop using it: they cease to value it. When the orders of the courts seem unjust or ineffective, people change the judges or they change the legal system: they no longer value the courts as they were.

An instrumental theory of value does not require the analyst to postulate an ultimate rationale or motive, whether "self-interest" or "greed," "cooperativeness" or "altruism." Neither does the theory of instrumental valuing require that individuals or groups strive to maximize or optimize. It does require limited choice. Certainly it raises no barriers to judgments in particular cases that some group of people strived for something because they were greedy, or even because they were indeed terribly nice people. Nor does the idea of instrumental valuing conflict with the idea of maximizing or optimizing where there is obserable evidence that such rules of mathematical logic are being applied by the decision-makers: for example, when a business firm in a commercial society—where the numbers generated by commercial processes are sufficient to make it possible to maximize—does in fact maximize; or when a peasant farmer—thinking about his experience of soils and seeds, manuring and weeding—says to himself, "There really isn't any way I can get more out of those fields without wrecking my life or my marriage."

Instrumental valuing will be rational, given the information, beliefs, and perceptions of the deciders, in that there will be a relating of means to ends and in that means and ends will be seen as causes-and-effects. Where alternatives are perceived, people will try to do better rather than worse, take the more rather than the less appropriate action. People try out an implement or an idea or a process. As the results become apparent they react: "Yes, this is rather what we wanted; let's go on using it," or "No, this isn't the sort of thing we had hoped for; let's quit, and maybe try something else." This wrench works better than that one; people take to using—valuing—this wrench rather than that one. The judicial system produces unjust decisions—the decisions are "unfair to wage earners," the sentences are "too brutal"—so new rules, new procedures are tried out to see if the consequences of the new ways of reaching judgments are in accord with the objectives of those who are valuing. If the consequences —*as they are experienced*—seem suitable, people continue to use the new practice. If the consequences are not in accord with the objectives, the judicial system changes again.

I began my argument by asserting that there was a chasm between the thinking of standard economists and the thinking of institutional economists; that this chasm was philosophical; and that this philosophical difference was highly correlated with something close to an acceptance of the philosophy of natural law by standard economists and a rejection of that tradition by institutional economists.

This proposition, long accepted by institutional economists, has not been understood by the generality of our profession. The failure to appreciate the philosophical origins of the conflict between standard and institutional economists probably accounts for the challenge often addressed to institutionalists by standard economists, to wit: "You criticize economic theory, but you do not provide an alternative theory." Institutionalists have indeed, since the very beginning, since Veblen, provided an alternative theory, even alternative theories: instrumental valuing, and historical and comparative analyses of the evolution of economic structures and practices. We thus feel frustrated when standard economists continue to ask us for an alternative theory. I submit that it is not the failure of institutional economists to provide an alternative, but rather that the demand for an alternative theory *implicitly*, and very likely unconsciously, includes a demand for an alternative that allows logical derivation of the necessary or the best. The standard economists are really asking for a theory of the natural order and ethics of economies. In the terms in which I have been speaking, they are asking us to slot alternative nouns into their noun slots, but institutionalists are *not* going to put *supreme court* into the present slot for *tastes*. Given that standard economic theory emphasizes nouns still carrying the genes of natural law, it is impossible for institutionalists, with their emphasis upon verbing and upon an instrumental view of people in action, to offer the kind of alternative theory for which our interlocutors ask. Our response to the challenge must therefore be, "No, we are *not* going to provide a *substitute* theory; we *are* providing a *different* philosophical foundation for theoretical analyses of the structure, functioning, and evolution of economies and of problems that arise in economic life and in the discipline of economics."

To argue that institutionalism is instrumentalism; that instrumentalism is right; and that there must thus be irreconcilable differences with those who follow in the traditions of natural law—these arguments are hardly new. Nor, among linguists, would what I have said be surprising, let alone sophisticated.

Rather, I hope that I have demonstrated that the absence of contexts restricting the meaning of words helps to explain why some primary concepts in economics—utility and choice, for instance, but probably not rent and investment—are incurably flawed by universalizing in violation of language's rules. I also hope that I have demonstrated how some explanations in standard economics are incurably flawed by confusing grammatical rules with what goes on "out there" in the world of human action. And I hope that, in the process, I have shown how these flaws have reinforced the tendency for elements of the philosophy of natural law to continue to permeate economic thought.

Institutionalists cannot have escaped—I doubt that anyone can escape—the dangers inherent in the temptation to generalize *a* meaning into a universal concept, or the dangers necessarily arising from the fact that all of us must speak in the grammar of some language. Nevertheless, in comparison with other kinds of economics, institutionalism has exhibited two great strengths: it has been relatively successful in restricting meanings within the referent contexts of circumstances and action that give meaning to speech; *and* it has emphasized verbing. I am struck by how much verbing runs through any exposition of instrumentalism and institutional economics: tasting, trying, learning, testing, experiencing. "Value is a *process of valuing*," said Commons.[9] The noun that sums it all up is a noun about verbing: *process.*

Notes

1. Nicholas Georgescu-Roegen calls this kind of concept "arithmomorphic." See his *Analytical Economics: Issues and Problems* (Cambridge: Harvard University Press, 1967), pp. 20–31, but especially pp. 21–27, for the basic argument; and pp. 35–36, 115–120, 124, 187, and 213 for applications and commentary. Georgescu-Roegen contrasts the *arithmomorphic* with the *dialectical*, which includes "the most vital concepts for human judgments, like 'good,' 'justice,' 'likelihood' (sic? livelihood?), 'want,' etc. They have no arithmomorphic boundaries; instead *they are surrounded by a penumbra within which they overlap with their opposites*" (p. 23, italics in original). He illustrates with comments upon the idea of "democracy."
2. New York: John Wiley & Sons, 1956.
3. For Wittgenstein's final position, see his *Philosophical Investigations* (Oxford: Basil Blackwell, 1953). For a remarkably clear presentation of the development of Wittgenstein's nonmathematical work in philosophy, see

Anthony Kenny, *Wittgenstein* (Harmondsworth, Middlesex: Penguin Books, 1973).

4. Although he comes from a quite different economic tradition (neoclassical/British/South African), Frankel's views on the issues discussed in this paper are very close to mine (or rather, mine are very close to his). See Essay II ("Some Aspects of Technical Change," pp. 19–28) and Essay III ("Concepts of Income and Welfare and the Intercomparability of National Income Aggregates," pp. 29–55), in S. H. Frankel, *The Economic Impact on Under-Developed Societies* (Cambridge: Harvard University Press, 1953); especially pp. 44–46, where Frankel cites Gilbert Ryle, *The Concept of Mind* (London: Hutchinson University Library, 1949).
5. Frankel, p. 46, again citing Ryle.
6. There are a number of works by Ayres and those who follow in his tradition. The most easily available is Clarence E. Ayres, *The Theory of Economic Progress*, 3rd ed. (Kalamazoo: New Issues Press, Institute of Public Affairs, Western Michigan University, 1978). Perhaps Ayres, in *The Industrial Economy* (Boston: Houghton Mifflin, 1952), especially chapters 1–4 and 12–16, provides a clearer exposition of his ideas in less space.
7. See John R. Commons, *Legal Foundations of Capitalism* (Madison/Milwaukee/London: University of Wisconsin Press, 1968 [c1924]), p. 6, and *passim* his work.
8. *Myself* (Madison: University of Wisconsin Press, 1964 [c1934]), p. 160.
9. *Legal Foundations*, p. 211, italics in original.

16

Linguistic Structure and Economic Method

Richard G. Fritz and Judy M. Fritz

The purpose of this article is to sample the literature and describe some of the impact that linguistic structure has had on the theory and methods of economic science. Lingustic studies have revealed the relation of language to perception, thought, and behavior. Incorporated into the structure of our unconscious, a language acts as a filter, conditioning not only what we are able to think or say but also what we are able to see.

The primary differences between languages are not in the symbols they use, or in the meaning expressed in the symbols, but in their structures. For the structure or syntax of two languages to be identical or isomorphic, one must be able to place their elements in a one-to-one (and onto) correspondence. The obvious differences between a natural language and mathematical language is in the richness of vocabulary and complexity of syntax of the former and the poverty of those in the latter. Marc Barbut [1970] argues that this opposition points up the enormous efficiency of mathematical models, a simplicity rarely encountered among the human sciences. The language of mathematics is employed at the expense of a reduction in phenomena to which those models may be applied. When reality is complex, symbolic language retains only certain characteristics of the mental model translated through the natural language system: those characteristics that matter most. The translation from one system into another calls for perception and judgment as to which characteristics matter most and brings into question the problem of ideology.

Thus, when the language used in communicating social, political, and economic ideas changes (that is, from verbal to static linear mathematics, or from verbal to dynamic nonlinear mathematics), this can affect the theoretical structure of the discipline in question. The concepts found in the previous language system do not receive equal "value" when translated into the new symbolic linguistic structure. What had been posited and affirmed in the luminous space of understanding in the previous system detaches itself from the squares it inhabits and is reformed under a new set of "signs" [Foucalt 1970, p. 217].

Many writers have attempted to attend to the epistemological questions concerning the role of language and mathematics and its affect on the progress of knowledge. A sample of this literature would include: Thorstein Veblen [1898], Clarence Ayres [1952], Paul Samuelson [1952], Robert Dorfman [1954], W. V. Quine [1960], Kenneth Boulding [1966], William Hardy [1978], Robert Lilienfeld [1978], Nicholas Georgescu-Roegen [1979], Daniel Fusfeld [1980], Ken Dennis [1982], Walter C. Neale [1982], John Blatt [1983], and Gerard Debreu [1984]. These authors (and many others) have recognized the constraints imposed by the variety of verbal and non-verbal language systems. Generally, the analysis is focused on the comparative use of natural verbal language systems rather than mathematical symbols. Attempts have been made to compare the relative versatility of natural languages versus symbolic language systems in evaluating and analyzing social systems. In practice, social system modelers seldom attend to the impact of linguistic structure on their working analytic paradigms. Even less attention has been applied to the comparison of various nonverbal linguistic structures employed in social system modeling. One notable exception is Donnella Meadows [1980], who without the use of explicit linguistic vocabulary covers several of the critical issues in her analysis of econometric models and system dynamic models.

This article will focus on the differences between language structures employed in economic analysis. The use of symbolic linguistic structure may inhibit progress in the evolution of economic thought as a result of the reduction in phenomena to which the knowledge is applied. Further, the use of the symbolic linguistic structure of mathematics masks (makes less apparent) the ideology of the author, as well as social meanings unconsciously marked in the structures of the text. This can result in the false appearance of promoting versions of economic theory as value-free scientific inquiry [Deane 1983, p. 6].

The history of economic thought may be viewed as one of alternative language systems, changing interpretations generated by structural shifts in the language used by mainstream economists. The first section of the article reviews the relation of language to the method of scientific inquiry. This includes a discussion of the debate over the problem of translating natural languages into symbolic languages for the purpose of evaluating policy alternatives of a social system. The final section of the study will review the impact of alternative language systems on interpreting economic phenomena.

Language and Epistemology

European epistemologists, notably the French, have contributed much to the understanding of the problem of scientific description. The relationship between the "truths" of a science and the descriptive schemata or "language" used to arrive at and to describe these "truths" has broad implications for the focus and direction of that science.

In practice, Anglo-American social scientists, being in the tradition of the epistemologists Karl Popper and Thomas Kuhn, have largely ignored this problem of language as they tend to view the direction of science as a result of the conscious choices of scientists. Some social system analysts have employed the refutationist approach developed by Popper in order to show that the method they employ offers a large number and variety of "points of contact" between theories and reality that represent genuine possibilities of exposing errors in the theory [Bell and Senge 1980], while others have employed the logic of Kuhn's paradigmism in an attempt to compare the problem-solving qualities of their method and other leading competitive alternatives to modeling social systems [Meadows 1980].

The French philosophers of epistemology, such as Gaston Bachelard, Georges Canguilham, and Michel Foucault, see the movement of science as a discursive process (moving from subject to subject in a rambling way, yet proceeding to a conclusion through reason rather than intuition), proceeding by reorganizations, ruptures, and mutations and inseparable from its cultural frame. Scientists are not the cause of scientific practice, only agents, subject to the external determinations—social, economic, ideological, and political. Bachelard maintains that the scientist constantly comes upon epistemological obstacles that are crystallized and systematized in philosophy and that produce braking effects in scientific practice. The epistemological obstacle emerges every time a pre-existing organization of thought is threatened, that is, it appears at a point where rupture with the past threatens. Its effect is to patch up, to displace the question before it is posed, to prevent the question from being posed. These obstacles are the perceptions, representations, values, and attitudes of a given society that intervene in science through language. The images, metaphors, or in Bachelard's terminology "traces" present in ordinary language inhibit the progress of science as they embody a certain representation of the real, a reality offered to investigation. Expressions such as "the rising/setting sun," remnants from pre-Newtonian science, permeate the unconscious and result in the substitution of imaginary questions for the real questions by which a science progresses. Bachelard states that the danger of metaphors for the formation of the scientific mind is that they are not always passing images; they press on towards autonomous thought.

Foucault, in the tradition of Bachelard, relates science and the discursive practice of a society at a given point in time. Discursive practice is the appropriation of a language system by a group resulting in a certain linguistic style. This style is dependent upon the types of relationships within the group, their extensions and the subject or content area that they are treating. Thus the conditions in which languages are used determines the discursive practice. Science is defined by the perceptual field of a given era—what is visible and invisible, thinkable and unthinkable, statable and unstatable. The objects that will or will not acquire scientific status are dependent upon an ensemble of interlocked and hierarchially structured discursive practices. As the discourse style of a given science or discipline acquires power and status, it affects the perceptual field of other disciplines. It begins to function as the norm, governing attitudes with respect to real objects and problems. When the science of medicine dominated the scientific scene, its discourse style acquired prestige, was adopted by other disciplines, and therefore influenced the scientific method of other disciplines. According to Foucault it is the structure and hierarchial relations of discursive practices, which he calls the discursive formation of an era, that assign the forms and limits to theory [Lecourt 1975]. The success of Newtonian physics, with its discursive practice characterized by algebraic representation and differential calculus, clearly influenced the scientific method adopted by economists in the late nineteenth century. The discursive formation of this area dominated by physics resulted in the assigned forms and limits for the theory of modern political economy.

The existence of a pure intellectual space in which the concepts of science are worked out by a body of scientists is pure fiction to these French epistemologists. The ideological values of the social formation in which the science is inscribed and the language through which these values pass permeate the consciousness of the body of scientists and restrict their choices to a limited set of predetermined paradigms.

Language, Thought, and Realty

To understand how language influences scientific investigation it is necessary to consider the relationship between language and perception, language and thought, and language and society. There is no pure act of perception without thought. The flux of experience must pass through the interpretative schemata of the mind. Language does not mirror the mind but rather gives structure and form to our thoughts. What we see and think tends to be limited to what we can say. Perceptions and thoughts are also socialized because the language that gives them form is immersed in the on-going life of a society and reflects the consciousness of that society.

> Languages are systems of categories and rules based on fundamental principals and assumptions about the world. These principles and assumptions are not related to thought: they are thought. Benjamin Whorf called these fundamental organizing assumptions a 'science' and a 'metaphysic,' that is, a systematic account of reality and the a priori assumptions on which that account rests. Such assumptions are embodied in language, learned through language and reinforced in language. . . . Institutional science and metaphysics require a professional class of scientists and metaphysicians to articulate their basic assumptions, but even professional thinkers use a language and through their prior use of its categories and processes these communal assumptions filter into their thinking. The interrelations between the two kinds of science and the two kinds of metaphysics makes an important subject of study [Kress and Hodge 1980, p. 5].

In the 1830s Wilhelm von Humbolt postulated that one thinks in forms limited and determined by the forms of one's native language. In the 1930s Benjamin Whorf [1956] linked the structure of language with a particular world view and sought to reveal the metaphysics implicit in the structure of Indo-European languages [Coetzee 1982]. "The Indo-European languages and many others give great prominence to a type of sentence having two parts, each built around a class of words—substantives and verbs. . . . The Greeks, especially since Aristotle, built up this contrast and made it into the law of reason. . . . Undoubtedly modern science, strongly reflecting western Indo-European tongues, often does as we all do, sees actions and forms where sometimes it might be better to see states" [Coetzee 1982 (citing Whorf), p. 4]. The tendency to perceive the universe as objects and actions rather than states is imposed by the use of a language that breaks down reality into subjects and verbs. The standard order so prevalent in English (Subject-Verb-Object) imposes the reading of causality and temporality into experience, whereas these meanings would not necessarily be transmitted in other families of languages. J. M. Coetzee affirms that the Subject-Verb order is metaphorical because it imposes a temporal-causal order over the syntactic order.

Modern science as we know it in the western world mirrors the structure and processes of Indo-European languages in that it seeks to give a systematic account of reality by linking events to a network of causal relations and to structures of objects and forces. Language provides a theory of reality superimposed on the scientific theory it helps to articulate.

Significant studies in physical science came after René Descartes developed his dualistic philosophical system in which he separated nature into two categories: mind (*res cogitans*) and matter (*res extensa*). With this distinction scientists were able to completely estrange themselves from the inert substance of matter. Upon this dualistic conception, Isaac Newton based his mechanics, the cornerstone of classical physics. The Newtonian universe was a product of a dualistic world view with a sharp "system/non-system" distinction, which fosters an absolute, as opposed to a relative, perspective. Space and time were invariant quantities, with "well-behaved" forces. The Indo-European linguistic structure imposed the reading of causality and temporality into the scientific system. Later, in Albert Einstein's formulation, space and time became inextricable partners in a four-dimensional continuum. An indication of the reorientation that the Quantum Revolution and Relativity Theory forced upon classical physics is provided by the noted physicist Niels Bohr: "For a parallel to the lesson of atomic theory, we must turn to those kinds of epistemological problems with which already thinkers like Buddha and Lao Tzu have been confronted, when trying to harmonize our position as spectators and actors in the great drama of existence" [Conceptual Monograph No. 2, 1980, p. 19].

There is evidence that Newton struggled with language while attempting to explain the law of gravitation. The ensuing controversy over this law (which became a cause celébre in the history of science) was a result of language. In using the standard syntactic order in English of Subject-Verb-Object, Newton was obliged to assign temporal-causal relationships to heavenly bodies.

> In his general law of gravitation, Newton states that every two particles of the universe attract each other with a force proportional to their respective masses and inversely proportional to the square of their distance apart. The key word is 'attract.' Apart from occasions where the law is expressed in mathematical symbolism, there is no statement of the law in Newton that does not include the word 'attract' or a synonym equally metaphoric. The controversy that broke out over the concept of gravity soon after the publication of the *Principia* was published in 1686 centered on this metaphor [Coetzee 1982, p. 5].

Newton was obliged to withdraw this first version and replace it with a more austerely mathematical treatment, "to prevent the disputes which might be raised" [Coetzee 1982, p. 7]. He used mathematics to circumvent the added meanings inherent in stating in natural language the relations between the elements of the universe, and to make his theory more acceptable to the professional thinkers of his day.

Newton attempted to eliminate metaphorical content in his scientific discourse by using two linguistic techniques. These techniques have been adopted by the modern scientific community and contribute to the scientific discursive style as we know it: the predominant use of passive constructions and nominalizations.

Passivization is a transformation of the basic transactive model (Subject-Verb-Object) in which there is a source, a verbal process, and an affected entity. The transactive model indicates clearly the causal process as all agents in the process are specified. When this model is transformed into a passive construction the source or agent of the process may be omitted. This information is lost or obscured. The passive construction enabled Newton to avoid philosophical questions about causality by omitting the syntactic agent. Nominalizations (nouning) reduce both agents, source and affected entity, and the process to a state, thereby eliminating all temporality and causality.

Take for example an active or transactive statement: "Police shoot blacks." Here the agent commits an act that affects an object: subject-verb-object. This statement may be transformed into a passive process: "Blacks were shot." In this passive form the object is acted upon but the agent is not explicit. The passive form may be stated with or without the explicit statement of an agent. When the agent is deleted, uncertainty is introduced which may result in obscuring the bias of the author. Nominalization may be achieved by transforming the original transactive statement: "Rioting occurred." This transformation reduces the process to a noun or state. In science the noun phrase replaces a "given" accepted by the discipline. The reduction of the process (nominalization or passivization) through transformation of the basic transactive linguistic structure imposes an epistemological obstacle. Information is lost and unavailable to both the initiator and the recipient of the communication. Nominalization and passivization may be achieved by transforming the syntactic order within a single linguistic system or it may result from translating one linguistic system into another, while simultaneously transforming the transactive process into a non-transactive structure.

The Translation Problems and Mental Models

In his attack on systems theory, Lilienfeld [1978] argues that the road to reality is traversed through everyday language. The major unresolved problem of epistemology is how we come to know our own mental life and that of others. Philosophers continue to debate how we come to be aware of physical objects and how far subjective elements enter into our experience of them. Symbolic structure to Lilienfeld represents outmoded thought patterns because one of the basic findings of "modern science" is that

> development and analysis of modern physics is the experience that the concepts of natural language, vaguely defined as they are, seems to be more stable in the expansion of knowledge than the precise terms of scientific language, derived as an idealization from only limited groups of phenomena. This is in fact not surprising since the concepts of natural language are formed by the immediate connection with reality; they represent reality. . . . On the other hand, the scientific concepts are idealizations; they are derived from experience obtained by refined experimental tools, and are precisely defined through axioms and definitions. Only through these precise definitions is it possible to connect the concepts with a mathematical scheme and to derive mathematically the infinite variety of possible phenomena in this field. But through this process of idealization and precise definition the immediate connection with reality is lost. The concepts still correspond very closely to reality in that part of nature which had been the object of the research. But the correspondence may be lost in other parts containing other groups of phenomena [Lilienfeld 1978, p. 251, quoting Heisenberg, p. 200].

Lilienfeld argues that all such systems approaches as *technique*—in their computer-based simulation models, in the mathematical foundations of cybernetics—are based on deterministic categories [Lilienfeld 1978, p. 256]. Accordingly, to Lilienfeld systems theory is an *ideology* that offers nothing new except a *new vocabulary*. Lilienfeld's conclusion that systems theory is neither a philosophy nor a science and thus on pragmatic grounds it appears to make no difference, ignores the contribution of the new linguistic structure. Even if his conclusions are correct, and there is much controversy over the issue, translation from mental models to some systems theory would "make the difference" if there is value in developing an alternative symbolic language system from which to translate the mental models social scientists have conceptualized in their natural language system.

The new vocabulary found in symbolic language systems fits the *doctrine of translation* identified and clarified by Ken Dennis [1982a]. This follows the development from the ninteenth century to the present of attempting to translate the concepts and propositions of economics into the symbols and formulas of mathematics. The doctrine has only limited credibility [Dennis 1982a, p. 697]. Mathematical symbols, formulas, and methods do enter into economic theorizing but not in such a way as to prove *behavioral* propositions about human beings and their economic actions. Mathematics as traditionally developed is the logic of numbers and number relations. It is not a logic about *events* and the *conditionality* of the *occurrence of events* [Dennis 1981, p. 107]. Even though number systems and measurement systems have been shown to be homomorphic relational structures [Krantz, et al., 1971], numerical functional formulas do not express behavioral propositions about events and the contingency of their occurrence [Dennis 1982b, p. 1058].

As Dennis points out, Paul Samuelson [1952, p. 59-60] incorrectly concludes that the transition of natural languages into mathematics can yield the logical identity of words and symbols. As a condition of translational adequacy [Rescher 1969, p. 322], a sentence must convey the same information as the original by expressing the same proposition. This requires the ability to shift back and forth between literary and symbolic forms of expression. The mere correspondence of synonymous words does not meet the necessary conditions of adequate translation. Thus translation may take on different degrees of translational rigor that may range from "naive" to "fair" to "strict" [Dennis 1982a, pp. 706-10]. Special symbolism is employed in scientific work primarily to achieve notational conciseness as an aid to logical manipulation. Abbreviation through linguistic symbolism does not afford greater degrees of precision than ordinary language, only clarity gained by the use of abbreviated symbolisms. Therefore translation of language systems may be of different quality with the highest quality resulting in symbolic notation that yields the most clarity in expressing the original propositions found in the natural language. When the propositions being translated are scientific argumentation, the translational adequacy may become a vital aspect of ensuring the logical rigor of the argument.

Translation, Transformation, and Syntactic Order

As an imposed value judgment, linguistic translations that result in nontransactive models, where transactive mental models were the goal, are categorized as "naive" translations. Natural language translated into symbolic systems that retain the original transactive model meet the *necessary* condition of "fair" translation. Here, Dennis's categories are adopted to fit this essay's theme. Note that "necessary" conditions may still not be "sufficient" for "fair" translation.

It has been argued that orthodox economics, relying on the logical positivism (empiricism) of statistical (econometric) modeling, achieves the passivization of theoretical discourse by "nouning" [Neale 1982]. Although Walter Neale's terminology is cumbersome, he succeeds in identifying the linguistic transformation problem.

> Nouning has contributed to confusion about meaning, and to confusing word order with cause. It is important to distinguish between value as a noun (thing), which it is not, and to *value* as a verb. The former generates a bunch of non-questions, such as . . . , "Why do diamonds have more value than bread?" Diamonds do not *have value*. They have mass, density. . . . Instead . . . one should be asking, "How do people value diamonds?" And answering by saying, "They value them by stealing them, buying them, insuring them, killing for them," and so on. Stealing, buying, . . . are how people value diamonds [Neale, 1982, pp. 362-63].

In orthodox economics, *nouns are explanations*: utility, preferences, tastes. These are not things but *verb processes*. Neale believes a clearer understanding of social systems is achieved by rejecting "nouning" and arguing for "processual verbing." Verbing influences our ideas about cause while nouns exist separately from their being or doing.

Broadly described, econometric models translate natural language systems into symbolic language systems, transforming the transactive structure into passive syntax. At first glance it appears that the causation analysis in the robust literature of probability theory is transactive. However, the question rests not with the power of statistical models but with what is the sentence (represented by an equation) saying. Are econometric models paraphrasing orthodox economics by avoiding the verb processes of the transactive structure?

Following the characteristics used by Meadows [1980, pp. 23-56], econometric models are based on the goal of detail decision making, product oriented, and structured as open systems requiring many exogeneous variables to drive the model. When two-way causation does appears, as in simultaneous-equation formulation, equilibrium is achieved without temporal analysis. The primary focus of econometric models is on the *noun* of the equation sentence. In the basic linear open model there is no feedback describing the temporal and causal path that represents the transactive Indo-European syntax of natural language structure. The result is similar to that of Newton adopting the non-transactive mathematical linguistic structure in order to avoid the debate over causal source. The reduced form estimation process means that econometric models tend to "represent surface phenomena only, with much causal structure implicit" [Meadows 1980, p. 52].

Mathematical modeling has benefited from the recent developments in the theory of measurement. In the modern literature, attention has focused on "the construction of homomorphous (scales) from empirical relational structures of interest into numerical relational structures that are useful" [Krantz et al. 1971, p. 9]. The relational concepts of structural identity (isomorphism) and structural similarity (homomorphism) are used to justify "the direct application of computational methods to the results of measurement" [Luce and Suppes 1968, p. 72]. The symbolic sentence: $x + y = z$ can serve the dual purpose of expressing z as the empirical result of measurement and the result of numerical computation, whereby the abstract operation of addition is performed upon the numbers x and y. The consequence of isomorphism between empirical and numerical relational structures is that the same symbolism may be adopted for both systems—thus the rationale for the use of numerical algebras to espouse and describe certain properties of empirical relation systems.

David Krantz et al. argue that the problem or representation is the heart of the measurement development: "When measuring some attribute of a class of objects or events, we associate numbers (or other familiar mathematical entities, such as vectors) with the objects in such a way that the properties of the attribute are faithfully represented as numerical properties" [Krantz et al. 1971, p. 1]. The problem of representation, while important, is not the source of concern in most social science theories. Most social policy analysis concerns causal connections (or patterns of connectedness) that are open to empirical inspection (corroboration or refutation). "The exploration of systems of causal connections relating distinct events or conditions seems not to have been a part of the agenda for theorists of measurement, even in chapters devoted to the measurement of probability involving an 'algebra of events' " [Dennis 1982b, p. 1058].

Linguistic Style, Theory, Ideology

When causal and temporal relationships are blurred through translation or transformation, discourse is vague or ambiguous as the source and consequence of phenomena. "The science that proceeds through non-transactive models will tend to be a large collection of particular facts about self-caused events which co-exist" [Kress and Hodge 1979, p. 39]. Gunther Kress and Robert Hodge maintain that such a style is functional for the community of scientists in that it allows one to avoid making distinctions when accounting for data beyond the scope of theory. Linguists believe that groups create language styles that serve to reinforce a sense of identity with the group members. A language style also sets up a barrier around the privileged knowledge of its community of specialists. The repetitive use of the expression "given" within current scientific discourse is a case in point. The expression suppresses the inclination to inquire. What is given? Who determines the goals? How is the theory defined? What is the status of the investigator? This common linguistic device can serve to remove important questions from public consideration [Kress and Hodge 1979]. Such an approach has been applied often in the positivist framework of Milton Friedman and the monetarists. In the positivist's methodology the only test of a theory is comparing its "predictions" with observations. The theorist's unrealistic assumptions about perfect competition, profit-maximization, and economic rationality are irrelevant. The "given" need not be realistic and is beyond analytical criticism [Dugger 1983, p. 83]. Theory is advanced by the logical positivists by emphasizing empirical tests. When the verification of assumptions is treated as an unnecessary and undesirable test of theory, the focus shifts to the scientific language used to produce the theory's "predictions." This constitutes a linguistic transformation.

Linguistic transformations are used to effect theoretical transformations and are not free of ideological determinations, according to R. Fowler, et al.: "Anomalies constantly face scientific theories and are resolved either by changing the theory or by reinterpreting the event. Awkward facts may be successfully denied, suppressed or reinterpreted (through linguistic devices). Anomalies are a challenge not simply to the ideology but to the legitimacy of the order" [Fowler et al. 1980]. Kress and Hodge maintain that linguistic transformations serve two functions: economy and distortion. Linguistic forms allow significance to be conveyed and to be distorted. In this way the hearer/reader may be manipulated and informed (p. 6). What is significant is the disappearance of deleted material and its non-recoverability in the text.

"Presenting anything in or through language involves selection—how the speaker/writer chooses to present reality" [Kress and Hodge 1979], p. 15). A profession is not self-contained. It has links with institutions, groups, and movements. Its credibility depends on which forces it gives expression to and which institutions or segments of society it identifies with, supports, and respects. Language serves to confirm and to consolidate the organizations that shape it, being used to manipulate people, to establish and maintain them in economically convenient roles and statuses, to maintain the power of state agencies, corporations, and other institutions [Fowler et al. 1980, p. 190; Mueller 1973, p. 64].

Linguistic styles are socially determined patterns of language. Preferred syntactical arrangements can encode a world view without the conscious choice of the speaker/writer. World view comes from relations to institutions and the socio-economic structure of society but is facilitated and confirmed by language use. "The systematic use of certain linguistic structures is connected to the texts' place in the socio-economic system and exists prior to the production of the text and our reception of it" [Fowler et al. 1950, p. 185]. We are socialized into holding theories and judgments because of their social meaning, reinforced in the lexical and syntactic structures we use.

It is unnecessary to assume that groups deliberately construct a syntax of mystification. Once a style comes into existence it becomes appropriate for expressing a given content. Groups do not consciously recognize the purposes they encode in language and that the aims that they mediate in their professional capacities may not coincide with their beliefs or sympathies.

Language is the product and producer of people as people are the product and producer of language. The diversity of ties that people have to their environment and the variety of their actions in the world affect language.

> The language of a tribe of Indians, making a living from agriculture in Central America, will not represent the same reality as that of Eskimos who hunt animals in the snow and break the ice for fishing. . . . Conversely, each language will impose, on those who use it, a particular way of viewing reality. As human experience finds its way into the vocabulary

and structure of the language, the latter orients the vision, predisposes the user to certain attitudes and behavior [Rambouillet 1973, p. 20].

Andre Rambouillet notes also that the way certain universal notions such as time and space are structured and therefore expressed within a language can influence the system of values, ideologies, and myths of a society. He maintains that the philosophy of Aristotle was shaped by the particular linguistic categories of the Greek language [Rambouillet 1973, p. 21].

Emile Beneveniste [1966] affirms that there is a hidden infrastructure that links language, culture, and the personality. When language is realized in oral or written discourse, the multiple interaction of linguistic, sociological, and psychological realities becomes apparent. "As soon as one produces an utterance one always says something other than what one/he wanted to say, even if one said exactly what he wanted to say" [Porcher 1980, p. 5]. When we speak something else speaks in us and for us—our own psychic history or unconscious, our culture latent in the structures of the language we use, and our social status.

Language is never neutral or socially unmarked. Subjectivity is inherent in the use of language. Pierre Bourdieu shows how social relationships are always present in discourse. Our status, roles, functions, and power govern our communication. Social position can always be discerned in oral messages in the intonation, rhythm, and accent as well as in the vocabulary and forms chosen. Traces of a writer's subjectivity are always present in the written document. Discourse analysis concerns itself with finding formal marks of the writer's intention that can be discerned in the very structure of the text. Ideology reveals itself not only in content matter but in the medium. Ideology, in turn, imprints itself on organizational behavior through the agencies of authoritative choice [Solo 1981, p. 37].

The interpretation of a written text is contingent on discerning the writer's "place of discourse" or ideological context. In natural language we can easily discern whether we share the author's presumptions and thus give the appropriate status or legitimacy to his or her document. The status and legitimacy of a text are indispensable to its comprehension and acceptance.

Natural Language Versus Mathematics

Adopting mathematics as an instrument of investigation and communication of scientific research does not negate the problem. Peter

Maher asserts that mathematics and logic are only "parasitic systems," outgrowths of the processes of natural language. He sees natural languages as palimpsests, as they bear the imprint of different eras. Language surface, its forms and structures, reflects not the present but the past. The grammatical system tends to persist indefinitely and will in time cease to symbolize the cultural forms that motivate its existence. "Surface structures are handed down from one generation to the next, while the underlying values are subject to revolutionary change" [Maher 1977, p. 5]. It is the juxtaposition between the surface structure and the shifting values that motivated it that creates the metaphor.

Mathematics is also metaphorical in that it grows out of abstraction. There is no pure abstraction as there is no pure perception. "The equation, the syllogism, all their superstructures . . . are intrinsically nothing but metaphors. The source of those metaphors is figure-ground differentiation of configuration, with abstraction of certain salient features, proceeding from other features of the bundle [Maher 1977, p. 8].

No matter what linguistic medium it adopts, scientific description will remain problematic. In reflecting on this problem one must consider two questions. What is the relationship between the linguistic medium and the material? and, What does this medium impose on the material?

A model is the expression of a theory. All suspects of phenomena are not represented in a model. One chooses properties that present a certain coherence and one negates the accessory. What the model retains and what it ignores poses the problem of what is pertinent and what is negligible. Judgment and interpretation are closely linked with perception, linguistic conditioning, and ideology.

A descriptive medium, whether natural language, logic, or fields of mathematics, has certain semantic limits that orient research within the boundaries of its own particular representation of the world. Scientific output may be viewed as a compromise between the necessities of the descriptive medium and those of the real. Much of the debate over the mathematical modeling methods used to represent social systems stems from the modeler's world view [Meadows 1980]. Institutionalists assume that economic systems are primarily closed, interacting with the social/political environment that influences them, and are interested in the evolutionary path of a response [Myrdal 1978]. Orthodox economics, through econometric models, assumes that the world is dualistic and open. This means that the environment (markets, government action, foreign influences) delivers inputs (exogenous) to which the system provides specific responses. Institutionalists believe the problems addressed are predominantly long-run issues, while the microscopic view of econometrics confines itself to the short run. Neale, Meadows, and Dennis summarize several characteristics useful for comparing modeling paradigms.

In order for the linguistic structures to matter between modeling methods, we must first show that they are different. That is, we must show that the mental model in our head is originally formed in a natural language system, then translated into a symbolic language structure consistent with the quantitative modeling tool. Further, the translation of the mental model differs, depending upon which symbolic language system is receiving the model.

Natural Language Systems, Mental Models, and Mathematics

By the end of the eighteenth century the Newtonian scheme had decisively convinced the world that nature is mathematically designed and that the true laws of nature are mathematical. Newton's amazing contributions were made possible by his reliance on mathematical description even where physical understanding was completely lacking. Newton placed mathematical description and deduction at the forefront of all scientific accounts and prediction.

While this position was attacked by David Hume and others, Immanuel Kant affirmed that all axioms and theorems of mathematics were "truths" [Kant 1781]. However, Kant argued that science was a world of sense impressions arranged and controlled by the mind in accordance with innate categories such as space, time, cause and effect, and substance. "The mind contains furniture into which the guests must fit" [Kline 1980, p. 77].

The development of non-Euclidean geometry finally led to the recognition that mathematics was not a body of absolute truths. The debate over the "anticipatory function" of the language of mathematics continues [Kuyk 1977, pp. 141-70]. That is, does the axiomatic language "run ahead" of verbal language such that the manipulation of a formula leads to a result that could not be thought to be true before the manipulation? Whether mathematics offers a more useful (powerful) linguistic structure for the social sciences is not the issue of this essay. However, those readers interested in the application of this problem in the language structure used in social system analysis are referred to the work of Jay W. Forrester on counter-intuitive behavior [Forrester 1971] and the recent Nobel lecture by Gerard Debreu [Debreu 1984].

The salient point is that orthodox economic analysis adopted the linguistic structure of differential calculus with the "marginalist" revolution in the late nineteenth century. The structure of the adopted calculus resulted in the dominant theoretical role played by a single economic agent. Ideologically, this shifted the focus away from the "political economy" of society to the "economics" of utility maximization by the individual. The new linguistic structure introduced new "words": *derivative* and *infinitestimal.* The marginalists used these to isolate relationships by the necessary linguistic constraint of assuming "other things remain equal," so that the changes in the economic variable on which they focused were not to be systematically related to the variation in the variables they were ignoring. As previously noted, simplification of the new symbolic language structure later supported the position that the assumptions of a theory could be removed from the ambit of criticism [Friedman 1953, p. 14]. Abstraction assumptions are not an element of the "axiomatic structure" of the theory for the positivist and therefore may be ignored by the formalistic language of the model. Some believe that the deterministic language of differential calculus and the "representative" individual economic agent were merely expository devices chosen because of their pedagogical utility [Gill 1981, p. 76].

The translators of classical economic theory into the calculus of exchange employed a new linguistic structure. In the new language system production relations, which had been a dominant feature of the mental models of the classical economists, became unnecessary elements. Carl Menger, W. S. Jevons, and Leon Walras stressed the notion of exchange as expressing the essence of the structural system: "Production to some extent appeared merely as an indirect way of exchanging initial holdings" [Arrow and Starrett 1973, p. 133]. Although there have been numerous attempts to define the complement of classical production within the new conceptual plane adopted by the marginalist, the theory of exchange exists in metaphysical space, cut off from reality by the absence of a theory based on real inputs and discrete capital goods [Fusfeld 1980].

> The effect of thus lifting the central body of economic theory out of the arena of ethical and political debate was twofold. It narrowed the scope of the theoretical core of the economists' research programme so that it was largely reducible to a theory of exchange under competitive conditions: and at the same time it took the passion and the point out of the debates on method that had characterized the 1870s and 1880s [Deane 1983, p. 6].

William Dugger argues that at the neoclassical core of economics is a faith in government's nonintervention in the economic process. This faith is supported by a set of assumptions [Dugger 1983, p. 75]. Dugger attacks the methodologies of Friedman's positivism and the Austrian School's subjectivism. These two conflicting methodologies conclude that neither qualitative historical evidence (positivism) nor quantitative prediction (subjectivism) can yield a scientific test of theory. "Serving economic science so poorly, why are these methodological positions gaining more and more adherents? One is tempted to conclude that the reason has more to do with economic ideology than with economic science" [Dugger 1983, p. 88].

Thus, the natural language system of the classical economists represented a different set of meta-assumptions (or methodological priors), compared to the symbolic language system of the marginalist economists. Translating mental models into the working models of the discipline led to differences in policy conclusions under the conceptual plane of calculus. While some authors have recognized that differences in analytic paradigms can lead to differences in policy conclusions [Anderson 1981; Neale 1982], they have not related the meta-assumptions back to linguistic structure.

Symbolic Structure, Institutionalism, and Non-Linear Symbolic Systems

As C. E. Ayres pointed out, when anthropologists study the economy of people quite different from themselves, they assume that rather than operating through self-interest, everybody does just what they are expected to do [Ayres 1952, p. 6]. But Ayres saw the modern foundation of economic ideas as influenced by the achievements of Isaac Newton. Newton's ability to explain the actions of the vast universe with the simplicity of the interaction of constituent particles was so dramatic that it dominated the world of scholarship. Ayres argued that a similarly mechanical conception of the human mind was being formed by pioneers such as John Locke [Ayres 1952, p. 7]. Lock proposed to explain "human understanding" as sensations through which the "primary qualities" of things interact upon the mind. Thus Locke laid the foundation for looking at the economy according to the organizing principle of "enlightened self-interest" and the "self-regulating market."

Ayres correctly saw language as a body of lore [Ayres 1952, p. 11]. Communication through use of language is a basic human activity, yet some language must exist for human communication. Language illustrates culture's existence independent of any particular human being.

> Economists of the highest standing still describe the economy as a sort of solar system, and sometimes even speak of current prices as 'gravitating about normal prices'; . . . the price system is the mechanism which holds the economy together: all this is economic orthodoxy; anything else is heresy [Ayres 1952, p. 14].
>
> Since all these situations are capable of diagrammatic and algebraic representation, an immense number of new formulas have been worked out, with all of which the professional economist is now expected to be conversant. The effect of this development has been to give an air of scientific precision [Ayres 1952, p. 386].

While there may be some examples of fair translations employing logical grammars in simultaneous equation econometric models, the dominant linguistic structure of econometric models transforms the transactive structure of natural langauge into a passive structure. Causality becomes the problem of the measurement of probability considered in an open structure [Granger 1969; Sims 1972]. However as Bell and Senge [1980] have pointed out, if a model includes multiple exogenous time series inputs, disentangling internally generated behavior from externally generated behavior may be difficult or impossible. From the viewpoint of linguistic structure, their conclusion is a logical outcome of avoiding the transactive model of natural language.

The institutionalists' model, based on endogenous explanations (verb processes), parallels the refutationists' insistence on causal explanations. The power of simulation testing to reveal flaws or corroborate assumptions is enhanced by employing endogenous explanations of behavior. Without exogenous time series inputs, an institutional model should generate the behavior of interest. The behavior arises from evolving feedbacks. The interactions necessary for understanding the causes of behavior are found within the model structure. This attends to the scientific goal of highly corroborative theories requiring multiple "points of contact" with reality [Bell and Senge 1980]. The refutationists' view of scientific method defines objectivity as the degree to which the theory presents opportunities to test it against reality.

The linguistic structure of institutional analysis provides increasing objectivity through refutability. Institutionalists have a strict syntax and structure [Neale 1982]. Their evolutionary models are also characterized by the property of *closure*. M. Ray Perryman [1982] has pointed out that evolutionary economists rarely employ econometric models, and econometricians are unwilling to accept the use of institutional results. While this explanation may be valid, it fails to note the differences in linguistic structure employed by competing symbolic language systems. Orthodox economists often translate from the natural language system into econometric models. The differential calculus, probability theory, and linear algebra dominating the symbolic structure of econometrics are not well-suited as a linguistic system to receive the translation of the evolutionary model. The calculus of integration with a nonlinear dynamic simulation process employed in control theory analysis yields a more sympathetic structure for translating the institutionalist's model. The similarity of the linguistic systems of institutionalists and system dynamics (employing control theory) implies that the synthesis between them is more likely than the synthesis reported by Perryman between econometrics and evolutionary economics.

The closure test for both evolutionary models and system dynamic models requires that starting from any point in the analysis it must be possible to return to that point by following the explicit or implicit direction of causation, in such a way as not to cross one's track [Coyle 1978]. "Closing the loop" can be accomplished only in a temporal setting with an explicit delay intervening between initial action and the resulting feedback [Roberts 1981, p. 7]. The syntactic structure of the variables (sentence components) is determined uniquely by the characteristic of each variable (nouns, verbs, or predictates). Evolution of the process is a necessary part of the model, which means that *time* is always considered as an integral component. As Dennis points out [1982b, p. 1060], "instantaneous process," a requirement in the symbolic structure of differential calculus, becomes a meaningless phrase of mathematical rigor. Time, feedbacks, and accumulating evolution are, however, a necessary part of other symbolic language structures, such as the control theory used in system dynamics.

R. Geoffrey Coyle outlines the relationships between the three variable types in nonlinear symbolic linguistic systems: rates (verbs), levels (nouns), and auxiliaries (predicates) [Coyle 1978, p. 523-28]. Level variables (an assumulation or integration over time) are stocks (nouns) that change as flows come into and go out of them. Rate variables are the flow, decision, action (verb), or behavior that changes over time as a function of the influence processes. Auxiliary variables are combinations of information inputs into concept (predicates) terms. Coyle explains the combinations of variables, but the syntactic order must remain transactive (Subject-Verb-Object) around the closed loop. This focuses the attention on the general reaction to disturbances and on the dynamic path of a response rather than its end state [Meadows 1980, pp. 227-28]. In Neale's terminology, system dynamics employs the linguistic structure of verb processes rather than "nouning" the hypothesis. The result may be a "fair" translation of the natural language system into a more concise symbolic language structure that may facilitate computer modeling of the causal relations described by the evolutionary process of institutionalists.

Language Structure and the Progress of Economic Theory

Ayres noted that Veblen's contempt for price theory produced among his followers a like contempt that led them to avoid "abstract" thinking and to concentrate their efforts upon studies of actual economic situations [Ayres 1944, p. 11]. Ayres asked, What are actual economic situations? "Taking problems as they come means taking them in the form they habitually assume, which means in the guise of the conventional way of thinking" [Ayres 1944, p. 12]. His argument against the futility of subtle mathematical analysis of imaginary price situations was based on the limitation it imposes on the range of economic studies. Maurice Dobb [1937] concluded that "so long as mathematical technique retains its servitude to a particular mode of thought, the concepts which it fashions are calculated to veil rather than reveal reality." More recently Robert Gordon [1976, p. 1] argued in his presidential address to the American Economic Association that "the mainstream of economic theory sacrifices far too much relevance in its insistent pursuit of ever increasing rigor."

Qualitative progress relies on novelty. No analytical model, oriented around mechanics and expressed in mathematical symbols, can deal with the emergence of novelty. Everything that can be deduced from an arithmomorphic system can concern only quantitative variations that are logically contained in its axiomatic basis. Dialectical reasoning however, treats concepts as distinct, but not discretely distinct. This allows concepts to overlap with their opposites: "their meanings slide into their opposites" [Georgescu-Roegen 1979, pp. 321-23].

Mathematical language is devoid of subjectivity. It neutralized and naturalizes the message by abstracting the writer's presence from the symbols. That is not to say that ideology is not discernible in a mathematical model, but it is not inherent in the model. From the orientation of mechanics, logical positivists combined pure theory with empirical testing of propositions. The new language of mathematical symbols replaced the old in order to establish a basis for scientific economics [Fusfeld 1980]. The empirical model includes three interrelated stages: first, construction of a theoretical model; second, hypotheses derived about reality from the theory; and finally, tests of the hypotheses made against empirical data. However, Popper [1965, pp. 42, 50, 82-83, 108] and others have argued that there is no scientific way to choose among competing theories that have equally sound logical foundations, with equal degrees of corroboration. Objective scientific analysis, where competing theoretic propositions exist, is transformed into a subjective choice by the individual scientist.

The logic through which the quantitative model is transcribed is carefully specified. The modeler achieves inference through the transformation of symbolic logic and mathematics. Statements are made by the author of the model in the form of formulas. Thus statements are logically derived through the authority of the author from other statements that need not have any meaning other than that of the prior statement. The "truths" of such models are completely self-contained and need not be relevant to anything else. Gödel's theorem stemmed from the use of axiomatic models as an avenue for developing a pure theory of economic science [Gödel 1930]. He proved that the consistency of a formal system adequate for number theory cannot be proven within the system itself. Thus unprovable propositions compromise the completeness of theoretical models. Within the language of mathematics, the knowledge derived from axiomatic systems must be imperfect, subjective, and problematic.

Formulation of ideas cannot be an independent process. Whorf [1956] argues that we dissect nature along lines laid down by our langauge structure. The world is presented in a flux of impressions organized in our minds by means of the linguistic systems in our minds. A critical contribution to the current understanding of the nature of knowledge has been made by the advances in understanding the role that language plays in the shaping of what is known [Cavallo 1979, p. 36].

In the days of the "literary" economists, the use of mathematics emphasised the potential for abstraction in the social sciences. Oversubscription to the linguistic structure of mathematics has resulted in the desocialization of economics as a social science. From a pragmatic perspective, Roger Cavallo believes, the resultant emphasis on sequential characterization of process description has had an unduly inhibitory effect on the investigation of the synchronic and mutually reinforcing aspects of processes. The greatest potential threat to economic science posed by the shift in linguistic structure is the real possibility of mathematical forms and techniques determining the substance and content of economic knowledge [Katouzian 1980, p. 168].

Conclusion

The translation of natural language systems into symbolic linguistic systems cannot produce isomorphic structures. Thus the problem is to minimize the loss of coherence that can result from the translation and transformation of the transactive structure of Indo-European language into the less causally and temporally explicit form of the non-transactive structures. Differences in analytic paradigms can lead to differences in policy conclusions. Some of these differences can be explained by the effect of linguistic structure on mental models and quantitative models.

As languages are not isomorphic, what is imposed on science by their linguistic structures will vary. Natural language as an abstract system of classification embodies a theory of reality in its forms and syntax. Groups of languages present a preferred model for interpreting and perceiving phenomena. However, these systems are made actual by human agents in social interaction and are negotiated in response to forces outside the language system.

Mathematics as an abstract system also imposes semantic limits that orient research. It may, as natural language, be manipulated to present certain points of view. The preference for mathematics over natural language to investigate and explain the forces of social science may be said to be in part ideoloogical. As in the case of natural language this choice may or may not be conscious.

When the discipline shifted linguistic systems from the natural transactive structure of Indo-European grammars to a non-transactive symbolic formalism, the cognitive structure of economics changed. This change tended to suppress ideological awareness and remove social relations from the analytical framework of the orthodoxy. Logical empiricism (positivism) surfaced as the dominant method following the developments in the natural sciences. The new structure was unable to incorporate the richness of the previous system and consequently contributed to a retardation of the progress of economic thought. Mathematical formalism became an end in itself and replaced dialectical reasoning. The open system approach of the calculus of exchange, as a cognitive structure, inhibited the progress of knowledge in economic analysis. The language systems of mathematics offer powerful descriptive devices but cannot perfectly map into a more robust linguistic structure useful for qualitative developments of theory.

Neale has characterized institutionalism as an interpretation of economic phenomena that uses a "verb process" linguistic structure, while orthodox economic theory imposes a "noun value" grammar on the system [Neale 1982, p. 363]. While it has not been the main objective of this article, we have noted that the verb process, closed system approach of the institutionalist is consistent with the symbolic language structure of control theory models. Orthodox economic analysis, which employs a non-transactive grammatical structure, fits the open system employed in econometric models. As such, control theory models may employ a linguistic structure that could potentially yield "fair" (in Dennis's terms) translation from the verb process structure of the institutionalist's natural language system.

This essay has attempted to enhance awareness of the placement of linguistic structure within the methodological critique of political economy. As Ayres noted, language is not an item of physical heredity. It is a social, or cultural, heritage. This heritage is not a faculty or function of the human body, but rather a body of action patterns that exists only by virtue of human beings and is perpetuated by human transmission [Ayres 1961, p. 74].

The early institutionalists clearly saw that the use of mathematics for the purpose of making orthodox theory more robust and hence more "scientific" was an illusion. Ayres concluded, "it continually widened the gap between the hypothetical world of mathematical price theory and the actualities of economic life" [Ayres 1952, p. 18]. This has had a retarding effect on the progress of economic knowledge for two important reasons. First, the often-noted divergence from reality has forced the debate into an unnatural world view of economic theory [Ayres 1952; Georgescu-Roegen; Fusfeld; Dennis 1981; Blatt 1983]. Second, as the main theme of this work points out, when translation and transformation of mental models into symbolic language takes place, the results differ according to the linguistic structure receiving the translation. Failure to understand and identify these differences in structure have resulted in miscommunication and lost effort. A normative judgment between different structures is not necessary. It is sufficient to note that the differences promote alternative cognitive processes that result in alternative interpretations of economic phenomena and thus competing policy promotions.

References

Anderson, David F. 1980. "How Differences in Analytic Paradigms Can Lead to Differences in Policy Conclusions." In *Elements of the System Dynamic Method*, ed. Jorgen Rander, pp. 61-74. Cambridge, Mass.: MIT Press.

Arrow, K., and D. A. Starrett. 1973. "Cost and Demand—Theoretic Approaches to the Theory of Price Determination." In *Carl Menger and the Austrian School of Economics*, ed. J. R. Hicks and W. Weber. Oxford: Oxford University Press.

Ayres, C. E. 1944. *The Theory of Economic Progress*. Chapel Hill: University of North Carolina Press.

________. 1952. *The Industrial Economy*. Cambridge, Mass.: The Riverside Press.

———. 1961. *Toward a Reasonable Society: The Values of Industrial Civilization.* Austin: University of Texas Press.
Bachelard, Gaston. 1938. *La formation de l'esprit scientific. Contribution a une psychanalyse de la connaissance.* Paris: Vrin.
Barbut, Marc. 1970. "On the Meaning of the Word Structure in Mathematics." In *Introduction to Structuralism*, ed. Michael Lane. New York: Basic Books.
Bell, James A., and James F. Bell. 1980. "System Dynamics and Scientific Method." In *Elements of the System Dynamic Method*, ed. J. Randers, pp. 3-22. Cambridge, Mass.: MIT Press.
Bell, James A., and Peter M. Senge. 1980. "Methods for Enhancing Refutability in System Dynamic Modeling." *Studies in the Management Sciences —System Dynamics* 14: 61-73.
Beneveniste, Emile. 1966. *Problems de linguistique generale.* Paris: Edition Gallimard.
Blatt, John. 1983. "How Economists Misuse Mathematics." In *Why Economics is Not Yet a Science*, ed. Alfred Eichner, pp. 116-86. Armonk, N.Y.: M. E. Sharpe.
Boulding, Kenneth. 1966. "The Economics of Knowledge and the Knowledge of Economics." *American Economic Review* 61 (May): 1-13.
Bourdieu, Pierre. 1977. "L'economie des echanges linguistiques." *Langue Francaise* 34 (May): 62-84.
Cavallo, Roger E. 1979. *The Role of Systems Methodology in Social Science Research.* Boston: Martinus Nijoff Publishing.
Chomsky, Noam. 1968. *Language and Mind.* New York: Harcourt, Brace and World.
Coetzee, J. M. 1982. "Newton and the Ideal of a Transparent Scientific Language." *Journal of Literary Semantics* 11 (April): 3-11.
Conceptual Monograph No. 2. 1980. "The Outward vs. Inward Paradigm and The Management of Social Systems." Cambridge, Mass.: MIT System Dynamics Group. #D-2456: 1-24.
Coyle, R. Geoffrey. 1978. "System Dynamics: An Approach to Policy Formulation." *Journal of Business Policy* 3 (Spring): 40-48.
Culler, Jonathan. 1977. *Ferdinand de Saussure.* New York: Penguin Press.
Deane, Phyllis. 1983. "The Scope and Method of Economic Science." *The Economic Journal* 93 (March): 1-12.
Debreu, Gerard. 1984. "Economic Theory in the Mathematical Mode." *American Economic Review* 74 (June): 267-78.
Dennis, Ken. 1981. "Provable Theorems and Refutable Hypothesis: The Case of Competitive Theory." *Journal of Economic Issues* 15 (March): 95-112.
———. 1982. "Economic Theory and the Problem of Translation." *Journal of Economic Issues* 16 (September): 691-712.
———. 1982. "Economic Theory and the Problem of Translation, Part Two." *Journal of Economic Issues* 16 (December): 1039-62.
Dorfman, Robert. 1959. "A Catechism: Mathematics in Social Sciences." *Review of Economics and Statistics* 36 (November): 374-77.
Dugger, William. 1983. "Two Twists in Economic Methodology: Positivism

and Subjectivism." *American Journal of Economics and Sociology* 42 (January): 75-91.

Forrester, Jay W. 1971. "Counterintuitive Behavior of Social Systems." *Technology Review* 73 (January): 1-16.

Foucault, M. 1970. *The Order of Things.* (New York: Vintage Books. Translation of *Les Mots et les Choses.*

Fowler, R., Robert Hodge, et al. 1979. *Language and Control.* London: Routledge and Kegan Paul.

Friedman, Milton. 1953. "The Methology of Positive Economics." In *Essays in Positive Economics.* Chicago: University of Chicago Press.

Fusfeld, Daniel. 1980. "The Conceptual Framework of Modern Economics." *Journal of Economic Issues* 14 (March): 1-52.

Georgescu-Roegen, N. 1979. "Methods in Economic Science." *Journal of Economic Issues* 13 (June): 317-28.

Gill, Flora. 1981. "Some Methodological Implications of the Marginal Revolution." *Australian Economic Papers* 20 (June): 72-82.

Gödel, K. 1930. "Gödel's Proof." In *The World of Mathematics,* vol. 3, ed. E. Nagel and J. R. Newman. New York: Simon and Schuster.

Gordon, Robert A. 1976. "Rigor and Relevance in a Changing Institutional Setting." *American Economic Review* 66 (March): 1-14.

Granger, C. W. J. 1969. "Investigating Causal Relations by Econometric Models and Cross-Spectral Methods." *Econometrics* 37 (July): 424-38.

Hardy, William. 1978. *Language, Thought and Experience.* Baltimore, Md.: University Park Press.

Hume, David. 1739. *A Treatise of Human Nature.* Oxford: Clarendon Press.

Jevons, W. S. 1871. *Theory of Political Economy,* 2d ed. London: Macmillan.

Kant, Immanuel. 1905. *Critique of Pure Reason.* Translated into English by F. Max Muller, 2d ed. New York: Macmillan.

Katouzian, Homa. 1980. *Ideology and Method in Economics.* New York: New York University Press.

Kline, Morris. 1980. *Mathematics, The Loss of Certainty.* Oxford: Oxford University Press.

Krantz, David H., et al. 1971. *Foundations of Measurement,* vol. 1. New York: Academic Press.

Kress, Gunther, and Robert Hodge. 1979. *Language as Ideology.* London: Routledge and Kegan Paul.

Kuyk, Willem. 1977. *Complementarity in Mathematics.* Boston: D. Reidel.

Labov, Wililam. 1973. *Sociolinguistic Patterns.* Philadelphia: University of Pennsylvania Press.

Lecourt, Dominique. 1975. *Marxism and Epistemology, Bachelard, Canguilhem, and Foucault.* London: Humanities Press.

Lilienfeld, Robert. 1978. *The Rise of Systems Theory.* New York: John Wiley and Sons.

Luce, R. Duncan, and Patrick Suppes. 1968. "Mathematics." In *International Encyclopedia of the Social Sciences,* vol. 10, pp. 65-76. New York: Collier-Macmillan.

Maher, Peter. 1977. " 'Upside-down' Language and Mind: The Linguistic Basis of Logical and Mathematical Formalism." *Language Science* 32 (December): 1-9.

Meadows, Donella H. 1980. "The Unavoidable A Priori." In *Elements of the System Dynamics Method*, ed. Jorgen Randers, pp. 23-56. Cambridge, Mass.: MIT Press.

Mueller, Claus. 1973. *The Politics of Communication*. New York: Oxford University Press.

Myrdal, Gunnar. 1979. "Institutional Economics." *Journal of Economic Issues* 12 (September): 773-74.

Neale, Walter C. 1982. "Language and Economics." *Journal of Economic Issues* 14 (June): 355-69.

Newton, Isaac. 1947. *Mathematical Principles of Natural Philosophy*. Translated into English by Andrew Motte, 1729, revised by F. Cajori. Berkeley: University of California Press.

Perryman, M. Ray. 1982. "Institutionalism and Econometrics: Toward a Meaningful Synthesis." *Journal of Economic Issues* 16 (June): 563-68.

Piaget, Jean. 1955. *Language and Thought of the Child*. Cleveland: Meridian World.

Phillips, Bernard. 1980. "Paradigmatic Barriers to System Dynamics." *Proceedings of the International Conference on Cybernetics and Society*. Cambridge, Mass.: MIT Press.

Popper, K. 1935. *The Logic of Scientific Discovery*. New York: Basic Books.

Porcher, Louis. 1980. "Parcours socio-pedagogiques." In *Signes de forces du renouveau actuel en D.L.E.*, ed. R. Galessin. Paris: C.L.E. International.

Quine, W. V. 1960. *Word and Object*. New York: John Wiley and Sons.

Quine, W. V. 1974. *Methods of Logic*, 3d ed. London: Routledge and Kegan Paul.

Rambouillet, Andre. 1973. *L'enseignement de la civilisation francaise*. Paris: Hachette.

Regnier, Andre. 1974. *La Crise du language scientifique*. Paris: Editions Anthropos.

Rescher, Nicholas. 1969. "Translation as a Tool of Philosophical Analysis." *Journal of Philosophy* 52: 152-55. Revised and reprinted in Nicholas Rescher, *Essays in Philosophical Analysis*. Pittsburgh: University of Pittsburg Press.

Roberts, Edward, ed. 1981. *Managerial Applications of System Dynamics*. Cambridge, Mass.: MIT Press.

Samuelson, Paul A. 1952. "Economic Theory and Mathematics, An Appraisal." *American Economic Review* 42 (May): 56-66.

Sims, Christopher. 1972. "Money, Income, and Causality." *American Economic Review* 62 (September): 540-52.

Solo, Robert. 1975. "What is Structualism? Piaget's Genetic Epistemology and the Varieties of Structuralist Thought." *Journal of Economic Issues* 9 (December): 605-25.

———. 1981. *The Positive State*. Cincinnati: South-Western.

Veblen, T. 1898. "Why Is Economics Not an Evolutionary Science." *Quarterly Journal of Economics* 12. Reprinted in *The Place of Science in Modern Civilization*. New York: Russel and Russel, 1961 [1919], p. 73-81.

Whorf, Benjamin. 1956. *Language, Thought and Reality*. Cambridge, Mass.: MIT Press.

PART IV

CRITIQUE OF ECONOMIC THEORY AS SOCIAL CONTROL AND A GUIDE TO POLICY

Introduction to Part IV

In the first three sections of this volume, the focus was mainly on philosophical, methodological, and historical differences between orthodox neoclassicism and institutionalism, with only occasional reference to their relevance and guidance for economic policy making. In this section, the question that before was incidental becomes central: which of the two perspectives is the more appropriate and successful in contributing to and guiding the formulation of policy to resolve problems that inevitably arise in the institutional structure through which real income is provided? Recall that, at the beginning of this volume, the claim was made that there is agreement among economists of all persuasions that the significance of economic theory is its demonstrated relevance for problem solving. The papers composing this section, then, offer a broad consideration of issues in the relationship between economics as a discipline and economic policy making. A multifaceted response is provided to the question of how institutional economists demonstrate the superior policy relevance of their own perspective.

The lead paper in this section, by J. Fagg Foster, sets a core analytical context to which the following papers relate, although in different ways and with divergent language. Foster's position consists of a series of logically sequential postulates for which generality is claimed: "Economics is and always has been concerned with the process of providing the means of human life and experience;" "The significance of [economic] inquiry lies in its applicability to the solution of real problems;" economics is "concerned with the institutional aspects of the productive process," that is, "with the prescribed patterns of human relations, patterns of correlated activities and attitudes, among groups of persons who are organized for the purpose of carrying on the process of providing the means of human life and experience." "A problem arises when that process ceases to be carried forward at the level of efficiency indicated by the current state of the industrial arts. It becomes an economic problem when that failure is caused by the failure of any one, or several, of those patterns to contribute to the economic process." That is, "effective correlation of institutional structures" can be accomplished only "by the modification of some part or parts of the structure." Economic policy is addressed to the formulation and implementation of that modification. Thus, "the economic general theory must be the theory of institutional adjustment." Since the identification of an economic problem requires the "recognition of a discrepancy between 'what is' and 'what ought to be,'" it follows that a theory of social value, a criterion to distinguish between "is" and "ought," must be an integral part of economic analysis. But the resolution of problems residing in structure requires that the "criterion of what ought to be" lie "outside the pattern of institutional structure." The "substance of that criterion is the instrumental efficiency of the economic process." Herewith, then, is a principle of social value for choosing appropriate economic policy. Given, existing, or proposed institutional structure is not part of this criterion. Foster concludes his paper with a critical assessment of neoclassicists who try to avoid social value analysis in economic inquiry by (1) "defining economics as analysis of the process of providing the means of life within a given institutional structure and (2) by identifying price and value and thus demanding that economic analysis be restricted to price."

Turning now to a specific area of problem analysis and policy, David Dale Martin asks, "What has happened to [orthodox] economic theory since 1890 to keep it relevant to questions of social control of business? Most of us would admit . . . that very little has happened to the theory to reflect the radical changes in the structure of control. . . . economic theory remains fundamentally a theory of conflict resolution among maximizing entities brought about through voluntary market transactions." Martin sees the actual structure of the economy as being very different "from the skeleton laid bare in economic theory." Martin is concerned in particular with some "characteristics of our society, neglect of which is likely to result in abuse of economic theory by those citizens participating . . . in developing the legal rules through which society at large attempts to control . . . business."

Three such attributes are: "(1) the necessity of unneutral mechanisms to achieve redistribution of income and wealth; (2) the role of business in the determination of relative degree of scarcity; and (3) the consequences of 'combinations in the form of trust or otherwise' for the existence of maximizing entities resolving conflict through market mechanisms." With regard to the first, Martin argues that the conventional "efficiency" arguments of orthodoxy must not interdict redistribution. "In a market system, the rich will get richer unless the political conflict resolution mechanism redresses the balance. . . . Today's wealth and income distribution is the result of yesterday's power struggles." With regard to the second, he contends that corporate business uses its power heavily to influence the character and extent of consumer preferences. It is an abusive usage of standard theory to deny a governmental role in helping to inform preferences and to oppose "restraints of trade," which generate "contrived scarcities." With regard to the third, Martin shows, through reference to economic history, that traditional theory has never really adapted "its premises to take into account the rise of the corporate form." Accordingly, when the need for social control of business is approached through the orthodox tenets, the latter fails adequately to inform the process of generating legal constraints.

In the next paper, William H. Melody laments the fact that there has been in this century no revolution at the microeconomic level comparable to that of the Keynesian revolution at the macroeconomic level. While orthodox economists have increasingly assumed consulting or advisory roles in policy deliberations, public and private, Melody contends that the microeconomic theory of the firm "has very little to say on matters of microeconomic policy." The theoretical world does not approximate the real world. In consequence, "all issues of microeconomic public policy involve problems that turn out to be *exceptions* to the general neoclassical theory." More disturbingly, Melody contends, orthodox economists hired as advisors of clients must generally serve that client's purposes and the preservation of whatever economic power that client has achieved. Where standard theory is used by such economists, in deliberations on public policy affecting the client's power and income interests, it becomes "cannon fodder for vested interests, a role that only can serve to reinforce the inherited structure of economic institutions and the maintenance and extension of monopoly power." Melody then turns to a consideration and critique of the use of neoclassical marginal analysis in policy formation. He argues that marginal analysis provides "an elegant framework from which economists can advise that decision makers should look to the marginal conditions, most specifically marginal costs, in order to optimize their objectives. This general standard can be recommended sweepingly to all problems in all possible circumstances at all times." Accordingly, firms, government agencies, and regulatory commissions are all urged to use marginal analysis. The illusion is that, for example, government agencies, through the use of marginal analysis, can regulate large corporate firms so as to achieve the equivalent of the optimal outcomes of a free competitive system. "As a guide to public policy directed to encouraging efficient resource allocation," however, "the marginal cost standard of neoclassical theory has been a resounding failure. Its advocacy on public policy issues appears largely opportunistic, dictated primarily by firms with vested interests in certain public policies." Melody recommends a "return-on-investment" criterion in lieu of the "marginal-cost" criterion in policy deliberations.

The declining confidence in the policy relevance of neoclassicism is eroded even further by Harry M. Trebing. After noting that institutionalists through this century have "provided much of the intellectual rationale for public control" of business enterprise, he commends their contribution and application of the "public interest theory of regulation" as an appropriate "method for resolving conflicts and coordinating social objectives in an industrial economy and . . . as a means for curbing monopoly power and preventing the abuses associated with the unrestricted exercise of that power." The waning of popular and academic support for public regulation in the 1970s and after was rooted in claims that regulation generated "inefficiency [and] inflation," impeded innovation, and led to the "cartelization of industry." "For the neoclassicists, misguided government intervention is the culprit, rather than the monopoly power of the firm." The primary focus and content of this paper, then, is a presentation and critique of the neoclassical agenda for "reform" through deregulation of industrial and social control and the provision of an alternative institutionalist approach. That this neoclassical agenda places heavy reliance on alleged returns to market discipline for allocative efficiency gains, to profit motives as incentives, and to competitive or "contestable" markets and more open entry to set constraints on power will come as no surprise. With reference both to the areas of the economy affected with the deregulation efforts and to the specific reformistic claims of the orthodox pushers of the deregulation agenda, Trebing reviews and appraises these orthodox theoretical positions and the implications and probable consequences of adopting their policy recommendations. In general, he finds few gains from the deregulatory return to more market-deferential arrangements. For modern institutionalists, in contrast, the question of public control of enterprise must be seen in a context where the current economy is characterized by "continuous change, imperfect markets, uncompensated social costs, decision making based on partial information, and corporations and pressure groups that exercise discretionary power." Institutionalists take a pragmatic approach to public control, given this reality. Their position, in the construction of policy, is characterized by "a holistic view of the interdependence of market structure, the adequacy and availability of service, equity and distributional effects, social values, and industry performance on the one hand, and different regulatory options on the other."

Michael R. Carter, a John R. Commons-based institutionalist, offers an additional critique of neoclassical microeconomic theory, with special reference to its deference to the policy criterion of Paretian efficiency (optimality). He observes that "most neoclassical microeconomic theory has no institutional content beyond implicit assumptions about the existence of markets, enforceable contracts, and individuals free to choose." Carter sees R. H. Coase as a chief proponent of the view that institutional arrangements are generally irrelevant in microeconomic analysis. Coase argues that, "in the absence of transaction costs, the distribution of property rights . . . [as institutional arrangements] does not affect the allocation of resources." Carter would turn the Coase claim on its head and argue the converse, "namely, in the presence of transaction costs, property rights and institutional arrangements *do* affect resource allocation." "Property rights" he continues, "affects *whose* costs and benefits enter the calculations that determine resource allocation in a non-Walrasian world." These contentions are reinforced through a brief consideration of two case studies: The first involves Commons' consideration of yellow dog contracts and the demonstration that the possession of property rights may well lead to economic coercion. The second concerns the contractual interlinkage of tenet cultivation and credit access that may create "the trap of debt peonage" in underdeveloped agricultural sectors of various countries. Carter concludes the paper with a consideration of "the insufficiency of Pareto efficiency" as a judgmental criterion. What Carter shows is that Pareto efficiency and economic coercion may well go hand in hand. Instead of "exploitation *versus* efficiency," as implied in neoclassicism, Carter sees "exploitation *and* efficiency" in certain rural settings. Orthodoxy takes no account of "the evolution of institutional rules that determine bargaining power and alternate opportunity" that was the "centerpiece of Commons's institutional analysis." "The distribution of power and assets" is not "a stable and secure given." It is an anterior concern, unaddressed by neoclassicists and unjudged by Paretian criteria.

The character and relevance of the Paretian criterion is raised by Warren J. Samuels, a co-editor of this volume and series, in a larger context of pervasive economic controversy "over the social role of economists and the relation of economic theory (or science) to policy." As a tool with which to probe the character of such controversies, Samuels chooses "the basis status and relevance of the theory of free trade to policy." He documents the fact of such controversies by surveys of theoretical differences over free trade of historical and contemporary scholars. After reporting on and interpreting these evidences of controversy over free trade, Samuels concludes that "the central issues separating large groups of respondents was the epistemological status of the two principle lines of reasoning, namely, that free trade leads to the Pareto optimum, and that free trade results in the maximization of the value of the output." When the query is posed as to whether these are positive or normative lines of reasoning, Samuels suggests that the presumption of mutual exclusivity be shelved in favor of an inquiry "into the normative elements which define or limit the *sense* in which a proposition is positive." He then explores "normative elements which delimit and render *conditional* the positive character of the two lines of reasoning." When "the proposition that free trade leads to a Pareto optimal result" is considered, Samuels finds that "at least four normative elements are involved." (a) "The choice of Pareto optimality . . . is itself normative." Other criteria are excluded. (b) "Any move from a restricted to a free-trade policy is itself non-Pareto optimal. (c) "There is no one Pareto optimal solution. Each is specific to the power structure . . . from which it arises." (d) "The proposition that free trade results in a Pareto optimal solution is nonoperational, nontestable, and nonrefutable. It is a matter of logic."

He concludes that, "*given* these normative elements . . . the statement that free trade results in a Pareto optimal result is 'positive.'" A similar result is achieved in considering "the proposition that free trade will maximize the value of output." Samuels' consideration of free-trade theory indicates that "very little can be said with regard to free trade which does not have normative elements. The meaningfulness of otherwise ostensibly positive *is* propositions is conditional upon the identification of the normative elements."

John Adams continues the questioning of the relevancy of orthodoxy for problem solving by directly challenging the claims, made by Theordore W. Schultz in his Nobel lecture, "that peasants are as rational as the rest of us; that they respond to price, cost, and profit signals in the market place; and that, as a guide to policy, their responsiveness means that proper market signals are a sufficient condition for innovation in agriculture and agricultural development." Each of these contentions is found wanting: Adams contends that "the idea of 'rationality' is empty . . . it does not do justice to the multiplex character of the human mind, motivation, and social or economic condition." The presumption is that "in some underlying way all people are the same—they calculate their interests and act upon them." Through consideration of case studies involving infant health care, caste structure and implications, and "backward sloping supply curves" of farm labor, he argues that all are in some sense rational, but "everyone's behavior is conditioned by the interplay of cultural and attitudinal factors. There is no *content* in being rational. The content comes from the cultural and attitudinal realms" in interaction with actual economic circumstances. Adams mounts counter evidence to the claim that "peasants are price responsive." The orthodox studies are biased at the outset in choice of subject matter, and claims to generality simply cannot be supported. Instead, he argues that "peasant market behavior is contingent upon a variety of specific concerns, many of which have deep ecological and cultural roots." Moreover, the injection of the "risk factor" is an effort to salvage the "non-price-responsiveness" assertion does not succeed, according to Adams. "Risk is not culturally defined and . . . indigenous systems for risk-bearing are not understood." Accordingly, the Schultz-defended "rationality dictum . . . fails both at the level of understanding peasant behavior and as a theory of development." It ill serves as a basis for development policy.

David Hamilton, employing institutional analysis, vigorously rejects assaults from conservative economists on policies of the welfare state who, by reclaiming Malthusian ancestry, argue that "any welfare program, with the possible exception of that provoked by begging, corrupts its beneficiaries. It hurts them worse than it hurts the hesitant giver. Spare the charity and save the child?"

Hamilton, using both historical and anthropological examples demonstrates that "all societies are [and must be] systems of income maintenance." While previous societies have had their own special hazards and impairments to real income flows, industrial societies have developed particularly severe versions of economic insecurities to which policy, in the form of income maintenance programs, must be, and is, directed. Private and family support systems have long since become inadequate; new public support systems have become essential. For Hamilton, an obviously critical condition for an individual is the termination of money income flow from unemployment, old age, illness, or whatever. Given current levels of interdependence, only the public assumption of responsibility to sustain that flow of money income can significantly preclude mass poverty. Hamilton notes that patchwork programs in the United States have been increasing in magnitude over the last couple of decades, but that in recent years both the programs and the ideational and budgetary support for them have, unfortunately, come under serious and continuing attack. Hamilton concludes his article, drawing on Keynes and others, with an explanation of how economic instability could be substantially reduced through a program of income redistribution. Extremely uneven distribution of income keeps those with a high propensity to consume in a continuing income deficit thus impairing the economy's ability to maintain high national "income and employment and real capital accumulation." Income maintenance programs are not then a cost that has to be borne; they are "essential to real economic stability and growth." Accordingly, in Hamilton's view, adequate income maintenance programs are affordable, are necessary, and are an important contributor to economic stability. "Our limitations are institutional, not technological."

Wallace C. Peterson, with a similar focus and concern, analyzes the "essential structure of the U.S. 'welfare' state," and the "impact on this structure of the conservative counterrevolution that came to fruition" with the Reagan administration. He concludes with brief observations on the long-term implications of this counterrevolution. After broadening the concept of the "welfare state" to include all transfers of income (that is, where "governments do not require any product, service, or asset in exchange for the money paid out"), Peterson shows empirically how this federal function has increased over the last several decades to constitute over two thirds of federal spending. Interestingly, however, Peterson includes not only the usual transfers of social security, Medicare, aid to dependent children, food stamps, unemployment compensation, and the like. His "welfare state" concept includes, as well, interest on the federal debt, tax expenditures (subsidies through tax breaks), and other benefits for the middle and upper classes. From his empirical analysis, Peterson concludes that "the vast and complex redistributional machinery of the federal government does not simply rearrange incomes from the top downward . . . The pattern of redistribution is . . . skewed toward the middle and the top, once tax expenditures as well as transfers are taken into account." Ordinary transfers are progressive; tax expenditures are regressive. In sum, "the pattern noted in the distribution of benefits from both transfers and tax expenditures largely reflects the distribution of power in our society."

The impact of the Reagan-led counterrevolution has been to tilt "the redistributional machinery of the federal government . . . away from the poor and near poor . . . toward families higher up on the income scale," and to provide tax cuts that were "skewed heavily in favor of upper income groups." In consequence, poverty has increased and income distribution is more unequal. If the Reagan counterrevolution is sustained over time, the reduction in the nonmilitary role of the federal government and the greater inequality of income distribution can only make the resolution of problems in the future more difficult.

17

The Relation between the Theory of Value and Economic Analysis

J. Fagg Foster

In his teaching, Foster constantly confronted students with the problem of value theory. But in order to avoid starting each new discussion at the beginning, he felt the necessity to establish some basic propositions and to answer some recurrent questions about the problem. Such seems to have been the purpose of this paper, written in 1949. Foster argues that society, in actually applying the instrumental criterion of judgment, accredits economic inquiry with significance only as it contributes to solving real economic problems. These exist not in peoples' heads, but in situations in which existing patterns of human relations prevent full application of the existing state of the arts. Given such problems, solutions require identification of new behavior patterns that will permit "state-of-the-art" applications. This identification requires understanding what "ought to be" in the instrumental sense of patterns that in fact permit doing what is technically feasible. Consequently, economists are of necessity concerned with questions of the desirability of existing institutional patterns. This desirability must be appraised by a criterion that is not itself part of the existing pattern. Since prices are part of that pattern, they cannot be the criterion of judgment. Price cannot properly be identified as value. Prices have significance, but they cannot tell society what it ought to do. Ayres reached the same conclusion on somewhat different grounds in the addendum printed in the third edition of The Theory of Economic Progress.

The relation between value theory and economic analysis is simple and easily comprehensible. The difficulties that invariably arise when the problem is under discussion spring from sources other than novelty and complexity. Just what those sources are should become more nearly apparent as the discussion proceeds.

Economics is and always has been concerned with the process of providing the means of human life and experience. The concern of economics with that process is and always has been to explain it, to make it understandable to the community so that the community may proceed to a solution of its economic problems.

But economics is not and never has been concerned with the physical-engineering aspects of that process except insofar as those aspects are genetic to its institutional phases. Economic institutions are the area of focus. Economics, then, is an effort at rational inquiry into those institutions through which man provides himself with the means of life and experience.

But why study the economic process? Particularly, why study the institutional aspects of that process? Some individual economists profess to be motivated in that effort by what is called idle curiosity. Indeed, they may well be. But that pattern of motivation has never been considered sufficient reason for a community to set up institutional arrangements through which those individuals may apply their major effort and attention to that endeavor. It should be noted that it is by virtue of such arrangements that economists are enabled to proceed in the rational organization of their inquiry. The community has set up such arrangements because it is and always has been confronted by real economic problems and because it has supposed that extended inquiry might throw some light on them. Whatever the motivation of the individual student, the significance of his inquiry lies in its applicability to the solution of real problems. In fact, such is the case in all fields of inquiry. We learned long ago that because the applicability of a line of inquiry is not immediately obvious, it does not mean that application will not be discovered. We have learned to tolerate and even support inquiry the application of which is not apparent, either to current problems or to problems that conceivably may arise in the future. But our conception of what constitutes significance and importance still remains fixed on the possibility of solving real problems confronting real people, and we concede significance to any inquiry in any field only on the basis of that possibility.

The next logical step is to discern the character of an economic problem. It already has been noted that economics is, by universal consent, concerned with the institutional aspects of the productive process. That is to say, economics is concerned with the prescribed patterns of human relations, patterns of correlated activities and attitudes, among groups of persons who are organized for the purpose of carrying on the process of providing the means of human life and experience. A problem arises when that process ceases to be carried forward at the level of efficiency indicated by the current state of the industrial arts. It becomes an economic problem when that failure is caused by the failure of any one, or several, of those patterns to contribute to the economic process or when any institutional arrangement interferes with its on-going. That is to say, an economic problem appears when disrapport arises between two or more patterns of human activities that are supposed to be correlated toward the effective continuation of the productive process.

But how can effective correlation of institutional structures be attained? It goes almost without saying that such correlation can be brought about only by the modification of some part or parts of the structure. This is a truism. Since the significance of economic theory lies in its applicability to the solution of economic problems, and since economic problems are situations of instrumental dislocation, it follows that answers to economic problems must take the form of institutional judgment—modifications of prescribed patterns of human relations looking toward the instrumentally effective correlation of those organizational patterns with each other and with the noninstitutional aspects of the economic process.

It necessarily follows that the economic general theory must be the theory of institutional adjustment. Otherwise, economic theory can have no significance insofar as significance is a function of problem solving. It is quite clear that significance never has been allowed any other connotation, although many theories of how significance may be measured have clamored for attention.

The identification of an economic problem has been made in terms of the recognition of a discrepancy between "what is" and "what ought to be," between "what goes on here" and "what ought to go on here." The resolution of an economic problem has been identified as the destruction of that discrepancy. But such a resolution at first glance seemingly could be brought about by bringing either of the discrepants into conformity with the other. If the dictum that "whatever is, is right" holds true, then most certainly there could be no such thing as an economic problem. But the community finds repeatedly that the economic process does not go forward at the level of efficiency that the noninstitutional factors indicate is available. This situation becomes so apparent at times that even the intellectually most recalcitrant members of the community are forced to recognize it. The community judges its problems to be conjunctures of factual circumstances that cannot be gainsaid by any verbal devices whatever. Since the physical circumstances that converge to bring on an economic problem remain just what they are, there can be no way of resolving the problem except to adjust the institutional structure so as to bring the two phases into instrumental rapport. Otherwise, the problem remains as such, and the compulsions toward resolution remain until, as

Veblen would put it, the community has "made up its account" with the physical circumstances that have converged to bring on the problem.

The point is that the criterion of judgment of "what ought to be" lies outside the pattern of institutional structure. There is no way, short of forceful destruction, to prevent recognition of a discrepancy between "what is" and "what ought to be" in terms of the instrumental efficiency of the economic process. The reason for this impossibility is that the problematic situation is a matter of factual circumstances the human incidences of which cannot be escaped except by "making up our account" with those same physical circumstances. There can be no way of making up that account, again short of forceful destruction, except by adjusting the relevant institutional structures so as to remove the inefficiency; there is no other way to remove the human incidences that comprise the compulsions toward adjustment.

It becomes completely certain that a criterion of judgment independent of any particular institutional structure is necessary if an economic problem is even to be recognized as such. It also becomes increasingly clear that the substance of that criterion is the instrumental efficiency of the economic process.

Whatever the identification of the character of the criterion of judgment, it remains that economic problems cannot be conceived—and certainly cannot be solved—without the application of some criterion for judging between alternatives, that is, without applying some theory of value.

Thus, since "what ought to be" in economic affairs is nothing less than the application of a theory of value, and since no economic problem can be conceived or resolved without some comprehension of "what ought to be," it becomes clear that significant economic analysis necessarily involves the application of the theory of value. This is the simple and apparent relationship between value theory and economic analysis.

Some economists have sought to avoid the value problem. Their expedients toward that end have been many, but the most important ones are (1) defining economics as analysis of the process of providing the means of life within a given institutional structure and (2) identifying price and value and thus demanding that economic analysis be restricted to price.

The first of these two expedients hardly requires comment. If the resolution of economic problems necessarily involves institutional adjustment, an analysis that assumes a given institutional structure can be of little if any significance. And if economics is to be without significance, if it is to be reduced to pure scholasticism, then some other discipline must replace it. It goes without saying that the community cannot avoid formulating answers to the real economic problems with which it is confronted. The proponents of this expedient frequently take the position that economics cannot be concerned with economic problems, that economics may be occupied only with describing what goes on. But if economic problems are not to be considered in terms of economic theory, then in what terms are they to be considered? Whatever caption be given those alternative terms, it would necessarily replace economics if the latter be restricted to simple description.

The second expedient for avoiding the value problem requires more extended comment. It is through this expedient that the major confusion in contemporary theory arises. Many economists have striven to avoid the value problem by identifying price and value and at the same time by denying that they are concerned with the concept of value as the criterion of judgment in choosing between alternatives. The latter they refer to as the philosophical and sometimes as the ethical concept of value, and they insist on deferring to the philosophers on the matter. But to defer does not require disregard, and it most certainly does not require failure to recognize accomplishments that the philosophers have attained on the problem. It should be pointed out further that the theory of value pronounced in the present discussion is widely recognized as the most important modern philosophical development. The development of philosophy did not stop in the eighteenth century.

If there be the total disconcern, as claimed, with the philosophical meaning of value, then these economists have committed an etymological error. They have used a word universally understood and historically used to mean one sort of thing for quite a different referent, and one for which a very clearly understood term is available.

But this mistake is more than a tendency toward euphemism. Through this device recent economic orthodoxy has managed to lay claim to generality and foundation, to lay claim to significance and at the same time avoid all responsibility for doing more than describing relative prices. This conjoinment of unlimited significance and complete irresponsibility is accomplished by tacitly, and perhaps unconsciously, reversing the direction of identity between price and value, by asserting that value is merely another way of saying price, which means simply ratios of exchange, and then by proceeding as if price means value and therefore that price serves as the criterion of judgment in choosing between alternatives. It would seem that Oscar Wood was correct in saying that nothing quite equals economics in permitting the use of the same word to mean absolutely different things without being found out.

If the identification runs from price to value, and if price is used to mean simply and only ratios of exchange, then the identification has no significance beyond release from the tedium of a constant linguistic repetition. In that case no objection is warranted beyond the dislocational effect on the more broadly literate members of the community in their reading of economics literature. This defect would still be unwarranted, however unimportant.

But, in contrast with this situation, if the identification runs from value to price, then the equation takes on an importance that cannot be exaggerated. For, in the latter case, price would be held to represent real worth (under whatever definition), and there could then be no necessity for economic analysis to go beyond the determinants of price. This would be significant, indeed. For if price equals real worth, then the revelation of the principles of price determination and the pattern of their interworking, the general price theory, would be the general theory of the economic process. And the revelation of the determinants of price would, *ipso facto*, be the revelation of the fundamental determinants of the economic process. It is this significance that is imputed to the identification of price and value by the insistence that economics be restricted to price analysis. This is necessarily the case since under no stretch of the imagination could inquiry into the economic process be rationally restricted to price unless price reveals the real determinants of that process. It is nonsense to say that we shall explain the economic process but shall not consider the determinants of that process. It is more than a suspicion that, in the minds of those who insist that economics be restricted to price analysis, the intended identification of value and price runs from value to price, irrespective of strong protestations to the contrary. Certainly, there is no escape from the fact that the insistence that economic theory be restricted to price theory must be either (1) an abandonment of its function and therefore of its significance or (2) a claim that price measures real value.

Some of those who identify value and price take the position that there is no need in economic theory to bother with value because wants can be taken as given, and that, since relative intensities of wants are brought toward equilibrium in an open market, no investigation and no theoretical formulation beyond the market is necessary. But the things people want are a function of their social experience, and that is carried on through structural institutions that specify their activities and attitudes. Thus, the pattern of a people's wants takes visible form partly as a result of the pattern of the institutional structure through which they participate in the economic process. As we have seen, to say that an economic problem exists is to say that part of that structure, that particular pattern of human relationships, has ceased or failed to provide for the effective participation of its members. In so saying, we are necessarily in the position of asserting that the instrumental efficiency of the economic process is the criterion of judgment in terms of which, and only in terms of which, we may resolve economic problems. In fact, we either must accept economic efficiency, in the instrumental sense, as the criterion of judgment, or we must revise the universally accepted conception of what constitutes an economic problem. Between these alternatives, there is only one rational choice because an economic problem is a conjuncture of factual circumstances, the effects of which can neither be avoided nor denied.

The evidence thus drives us rationally to the inescapable conclusion that our only choice is to accept economic efficiency in the instrumental sense as our criterion of judgment, as our theory of value.

18

The Uses and Abuses of Economic Theory in the Social Control of Business

David Dale Martin

Economic theory consists of a body of propositions deduced from alternative sets of premises. Few, if any, of these propositions have been tested and accepted, even tentatively, as scientific laws in the sense in which the natural sciences have "discovered" laws of nature. The propositions of economic theory are statements about the behavior of human beings within a social structure. Those economists whose philosophical underpinnings permit an element of "free will" in human behavior are likely to consider even those empirically tested and accepted hypotheses to be limited to particular societies subject to change by human actions.

The philosophical proposition that mankind's nature gives rise to universally true and discoverable economic laws is perhaps gaining acceptance among economists. Even the purest positive economists, however, have come forth with so few persuasive claims of empirical verification that we will not be concerned here with the uses and abuses of economic science in that sense. Rather, this article addresses the question of the usefulness of the process of theorizing as generally practiced by those who "do economics."

The term *social control of business* is used in the title with the deliberate intent of conjuring up in the minds of those with long memories, or an historical bent, the literature of a bygone era.[1] Although a generation of economics graduate students has grown up with "industrial organization" labeling their specialty, social control of business never died as a characteristic of the society itself. With or without the participation of economists, society continues its attempts to control business, and, I might add, vice versa.

The topic, therefore, really does not require consideration of all the philosophical questions associated with the proper role of value judgments in economics.[2] The question is, rather, whether we gain useful insights or mislead ourselves and others when we use the tools of our trade as citizens participating in the political and governmental processes through which legal rules are developed and changed. And changes are advocated by almost everyone and perhaps most vigorously by those most committed to the withdrawal of government from what is called interference in private business decisions.

Those who have studied those ideas called "economic theory" that have evolved primarily over the past two centuries have something in common with each other. Essentially, there exists a common language, a language with which to think about certain aspects of human behavior. Economic theory consists of some "packages of logic." Conversations move along much faster if the conversing parties can make mutually acceptable "big leaps" in the logic. Economic theory is much like mathematics, except that the variables are much less abstract.

These packages of logic can be arranged under three main groupings: (1) a theory of maximizing behavior of households and firms; (2) a theory of conflict resolution through markets; and (3) a theory of aggregate economic activity within the system. Each is used in the social control of business. Some persons tend to use them dogmatically, and it is from dogmatic use that abuses arise.

The dogma of economic orthodoxy can be summarized in a few sentences, which should suffice to call to mind much more for anyone who has been exposed to a good principles course. Economic activity is directed by heads of households, or consumers with "given" preference functions, the nature of which is revealed by their behavior and determined by forces beyond the scope of economics. A subset of these households, singly or in combination, takes on the character of business firms that acquire the services of human and nonhuman agents, organize production, and distribute produced goods and services to households. Each household and each firm is a goal directed entity that maximizes its objective function subject to constraints placed on it by nature and all other entities. The entities deal with each other primarily through voluntary market transactions mutually agreed upon. Government and the political process are used for limited purposes to maintain the peace and keep the lighthouses lit for the fishermen. This dogmatic approach teaches that government intervention should meet the test of whether it makes someone believe he is better off without making anyone believe he is worse off. Although such questions are beyond the scope of economics, each citizen is free, in this scheme of things, to advocate government intervention to achieve a more equitable distribution of income and/or wealth so long as the transfer is not effected by means that interfere with incentives "at the margin."

Some adherents to the dogma would allow the "weak welfare principle," whereby even intervention that injures someone is welfare increasing if those gaining gain enough to compensate those losing from the government action.

If not applied dogmatically, these ideas can be helpful in searching for public policy proposals. It is good politics and good government, as well as good economics, to do good whenever possible without incurring anyone's wrath. The packages of logic on which these welfare principles are based, however, include a number of specific premises of which we need to be aware when jumping to conclusions about the "efficiency" effects of alternative public policy proposals. Because I treat the body of theory as theory rather than as a set of empirically verified propositions of economic science, I am unwilling to accept the irrelevance of testing the premises.[3]

The structure of the society in which we live differs in many important respects from the skeleton laid bare in economic theory. With no attempt to be exhaustive, this article will consider a few characteristics of our society, neglect of which is likely to result in abuse of economic theory by those citizens participating (qua economist or otherwise) in developing the legal rules through which society at large attempts to control that subset of itself we call business. These characteristics are: (1) the necessity of unneutral mechanisms to achieve redistribution of income and wealth; (2) the role of business in the determination of relative degree of scarcity; and (3) the consequences of "combinations in the form of trust or otherwise" for the existence of maximizing entities resolving conflict through market mechanisms. The last of these has to do with the failure of economic theory in the past century to adapt its premises to take into account the rise of the corporate form of business organization.

Mechanisms for Income Redistribution

The most powerful argument brought to bear on government policy makers by economists is the efficiency argument. Almost all proposals to change legal rules are perceived by some groups as damaging to their own interests. Advocates of change often are motivated by a desire to enhance the welfare of a subgroup of which they are members. Each side gains strength in the political conflict resolution system by showing that its own interests are really consistent with the public interest.

The *public interest* is not easy to define. Most of us hold values that prevent us from accepting a simple majority rule. We not only do not wish to risk being in the minority in such a system, but also, I think, we are unwilling to be part of a 51 percent majority that enslaves the other 49 percent. Our democratic principles of government rest very much on legal rules designed to protect the "civil liberties" of each individual. Perhaps the greatest threat to democracy is use of the majority rule principle in matters affecting the vital interests of individuals. A decentralized, competitive market system offers much to a society desiring to assure individual freedom.

Freedom, however, is multidimensional. Freedom from want as well as freedom from fear are important to us. Each person is born into a society in which wealth and income are, in fact, distributed. He does not start in a new game. Each new baby is part of a family whose older members have been participating in the struggle against scarcity. Their status very much affects the economic prospects of the new family member. Those who enter the on-going economic system as part of a family with a relatively larger stock of material, legal, and intellectual capital are doubly blessed.[4] They not only are better off, but also have the means to defend and enhance their advantages and those of their children. In a market system the rich will get richer unless the political conflict resolution mechanism redresses the balance.

Will Rogers is alleged to have told a group of Boston bankers that if they did not give back about half of what they had stolen they would lose it all. Voluntary restraint in the uses of power may help preserve it, if not carried too far.

What role does economic theory play in conflict over legal rules? Sometimes economists are able to help decision makers assess the claims of interested parties by forecasting the true consequences of alternative actions, not only on the active participants in the dispute, but also on other parties. Skill in such forecasting, however, is not limited to economists. Indeed, in most specific cases, engineers or businessmen are more likely than economists to have command of the facts necessary to judge consequences.[5]

Unfortunately for policy makers, the best qualified forecasters are likely to be interested parties. For this reason adversary proceedings play an important role in the nonmarket conflict resolution system. Third parties tend to be left out, however, and that gap is beginning to be filled by the developing public interest pressure groups. Public servants, of course, also are supposed to look after the public interest, but in many cases they operate under rules requiring them merely to resolve conflict between two contending parties.

Economic theory is useful in forecasting, if it is used flexibly. Its practitioners, however, often tend to use it dogmatically. The easy way to measure the effect on the public is simply to ask whether a government action would interfere with the market's "Pareto-optimal" results. If so, it lessens "efficiency." But what about the effect on the distribution of income, wealth, and power? A dogmatic economist will wash his hands of that matter and say: "You can do anything you wish with the income distribution so long as you do not use a government measure that is inefficient." All government measures to redistribute income and wealth, however, are inefficient when judged in terms of the economist's welfare criterion. No one has yet devised a neutral tax and spending scheme.[6]

Dogmatic use of economic theory, therefore, is inherently conservative. It comes down on the side of the status quo. That may not be a truly conservative position, of course, if Will Rogers was right. Perhaps that fact accounts for the existence of an "Eastern liberal establishment."

The distribution of wealth did not arise from economically efficient public policies in an egalitarian society of the past. Today's wealth and income distribution is the result of yesterday's power struggles. Measures used by our ancestors as participants in those power struggles included war, enslavement, and forced migrations; industrial sabotage, strike breaking, monopolization, restraint of trade, and unfair methods of competition; and manipulations of government policy. To accept the distribution of wealth, income, and power now existing, and to argue that measures to redress the unbalance must be consistent with the Pareto optimality condition or else be economically "inefficient," are, to me, abuses of economic theory. To invoke that proposition as if it were a scientific finding devoid of value judgment is at best a delusion. As a minimum, a positive economist should ask: What is the next best method actually available for achieving redistribution of income?

Business Power and Relative Scarcities

A fundamental weakness in economic theory as a guide to government policy is its premises of "given" consumer preferences, "given" technology, and "given" resources. Economic theory abstracts from all the institutional characteristics those forces that determine the manner in which consumer preferences are brought into consistency with relative scarcities. In so doing, the theory focuses on only a small part of the actual role played by both business and government in the workings of the economic system.

That "business" plays a major role in the determination of household preferences has been clearly recognized.[7] Household preferences not only are influenced by advertising, but also in many ways by public policies and legal rules that are determined in large measure by business participation in the political process.[8]

Perhaps more important is the failure of the theory of consumer behavior to take into account the learning process. Each person's preference function in reality is very much influenced by his pattern of want, satisfaction over time, and even by his family's pattern before his birth. Preference itself evolves within a social system in which the degree of scarcity and the distribution of power in past periods play a major role.

One might dismiss the relevancy of this evolving nature of consumer preferences with the observation that, however determined, today's preferences are all we have with which to judge what is good or bad, and each person's current preferences can be known collectively only through the market process without government intervention. That argument is very persuasive. Yet, today's public policy issues very often have to do with the distribution of power to affect tomorrow's preferences.

Business power affects the demand side of relative scarcities other than by its effect on consumer preferences. In spite of the derived nature of the demand for goods and services by governments and businesses, much opportunity exists for business intervention in the processes of derivation of demand for such intermediate goods and services. Mention of a few such opportunities will suffice to suggest the nature of this problem.

Reciprocity is a term well known to businessmen and antitrust experts but not often used in economic theory. The multiproduct, multimarket firm may have opportunities to tie its transactions in some markets to its bargaining in other markets in ways that distort the demand for its outputs or the prices of its inputs. Both offers of rewards and threats of retaliation in unrelated markets can be used in negotiation of terms in a particular transaction.

Standards for product design are set by processes given very little consideration in the literature of economic theory.[9] Products as well as preferences for them usually are assumed to be given.[10] Yet decisions about standards play a major role in the determination of relative demands for intermediate goods as well as in determining the set of products among which consumers may choose to allocate their budgets.

Standards often are reversible only at great cost because of the necessity of either scrapping useful equipment or multiplying the varieties during transition. For example, any change in television transmission processes that requires a change in television receivers could make obsolete the existing stock of receivers and perhaps even require duplication of equipment at both ends. Standards are set by a wide variety of decision-making processes ranging from completely governmental to completely private, but in most cases the process involves interaction among governments and businesses. Economic theory is abused, it seems to me, if it is used to denounce the governmental role in standardization without adequate consideration of the relative power of the business participants in any nongovernmental alternative standard setting mechanism.

For example, those who criticize the recently growing role of the federal government in automobile design should, at least, apprise themselves of the structure of control of the Society of Automotive Engineers, its role in years past in deciding such things as the design of bumpers, and the consequences of bumper design on the demand for "crash parts" and the rate of scrapping vehicles.[11]

Technological change effects relative scarcities on both the demand and the supply side. All goods and services are substitutes for or complements to other goods and services to some degree. Technical change, like standardization, affects both demand and supply of all products in, or potentially in, the system. The course of technical change may be exogenous to the theory of markets, but it is not exogenous to the structure of control of industry. A major role of business management is in making decisions concerning not only the allocation of research and development budgets but also the many questions associated with innovation. The existing structure of power affects, for example, whether resources are devoted to such energy demand reducing research as that on windmills or sailboats. The degree of vertical integration plays a major part in determining whether "creatively destructive" technical changes will be adopted.

A basic paradox of economic activity is that the ultimate achievement of the goal of economic growth would reduce GNP to zero and destroy all capital values. Without scarcity, market values do not exist. Therefore, a social system that encourages individuals, acting alone or in coalition, to enhance the value of their property, also may encourage actions that increase scarcity for society as a whole. A theory that takes the degree of scarcity as "given" must be used very carefully as a guide to government intervention in a business system in which business firms can gain by restricting the supply of productive services. Contrived scarcity is the basic issue of antitrust. The purpose and the effect of restraint of trade is literally to restrain trade. To the recipient, rent is income whether or not it results from contrived scarcity.

Unfortunately, the distinction is very difficult to make in practice between scarcity that stems from the niggardliness of nature and that which results from such practices as the ancient crimes of forestalling, regrating, and engrossing. The contriving that takes place in a highly industrialized, corporately organized, "new industrial state" is particularly difficult to identify. Only decentralization in the structure of control can offer much assurance that perceived scarcity reflects the state of nature sufficiently accurately to warrant a laissez-faire policy.

The effects of centralization of control of pricing and output decisions in particular markets have, of course, been the subject of much of the literature of microeconomic theory. Much less attention has been given, however, to the centralization of investment decisions or the preemption of resources.[12] In the short run, scarcity in plant capacity is very real whether or not contrived. Government failure to intervene to prevent contrived scarcity of either resources or capital equipment vitiates any economic grounds for a government hands-off policy in the future short-run price-output decision process. The current controversy over deregulation of natural gas pricing is a good case in point.[13]

The fact that scarcity is, in part, contrived gives rise to three additional common abuses of economic theory that will be mentioned here with little elaboration. One is the tendency to cope with the very real unemployment-inflation dilemma by defining full employment to be whatever level results from monetary and fiscal policies restrictive enough to stabilize average prices. The theoretical foundations for concluding that appropriate macro policies can be found to achieve simultaneously full employment and price level stability include the assumption that all particular markets are adequately decentralized in structure to be competitive. Rather than simply assuming that condition to hold and defining full employment to be that level that results from the workings of the system with price-level stabilizing monetary and fiscal policies, an economic scientist could as easily view the fact of unemployment with price stability as empirical evidence that competition is inadequate.

If one's economic theorizing leads him to the latter conclusion, it can be very useful in suggesting policy measures to achieve the macroeconomic goals without the necessity of direct government intervention in short-run price and allocation decisions.[14]

The fact that scarcity is, in part, contrived, if ignored, also can mislead a policy maker into believing that government intervention would interfere with "efficient" location of economic activity. Much recent controversy over U.S. foreign trade policy stems from dissatisfaction with the market system dominated by giant multinational firms as an appropriate way to determine the location of plants and jobs. Economists tend to use their theory to come down on the side of no government intervention without any concomitant opposition to essentially nonmarket "private government" regulation of international trade by multinational corporations with power surpassing that of many national governments.

For example, writing in the magazine for Volkswagen owners in the United States, Paul A. Samuelson very persuasively makes the comparative advantage case for free trade and argues against the need for government quotas, tariffs, and surcharges to maintain employment in the United States. He says: "The give and take of international competition can be a great policer of monopoly. It has been well said in our political history: The tariff is the mother of trusts.[15] No mention is made of international cartels, "voluntary" export restraint arrangements, or multinational corporations. Yet, a U.S. Department of Commerce survey for 1970 showed that 298 responding "American" multinational corporations accounted for over one-third of all U.S. imports, and 46 percent of those were transfers from majority-owned foreign affiliates.[16]

A third example of the policy implications of applying economic theory as if no scarcity were contrived has to do with the tendency of antitrust economists to first define markets and then look for evidence of monopoly. The notion that products and markets are "given" is so deeply rooted in economic theory that it is easy to ignore the fact that those with power to contrive scarcity often have the power to determine the extent of the market. Specifically, we can expect a monopolist to raise his price high enough to invite competition from greater spatial distance and greater "distance" in the spectrum of product qualities than would be the case if no monopoly power were exercised. This simple fact was obvious to William Howard Taft when he wrote the lower court opinion in 1898 in the Addyston Pipe and Steel case.[17] Yet, economists still suggest that courts should ascertain the boundaries of a market before asking whether the structure is competitive, or argue that interindustry or international competition is adequate to protect the public interest from contrived scarcity.[18]

Combinations: Trusts or Otherwise

The method of economic theorizing is to abstract from the multifaceted and rapidly changing social structure those few more or less persistent characteristics thought to be crucial in the ordering of economic activity.[19] If the theory attempted to tell the truth, the whole truth, and nothing but the truth, it would not be a theory. The resulting description of the economic system would be as complex as the social structure itself, and no useful insight would result. Economic theory should not be criticized for abstraction; rather, it should be questioned from time to time about the continuing appropriateness of its choice of premises.

By 1874, with the publication of Léon Walras's general equilibrium theory, economics had taken on those essential characteristics that give it an identity separate from other branches of philosophy.[20] Economists have taken ever since a "systems approach." The theory has sought to explain not only the behavior of producers and consumers, but also their interrelationships with each other as part of a system of economizing in the use of scarce resources and distributing the scarce goods and services among the members of society. The foundations of economic theory were then and remain today in the hedonistic psychology of Jeremy Bentham.[21] Each person is assumed either to be a maximizing entity or to have all decisions made for him by such an economic animal. Resolution of conflict about goals within the household or family was considered "home economics" and was not the concern of political, social, or national economy.

The economic system all along has been viewed by economists as a social structure that accomplishes peaceful resolution of conflict among the separate and clearly defined households and firms. Although the theory of household behavior and the theory of the firm were not brought together explicitly until Samuelson's *Foundations* was published in 1948, the method of economics all along was to explain the maximizing behavior of only those entities characterized by what Jacob Marshak called "solidarity" and to explain conflict resolution only in terms of the theory of markets.[22]

Most teachers of microeconomic theory, I conjecture, would be very happy to have their undergraduates understand the market system as well as Alfred Marshall did in 1890 when the first edition of the *Principles of Economics* was published.

What has happened to the actual structure of control of the American economic system since the basic underpinnings of the theory were settled upon?

Something other than competitive market structures had, in fact, evolved as a major part of the conflict resolution mechanism as early as the 1870s with the rise of the trusts as a device for forming coalitions among small numbers of wealthy capitalists. The trusts were outlawed by the Sherman Act in 1890. Despite the statute's use of the phrase "in the form of trust or otherwise," combinations have persisted and grown in importance as part of our system's conflict resolution mechanism.

In 1887 the New Jersey legislature enacted a statute providing "that it shall be lawful for foreign corporations to acquire, hold, mortgage, lease, and convey such real estate in this state as may be necessary for the purpose of carrying on . . . business."[23] In 1889 New Jersey's general incorporation law was further amended to provide that "any company . . . may carry on part of its business out of state, and have one or more offices and places of business out of this state, and may hold, purchase and convey real and personal property out of this state the same as if such real and personal property were situated in the state of New Jersey."[24]

In 1893 New Jersey specifically authorized horizontal mergers without limit.[25] In 1888 the New Jersey legislature had authorized its corporations, for limited purposes, to purchase and hold stock in other corporations. In 1893 all limitations were removed, and the New Jersey holding company was born.[26] One week later, the legislature removed New Jersey's last obstacle to unlimited centralization of control of the world's economy by providing that "subscriptions to the capital stock . . . may be paid wholly or partly in cash, or wholly or partly in property."[27] The medium of exchange with which a New Jersey holding corporation could acquire ownership of other corporations, without limit, was not only money, but also its own stock certificates, which could be issued in unlimited numbers.

In 1895 the United States Supreme Court, in the sugar case,[28] held that the Sherman Antitrust Act did not prohibit any combinations created under the authority of and with the legal sanction of a state legislature. Between the E. C. Knight decision in 1895 and the Northern

Securities Company dissolution in 1904, no legal constraints limited consolidation of control for purposes of market control, and the structure of control of the American economy underwent revolutionary changes. These changes by coincidence took place at the time when the number of years since the birth of Jesus rolled over from 1899 to 1900 and, in our conventional reckoning, the twentieth century arrived and the third millenium began. But we should guard against the very strong temptation to conclude that big business, the corporate revolution, and the new industrial state were caused, therefore, by "modern technology." The legislature of New Jersey and the United States Supreme Court—the same Court that sanctioned racial segregation—with deliberate speed overrode the policy embodied in the Sherman Act and set us on the road to the corporate state. The full implications of the change in the structure of control of the economy have taken some years to work out. The slow but steady decline in the relative magnitude of the agricultural sector has played a major role, it seems to me, in delaying until recent years some of the inevitable consequences of the structural changes that occurred three-quarters of a century ago.

What has happened to economic theory since 1890 to keep it relevant to questions of social control of business? Most of us would admit, it seems to me, that very little has happened to the theory to reflect the radical changes in the structure of control. Despite the contributions of E. H. Chamberlin, Joan Robinson, J. M. Keynes, and John von Neumann, economic theory remains fundamentally a theory of conflict resolution among maximizing entities brought about through voluntary market transactions.

Despite the antitrust laws in the United States and similar restrictive practices laws in many other countries, corporations have made possible the evolution of very complex organizations that overlap and interrelate with each other and with governments. Some corporate groups have taken on characteristics very much like those we generally attribute to governments. Meanwhile, the proliferation of nation states and the development of socialist economic systems have given to many governments the characteristics generally attributed to business firms. The behavior of the existing economic system of the world cannot be understood adequately with a theory that treats giant multinational corporations and complex financial interest groups as if they were "ma and pa" grocery stores.

Society still controls business largely through law, and vice versa. Economic theory is useful to those persons who share in the responsibility for development of the law as it relates to the structure of control of economic activity. To some extent each member of society shares that responsibility—even the positive economists. Citizens participating in the development of the law as it affects the constraints under which business managers, qua manager, make their decisions undoubtedly are helped by knowledge of the probable consequences of alternative legal rules. Because false knowledge may be worse than none, however, we must ask whether economic theory helps those who have knowledge of it. Some wise man once said: "It is better to not know and know you do not know than to not know and think that you do." Economic theory is more useful to those who know its weaknesses than it is to the true believers. The process of theorizing is more useful than the propositions of economic theory, if those propositions are misconstrued to be laws of nature.

Notes

1. See J. M. Clark, *Social Control of Business,* 2d ed. (New York: McGraw-Hill Book Co., Inc., 1939).
2. This author's views have not changed on this fundamental issue since writing "Value Judgments in Economics: a Comment," *Southern Economic Journal* 23 (October 1956): 183-87. See also John Dewey, "Theory of Valuation," *International Encyclopedia of the Unified Science,* vol. 11, no. 4 (Chicago: University of Chicago Press, 1939); and Gunnar Myrdal, *Objectivity in Social Research* (New York: Pantheon Books, 1969).
3. See Fritz Machlup, "The Problem of Verification in Economics," *Southern Economic Journal* 22 (July 1955): 1-21.
4. By assuming that each new consumer enters the economy with an exogenously determined set of attributes, economic theory abstracts from all those forces through which new members of society are related to their families and to larger social groups. Much recent literature in psychiatry and social psychology focuses on the importance of family systems in individual behavior. See Jack Oldham Bradt, M.D., and Carolyn Johnson Moynihan, ACSW, eds., *Systems Therapy; Selected Papers: Theory, Technique, Research* (Washington, D.C.: Groome Child Guidance Clinic, 1971).
5. For example, the author's work on the problem of seasonal unemployment in the construction industries led him to engineers, architects, contractors, and labor leaders for judgments on the consequences of alternative policy proposals. See David D. Martin, "Construction Seasonality: The New Federal Program," *Construction Review* (May 1970): 4-7.
6. See Paul A. Samuelson, "The Pure Theory of Public Expenditure," *Review of Economics and Statistics* 36 (November 1954): 387-89; and George M. von Furstenberg and Dennis C. Mueller, "The Pareto Optimal Approach to Income Redistribution: A Fiscal Application," *American Economic Review* 61 (September 1971): 628-37.
7. The consequences of advertising have been well treated in the literature

at least since the appearance of Edward H. Chamberlain, *The Theory of Monopolistic Competition* (Cambridge, Mass.: Harvard University Press, 1933). The implications for welfare theory of corporate power to influence public policy, technological change, and the social context in which consumer preferences are formed more recently has been articulated in John Kenneth Galbraith, *The New Industrial State* (Boston: Houghton Mifflin, 1967); and Kenneth Boulding, *Economics as a Science* (New York: McGraw-Hill, 1970). Also see Philip Klein, "Demand Theory and the Economist's Propensity to Assume," *Journal of Economic Issues* 7 (June 1973): 209-40. But little has been added to the contributions contained in C. E. Ayres, *The Theory of Economic Progress* (Chapel Hill: University of North Carolina Press, 1944), chap. 4.

8. Undoubtedly, consumers have interacted with government as well as business in recent years in forming preferences for such goods as cigarettes, drugs, pollution control devices, and rapid transit facilities. Market and nonmarket information flows are treated in Joseph F. Brodley, "Massive Industrial Size, Classical Economics, and the Search for Humanistic Value," *Stanford Law Review* 24 (June 1972): 1155-78.
9. See Edward H. Chamberlin, "The Product as an Economic Variable," *Quarterly Journal of Economics* 67 (February 1953): 1-29; David D. Martin, "Monopoly Power and the Durability of Durable Goods," *Southern Economic Journal* 28 (January 1962): 271-77; and Peter L. Swan, "Durability of Consumption Goods," *American Economic Review* 60 (December 1970): 885.
10. But see Kelvin Lancaster, "A New Approach to Consumer Theory," *Journal of Political Economy* 74 (April 1966): 132-57; and Irvin M. Grossack and David D. Martin, *Managerial Economics, Microtheory and the Firm's Decisions* (Boston: Little, Brown and Company, 1973), chap. 8.
11. See Motor Vehicle Information and Cost Savings Act, Public Law 92-513, 92nd Congress, 20 October 1972; Donald A. Randall and Arthur P. Glickman, *The Great American Auto Repair Robbery* (New York: Charterhouse, 1972), chap. 7, "High Repair Costs by Design"; and Subcommittee on Antitrust and Monopoly, Committee on the Judiciary, United States Senate, 91st Congress, 1st sess., Hearings, *Automotive Repair Industry* Part 3, 6, 8, 9, 14, and 16 October 1969.
12. See David D. Martin, "Resource Control and Market Power," in *Extractive Resources and Taxation*, Mason Gaffney, ed. (Madison: University of Wisconsin Press, 1967), pp. 119-37.
13. Subcommittee on Antitrust and Monopoly, Committee on the Judiciary, United States Senate, 93rd Congress, 1st sess., Hearings, *Natural Gas Industry*, 26, 27, and 28 June 1973.
14. See *Studies by the Staff of the Cabinet Committee on Price Stability* (Washington, D.C.: Superintendent of Documents, January 1969); Subcommittee on Antitrust and Monopoly, Committee on the Judiciary, United States Senate, 92nd Congress, 2d sess., Hearings, *Symposium on the Economic, Social and Political Effects of Economic Concentration*, 18, 19, 20, and 21 January 1972; and *Congressional Record*, 92nd Congress, 2d sess., 24 July 1972, remarks by Senator Philip Hart and text of the Industrial Reorganization Act, pp. S. 11494-505.
15. Paul A. Samuelson, "Imports and America's Prosperity," *Small World*, Fall 1973.

16. See Betty L. Barker, "U.S. Foreign Trade Associated with U.S. Multinational Companies," *Survey of Current Business* 52 (December 1972): 20–28, Table 2, p. 23.
17. *United States* v. *Addyston Pipe and Steel Co.*, 85 Fed. Rep. 271 (1898).
18. See Bryce J. Jones, "The Brown Shoe Case and the New Antimerger Policy: Comment," and David D. Martin, "Reply," *American Economic Review* 54 (June 1964): 407–15.
19. The notion that economic principles were useful abstractions rather than laws of nature was first brought home to this writer upon first reading Frank Knight's *Risk, Uncertainty, and Profit* (Chicago: University of Chicago Press, 1921).
21. Léon Walras, *Éléments d'économie politique pure* (Lausanne: L. Corbay & Cie, 1874).
22. See W. Stark, *Jeremy Bentham's Economic Writings* (London: George Allen & Unwin Ltd., 1952).
23. Jacob Marschak, "Towards an Economic Theory of Information and Organization," in *Decision Processes*, R. M. Thrall, C. H. Coombs, and R. L. Davis, eds. (New York: 1954), pp. 187-220.
24. *Acts of the One Hundred and Tenth Legislature of the State of New Jersey, and Forty-Second under the New Constitution*, C. 124, 11 April 1887.
25. *Acts*, C. 265, 9 May 1889
26. *Acts*, C. 67, 8 March 1893
27. *Acts*, C. 171, 14 March 1893
28. *Acts*, C. 254, 21 March 1893
29. *United States* v. *E. C. Knight*, 156 U.S. 1, (1895).

19

The Marginal Utility of Marginal Analysis in Public Policy Formation

William H. Melody

In times past, neither the development of economic theory nor the activity of economists took place in an environment where there was a direct involvement in the formulation of economic policies by government and business. For the most part, economists and their theories stood outside the real world of practical decision making as exogenous observers and descriptions of economic behavior. However, over the past generation or so, both economists and their theories have become increasingly involved—for better or worse—in the economic policy decisions of government and business. The involvement has been most obvious and direct in macroeconomics and the formulation of aggregate economic policies by national governments. The Keynesian revolution virtually required involvement, and economists have been placed in positions where they are responsible, and sometimes held accountable, for the development and application of economic policies.

At the microeconomic level, there has been no Keynesian revolution that has thrust microeconomics into an equivalent role in the formulation of real world economic policies. Nevertheless, a marked increase in the involvement of the profession in the microeconomic decisions of government and business has occurred, either by means of direct employment of economists by government and industry, or through consulting and advisory relationships.

The neoclassical theory of the firm has provided economists with very little to say on matters of microeconomic policy. Given an optimal income distribution and perfect knowledge, counsels the theory, optimal resource allocation and maximum consumer welfare will be achieved in a perfectly competitive market system where the government follows a policy of laissez-faire. But a moment's observation clearly demonstrates that there are no real markets approximating perfect competition; many markets are heavily concentrated oligopolies; some are monopolies; many goods and services are not supplied through traditional market mechanisms; and government involvement in many areas of economic activity is extensive. In the face of a clear contradiction between theory and practice, what can economists say to policy makers on microeconomic problems?

Some economists continue to recommend laissez-faire, extending the tradition of earlier economists who counseled Say's Law at a time of world-wide economic depression. Others recommend a more vigorous application of antitrust policy to bring the structure of real markets closer to the perfectly competitive structure of neoclassical theory. Still others conclude that the theory is irrelevant to policy issues and it should be abandoned as being more harmful than helpful.[1]

Unfortunately, as the involvement of economists in real world microeconomic problems has increased, most theoretical work has become directed more and more narrowly, as if to attempt to save the theory by means of more elaborate and elegant "proofs." But this pursuit of positivism through rigor has tended to foster more rigor mortis than enlightenment. The result has been that all issues of microeconomic public policy involve problems that turn out to be *exceptions* to the general neoclassical theory. Recommended policy solutions depend upon how much, if any, weight is given to selected elements of the neoclassical theory. Hence, there are no standard theoretic solutions to microeconomic policy issues.

At the microeconomic level, economists are seldom in positions where they are responsible and accountable for the development of public policy. They are almost universally advisers who generally take great pains to separate their pure economics from areas where societal value judgments are involved. Yet, we must recognize that advisers are hired by clients with vested interests who have a very good idea of what any adviser is going to say on any particular public policy issue and what the consequences are likely to be for the client. Thus, both the economic theories and the economists selected become part of the advocacy of a client's position. The aggregate strength of that advocacy depends upon the significance of the policy issue for the client and its position of economic and political power. Disturbing for economics is the fact that its use in such public policy formulation is primarily as cannon fodder for vested interests, a role that only can serve to reinforce the inherited structure of economic institutions and the maintenance and extension of monopoly power.

Marginal Analysis

The major area of microeconomic public policy development has been in the social control of business, either by means of antitrust policy or direct governmental regulation of firms and industries uniquely "affected with a public interest," such as public utilities and transportation. Most public policy issues are heavily involved with problems relating to pricing, costing, or profits. Although these firms and industries are clear exceptions to the neoclassical theory, the theory has provided an elegant framework from which economists can advise that decision makers should look to the marginal conditions, most specifically marginal costs, in order to optimize their objectives. This general standard can be recommended sweepingly to all problems in all possible circumstances at all times. Firms can use marginal analysis as a means of maximizing profits. Government agencies can maximize net social benefits. Regulatory agencies can force regulated firms to set prices so as to optimize resource allocation and maximize consumer welfare.

A recommendation that decision makers employ the mathematical methods of optimization may not be viewed as containing a high level of economic content. Indeed, the economic substance of the matter does not begin until the economist begins to define his terms in light of the public policy issue at hand, to place values on alternative courses of action, and to pour content into the empty mathematical functions. Unfortunately, economic theorists generally have declined to assume the responsibility for providing the economic substance, leaving the factual calculations on these matters to the specialists who are familiar with operational details. As a result, the marginal principles have acquired the status of doctrinal slogans, so internalized to economic thinking that failure to employ them calls for a brief recitation on the mathematics of optimization.

Economists have not been much concerned about what practitioners actually do, or how they go about actually trying to measure such things as marginal cost. Rather, the important thing has been what they say. Concern has been devoted almost entirely to the terminology that practitioners use. Failure to adopt the terminology of marginal analysis elicits the appropriate reflex response. But, as Gunnar Myrdal has observed, "terminology, and the meaning given to terms, do matter. They represent, if not subjected to continual scrutiny, temptations and opportunities for the logical gliding of our thinking in unrealistic directions."[2]

Claimed applications of the marginal analysis have been guided generally by a series of mythological impressions about the meaning of the term and the nature of its applications. The myths are created both by economists, in their careless or expansive interpretations of the theoretical concepts when attempting to apply them to real world problems, and by practitioners, in developing methodologies directed toward the calculation of desirable results. The logical gliding of thinking on marginal analysis in public policy formulation seems to have glided quite far in unrealistic directions, despite its limited use in the application of public policy.

Resource Allocation: Theory and Practice

Alfred Kahn has observed in his recent work, *The Economics of Regulation,* that "the central policy prescription of microeconomics is the equation of price and marginal cost. If economic theory is to have any relevance to public utility pricing, that is the point at which the inquiry must begin."[3] Yet, inquiry by corporate managers and government regulators has seldom, if ever, attempted to begin at the point where price equals marginal cost. Resource allocation in practice is characterized by the almost complete absence of prices set equal to marginal costs. Moreover, in an economy characterized by imperfect markets where, according to neoclassical theory, all prices should be expected to deviate from their respective marginal costs, neoclassical economists rarely recommend that prices be set equal to marginal costs. Even in the directly regulated public utility sector, economists seldom recommend that marginal cost pricing be employed. Rather, they recommend that marginal costs, however defined, be used as reference points from which optimal deviations of prices from marginal costs can be calculated.[4] In essence, they recommend that the inefficient deviations of prices from the theoretical marginal cost optima be minimized.

But why should public policy depart from a theoretical optimum and attempt to achieve inferior results that only can be calculated by reference to that optimum? What overriding constraint possibly could be acceptable as a legitimate cause for injecting such allocational inefficiency into an optimal pricing system? The overriding constraint is the financial revenue requirement of the firm. In the real world, those who actually allocate resources base their decisions upon financial parameters such as rate of return on investment. Public policy makers also have directed their attention to these financial parameters as a principal basis for policy decisions.

Yet, what is it about the nature of marginal cost that tells us that marginal cost pricing will yield a deficient amount of revenue to the firm? It is the overwhelming assumption that the firm is operating under continuous long-run decreasing costs within the static framework of the neoclassical model. However, such an assumption has no validity as a basis for public policy analysis of real world problems. As Ralph Turvey has stated, "an a priori statement about the relationship between long run marginal cost and total cost is possible only if the system lacks history—i.e., in practically no real system. Thus, simple statements of the sort that, since the industry is one of increasing returns, marginal cost pricing would involve a deficit, are irrelevant."[5]

The assumption that marginal cost pricing *in reality* would involve a financial deficit reflects an imposition of the artificial limitations of theory upon the policy issue under examination. In addition, this assumption has fostered the myth that marginal costs are always lower than average or fully distributed costs. Indeed, Kahn has noted that a lesson to be learned from our long experience with intercarrier competition is that "not all rates will be set as low as long-run marginal costs, because competitive pressures will differ between different customers, classes of service, and localities; nor can all rates be set as low as LRMC and still cover average total costs."[6] Under this set of circumstances, however, the neoclassical theory would lead us to conclude that all firms in the economy would suffer financial deficits if they employed marginal cost pricing. Moreover, it would tend to indicate that the most efficient allocation of resources could be achieved by having a single firm supply all goods and services in the industry, if not the entire economy. Clearly, one cannot begin the analysis of public policy issues with a presumption that the marginal costs of neoclassical theory are necessarily less than average costs, or that marginal cost pricing would yield a financial deficit, without adopting an enormous unjustified bias in the approach.

Nevertheless, there is no *a priori* reason to believe that the marginal cost standard for resource allocation would yield results similar to the return on investment standard. This raises the question: Which standard is superior as a guide to efficient resource allocation? The return on investment standard is viewed almost universally in practice as the appropriate economic one for allocating resources, especially when a firm is attempting to attract capital in competitive capital markets. Capital is allocated to applications that offer higher rates of return and away from applications that only offer lower rates of return. Those users that cannot earn rates of return sufficient to cover their respective costs of capital do not obtain the resources.

Both the rate of return on investment standard and the marginal cost standard are founded upon the basic economic idea of opportunity cost. Neoclassical theorists generally approve of a rate of return standard for allocating resources among industries and among firms within an industry. However, in allocating resources among product lines or services within the firm, the marginal cost standard is viewed as crucial, while the return on investment standard, which now has become labelled as a fully distributed cost standard, has sunk to the depths of "arbitrary allocation." According to neoclassical economics, if services A and B are supplied by different firms, then a return on investment standard is an acceptable basis for efficient resource allocation. But if services A and B are supplied by the same firm, the return on investment standard is in error. Marginal cost becomes the standard for efficient resource allocation within the firm.

This dividing line between the rate of return on investment and marginal cost standards at the level of the firm is not justified by any economic criteria. Indeed, the neoclassical theory states quite clearly that all prices should equal marginal costs for optimal resource allocation. Rather, advocates of the neoclassical theory have fallen back to the level of the firm in advocating marginal cost and have accepted any revenue requirement constraints imposed by return on investment criteria at higher levels of resource allocation.

It must be emphasized also that the return on investment criterion is applied where there is a market exchange of resources between firms and suppliers of resources. The marginal cost standard is advocated most strongly for intrafirm product line or interservice resource allocation, which does not require submission to an external market test. Hence, marginal cost is advocated principally where real resource allocation decisions are not at issue because the firm acts as a single unit in attracting resources. Individual products and services do not have to attract resources from external markets on their own merits. The internal issue is the distribution of resources attracted by the firm among the products or services.

As a practical matter, tests of the efficiency of resource allocation have tended to apply the return on investment standard to intrafirm as well as interfirm decisions. Most firms have established product line, cost responsibility center, or profit center classifications as a means of measuring and comparing the profitability of particular products or services within the firm. Similarly, government policy makers have tended to rely on the return on investment criterion for policy relating to intrafirm resource allocation decisions. Moreover, such a criterion has been recommended by economists directly involved in public policy analysis. This author concluded that if the Federal Communications Commission is to fulfill its regulatory responsibilities, it must adopt a return on investment standard as a basis for reaching policy decisions relating to efficient resource allocation among the Bell Telephone System's major interstate service classifications.[7] Recently, the Bureau of Economics Staff of the Federal Trade Commission proposed an annual line of business report program for large corporations as a means of determining relative returns on investment. In its Statement of Purpose, the staff stated:

> Given the purpose of the FTC, a guiding principle in providing solutions to the allocation problem is that all costs must be finally allocated. . . . The reason for this necessity is that a major concern of the Commission is the overall allocation of society's resources in such a way that the benefits to society are made as large as possible. Without descriptive data on how the totality of the pool of resources at the disposal of society have been allocated, it would not be feasible to comment meaningfully on how well resource allocation has been carried out. Nor would it be possible to analyze the effects of changes in underlying structural or behavioral characteristics of the economy on the allocation of resources.[8]

In sum, as a guide to public policy directed to encouraging efficient resource allocation, the marginal cost standard of neoclassical theory has been a resounding failure. Its advocacy on public policy issues appears largely opportunistic, dictated primarily by firms with vested interests in certain public policies. Regulated firms prefer a return on investment standard for determining their profit levels and revenue requirements. But marginal cost, as the standard for pricing individual services, preserves maximum flexibility to the firm in pricing its individual services. This flexibility does not derive from the neoclassical theory of marginal cost, but from the mythology of marginal cost and from a recognition by the regulated firms that they will have complete control over the calculation of the marginal cost values. It is a tribute to public policy makers that they generally have not succumbed to the superficial rationality of the neoclassical model and the marginal cost slogan.

Marginal Cost: Theory and Interpretation

Kenneth Boulding has observed that the essential principles of marginal analysis are almost trite. The firm in neoclassical theory is viewed essentially as an input-output process where, given the principle of maximization of something, the marginal conditions follow as simple mathematical tautologies. Boulding has stated: "The firm is thus an aggregation of capital and labor rather than an organization, and most of the problems which are connected with it simply do not arise."[9] Thus, criticism of the neoclassical theory and its applicability as a guide to public policy is not directed to pointing out logical flaws in its analysis but rather to demonstrating that the enormous constriction of its explicit and implicit assumptions renders it, for the most part, irrelevant for solving the economic problems of the real world.

The term *marginal cost* is so general that the variety of interpretations of its meaning is virtually infinite. To give it a somewhat more specific content, economists must apply further definitional restrictions such as *short run* and *long run*. But even these terms do not provide restrictions upon the interpretation, selection, and valuation of marginal costs. There are as many marginal costs as there are conceivable sets of alternatives to be considered, and their values can range from very high to extremely low. The important issue in marginal analysis is always the *selection* of the alternative courses of action between which the marginal conditions will be measured.

One is reminded of the story of the young man who told his father that he had walked home from school instead of taking the bus and saved $.25. The father replied that his son should have walked home instead of taking a taxi because then he would have saved $3.00. The son's marginal cost was $.25; the father's was $3.00. Had the son evaluated the alternatives of taking the bus home instead of a taxi, he would have concluded that the marginal cost of taking a taxi was not $3.00, but $2.75. If he considered a limousine ride at $5.00, he would have concluded that the marginal cost relative to walking was $5.00; the marginal cost relative to taking the bus was $4.75; and the marginal cost relative to taking a taxi was $2.00. The marginal cost depends crucially on the relevant decision alternative that will *not* be followed. He who selects this decision alternative will determine the marginal cost. Clearly, public policies affecting vested interests cannot be based upon such subjective assessments by vested interests.

In addition, the framework for marginal cost analysis assumes a planning horizon sufficiently distant that all the effects of all alternative decision possibilities can be taken into account. But all of this information is hypothetical and subject to the forecasting ability of the decision maker. Once the optimum alternative is selected and pursued, the firm must await the judgment of reality to see if its decision was good or bad. If the firm correctly perceived and made perfect forecasts for all alternative decision possibilities, its decision indeed will have been optimum. If it did not, its marginal cost calculations will have been inaccurate. As a practical matter, we know in advance that our hypothesis of optimization will be disproved by reality.

As a theoretical construct, the long-run marginal cost concept does not come to grips with the problems created by the continuity and incomplete nature of the firm's activities. The concept assumes that the decision to be made involves a single complete venture. At the time the decision is to be made, there are no constraining conditions of past decisions and events that will influence the decision alternatives. The firm is in a completely uncommitted state. Moreover, the evaluation of the alternative decision possibilities reflects all effects through the completion of the activity under consideration. Hence, the framework for decision is closed. The firm is considering a venture in which it can both start fresh and complete the activity. At this theoretical level, there is no need for an evaluation of the state of affairs before the effects of the decision are complete. There will be no modification of the decision as reality unfolds. An accounting is required neither during nor at the completion of the venture.[10]

Indeed, theoretical optimization can be a very misleading concept. In the neoclassical model, the decision maker is deemed to have optimized if he does what he thinks is best in light of the alternatives he perceives. But if his best turns out to be in reality an obviously wasteful investment that has no use whatsoever, the decision was still optimal according to the marginal criteria. For most matters of public policy, a static mathematical test that asks whether management believes that it did what it thought was best on the basis of what it knew at the time is not a relevant policy standard. What is generally more important is the market test of whether management decisions made in an uncertain environment with limited information turned out to be prudent, responsive to consumer demands, and tolerably efficient in light of the reality that developed. Rate of return on investment is such a test that can be applied not only prospectively for planning purposes, but also retrospectively for purposes of tracking, accountability, and improved future decision making.

At any point in time, a real firm is highly constrained by its past decisions. It is a going concern involved at different stages of decision making with respect to many interrelated and interdependent investment decisions that relate to different combinations of output for various services in different localities. The characteristics of the investments, including the amount of the expenditure, the types of facilities to be added, and the timing of additions, depend directly upon the quantity and structure of the capacity elements inherited from the past as well as plans for related investments in the future. The firm is in a continuous process of partial adaptation to changing events, and its planning into the future is severely limited by its inability to forecast future events accurately and to perceive all the effects of its alternative investment possibilities.

In any real world situation, the firm has an infinite variety of marginal costs, marginal cost functions, and families of marginal cost functions with values covering a wide range of cost variation. Different marginal costs can be derived for every pair of alternatives being considered; for every conceivable increment in output; for every difference in the amount and/or structure of inherited capacity; for every difference in the actual planning period employed in the analysis; for every change in the relative proportions of the various products or services being supplied; for every different forecast of future events; and for every different perception of the timing, location, and impact of the marginal effects. In addition, since units of output are far from homogeneous, different marginal cost functions will be obtained as the dimensions of the output unit are varied.

In the final analysis, it must be recognized that marginal costs (as well as revenues) are entirely bound up in the personal judgment of the analyst, the "arbitrary" decisions that he makes in defining his problem, and his changing expectations. In fact, we should expect that the optimists in a firm could have quite different marginal costs than the pessimists. Marginal costs cannot be viewed as facts for which objectively valid values can be known. The marginal cost values will depend upon who applies the theory and the incentives under which he works in the environment in which it will be applied. The nature of marginal cost illustrates Myrdal's conclusion that "valuations determine not only our policy conclusions but all our endeavors to establish the facts, from the approaches chosen to the presentation of our results."[11]

In addition, it should be noted that the information requirement for measuring marginal costs in imperfect markets and multivariable production functions is overwhelming. Boulding has observed: "As a theory which purports to represent actual behavior, the maximization theory suffers from the almost fatal defect of failing to consider the information which is available to the decision maker. A theory that assumes knowledge of what cannot be known is clearly defective as a guide to actual behavior.[12] Finally, there is no indication that consistent measurements over time of any single definition of marginal cost by the same individual would have any degree of necessary *stability* from one measurement to the next.

Marginal Cost and Industry Structure

The neoclassical theory of the firm provides no *a priori* basis for concluding that any particular marginal costs are lower than, higher than, or equal to the firm's total cost or revenue requirement. The theory illustrates situations where short-run marginal cost may be higher than short-run average cost, long-run marginal cost, and long-run average cost. The only real constraining relationship is that short-run average costs never can be less than long-run average costs. Moreover, none of the theoretical cost functions have any necessary relationship to actual expended costs that are recorded in the books of account.

Nevertheless, when it comes to measuring marginal costs, practitioners almost invariably address their attention to the books of account, allocating the firm's total costs between fixed and variable. The variable costs are classified as short-run incremental costs. The addition of some fixed capacity costs raises the figure to the level of long-run incremental costs. The inclusion of all costs raises the figure to average total costs. The incremental unit cost figures are deemed applicable to *all* relevant output increments. This additive methodology reinforces the myth that marginal costs are always lower than average costs because you do not allocate the common overhead costs to the former. Under this methodology, all incremental and marginal cost estimates must be less than their companion average cost estimates, a circumstance that can find no support in the neoclassical theory.

The theory of the firm does not directly address the issue of determining the optimal industrial structure. Rather, it is accepted as given for purposes of the marginal analysis. The rationale described above, that marginal cost is always lower than average cost, provides large firms with substantial ammunition, in the name of theoretical economic efficiency, to thwart the entry of potential competitors into their markets, to justify extension of their markets, and to support discriminatory pricing practices. In the communications industries, the American Telephone and Telegraph Company is attempting to reestablish, and the United States Postal Service is attempting to maintain, public policy prohibitions against the entry of competition into some of their traditional monopoly markets. Their principal argument is that their relatively low marginal costs demonstrate that economic efficiency rests in monopoly and not competition. Moreover, since they are using the "correct" terminology from microeconomic theory, their assessments become "generally acceptable" to theorists. Somehow forgotten is the fact that the implementation methodologies adopted would require very low marginal cost calculations when applied anywhere. And the fact that economic entities with vested interests to protect, and with powerful economic incentives to arrive at very low marginal cost figures, are doing the calculating on the basis of personal, subjective valuations for which there can be no accountability is naïvely assumed away.

On matters of competition and industry structure in regulated industries, policy change often occurs when the burden of proof is shifted from one opposing position to another. For example, historically in telecommunications, a new firm could not obtain entry to a communications market without first demonstrating that the existing certified carrier, usually a telephone company monopoly, could not, and would not, provide the service. There was no entry. In its landmark decision permitting the entry of new certified carriers into data and other specialized telecommunications markets,[13] the FCC shifted the burden of proof to those who would oppose the entry of new firms. Now the established carriers must prove that specific entry applications are not in the public interest if new entrants are to be denied certification.

Competitive rate reductions based upon the established firm's assessment of its own relevant marginal cost, in a market environment where traditional monopoly services automatically will provide all residual revenue requirements, has proven to be an effective tool for the established monopoly to take the industry structure policy away from the regulatory authority. The established monopolist assesses its relative efficiency in the market and implements its industry structure policy through its marginal cost determinations. If and when new entry begins to threaten the established market structure, new valuations are placed on new alternative prices, and new marginal costs are calculated. Marginal cost of neoclassical theory provides an effective weapon by which the regulated monopolist can usurp the real power to make the relevant judgments necessary to the implementation of public policy. Thus, the significance of economies of scale, the scope of natural monopoly, and the dimensions of competition become determined by the monopolist, whether natural or unnatural.

Despite their claims of economies of scale as a substantial efficiency advantage, both AT&T and the Postal Service appear to fear a market test of these claimed efficiencies as something equivalent to the bubonic plague. They continue to petition for policy barriers to entry, lest a real market test embarrass them. In sum, the myths of marginal cost have provided a universally applicable efficiency rationale for the preservation and extension of concentrations of economic power in the creep toward monopoly structures in many industries.

Conclusion

It is somewhat ironic that the marginal analysis of neoclassical theory, which was developed to explain how perfect competition could provide optimal resource allocation, has been adopted principally by monopolistic firms to thwart competition and justify the allocational efficiency of monopoly. From a public policy viewpoint, the economic substance of the economic opportunity cost notion has been wrung out of the terminology of marginal analysis. What remains is sterile terminology available for appropriation and implementation in an unlimited variety of applications.

Moreover, the mythology surrounding the terminology of marginal analysis has made it extremely vulnerable to misapplication. We clearly have passed the point of diminishing returns in terms of the benefits of the marginal analysis to effective public policy formulation, and we probably are operating in the area of negative returns. It is time to dispense with the slogans of marginalism. General sweeping recommendations for the use of marginal cost or marginal analysis must be recognized as nothing more than the exhortation of neoclassical theory for decision makers to do their best. The neoclassical theory of the firm should be recognized as essentially irrelevant to the analysis of public policy issues. Economic analysis must return to the rudiments of the opportunity cost concept and its specific meaning for particular public policy issues in an environment of uncertainty, incomplete information, and monopoly power, where the largest constraints on today's policy decisions are the conditions inherited from the immediate past.

Finally, if economic theory is to approach that dangerous area where it would be really useful in the formulation of public policy, it must go beyond the task of providing terminology that is supposed to help decision makers select what they think is best from a predetermined number of alternatives. It must provide a basis for the improved assessment of the efficiency of decisions in light of the market reality that develops. The ultimate economic test is not whether decision makers state (or believe) that they have done their best; it is whether their best is an efficient allocation of resources in the satisfaction of consumer demands. Without accountability, public policy is a sham.

Notes

1. See, for example, John Kenneth Galbraith, *Economics and the Public Purpose* (Boston: Houghton Mifflin, 1973), and "Power and the Useful Economist," *American Economic Review* 63 (March 1973): 1-11.
2. Gunnar Myrdal, *Against the Stream: Critical Essays on Economics* (New York: Pantheon, 1973), p. 159.
3. Alfred E. Kahn, *The Economics of Regulation: Principles and Institutions* (New York: Wiley, 1970), p. 65.
4. See, for example, W. J. Baumol and D. F. Bradford "Optimal Departures from Marginal Cost Pricing," *American Economic Review* 60 (June 1970): 265-283. See also testimony of Baumol on behalf of the American Telephone and Telegraph Company in FCC Docket 16258, 1968; and testimony of W. Vickrey for the United States Postal Service before the Postal Rate Commission, 1973.
5. Ralph Turvey, *Optimal Pricing and Investment in Electricity Supply* (Cambridge, Mass.: The MIT Press, 1968), p. 59.
6. Kahn, *Economics*, p. 160.
7. See W. H. Melody "Interservice Subsidy: Regulatory Standards and Applied Economics," in *Essays on Public Utility Pricing and Regulation*, H. M. Trebing, ed. (East Lansing: Institute of Public Utilities, Michigan State University, 1971), pp. 167-210.
8. "Statement of Purpose, Annual Line of Business Report Program," Bureau of Economics Staff, Federal Trade Commission, 1973.
9. K. E. Boulding "The Present Position of the Theory of the Firm," in *Linear Programming and the Theory of the Firm*, K. E. Boulding and W. A. Spivey, eds. (New York: MacMillan, 1960), p. 1.
10. Melody, "Interservice Subsidy," pp. 181-86.
11. Myrdal, *Against the Stream*, p. 54.
12. Boulding, "Present Position," p. 5.
13. First Report and Order, Docket 18920, 29 FCC 2d 870 (1971).

20

A Wisconsin Institutionalist Perspective On Microeconomic Theory of Institutions: The Insufficiency of Pareto Efficiency

Michael R. Carter

Microeconomic analysis of institutions has found a secure place in the economics literature. In development economics, for example, the last few years have seen a proliferation of studies trying to explain the tenure, credit, and labor institutions that dot the rural landscape of the developing world. This essay reflects on the nature of institutional analysis in contemporary microtheory: when institutions matter; and when they matter, how they are studied. The perspective of current micro institutional analysis is contrasted with the institutional economics of John R. Commons and the Wisconsin School. It will be argued that the John R. Commons point of view makes clear the insufficiency of microeconomic Pareto efficiency as the sole basis for institutional analysis.

This article is divided into three parts. The first will introduce the entry points for institutional analysis in microeconomic theory. It will be shown that institutions can be introduced at both general equilibrium and partial equilibrium levels, although only the latter has really been explored. The second section will tell the tale of two contracts. It will present Commons's analysis of "yellow dog" labor contracts and A. Braverman and J. Stiglitz's analysis of the institutional puzzle of interlinked tenure-credit contracts. Both examples have been chosen to typify their respective regimes of institutional analysis. The third and final section will construct the theme of the insufficiency of Pareto efficiency as the basis of institutional analysis.

The Appearance of Institutions in Microeconomic Analysis

It is probably fair to say that most neoclassical microeconomic theory has no institutional content beyond implicit assumptions about the existence of markets, enforceable contracts, and individuals free to choose. The apotheosis of the general irrelevance of institutional arrangements is R. H. Coase's essay "The Problem of Social Costs." There Coase argues that in the absence of transaction costs, the distribution of property rights (which we will interpret broadly as meaning institutional arrangements) does not affect the allocation of resources. If the benefits of clean air exceed the cost of pollution control equipment, then there will be clean air regardless of whether society has defined a right to clean air or a right to pollute. In the first case, polluters would find it cheaper to install pollution control equipment than to buy out citizens' rights to clean air. In the second case, polluted citizens would be willing to band together to buy out polluters' right to pollute. Either way, pollution control equipment is installed, the air is clean, and, ignoring distributionally induced shifts in demand, the allocation of resources is the same.

Perhaps more interesting than Coase's theorem itself is its converse. Namely, in the presence of transaction costs, property rights and institutional arrangements *do* affect resource allocation. In the previous example, if there is some impediment to the citizens banding together and completing the transaction with the polluter, then air quality and resource allocation could be quite different under the alternative institutional scenarios. Impediments could appear in the form of informational costs and uncertainties (what are the benefits of clean air?), bargaining costs and enforcement costs. Such impediments to exchange in the form of transaction costs are the stuff of any interesting externality problem.[1]

In fact, if transaction costs are as ubiquitous as they seem, Coase's converse provides a wide basis for the microeconomic study of institutions. Starting from Coase's converse, there is both a general equilibrium and a partial equilibrium direction for institutional research. I will briefly review the general equilibrium direction before moving toward the partial equilibrium variant, which forms the basis for the rest of this article.

Externalities and interesting institutional problems arise when some market fails to clear neoclassically[2]—perhaps Walras's auctioneer does not bother to organize and clear markets in pollution side payments. But given that the auctioneer is only a heuristic device, it is quite reasonable to ask how many decentralized markets can clear neoclassically. The great irony of general equilibrium theory is that it relies on the *centralized* device of the fictive auctioneer to explain equilibrium in a *decentralized* system of markets. Axel Leijonhufvud [1968] makes the information and transaction cost problems of an auctioneer-less market system into a basis for Keynesian economics. Spawned from Leijonhufvud's analysis has been a generation of neo-Keynesian disequilibrium theory (for example, Cuddington et al. [1984] extend disequilibrium theory to open economy analysis and also provide a succinct review of prior literature).

From the point of view of institutional analysis, the exciting thing about neo-Keynesian price theory is that it sweeps away the Walrasian world in which institutions do not matter. Once resource allocation is freed of its predestination with the Walrasian general equilibrium, property rights and institutional arrangements can affect the pattern of rationing and resource allocation. As I argue in a preliminary work [Carter 1983], property rights affect *whose* costs and benefits enter the calculations that determine resource allocation in a non-Walrasian world. In particular, economic development under capitalist property rights creates an identifiable class of losers who are rationed out of the general (dis)equilibrium.

The potential for institutional analysis once Coase's converse has been used to unseat Walrasian price theory is enormous.[3] John Eatwell (of Cambridge, United Kingdom) remarked to two anxious young would-be Wisconsin institutionalists that the institutionalists were always getting "beat up" because they lacked a firm theoretical foundation. Non-Walrasian price theory offers that missing foundation on which institutional analysis can rest secure from Coase's theorem, which otherwise threatens intellectually to undermine it.

While perhaps potentially the most interesting, the general equilibrium direction for microtheoretic institutional analysis is also relatively unexplored. To date neo-Keynesian disequilibrium models have put their effort into understanding market interrelationships *given* a non-Walrasian price vector. Little attention has yet been given to the actual price adjustment process, its basis in transaction costs, or the importance of institutions in this context. A. K. Sen's analysis of the 1944 Bengal famine is perhaps the one outstanding example of general equilibrium institutional analysis [Sen 1977]. Sen makes three basic points about this famine that claimed several million lives: (1) On a per-capita basis, there was sufficient food available so that no one technically had to starve. (2) Because traditional institutions and entitlement rights had eroded, and the safety net of the modern welfare state was not fully in place, there existed a wage labor class completely dependent on the efficiency of the price mechanism for access to subsistence. (3) Relative prices got badly out of line and sales constraints existed in labor markets. The opportunity to sell (or implicitly sell) labor was not price rationed, but was instead rationed on the basis of direct access to means of production. Those without such access, the free wage laborers, were rationed out of the (dis)equilibrium and disproportionately filled the ranks of those who died.

As this case makes clear, outside the realm of Walrasian general equilibrium, institutional rules establish rationing priorities and affect resource allocation as well as the distribution of the costs of economic disequilibrium. But as Sen parenthetically recognizes, a good deal more work needs to be done on institutions in general equilibrium.

In contrast, what might be called partial equilibrium extensions of Coase's converse are better developed.[4] Recognition of information, bargaining, and enforcement costs that inhibit transactions in specific markets has led to a renewed interest in economic institutions. The hierarchically organized firm, for example, is seen to arise because of transaction costs that block coordination and control of the work process through conventional exchange transactions.[5] More generally, asymmetrically distributed information (where one party to a contract can neither directly control or observe behavior and circumstances that affect contract fulfillment) has been shown to inhibit contractual enforcement and conventional market exchange in a number of areas, and has been used to propose and explain a number of alternative institutional arrangements.[6]

Partial equilibrium micro-institutional theory is perhaps best described as analysis of "voluntary exchange by non-conventional means." Institutions are modeled as elaborate contracts and the question posed by the analysis is whether the implicit exchange is Pareto efficient. The hierarchical firm, for example, is thus explained as the equilibrium contractual outcome of a Pareto efficient exchange in an informational environment that prevents enforcement of conventional trade agreements.

This "institution as Pareto efficient contract" approach will be evaluated in the third section of this article. Before that, however, the second section will tell the tale of two institutional arrangements—one taken from the work of John R. Commons, and the other from contemporary micro-institutional theory. The contrasts between the two tales—the way they are told, the questions that are asked—will provide the basis for the third section's discussion of the insufficiency of the Pareto efficiency approach to institutional analysis.

A Tale of Two Contracts

Tucked into the pages of *Legal Foundations of Capitalism* is Commons's discussion of "yellow dog" contracts—contracts signed by employees in which they promise not to join a union as a condition of employment. The microeconomics of yellow dog contracts are simple, and uninteresting. There is no maze of information asymmetries nor transaction costs to figure out. Yet yellow dog contracts represent the type of institutional problem that Commons found interesting and important. *Because* of their microeconomic simplicity, yellow dog contracts make a good study in Commons's institutional analysis and its distinctiveness from contemporary microtheoretic analysis.

In contrast, the second type of contract discussed in this section represents a genuine microeconomic puzzle. The interlinkage of tenure and credit contracts in "backward" agriculture is the second contract tale to be examined here. After an introduction to the empirical reality of interlinked tenure-credit contracts drawn from work on the post-bellum southern United States, the microeconomic analysis of Braverman and Stiglitz [1982] will be presented. First, however, we present John R. Commons's analysis of yellow dog contracts.

Yellow Dog Contracts and the Explanation of Institutional Evolution

Commons's discussion of yellow dog contracts centers about the case *Coppage* v. *Kansas*, brought before the U.S. Supreme Court in 1915. The facts of the case were simple: "Coppage, a superintendent of a railway company, had requested Hedges, a member of the switchmen's union, to sign [a yellow dog contract], at the same time informing him that if he did not sign it he could not remain in the employ of the company. Hedges refused to sign, or to withdraw from the union, and Coppage discharged him" [Commons 1924, p. 289]. Suit was brought against Coppage under a Kansas law forbidding yellow dog contracts, and eventually the Supreme Court declared the Kansas law unconstitutional because it violated freedom of contract.

From Commons's point of view, there are two interesting aspects of this case that illuminate the institutional explanation and evolution of yellow dog contracts. First is the issue of economic coercion and the "power which property has by merely withholding from others what they need but which does not belong to them" [Commons 1924, p. 64]. In *Coppage*, the Court found that there was no legal basis for outlawing yellow dog contracts as coercion. Interestingly, in the case, Hedges found himself in court facing Coppage, a person like himself, rather than the railway "Leviathan controlling twenty-thousand jobs" (p. 292) that had been formed by a corporate union of property owners. The Court applied the legal standard appropriate to personal coercion or holdup, and found no evidence of coercion because Coppage had not threatened Hedges with either physical violence or with retention of property belonging to Hedges. Coppage had simply threatened to take away Hedges's job—something that Hedges needed, but which was not his legal property. This economic coercion, or power of property, was found to be legal in this case. Coppage had simply presented Hedges with an opportunity to make an exchange, and Hedges could voluntarily decide to make trade or not. In *Coppage* v. *Kansas*, the Court majority fell behind earlier rulings that had found that it was legally permissible to regulate economic coercion by outlawing certain types of contracts. For example, in the 1898 case *Holden* v. *Hardy* the Supreme Court had upheld a law forbidding economically coercive contracts for more than a ten-hour working day.

The ruling to permit restriction of economic coercion in cases like *Holden* v. *Hardy* can be traced to the Court's recognition of the institutional change that had overtaken the early industrial United States. Commons describes the change:

> Where production was isolated or the owner held under his control all of the material things as well as the laborers necessary to the support of himself and dependents, the concept of exclusive holding for self was a workable definition of property. But when markets expanded, when laborers were emancipated, when people began to live by bargain and sale, when population increased and all resources became private property, then the power to withhold from others emerged gradually from that of exclusive holding for self as an economic attribute of property. The one is implied in the other, but is not unfolded until new conditions draw it out. Just as the scales of the reptile become the feathers of the bird when the environment moves from land to air, so exclusive holding for self becomes withholding from others when the environment moves from producing to marketing. The transition was hardly noticeable as long as the merchant, the master, the laborer, were combined under small units of ownership, but becomes distinct when all opportunities are occupied and business is conducted by corporations on a credit system which consolidates property under the control of absentee owners. Then the power of property *per se*, distinguished from the power residing in personal faculties or special grants of sovereignty, comes into prominence [Commons 1924, p. 53].

In this quotation, Commons describes what Karl Marx [1859] calls the separation of labor from the means of production, and Karl Polanyi

[1944] studies as the destruction of the natural or socially embedded economy. Capitalism at its nadir meant free, propertyless wage labor: individuals without any direct access to means of production or income, and completely dependent on market exchange opportunities. Such individuals are without exchange entitlements in Sen's language, and Sen dubs such a pristine capitalist economy a "PEST" (Pure Exchange System in Transition) [Sen 1977].

Commons *explains* the emergence of yellow dog contracts through these new economic circumstances of liberal economy that created propertyless wage laborers and gave them the choice to accept such contracts or to accept poverty.[7] In Commons's view, this was a coerced and not a free choice—it was an "economic hold-up."[8] Property owners possessed the jobs (the access to means of production and income) that individual laborers had to have to survive. Moreover the legal system permitted property owners to monopolistically band together in the corporate form in order to improve their terms of exchange.

In Commons's analysis, the "Pareto efficient" yellow dog contract is not the institution of interests. Instead the contract itself is explained by the larger political-legal institutional environment. The structure of property rights, as legally defined and enforced, establishes the entitlements, powers, and alternative opportunities that structure the environment in which contractual bargaining occurs. Commons's institutional economics concerns the formation and transformation of the institutional environment understood in this broader sense.

In cases like *Holden* v. *Hardy*, the Court had recognized the public interest in regulating purely economic power (that is, the bargaining power that results in being able to withhold means of production from the market), just as courts had earlier regulated physical violence and coercion. What then explains the court's refusal in *Coppage* v. *Kansas* to permit regulation of the economic coercion implicit in yellow dog contracts? This question introduces us to the second aspect of this case, which further explains the persistence (in 1915) of yellow dog contracts and illuminates Commons's institutional analysis.

The legal issue involved in this second aspect of *Coppage* ("whether the legislature can be permitted to create and protect a right of association of persons as against an association of property owners" [Commons 1924, pp. 289-90]) is somewhat complex and only obscures Commons's analysis. In Commons's words, the Court's decision can be explained "not as a matter of logic but as a matter of beliefs and this belief is none other than the habitual wish of the judge who decides and who, in three hundred years since the beginning of the business revolution, can always find precedents and logic to back up what he wishes. It is the judge who believes in the law and custom of business and not the judge who believes in the law and custom of labor, that decides" [Commons 1924, p. 298].

Yellow dog contracts exist because of economic coercion created by the institutional structure of the capitalist economy, and they persist because of a class-based legal system. Yet, it would be wrong to impute to Commons an "executive committee of the ruling class" theory of the state. He saw the apparatus of the Anglo-Saxon state as being somewhat responsive to the needs of its citizens and definitely responsive to the pragmatic need for industrial peace. Commons himself was one of those who pushed the state to extend protection from economic coercion to its citizens. His cynical analysis of the anti-labor bias of the Supreme Court is written in the confidence that the court would eventually change and constitutionalize labor associations as legitimate, and socially useful, bodies of countervailing power. As J. Barbash [1976] indicates, Commons was correct in that confidence.[9] In the context of our interest in the economic analysis of institutions, Commons's confidence marks his understanding, his "prediction," about the evolution of the yellow dog contract. We turn now to our sale of interlinked tenure-credit contracts.

Interlinked Tenure-Credit Contracts and Pareto Efficiency

Contractual interlinkage occurs when several interdependent exchanges are made simultaneously. Examples of interlinkage abound from across the time and space of the world's underdeveloped agricultural region. For example, D. McCreery [1983] describes interlinkage of labor and credit contracts in rural Guatemala from 1876 to 1936. P. K. Bardhan and A. Rudra [1978] describe various sorts of interlinkages uncovered in surveys of contemporary India. R. Ransom and R. Sutch [1977] provide a fascinating and well-documented description of interlinkage in post-bellum southern U.S. agriculture. This latter case will be used here to establish a frame of reference for the review of microtheoretic analysis of the institution of interlinkage. There is of course no intention of implying that the particulars of the southern U.S. experience are representative of interlinkage elsewhere.

What Ransom and Sutch describe as "the trap of debt peonage" was built on interlinked transactions in land and credit markets. To meet subsistence needs, the sharecropper was dependent on credit from the local merchant (who typically was his landlord).[10] To receive credit, the sharecropper had to plant cotton, with the crop standing as a lien for the credit advanced.

The impact of this system is visible in the marked decline in food production in the post-bellum South, and in the high percentage of farms that exhibited deficits of grain consumed over grain produced. The trap identified by Ransom and Sutch was the perpetual seasonal indebtedness of the sharecropper. Specialization in cotton meant that there was never enough food to carry over to cover the next season's subsistence needs and to break out of the cycle of credit dependence. And the cotton lien meant that the necessary credit could never be received without planting the cotton crop sure to guarantee the need for consumption credit again in the following year.[11]

By Ransom and Sutch's calculation, this interlinked system was quite effective at extracting income from the tenant. Implicit annual rates of interest on consumption credit hovered in the range of 60 percent in an era when urban short-term interest rates were in the 4 percent to 6 percent range. The net impact on tenant living standards was a rate of exploitation of 13.5 percent.[12] While this 13.5 percent rate left tenants with a living standard about 29 percent above that of *ante-bellum* slaves. Ransom and Sutch do not find an exploitation rate less than that of slavery to be much of a recommendation for debt peonage interlinkage.[13] With the Ransom and Sutch presentation of interlinked southern sharecropping as admittedly selective background about rural transactions interlinkage, let us now turn to examine the current microtheoretic explanation of this somewhat peculiar institution.

Braverman and Stiglitz's "Sharecropping and the Interlinking of Agrarian Markets" is a classic piece of microtheoretic institutional analysis. The authors begin by noting that prior literature (for example, [Bharduri 1973]) had basically viewed interlinkage as a tool used by the strong to exploit the weak. Braverman and Stiglitz ask whether interlinkage can be properly understood as a mode of appropriation and exploitation. If exploitation were the issue, they ask, why could not the landlord simply manipulate the sharecrop parameter to achieve the desired income extraction from the tenant? As an alternative explanation of interlinkage, Braverman and Stiglitz suggest that transaction costs and constraints are the key to understanding interlinkage. They propose to explain interlinkage as a Pareto efficient outcome of an appropriately constrained voluntary exchange. As the section below discusses, the relationship between their explanation and exploitation is obscure (and obscurantist). The remainder of this section will present the Braverman-Stiglitz explanation of interlinkage.

At the heart of the Braverman-Stiglitz model is an assumption of asymmetric information. Labor inputs in agriculture cannot be directly measured, nor can they be accurately imputed from output because of unobservable stochastic inputs that affect production (for example, weather). The seller of labor knowns his input, but the buyer cannot. This asymmetric distribution of information means that conventional commodity contracts for labor inputs are not enforceable. As the literature on sharecropping has shown (for example, [Stiglitz 1974]), sharecropping is in general Pareto superior to either wage labor or fixed rent tenancies. Sharecropping is superior to wage labor because under the latter the individual has no incentive to effectively supply labor. It is superior to a fixed rent tenancy because it divides risk between tenant and landlord, whereas fixed rent tenure places all risk on the tenant. (This argument of course assumes risk-averse tenants.) But while it is superior to these two institutional alternatives, the measure of insurance provided by sharecropping is subject to a moral hazard, or free rider problem. The sharing of risk also partly shields the tenant from the expected consequences of his (in)actions, and his labor input is consequently less than it would be in an informationally perfect world.

It is in this context that Braverman and Stiglitz demonstrate the usefulness of interlinkage. The landlord can improve performance in sharecropping burdened by moral hazard by linking the tenant's behavior to a second transaction. The second transaction then becomes an instrument of indirect control in the moral hazard-burdened tenancy market, and equilibrium can be moved toward the informationally perfect first best allocation.

The logic can be easily explained. The landlord, for example, requires the tenant to take a consumption loan as a condition of tenancy. The penalty for non-repayment of the loan is severe (for example, the landlord's thugs break the tenant's knees). The tenant subsequently has incentives in addition to those provided by the share contract to supply labor effort in order to reduce the probability that production and his share is insufficient to repay the consumption loan.

The formal structure *per se* of the Braverman-Stiglitz model is informative from the perspective of this essay. The landlord maximizes his wellbeing over contractual terms subject to the constraint that the expected uility of the contract yield the tenant a given reservation expected utility level, $\bar{U}$. This level $\bar{U}$ can be interpreted as either a competitively determined level that equates supply and demand of tenants, or some subsistence utility floor to which the monopolistic landlords can push tenants.[14] The Pareto efficiency of interlinkage emerges directly from the structure of the problem when the optimal contract terms are shown to include interlinkage.

Braverman and Stiglitz embellish their model with detail beyond that just outlined. However, the basic model nicely illustrates the nature of microeconomic institutional analysis. An apparently peculiar institutional form is explained as a Pareto efficient response to a transaction cost constrained environment. In an informationally perfect environment, there would be no need for interlinkage. Asymmetric information, not exploitation, therefore explains tenure-credit interlinkage in Braverman and Stiglitz's analysis.

The distance between Commons's analysis of yellow dog contracts and Braverman and Stiglitz's analysis of interlinkage is perhaps so large as to be overwhelming. The final section will now try to draw the two together into an informative evaluation of microeconomic theory of institutions.

The Insufficiency of Pareto Efficiency

A microtheoretic analysis of yellow dog contracts might offer the following proposition: "The fact that individuals signed yellow dog contracts without non-economic coercion indicates that the utility value of the union to the worker was less than the cost of the union to the firm. Otherwise, workers would have counteroffered a contract permitting unionization but with a wage sufficiently low to offset the cost of unionization to the firm. Moreover, assuming that appropriate markets exist and function, it would not matter whether workers have a right to unionize or firms have a right to be free of unions."

Whatever the merits of that hypothetical analysis, and one could quibble about market structure and transaction cost issues that it ignores, it might be reasonable to ask, "Who cares?" Commons does not dispute the Pareto efficiency of yellow dog contracts, nor does he seem to consider it an interesting question. From Commons's perspective, yellow dog contracts came into existence because of the evolution of the economy that stripped workers of entitlements, that gave workers a lousy "$\bar{U}$." The fact that individuals signed yellow dog contracts without physical duress does not *explain* that institution anymore than a crime is explained by the robbery victim voluntarily saying "my money" when presented with the choice, "your money or your life."

The interlinked tenure-credit contracts studied by Braverman and Stiglitz are a more complex form of exchange, and their analysis is genuinely insightful. Yet, their finding that interlinkage can be Pareto efficient in an environment of asymmetric information neither proves nor disproves the existence of exploitation. Braverman and Stiglitz's analysis is quite compatible with Ransom and Sutch's debt peonage interpretation of interlinkage. One might properly say that interlinkage makes for "very efficient exploitation." Interlinkage indirectly coerces the tenant into working inordinately hard on shares, and the landlord still extracts everything above subsistence.

While this exploitation *and* efficiency interpretation is logically quite consistent with Braverman and Stiglitz's analysis, it represents a shift away from the "exploitation *versus* efficiency" spirit of the neoclassical microtheoretic approach to interlinkage. Bardhan and Rudra [1978], for example, pronounce that their survey of interlinked contracts in India found no significant pattern of non-economic coercion. It is hard to know what to conclude from this piece of evidence, but Bardhan and Rudra seemingly think that the evidence somehow discounts the exploitation view of interlinkage. One problem with the microtheoretic analysis of interlinkage is that its emphasis on Pareto efficiency obscures the fact that beneath a superficial equality of exchange, there can be exploitation.[15] This view that the appearance of voluntary exchange mystifies the reality of exploitation was of course central to Marx's thought. As seen in Commons's analysis of yellow dog contracts, Pareto efficiency and economic coercion can go hand in hand. The ability to contract without physical duress is just "one kind of freedom," as states the title of Ransom and Sutch's study.

Commons's approach illuminates a second, more significant shortcoming of microeconomic analysis of interlinkage and of institutions in general. As seen in the case of yellow dog contracts, Commons was not preoccupied with the question of whether exchange was Pareto efficient. The more salient question from Commons's point of view is, What determines the reservation utility $\bar{U}$? What evolution of ownership over means of production explains the given alternative opportunities that are the datum of the microtheoretic approach? From this point of view, the Pareto efficiency of the exchange implicit in an institutional arrangement does not suffice to explain the institution. The evolution of institutional rules that determine bargaining power and alternative opportunity is the centerpiece of Commons's institutional economic analysis.

This perspective suggests several immediate questions about interlinkage—questions that do not occur within the neoclassical context. For example, why is it that tenure-credit interlinkage seems to be significant only in low-income agriculture? Perhaps interlinkage occurs only when there is a class of dispossessed agricultural laborers? Their lack of assets and their lack of risk-bearing capacity prevents them from being able to achieve independent standing in either land or credit markets. Their options are limited, and their vulnerability within an exchange economy leaves them little choice but to assent to isolated, interlinked tenure and credit contracts.[16]

Proper answers to these questions and a satisfying explanation of interlinkage requires research into the evolution of power and assets, and "$\bar{U}$." (J. M. Rao [1980] makes essentially this point.) It is the type of research at which Commons excelled, but which is of little interest to the microtheoretic approach because it probes into phenomena taken as safely and securely given.[17] But is the distribution of power and assets really a stable and secure given? What would Commons's common law courts say about the economic extortion often associated with interlinkage, at least if they recognized tenant farmers as citizens of the commonwealth?

This last question introduces a third and final difference between the institutional analysis of Commons and that of the microeconomic approach. They differ not only in their static explanation of what is, but also in their dynamic prediction about what will be. The alternative opportunities that the microtheoretic approach takes as given are seen by Commons to be very much in flux and subject to systematic regulation. An outraged exploited sharecropper is presumably not quieted by the information that the market at best offers him only utility equivalent contracts—presumably he knows that! Similarly, Commons's progressive liberal commonwealth is not content to expose its citizens to economic extortion, if only because class warfare is judged too costly.

Commons's institutional analysis reveals a level of analysis that, if the practitioners of microtheoretic analysis see at all, they ignore. It is perhaps because economists take the distribution of power and assets as settled and given that economists seem to lag behind lawyers and politicians, as K. H. Parsons [1985] remarks.

In summary, these comments are not meant to disparage microeconomic analysis of institutions. The Braverman-Stiglitz analysis is insightful, and usefully analyzes issues such as the impact of banning interlinkages, assuming that the opportunity alternatives $\bar{U}$ were not perturbed. But their analysis can provide only a very partial understanding of the existence and likely persistence of peculiar contractual interlinkages. Improperly handled, it may also tend to mystify an economically coercive reality with the appearance of voluntary exchange of equal values. In this respect, the Braverman-Stiglitz analysis reflects the more general limitations of microeconomic theory of institutions. It also reflects the incompleteness and the insufficiency of Pareto efficiency explanations of economic institutions.

Notes

1. The remarks here are very much in the spirit of Calebresi and Melmed [1972]. It is worth noting along with Dahlman [1979] that the same costs that impede market allocation may also hinder the operation of some alternative allocational mechanism.
2. In this context it would be more correct to say "clear in a Walrasian fashion."
3. It might be noted that any alternative price theory opens economic analysis to see the impact of institutions, not just the so-called neo-Keynesian disequilibrium analysis. The latter is just another variant of "bastard Keynesianism" to the Cambridge School, which places its analysis on a Ricardo-Sraffa foundation. Ricardian theory could also provide a basis for institutional analysis.
4. They are equilibrium because they refer to a transaction cost that afflicts a particular market, rather than costs endemic to the market system as a whole.
5. Coase's [1937] own work on this subject is seminal. Also see Alchian and Demsetz [1972] and Williamson [1975].
6. For several Wisconsin examples see Segerson [1985] and Carter [1985].
7. Marglin [1973] and Gintis [1976] give a similar explanation of the rise of the hierarchical firm. They explicitly contrast their explanation with that of the Coase microtheoretic school.
8. C. B. MacPherson's [1973] essay, "Elegant Tombstones: An Essay on Friedman's Freedom," captures this notion better than any other piece I know.
9. How elastic the liberal state is within the confines of private capitalist ownership of the means of production is an open question. Wolfe [1977] writes that the liberal state has reached the "exhaustion of political alternatives"—implying that Commons's pragmatism has reached the end of the line and that only a transformation of the structure of ownership can resolve the system's problems.
10. Ransom and Sutch are unable to calculate with any precision to what extent consumption loans were actually given by the sharecropper's landowners. In instances where the landlord and merchant were different individuals, Ransom and Sutch suggest that an identity of class interest suppressed any conflict of interest that might arise between landlord and merchant. As our use of Ransom and Sutch is only illustrative, complications introduced by the lack of identity between merchants and landlords is unimportant.
11. Implicit in this discussion of debt peonage is the issue of whether the decision to plant cotton was economically suboptimal. Ransom and Sutch [1977, p. 165] say that it was. The issue of interlinkage causing inefficient exploitation of resources has been debated in the literature on India (see, for example, Bhaduri [1973] and Newberry [1975]). While this issue is of obvious significance, this essay can proceed without resolving it.
12. Ransom and Sutch define exploitation as the gap between actual income

received by the tenant and what can be called the competitive labor share. See their Appendix A for details.

13. Nor were contemporary observers impressed by the system. One of them wrote that the "vast credit system whose tremendous evils and exorbitant exactions have brought poverty and bankruptcy to thousands of families . . . crushed out all independence and reduced its victims to a coarser species of servile slavery" (quoted in Ransom and Sutch [1977, p. 104]). Ransom and Sutch also cite similar evaluations from less passionate observers.
14. The ultimate irrelevance of the market power of the landlord to the analysis is symbolized by Mitra's [1982] demonstration that a village cooperative authority interested solely in the welfare of villagers would employ market interlinkages.
15. Exploitation is maybe best described by Justice Potter Stewart's comment on pornography: "I can't define it, but I know it when I see it." Scott's [1975] analysis of the breakdown and delegitimization of peasant economies dresses up Stewart's comment into a definition of "phenomenological exploitation." By phenomenological exploitation, Scott simply means that if a relationship is perceived as exploitative by actors in the situation, then it is effectively exploitative. This approach sidesteps the contentious debate in Marxism about objective exploitation and the problem of class consciousness. Roemer [1982] gives an interesting array of (objective) definitions of exploitation under alternative modes of production. For purposes here, the Potter Stewart approach suffices, and indeed matches well with Commons's emphasis on the legal system as mover (or at least ratifier) of social change.
16. Basu [1983] notes that even competitive interlinkage situations are characterized by elements of monopoly. The tenant-borrower cannot search for a better credit contract alone. In that sense, his landlord is a credit monopsonist. At the same time, the tenant-borrower can perhaps search out a better tenancy-credit package. Basu suggests the term "isolated" to describe these markets, which are a mixture of competitive and monopolistic features.
17. "Economics became the queen of social sciences by dealing only with solved political problems" (source of quotation unknown). Perhaps the quote should be modified to say "by dealing only with what it *pretends* are solved political problems."

References

Alchian, A., and H. Demsetz. 1972. "Production, Information Costs, and Economic Organization." *American Economic Review* 43 (December): 777-95.

Barbash, J. 1976. "The *Legal Foundations of Capitalism* and the Labor Problem." *Journal of Economic Issues* 10 (December): 799-810.

Bardhan, P. K., and A. Rudra. 1978. "Interlinkage of Land, Labour, and

Credit Relations: An Analysis of Village Survey Data in East India." *Economic and Political Weekly* 13 (February): 367-84.

Basu, Kaushik. 1983. "The Emergence of Isolation and Interlinkage in Rural Markets." *Oxford Economics Papers* 35: 262-80.

Bhaduri, A. 1973. "Agricultural Backwardness Under Semi-Feudalism." *Economic Journal* 83 (March): 120-37.

Braverman, A., and J. Stiglitz. 1982. "Sharecropping and the Interlinking of Agrarian Markets." *American Economic Review* 72 (September): 695-715.

Calebresi, G., and D. Melmed. 1972. "Property Rights, Liability Rules, and Inalienability: One View of the Cathedral." *Harvard Law Review* 85 (April): 1089-1130.

Carter, M. R. 1983. "Development Losers: Towards Some Price Theoretic Foundations for Institutional Content in Development Models." Mimeograph. Department of Agricultural Economics, University of Wisconsin-Madison.

Carter, M. R. 1985. "Changing Roads in Agrarian Reform Agriculture: Parcelization and Dilemmas of Risk Sharing and Incentives." Mimeograph. (Revised version University of Wisconsin Agricultural Economics Staff Paper 224).

Coase, R. H. 1937. "The Nature of the Firm." *Econometrica* 4 (December): 386-405.

Coase, R. H. 1961. "The Problem of Social Cost." *Journal of Law and Economics* 3 (March): 1-60.

Commons, J. R. 1924. *Legal Foundations of Capitalism.* University of Wisconsin Press, 1957.

Cuddington, J., P. Johanson, and K. Lofgren. 1984. *Disequilibrium Macroeconomics in Open Economies.* New York: Basil Blackwell.

Dahlman, C. J. 1979. "The Problem of Externality." *Journal of Law and Economics* 23 (May): 141-62.

Gintis, H. 1976. "The Nature of Labor Exchange and the Theory of Capitalist Production." *Review of Radical Political Economy* 8 (Summer): 36-54.

Leijonhufvud, A. 1968. *Keynesian Economics and the Economics of Keynes.* Cambridge: Cambridge University Press.

Marglin, S. 1974. "What Do Bosses Do?" *Review of Radical Political Economy* 4 (Summer): 33-60.

McCreery, D. 1983. "Debt Peonage in Rural Guatemala, 1876-1936." *Hispanic American Historical Review* 63: 735-759.

MacPherson, C. B. 1973. "Elegant Tombstones: An Essay on Friedman's Freedom." In *Democratic Theory: Essays in Retrieval.* London: Oxford University Press.

Marx, K. 1859. *Pre-Capitalist Economic Formation.* New York: International Publishers (1964).

Mitra, P. 1983. "A Theory of Interlinked Rural Transactions." *Journal of Public Economics* 20 (March): 167-91.

Newberry, D. 1975. "Tenurial Obstacles to Innovation." *Journal of Development Studies* (July): 263-77.

Parsons, K. H. 1985. "John R. Commons: His Relevance to Contemporary

Economics." Mimeograph. Department of Agricultural Economics, University of Wisconsin-Madison.
Polanyi, K. 1944. *The Great Transformation*. Boston: Beacon Press (1957).
Ransom, R., and R. Sutch. 1977. *One Kind of Freedom: The Economic Consequences of Emancipation*. Cambridge: Cambridge University Press.
Rao, J. M. 1980. "Interest Rates in Backward Agriculture." *Cambridge Journal of Economics* 4: 159-167.
Roemer, J. 1982. "Exploitation, Alternatives, and Socialism." *Economic Journal* 92 (March): 87-107.
Scott, J. C. 1976. *The Moral Economy of the Peasant*. New Brunswick: Yale University Press.
Segerson, K. 1985. "Economic Incentives for Control of Nonpoint Pollution." Mimeograph. Department of Agricultural Economics, University of Wisconsin-Madison.
Sen, A. K. 1977. "Starvation and Exchange Entitlements: A General Approach and its Application to the Great Bengal Famine." *Cambridge Journal of Economics* 1 (March): 33-59.
Stiglitz, J. 1974. "Incentives and Risk Sharing in Sharecropping." *Review of Economic Studies* 41 (April): 214-55.
Williamson, O. 1975. *Markets and Hierarchies*. New York: Free Press.
Wolfe, A. 1977. *The Limits of Legitimacy*. New York: Free Press.

21

Economics as a Science and Its Relation to Policy: The Example of Free Trade

Warren J. Samuels

Economic controversy has centered on questions of substantive doctrine, the conflict of schools and ideologies, and issues of scope and method. Somewhat more peripheral but no less fundamental in importance have been controversies over the social role of economists and the relation of economic theory (or science) to policy. These have involved the tension between the desire for analysis free of ideology or values, on the one hand, and the more or less reluctant belief in the inevitability of ideological or valuational elements, on the other;[1] whether economic principles are independent of practical affairs or are applicable, directly or indirectly, to matters of policy; whether economic theory is an engine of inquiry or a corpus of truth; and, in general, the nature of economics as a science and its relation to policy. In all these and other respects, there have been considerable diversity, ambiguity, and conflict of views.

Recently, I have been studying in some depth the period 1870–1914 to understand the factors and forces which produced the combination of mainstream and diversity in twentieth-century economics, principally, of course, neoclassicism. All the controversies noted above were present then and persist to the present day, as evidenced in part by the numerous articles during the past decade which have criticized the status of economic knowledge from within orthodox ranks.

With these considerations in mind, it seems useful to probe the belief structure of contemporary economists in order to reject or confirm (and if so, spell out in some detail) the diversity, ambiguity, and conflict of views bearing on the controversies noted above. My inquiry posed a basic question with regard to a doctrine which I believed would command widespread if not fundamental assent and which thus would not introduce complicating substantive issues. The principle of free trade was chosen. Not unsurprisingly, the doctrine was generally adhered to by those questioned. Although its use introduced no needless controversy, it was found that the basic status and relevance of the theory of free trade to policy is perceived with enormous diversity among contemporary economists.

This article reports on and interprets that probe. It also suggests certain lines of possible resolution of the conflict and the ambiguity. At the least, it may help clarify the issues and the positions taken. The first section outlines the free trade controversy as it began to develop a century ago. The second section reports on the responses to my inquiry. The third discusses a seminar which focused on the subject. The concluding section attempts a limited resolution, perhaps only an interpretation, of the issues. The relation to policy of economics as a science is addressed in terms of resolving the positive-normative controversy, specifically, the varying *senses* in which certain propositions are positive and normative.

A Retrospect

It will be useful, if not also comforting,[2] to examine briefly the period 1870–1914, roughly midway between our own day and the times of Adam Smith and David Ricardo. During those decades prior to World War I, economics as a discipline often was identified in the public mind with free trade, but there was considerable diversity among professional economists as to both the scientific status and the policy merits of free trade. For example, in the early twentieth century, there was marked disagreement among some theoretical economists supporting free trade and some historical economists favoring protection in one form or another. C. E. Collet has cited Herbert Somerton Foxwell's reservations (to put it mildly) about what we might call the Pareto-optimal character of free trade: "What were somewhat floridly described as the 'bloodless victories of Free Trade,' often left such a train of suffering behind them that the epithet applies less truly to the victories than to their victims."[3]

Shortly before the turn of the century, in speaking of the Manchester

School, but making a point applicable to many if not most contemporary economists, Frank W. Taussig noted the predominant strong *faith* in the effects of international free trade.[4] Narmadeshwar Jha, writing of the period after 1890, the age of Marshall, argued that the main trend in the development of international trade theory (F. Y. Edgeworth, H. H. S. Cunynghame, and C. F. Bickerdike) was an undermining of faith in the theoretical case for free trade. Jha added that "these theoretical developments did not in any way weaken the faith of the majority of British economists in the policy of free trade as the best one for England and other industrially advanced countries."[5] Joseph Schumpeter wrote of Marshall that "his success was as great as A. Smith's, if account be taken of the facts that a science must inevitably grow less accessible to the general public as its techniques develop and that Marshall had no winning political horse to back, such as free trade had been in its prime."[6] Edgeworth remarked, with respect to Marshall's work on foreign trade, that "he feared that if separated from all concrete study of actual conditions, it might seem to claim a more direct bearing on real problems than it in fact had."[7]

Arthur Latham Perry's affirmation of the scientific character of the free trade doctrine will be referred to in the next section. That view had widespread sympathy among his contemporaries. Leslie Stephen seemingly echoed the views of many, however, when he declared that "the free trade argument is perfectly conclusive in a negative sense. It demonstrates, that is, the fallacy which lurks in the popular argument for protection."[8] He did add that there were extra-economic considerations which also had to be considered, with "arguments which, good or bad, are outside the sphere of economics proper."[9] Perhaps his principal methodological argument was that economics as a science was not fully able to "deduce from the laws accepted by Economists the necessary working of any given measure—say, the effect of protection or free trade."[10]

A quite different but nonetheless complex approach was taken by Charles Dunbar. He argued that the "problem is to determine the mode of action of the reciprocal demands made by two trading countries" as these attempt to "satisfy certain wants with the least effort." The introduction of protection in one form or another "would obviously bring in a new element, not necessary to the essentials of the problem, and of infinitely variable action and intensity." Dunbar, however, was unwilling to treat the simpler case as the basis for normative policy analysis: "But, plainly, the question whether competition may be restricted by law or by combination, or should be free, must be answered by entirely independent reasoning. No answer is implied, or is approached, by that reasoning which merely seeks to ascertain the normal effects of the primary forces with which political economy has mainly occupied itself." Seemingly cognizant that the free trade doctrine is a surrogate for free market doctrines in general (that is, domestic policy as well), Dunbar stated: "It seems, then, that *laissez faire* is no part of the logical structure of the old economic doctrine. . . . It is plain, in short, that, not only logically, but according to the practice of leading economists, the maxim *laissez faire,* whatever validity we assign to it, has to do only with the practical applications of economic reasoning, and has no place as a part of the reasoning itself." He did not leave the matter at that: "It is no doubt true that, for various reasons, the great majority of economists of the deductive school have in fact given so much effect to the maxim as to recognize a presumption in favor of non-interference, to be set aside only for strong reasons."[11]

In 1891, Dunbar wrote that the conflict between free trade and protection

> as a political question, . . . is often treated by partisans in the heat of discussion as if its solution were the chief, and sometimes as if it were the only, aim of political economy. . . . The call for exceptional treatment of the question between protection and free trade is, in effect, a demand that upon a controverted point, as to which scientific opinions are not at one, political economy shall be made to give its answer in a particular, predetermined sense. . . . In short, the attempt was made to judge of a body of scientific inquirers by references, not to their processes, but to their opinions upon questions still *sub judice.* This was not far different from requiring of them the profession of a creed.[12]

In 1889, Francis A. Walker had declared it unfortunate that economists had become "divided early and decisively on the issue, largely a false issue, between so-called protection and free-trade. Ethical and political considerations were held to require that an economist should, first of all, range himself as a protectionist or as a free trader."[13]

Some years later, in a lecture entitled "Government is Founded on Opinion," James Bonar wrote: "There are parts of the economic system hardly now influenced by public opinion," such as the areas covered by the principles of exchange and division of labor, value, currency, and credit. "To that extent economic theory is also superior, or if you like anterior, to public opinion. But economic *policy* depends as we all know very largely on public opinion; and, as theorists are human, and even man is influenced by his atmosphere, economic theory is influenced by it too, as soon as the first elementary principles are passed and the question is of their further applications." Thus, said Bonar, "when free trade is alleged to be a development of division of labor [the principle of division of labor being one which "no economist would repudiate"] there may be a bias in our attitude, hostile or favourable, towards the allegation."[14] It may be noticed that the thrust of Bonar's point that theory is anterior to but not conclusive with regard to policy has the same effect as Dunbar's point that the analysis of the "primary" effects of the normal operation of markets in the abstract has no logical connection with policy doctrines. But that effect was not agreed to by all in any pristine form; as Dunbar also said, economists largely continued to recognize a presumption in favor of free trade.

Stephen's affirmation of a negative role for the free trade doctrine is echoed in Schumpeter's treatment.[15] But exactly how far either the negative or the positive role should be carried was questioned by Bernard Moses:

> The earlier thought, that there was an art of political economy, and the disposition of certain economists to make it stand for what the art of social control now signifies, have done much to cast doubt on the wisdom of economic teaching when applied to practice. These economists have taken strictly economic principles, and inferred from them alone [?] the propriety of a line of conduct, without appreciating the fact that this line of conduct, before being definitely accepted as a rule for social control and guidance, should be modified and corrected by the principles of the other social sciences. They have vigorously affirmed the advisability of freedom in international trade, because their special science has indicated that under freedom the maximum gains of trade may be realized. With our present view of the relation of practical economics to politics and ethics, we might accept the truth of the economic conclusion, and still find it not advisable to adopt a practical policy of freedom, because of the corrective which political considerations furnish. Our rule of social conduct, whether in national or local affairs, is not identical with the indications of economics, but is, in some sense, the resultant of the principles of all of the social sciences.[16]

From this cursory review, it is apparent that, with respect to free trade, the critical issue of the relation to policy of economics as a science (that is, the social role of economists, the relation of and possible hiatus between the province and reach of economic theory and science and the requirements of policy, and the faith in the presuppositions of economic analysis and its uses) were pervasive and unsettled. I now turn to the present situation.

A Probe of Present Beliefs

In October 1977, members of the departments of economics and agricultural economics at Michigan State University were sent the following letter.

Dear Colleague:

I would appreciate your thoughtful answer to a question which has arisen in my research.

As you know, economists long have both lauded the scientific character of their discipline and praised free trade, as opposed to protectionism, although often with qualifications.

Speaking of Arthur Latham Perry in the late nineteenth century, Joseph Dorfman wrote: "Perry valiantly stood his ground and declared that at Williams free trade was taught. Those college professors who proclaimed that they taught neither protection nor free trade, he said, were at best foolish, because this in fact denied that the science they professed to teach was a science at all" (*Economic Mind of American Civilization,* vol. 3, p. 61).

My query is this: What do you think is the relationship between the pro-free trade position and the status of economics as a science?

Warren J. Samuels

Eighteen (of thirty-six) replies were received from the economics department and nine (of forty-one) from the agricultural economics department. There were no obvious major differences in positions taken between the two departments or on the basis of age (nine respondents were under and eighteen over age 40). Responses quoted below are labelled E (economics) and AE (agricultural economics). To assure anonymity, respondents were numbered (one through twenty-seven). In some cases, follow-up inquiries were used to clarify answers. Responses were quite divergent in substance, direction, and tone.[17] It is more than likely that different persons may interpret them, singly and in the aggregate, quite differently.

One group of respondents affirms that the position in favor of free trade is grounded in economic science. One writer said that "under certain ideal assumptions (perfect competition, no externalities, etc.), free trade yields a Pareto optimum. This statement is no less scientific than any other in economics." The respondent added that his view was positive, not normative, economics and that "free trade yielding a Pareto-optimum" is "a justification of free trade" but it would be "perhaps too strong" to consider that it affirms the pro-free trade position (1E). This general view was repeated by another respondent, who said that the statement "under certain conditions free trade leads to a Pareto optimum" is "about as strong a scientific justification for the free trade position as exists in economics" (2E).

Another respondent (3AE) qualified his position: "In static analysis the proof of the benefits of free trade are scientifically provable, however, in a dynamic growth framework the modifications of free trade theory which may be needed have not been sufficiently explored, probed or presented concisely." This statement could be interpreted as akin to the opinions of respondents 20–24, who in general state that economic science cannot advocate free trade but can describe the consequences—here the "benefits"—of free trade. It also is similar to the assertion by respondents 8–10 that the pro-free trade position in principle could be but is not (yet) grounded in economic science. Indeed, respondent 3AE agreed with the latter point, adding that "it appears to me that in the economic growth context the free trade position is likely to be able to be demonstrated as contributing to higher income as a general proposition, but that under many particular country circumstances the position might not hold during particular time periods due to major variables not normally included in economic analysis. The above has not been yet clearly demonstrated." Apropos the position taken by respondents 20–24, respondent 3AE wrote: "I do not think we can advocate absolute free trade (no tariffs, etc.) at all times and places. Economists certainly can indicate the likely effects of trade barriers, which can then be balanced in a political economy framework against any possible benefits of barriers."

Respondent 4E simply wrote that on theoretical grounds free trade should be espoused by economists, although practically it may be a dying cause.

A somewhat circumspect respondent (5E) wrote that Paul Samuelson "has proven beyond doubt that some trade is better than no trade . . . and the result is arrived at under a general set of assumptions. Of course, the real world situations are not exactly identical to Samuelson's assumptions."[18] When asked whether the Samuelson position means that economics as a science thereby supports free trade and about the significance of the fact that real world situations are not identical to Samuelson's assumptions, respondent 5E replied that a change in social goal (welfare function) or real world situation at variance with Samuelson's assumptions precludes the pro-free trade conclusion. Respondent 5E believes the pro-free trade conclusion is scientific insofar as it follows from the assumptions. He also feels that all such analysis is strictly normative economics, inasmuch as it involves goal functions and judgments as to who is made better or worse off.

Respondent 6E said that economics is a science with propositions or hypotheses (imperfectly) capable of being refuted and, therefore, "any stance on free trade is consistent with economics as a science." By "any stance" he meant "any hypothesis concerning benefits of trade; i.e., any refutable position." With regard to the question of support for the free trade position, "if by 'support' one means 'tangible' evidence indicating free trade maximizes some objective (life efficiency, etc.), then 'support-evidence' is positive. However, if given some (positive) evidence, some actor (policy maker, etc.) 'supports' free trade then 'supports' is normative, i.e., based on available positive findings the actor feels free trade ought to exist."

Quite a different view of science is taken by respondent 7AE. In his conception, "economics is a science insofar as its practitioners use methods which exhibit internal clarity and coherence of analysis and external correspondence with other practitioners' experiences or theory. As such, economics does not avoid being influenced by values; indeed, such influence is, I expect, inevitable." He therefore considers pro-free trade arguments by economists "scientific insofar as they are clear, coherent and correspond to other neoclassical economic theory and empirical conclusions." But a similarly qualified position different from the strict pro-free trade position would be "no less scientific."

Respondent 8E in effect takes issue with the reliance by the first two respondents on the significance of the Pareto criterion:

1. Any science worthy of the name is grounded in "values." (T. Kuhn, B. Ward, etc.)
2. An alleged "value" of economic science is the Pareto Criterion.
   a. The Pareto Criterion is one of the key assumptions of welfare theory.
   b. The Pareto Criterion is especially important because it is used to exclude other stronger value judgments at a crucial stage of the analysis (work of Arrow notwithstanding).
3. Welfare theory shows that competition can lead to an equilibrium which is Pareto optimal.
4. This conclusion is often carried over into the theory of trade, and used to justify a free trade position.
5. A careful analysis of welfare theory would show that most real-world policies which allege to move in the direction of free trade cannot be justified under the Pareto Criterion alone.
6. Thus the free trade position goes beyond economic science in the sense that it requires stronger value judgments than are usually admitted by the running dog lackey practitioner of the science.

This respondent believes that it is normative economics to base the pro-free trade position on the Pareto criterion.

A similar position is taken by respondent 9E, who suggests that second best considerations require the conclusion "that the intransigent advocacy of the market allocation in any and all circumstances is not supported by the 'science' of economics." Moreover, "free trade may indeed be the second best policy, but that determination depends on empirical work and analysis which has not yet been done and certainly hadn't been done by the late nineteenth century." Stating that "a conclusion of the form 'free trade is optimal' either as a first or second best result would be a result in normative economics," 9E also believes that "it is possible in principle . . . for a combination of artful a priori analysis and solid empirical results to generate a normative implication which would be desirable from the point of view of any social welfare function which satisfies certain conditions. One possible result of this sort might be 'don't interfere in any markets.' " Interestingly, with regard to empirical research, 9E says that "this work has not been done, and while possible in principle, I doubt whether it will be done, simply because I don't believe that 'free trade' is optimal."

Another respondent (10E), who believes the pro-free trade position is not fully grounded in economic science, also says that it is a plausible but not conclusive jump to the pro-free trade conclusion.

1. The pro-free trade argument in its simplist form—two nation, two commodity, static—has a pretty strong basis in logic. But it is a conclusion drawn from an abstraction in the extreme. Further, it is based on an implicit assumption regarding the joint welfare of the two countries.
2. There is an understandable tendency to generalize to the real world from this simple abstraction—multiple products, multiple nations, unequal parties, confused national priorities.
3. There is no comparable, neat logical model which points toward protection as a desirable policy even in the simple or more complex cases.
4. The logic of the simple case fits mostly the biases of economics and economists; thus it was easy for them to jump quickly (and perhaps in error) from the "provable" simple case to the conclusions they wanted (expected) in the general case.
5. "Free trade" provides *an* answer. No set of policies suggests *complete* protection; it was considerably easier to go with *a* plausible answer rather than be faced with defining an optimum level and type of protection.
6. As "science," this suggests a high degree of inexactness and some unscientific jumping-to-conclusions. A great deal has been done to try to spell out the meaning of assumptions, the distribution of the benefits, the changes wrought if explicit voting priorities are entered. These seek modification to the imperfect first approximation. They don't make for "more" scientific conclusions but "better" conclusions as they derive from better science.

When asked whether the foregoing is positive or normative economics, 10E wrote: "I think that it probably starts out positive (i.e., simple 2x2 model). But as it progresses to the more complex real world and skips from both may benefit to both do benefit, then the conclusions read are those which fit the values of the expounders rather than the elucidation of all possible outcomes. It is positive in a loose sort of way at the outset, becoming more sloppy and more value-determined as the logical niceties are relaxed. Not a very tight answer."

A group of respondents quite in conflict with the first seven argues that there is no possible justified and conclusive relation between the pro-free trade position and economics as a science. Respondent 11AE says that "economics is concerned with the allocation of scarce resources among competing ends. The science of economics does not define the end. Equation of economics as a science with free trade implies that maximum 'output' is the only valid end." Two others claim that no science can be identified with a particular paradigm (12AE) or with a particular doctrinal position (13E), the latter saying that "no one 'position' is the 'scientific position.' " Respondent 12AE writes: "It appears to me that if the status of any science—as a science—is dependent upon specific paradigm being embraced, the claim of scientific inquiry is in fact negated. My conception of science follows closely the ideas of Leslie White, John Dewey, Jacob Bronowski, Thomas Kuhn, et al. . . . Science, in this context, is thought to be an activity wherein the most important component is the need for continual re-evaluation and, if appropriate, rejection of existing paradigms. The failure to reject concepts and ideas which have outgrown their usefulness leads to the establishment of a religion—not a science." Respondent 13E stated that "a case can be made effectively that free trade doctrines are of a particular time."

The two previous writers are echoed in respondent 14E's statement that he disagrees with any view which "suggests that 'free trade' is the only sound position for an economist. . . . To teach 'free trade' to the exclusion of any other position is no more sound than to teach only one side of any question which is controversial or debatable. It also does not take account of the world as it exists today." A quite different position, but to the same negative effect, is taken by respondent 15E: "Economics is a science only to the extent that it can predict and 'explain' observable phenomena." (This view is also close to that of respondents 20–24. Compare it, however, with that of respondent 6.) Another writer (16E) replies simply: "No relationship." Much stronger views are offered by one respondent (17E), who writes: "You give a curious and telling example of the perennial character of neo-classical economics: the effort to dress up an ideology with the garb of pure science—with no real idea of the character of science, but only of its superficial forms. Thus mathematizing of the discipline today." Another (18E) is of the view that "Perry was engaged in 'scientism' not science." He does not believe that a study of economics proceeding upon an assumption of protection is any less scientific than that of free trade.

One respondent (19E) would have nothing directly to do with the relation of free trade and economics as a science. Nevertheless, his position is clear: Arguing that Samir Amin's *Accumulation on a World Scale*[19] presents "a definitive explanation of world trade (neoclassical style) as world exploitation," 19E believes that neoclassical trade theory fails to capture or explain the forces operative in international trade in a world of state and corporate imperialism.

Another major group of respondents, concentrated in agricultural economics, takes the general position that economics cannot advocate a position but can describe the likely consequences of alternative policies, a view compatible with several earlier responses. Respondent 20AE writes: "Free trade like any welfare economics proposition is value selective and presumptive. To describe the distributive consequences of free trade is scientific. To advocate free trade without making explicit the interests to be counted is not scientific." (Also see responses 25–27.) A similar view is stated by respondent 21AE: "As a science economics should strive to identify the magnitude and distribution of benefits and costs associated with different institutions regulating trade under different situations. There is no scientific—that is, objective—basis for a universal conclusion favoring free trade. Teaching free trade would thus be inconsistent with the values we usually associate with science." Respondent 22AE believes that educators (even those who favor free trade) should present the arguments for both sides. He also feels that the economist can explain, presumably scientifically, why protectionism is so widespread (largely, he feels, because producer interests are so politically powerful). "This is not necessarily an argument for protectionism, although economists should be able to analyze the cost of the [protectionist] status quo versus free trade and let the general public and elected officials decide on the trade-offs." A similar role is advocated by respondent 23AE, who adds that extreme partisanship by economists would render them useless in the evaluation of policy alternatives and would not make "full use of our talents as economists." The last of this group (24E) writes as follows:

> Where some policy goals clearly favor free trade, economic science helps by exposing the self-serving role of trade restraints and how it favors the

> selected. But there are goals which conflict with free trade, and ignoring them or saying they should be consigned to the dustbin makes free trade a normative prescription and a religion.
>
> The role of economic science is merely to illuminate the consequences of changes in trade restrictions—consequences as one proceeds towards more and more liberalization or as one becomes more and more protective. Addiction to some normative goals has generally hindered the process.
>
> Even the word "free" trade, like "free" collective bargaining, hinders science and objective discussion because things get loaded. Nothing is really "free" except within a framework of initial endowments, etc. The word is best left out if economics is to progress as a science. (I write as a man strongly in favor of liberalization of trade, etc., particularly among LDCs.)

Two respondents focused on the recognized and not-so-neat distinction (as one of them puts it) between exposition and advocacy (a distinction present in several earlier responses). Respondent 2E declared:

> I start from the position that economics isn't a science, because in economics we are unable to conduct controlled experiments with which we can test hypotheses and establish theories and laws. We come close, to be sure, in that we can observe behavior and state hypotheses and tentative generalizations. Our predictive power, unlike that of a bona fide science, is not impressive.
>
> Assuming that economics aspires to be a science, one supposes that an important aspect of economics would be that it be value-free. From that it would seem to follow that if an economist examined the effects of free trade upon the world-wide level of output from available resources and concluded that free trade would yield optimal allocation of resources and consequently optimal output, then the economist would become an expositor of the advantages of free trade, but not an advocate of it.
>
> Advocacy of a position does not seem to be consistent with scientific inquiry, as I understand the nature of science.
>
> I should think that an economist would stand on firm ground as a student of economic relationships if, as Keynes did, he or she pointed out the short-run sacrifices espousal of free trade would expose a nation to if other countries were exporting their unemployment. In such a case, the economist, while explaining the ramifications of a free trade position under those particular circumstances, provides ammunition to the soldiers in the protectionist army. But that's not the same thing as teaching/advocating protectionism.

The other respondent (26E) wrote: "What the scientist can say is that free trade is a precondition to maximizing the value of output from given resources and techniques (for the country and for the world), under certain conditions which are not too hard to approximate in the real world. Interferences with free trade can benefit certain groups, but at the expense of other groups and of the total value product. Is this being pro-free trade?"

Only one respondent (27AE) analyzed the relation of free trade to economics as a science in terms specifically of the conflict between positive and normative economics and also of the conditional nature of propositions.

> Are free trade advocacy and economics as science incompatible?
>
> Light can be shed on this question from two directions. First is the purely philosophical and second is the philosophical combined with economic theory.
>
> An economist whose philosophical stance is positivism would argue that any normative position (advocacy or otherwise) is nonobjective and therefore nonscientific. The true positivist, who argues that normative facts and experience simply do not exist, would also reject that part of the economics discipline known as welfare economics. To be true to his position he would also need to reject normative economic theories of behavior and value concepts such as prices. Thus to the strict positivist economist free trade advocacy and scientific economics are incompatible. But such a philosophic position for an economist, particularly a policy economist, is sterile.
>
> An economist willing to embrace normativism at least to the extent of recognition of the existence of normative facts and experience (i.e., facts and experience about values) has a somewhat different perspective. He along with his positivist brother would argue that under perfectly competitive conditions, free trade by all nations provides the most efficient allocation of resources to productive activities. He would go on to say that if performance criteria [are] based on allocative efficiency alone then free trade conditions by all nations [are] (along with perfectly competitive domestic economies) the way to achieve the allocative efficiency objective. In addition, since the normativist will recognize welfare economic theory as valid, he must conclude that equity objectives may or may not be served by free trade per se. And even more difficult is the question if (as in the real world) the starting point is one in which various nations are engaging in some form of protectionism. Then, any movement from the status quo either toward protectionism or toward freer trade by one or many nations will leave some nations and some individuals within nations worse off than they were before. The economist can assess the costs and benefits of a movement from the status quo using a common denominator—the poli-

tician must determine the weights to place on that common denominator for interpersonal validity and to determine the net welfare changes.

Are free trade advocacy and economics as a science incompatible?

Yes, if you are a positivist.

No, if you are a normativist and allocative efficiency is your only criterion.

Maybe, if you are a normativist and your criteria are both allocative efficiency and equity.

But in your advocacy you step outside the bounds of what you can objectively say about the specific case using knowledge from economic theory including welfare economics.

Seminar Reactions

In April 1978, the responses to my inquiry, plus a preliminary version of the next section of this article, were presented to a faculty-student seminar at Michigan State University. Discussion was held after each phase of the presentation. Most comments centered on the responses and on an effort to pose scientifically meaningful propositions about free trade.

Numerous points were raised about the original query itself. Some remarked that since there was likely to be great variability of individual views on the subject over time, some idea of distribution (with an indication of central tendency) would have been preferable to single-headed responses. Others noted that semantic differences may obscure greater unanimity than appeared in the responses. Some suggested that the query itself should have been more specific, to preclude respondents' answering, in effect, different questions. Several said that the responses to the single query, while interesting, were limited in significance given the complexity of the issues involved and the smallness of the sample. All who participated in the discussion indicated an awareness of the profound importance of the general question of the nature of economics as a science and its relation to policy matters. Some seemed determined that economics be considered a science; others were less concerned with the point; a few insisted to the contrary. Despite substantive disagreements, they seemed to concur that the query had elicited most if not all of the considerations entering into the matter.

Seminar discussion on the nature of science was sporadic and largely subordinate to the question of the possibility and substance of purely positive statements. Among the aspects attributed to "science" were: internal logic and coherence, predictive ability, dealing with universals, if-then relations, if-then relations "which people don't burst out laughing about," explaining a system on its own terms, empirical analysis, alternative inferences from alternative premises, a set of tools, and knowledge of what is impossible and of the effective means of achieving goals. There was little argument as such over these characteristics of science but clear disagreement as to their present applicability and as to whether free trade analysis qualified as science according to any or all of them. The view was expressed by one person (and perhaps silently held by others) that economists should do their work, not worry about being scientific, and certainly not engage in self-flagellation over it. This opinion diverged sharply from the apparently widespread concern in the seminar that economics be recognized as science. The general focus of this disagreement was the question of whether free trade statements were scientific.

Some discussion centered on the claim that the Pareto optimal exposition of free trade was positive economics: There were a set of Pareto optimal results, free trade leads to one optimal result, and free trade plus lump-sum transfers leads to another. Some felt that Pareto optimality itself was normative; others felt that although that was true, propositions which stated that an arrangement was or led to a Pareto optimal result were positive and scientific. There seemed to be agreement that, regardless of that divergence, to go beyond such a proposition and advocate free trade was normative. But there was ambiguity with regard to whether or not and in what sense such a proposition itself justified free trade.

Contention arose over the proposition that free trade leads to the maximization of the value of output (in the GNP sense of goods with prices attached) as opposed to the advocacy of free trade (say, because it maximizes the value of output). Some viewed the former as positive and scientific, the latter as normative, requiring an additional normative premise. Most of this discussion dealt with whether value maximization was a value. Some believed that statements of the form "free trade leads to such and such results" were positive and scientific, not normative. Others believed that value-maximization statements are normative. They argued, first, that *maximization* per se is normative, involving interpersonal utility comparisons and adoption of value of output maximization as the social welfare function. Second, *value* maximization (1) as the object of economic science is normative (even if not the value of the analyst); (2) is not unequivocally the object of the economic system; (3) as the choice of model or paradigm for analysis is normative; and (4) can be interpreted as a mask for bourgeois domination of the world economy, or as functioning to obscure the dependence of resource allocation upon income, wealth, and power distributions. Third, both the definitions and weighting of output by utility functions are a function of rights and are normative. Fourth, value maximization, therefore, is conditional upon and tautological with certain inevitable normative premises, such that the proposition that free trade leads to the maximization of the value of output is normative.

Seminar participants also were asked whether the proposition that "a tax cut will have a change of a certain probable magnitude on investment" is positive in the same sense that "free trade will result in the maximum value of output" is positive (given their different testability). Some believed that the two statements were epistemologically identical; others thought that the latter was distinctively normative for the reasons given above, particularly because it dealt with maximization. The issue seemed to reduce to this: Are prices purely descriptive subject to initial resource distributions, power, and so forth? Is the following a scientific, positive proposition: Given weights and prices, free trade will maximize the value of output.

Interpretation

Economics is much more a system of belief than it is a corpus of verified logical positivist knowledge. What economists actually believe is no less important than what they "should" believe on the basis of verified fact and/or methodological or normative principle. Indeed, it may be more important; they think, research, consult, and advise on the basis of actual belief, however grounded or substantiated.

The responses to my query, *qua responses*, can be interpreted as follows. First, no single or stylized answer was given. Rather, there was considerable diversity, especially regarding arguing with respect to policy on a "scientific" basis. This diversity echoes that of the 1870–1914 period, although the latter-day responses are somewhat more sophisticated.

Second, there is considerable explicit and implicit diversity as to the meaning of economics as a "science." Five points may be made in this respect. (1) Among the various conceptions are deductive theory, predictive empiricism, the combination of these two (logical positivism), and something best termed "specialized intensive study."

(2) Interestingly, only one respondent invoked and applied the specific distinction between positive and normative economics. Several others took positions on this point when queried further, but only respondent 27 explicitly introduced this consideration. The overwhelming majority did not appear to think of the relation between free trade doctrine and economics as a science in terms of this distinction, although the stress by many

upon the inability of economics properly to do more than describe the performance consequences of various policies may constitute an implicit emphasis.

(3) The great majority (but not all) of the respondents seem to be saying that the free trade position is not positive but normative economics. Even among those who believe that the pro-free trade position is grounded in economics, not all think that the grounding is in positive economics. The question is, of course, of enormous epistemological importance for the probative or truth value of a doctrine.

(4) With regard to the refutation criterion of scientific work, some seem to believe that economists can rely upon economic science to support free trade precisely because it *is* a refutable positive science. Others believe that economists cannot so rely upon economic science precisely because it is *only* a refutable positive science and nothing more, that is, it does not permit the normative leap from explanation of what is to prescription of what ought to be.

(5) A further and extremely important question concerns the identity of *normative economics* as a *science*. It would appear that about 80 percent of respondents believe that economics, either generally or in relation to the free trade doctrine, is a normative and not a positive science. But such emphasis on the normative character of economics must lead to exploration and explication of the grounds on which normative economics is to be differentiated from "lay" views on policy. Presumably, the difference lies neither in the superiority of economists' normative insights nor in the strictly positive nature of economic doctrine, but in the advantage of specialized intensive study accruing to professional economists. But is normative economics *science,* and if so, in what sense? Thus, on both questions —whether economics in relation to the free trade doctrine is positive or normative economics, and whether normative economics is a science— there seems to be considerable diversity of opinion among respondents. To the extent that specialized intensive study constitutes the *differentia specifica* of normative economics as a science, then it would appear that the combination, *inter alia,* of professional training (investiture in a particular mode of belief or paradigm) and social acculturation produces a general belief system to which the substance of formal economic analysis (by whatever specific definition) relates as reinforcing cause and consequence. There clearly is tension between the obligation of economists to apply the results of their disciplined study *and* their perception and felt obligation of objectivity as the crux of positive science. The predominant view seems to cast serious doubt on the viability, recommendatory force, relevance, and meaningfulness (in accordance with the belief system of

economists themselves) for policy of wide ranges of normative economics. Much implicit doubt is cast on the practice of seeking "optimal" solutions. Many uses of normative economics, perhaps the entire corpus of the subject as such, may represent only the clothing of normativism with the garments of science, confusing the social role of analyst with that of moral teacher, priest, and advocate.

Third, there are obvious differences among the respondents as to the proper social role of economists, although most seem to favor a relatively active role in one form or another. Some distinguish between description and advocacy; others do not. There is wide acceptance of the view that economic analysis can (only) describe the likely consequences of various policies without directly assessing their merits. There is much less acceptance of, and some marked opposition to, the view that economists should support the free trade doctrine as a matter of scientific or professional obligation.

Finally, as to the relation of the pro-free trade position and the nature of economics as a science, there is broad disagreement as to the authoritativeness and confidence with which an economist can speak to the free trade issue as a policy question. There are enormous differences as to whether economics can properly address the policy issue at all; what economics can say on the issue, assuming it can speak to it; what considerations are relevant; and, *inter alia,* the substance of any value premises involved. Among those who believe that economics properly can directly address the policy issue, there are quite different grounds for finding that economics as a science supports the free trade position. Most if not all respondents seem to recognize the real world limits to the usefulness of theory for policy (for example, second-best considerations).

In sum, economists as a group apparently are much more circumspect and their views on the scientific status of free trade much more heterogeneous than the doctrinal position with which they generally are identified would lead one to believe.

It would appear that economics is a system of belief, far from homogeneous. It might behoove individual economists, if only to communicate better among themselves, to clarify the sense in which they adhere to certain concepts, such as positive and normative economics, science, and world value-of-output maximization through free trade.

The central issue separating large groups of respondents was the epistemological status of the two principal lines of reasoning, namely, that free trade leads to the Pareto optimum and that free trade results in the maximization of the value of output. The usual procedure is to ask whether these statements are positive or normative. Such a query inevitably seems to place the believer in their positive status on the defensive, as whatever positive qualities the statements may have are threatened. Positive and normative are considered mutually exclusive categories with regard to particular propositions. It would seem preferable to inquire, instead, into the normative elements which define or limit the *sense* in which a proposition is positive. The problem of identifying normative elements long has been neglected and is fraught with difficulties, in part due to the disagreement about the ways in which normative elements enter into positive propositions.[20] In the remainder of this article I shall suggest the normative elements which delimit and render *conditional* the positive character of the two lines of reasoning.[21]

Conclusion

Let me specify the use of certain terms. A statement is *positive* if it is (an attempt at) objective, confirmable, and descriptive of *is* knowledge. A statement is *normative* if it contains an element of choice and in some respects this incorporates an *ought* element. The statement, for example, that "consumers have such and such preferences" is a positive proposition. Preferences are themselves normative (a matter of choice), but the observer-analyst can treat them as an object of positive knowledge. Similarly, the economy operates to allocate resources (which is normative, a matter of choice), but the observer-analyst can treat its operation and the resultant allocation as an object of positive knowledge. From the point of view of the consumer-participants, the preferences and the allocation are normative, a matter of choice. The observer can analyze in a positive manner the prices which emerge in the market; for the analyst, the prices are objective givens, but price data as such are normative. From the point of view of the economy, the prices are normative: They emerge, in part, from the interplay of consumer preferences and represent, in Joseph Schumpeter's words, coefficients of choice. Given the sense(s) in which preferences, allocation, and prices are normative (not all of which are noted above), the positive economist must be careful in formulating statements. Normative elements readily enter, and they are of at least two kinds: those analytically a part of the proposition, and those which tend to accrue to the meaning attached to the proposition by the nature of its use.

Let us consider the proposition that free trade leads to a Pareto optimal result. At least four normative elements are involved. First, the choice of Pareto optimality as the relevant (normative) category is itself normative. The statement establishes a normative category (Pareto optimality) and identifies (within the limits of its technical assumptions, for example, second-best considerations, and its nature as a paradigm or model) something as coming within or leading to it (free trade). The systematic use by economists of Pareto optimality excludes (and may obscure) other normative categories (and can be manipulated to do so in a selective way). The Pareto criterion is not "minimally" normative, as is sometimes alleged; it is no less normative than any other rule; it has a distinctive normative thrust in favor of the status quo in which its use is (selectively) made.[22] The Pareto optimum character of free trade can, in fact, coexist with lines of reasoning in which free trade is identified as part of a system of power and domination; that is, both the Pareto optimal character of the voluntary exchange under free trade and the nature of free trade as an instrument or adjunct of international power play can be simultaneously positive (and, *arguendo,* true) propositions. Emphasis on one to the exclusion of the other is itself normative. Pareto optimality analysis expresses a point of view, or certain values, and functions as a guide to conduct (policy), especially when used exclusively. The very use of the Pareto criterion as the relevant frame of reference (say, in contrast to the Pigovian approach) *tends* to lead to assuming the propriety of the status quo power structure within which voluntary exchange takes place and thereby to reinforcing same.

Second, any move from a restricted to a free trade policy is itself non-Pareto optimal.

Third, there is no one Pareto optimal solution. Each is specific to the power structure (set of entitlements) from which it arises. Different power structures may adopt free trade, and each will yield a different Pareto optimal solution. Different power structures may adopt a regime of lump-sum transfers (and so on), and each will yield a different Pareto optimal solution. In order for any specific such solution to have recommendatory force, there must be an additional normative premise relating to the propriety of the initial and resultant distributions of income, wealth, and power.

Fourth, the proposition that free trade results in a Pareto optimal solution is nonoperational, nontestable, and nonrefutable. It is a matter of logic. Pareto optimality is one characteristic of an equilibrium solution in which voluntary exchange exists. Both free and unfree trade (say, with tariffs, quotas, and lump-sum transfers) involve voluntary exchange. Given the assumption of constrained maximization (rationality) by economic actors, trade will be conducted up to the point at which there are no further mutual gains from trade and one person can gain only with a loss to another. Thus, the Pareto optimal result of free trade is implicit in the premises of voluntary exchange and constrained maximization; there is thus a logical implication or a tautology. In either case, it is nonrefutable.

I conclude that *given* these normative elements and the technical limits of the statement, the statement that free trade results in a Pareto optimal result is "positive." (Notice that I also have abstracted from an array of technical assumptions, including an implicit assumption concerning the marginal utility functions of persons in the different trading nations.) Free trade *does* result in a Pareto optimal solution. The significance of that proposition/assertion is constrained and made conditional by the factors added above which delimit the sense in which an efficient solution is efficient.

Let us now consider the proposition that free trade will maximize the value of output. What are the normative elements which constrain and make conditional the positive content of the proposition? (1) The choice of maximization of value of output as the presumed objective of the economic system is normative. (2) There is no one maximum value of output. It varies, and noncomparably, with price structure and output definitions. These latter and the weighting of output by utility functions are dependent upon and generally specific to rights and are normative.[23] The price structure is a function of and specific to the income, wealth, and power structures of society and is normative. Maximization within and specific to the income, wealth, and power structures which produce specific prices for specific output definitions is normative. (3) Maximization of the value of output involves index number problems whose solutions are normative. (4) The income, wealth, and power consequences of value of output maximization are normative. (5) Maximization of the value of output is a deductive implication which is nonoperational, nontestable, and nonrefutable.

I conclude that *given* these normative elements and the technical limits of the statement, the statement that free trade results in a maximum value of output is "positive." *Given* normative prices, *inter alia,* free trade *does* maximize the value of output. The significance of that proposition/assertion is constrained and made conditional by the factors adduced above which delimit the sense in which value maximization takes place.

It is obvious that economists will differ in the recommendatory force which they attribute to the two propositions, given the conditional impact of the normative elements.

In conclusion, it would appear that there inevitably are normative facets to social science propositions.[24] Very little can be said with regard to free trade which does not have normative elements. The meaningfulness of otherwise ostensibly positive *is* propositions is conditional upon the identification of the normative elements. I suspect that if economists recognized and engaged in the practice of specifying those normative elements which condition the positive status of propositions, there would be somewhat, perhaps considerably, less diversity of views as to the relation of economic analysis to policy. Moreover, they would acquire the habit of recognizing the *senses* in which propositions are positive and normative, respectively.

Notes

1. See Warren J. Samuels, "Ideology in Economics," in *Modern Economic Thought,* edited by Sidney Weintraub (Philadelphia: University of Pennsylvania Press, 1977), pp. 467–84.
2. It is comforting to remember that our problems were shared by our predecessors, but possibly discomforting to recognize that we may have progressed no farther.
3. C. E. Collet, "Professor Foxwell and University College," *Economic Journal* 46 (December 1936): 616. Collet is quoting from notes made during a lecture by Foxwell.
4. Warren J. Samuels, "Ashley's and Taussig's Lectures on the History of Economic Thought at Harvard, 1896–1897," *History of Political Economy* 9 (Fall 1977): 405.
5. Narmadeshwar Jha, *The Age of Marshall,* 2d ed. (London: Cass, 1973), p. 200.
6. Joseph A. Schumpeter, *History of Economic Analysis* (New York: Oxford University Press, 1954), p. 830.
7. F. Y. Edgeworth, "Reminiscences," in *Memorials of Alfred Marshall,* edited by A. C. Pigou (London: Macmillan, 1925), p. 67.
8. Leslie Stephen, *Social Rights and Duties* (New York: Macmillan, 1896), p. 113; see pp. 113–14, 123–24.
9. Ibid., p. 114.
10. Ibid., p. 127.
11. Charles F. Dunbar, "The Reaction in Political Economy," *Quarterly Journal of Economics* 1 (October 1886): 20–23.
12. Charles F. Dunbar, "The Academic Study of Political Economy," *Quarterly Journal of Economics* 5 (July 1891): 403–404.
13. Francis A. Walker, "Recent Progress of Political Economy in the United States," American Economic Association, *Publications, First Series,* vol. 4 (1889), p. 19. "The economist is now known to all as an economist, on whichever side of the Atlantic Ocean or of the British Channel he may live, or whatever views he may hold as to free trade or protection" (pp. 22–23).
14. James Bonar, *Disturbing Elements in the Study and Teaching of Political Economy* (Baltimore: Johns Hopkins University Press, 1911), pp. 53–54. On the broader issue, see Henry Sidgwick, *The Principles of Political Economy*, 2d ed. (New York: Macmillan, 1887), p. 13, note 1: "I think it may be said that, at least in nine cases out of ten, when reference is made by public speakers or journalists to the laws of Political Economy, it is

implied that Political Economy *prescribes* 'freedom of contract,' and does not merely assume it as a condition of the applicability of its conclusions." See also pp. 23–24.

15. Schumpeter, *History of Economic Analysis,* pp. 806–807.
16. Bernard Moses, "Certain Tendencies in Political Economy," *Quarterly Journal of Economics* 11 (July 1897): 380–81.
17. The responses have been subject to minor editing. See also the third section of this article.
18. Respondent 5E cites Paul A. Samuelson, "The Gains from International Trade," *Canadian Journal of Economics and Political Science* 5 (May 1939): 195–205.
19. In two volumes (New York: Monthly Review Press, 1974).
20. See Samuels, "Ideology in Economics," and book review of Glenn L. Johnson and Lewis K. Zerby, *What Economists Do about Values* (East Lansing: Center for Rural Manpower and Public Affairs, Michigan State University, 1973), *Journal of Economic Issues* 11 (December 1977): 901–903.
21. The nature of conditional normativism is developed in Johnson and Zerby, *What Economists Do*; see Samuels, book review.
22. See Samuels, "Ideology in Economics," and "Welfare Economics, Power and Property," in *Perspectives of Property,* edited by Gene Wunderlich and W. L. Gibson, Jr. (University Park: Institute for Research on Land and Water Resources, Pennsylvania State University, 1972), pp. 61–148.
23. Output definitions as a function of rights (power) are discussed in Warren J. Samuels, "Normative Premises in Regulatory Theory," *Journal of Post Keynesian Economics* 1 (Fall 1978): 100–114.
24. A further example: Consider the two propositions that "markets allocate resources" and that "markets produce an optimal allocation of resources." Both, although in the "is" form, are normative in the sense that they abstract from or exclude consideration of the power (income, wealth, rights) structure which operates through the market to produce an allocation specific to the power structure. The latter is also normative in the sense that it adopts a particular normative category (as discussed earlier in the text). There is a marked tendency in economics to treat as positive those propositions which deal with allegedly unambiguous welfare gains within the ambit of Pareto optimality. This is normative in the senses noted above in the text.

22

The Emptiness of Peasant "Rationality": "Demirationality" as an Alternative

John Adams

In his Nobel lecture, entitled "The Economics of Being Poor," Theodore W. Schultz said, "Poor people are no less concerned about improving their lot and that of their children than rich people are." He also said, "It is now well documented that in agriculture poor people do respond to better opportunities."[1] In other portions of his talk Schultz covered familiar Schultzian ground. He stressed the importance of the qualitative aspects of labor and lambasted "government-induced distortions," especially in the agricultural sector. The main theme, however, is the price and profit responsiveness of peasants and their entrepreneurial capabilities. It is probably too late to ask the committee to repossess the award, and in any case it is no more curious than a number made since the institution of the economics citation. But it is not too late to take a hard look at the Schultzian doctrine and its policy import.

Schultz's claim is that peasants are as rational as the rest of us; that they respond to price, cost, and profit signals in the market place; and that, as a guide to policy, their responsiveness means that proper market signals are a sufficient condition for innovation in agriculture and agricultural development. I would like to challenge each of these propositions in turn and also confront some of the evidentiary bases upon which they rest. I would argue that peasants *are* as rational as the rest of us but would insist that in all cases—us and peasants—one can at best talk about a qualified *in situ* economic rationality, which for want of a better term I will call "demirationality." By demirational I mean not exactly half rational but something less than purely rational, and that economic rationality must be considered in context; there is an economic interest but it flickers like a candle, sometimes burning intensely, sometimes waning. I would argue secondly that the price responsiveness studies on which Schultz and others have relied to make their claims of rationality are flawed, mixed in results, and essentially irrelevant even if taken at face value. Lastly, I would assert that as a basis for policy formulation in agriculture and as a theory of development the rational peasant view fails.

Let me begin the case by reciting at some length three reports from field workers about behavior in peasant societies.

Case #1: Treatment of Diarrhea in South India

In South India childhood diarrhea is associated with infant ingestion of "hot" foods, such foods not being either physically warm or spicy but rather classified as such according to an elaborate belief system that touches many other parts of society. Restoration of health can be achieved by taking in a balance of "cold" foods or drinks. A drink of sugar water would be a readily available therapeutic but sugar is classified as "hot." Severe diarrheal dehydration is recognized as a separate condition that results when a mother feeds her baby after seeing, perhaps unknowingly, a woman who has had a miscarriage. In this instance chants and thread-tying are indicated.

An impasse between modern and traditional belief systems led to the following story:

> An 11-month child began having frequent watery stools and occasional vomiting . . . . The next day the child was brought to the clinic and given sugar water with salt. (Later) the child was taken to a traditional medical practitioner, who concluded that the infant's condition resulted from the mother's breast feeding of the child after she had seen a woman who had a miscarriage. He said some chants, did a thread-tying procedure, and recommended that the baby remain at home. The child continued to vomit and pass watery stools. (Five days later) the baby became very restless, hitting his head against the floor and grinding his teeth. At about 8:00 p.m., the mother found him dead.[2]

Case #2: Caste Structure of Villages and Agriculture

Caste ranking in India depends on the numerical size of the membership (since force ultimately matters in disputes), on social position as defined by Hindu doctrine and pollution rules, and on the caste's economic base: land, water, herds, skills, and other assets. It is generally recognized that different castes and villages with different caste structures respond differently to innovation opportunities, as the following report based on field research attests:

> All three attributes of caste dominance—numerical, hierarchical, and economic—have relevance for agricultural development. Numerical dominance contributes to the homogeneity of the village population in terms of caste and ritual status which in turn insures close interaction and diffusion of innovative ideas. The ritual status of upper castes makes their members shun direct involvement in agriculture in terms of management and labor. The castes with low ritual status lack skill, motivation, and capital to invest in agriculture. The agricultural castes, on the other hand, have both capital, although of a limited scale, and skills and interest to achieve maximum return. Their position in the caste hierarchy enables them not to consider manual labor as demeaning to their socioritual status. Finally, their economic dominance, in terms of ownership of a large share of locally available land and large-sized farms, contributes to relatively more efficient use of land and higher agricultural productivity.[3]

Case #3: Backward-Bending Supply Curves in Malaysia

A report on the behavior of three sets of rice farmers in Malaysia concluded:

> The results indicate that in a subsistence economy farmers tend to behave in such a manner that their incomes gravitate toward a minimum-subsistence level. In this sense they are behaving according to a backward-bending supply curve notion. Under these circumstances, it is possible to explain why yields and intensity in use of inputs varies from farm to farm, thus, one could simultaneously observe low marginal productivities and high ones in the same area. . . . [T]his paper has tried to indicate how socioeconomic factors such as farm size, tenancy, and 'subsistence needs' could influence input usage and thus affect productivity.[4]

This selection of three items from many hundreds of field reports is sufficient to show the kinds of complexities involved in studying behavior in peasant societies. Systems of folk thought touch not only medicine but also agriculture. Caste in South Asia, the latifundia system of Latin America, and communal tribal property rights in pasturage and tillage in Africa are important systems that impinge upon farming practices and farmer innovativeness. Risk and subsistence needs are powerful constraints on the willingness of self-reliant peasants to enter world markets in grains and commodities.

In saying that the idea of "rationality" is empty, what is meant is that it does not do justice to the multiplex character of the human mind, motivation, and social or economic condition, as depicted in these three cases and many others. The strength of the concept is perhaps that it insists that in some underlying way all people are the same—they can calculate their interests and act upon them. This is a welcome alternative to many colonial racial doctrines and to many early views in development economics of the peasant as a hopelessly inert drudge, to be saved only by being pulled headlong into industry down the Fei-Ranis labor conveyor belt. Still, in making this simplification all has been lost of what might most directly be called the "cultural content" of peasant life. The woman whose baby died was no less concerned about its recovery than would be a mother who believed sufficiently in the modern clinic. Neither understood the fundamental science at work, but an in-depth interview or questionnaire might well have shown underlying educational, attitudinal, or value differences between the two. Similarly, caste relates to too many things in rural India not to be implicated in sensitivity to and control of innovation possibilities. The farmer with the backward-bending supply curve behavior in Malaysia is trying to cope as best he can even if he is doing it differently than his neighbor who raises cash crops. Everyone is thus rational but everyone's behavior is conditioned by the interplay of cultural and attitudinal factors. There is no *content* in being rational. The content comes from the cultural and attitudinal realms and it is the interaction of those realms with specific economic circumstances that gives rise to observable behaviors about which something useful can be said.

An important illustration of the emptiness of the concept of rationality arises in field work when the question is faced as to what is being maximized. It is difficult to say when a peasant is maximizing profit since his land, labor, and other inputs are often not priced. Does he maximize his cash income, his vendable "surplus," or as one economist has curiously said, "his position?" One anthropologist found her peasants were maximizing their marginal revenue. Schultz himself said, as quoted above, that peasants "respond to better opportunities." (Is there a case where people have responded to "worse" opportunities?) Tautology or self-fulfilling premises are simply piled one upon the other. It is not sufficient as an escape hatch to say that peasants are maximizing utility in a complex equation that can include such things as status or power since there is no way to test such a statement, even indirectly. One can be aware of the calculus of constrained optimization and of simultaneous consideration of multiple desiderata and still not see these as solutions. Even D. Hopper's original statement upon which Schultz relied so heavily said that "in general each man comes close to doing the best he can with his knowledge and cultural background."[5] Is not this what we all do, even on our bad days? And so does my cat.

A major prop of Schultz's case has been a spate of studies showing that peasants are price responsive. My colleague Walter Neale likes to point out that such studies are biased in any case at the beginning because they after all select markets to study, and how could one have a market without supply and demand responses of some form?[6] Michael Lipton has noted that a peasant may make a rational at-the-time planting decision only to find himself the victim of lower, perhaps disastrously lower, income at harvest.[7] In an earlier review of the price responsiveness literature I remarked upon the patchwork character of the various findings.[8] Dependent variables cover the range from output and crop sales to acreage shifts. Explanatory variables include own prices with various lags, crossprices, and exogenous variables to control for such items as rainfall, irrigation, high yielding seeds and other innovations, and crop pests. Raj Krishna, upon whose work Schultz relied heavily, was quoted as summarizing thusly:

> Our results show . . . that in the determination of acreage, price alone was the important factor identified in the case of maize and sugarcane; price was a more important factor than yield (in terms of elasticities) in the case of cotton (desi); irrigation capacity was more important than price in the case of cotton (American), bajra and wheat (irrigated); yield was more important than price in the case of rice; and rainfall was almost all-important in the case of unirrigated wheat, barley, and gram.[9]

When one multiplies such findings by two dozen, trying to make any general sense is impossible. A valid conclusion is that Indian farmers do respond to price in the normal way under certain conditions, in certain periods, at certain times, for certain crops. What then might be drawn from this welter of findings for a priori use in theorization or for policy formulation is most unclear. The results are consistent, however, with the proposition that peasant market behavior is contingent upon a variety of specific concerns, many of which have deep ecological and cultural roots, varying by crop, and is also subject to short-run considerations such as a runaway boom in a new export crop—cotton, jute, or cocoa being cases in point in India and Africa. Exactly what one does about the instances where peasants may supply more at lower prices to keep incomes constant or not respond at all if risk is feared to a subsistence base—both in some sense rational reactions—is not clear. Nor is it clear what size a coefficient should be—usually statistical significance is taken as sufficient to prove the case—but what makes a Gujarati cotton supply response less than a Maharashtrian or Mississippian? To my knowledge no one has treated the supply elasticities themselves as dependent variables to be explained.

One way of alibi-ing for non-price-responsiveness has been to inject the risk factor. There is no doubt that this has been an important effort to put content into the hollow rationality construct. Risk is after all subjective but can be made objective to the degree that it relates to visible aspects of one's situation. There is some point in connecting observable risks with farmers' behavior. If farmers are taken as risk-averse or risk-takers for subjective reasons, however, we are once again plunged back into the projection of mentalistic constructs and taken away from the behavioral realm.

Furthermore, the rationalistic risk analyses never specify the precise risks involved. They operate in a simple, possibly Malthusian world in which subsistence economic man faces death by starvation if his crops (or labor) cannot bring in enough to survive. This fate could result from bad chance in the form of locusts or poor rainfall or could be due to miscalculation. The peasant does not take chances with his family's livelihood because his tried-and-true practices give him the best hope of survival. Only the most powerful inducements in the form of market prices and profit will draw him forth into the marketplace.

The two problems with this line of thought are that risk is not culturally defined and that indigenous systems for risk-bearing are not understood. It is probably principally in market systems of the capitalist sort that persons are permitted to fall out of the system at first mischance. In Africa peasants were generally considered as tribal members to have rights to cultivation and grazing irrespective of their efficiency or luck in using resources. Similarly, in India members of a cultivating caste were buoyed up by the general power and control over land and other assets of the caste as a whole. Non-landed persons in the village had some claims to support in bad times from what might most widely be called patronage. Even in a semi-commercial setting a farmer had recourse: selling jewelry or livestock, shifting from landowner to tenant, or even borrowing from a moneylender were options. (It is an often forgotten result that at least some of the time moneylenders must be paid back and peasants freed of temporary debt.) Grain was stored against hard times and the human body is capable of riding out a certain period of undernourishment. What failing in the traditional context meant was only the possible risk of slipping somewhat down the social and economic ladder, not Malthusian death. The fear is loss of face or place, not loss of life. Again, it is the social that is important, not the simple economic calculus. The lesson is, of course, that pushing innovation becomes a matter not of mere economic return but of the provision of modern insurance and social safety-net schemes as alternatives for those traditional ones lost with the move to the market.

Perhaps the best way to challenge the Schultzian stress on market rationality is to show that even if peasants are market responsive this is an insufficient base for economic development. Markets carry only one kind of information: price information. Price responsiveness is no guarantee of technological innovation since technological information must come through some other source or sources. As Yujiro Hayami and Vernon W. Ruttan argue, the American and Japanese experiences of agricultural development were predicated on massive public sector provision of research and extension services.[10] Their mass of related books and articles is both a critique of the simple Schultzian faith in the efficacy of markets and, to some extent, a reassertion of the importance of prices since relative factor scarcities thereby generate land-saving or labor-saving innovation. Nonetheless, it is plain that a vast public sector enterprise is needed to provide an administrative infrastructure within which agriculture can innovate. This is certainly the lesson of India's green revolution and of other Third World success as well. Incidentally, Hla Myint's discussion of the impact of markets on colonial economies following export booms in peasant and commercial crops reaches the same point: markets alone are not sufficient to generate and diffuse technological innovation.[11] At the end of the Cancún summit between leaders of the rich and poor lands, Julius Nyerere responded to Ronald Reagan's plea for unfettered free enterprise with the remark that American agriculture was the most heavily subsidized in the world. Others know us and our history better than our Presidents and Laureates sometimes do.

The rationality dictum thus fails both at the level of understanding peasant behavior and as a theory of development. Let us agree that we are all equally rational, given our time, place, and circumstances, and get on with understanding the variation in human behavior, even in the cheek-by-jowl neighborhoods of Indian farmers. Why is brother number one innovative and productive, a model farmer, and why is brother number two a profligate wastral, content to rackrent a succession of hapless tenants? Let us all agree that peasants, like us, are wise and foolish, sentient and blind, workaholics and sloths, risktakers and scared silly, entrepreneurial and gridlocked. We none of us work hard enough (said writing this on Sunday morning) or use our resources efficiently. Most are terminally X-inefficient and just plain inefficient besides. We do have an economic interest and it sometimes matters, at other times not. We have none of us given our babies all the sugar water they needed and are poorer than we see ourselves in our dreams, yet satisfied to be as well off as we are. We are dimly rational or demirational.

Whether India or another country experiences technological progress in its rural areas depends not exclusively on the play of economic interest but upon the relationship between technology and institutional and attitudinal systems. Hayami and Ruttan stress the public and political nature of the innovation process, but it is more vital to understand innovation as an individual confrontation between a new piece of technology and the peasants' varied views of and feelings about the social, economic, and ecological systems of which they are part and into which they each fit differently. This amounts to an evolutionary or instrumental view of peasant behavior. The peasant is perceived as responding in an active, individualistic way—with adroitness, sense, and judgement—to evolving systems around him. He is bound by habitual customs and habitual modes of thought but he is also "capable of intelligent response to changing realities."[12]

None of this denies the importance of positive or negative incentives or the sometime importance of the material interest. Neale says, "Of course new knowledge, inputs, technologies, and agencies are needed; and there must be incentives buttressed by appropriate opportunities. But these must fit into the existing if evolving institutions, or new institutions with quite different working rules must emerge—in either case, what is new must be provided according to the rules of *a* particular game, and the rewards (and the punishments) for plays of that game must be ones which lead to the effective adoption and adaptation of the new knowledge, inputs, technologies, and agencies."[13]

Kusum Nair has argued that cultural systems and subsystems do result in substantially different levels of efficiency across farmers and regions and similarly cause differential rates of innovation, not always in expected directions. In her recent book, *In Defense of the Irrational Peasant*, she compares the efficiency of Punjabi and Bihari agriculturalists. I will leave to the interested the pleasures of her trenchant volume but will end with a summary of her argument and three quotations.

Nair believes that inefficiency is built into much of Indian agriculture. How else to explain how some states do so much worse than others and so many individual farmers so much worse than others—who may do as well as the best in the world? She rejects the Schultzian reliance on simple market incentives: "Needed is an entirely different approach based on empirically proven premises and recognition of (a) the infinite diversity of factors that determine expressed behavior; and (b) the fact that the socio-psychological (and metaphysical) environment under which farmers live and work can never be cleansed of all constraints, especially in large heterogeneous societies. It cannot be done."

She argues for a system of incentives and disincentives that would induce those in agriculture to utilize their land and resources up to a reasonable standard:

> Instead of trying to orchestrate appropriate responses to national needs, priorities, and programs, by juggling the monetary incentives, the strategy would be to use the conventional market mechanisms, prices and taxes, to make it reasonably profitable, but also economically imperative at least for landowners who have the basic resources to cultivate the soil intensively and efficiently, even if the environment is not ideal—under less-than-optimal conditions. It would make it too costly, for instance, uneconomic for them *not* to sow on time; *not* to dig well and on-farm ditches for irrigation and drainage; *not* to water and fertilize the soil adequately—that is, *not* do all they can to maximize crop yields and yet survive as farmers and retain possession of the land.

Finally, I conclude as she concludes her Preface:

> Max Planck, the originator of the quantum theory in physics, once said that science makes progress funeral by funeral—the old are never converted by a new doctrine; simply replaced by a new generation. In the social sciences it often takes several generations to dislodge obsolescence. In the meantime, serious mistakes can be, and are made, hurting the lives of millions of hapless people. In poor countries, like India and Pakistan, the mistakes can be costly. And the funerals premature and unnecessary—funerals, not of social scientists, who usually operate from a secure haven, but of the designated beneficiaries of development policies formulated on the basis of faulty premises and paradigms.[14]

Notes

1. Theodore W. Schultz, "Nobel Lecture: The Economics of Being Poor," *Journal of Political Economy* 88 (1980): 639, 643.
2. Betsy Lozhoff et al., "Infection and Disease in South Indian Families: Beliefs about Childhood Diarrhea," *Human Organization* 34 (1975): 353–358.
3. Satadal Dasgupta, "Caste Dominance and Agricultural Development in Village India," *Human Organization* 34 (1975): 400–403. The selection of reports by Lozhoff et al. and Dasgupta from the same issue of the same journal was fortuitous and signifies neither the abundance nor scarcity of such reports.
4. Yukon Huang, "Backward-Bending Supply Curves and Behavior of Subsistence Farmers," *The Journal of Development Studies* 12 (1976): 191–211.

5. D. Hopper, "Allocation Efficiency in Traditional Indian Agriculture," *Journal of Farm Economics* 47 (1965): 611.
6. At some uncertain time and place and more than once thereafter.
7. Michael Lipton, "Should Reasonable Farmers Respond to Price Changes?" *Modern Asian Studies* 1 (1967): 99.
8. John Adams, "The Analysis of Rural Indian Economy: Economics and Anthropology," *Man in India* 52 (1972): 1–20. Bibliography A lists 26 price responsiveness studies for South Asia alone; there have been many others since and there are many from other regions.
9. Quoted in ibid.
10. Yujiro Hayami and Vernon W. Ruttan, *Agricultural Development: An International Perspective* (Baltimore: The Johns Hopkins University Press, 1971).
11. Hla Myint, *Economics of the Developing Countries* (London: Hutchinson, 1980; fifth ed., first published 1964).
12. James H. Street and Dilmus D. James, "Institutionalism, Structuralism, and Dependency in Latin America," Twelfth Atlantic Economic Conference, New York, New York, 8–11 October 1981, p. 1.
13. Walter C. Neale, "Institutional Analysis of the Development of South and Southeast Asia," Twelfth Atlantic Economic Conference, New York, New York, 8–11 October 1981, p. 7.
14. Kusum Nair, *In Defense of the Irrational Peasant: Indian Agriculture after the Green Revolution* (Chicago: University of Chicago Press, 1979), pp. xx–xxi, viii–ix.

23

The Myth is not the Reality: Income Maintenance and Welfare

David Hamilton

Fashions in economics are almost as fickle as those in dress and automobiles. Many of the economic ideas prevalent in the 1960s, and which admittedly had positive economic effects, such as those following the 1964 tax cut, are said today to be old hat. Economic and social conditions have in some mysterious manner in the intervening years so changed that what was once a feasible economic strategy is now held to be passé.

No evidence is brought forth to substantiate such a claim. It is based on strong assertion rather than on strong demonstration. The new ideas, just as in fashion, turn out to be those of five or six decades or even of a century and a half ago. J. M. Keynes is dead! Long live Adam Smith, J. B. Say, Jeremy Bentham, Herbert Spencer, and laissez faire!

So be it with the matter of income maintenance. The fond hopes of eliminating utter degrading poverty, expressed in the mid-sixties, have given way to the meanness that characterizes social welfare administration and what was more properly known as "charity" in the nineteenth century and before. Those notions have been refurbished and put forth as something newly discovered.[1] All of us in the long sweep of history have but a momentary appearance and, hence, of necessity a short memory: with a sense of history learned rather than experienced we are perfectly set up for the latest in fashion. Our shapers of public opinion at the moment are shaping public fashion, not the long-range public mind. But to deal with real problems we must strip them of the fashionable myths and humbug that hide their stark reality.

The popular myth of the time leads us to believe that income maintenance, a large component of the welfare state, is a function of misplaced sentiment for the welfare of the poor. And, although well meaning, it is misplaced because it worsens a problem that lies in the flawed characters of the victims. It is the victims who are responsible for bringing on their own downfall, much as it is alleged that rape victims provoke their attackers.[2] For every one of those who take the term "welfare mess" to mean that welfare is poorly administered and mean in spirit, there are two or more who interpret the phrase to mean that the mess is inherent in the concept of welfare itself. The latter critics do not differ in outlook more than a hair's breadth from the Malthusian and Ricardian critics of the poor laws more than a century and a half ago. Both argue in essence that any welfare program, with the possible exception of that provoked by begging, corrupts its beneficiaries. It hurts them worse than it hurts the hesitant giver. Spare the charity and save the child!

Both the past and the present critics have a wholly distorted picture of just how income maintenance systems came to be in an industrial economy—or in any economy for that matter. In one sense all societies are systems of income maintenance, tribal societies with a paleolithic industrial art no less so than contemporary mass societies with machine, or perhaps computer, industrial art. There are not orphans in the Highlands of New Guinea. Their kinship structure is such that no one is left without some income, whether able to participate actively in the work force or not.

Sometimes in the popular treatment of such matters myth and fancy serve in the place of knowledge. From time to time we are treated to the Eskimo-elder story. We are told that the Eskimos leave an elderly kinsman blocked up in an igloo with two (sometimes three, depending upon the teller) day's supply of blubber. And indeed in some of the recordings of Eskimo culture such events are noted. But the true circumstances are otherwise. The Eskimo peoples followed the caribou and when the caribou went south, to elude the suddenly freezing winters, the Eskimo went south. Sometimes, an elderly and very feeble member of the tribe, feeling unable or unwilling to make one more move, would plead to be left behind. To go, slowing the journey of the others, would have jeopardized the entire family unit.[3] Only under these circumstances did the Eskimos ever leave the elderly and it was with flagging hearts that they did no. The Eskimo, no less than any other society, was an income maintenance system.

Our distortion of medieval feudalism also leads us astray in interpreting that society. We emphasize the "bound" nature of serfdom, not realizing that everyone in a feudal society was "bound," king no less than serf—albeit if one is "bound" 'tis much better to be so in kingly than in serfly style. George Homans, in his *English Village Life of the Thirteenth Century*, reproduces some written agreements between sons and fathers, both serfs, in which the son agrees to tend to the father's and mother's needs until death do them part on the condition that the father give to the son his rights in the manor.[4] On this condition the son could secure the permission of the lord to marry. Viewed from another perspective, it was a system of social security or income maintenance by kinship and feudal right.

This kinship system of security was built right into rural architecture in the United States. As Clarence Ayres noted long ago in *Science, The False Messiah*, those elegant old homes in rural New England with their seemingly infinite attachments represented an accommodation to an extended family—a family that provided economic security to the lame, halt, and blind, as well as to able-bodied family members.[5] The rambling nineteenth-century adobe structures found in rural New Mexico are similar physical testimony to a family-oriented system of social security that characterized not only New England and New Mexico, but almost all of the rural United States.

Being that people then did not live as long as people do today (so that there were fewer old people), that what old people there were held title much as old people in medieval society held rights, that high infant mortality kept down, to some extent, the number of dependent children, and that the real income on a farm had an elasticity that does not characterize urban cash income, security vested in the family was a feasible way to meet the economic needs of an agrarian-based population.

When we look at longevity figures from New Guinea, from medieval Europe, from rural nineteenth-century New England and New Mexico, in comparison with those of the industrial economy of today, we cannot help but surmise that life today is much more secure than it once was. The industrial economy is more secure in general as evidenced by such measures as infant mortality, longevity, disease, general health, etcetera, than in previous orderings of society. Machine technology means abundance, not in the sense of limitless goods and services, but in the sense of better health and nutrition, greater literacy, more varied lives. But, nevertheless, it does have some inherent insecurities that were not a part of the older order of life.

For one thing, the extended family has largely disappeared. The nuclear family, an adult or adults with dependent children, has displaced the extended family. Kinship ties, although most certainly still recognized and honored, cannot make the demands in an urban society with two thousand miles separating the related nuclear units that they do in an agrarian economy. The family unit living in a rather small apartment in Manhattan can hardly be called upon to meet the demands of grandfather and grandmother for physical security and income maintenance.

Granted that major changes in the social fabric are the root cause of the development of the welfare state, our argument can be stated more generally. All societies are bound by ties of reciprocity. Social interaction involves two or more individuals, and reciprocity means that anything done by one individual on behalf of another calls for a reciprocal action of equal social worth, by the original beneficiary on behalf of the original giver. The matter of social worth is determined in a rough and ready manner by the society itself. The customs and practices of each tribe define how these interactions shall be settled.

In industrial economies the matter of reciprocity sets up two circular flows, one of goods and one of whatever is defined as money—a standardized unit socially acceptable to settle reciprocal obligations, today ranging from metal coins and paper dollars to simple symbols on a computer printout.[7]

The goods flow represents our technological interdependence.[8] As economists put it, we are all busy doing one another's wash. The money flow represents the ceremonial recognition of that technological interdependence.

In our industrial society, lack of money with which to settle reciprocal obligations mandated by technological interdependence puts a person out of the mainstream; it disallows any access to the technological process by virtue of which the life process is sustained. One of the risks of the industrial society is disruption of the pecuniary flow either socially or to individuals, through all kinds of unforeseen and unplanned circumstances—unemployment, disability, lack of parents through which one can establish a claim, aging and involuntary retirement, injury.

To the two traditional and accepted flows of pecuniary income, that from ownership of property allegedly having some productive efficacy, and that from some alleged direct participation in the work force also having some imputed productive efficacy, we have been adding a third stream, independent income. It is independent in the sense that it does not rest on any imputed productive efficacy, although, as we shall argue, it may be very efficacious in supporting the two traditional flows of income.

The industrial economy as noted has any number of insecurities built into it by virtue of its major characteristics. We have recognized these insecurities by building, over the last six or seven decades, systems that circumvent stoppages in the usual pecuniary flow. The problem in general in an industrial economy is the termination of cash income for whatever reason.

On the individual level such termination disrupts or forbids meaningful participation in the life process of the group. On the social level massive breakdowns in money flows are allowed to so impede the productive process that the very economic and social well-being of the entire group may be threatened. We have the ironic spectacle of want and deprivation in the midst of potential relative abundance. It would be an eloquent person indeed who could explain to an elder of the Mafulu Mountain Folk just why some substantial part of the population had to be without "shoes" because we had produced too many "shoes," or because we were forced to preserve something sacred, the "purchasing power" of the dollar as it was held to be sometime in the past.

One of the first of these terminations that we recognized and accepted at a community, rather than as a family or an individual responsibility, was industrial accidents culminating either in death or in temporary or permanent disability. Workmen's compensation was devised in the second decade of this century to offset the loss of family income from death or injury. This was a feeble beginning in our recognition of a more general problem, but nevertheless a beginning that clearly reveals its origins in the machine process.

In the 1930s we recognized that income could be terminated by involuntary unemployment and recognized this, too, as a cost of industry. And in the horrendous social conditions of that era we finally recognized that the family unit and private charity could not cope with dependent children, the blind, the disabled, and the aged. The Social Security Act of 1935 included provision for all of these economic insecurities. Although provision for health care was originally a part of the Social Security Act, that feature was removed for political reasons. The provisions of the bill were viewed as "revolutionary" enough and any more social change was more than the populace, as represented by their elected spokespersons the politicians, would tolerate. We had to wait another thirty years to get the modest medical care for the elderly that we have today.

That the welfare state is a response to the insecurities of an industrial economy is proven by the fact that every industrial nation has been forced to establish some system—and for the same reasons that we belatedly responded to the same forces—to establish some system of income maintenance and security. It has often been remarked that we in the United States were retarded in our response to those forces, and much is made of the fact that the German system of social security was originally sponsored by Bismarck, and precedes that of the United States by more than fifty years.

A better explanation, perhaps, is that the industrial revolution that provoked the social changes to which the welfare state is a response affected Germany before it did the United States, as it most certainly did Great Britain.[9] In any event, leads and lags notwithstanding, every industrial nation has been forced to come to grips with the insecurities peculiarly associated with that form of economic organization.

For most people this analysis of the rise of and necessity for the welfare state is sufficient unto itself. However, to the conventional economic mind it was always troublesome. Since the conventional wisdom envisioned an economy in which the market was responsive to human need, these welfare measures seemed to be exogenous intrusions. The market produced goods and services in just the quantity and quality that consumers indicated by their bids that they desired them, and their bids reflected the distribution of income, an income distributed in the same ratio as each had contributed to the final product. It was the best of all possible worlds, almost biblical in that it appeared that people ate bread in proportion to the sweat on their brows.

Since this analysis was held to be a reasonable presentation of actuality, the welfare state and income maintenance programs were taken to be aberrations. Admittedly the system did not always work in such perfect fashion. Some people did, through adversity, fall outside the system. And some had such personalities that they could find no reasonable niche. Hence, for the former, the worthy widows, the orphans, the non-drinking very old, there was private charity, augmented where necessary by some minimal public contribution. For those in the second category, the "sturdy beggars," there was nothing other than a Greenriver ordinance. But anything done even for the worthy poor should be minimal because generosity, even though well intended, always bore the danger of debauching the poor. Neither private nor public charity should become a way of life.

The problems of the welfare state were viewed as outside the economic system—until the great depression of the 1930s. That event was indeed a great eye-opener to those with eyes that could be opened. By its sheer intensity it made manifest to perceptive people the insecurities that were an integral part of the industrial economy. And it provoked an economic theory that could view these economic insecurities as a part of the system, as endogenous rather than exogenous.

Many people totally missed one of the major messages in the back of J. M. Keynes's *General Theory*. In his almost afterthoughts he remarked that two major flaws existed in a capitalist economy: the first was its tremendous instability and the second its very unequal distribution of income. And he argued that mitigating the second flaw, the uneven distribution of income, would go a long way toward remedying the first, the instability.[9]

Income maintenance, from being an exogenous problem, was brought into the main corpus of economic theory. The message was loud and clear for those who cared to hear. In classic theory the extremely uneven distribution of income, particularly apparent in the late nineteenth century, was essential for rapid accumulation of capital. Only by such a distribution of income could the "lower orders" be saved from poverty. Even though the poor might misunderstand, the riches of the rich were in the long run more beneficial to the poor than to the rich. All savings were realized in real investment. The rich, by virtue of their saving, were public benefactors. Any kind of income maintenance, some of which might be essential for purely humanitarian reasons, represented a cost. If funded by transfer from the affluent, it would reduce savings and hence capital accumulation.

The contrary message from Keynes was quite clear. Extremely uneven distribution of income, far from advancing the general level of income, impaired the maintenance of income and employment and real capital accumulation. The very rich, far from being public benefactors, impaired economic progress by attempting to accumulate savings that were never realized. Saving was a result of income, not a cause of income. Income maintenance programs that registered in a Lorenz curve as a move in the direction of more income equality were not a cost that had to be borne. They were essential to real economic stability and growth. Such a message ran counter to long-held economic theory as well as to long-established economic practice. The traditional theory made of practice a convenient social virtue, to borrow a Galbraithian term. A system of income distribution in accordance with a system of social status had the endorsement of the keepers of the higher economic verities.[10] Is it any wonder that the strategies suggested by Keynes did not survive long in the post-World War II world? Viewing the welfare state as an instrument for maintaining economic stability was threatening to the economic theorist as well as to those whose incomes were unconsciously(?) justified by the theorist. In the past two decades income maintenance has once again come to be viewed as almost solely an economic cost. Somehow, in what is referred to as the neo-classical synthesis, in which the fallacy of composition endemic to micro-economics was glossed over, only the Keynesian mechanics were left. The message in the back of the book was lost.

If we view the welfare state as a monstrous growth, as more or less an economic cancer that has grown on an otherwise well-articulated system, then we most certainly must view it as a cost. But if we view it as a means of resolving the inherent problems of a system flawed by an inability to distribute income in a manner that will sustain income and employment, then we must consider it a strategy to balance an unbalanced system.

In the period immediately after World War II the latter view predominated. William Beveridge, in his *Full Employment in a Free Society*, taking up on Keynes, argued for security from the cradle to the grave as not only a matter of humanity, but as a means of economic stability.[11] In this country Alvin Hansen, although more or less insisting that our major emphasis should be on government investment to compensate for insufficient private investment, when getting down to naming those public investments named categories clearly consummatory in nature—education, parks and recreation, and public facilities whose major impact would show up in a consumer budget.[12]

Public investments would represent direct contributions to raising the general level of living, but the contribution to the lower income groups would be much greater than they would be to the rich. Late in the 1950s in *The Affuent Society* Galbraith put the argument for public expenditure in just that way. By redressing the balance between public and private expenditure in favor of the former, more would be done to lift the levels of living of the lower income groups than of the rich.[13] However, Keynes's emphasis on economic stability was lost or at least weakened by the manner in which Galbraith stressed the existence of affluence in the private sector. To a great extent he also downgraded the necessity for economic stability, which had been Hansen's major emphasis.

Two other books published after World War II, one by H. Gordon Hayes, *Spending, Saving, and Employment*, and one by C. E. Ayres, *The Divine Right of Capital*, directly connected public spending as an instrument to redress the balance between public and private spending and at the same time resolve the problem of economic instability.[14] Both authors argued that our system of income distribution, by maintaining a weak propensity to consume, constantly threatened the ability of the economy to operate at full capacity. Both argued for active governmental policy that would alter the pattern of income distribution in favor of the lower income receivers. In so doing, they lent support on this side of the Atlantic to the Beveridge program.

Such a conscious use of welfare measures to maintain economic stability was never implemented. Yet a belief that it had been accomplished underlay the myth of the "affluent society" so prevalent in the fifties. People firmly believed that there had been a rather large shift in income distribution during the thirties and forties. This shift in income distribution was alleged to be a function of two actions. One was the establishment of welfare state programs in the 1930s. The other was the extension of the income tax during World War II, so that a larger proportion of higher incomes was taken in taxes than had previously been the case. The evidence that this shift in distribution, attributable to the welfare state and the income tax, was a meaningful one in real terms and real well-being was that our productive capacity had greatly enlarged during World War II. The argument made throughout earlier times that redistribution of income was hazardous for all, because such a redistribution would do relatively little for the poor while reducing the well-being of the rich, came to seem irrelevent because of the large increase in real per capita income.

Government leaders of the times did come to the stabilizing effect on the economy of income maintenance programs. During the Eisenhower administration the allegedly stabilizing character of our limited welfare state was acknowledged in the term "built-in stabilizers." It was noted that the budget effect of these programs, partially by virtue of the manner in which they were financed, was to contribute to an unbalanced federal budget during a recession. Outlays to meet claims for social income and welfare increased during a depression while the revenues from social security and unemployment compensation taxes, as well as from the income tax and other conventional taxes, fell. The administration of that era viewed depressions with some equanimity having recognized this budgetary phenomenon.

It cannot be argued that the United States made a conscious attempt to follow a Keynesian strategy, raising the propensity to consume or using the consumption function as a device to partially offset the savings gap by an enlarged stream of consumption expenditure at any level of income, full-employment or partial-employment level. The level of unemployment tolerated as well as the amount of persistent poverty is testimony that such a strategy was not followed at any time after World War II. And certainly no such strategy is being attempted today. Indeed, quite the contrary!

But despite the fact that we have not created a welfare state based upon any consistent economic philosophy or theory, we do have a crazy quilt welfare state with here a patch, there a patch, everywhere a patch. It came into being as we recognized specific problems of income insecurity in an industrial economy. Taken as a whole the patchwork does provide for a guaranteed income of sorts. To the extent that very few can possibly fall through the welfare net, we have managed to build an income floor corresponding to a guaranteed income in a rough and ready way. However, that floor is so low that a person can take an almost death-dealing fall before finding support. Any review of the average payments under many of our programs quickly disabuses all but the most calloused of the notion that our income maintenance programs provide for the rich life.

Table 1 below shows average payments nationwide under various support programs.

Table 1. ***Average Monthly Payments on Income Maintenance Programs.***

	1979	*1980*
Retired Worker	$294	$341
Disabled Worker	322	371
Widows and Widowers	270	311
Unemployment Compensation	388.57	428.39
% of Weekly Wage	35.9%	37.5%
Aid to Families with DC	123.00	128
Aid to Aged SSI	123.00	128
Aid to Disabled SSI	182.00	198

SOURCE: *Statistical Abstract of The United States*, 1981, pp. 329, 340, 343.

The minimums that we have established under our income maintenance programs almost insure that the recipients will fall below the poverty line. In other words, poverty is written into the system and almost legitimized by virtue of the governmental payment. We do indeed have a welfare state, but it is a welfare state that goes it on the cheap.

Despite the low level of support for welfare, we are told (and it is rather widely believed) that our welfare state has been growing at such a monstrous rate that is it a threat to general well-being. This belief is based on some elementary statistics allegedly showing that we are about to be overwhelmed by the costs of the welfare state.

Welfare costs, according to this legend, have been growing by leaps and bounds, particularly since the mid-sixties when the Great Society doctrine prevailed. On first examination the numbers seem to warrant the alarm. In Table 2 we show figures for social welfare expenditures for the period

Table 2. ***Growth in Social Welfare Expenditures, 1960-1979.***

	1960	*1970*	*1979*
Social Insurance	$19,306	$54,692	$193,588
Public Aid	4,101	16,488	64,649
Health and Medical Programs	4,464	9,907	24,496
Veterans Programs	5,479	9,078	20,456
Education	17,626	50,846	108,279
Housing	177	602	6,226
Other Social Welfare	1,140	4,145	10,641
Total	52,294	145,856	428,333

SOURCE: *Statistical Abstract of the United States*, 1981, p. 318.

1960-1979, the period during which the Great Society programs are supposed to have taken hold and mushroomed.

These are numbers that those wholly opposed to social expenditure can use to advantage. But they are not nearly so alarming when we examine the total context in which they exist. For one thing, if put in constant dollars, thus adjusting for inflation, the sheer magnitude of the growth is severely diminished. But it is even better for relieving anxiety if we examine more carefully the various categories that make up the total.

If we remove social insurance and education, items that are not exactly welfare or income maintenance, we have a total expenditure in 1979 of $126.466 billion. Public aid, one of the more controversial of our income maintenance programs, constituted one percent of the GNP in 1960; in 1979 it was 2.5 percent, which does represent an appreciable relative growth, but certainly nothing alarming. The items accounting for the largest relative growth are food stamps and Medicaid, neither of which was significant in 1960. The conventional "welfare" part of this expenditure was .7 percent of GNP in both 1960 and 1979.

We can take another look at the impact of our "welfare state" on both state and federal government in Table 3, where we give the total expenditures as a percentage of total government expenditures as well as a percentage of GNP.

Table 3. ***Growth in Social Welfare Expenditures as Percent of GNP of all Government Outlays.***

Year	*% of GNP*			*% of Government Outlays*		
	Total	*Federal*	*State & Local*	*Total*	*Federal*	*State & Local*
1960	10.5	5.0	5.5	38.4	28.1	60.1
1970	15.2	8.1	7.1	48.2	40.1	64.1
1979	18.5	10.1	7.1	56.8	55.0	60.4

SOURCE: *Statistical Abstract of the United States*, 1981, p. 317.

We must again interpret these numbers with some caution. The largest contributors to these percentages are social insurance and education, items available and open to all persons regardless of income. More than one half of all state level expenditure for social welfare is accounted for by education. Certainly these numbers taken as a whole indicate that social programs, not all income maintaining by any means, are a larger part of our economy today than they were twenty years ago. But only those who are deliberately alarmist would project on the basis of this twenty-year experience that they were about to overwhelm us. It is possible, of course, to project their growth into the infinite future so that they constitute all of the GNP. That is a statistical possibility; it is not a statistical probability.

The whole matter of income maintenance and welfare is obscured by the money illusion. When we relate it to the pecuniary measure of gross national product and to governmental expenditure we see only its pecuniary side. We need to view it in real terms. How much of that ongoing flow of real goods and services are we going to allocate to the lame, the halt, and the blind? The questions over money are matters of bookkeeping. Not that bookkeeping does not have its effect on individuals and how much we are going to allot to each. But when we view the problem in real terms it becomes quite apparent that we can afford the "welfare state." In fact when we see it as an answer to income insecurities in an industrial economy we know that we cannot afford to be without it.

Our limitations are institutional, not technological. This fact should be apparent from the Brookings Institution studies of the performance of the U.S. economy in the 1920s.[15] In that now long-forgotten study, the Brookings Institution argued that had we produced the additional 19 percent of industrial output of which we were then capable, and had we distributed this additional 19 percent to those spending units at the bottom of the heap, no American family would have been below $2,000 in annual income. In today's (1982) dollars, that would amount to $11,251. This amount is approximately $2,000 above the poverty line for a family of four in 1982. While not lavish it means that our economy as early as 1929 was capable of eliminating utter degrading poverty. It also means that today we are even more capable of sustaining income maintenance programs well above the poverty lines—even more so than in 1929, a year in which our real per capita disposable personal income was considerably less than half of what it is today.

The irony of the present malaise concerning the welfare state is the widespread belief that we somehow cannot afford it even in the face of overwhelming evidence that we can. Unless one assumes that the involuntarily unemployed, the untended dependent children, the elderly, the injured and disabled can be made somehow to disappear, we would have to maintain some kind of minimum income even if economically strained in doing so. Sometimes we try to wish these problems away by assuming some natural rate of unemployment or by arguing that all involuntary unemployment is in fact voluntary or by arguing that the welfare system itself provokes personal habits that create dependent children. These are all verbal solutions to real problems that will not vanish by wishing them away. Since we obviously can and we obviously will maintain our welfare state, what are the real rather than the imagined problems? First and foremost is our understanding of the welfare state and how it came into being. The belief persists that it was all somehow the creation of "liberals" rather than the product of hard answers to social realities. We need to become fully aware that it is not something that we can do away with any more than we can do away with urban water systems. Both are essential parts of urban and industrial culture. Far from being social luxuries that we can ill-afford, we must somehow begin to understand that the multitude of programs identified with the welfare state are essential to both social and individual income levels. The tendency of the pecuniary aspects of the industrial economy to impede the operation of the industrial side through inadequate flows of income must be acknowledged. The notion that the system automatically operates to create just such reciprocal flows of goods and monies (Say's law), that depression cannot occur, is theology, not science, no matter the credentials of those who see fit to purvey it.

Second, which also requires a change in the conventional outlook, we need to see income maintenance not as a cost, but as a necessary part of the economy. Having a healthy, well educated, and working populace, far from being costly, is a dire necessity. The whole message of Harrell R. Rogers's book is that the real cost of human neglect is one that we cannot afford. Economic stability is encouraged, not hampered, by effective income maintenance programs.

Healthy mindedness on welfare is essential to solving what administrative problems actually do exist. The funding of social security is one of these. That we can afford it and that it is not going "broke" is readily apparent. The problem, if there is one, is our insistence on funding it with an earmarked tax. We are the only industrial nation that does this. This manner of financing almost ensures that the system will be constantly on the edge of going "broke." It is a system well designed to perpetuate paranoia among those who depend on it for income security.

We have been modifying some of our social security legislation to conform with the new family styles that have come to prevail in the second half of the nineteenth century. The original social security act was designed to aid the then-current conception of a "normal" family. That "normal" family consisted of two married parents, one of whom, the female, remained in the household, and two children, preferably a boy and a girl. Increasingly that is no longer the typical family. As a matter of fact, it could perhaps be said today, with some justification, that there is no typical family. We need to modify our social security legislation to secure for each individual benefits as a right and as a social necessity.

Overall, every one of our income maintenance provisions needs to be constructed so that it has at least a minimum payment no lower than the poverty line. That we could eliminate poverty, as currently defined, in one fell swoop was evident in 1966 when it was estimated that it would have taken approximately $11 billion dollars to have raised everyone below the poverty line to that level; in 1966 the gross national product increased more than five times this amount. But we cannot do so when our income maintenance programs are pitched at the meager levels they are today.

Although it is not within the scope of this article, we need to take seriously the aims of the original Employment Act of 1946. We cannot resolve even the administrative problems of our "welfare" state with vast amounts of unused resources. With these resources fully employed we can easily maintain the "welfare state" at decent levels of funding. So long as inflation is viewed as an intolerable problem of first magnitude while unemployment is viewed as a device for curing inflation, the welfare state, composed of all of our income maintenance plans, does indeed place both a pecuniary and a real strain on the performance of the economy. It does so in several ways. When the economy operates with substantially less than full employment it means that Adam Smith's product of the "annual labor" is smaller. The pile of real goods and services from which must come the contribution to the "lame, the halt, and the blind" is in real terms smaller. Second, on the funding side there are fewer government revenues from which to make income maintenance payments. The government has fiscal problems in managing welfare state payments in chronic depression conditions. From 1949 to 1983 unemployment has been below 4 percent in only seven years. Viewed from the immediate post-World-War-II outlook, this is chronic unemployment and chronic lingering depression.

If we were to face the problem of unemployment with the same dedication given to national defense there is no reason we could not achieve the unemployment rates of two and three percent that we once identified with full employment. As such levels we would generate a much larger real output within which the transfer for income maintenance would take place; simultaneously we would reduce the size of those needed transfers. If achieving this takes wage and price controls, so be it. The opposition to such controls is an emotional one, not a reasoned one. The argument that they require a huge bureaucracy is denied by the experience we have had with their administration in the past. The argument that they "distort the market" presumes that private price making has not already "distorted" that idyllic condition and figment of the mythopoeic imagination. This argument also fails to note that public price controls inject the public interest into what heretofore has been viewed as strictly a private matter by a large segment of the economy, that 70 percent dominated by the *Fortune* 500. Just as feudal lords were outraged by the intrusions of the king, so we can always anticipate such outrages from the corporate principalities that govern various segments of the U.S. economy. Lastly, the argument that price controls will not work because prices soar when they are removed is a weak argument. All it says is that prices are relatively stable with price controls; in their absence return the very conditions that recommend them in the first place.

In summary, we are capable of eliminating poverty and of providing a decent standard of living for all who have been left out in the industrial economy. That we have not chosen to do so is largely attributable to institutional inhibitions that perpetuate a system of income distribution in accordance with status. Our rising "welfare costs" in recent years, rather than being reason for alarm, are evidence that we had been going in the right direction. The problems that agitate us most are bookkeeping problems. These are most certainly surmountable. But before we can successfully solve even the nit-picking problems we must transform our conception of income maintenance programs. We need to view them as essential to a healthy and thriving economy.[16] Until there is such a transformation, we can expect only a hard life for those who have been passed over by our economy.

Notes

1. George Gilder, *Wealth and Poverty* (New York: Bantam, 1982).
2. William Ryan, *Blaming The Victim* (New York: Vintage Books, 1971).
3. Peter Freuchen, *Book of The Eskimos* (New York: Fawcett Premier Books, 1961); see especially chap. 8, "The Eskimo Mind." See also Wilhjalmur Stefansson, *My Life With The Eskimo* (New York: Collier Books, 1962).
4. George Homans, *English Villagers of the Thirteenth Century* (Cambridge: Harvard University Press, 1941).
5. C. E. Ayres, *Science, The False Messiah* (Indianapolis: Bobbs-Merrill, 1927), pp. 100-102.
6. Marcel Mauss, *The Gift* (Glencoe, Ill.: The Free Press, 1954); and Bronislaw Malinowski, *Crime and Custom in Savage Society* (Paterson, N.J.: Littlefield, Adams, 1959).
7. Emile Durkheim, *The Division of Labor in Society*, Book I (New York: The Free Press, 1966 printing); David Hamilton, "Interdependence in Economics," in *Interdependence: An Interdisciplinary Study*, ed. Archie Bahm (Albuquerque: World Books, 1977).
8. Harrell R. Rogers, Jr., *The Cost of Human Neglect: America's Welfare Failure* (Armonk, N.Y.: M. E. Sharpe, 1982); see especially chap. 4.
9. J. M. Keynes, *The General Theory of Employment, Interest, and Money* (London: Macmillan, 1936), pp. 372-81.

10. Barbara Wootton, *The Social Foundations of Wage Policy* (London: George Allen & Unwin, 1955). This book has not received the attention that it warrants. After indicating the weaknesses of conventional wage theory in a very thoughtful way, Ms. Wootton went out to see how wages were in fact determined in Great Britain. The results strongly suggested that wages were determined in accordance with an established system of status.
11. William Beveridge, *Full Employment In A Free Society* (New York: W. W. Norton, 1945), pp. 90-104 and Part IV, Sections 1 and 2.
12. Alvin Hansen, *Economic Policy and Full Employment* (New York: McGraw Hill, 1947); see especially chap. 16, "Public Investment." See also his later *The American Economy* (New York: McGraw Hill, 1957), especially chap. 8, "Standards and Values in a Rich Society."
13. J. K. Galbraith, *The Affluent Society* (Boston: Houghton Mifflin, 1958). Also see the "Introduction to the Third Edition," in *The Affluent Society*, 1977.
14. H. Gordon Hayes, *Spending, Saving, and Employment* (New York: Alfred A. Knopf, 1945), especially Part II; C. E. Ayres, *The Divine Right of Capital* (Boston: Houghton Mifflin, 1946).
15. The relevant volumes are Edwin G. Nourse, *America's Capacity to Produce* (New York: Review of Reviews, 1934), and Maurice Leven, Harold G. Moulton, and Clark Warburton, *America's Capacity to Consume* (New York: Review of Reviews, 1934).
16. Benjamin I. Page, *Who Gets What From Government* (Berkeley: University of California Press, 1983). This whole book is an assessment of public expenditure fiscal policy, but is especially a critical examination of our notion that we have an effective welfare state.

24

The U.S. "Welfare State" and the Conservative Counterrevolution

Wallace C. Peterson

This article has three major objectives. The first is to examine the essential structure of the U.S. "welfare" state, a term given in this essay an expanded and more controversial interpretation than is usually the case. The second is to analyze the impact on this structure of the conservative counterrevolution, a counterrevolution that came to fruition with Ronald Reagan's election to the presidency in 1980. The full philosophical and economic dimensions of the Reagan counterrevolution are found in two basic documents, the 1982 *Economic Report of the President*, especially Chapter 2 of the *Annual Report* of the Council of Economic Advisers, and the president's *A Program for Economic Recovery*, transmitted to the Congress on February 18, 1981. Third, the article concludes with some observations on the probable long-term consequences of these developments.

On the Meaning of the "Welfare State"

It is uncertain as to exactly when and how the phrase "the welfare state" was first used, although the concept in its modern form is thought to have originated with the Beveridge Report on social insurance, presented to the British government in November 1942.[1] This document was the basis for the development of the post-World War II "welfare state" in Great Britain, a major part of the sweeping reforms undertaken when Winston

Churchill was defeated in 1945 and the Labour Party took power in the House of Commons with a nearly 150-seat majority.

As set forth in the Beveridge Report, the prime objective of social policy in the post-war world was to be "the abolition of want." The main means of attaining this end was to be a comprehensive system of "social security" or "social insurance"—the terms are used more or less interchangeably—which would protect the family against any interruption of earnings as a result primarily of unemployment, sickness, old age, or death. Also there was to be a second and continuous adjustment of earnings through a system of allowances for children. In effect, the Beveridge Report argued that the abolition of want in post-war Britain required a "double re-distribution of income through social insurance and children's allowances."[2]

This is largely what the term the "welfare state" has come to mean within the context of modern industrial society. Whether "social security" or "social insurance" is the phrase used to describe this phenomenon is unimportant. What is important is that the term applies to a phenomenon that has become a major feature of contemporary systems of market capitalism: the use of the power of the central government to protect people from income losses inherent in an industrial society—especially those arising out of unemployment, accidents and illness, and retirement—and to provide for a minimum standard of economic well-being for all citizens, irrespective of circumstances. Taxes and transfers are the primary instruments used by modern governments to construct and administer a "welfare state."

The foregoing represents the traditional—perhaps one might say even classical—definition of the welfare state. Though not always explicitly stated, this definition implies that the basic benefit structure of the welfare state ought to be progressive—which is to say that most of its benefits should be channeled toward those at the lower end of the income scale since this is where one finds most of the people who suffer a loss of income through forces over which they have no control. On the taxing or financing side, the matter is less clear, since most schemes of social insurance, here and elsewhere, require a flat contribution by the employed (including the self-employed) persons who are also the ultimate beneficiaries of the system. This may introduce a regressive element into the tax part of the structure of the welfare state, as in the United States, where there is an upper limit on the amount of earned income subject to the Social Security tax. Nevertheless, the use of taxes to finance transfer payments that provide some minimum of income security constitutes the essence of the traditional definition of the welfare state.

The U.S. welfare state was created in two separate stages, three decades apart. The system for old age and disability income and unemployment compensation originated in Franklin Roosevelt's New Deal administration during the 1930s. In the 1960s Lyndon Johnson's Great Society programs added medical insurance and assistance for the aged (Medicare) and for the poor (Medicaid), while vastly expanding public assistance programs aimed at poor families, especially in the form of foodstamps, Aid to Families with Dependent Children (AFDC), other forms of public assistance, and job training. There have been no major innovations in this structure since the mid-1960s. Under the Reagan administration, some programs like the Comprehensive Employment Training Act (CETA) have been eliminated, while others have suffered sharp cutbacks in their rate of funding increase, especially housing assistance, AFDC, and foodstamps.[3]

A Broadened Interpretation of the Welfare State

By way of introduction to the much broader interpretation of the "welfare state" as this concept is used in this article, comments are in order on the two basic, but fundamentally different, ways in which governments spend money. This distinction is crucial to an understanding of the real role that the federal government now plays in the nation's economic life.

The first way in which governments spend money centers on those tasks that the word "government" suggests for most people—maintaining armed forces, building roads, running school systems, delivering the mail, constructing dams and parks, and undertaking a variety of other activities not usually done by private business. To do these things governments need resources, just as do private firms when they produce goods for sale in the market. The goods and services, including labor, that government buys from the private economy constitute the resource inputs necessary to the "social" or "collective" output of the public sector. The sum total of spending for goods and services by all levels of government—federal, state, and local—measures how much of the economy's total output (GNP) is being used by government for the kinds of tasks described above.[4] The major way in which governments in this context differ from private firms is that they get the money to purchase their resources primarily from their taxing powers, whereas the private firm depends upon the sale of its output for money needed to acquire the resources necessary for production. Of course, both governments and firms also get money through borrowing, as do households and consumers in general, although borrowing can never be the major, long-term source for most spending, either public or private.

The second fundamental category of spending is what economists call "transfer payments," an aptly descriptive term. The purpose of this type of spending is to provide income to a person, a business firm, a non-profit organization, or even another unit of government, either in the form of money or "in kind," by which is meant some form of service. What distinguishes transfer spending from spending for goods and services is that governments do not require any product, service, or asset in exchange for the money paid out or the service provided. There is no *quid pro quo.* The unemployment check a jobless worker receives is a well-known example of a transfer payment. The government does not require that the person receiving the check perform any work for the government, nor does the jobless person have any obligation to repay the government when he or she goes back to work.

What is involved in transfer spending is exactly what the word "transfer" implies. The government is, in effect, the instrument through which income is obtained from some or all citizens—normally through taxation—and transferred to other citizens or organizations in the economy. An equally important fact about transfers is that they have the effect of rearranging the pattern of income distribution in society by increasing the income of some and reducing the income of others. Of course, one can argue, as some economists do, that *all* taxing and spending by government does this—that no governmental activity is neutral as respects the distribution of income and wealth. This may be true, though probably impossible to measure. But what is unique about transfers is that they are undertaken with the *deliberate* intent of affecting incomes somewhere in the economy. It is important to keep this in mind.

Throughout most of the period after World War II, the public's interest in government—especially the federal government—focused largely on the stabilizing role government is supposed to play in the management of the economy. In a nutshell, this was the Keynesian "revolution." By the judicious and timely use of its fiscal and monetary powers, the federal government was supposed to offset fluctuations in the private economy, keeping unemployment low, prices stable, and the economy growing. During this same period, however, another sort of governmental "revolution" was taking place, one not much noticed until recently by either scholars or the general public. This was the persistent, steady growth in the government's role—mostly at the federal level—in providing income directly to an ever-widening segment of the population. As a consequence there now exists in the United States a vast and complicated income maintenance system, the dimensions of which are barely known or understood by most citizens. Even though this transfer "revolution" has been going on since the 1930s, its acceleration during the last two decades justifies our speaking of a "transfer explosion."[5] The practical consequence of this "explosion" has been to involve the federal government in the *direct* provision of money income to people on a scale unprecedented in our history. In 1983, for example, 14.8 percent of personal income came from transfers. In contrast, in 1939 only 4.1 percent came from this source, and a mere 1.8 percent in 1929.[6]

The full dimensions of the foregoing phenomenon are found in Table 1, which shows for the period 1948 through 1983 both the dollar value and these as percentages of the GNP of total government spending, government spending for goods and services, and government transfer spending. The data pertain to spending by *all* governments in the economy, showing annual averages for the post-war decades of the 1950s, the 1960s, and the 1970s plus the first four years of the 1980s.

The relatively simple statistical averages found in this table tell us some very important things about what has been happening in the society. The figures in columns (1) and (2) are the kind that get the most attention today, since they seem to show that government is not only big, but getting bigger all the time. In the period 1948-1959, for example, total government spending at all levels averaged 25.7 percent of the GNP. By the 1980s, this percentage had jumped to 37.2, an increase of 11.5 percentage points. The erroneous interpretation given to these figures, especially by those hostile to government, is that governments—federal, state, and local—are now "taking" more than one-third of the nation's output. But this is not correct. As indicated earlier, the appropriate measure of the part of the nation's output being used by the governmental sectors for public purposes is the spending for goods and services alone, not the total of government spending for all purposes. This is shown in its dollar value in column (3) and as a percent of the GNP (decade averages) in column (4). The latter figure tells an interesting story, for the size of government from this perspective has not changed significantly in the whole of the post-war period. Year in and year out approximately one-fifth of the GNP is used for public purposes. Although the data in Table 1 do not reveal this, a look behind these figures shows that during this whole period the size of the federal government *declined relative* to the size of state and local government. In 1948, for example, state and local spending for goods and services totaled 5.9 percent of the GNP, but by 1983 this percentage had more than doubled, to 12.5. In the same period federal spending for goods and services as a share of the GNP went from 6.4 to 8.3 percent, showing that now the federal government absorbs a smaller proportion of the national output then do state and local governments.[7]

What accounts for the relatively large jump in total government spend-

Table 1. ***Government Spendng and the Economy: 1948-1983 (annual averages for indicated period).***

Period	*Total Spending** (1) Dollar Value**	*Total Spending** (2) Percent of GNP	*Total Spending for Goods and Services* (3) Dollar Value	*Total Spending for Goods and Services* (4) Percent of GNP	*Nonmilitary Spending for Transfers* (5) Dollar Value	*Nonmilitary Spending for Transfers* (6) Percent of GNP
1948-1959	$ 93.2	25.7%	$ 69.6	19.5%	$ 23.6	6.2%
1960-1969	198.9	28.7	146.3	21.2	52.6	7.5
1970-1979	506.1	32.1	328.6	20.8	177.5	11.3
1980-1983	1,115.1	37.2	618.2	20.7	496.9	16.5

*Goods and Services plus transfer-type expenditures.
**Dollar values are in billions of dollars.
SOURCE: *Economic Report of the President* (Washington, D.C.: U.S. Government Printing Office, 1984).

ing as a share of the GNP is, of course, the growth in transfer spending. This change is shown in columns (5) and (6) in the table. The essence of the "transfer explosion" is found in column (6), which shows transfers as a percent of the GNP. Here the percentages have gone from an average of 6.2 percent of the GNP for the 1948-59 period to an average of 16.5 percent in the first four years of the current decade. This is the truly revolutionary change that has taken place in the government's role in the economy in the post-war period, and not, as is perhaps popularly believed, a drastic expansion in government's more traditional functions.

It is also important to note at this juncture that the growth in transfer spending has been primarily at the federal level. Between 1960 and 1983, for example, federal transfer payments in all forms grew by a factor of 14. State and local governments also engage in transfer spending, although not on such a massive scale as the federal government. Moreover, much of their transfer spending must be traced back to the federal government simply because a sizeable portion of the revenue for the states and lesser units of government comes from the federal government. In 1983, for example, state and local governments got $86.5 billion in grants from Washington, a sum that accounted for 18 percent of their total income.[8]

Even more significant than the explosive growth of transfer spending at the federal level is the profound change that growth has brought about in the role played by the federal government in our society. This change is documented in Table 2, which shows for the same time periods as Table 1 federal spending for goods and services, military spending by itself, and federal transfer spending as percentages of total federal spending. As in Table 1 the percentages are averages for the periods indicated.

Table 2. ***Purchase of Goods and Services, Military Spending, and Transfer Payments as a Percent of Federal Outlays: 1948-83 (annual averages for indicated period).***

Period	*(1) Purchase of Goods & Services*	*(2) Military Spending*	*(3) Transfer Payments*	*(4) Column 2 Plus Column 3*
1948-1959	63.2%	53.6%	36.8%	90.0%
1960-1969	55.1	43.0	44.9	87.9
1970-1979	36.1	24.9	63.6	88.5
1980-1983	33.2	23.0	66.7	89.7

SOURCE: *Economic Report of the President* (Washington, D.C.: U.S. Government Printing Office, 1984).

These are simple figures but they carry a powerful message. They tell us, in effect, that the single most important function of the federal government is the shifting of income from person to person and group to group. It was not always thus, because in the late 1940s and 1950s only about one-third of federal spending could be classified as "transfers." Now the proportion has climbed to two-thirds, an ironic twist given the Reagan administration's hostility to the growth of federal spending in general and social spending in particular. Beyond the numbers and the sheer magnitude of transfers in the federal budget—in 1983 transfer spending for all purposes totaled $551 billion—the basic meaning of the transfer explosion is that increasingly people, either as individuals or as members of organizations, are unwilling to accept the verdict of the market in the determination of their incomes. If they cannot organize successfully outside of government to modify the terms on which they get income from the market, they turn to government to accomplish the same objective. This is the real significance and explanation for the transfer explosion.

The other dominant activity of the federal government is, of course, military spending. The only surprise in this respect is the fairly steady decline since the early 1950s in the *relative* share of military spending in the federal budget, a decline accounted for by the continued—and, after 1965 explosive—growth in transfer spending. This trend has been reversed by the Reagan administration, as its avowed aim is to boost military spending both absolutely and relatively as a part of its drive toward military supremacy over the Soviet Union. By 1983 military spending had climbed to 24.2 percent of federal spending in contrast to 21.8 percent in 1980, the last year of the Carter administration.[9]

If, as is done in column (4) Table 2, the averages for transfers and military spending are combined, we get a rather remarkable statistic. This combined percentage figure indicates that ever since World War II, narly 90 percent of the activity of the federal government—insofar as activity is measured by spending—consists either of rearranging incomes in society, or nourishing the military economy. Barely 10 percent has gone for what we described earlier as what people conventionally believe that governments do. This hardly adds up to a picture of an ever-expanding federal government, hungry for more power and direct control over the economic lives of Americans.

This brings us finally to the main objectives of this section, namely a broadened definition of the "welfare state." A key argument of this article is that the essential, bedrock characteristic of the welfare state lies in the use of the powers of that state as an instrument for the transfer of income within society. Because the explosive growth in transfer expenditures that has characterized the U.S. economy since the mid-1960s extends well beyond transfers that, in the classic concept of the welfare state touched upon earlier, protect people from the economic risks inherent in an industrial society and provide a minimum level of material well-being, the concept of the welfare state must be broadened to take into account the distributional effects of *all* transfer spending by the central government. The term "welfare state" is not really adequate as a description of the magnitude of the income transfer system that has emerged in the U.S. economy. In the absence, however, of a more satisfactory term to describe this phenomenon, we apply the phrase "the welfare state" in this article to the entire array of transfer spending undertaken by the federal government. This is the structure we examine next.

The Structure of the U.S. Welfare State

On the basis of this broadened definition of the "welfare state," we turn now to analysis of the entire range of transfer spending by the federal government. Specifically, in this section we shall, first, analyze in a general way the major categories of federal spending coming under the rubric of "transfers," and, second, examine in detail transfers that go directly to people. Most of the analysis centers on transfers to people in part because they account for the major portion of federal transfer spending. More important, however, is the fact that transferring income to people is the ultimate *raison d'etre* of the welfare state. Thus it is logical that transfers to people should be the major focus of our analysis. Once we have obtained a more detailed understanding of the structure of federal transfers, we can answer two important questions: First, who, ultimately, are the real beneficiaries of the massive income-redistributional activities of the federal government? and second, How has transfer spending affected the poverty level, as well as the overall distribution of income in the U.S. economy? Answers to these questions, which will be sought in the next section, set the stage for our analysis of the impact of the conservative counter-revolution on the U.S. welfare state.

The data in Table 3, drawn from the national income and product accounts, show that transfers fall into five major categories, of which transfers to people are the most important, now accounting for nearly two-thirds of all transfer expenditures. Actually this percentage is even higher, as will be seen subsequently when we make some necessary adjustments for a more detailed analysis, adjustments reflecting the fact that some of the transfers falling into the other categories in the national income and product accounts actually go to people. Grants to state and local govern-

Table 3. ***Federal Transfer Expenditures by Major Category as a Percentage of Total Transfer Expenditures: 1950-83 (annual average in percent).***

Period	*(1)* *Transfers to people*	*(2)* *Grants to state and local governments*	*(3)* *Net interest*	*(4)* *Subsidies*	*(5)* *Other**
1950-59	51.5%	14.3%	19.4%	6.2%	8.7%
1960-69	54.6	19.7	14.5	7.3	3.9
1970-79	59.9	24.1	11.1	3.5	1.4
1980-83	61.2	18.1	16.4	3.2	1.2

*Primary transfers to abroad (that is, foreign economic aid).

SOURCE: *Economic Report of the President* (Washington, D.C.: U.S. Government Printing Office, 1976, 1984).

ments, followed by net interest, subsidies, and the general category of "other" (mostly transfers to foreigners) are the other major forms of federal transfer spending.

If we look overall at the period 1950 through 1983, three major trends are apparent. First, transfers to people have been growing steadily in relative importance, increasing from an annual average of 51.5 percent of all federal transfer payments in the 1950s to 61.2 percent in the first four years of the 1980s. It remains to be seen whether the Reagan administration's efforts to constrain social spending will significantly alter this trend. To date this has not happened. In 1983 transfers to persons on the national income and product accounts totaled 61.5 percent of all federal transfers, up slightly from 60.8 percent in 1980.[10]

The second important trend concerns federal grants to state and local governments. For the first three post-World War II decades—the 1950s, 1960s, and 1970s—federal "grants-in-aid to state and local governments," as they are formally called, also increased steadily as a relative proportion of all federal transfers. They rose from 14.3 percent in the 1950s to 24.1 percent in the 1970s. Under the Reagan administration, however, this trend has been reversed, the proportion falling to 18.1 percent. An examination of the detailed data on fedral grant-in-aids to state and local governments in the July 1984 *Survey of Current Business* indicates that the relative decline in this category of transfers in the overall picture came from major reductions in two types of federal grants to the states and localities, namely "Labor Training and Service" and "Revenue Sharing." Between 1980 and 1983 federal grants in the Labor Training and Service category were reduced by $4.2 billion and grants for Revenue Sharing by $2.2 billion. In all other major subcategories of federal transfers to state and local governments there were increases. Overall, the total of grants-in-aid to state and local governments dropped from $88.7 billion in 1980 to $86.3 billion in 1983.[12] The elimination of the CETA public service jobs program accounts for a major part of the decline in federal grants under the "Labor Training" rubric, but the reasons behind the decline in federal revenue sharing are unclear, especially since enlargement of federal grants to state and local governments without any strings attached was one of the prouder achievements of the Nixon government.

Finally, we must look at what has been happening to interest on the federal debt. This has been the third most important category of federal transfers. For this form of transfer spending the trend runs exactly counter to that for federal grants to state and local governments. In the three decades from 1950 to 1979 the net interest share of total federal transfers steadily declined, going from 19.4 percent in the 1950s—when interest on the debt represented the second largest category of transfers—to 11.1 percent during the 1970s. The primary reason for this relative change was the decline over the same period in the ratio of the outstanding federal debt to the GNP, a shrinkage resulting from the fact that during these three decades the GNP grew more rapidly than total debt. Specifically, the ratio of the total federal debt to the GNP dropped from 89.6 percent in 1950 to 34.4 percent in 1980.[13]

Now there has been a sharp reversal of this trend. For the 1980-83 period, interest on the debt averaged 16.4 percent of all federal transfers. The average for this period conceals how sharp the relative increase has actually been in this category of transfers. In 1980 the share was 13.2 percent; by 1983 it had jumped to 17.5 percent.[14] We have come full circle since the 1950s with interest on the debt once again becoming the second largest category of transfer spending. In 1983 interest on the debt totaled $94.2 billion, as compared to $86.3 billion for federal grants to state and local governments.[15] The reasons for this change are easy to understand. It resulted, first, from soaring federal deficits, a development that pushed the federal debt-GNP ratio to 41.6 percent in 1983.[16] A second factor has been the failure of interest rates to fall since 1980 to the same degree as the overall decline in the inflation rate, a development contributing to the growth in servicing costs for the federal debt.

The full, long-term effects of this rise in the relative share of interest payments in the total of federal transfer spending are by no means clear, although by no stretch of the imagination can it be described as healthy. In *The General Theory*, J. M. Keynes spoke of the "euthanasia of the rentier," which would end the "oppressive power of the capitalist to exploit the scarcity-value of capital." "Interest," he went on to say, "to-day rewards no genuine sacrifice, any more than does the rent of land."[17] Far from being euthanized, the social-economic class that Keynes saw as getting income without any genuine sacrifice is being re-born. It does not bode well for the future of the economy that the beneficiaries of what is now the second largest category of federal transfer spending are almost overwhelmingly concentrated in the upper ranges of the income scale. In 1976, the latest years for which data are available, 46 percent of all bonds (private and public) were owned by the top 1 percent of all persons; this is the highest percentage for any form of personal wealth held by the upper 1 percent.[18]

The Anatomy of Transfers to People

Now that we have taken an overall look at the basic kinds of income transfers made by the federal government, the next step is to focus on the largest single category of transfers, namely those going to people. We shall examine both the magnitude and the precise kinds of transfers aimed directly at people. In order to do this, however, we need to make two adjustments in the figure labeled "transfer payments to persons" in the national income and product accounts. First, some of the spending shown in the national income and product accounts under the rubric "grants-in-aid to state and local governments" provides income directly to people, the reason being that some social programs are financed (in whole or in part) by the federal government, but administered by the states and cities. Among the most important of these are Medicaid, a part of AFDC (Aid to Families with Dependent Children) payments, some unemployment insurance, children's nutrition, and other forms of public assistance.[19] In 1980, for example, estimated transfers going directly to people —but appearing in the accounts as grants to state and local governments— totaled $34.9 billion; in 1983 this total was $42.4 billion.[20] The second adjustment to transfers as shown in Table 3 is to add to "transfers to people" the portion of "net interest" outlays paid to individuals. The national income and product accounts do not provide this information, but it can be estimated reasonably well on the basis of ownership of the privately held portion of the federal debt.[21] In 1980 $11.3 billion of "net interest" outlays went to persons, but by 1983 this figure had climbed to $19.7 billion.[22]

Table 4 contains a detailed breakdown reflecting these adjustments of transfers to people for 1980, the last year of the Carter administration, and for 1983, the most recent year for which data are available that re-

Table 4. ***Federal Transfer Expenditures to People by Major Subcategory: 1980, 1983 (in billions of dollars and in percent).***

	1980 Dollar Expenditures	*Percent of Total*	*1983 Dollar Expenditures*	*Percent of Total*
Social Insurance Programs				
Social Security and Distability	118.6	40.5%	164.4	41.0%
Other Retirement and Disability				
Military	12.5	4.3	16.3	4.1
Civil Service	15.5	5.3	21.2	5.3
Railroad Pensions	4.8	1.6	6.0	1.5
Subtotal	32.8	11.2	43.5	10.9
Medicare	35.6	12.2	57.2	14.3
Unemployment Insurance	18.6	6.4	28.5	7.1
Veterans' Benefits (Service Related)	8.1	2.8	9.7	2.4
Black Lung Disability	1.8	0.6	1.7	0.4
Total for Social Insurance	215.5	73.7	305.0	76.1
Income Assistance Programs				
Public Assistance ("welfare")				
AFDC	7.4	2.5	7.9	2.0
Medicaid	14.3	4.9	19.1	4.8
Subtotal	21.7	7.4	27.0	6.7
Supplemental Security Income	5.9	2.0	7.4	1.8
Food Stamps	8.2	2.8	11.1	2.8
Veterans (non-service related)	6.9	2.4	8.0	2.0
Earned Income Credit	1.3	0.4	1.2	0.3
Other*	21.7	7.4	21.5	5.4
Total for Income Assistance	65.7	22.4	76.2	19.0
Interest on the Public Debt				
Payable to Individuals	11.3	3.9	19.7	4.9
Total Transfers to People	292.5	100.0%	400.9	100.0%

*Consists primarily of grants to non-profit institutions, basic opportunity grants, children's nutrition, and grants for social services and human development services.
SOURCE: *Survey of Correct Business*, July 1983, 1984.

flect the impact of the Reagan administration's cutbacks in spending and spending priorities for transfer payments going to people. This is a key table in this article. The 1980 figures on transfers to persons shows the detailed "anatomy" of these transfers prior to the beginnings of the conservative "counter-revolution." We shall also use these data to develop a broad picture of the beneficiaries of federal largesse in the form of transfers, especially where these beneficiaries are found in the income scale. Subsequently, the 1983 data will be drawn upon for an analysis of the impact of the "counter-revolution" on this structure.

Transfer spending directed to people in Table 4 is divided into three major categories. The first of these is labeled *Social Insurance Programs.* Broadly speaking, these are programs also known as "Entitlements," the reason being that they involve income claims and benefits deriving from disability, unemployment, retirement, the death of a spouse, or, in the case of persons 65 years of age or older, from illness. They are programs that the Reagan administration has described as falling within the "Social Safety Net."[23] The Joint Economic Committee of the Congress describes these programs as "Employment-Related, Non-Income Tested," which means, when stripped of bureaucratic jargon, that the benefits paid to people relate in some way to prior work (or age in the case of medical help).[24] Having a low income *is not* a prerequisite for receiving benefits under these programs.

The second category in the table is *Income Assistance Programs.* Spending under this category is probably what most people have in mind when they use or hear the word "welfare," because it is here that we find such well-known programs as foodstamps, AFDC, and Medicaid. These programs are designed to help low-income people or persons not getting sufficient income from the Social Insurance Programs even when they are eligible for the latter. The Joint Economic Committee describes these programs as "Income-Tested Cash and In-Kind Programs," which means, first, that a "means" test is applied, and, second, that the benefits are not tied to prior income or work status, or to age. These are the transfers aimed directly at the poor. The last major category in the table is the portion of interest on the public debt payable to individuals. As already indicated, this figure is based upon that portion of the debt owed by individuals.

What do these data tell us about what the federal government is doing? Several things. By re-arranging the national income and product data to better reflect the transfers actually going to people, we find, for example, in 1980, that 72.2 percent rather than 60.8 percent of all federal transfers go directly to people. For 1983 the respective percentages are 72.6 rather than 61.5. A second—and truly major—point is that only a small proportion of the total of transfers to people are targeted directly at low-income people, persons who in the public mind fit into the "welfare" category. This, of course, is that part of the total falling under the heading of "Income Assistance Programs." This is not to say that no low-income people benefit from the other programs—they do—but the programs that account for the bulk of transfers or social spending are in the "Social Insurance Category." Because of the link between these programs and work or prior income, they are transfers that go to a large extent to the middle and upper middle classes. This matter will be examined more thoroughly when we look at the distribution of these benefits by income class. Interest payments, as we shall also demonstrate more precisely, go largely to those in the upper reaches of the income scale. Finally, if we compare 1980 and 1983 data we see that the overall tilt of federal transfers to people away from the lower income ranges has become even more pronounced. Income Assistance Programs are now responsible for only 19 percent of total transfers, compared to 22.4 percent just four years earlier. Federal transfers to people as defined earlier in this section totaled 13.5 percent of personal income in 1980, and 14.6 percent in 1983, a trend that has risen steadily in the last half-century.[25]

Federal Transfer Payments and the National Income

Another useful way to look at what the federal government is doing is to compare the total of transfer spending to the national income. Why the national income? It is the best single measure that we have of the income people get from the market by virtue of ownership of the economic resources that enter into production—namely, labor, capital and land. By comparing the national income to transfers in different years, we get a useful measure of the overall amount of income earned through the market process that is being rearranged by the mechanisms of the federal government.[26] In 1983, the total of federal transfers for all purposes was $551.0 billion. In the same year the national income totaled $2,646.7 billion. Transfers were thus equal to 20.8 percent of the national income, a figure which means that one-fifth—one dollar out of every five—of income determined by market processes is being rearranged by action of the federal government.[27] In the last half-century this particular percentage has been rising steadily. For example, in 1929 transfer spending by the federal government was equal to a mere 1.4 percent of the national income. By 1939 this percentage had climbed to 5.2. After World War II, federal transfers as a percent of the national income continued to increase, reaching 9.3 in 1950, 9.5 in 1960, 13.4 in 1970, and, finally in 1983, the current figure of 20.8 percent. The meaning of this trend is clear: the federal government is increasingly involved in determining the ultimate distribution of income earned through production.

Since the amount of money flowing through the federal government in the form of direct transfers to lower income groups (persons benefitting directly from the Income Assistance Programs shown in Table 4) is relatively small—both as a part of total transfers and in relation to the national income—it is obvious that the transfer "explosion" of the last couple of decades has involved the federal government in rearranging incomes to a far greater extent than would be the case if its transfer activities were more or less limited to those implied in what we earlier called the traditional—or classic—definition of the welfare state. To illustrate, transfer spending in 1983 under the "Income Assistance" rubric amounted to a mere 2.7 percent of the national income. Clearly, the American "welfare state" has exploded far beyond the earlier—and perhaps original—meaning of the concept. Thus, it is essential that we try to determine as fully and as accurately as possible who are the ultimate beneficiaries of the vast structure of transfer spending that dominates the federal government.

Tax Expenditures: Another Form of Transfers

Before we can turn to the above task, the picture of the redistributional role played by the federal government will not be complete until we examine another important phenomenon, one the public is probably less aware of than it is of transfers. This is "tax expenditures," a concept that first surfaced in the waning days of the Johnson administration. The concept of "tax expenditures" has not been fully or uncritically accepted even among economists. Nevertheless, it is a notion that provides important and additional insight into how the power of the federal government is being used to determine who gets what in the way of money income in the economy.

One aspect of tax expenditures differentiates them from transfers in general: they are defined by statute, which is not the case with transfer payments. The 1974 Congressional Budget Act identifies tax expenditures as "those revenue losses attributable to provisions of the federal tax laws which allow a special exclusion, exemption, or deduction from gross income or which provide a special credit, a preferential rate of tax, or a deferred tax liability."[28] Simply put, tax expenditures are revenue losses resulting from special or selective tax relief for persons or businesses. They are called "expenditures" because their economic effects are quite like transfer payments made by the government, except that they come about through a reduction in the taxes people pay rather than through their being the beneficiaries of federal spending.[29] As with transfer payments, income is different from what it would have been in the absence of such payments; thus they are an important part of any picture of the redistributional activities of the federal government.

Just as there has been an "explosion" in transfer spending by the federal government, there has been an equally important "explosion" in tax expenditures. The latter, however, is much more recent and far less known to the public than the growth in transfer spending. But the implications of the tax expenditure "explosion" both for the federal revenue system and for the role of the federal government in determining the distribution of income are profound and far-reaching. Tables 5 and 6 tell the dramatic story of this development.

Table 5. ***Total Federal Taxes and Tax Expenditures: 1975-1983 (billions of dollars).***

Year	*Total Taxes*	*Total Tax Expenditures*	*Ratio**
1975	$283.4	$ 92.9	32.8%
1976	314.9	97.4	30.9
1977	365.9	113.5	31.0
1978	414.3	123.8	29.9
1979	480.8	150.1	31.2
1980	529.9	181.5	34.3
1981	610.3	228.6	37.5
1982	627.8	266.3	42.4
1983	630.7	306.4	48.6

*Tax expenditures divided by total taxes.

SOURCES: Congressional Budget Office, *Tax Expenditures*, September, 1981; *Economic Report of the President*, 1984. All figures are on a fiscal year basis.

In Table 5 are shown since 1975 total taxes collected by the federal government, total tax expenditures, and the ratio of the latter to the former. Up until 1980 tax expenditures averaged roughly 31 percent of tax collections, but in the latter year the ratio of tax expenditures to taxes began to rise rapidly. By 1983 tax expenditures amounted to nearly half the amount of taxes actually collected. The actual figure was 48.6 percent.

The story told by the data in Table 6 is even more dramtic. Tax expenditures are of two basic kinds, those benefitting corporations and those benefitting individuals. In this table we show for the last four years the total of individual and corporate income taxes paid in comparison to tax

Table 6. ***Federal Individual and Corporation Income Taxes and Tax Expenditures: 1980-1983 (billions of dollars).***

	Individuals			*Corporations*		
	Taxes Paid	*Tax Expenditures*	*Ratio**	*Taxes Paid*	*Tax Expenditures*	*Ratio**
1980	$250.4	$137.4	54.9%	$69.9	$44.1	63.1%
1981	289.4	179.8	62.1	69.3	46.8	67.5
1982	311.4	214.2	68.8	50.9	52.1	102.4
1983	294.1	248.2	84.4	53.8	58.2	108.2

*Tax expenditures divided by total taxes.

SOURCES: Congressional Budget Office, *Tax Expenditures*, April, 1980, September, 1981; *Economic Report of the President*, 1984. All figures are on a fiscal year basis.

expenditures for individuals and corporations. As far as individuals are concerned the ratio of tax expenditures to income taxes collected has soared from 54.9 percent in 1980 to 84.4 percent in 1983. What this means is that for every dollar of the tax base—that is, for every dollar of income subject to taxation—84.4 cents is not subject to taxation. An even more dramatic change has taken place with respect to the corporate income tax. For this tax the ratio of tax expenditures to taxes paid by corporations has gone from 63.1 percent to 108.2 percent, meaning that for every dollar of corporate income constituting the corporate tax base, $1.08 of income is not subject to taxation. These figures offer additional evidence of the atrophy of the corporate income tax, which now (1983) accounts for only 9.3 percent of federal revenue, in contrast to 12.9 percent in 1980 and 22.3 percent in 1960.[30] As corporations pay less and less of federal taxes—since 1980 both the absolute amount and relative share of the corporate income tax has declined—the tax burden is being shifted to individuals, particularly in the form of rapid increases both absolutely and relatively in payroll (Social Security) taxes. This development has made the federal tax structure less progressive.

The Combined Effect of Transfers and Tax Expenditures

Earlier we pointed out that by 1983 total transfer spending by the federal government was equal to 20.8 percent of the national income, a percentage meaning that federal government activities redistribute one dollar out of every five of earned income. This percentage jumps significantly if we add tax expenditures to transfer payments. In 1983 the combined total of tax expenditures ($306.4 billion) and transfers of all kinds ($551.0 billion) was $857.4 billion. This amounts to 32.4 percent of the 1983 national income of $2,650.2 billion. Approximately *one* dollar out of every *three* is subject to redistribution. The dollar amount and the percentage figure are measures of magnitude. They do not tell us whether the activities they reflect are worthwhile, nor do they describe the major beneficiaries of either transfer payments or tax expenditures. The latter is a task undertaken in the next section. But the combination of transfer payments and tax expenditures adds up to an "income transfer system" at work in the U.S. government, the scale of which truly staggers the imagination. The "system," if we want to designate it thus, has come into existence in piecemeal fashion over the last half-century. Probably most members of the public, not to mention more sophisticated observers, have only a faint understanding of the variety of ways in which governmental power directly affects the income people get. But the system exists.

Transfers and Tax Expenditures: Who Are the Beneficiaries?

Now that we have established the existence in the U.S. economy of a vast and complicated income redistributional system, we need to answer these key questions: (1) Who are the prime beneficiaries of this system? (2) How is the poverty level affected by the structure of transfers and tax expenditures? and (3) How is the distribution of income affected by this same structure? The answers to these questions will yield significant insights into the overall impact of this system on the U.S. economy and the way it works. Unfortunately, it is virtually impossible to obtain wholly definitive answers to these questions, given the complexity of the subject and the elusiveness of available data. Nevertheless, some tentative conclusions firmly grounded in available data are possible.

First, let us examine the question of who are the beneficiaries of income transfers to persons found in Table 4. Table 7, using data from the Cur-

Table 7. ***Distribution of Families, Earned Income, Property Income, Social Security Income, and Public Assistance: 1982 (in percent).****

Income Range	*All Families*	*Earned Income***	*Property Income*	*Social Security*	*Public Assistance*
0-$9,999 (Poverty)	16.6%	1.6%	1.8%	17.8%	77.4%
$10,000-$19,999 (Near Poor)	24.6	11.0	10.9	38.1	22.5
$20,000-$29,999 (Lower Middle Class)	23.0	20.8	16.2	21.6	—
$30,000-$39,999 (Middle Class)	15.8	21.3	15.6	11.3	—
$40,000-$59,999 (Upper Middle Class)	13.8	26.0	21.6	7.4	—
$60,000-$74,999 (Affluent)	3.2	8.2	10.1	1.9	—
Over $75,000 (Rich)	3.0	11.1	23.9	1.9	—
	100.0	100.0	100.0	100.0	100.0

*Details may not add to 100.0% because of rounding.

**Employment and self-employment income.

SOURCE: U.S. Department of Commerce, Current Population Reports, *Money Income of Households, Families, and Persons in the United States: 1982*, February, 1984.

rent Population Reports of the U.S. Department of Commerce, divides the population into seven social-economic "classes," ranging from "Poverty" and "Near-Poor" at the lower end of the income scale to "Affluent" and "Rich" at the top. This is done to provide a rough guide to how the different kinds of income, including transfers, are divided among families in different income ranges.[31] If we look, first, at the proportion of Social Security income and Public Assistance going to families in the "Poverty" range, and apply these proportions to the 1980 figures in Table 4, it works out that about 25 percent of all transfer income goes to those in the lowest income range. The data in Table 4, it will be recalled, show that a little more than 22 percent of all transfers to people were targeted at the poor (the "Income Assistance" category), but since some of Social Security income also goes to people in the poverty range (17.8 percent, according to Table 7), the 25 percent figure for the overall proportion of transfer spending going to the poor is no doubt accurate. If we add to the picture the proportions of Social Security and Public Assistance Income going to families in the "Near-Poor" category in addition to those in the "Poverty" classification, it works out that approximately 52 percent of all transfers (1980) go to families with incomes of $20,000 or less. The "Near-Poor" category would include the "working poor," as evidenced by the percentages of earned and property income going to this group, as well as some retired persons and families getting public assistance. So what is our basic conclusion? Although most of the transfers to people as defined and shown in Table 4 are not targeted to the poor, there is a mild degree of progression in the distribution of transfer income. Table 7 shows that roughly 17 percent of families are in the "Poverty" income range, and, according to our calculations, they got about 25 percent of all transfer income in 1980. If we include the "Near-Poor" as well as "Poverty"-level families, then 41 percent of all families receive 52 percent of transfers.

If, as the foregoing figures indicate, there is some mild progression in the structure of transfer payments, the same thing cannot be said about tax expenditures. Unfortunately, there is an extreme paucity of data on the incidence of tax expenditures, even though the Congressional Budget Office reports annually in great detail on the specific items entering into the totals flowing to both corporations and individuals.[32] The situation is not hopeless, however. At the request of two members of the Congress,[33] the Treasury Department undertook two studies—one in 1974 and the other in 1981—that developed estimates of the benefits that individuals by adjusted gross income class received from the major tax expenditures. By combining these two studies, we obtain a reasonably accurate picture

Table 8. *Major Tax Expenditures* by Type and by Income Class (in percent).*

Tax Expenditure By Type and Rank	*INCOME CLASS* 0-$9,999 (Poor)	$10,000-$19,999 (Near Poor)	$20,000-$49,999 (Middle-Class)	$50,000-$99,999 (Affluent)	Over $100,000 (Rich)
Employer Contributions to Pensions	9.3%	35.8%	36.8%	12.6%	5.5%
Mortgage Interest on Owner-Occupied Homes	1.1	6.3	62.6	23.8	6.1
State and Local Taxes	0.7	4.1	48.0	28.3	19.0
Capital Gains	3.2	5.2	28.0	24.0	39.5
Employer Contributions to Medical Insurance	6.5	19.5	61.1	10.6	2.2
Charitable Contributions	0.4	4.3	40.0	23.9	31.4
Social Security and Pension Income	70.4	18.5	8.5	1.8	0.8
Property Taxes on Owner-Occupied Homes	1.2	6.3	54.7	26.4	11.4
Interest: Consumer Credit	6.8	41.8	42.7	7.1	1.9
Interest on Life Insurance	19.7	26.1	29.6	13.7	10.9

*Ten largest types of tax expenditures, ranked by size in 1983.

SOURCE: U.S. Treasury, Reports compiled for former Senator Walter Mondale and U.S. Representative Henry S. Ruess.

Table 9. ***Distribution of Tax Expenditures,* Tax Returns, and Taxes Paid By Income Class (in percent).***

	INCOME CLASS				
Distribution of:	*0-$9,999 (Poor)*	*$10,000-$19,999 (Near Poor)*	*$20,000-$49,999 (Middle-Class)*	*$50,000-$99,999 (Affluent)*	*Over $100,000 (Rich)*
Tax Returns	36.9%	26.0%	32.7%	3.7%	0.7%
Taxes Paid	2.2	13.9	51.1	18.3	14.6
Tax Expenditures	4.5	10.2	45.5	25.1	14.7

*Distribution of the total or tax expenditures for the ten items in Table 8. This total accounted for 74.6 percent of all tax expenditures in 1983.

SOURCE: Same as Table 8.

of distribution of tax expenditures by income class. This is done in Tables 8 and 9. In Table 8 are listed in order of magnitude using 1983 data the ten largest tax expenditure items, which, in total, accounted for in this year 74.6 percent of all tax expenditures going to individuals. For each type of tax expenditure the proportion going to the indicated income class is shown. The percentage figures in italics in the table indicate which income class is the main beneficiary for that particular type of tax expenditure. For some types of tax expenditures, as with "Employer Contributions to Pensions," two of the percentage figures are shown in italics. This simply indicates that two income classes rather than one should be regarded as the primary beneficiaries of the tax expenditure in question. On this basis, the "Poor" are the prime beneficiary for only one kind of tax expenditure, the "Near-Poor" have this status in two cases, the "Middle Class" in six instances, the "Affluent" in four, and the "Rich" in two. The italics serve to show in a rough visual way how tax expenditures are skewed toward the upper ranges of the income scale.[34] Scrutiny of the percentage data in the table reinforces this perception. Table 9 provides more complete statistical verification for this. This table shows the distribution among the same income classes of total tax returns, total taxes paid, and total tax expenditures. If we lump together taxpayers classified as "Rich" and "Affluent," these two income classes represent only 4.4 percent of the taxpayers, but benefit from 39.8 percent of tax expenditures. The "Middle Class" gets 45.5 percent of all tax expenditures, while accounting for 32.7 percent of all tax returns. At the lower end of the income scale, the "Poor" and the "Near-Poor" file 62.9 percent of all tax returns, but get only 14.7 percent of the benefits from tax expenditures. Thus tax expenditures are skewed heavily toward the middle and upper ends of the income scale.

If we draw together all the findings contained in previous paragraphs in this section, what should we conclude at this point? On the basis of the foregoing data and findings, imperfect as they may be, it is clear, first, that the vast and complex redistributional machinery of the federal government does not simply rearrange incomes from the top downward, leaving those at the top with less income and assuring that those at the bottom always have more. The pattern of redistribution is much less clearcut, much more complex, much more skewed toward the middle and the top, once tax expenditures as well as transfers are taken into account. This should not be surprising. As asserted earlier in this article, a major reason for the explosive growth in transfer spending in the U.S. economy is the unwillingness of large numbers of people to accept the verdict of the market in the distribution of income. Hence, they turn to using the power of the state to alter income distribution in their favor. Something similar to this has been going on with respect to the tax system, for tax expenditures, in the final analysis, are nothing more than a reflection of the same kind of power. Our basic conclusion is this: the pattern noted in the distribution of benefits from both transfers and tax expenditures largely reflects the distribution of power in our society. Those with power, found primarily in the upper and middle parts of the income scale, have the most ready access to federal largesse, and those with little or no power, found mostly toward the bottom, are far less successful in bending the redistributional machinery of the federal government to their advantage. None of this can be measured with the statistical precision we might desire, but overall the statistical evidence we can muster supports this conclusion. It will be reinforced when we examine the results of the Reagan counterrevolution.

The fact that the mildly progressive character of transfer payments, when combined with the regressive nature of tax expenditures, tilts the federal income redistributional system toward the middle and upper classes helps explain an important paradox, one having to do with the second and third questions posed at the beginning of this section. These, it will be recalled, involved the impact of the federal redistributional system on poverty and the distribution of income. The paradox is this: How was it possible to bring about a substantial reduction in the number and percent of families living in poverty in this country, while at the same time leaving the distribution of income virtually unchanged?

Consider the following facts. In 1960, the percentage of all Americans living below the poverty line was 22.2; by 1973 this percentage had fallen to 11.1, the lowest point since the beginning in 1965 of President Johnson's "War on Poverty."[35] There is a rough correspondence between the progress against poverty and the explosive growth in transfer spending. The Congressional Budget Office reported in the late 1970s that without transfer income, more than 25 percent of U.S. families would fall below the poverty line.[36] During this same period, however, there was practically no change in the distribution of family income in the United States. In 1965, for example, families in the lowest fifth of the income scale got 5.2 percent of aggregate money income; those in the highest fifth got 40.9 percent. Twelve years later, in 1977, the lowest fifth was still getting 5.2 percent, while the top fifth had increased its share slightly to 41.5 percent.[37]

The paradox of a declining poverty rate and a static distribution of income is explained by the fact that as transfers grew and contributed directly to a reduction in poverty, the growth in tax expenditures had the opposite effect since they were skewed toward the upper end of the income scale. These two tendencies offset one another—the thrust toward greater equality brought about by the transfer explosion being nullified by the thrust toward less equality resulting from an equally explosive growth in transfer expenditures. This conclusion is verified by the experience of the last three years as the economy began to absorb the effects of the Reagan counterrevolution. For the first time since World War II there has been a decided shift in the pattern of income distribution toward the direction of greater inequality. As we shall see in the next section, this is largely accounted for by the Reagan administration's tax and spending policies.

The Conservative Counterrevolution

Ronald Reagan's victory in the 1980 presidential race brought more than the normal postwar swing from a mildly liberal Democratic administration to a mildly conservative Republican administration. Unlike the preceding Nixon and Ford administrations, President Reagan in his first month in office challenged directly the basic consensus that had set the bounds for policy making since the end of World War II. This consensus involved, first, an acceptance of the broad contours of the U.S. welfare state as it had evolved since the end of World War II, and, second, active demand management policies to promote economic stability and growth within this framework. The Reagan administration set out to dismantle this consensus, its primary objective being to bring about a radical shift in the role played by the federal government in the economy. In this section we shall examine how well the administration's counterrevolution has succeeded, particularly with respect to the impact that the administration's policies have had on the income redistributional system analyzed earlier in this paper.

President Reagan's counterrevolution involved a four-fold strategy. First, there was to be a substantial reduction in the rate of growth of federal spending, a reduction that would also scale back sharply the *relative* size of the federal government. Federal spending relative to the GNP was scheduled to fall from 23.0 percent in 1981 to 19.0 percent by 1986.[38] This reflected the Reagan administration's belief that federal spending along with federal taxes were the major causes of the nation's economic difficulties. Since the administration planned a major build-up in military spending, overall cutbacks in federal outlays could come only at the expense of social spending. This is what has happened. The second element in the Reagan program was a major, across-the-board reduction in personal income taxes plus major tax relief for business, primarily through accelerated depreciation. Supply side economics, with its belief that incentives to work, save, and to invest are badly hurt by taxes, provided the necessary intellectual rationale for the massive tax cuts ultimately enacted.[39] The intent was to shift the tax burden away from business and the upper income groups generally, an intent that largely succeeded. The two remaining elements in the Reagan program involved scaling back the regulatory functions of the federal government and getting strong monetary support from the Federal Reserve as the fiscal elements in the program became operative. To the dismay of the administration, tighter money in 1981 overshadowed the supply-side impact of the tax cuts, plunging the economy into the deepest recession since the 1930s.[40]

Before turning to specific impacts of the administration's policies on the U.S. welfare state (as we have been using this term), as well as on the distribution of income, a few comments are in order on the overall results of the Reagan program. Table 10 shows projected and actual results for five key variables: (1) federal spending as a percent of the GNP; (2) the federal deficit; (3) the rate of growth of GNP; (4) the inflation rate; and (5) the unemployment rate. As these data indicate, the results are mixed. The goal of shrinking the relative size of the federal government is further away than it was when the administration came into office. Federal spending has reached the highest percent of GNP (an estimated 24 percent in 1984) in any year after World War II. The severity of the recession plus the rapid military build-up is responsible for this. The supply-side illusion that growth would be so rapid following the tax cut that the deficit would be eliminated by the end of this year proved to be just that—an illusion. Deficits now have reached record levels, even under current boom conditions, and there is little expectation that they will be reduced significantly in the foreseeable future. The ultimate impact of deficits of this magnitude on the economy's future performance remains unknown, although there is little doubt that they provided a major Keynesian-style stimulus to the economy, bringing about the 1984 boom. The administration's primary success was in bringing down the inflation rate at a far more rapid pace than was foreseen in the president's 1981 forecasts. This is, of course, a major plus for the administration, though achieved at the cost of a severe recession.

The record on unemployment is mixed, as it has failed to drop as rapidly as anticipated. It now stands about where it was when the administration took office in 1981, although it rose to record post-World War II levels during the recession. In fairness, it should be noted that the Reagan experience with unemployment is not significantly different than that after prior recessions. It has been extremely difficult after any reces-

Table 10. ***Key Objectives of the Reagan Administration: Projected and Actual Results: 1981-1984.***

Year	*Federal Spending as Percent of GNP*		*Federal Deficit*[1]		*Rate of Growth of GNP*		*Inflation Rate*		*Unemployment Rate*	
	Projected	*Actual*	*Projected*	*Actual*	*Projected*	*Actual*	*Projected*	*Actual*	*Projected*	*Actual*
1981	23.0%	22.2%	$–54.5	$–57.9	1.1%	2.5%	11.1%	8.9%	7.8%	7.5%
1982	21.8	23.7	–45.0	–110.6	4.2	–2.1	8.3	3.9	7.2	9.5
1983	20.4	25.7	–23.0	–195.4	5.0	3.7	6.2	3.8	6.6	9.5
1984	19.4	24.0*	0.5	–177.8	4.5	5.3*	5.5	4.2**	6.4	7.5**

[1]Billions of current dollars.

*Estimated.

**Average for first 9 months, 1984.

SOURCE: *Current Economic Indicators*, July, 1984. (Federal spending as a percent of GNP and federal deficit are fiscal year data.)

sion to get the unemployment rate back down to where it was before the recession. Since the end of the 1960s there has been a secular upward drift in the unemployment rate, a development for which there is not a clear explanation. The growth record is also mixed, embracing a sharp fall in the rate of growth during the 1982 recession, but a solid recovery and strong boom in 1983 and 1984.

So much for the general picture. What has been the impact of the Reagan program on the U.S. "welfare state" and the distribution of income in our society? These are the "bottom line" questions. From the mass of statistical data now available concerning actions of the administration since 1981, two clear findings emerge.

First, the administration's cutbacks in social spending (transfers to persons) has tilted the redistributional machinery of the federal government—already weighted in favor of the middle class—further away from the poor and near poor and toward families higher up on the income scale. To the extent that the U.S. "welfare state" before Reagan was primarily a middle class-based welfare state, the Reagan administration policies have made it more so. If, as indicated earlier, the structure of federal transfer was mildly progressive in 1980, it is now less so. Table 11 documents this shift, showing in real terms (1972 dollars) federal transfer spending to people for the same major categories initially analyzed in Table 4. In real terms *all* of the reductions in social spending are to be found in the Income Assistance Category, which are the programs targeted to the poor and near poor. Overall, these programs were reduced by 3.8 percent, whereas real spending for the essentially middle-class programs found under the Social Insurance rubric rose by 17.2 percent. Real transfers to persons through interest on the public debt jumped by an astounding 44.4 percent.

Recent studies by the Congressional Budget Office and the Urban Institute confirm the regressive character of the Reagan administration cuts in social spnding. Table 12 documents by income range the amount of cash and "in kind" benefits lost per household in each income range for 1984. Figures in the table are in 1982 dollars. Families with incomes below $10,000 (poverty level) have been hardest hit by the Reagan programs, having their incomes reduced on the average by $375 or 7.5 percent. At the upper end of the scale, families with incomes of $80,000 or more lost only $131 or less than 0.1 percent of their income. The Urban Institute has pointed out that if the Congress had enacted all of the *proposed* budget reductions of the Reagan administration, the losses would have been more than twice as large and even more heavily concentrated on the low-income assistance programs.[41]

Table 11. ***Federal Transfer Expenditures to People by Major Subcategory: 1980 and 1983 (in billions of 1972 dollars).***

Social Insurance Programs	*1980*	*1983*	*Percent Change*
Social Security and Disability	$ 66.5	$ 76.3	14.7%
Other Retirement and Disability			
Military	7.0	7.6	8.6
Civil Service	8.7	9.8	12.6
Railroad Pensions	2.7	2.8	3.7
Subtotal	18.4	20.2	9.8
Medicare	20.0	26.6	33.0
Unemployment Insurance	10.4	13.2	26.9
Veterans' Benefits (service related)	4.5	4.5	—
Black Lung Disability	1.0	0.8	-20.0
Total for Social Insurance	120.8	141.6	17.2%
Income Assistance Programs			
Public Assistance ("welfare")	4.1	3.6	-12.2%
AFDC	8.0	8.9	11.1
Medicaid	12.1	12.5	3.3
Subtotal	3.3	3.4	3.0
Supplemental Security Income	4.6	5.2	13.0
Veterans (non-service connected)	3.9	3.7	-5.1
Earned Income Credit	0.7	0.6	-14.3
Other	12.2	10.0	-18.0
Total for Income Assistance	36.8	35.14	-3.8
Interest on the Public Debt			
Payable to Individuals	6.3	9.1	44.4
Total Transfers to People	163.9	186.1	13.5%

SOURCE: *Survey of Current Business*, July, 1983, 1984.

Second, the 1981 tax cuts—the centerpiece of the Reagan administration's recovery program—were skewed heavily in favor of upper income groups. Table 13 contains estimates made by the Congressional Budget Office of tax changes per household for different income brackets for the years 1982 through 1984. These are tax changes resulting solely from the Economic Recovery Tax Act of 1981, the act that incorporated the basic tax cut proposals of the Reagan administration. Overall, the tax savings flowing to the highest income category—households with incomes in excess of $80,000—exceeded $21,000 over the three-year period, while households in the lowest income category, namely those with incomes of less than $10,000, had tax savings of only $60. This kind of an outcome

Table 12. ***Reduction in Benefit Payments per Household in Fiscal Year 1984 (in 1982 dollars).***

	Household Income					
	Less than $10,000	*$10,000–20,000*	*$20,000–40,000–*	*$40,000 80,000*	*$80,000 or More*	*All Households*
Cash Benefits[a]						
Reductions (in dollars)	$217	$154	$ 67	$ 41	$ 85	$112
Reductions as a % of Household Income	4.3	1.0	0.2	0.1	c	0.5
In-Kind Benefits[b]						
Reductions (in dollars)	$158	$ 84	$ 46	$ 56	$ 46	$ 84
Reductions as a % of Household Income	3.2	0.6	0.2	0.1	c	0.4
Total Benefits						
Reductions (in dollars)	$375	$238	$113	$ 97	$131	$196
Reductions as a % of Household Income	7.5	1.6	0.4	0.2	c	0.8

[a] Includes Social Security, Railroad Retirement, Civil Service Retirement, Veterans' Compensation, Veterans' Pension, SSI, Unemployment Insurance, AFDC, and Low-Income Energy Assistance.

[b] Includes Food Stamps, Child Nutrition, Guaranteed Student Loans, Student Financial Assistance, Medicare, Medicaid, and Housing Assistance.

[c] Less than 0.1 percent.

SOURCE: The Uurban Institute, ***The Reagan Record***, 1984.

Table 13. ***Individual Income Tax Changes Per Household by Income Category: 1982-1984 (in current dollars).***

Calendar Year	*Household Income Range* *Less Than $10,000*	*$10,000 to 20,000*	*$20,000 to 40,000*	*$40,000 to 80,000*	*Over $80,000*
1982	–$10	–$130	–$460	–$1,170	–$5,100
1983	–$20	–$240	–$910	–$2,260	–$7,510
1984	–$30	–$290	–$1,130	–$2,870	–$8,750
Total: 1982-84	–$60	–$660	–$2,500	–$6,300	–$21,360

SOURCE: Congressional Budget Office, *Staff Memorandum*, March, 1984.

was inevitable, given the across-the-board structure of the tax cut. The disequalizing impact of the change was increased by the reduction in top rate on unearned income (that is, property income) from 70 to 50 percent, a change that also had the effect of reducing the maximum rate on capital gains from 28 to 20 percent.[42] The shift in the overall tax burden away from the upper income groups was deliberate, reflecting in part the extreme supply-side view that *all* taxes impede incentives, and the more traditional conservative view that taxes on income from capital depress personal saving and business investment. As the Council of Economic Advisers said in its 1982 *Report*: "The Economic Recovery Tax Act of 1981 has changed the basic character of the tax system by shifting the burden of taxation away from capital income, thereby providing substantially greater incentives for capital investments and personal saving."[43]

One significant result of these changes was a slight reduction in the progressivity of the federal income tax. According to an analysis of changes between 1980 and 1984 made by the Urban Institute, families in the lowest fifth of the income scale had an increase in their effective tax rate from 0.5 percent of pre-tax income in 1980 to 1.2 percent in 1984. Families in the top fifth, however, enjoyed a reduction in the effective rate on their income from 19.5 percent in 1980 to 18.9 percent in 1984. If changes in the payroll tax over this period—1980 to 1984—are taken into account, the shift toward a relatively higher burden on the lower-income groups is more pronounced. The changes for families in each income quintal for both federal income and payroll taxes as a percent of pre-tax income are summarized in Table 14. With payroll taxes added in, there was no reduction in the overall combined tax rate for all families, though the overall structure became slightly less progressive.

As one might readily surmise, the combination of the Raegan administration's social spending cuts and tax reductions has had two major con-

Table 14. *Federal Income and Payroll Taxes for Families by Quintiles: 1980 and 1984 (percent by pre-tax income).*

	Poorest Fifth		*Second Fifth*		*Third Fifth*		*Fourth Fifth*		*Wealthiest Fifth*		*All Families*	
	1980	*1984*	*1980*	*1984*	*1980*	*1984*	*1980*	*1984*	*1980*	*1984*	*1980*	*1984*
Federal Income Tax	0.5%	1.2%	6.3%	6.0%	10.5%	9.4%	14.0%	12.6%	19.5%	18.9%	13.9%	13.4%
Federal Payroll Tax	3.2	3.7	4.6	5.2	5.3	5.8	5.3	5.9	4.5	5.0	4.8	5.3
Total	3.7	4.9	10.9	11.2	15.8	15.2	19.3	18.5	24.0	23.9	18.7	18.7

SOURCE: The Urban Institute, *The Reagan Record*, 1984.

sequences. First, the proportion of persons and families below the poverty line has risen, and, second, there has been a slight but decided change in the distribution of family income in the direction of greater inequality. These are the major changes brought about by this administration, changes that must be weighed against the other and more positive accomplishments of this administration, especially the progress against inflation.

Tables 15 and 16 document these important consequences of the conservative counterrevolution. Table 15 shows for both individuals and important family categories what has happened with respect to poverty

Table 15. ***Persons Below the Poverty Level, Selected Categories and Years: 1960-1984.***

	Persons			*Families*			
Year	*All Persons*	*Over 65*	*Children*	*All Families*	*Black*	*Female Head*	*Unrelated Individuals*
1960	22.2%	NA	26.5%	20.7%	NA	48.9%	45.2
1966	14.7	28.5	17.4	13.1	40.9	39.8	38.3
1970	12.6	24.5	14.9	10.9	32.2	38.1	32.9
1975	12.3	15.3	16.8	10.9	30.1	37.5	25.1
1980	13.0	15.7	17.9	11.5	31.1	36.7	22.9
1981	14.0	15.3	19.5	12.5	33.2	38.7	23.4
1982	15.0	14.6	21.3	13.6	34.9	40.6	23.1
1983	15.2	14.1	21.7	13.8	34.7	40.2	23.4

SOURCE: Current Population Reports.

in the United States in recent years, while Table 16 does the same thing for the distribution of income to families. The significant finding in Table 15 is that there has been a sharp increase in the poverty rate for all of the categories shown, save persons over 65. In the latter case, the poverty rate continued to fall even during the 1981-82 recession. This has resulted from a combination of a decline in the rate of inflation and *real* increases in Social Security benefits, the latter being tied to the indexing of such benfits. As we have already seen (Table 11), Social Security outlays in real terms grew by 14.7 percent between 1980 and 1983. Social Security, largely because of the voting strength and political sophistication of the over-65 population, is nearly sacrosanct, something that cannot be said with respect to the Income Assistance programs. Thus the Ragan administration was able without fear of polical retribution to concentrate cuts in social spending on programs mainly affecting the poor and near poor.

Table 16. ***Real Disposable Family Income: 1980 and 1984 (in 1982 dollars).***

	1980		*1984*			
Quintal	*Average Disposable Income*	*Percentage Share*	*Disposable Income*	*Percentage Share*	*Percent Change**	*Attributable to Reagan Policies*
Poorest	$ 6,913	6.8%	$ 6,391	6.1%	–7.6%	–4.1%
Second	13,391	13.2	13,163	12.5	–1.7	–3.0
Third	18,857	18.5	19,034	18.1	0.9	–1.7
Fourth	24,866	24.5	25,724	24.5	3.4	–0.6
Wealthiest	37,618	37.0	40,880	38.9	8.7	1.6
All Families	$20,333	100.0	$21,038	100.0	3.5%	–0.5

*1984 Real Income over 1980 Real Income.

SOURCE: The Urban Institute, *The Reagan Record*, 1984.

The latter simply do not vote in anywhere near the proportions of persons higher up on the income scale.[44]

For all the other categories shown in the table, including *all* persons and *all* families, the poverty rate has risen steadily over the 1980-1983 period. As a matter of fact, the low point for both persons and families in the "war on poverty" was reached in 1973, when the index for all persons had fallen to 11.1 percent (from 22.2 percent in 1960), and for all families to 9.7 percent (from 20.7 percent in 1960).[45] From that point on, the poverty index rose slowly through 1979, and then accelerated sharply upward from 1980 onward. What is especially shocking about these data are the figures for children, black families, and families headed by women with no male present. In all three cases, the poverty rate is not many percentage points below the rate that prevailed in 1960, thus indicating that much of the gain made in the "war on poverty" between 1965 and the early 1970s has been wiped out. Children, women, and minority families are the particular victims of the latest upsurge in poverty in this country. Some of the blame for this must be attributed to the severity of the 1981-82 recession, but the continued rise in the poverty rate in the face of the strong 1983 recovery has to be accounted for by the change in social spending priorities established and carried out by the Ragan administration. Since the sharp reduction in the poverty rate in the U.S. economy between 1965 and 1973 is accounted for almost wholly by the growth in federal transfers, it also follows that the cutbacks in real terms in social spending targeted primarily at the poor are responsible for the sharp increase in the poverty rate over the last four years.[46]

The other significant consequence of the conservative counterrevolution is the definite change in the distribution of family income in the U.S. economy. This change, which is in the direction of more inequality, may have even greater long-run significance than the rise in the poverty rate. Table 16, which is taken from the Urban Institute's wide-ranging and thoroughly documented study, *The Reagan Record*, shows what has happened to family real disposable income—after-tax income. Families are arrayed by quintals, from the poorest to the wealthiest. This table, because it measures income after taxes, yields a better picture of the combined impact on families of the Reagan administration's social spending cuts and tax changes than does the Current Population Reports data on income distribution, since the latter are normally before taxes. What is most striking about these data is the magnitude of the shift in income distribution that has taken place in such a short period. This change has to be viewed against the fact that for all practical purposes, the pattern of income distribution for families by quintals changed very little over the whole of the post-World War II period.[47] The degree to which the distribution has been tilted toward the top is indicated by the fact that the share of the three poorest quintals dropped between 1980 and 1984, the share of the fourth wealthiest was unchanged, while the share of the wealthiest fifth increased by 1.8 percentage points, or 5.1 percent. Looked at in another way, in 1980 the average disposable income in the wealthiest fifth of families was 5.4 times larger than the average for families in the poorest fifth. By 1984, however, families in the wealthiest fifth had an average disposable income 6.4 times larger than families in the poorest fifth. In fairness, it should be pointed out that not all of these changes are the result of Reagan administration policies. The Urban Institute has estimated the proportion of the overall changes that can be attributed directly to the administration's policies as contrasted to the changes that probably would have taken place under an alternative scenario involving smaller cuts in both social spending and in taxation.[48] These figures are shown in the last column of Table 16.

Some Concluding Observations

It is clear from the data examined in this article that the Reagan-led conservative counterrevolution has been a major factor in both the rise in the poverty rate and the tilt in income distribution in the direction of greater inequality. The former was not supposed to happen, while the latter was the intended outcome of administration policies. Cutting taxes for those in the upper brackets is supposed to stimulate work, saving, and investment, but providing income without work (that is, welfare) to those at the lower end of the income scale promotes and perpetuates idleness. This is the basic thrust of supply-side economics, the theoretical rationale for the Reagan program. The justification for the differential treatment of the rich and the poor is the belief that ultimately everyone, rich and poor alike, will be better off because of the stimulus to growth provided by the supply-side approach. It remains to be seen, of course, whether this will ever happen.

Beyond the fact of the immediate rise in the poverty rate and shift in income distribution in the direction of greater inequality, the full, long-term consequences of the Reagan counterrevolution are not readily apparent. As Keynes pointed out in *The General Theory*, making long-term forecasts for investments, let alone the state of the whole economy, is a risky undertaking.[49] Nevertheless, there are some things that can be said with reasonable assurance about the impact of the Reagan program on the economy's future. Several interrelated points are important.

First, the Reagan administration has succeeded in bringing about a major shift in the role played in the economy by the federal government, a shift that may not be nearly so far-reaching as that which accompanied the "New Deal," but one that is, nevertheless, real. It will not be easy for any future administration, especially one of a liberal propensity, to bring public policy back to a pre-1980 course. This is true in spite of the fact that the administration has not succeeded in shrinking the size of the federal government as measured by federal spending in relation to the GNP. Two factors will seriously inhibit, if not prevent altogether, any major reversal of the cutbacks in social spending—especially such spending for the poor—initiated by the Reagan administration. They are, first, the enormous build-up in military spending, which by now has acquired such a momentum that it may be beyond the effective control of *any* administration, liberal or conservative.[50] Second, and even more important, there is the prospect of deficits in the $200-billion plus range extending into the foreseeable future. No new spending initiatives nor significant spending restorations are likely in the face of such deficits. Given, too, the anti-tax mood of the nation, it is unrealistic to expect any major reductions in the deficit through tax increases, even if this were desirable. On a practical level, a major consequence of the 1981 tax cuts and the ensuing deficits has been the weakening of fiscal policy as an instrument for managing the economy. There simply is no longer any margin for either tax or spending changes for this purpose. This, of course, is not an unwelcome result as far as the administration is concerned, since it does not believe in an active management policy, especially in attmpting to "fine-tune" the economy.[51]

A second point concerns the shift in income distribution in the direction of greater inequality. It is too early to say whether this trend will continue as a result of the forces let loose by the conservative counterrevolution. Nonetheless, it is hard to see, supply-side rhetoric to the contrary, that such a change bodes well for the economy's future. We should not overlook the fact that the highly unequal distribution of income that prevailed in the 1920s was a major factor in the collapse that began in October 1929.[52] We are, of course, a long way from that era, when the wealthiest 5 percent of families received 30 percent of the income. Even so, an increase in the income share in three years (1980-1982) of the wealthiest 5 percent of families from 15.3 to 16.0 percent should not be dismissed lightly. More instability rather than less is a likely by-product of more inequality in the distribution of income. Given the crippling of fiscal policy as a consequence of the 1981 tax cuts, this growth in income inequality is not a favorable development, especially in view of the fact that there is no serious evidence that the supply-side formula really works.

Finally, and related to the foregoing, there is the question of the contribution of the Reagan administration's policies to the highly publicized and much-debated issue of the "shrinking middle class." So far the evidence of such a shrinkage is fragmentary at best, but there is cause for concern. Between 1980 and 1982—a three-year period—the middle fifth on the income scale saw its share shrink from 17.5 to 17.1 percent, a small change statistically. More to the point, perhaps, is that between 1980 and 1983 both interest and transfers as sources of personal income grew much more rapidly than did wages and salaries.[53] Interest income in 1983 accounted for 13.4 percent of all personal income as compared to 6.2 percent in 1960, while the percentages for transfers were 14.7 in 1983 and 7.2 in 1960. Thus, one might argue that two non-working classes at the opposite ends of the income scale—the rentier and the poor—have grown at the expense of the wage-earning middle. Since this change has been relatively rapid over the last four years, there is some justification for the fears expressed concerning a "shrinking" middle class.

Notes

1. Sir William Beveridge, *Social Insurance and Allied Services* (New York: Macmillan, 1942).
2. Ibid., p. 8.
3. Frances Fox Piven & Richard A. Cloward, *The New Class War* (New York: Pantheon Books, 1982), pp. 15ff.
4. This might be called the "Smithian" concept of government, after Adam Smith (*The Wealth of Nations*), who saw the government as having but three principal duties: (1) to protect society from the "violence and invasion of other independent societies"; (2) to protect every member of society "from the injustice of oppression of every other member"; and (3) to erect and maintain "those public institutions and public works . . . which are of great benefit to society but are too costly to be maintained by any individual or group of individuals."
6. *Economic Report of the President* (Washington, D.C.: U.S. Government Printing Office, 1984), pp. 246, 247.
7. Ibid., pp. 220, 221.
8. Ibid., p. 309.
9. *Current Economic Indicators*, July, 1984, p. 1.
10. Ibid., p. 34.
11. *Survey of Current Business*, July, 1984, p. 36.
12. Ibid.
13. *Economic Report of the President*, 1964, 1984.
14. Ibid., 1984, p. 309.
15. *Current Economic Indicators*, October, p. 34.

16. Ibid.
17. John Maynard Keynes, *The General Theory of Employment, Interest, and Money* (New York and London: Harcourt Brace Jovanovich, 1964), p. 376.
18. *Statistical Abstract of the United States* (Washington, D.C.: U.S. Government Printing Office, 1983), p. 481.
19. Medicaid payments are treated as payments to people, even though this is not strictly correct as they are paid to the suppliers of the medical services. The assumption here is that the value of the "in kind" medical services provide low-income persons is equal to the expenditures under the Medicare rubric.
20. *Survey of Current Business*, July, 1984, p. 36.
21. *Statistical Abstract of the United States*, 1983, p. 324.
22. *Survey of Current Business*, July, 1984, p. 36.
23. *A Program for Economic Recovery* (Washington, D.C.: The White House, 18 February 1981), p. 13.
24. U.S. Congress, Joint Economic Committee, Studies in Public Welfare, Paper No. 2, *Handbook of Public Income Transfer Programs* (Washington, D.C.: U.S. Government Printing Office, 1972), pp. 8-19.
25. *Current Economic Indicators*, July, 1984, p. 5.
26. The word "earned" is being used in this context in the economist's sense of a payment to an owner of an economic resource, namely land, labor, or capital. It does not imply whether the income is "deserved" or "earned" in a broader, more philosophical sense.
27. *Current Economic Indicators*, July, 1984, p. 4.
28. U.S. General Accounting Office, *Tax Expenditures: A Primer* (Washington, D.C., 1979), p. 7.
29. Ibid.
30. *Economic Report of the President*, 1984, p. 309.
31. U.S. Department of Commerce, Current Population Reports, *Money Income of Households, Families, and Persons in the United States*, 1982 (Washington, D.C.: U.S. Government Printing Office, 1984), p. 29.
32. In 1983 total tax expenditures of $306.4 billion were made up of 103 separate items.
33. Former Senator Walter Mondale in 1975 and Representative Henry S. Ruess in 1982.
34. These income classes differ in the upper ranges from those shown in Table 7, the reason being that the income classes shown in Table 8 are drawn from the tax and tax expenditure data contained in the Mondale-Ruess reports.
35. U.S. Department of Commerce, Current Population Reports, *Characteristics of the Population Below the Poverty Level: 1982* (Washington, D.C.: U.S. Government Printing Office, 1984), p. 7.
36. Congressional Budget Office, *Poverty Status of Families Under Alternative Definitions of Income* (Washington, D.C.: U.S. Government Printing Office, 1977), p. xv.
37. U.S. Department of Commerce, *Money Income of Households, Families, and Persons in the United States*, p. 47.
38. *A Program for Economic Recovery*, p. 11.

39. The original Kemp-Roth proposals was for a 10 percent across-the-board reduction each year for three straight years.
40. The expected supply-side effects of more saving, rising productivity, and higher investment simply did not materialize during either 1981 or 1982.
41. John I. Palmer and Isabel V. Sawhill, *The Reagan Record* (Cambridge, Mass.: Ballinger, 1984), p. 324.
42. Ibid., p. 326.
43. *Economic Report of the President*, 1982, p. 109.
44. Thomas Byrne Edsall, *The Politics of the New Inequality* (New York: W. W. Norton, 1984), p. 180.
45. U.S. Department of Commerce, *Characteristics of the Population Below the Poverty Level: 1982*, p. 7.
46. John E. Schwarz, *America's Hidden Success* (New York: W. W. Norton, 1983), pp. 32ff.
47. From 1947 to 1979 the Gini Index of Concentration declined by only 2.9 percent, indicating a move toward slightly less inequality. But from 1979 to 1982, a three-year span, the index rose by 4.4 percent, a move toward greater inequality.
48. Palmer and Sawhill, *The Reagan Record*, chaps. 3, 10.
49. John Maynard Keynes, *The General Theory*, p. 149.
50. The build-up actually began in 1979. The rate of growth in military spending in real terms since then has been: 1979, 2.6 percent; 1980, 3.9 percent; 1981, 4.9 percent; 1982, 7.6 percent; and 1983, 7.1 percent.
51. *Economic Report of the President*, 1982, p. 36.
52. John Kenneth Galbraith, *The Great Crash of 1929* (New York: Time, 1962), p. 179.
53. Wages and salaries grew by 34.5 percent in this period, as compared to 67.5 percent for interest income and 61.2 percent for transfers.

25

Public Control of Enterprise: Neoclassical Assault and Neoinstitutional Reform

Remarks upon Receipt of the Veblen-Commons Award

Harry M. Trebing

No one can dispute that Thorstein Veblen and John R. Commons stand as the twin pillars of institutional economics. Both had serious misgivings about the workings of the unbridled market and the potential abuses inherent in uncontrolled economic power. The growth of economic and social regulation follows logically from their work, and their vision continues to serve as an inspiration to that stalwart band of neoinstitutionalists who seek to prove that government can play a purposeful role in the control of economic activity. To all of us who hold this view, the Veblen-Commons Award has a very special significance, and I deeply appreciate the honor that my colleagues in AFEE have conferred upon me.

The historical development of government regulation of business enterprise has been closely associated with the work of many institutional economists. Henry Carter Adams, John R. Commons, J. M. Clark, Martin Glaeser, James Bonbright, I. Leo Sharfman, and Eli Clemens were among those who provided much of the intellectual rationale for public control. Regulation was viewed as a method for resolving conflicts and coordinating social objectives in an industrialized economy and, more importantly, as a means for curbing monopoly power and preventing the abuses associated with the unrestricted exercise of that power. This perception of government intervention became known as the public interest theory of regulation.

By the 1970s, however, popular and academic dissatisfaction with regulation had increased to a point where the earlier public consensus regarding the desirability of public control was severely shaken. Economic regulation (control over prices, earnings, entry and exit of firms) was blamed for inefficiency, inflation, impeding innovation, and the cartelization of industry. Social regulation (control over factors affecting environment, health, safety, and the workplace) was blamed for the noncompetitive posture of major U.S. industries (such as steel, copper, textiles, and drugs), unemployment, inflation, and the growing trend toward off-shore procurement. Even those groups that might have been expected to support regulation became increasingly skeptical in the face of price increases for energy that outpaced the Consumer Price Index and the worsening plight of the low-income consumer. More and more, consumer activists and environmentalists took the view that regulation was at best a feeble source of protection.

Neoclassical, mainstream economists have played a significant role in the growing movement to limit the nature and scope of public control and to deregulate entire industries. Indeed, the neoclassicists have played a reformist role similar to that of the earlier institutionalists. However, there are significant differences. For the neoclassicists, misguided government intervention is the culprit rather than the monopoly power of the firm. Regulation is accused of promoting inefficiency, of sending the wrong signals to consumers and management, and of frustrating market prices. Corporate power is dismissed as transitory or largely ineffectual.

It would, of course, be an oversimplification to argue that institutionalism has meaning only in the context of the earlier movement to regulate, and that neoclassical activism is synonymous with deregulation. Many neoclassicists accept the existence of externalities and natural monopolies as a basis for government action, but their view of the prevalence of these conditions and the appropriate response differs significantly from that of the institutionalists.[1] Given the ascendency of neoclassical thought among policy makers in government, it is important to examine the neoclassical approach to regulation in greater detail, including its salient features, its successes, and its failures.

The Neoclassical Agenda for Reform

The movement to constrain economic regulation in surface transportation took a significant step forward with passage of the Railroad Revitalization and Regulatory Reform Act of 1976 and the Staggers Rail Act of 1980, while economic regulation of the airlines effectively ended with implementation of the Airline Deregulation Act of 1978. The movement toward deregulation in energy and telecommunications has had a more checkered legislative history (except for new gas production), and much of the initiative for decontrol has come from federal commissioners and senior staff members in the late 1970s and 1980s who were unsympathetic to the traditional goals of regulation.[2] Alfred Kahn occupies a unique role in the deregulation process, first as chairman of the Civil Aeronautics Board where he championed decontrol of air carriers, and more recently as a leading spokesman for abolishing the rate base regulation of public utilities. The attack on social regulation was spearheaded by Charles Schultze, who, as chairman of the President's Council of Economic Advisers, created the Regulatory Analysis Review Group (RARG) and the Regulatory Council, which sought to impose stringent benefit/cost criteria on both existing and new regulations. The Reagan administration disbanded RARG but the Office of Management and Budget continued to apply strict benefit/cost criteria in a fashion designed to overturn and discourage social regulation. This application was sufficiently restrictive to prompt Mark Green's observation that neither the child labor laws or the abolition of slavery could have passed such a test.[3]

Five features of the neoclassical assault on economic and social regulation deserve attention. First, the promotion of economic efficiency has become the major policy objective. This inevitably shifts attention toward a greater reliance on market forces through deregulation, the limiting of regulation to residual monopoly markets, and the creation of efficiency maximization rules. Equity issues are explicitly or implicitly treated as trivial, except for demonstrable cases where low-income consumers are denied service because of price.

Second, the formulation of rules for maximizing efficiency has become a major task for economic analysis. These rules typically take the form of pricing criteria, optimum departures from marginal cost pricing, tests for cross-subsidization, predation, and measures of changes in welfare. In practice they have been embodied in peak pricing based on marginal cost, Ramsey pricing (or the inverse elasticity rule), the burden test for judging cross-subsidization, and an adherence to consumer and producer surplus as the test of net changes in welfare.

A third feature of the neoclassical approach has been the effort to develop remedial measures that correct for cases of market failure by relying on the profit motive. For example, the existence of natural monopoly would be handled by franchise auctioning rather than by direct price/earnings controls. A public resource such as the radio frequency spectrum would be allocated through competitive bidding, and the control of pollution would be achieved through effluent charges that impact on profits rather than through the direct prescription of pollution standards.

A fourth feature has been the simplified approach to the market structure of industries subject to economic regulation. Typically, the neoclassicists have drawn a distinction between natural monopoly and competitive industry structures, which minimizes the need to explore a role for public control in treating the problems posed by oligopoly, imperfect competition, and corporate strategies to maintain market dominance. The best example of this distinction is William Baumol's definition of natural monopoly markets and contestable markets.[4] A sustainable natural monopoly is one where entry is foreclosed by virtue of the fact that the established firm is the least-cost supplier. But if Ramsey pricing results in high mark-ups in inelastic markets, the firm may be vulnerable to entry and creamskimming. Under these circumstances, social policy should foreclose entry and prevent the wasteful duplication of capital. In contestable markets potential entry will eliminate monopoly profits, cross-subsidization, and predation so that no government intervention is required.

Finally, the neoclassical analysis of regulatory behavior has produced theories of regulation that are essentially negative, with few insights into opportunities for reform and little basis for optimism. In the work of George Stigler, Sam Peltzman, Milton Russell, and Robert Shelton, regulators emerge as vulnerable to capture and manipulation, or as bureaucrats seeking to build empires by the distribution of favors through artificially low prices to special constituents. At best, regulation is portrayed as a faltering political effort to replace efficient markets with ill-defined equity goals.

A Critique of the Neoclassical Contribution

The neoclassical challenge to public control of enterprise has been premised on the belief that much regulatory activity and practice constitutes a barrier to economic efficiency. The proper remedy involves the introduction of pricing reforms and related market-oriented efficiency rules, and the encouragement of programs that would circumscribe or erode regulatory authority. These proposals have received widespread acclaim in academic and political circles, yet it is premature to conclude that the neoclassical solutions have been successful when applied or that they provide the best guide for future public policy.

Neoclassical analysis has achieved its greatest success in the reform of price structures and rate designs. A large body of literature has shown that peak, off-peak pricing differentials are the most effective method of sending price signals to consumers that reflect current resource costs. Furthermore, peak pricing will constrain the cross-subsidization inherent in undercharging peak customers and overcharging off-peak customers. It will also eliminate artificial incentives to expand plant capacity that stem from declining block rates (or, more correctly, from second and third degree price discrimination) and flat rates. The growing acceptance of time-of-day and time-of-use in electricity and telecommunications is evidence of commission recognition of the inducement to efficiency inherent in this form of pricing.

However, the neoclassical victory in peak pricing is far from complete. At best, such pricing can send price signals and it has only limited success in actually reshaping usage patterns. Econometric studies of price elasticities of demand for peak and off-peak periods, as well as cross-elasticity estimates of shifts between the peak and off-peak consistently reveal numerical values far below unit. In addition, an intense debate has arisen regarding the transferability of the results of one pricing experiment to another market—suggesting that *ex ante* generalizations about the benefits of pricing reform are very hazardous.[5]

The implementation of peak pricing is further complicated by the lack of agreement over the proper method for measuring marginal capacity cost. Proponents champion such diverse approaches as the peaker method and the expansion-of-plant method, demonstrating that estimates of long-run marginal cost in the real world are no less arbitrary than those of fully distributed cost. Peak pricing must also contend with the revenue reconciliation problem, which requires that sales revenues from prices based on incremental costs be reconciled with a revenue requirement based on rate base regulation (which is heavily influenced by sunk costs). The theoretical solution suggested by the inverse elasticity rule involves price markups or mark-downs in the inelastic markets, while prices remain set at marginal cost in elastic markets. Clearly, this solution has substantial distributional consequences and it can be shown that under certain assumptions, it can result in price reductions in peak periods in the face of rising marginal costs.[6]

But perhaps the biggest shortcoming of the neoclassical peak pricing solution is that it has relevance only under a specific set of assumptions, and that it may become irrelevant in an evolving context of structural and institutional change. To illustrate, when a system of electricity supply operates at or near capacity and the growth of peak demand requires the progressive shift from low-cost base load generation to high-cost cycling and peaking units, peak pricing is rational and conducive to efficiency. But when the system has reserve margins of 40-50 percent, indicating massive excess capacity, and when cost overruns for new base load plant indicate that such units will cost more than twice the price per kwh of cycling and peaking units, then the application of the peak pricing model will have a perverse effect on both efficiency and income distribution. In short, the neoclassical model is not an all-events, universal solution to the problem of efficient pricing, but rather a model that was much more appropriate to conditions in the 1970s than in the 1980s.

There are at least two sectors where it is too early to judge whether neoclassical reforms have enhanced the general welfare. These include the deregulation of airlines and the promotion of competition in interexchange telecommunications markets.

Deregulation of the airlines has produced price volatility, a reshuffling of carriers between routes, the entry of new firms, pressures for wage reductions, and bankruptcies. But at this point it is difficult to discern whether this represents the shift from cartelized to competitive markets or a high degree of instability that will terminate in mergers, increased market concentration, and conscious parallelism among rivals. It is even more difficult to determine whether the reduction of service on thin routes will result in a lower quality of life among those living in the affected communities. A new form of social cost could emerge if the deterioration in airline service left a city stranded, and if business activity and employment declined as a consequence, resulting in a lower standard of living for people with no immediate or direct contact with the carrier that failed or abandoned service.

In telecommunications, the promotion of liberalized entry into interexchange markets began in 1969 and was broadened in 1977. Yet it has not produced a decline in market shares of the dominant firm to a point sufficient to curtail profits.[7] Indeed, AT&T's share of the intercity private line market actually increased from 81 percent in 1968 to 85 percent in 1980. In addition, there is some question whether competition will be a self-reinforcing force. Recognizing that firms such as Xerox have withdrawn from telecommunications markets, MCI, GTE-Sprint, and others may well consider the wisdom of a policy of coexistence and non-price rivalry if the rate of growth in the message toll telephone service (MTS) declines and price differentials between AT&T and its rivals begin to narrow. Similarly, much of the discussion of bypass of the interexchange and local exchange markets by new service offerings fails to distinguish between the loss of business to new entrants and efforts by established telephone companies to bypass their own traditional services with new offerings in order to retain customers. The latter hardly qualifies as a viable long-run competitive force.

Deregulation in both airlines and intercity telecommunications involves two additional fundamental questions that still have to be resolved: (1) Will prices gravitate toward cost, and (2) Will deregulation actually reduce the size of the market accessible to consumers? There can be little doubt that price structures will become more complex, but it is too early to determine whether they are moving toward a more sophisticated form of price discrimination. For airlines, prices are no longer proportional to distance. Instead, they tend to reflect the presence or absence of competition on a route-by-route basis, and the carrier emerges as a multiproduct firm serving markets of differing price elasticities. Whether competition will erase these differences remains to be seen. In telecommunications, liberalized entry has been conducive to limit entry pricing and non-compensatory price reductions in potentially competitive markets that are offset by higher prices in residual monopoly markets. More recently, AT&T's new experimental rate structures in the MTS markets feature minimum bills and significant volume discounts that are largely insensitive to distance. Such price structures, when combined with traditional MTS rates, exploit demand elasticities for occasional customers as well as for the most elastic volume customers. The interaction between price and market structure is further complicated in both air transport and telecommunications by the need to price access to airports and local exchanges. Failure to impose adequate peak period charges for airports will encourage overexpansion at large metropolitan centers and the diversion of carriers from other markets. Large volume discounts for access to the local exchange that are not cost justified will bestow significant benefits on AT&T at the expense of its smaller rivals.

The impact of deregulation on the size of the market accessible to consumers is a more elusive problem. Essentially, with deregulation a carrier or a utility has an incentive to discontinue joint services and other intersystem services that involve any potential diversion or sharing of traffic. The objective is to confine the customer to the offerings of that carrier wherever possible. The outcome could be a restriction on the number of service combinations available to individual customers, a reduction in the number of interconnected offerings, and a tendency toward Balkanized systems. Such actions could result in a reduction in overall network reliability and a loss in economies of scope, scale, and joint production. For a parallel situations, one can look at the telephone industry prior to 1914, when AT&T refused to interconnect with rival local exchanges.

Finally, there are at least five areas where the analysis and policy recommendations of the neoclassicists have failed to make a significant contribution toward resolving the major policy issues that affect public control of enterprise. First, neoclassical analysis has been particularly disappointing in its failure to establish generally acceptable guidelines for judging the presence or absence of cross-subsidization, limit entry pricing, and predation. The proposed solutions for controlling cross-subsidization have included the burden test, the inverse elasticity rule, and the stand-alone test. The burden test suffers from a number of deficiencies, including the fact that its calculation is so arbitrary that it gives the firm excessive latitude in setting prices. These deficiencies led to its rejection by the FCC in 1976.[8]

The inverse elasticity rule is severely handicapped when marginal cost is indeterminate, when demand in two or more markets is highly inelastic, and when controls over revenue requirements are weak or incomplete.[9] The inverse elasticity rule is also deficient because it is incapable of establishing a cost-based ceiling in the inelastic markets, which are the most vulnerable to price discrimination.

Baumol has suggested that the cost of a stand-alone system to serve the inelastic residual monopoly market could serve as the basis for setting ceiling prices in that market.[10] He argues that the firm will be charging a price equal to the stand-alone cost if the firm earns only a normal overall rate of profit and if prices for products sold in competitive markets are set at compensatory levels. A price greater than the stand-alone cost will result in excessive profits or in the sale of competitive output at prices below compensatory levels. There are serious problems with this approach to implementing the stand-alone concept. The most important is that it denies all economies of scope and joint economies of production to the residual monopoly market. Instead, it assigns these economies to competitive elastic markets. Furthermore, this approach assumes that there is a consensus regarding criteria for determining minimum compensatory prices. In fact, there has been an extensive debate in the neoclassical literature over the proper criteria for judging the existence of predatory pricing. As a result, standards for evaluating limit entry pricing, predation, and the reasonableness of minimum prices remain indeterminate. One is free to select from a range of tests that extend from short-run marginal cost to fully distributed cost. The former is, of course, hardly appropriate for evaluating minimum prices in a capital-intensive public utility.

Second, neoclassical judgments regarding net changes in welfare typically rely on net changes in consumer surplus, and suffer from all of the shortcomings inherent in that concept. Since Wendell Gordon has examined the difficulties of applying this concept as a measure of social welfare,[11] it is sufficient at this point to mention some of the applied problems that arise when the concept is used to evaluate the impact of economic regulation. Efforts to quantify consumer surplus often make heroic assumptions based on little or no supporting evidence. It is not uncommon for such estimates to assume constant returns to scale, a linear demand function, and price elasticity estimates that are open to serious question. A change in any one of these assumptions will result in wide swings in the net gain or loss in welfare.

Third, neoclassical policy recommendations are often biased by the desire to apply profit-oriented solutions to cases of market failure. In many instances, such solutions are too confining or too cumbersome to administer. For example, franchise auctioning may be a feasible method for limiting the profits of a localized enterprise serving a homogeneous group of customers at a single price, but the auctioning process and the administration of the franchise become hopelessly complicated as a method for limiting profits for a large regional energy or telecommunications system serving many customer classes in a variety of different markets. By the same token, franchise auctioning is largely ineffectual as a constraint on price discrimination. In addition, while an effluent charge may impact on the profit calculations of the firm, there is no assurance that the firm's decision will reflect social values or that these values can be adequately incorporated in a single charge.

Fourth, the neoclassical treatment of economic regulation has not been successful in coming to grips with the problems of market structure and corporate power in a deregulated environment. A number of the unresolved issues have already been mentioned with respect to the deregulation of airlines and the promotion of free entry into interexchange telecommunications, but the problems become even more difficult when one turns to electricity, gas, and telecommunications as whole. There is a clear basis for skepticism whether highly concentrated markets will become competitive and whether competitive pressures will be sufficient to constrain the strategies of the dominant firm. The problem is further complicated by the interdependent relationship between firms in both energy and telecommunications arising from the frequent need for technical interconnection, joint planning, and revenue sharing. Horace M. Gray, an institutional economist critical of economic regulation, expressed this concern over the adequacy of competition in deregulated markets, noting that deregulation may be little more than a propaganda slogan to permit the firm to enjoy even more power and privilege than it had under commission regulation.[12]

It is difficult to be sanguine about the options for market structure analysis provided by much of the economic literature. Neoclassical oligopoly analysis remains essentially static and limited, while the industrial organization paradigm gives few insights into the sources of potential competition. Acceptance of the sustainability thesis for natural monopoly relegates government to the negative role of foreclosing entry except in cases where the new entrant offers a new technology or a new product. Acceptance of the theory of contestable markets will also deny government any positive role since potential entry will discipline the established firms. As a consequence, it could be argued that high concentration ratios are meaningless in contestable markets, and that the power of the dominant firm is illusory. The flaw in this argument is that the heavy capital requirement associated with entry in the public utility industries and the prospect of a substantial capital loss should the venture fail make potential hit-and-run entry largely irrelevant.

Fifth, the neoclassicists have essentially disregarded equity and distributional effects, and have failed to establish a framework for examining social values. Three sets of equity and distributional issues have emerged in those industries subject to economic regulation: (1) the need to assure minimum service to low-income customers and rural or thin markets; (2) the incidence of economic rents associated with low-cost gas and electricity in the face of rising energy prices; and (3) the distributional impact of technological change and increased uncertainty in telecommunications and energy. Each of these issues involves billions of dollars and intense controversy between consumer groups, management, shareholders, different geographic regions, and different industries. The eventual solutions will determine who captures the economic rents from low-cost gas, who receives the benefits from technological advance in telecommunications and who bears the burden of accelerated obsolescence, and who bears the burden of excess capacity, cost overruns, and nuclear power plant terminations. For its part, neoclassical analysis confines itself largely to endorsing transfer payments to the poor as the preferred option for assuring adequate service with minimum disturbance to the price system and free consumer choice. However, even this solution ignores the high cost of administering such welfare programs and their vulnerability to legislative budget cutting.

The failure to develop a framework for delineating social values has raised serious doubts about the validity of the efforts of neoclassical economists to constrain social regulation through the imposition of stringent benefit-cost ratios. The difficulty arises because of the inherent tendency to underestimate social benefits. It is comparatively easy to estimate the administrative and compliance costs associated with social regulation, but much more difficult to define and measure those market and extramarket values that constitute the gains to society. Furthermore, when these gains arise over time, some decision must be made about the appropriate rate of social discount. There is, of course, no assurance that the optimal social discount rate corresponds to the yield on long-term Treasury bonds. Yet the application of this rate, at current high market yields, could terminate many health and environmental protection programs. Proponents of social regulation are left with little more than recourse to case studies and anecdotal evidence to support their position, while critics can limit the discussion to market-oriented benefits and costs—supported by occasional references to externalities.[13]

Neoinstitutionalism and Reform

In contrast to the neoclassicists, the current generation of institutional economists views the problems of public control of enterprise within the context of an economic system characterized, more often than not, by continuous change, imperfect markets, uncompensated social costs, decision making based on partial information, and corporations and pressure groups that exercise significant discretionary power. It is therefore not unexpected that neoinstitutionalists believe that major public policy decisions do not involve simply a choice between deregulating markets that are inherently competitive and retaining flawed regulatory institutions.

A strong tradition of pragmatism is reflected in the neoinstitutionalists' effort to define the form of public control in terms of the perceived task of regulation. The public utility industries provide an example of this approach to reform. For telecommunications, new technology is creating new markets, new sources of supply, falling incremental costs, and accelerated obsolescence. For electricity and gas, new technology is creating increased financial risk, rising incremental costs, and uncertainty regarding the treatment of social costs such as nuclear waste disposal and acid rain. The regulated firm will seek to reposition itself in the face of these changes through strategies designed to maintain its status as a going concern. Three sets of strategies will contribute to this objective.

First, the firm will seek to maintain hegemony in its principal markets through rates designed to prevent bypass, customer diversion, loss of high-volume users, and new entry. This can be accomplished through high minimum bills, volume discounts, and selective promotional rates. Hegemony can also be maintained through market structure practices that block entry and reduce customer options. These involve refusals to wheel and transport, refusals to interconnect, tying arrangements, and territorial allocations.

Second, the firm will seek to minimize risk in the face of increased uncertainty and accelerated obsolescence. This requires the promotion of accelerated depreciation, increased cash flow, phase-in programs for high-cost plant, various automatic passthroughs, and tax normalization.

Third, the firm will endeavor to maximize the overall rate of return by abandoning less attractive markets, entering new markets (whether regulated or nonregulated), and endeavoring to weaken rate-of-return constraints in regulated markets. This can be accomplished by creating separate subsidiaries, creating new holding companies beyond the jurisdiction of the regulator, securing repeal of the Holding Company Act of 1935, and introducing adjustments to inflate revenue requirements.

Paralleling these actions by the firm are the strategies of consumer groups to impede price increases, obtain access to alternative sources of supply, or extract special price concessions. New entrants seeking a foothold in the market will press for full-cost pricing for the established firm and freedom to interconnect or wheel.

The challenge for neoinstitutionalists will be to reconcile these changes and strategies with a program of public control that promotes the general welfare. This requires a holistic view of the interdependence of market structure, the adequacy and availability of service, equity and distributional effects, social values, and industry performance on the one hand, and different regulatory options on the other. It is no longer sufficient to view the task of regulation largely as one of controlling earnings and reviewing the legitimacy of expenditures. In markets that are potentially competitive there will be little need for regulatory intervention in earnings and prices when free entry can control price discrimination and cross-subsidization. In such cases, government may be able to confine itself to an oversight function, monitoring the adequacy of service and potential collusive behavior. In highly concentrated markets, a much broader approach to regulation will be necessary. Regulation will control earnings and prices, but will also have to prevent attempts to shift risk forward to the consumer. The method of regulation should tie risk to shareholder return in order to establish proper accountability for management error or miscalculation. Otherwise there will be a strong tendency toward overinvestment, higher prices, and the monopolistic transfer of income from consumers to shareholders.

Broadened regulation will also have to experiment with new methods for determining costs and earnings by class of service. In some cases fully distributed cost may be appropriate, while in others experiments such as those by William Melody and Richard Gabel to establish price ceilings in inelastic markets are necessary.[14] As neoinstitutionalists, Melody and Gabel are free from the strictures of orthodox economics, and they proceed to devise a method for controlling cross-susidization by assigning to basic telephone service only those costs appropriate to that service, while so-called enhanced services (teleconferencing, data transmission, MTS, etcetera) are expected to pay the higher costs of the more sophisticated system required to provide these services. This involves a redefinition of markets, plant, and facilities, and an allocation of joint costs that would be abhorent to neoclassicists. If successfully applied, the Melody-Gabel approach could improve efficiency, curtail cross-susidization, and prevent the firm from burdening basic-service customers with unwarranted cost increases.

Broadened social control must also consider the potential consequences of other strategies employed by participants in the regulatory process, particularly diversification and joint ventures. The incentive to diversify could foster disinvestment in utility plant and facilities that, in turn, could have adverse social effects by denigrating the quality of basic service. This incentive would increase if the cost of any failure at diversification could be charged off against utility customers. But even if accounting controls were adequate to prevent this abuse, a diversification effort that failed would still increase risk and raise the overall cost of capital, thereby burdening utility customers. Once again, neoinstitutionalists are confronted with the need to devise new arrangements that simultaneously curb market power as well as adverse distributional effects. Joint ventures pose a problem when, as David Schwartz has pointed out, they diminish arms-length bargaining between the regulated firm and its suppliers, and eliminate any incentive to hold down costs. Schwartz has repeatedly shown how the absence of incentives on the part of pipelines and distributors involved in joint ventures to bargain aggressively to hold down the price of gas has resulted in field contracts that escalate prices and burden retail customers.[15]

Other features of the neoinstitutionalist approach have been the willingness to explore shortcomings in the existing commission system and to advocate far-reaching reforms that transcend the traditional distinction between regulated and nonregulated markets. Since neoinstitutionalists are not inclined to think of regulation and competition as mutually exclusive concepts, it is not surprising that such economists consider the use of regulation to promote competition in submarkets as a means of enhancing the overall effectiveness of public control. The best example of this type of reform involves the use of regulatory intervention to neutralize barriers to the creation of an interconnected transmission network capable of bringing together many more buyers and sellers in the bulk power and wholesale gas markets.[16]

Much work needs to be done in examining the immense array of problems that confront economic and social regulation. Deregulation in an imperfect market setting will resolve many of these problems by transferring the burden to those consumers who have no alternative sources of supply. One hopes that the neoinstitutionalists will be able to provide solutions that are more insightful and humane.

Notes

1. The neoclassical literature is generally critical of regulation, even though it recognizes that the need for government intervention may be justified by cases of market failure or the existence of public goods and common property resources. J. D. Tomlinson has characterized much of this literature as the "anti-regulatory economics of regulation." See J. D. Tomlinson, "Regulating the Capitalist Enterprise: The Impossible Dream?" *Scottish Journal of Political Economy* 30 (February 1983): 54-68. D. Needham and L. W. Lee have sought to broaden the treatment of regulation to recognize behavioral factors and "fairness" while retaining a neoclassical framework that focuses on efficiency. It is too early to judge the outcome of these efforts. See D. Needham, *The Economics and Politics of Regulation—A Behavioral Approach* (Boston: Little, Brown, 1983); and L. W. Lee, "A Theory of Just Regulation," *American Economic Review* 70 (December 1980): 848-62.
2. The recent decision by the U.S. Court of Appeals in the Williams case appears to challenge FERC's effort at administrative deregulation. The Court stated: "We believe that this apologia for virtual deregulation of oil pipeline rates oversteps the proper bounds of agency discretion under the 'just and reasonable' standard." U.S. Court of Appeals for the District of Columbia, No. 82-2412, Farmers Union Central Exchange, Inc., et al., v. Federal Energy Regulation Commission, 9 March 1984, preliminary print, p. 43.
3. Quoted in S. J. Tolchin, *Dismantling America—The Rush to Deregulate* (Boston: Houghton Mifflin, 1983), p. 22.
4. W. J. Baumol, "Contestable Markets: An Uprising in the Theory of Industrial Structure," *American Economic Review* 72 (March 1982): 1-15.
5. For a review of empirical findings regarding price elasticities, see A. Faruqui and J. R. Malko, "Time-of-Use Rates and the Modification of Electric Utility Load Shapes," *Challenges for Public Utility Regulation in the 1980s*, ed. H. M. Trebing (East Lansing: Michigan State University, 1981), pp. 617-34. For a discussion of the transferability problem see D. W. Caves, L. R. Christensen, A. Faruqui, and J. A. Herriges, "Transferability of Residential Response to Time-of-Use Electricity Rates," *Adjusting to Regulatory, Pricing, and Marketing Realities* (East Lansing: Michigan State University, 1983), pp. 632-41.
6. Assume that demand during the peak period is price inelastic, that demand off-peak is elastic or unit elastic, and that incremental cost is rising. Prices set on the basis of incremental cost will produce total revenues greater than the revenue requirement. According to the inverse elastic rule, price would be marked down in the inelastic market to reconcile

revenues with the revenue requirement. This means that peak prices will be reduced in the face of growing demand and rising incremental cost.

7. The relationship between changes in market shares and control of the level of profits through entry is discussed by Shepherd. See W. G. Shepherd, "General Conditions of Entry," *Regulation and Entry*, ed. M. W. Klass and W. G. Shepherd (East Lansing: Michigan State University, 1976), pp. 48-49, 55-60. Also see H. M. Trebing, "A Critique of Structure Regulation in Common Carrier Telecommunications," *Telecommunications Regulation Today and Tomorrow*, ed. E. M. Noam (New York: Harcourt Brace Jovanovich, 1983), pp. 137-142.
8. The burden test involved a comparison of the revenue from service *x* with the incremental cost of service *x* and the diversion of revenues (revenue loss) from other services. The FCC rejected the burden test in FCC Docket No. 18128, 1976.
9. If demand in two or more markets is highly inelastic, then the mark-up or mark-down to achieve revenue reconciliation will be arbitrary. Further, if much of the plant is obsolete or redundant so that book values bear no relationship to market values, application of the rule may allow the firm to earn a return on the impaired book values.
10. W. J. Baumol, "Minimum and Maximum Pricing Principles for Residual Regulation," *Current Issues in Public Utility Pricing*, ed. A. L. Danielson and D. R. Kamerschen (Lexington, Mass.: Lexington Books, 1983), pp. 177-96.
11. W. Gordon, "Welfare Maxima in Economics," *Journal of Economic Issues* 17 (March 1983): 1-16.
12. H. M. Gray, "The Sharing of Economic Power in Public Utility Industries," *Salvaging Public Utility Regulation*, ed. W. Sichel (Lexington, Mass.: Lexington Books, 1976), pp. 5-19.
13. There are numerous examples of the benefits of social regulation, but these are difficult to aggregate and quantify. Sulfur emissions have declined by 17 percent in the last ten years and significant progress has been made in restoring the Great Lakes. Safer cribs have reduced infant injuries by 44 percent since 1974. Seat belts have reduced deaths by 20 percent and injuries by 34 percent over an eight-year period. A Food and Drug Administration inspector held up approval of Thalidomide, thereby sparing the United States the birth defects that plagued Europe. For a further discussion, see Tolchin and Tolchin, *Dismantling America*, pp. 23-28, 133-37.
14. See W. H. Melody, "Cost Standards for Judging Local Exchange Rates," *Diversification, Deregulation, and Increased Uncertainty in the Public Utility Industries* (East Lansing: Michigan State University, 1983), pp. 474-95. Also, "Allocation of Telephone Exchange Plant Investment," *Adjusting to Regulatory, Pricing, and Market Realities*, pp. 452-82.
15. D. Schwartz's testimony before various congressional committees has dealt with these problems at length. For a summary of his views on joint ventures and the exercise of economic power in the natural gas industry, see D. S. Schwartz, "Recent Developments in the Natural Gas Industry—A New Perspective," *Public Utility Regulation*, ed. W. Sichel and T. G. Gies (Lexington, Mass.: Lexington Books, 1975), pp. 21-51.

16. For a neoinstitutionalist's thoughts on one aspect of the reform of the commission system, see J. C. Spychalski, "The NARUC: Contributor to Effective Regulation? A Retrospective and Prospective Critique," *A Critique of Administrative Regulation of Public Utilities*, ed. W. J. Samuels and H. M. Trebing (East Lansing: Michigan State University, 1972), pp. 89-135. For a neoinstitutionalist's thought about the problems of creating a competitive bulk power market and the persistence of market power in the face of structural change, see E. S. Miller, "Is There a Meaningful Role for Economic Regulation in a Supply-Side World?" *Adjusting to Regulatory, Pricing, and Marketing Realities*, pp. 3-12.

PART V

TOWARD A MEANINGFUL POLITICAL ECONOMY

Introduction to Part V

We conclude this anthology with three papers that, in somewhat different ways, are intended to suggest "which direction is forward." Having already addressed basic differences between neoclassical orthodoxy and contemporary institutionalism with regard to philosophical constructs, modes of inquiry, and derivative approaches to policy analysis and formulation, the papers that follow suggest both the need for, and something of the character of, a comprehensive shift from neoclassical orthodoxy to an institutionalist-instrumentalist perspective that is at once more germane and more productive of insights and understanding.

The envisioned shift is literally a supersession—the abandonment of the old in favor of the new. As we have observed in the preceding papers, the institutionalist perspective is fundamentally different from that of its orthodox predecessor. It is holistic, rather than narrow, in scope; it is normative, as well as positive; it is both inductive and deductive; it does not sacrifice relevance for rigor; it is policy- and goal-focused, not market deferential; it is pragmatic and behavioralistic, not analytically austere and a prioristic; it is a version of open-ended inquiry, not a dogmatic model; it is addressed to problem solving, not to logical elegance and model sophistication; it is in quest of understanding rather more than prediction; it reflects both evidential grounding and logical consistency; it encompasses truth as derivative and provisional, not as given and eternal; it reflects Albert Guerard's admonition: "By thought ye shall seek the truth; and the quest shall make you free," providing "thought" is taken to mean a running dialogue between reason and experience. The papers that follow, of course, also reflect a number of these distinctions and, given this characterization of the institutionalist perspective, suggest how the social and economic order of the future may be addressed and how its inevitable problems may be made the object of increasingly productive inquiry.

The lead paper, by Robert L. Heilbroner, offers an analysis of the increasing irrelevance of conventional economics and, more important, a suggestion of the direction in which economics must move if it "is to regain a sense of relevance." It is a comment on our times to note that this paper, written nearly two decades ago, retains much of its vitality and pertinence as a comment on the inadequacies of orthodoxy and as an advocate of paradigmatic supersession. For Heilbroner, the relevancy shortfalls of orthodoxy include a failure of its major proponents "to interest themselves in any deep criticism of our present social and economic order." Given their "conservative political orientations," they "do not which to investigate" critical questions. Furthermore, the subject itself, as perceived, does not contain "the appropriate tools . . . in that famous tool kit" to resolve certain critical problems. Lacking is "a consistent or integrated model of the economic system in the terms in which that system is usually perceived," "an adequate theory of the major agent of contemporary capitalism—the corporation," and "the validity of certain prime constructs of economic thought, such as 'capital' or 'welfare,'" among others. "Economics," Heilbroner says, "no longer asks the questions that are of greatest concern for contemporary society . . . Irrelevance springs from the intellectual mistake of first wrenching the 'economy' from the 'society,' and thereafter treating the abstractions of economics without regard for their inextricably linked noneconomic causes and consequences." It cannot be characterized as political economy; it is not holistic. Heilbroner's alternative paradigm is an "instrumental reformulation." "The new paradigm . . . consists in an abandonment of the view of social analysis as that of determining the immanent destination of a universe of goalless particles, and substituting a view of social science as the search for the means by which social goals can be attained. . . . It elevates a desired terminus of the social process—steady growth, ecological balance and so forth—to the status of the initial premise of economic analysis." "The purpose of instrumentalism . . . is not so much to achieve an easy mastery over social processes as to free our minds from ways of thinking that prevent us from making our theories 'relevant' to the problem of purposeful social change."

Philip A. Klein says there is a special need to "free our minds" of the current conception of the public sector in political economy and of the character and significance of its roles. He offers a fresh and definitive institutionalist theory of the public sector, showing how economies can move forward by defining and redefining the "collective ought." Through a running dialogue with orthodox economists, Klein shows that neoclassical microanalysis really does not offer a credible theory of the public sector; "mainstream economists are hard-pressed to state . . . policy objectives, because market-clearing equilibrium finesses most of the difficult questions presented by the real world." Macroeconomics, on the other hand, reflects

Keynes' virtual abandonment of the normative-positive dichotomy [an underemployment equilibrium is not a good thing] and his recasting the conception of the public sector, in *The General Theory*, to specify a continuing and conpensatory macromanagement role for the central government. Going beyond Keynes, Klein contends that "economists *qua* economists . . . must be concerned about where the economy is going, how basic economic decisions are made, and about the essential allocative thrust of the economy." Continuing, he observes that "institutionalists are neither for nor against [governmental] intervention *per se*." Rather, "they are concerned with assessing the emergent values of the economy itself and the role of the public sector in partially shaping those values as well as in transmitting them through allocation."

Institutionalists assign two central tasks to the public sector: the first "is to monitor the allocative results flowing from private markets;" the second "is to create some resources for allocation and to directly undertake and direct some part of the allocating." But in any such allocation, the explicit normative focus, the "collective ought," is central. As Klein summarizes, "all economies" in some degree exhibit goals of "efficiency, equity, freedom, security, and compassion." A task for the public sector is to "judge *the higher efficiency*—the degree to which our economy diverges from the kind of adherence to these characteristics which ideally its participants currently prefer. The particular mix of these characteristics currently collectively chosen is . . . the *value floor*." The other task of the public sector is to "provide that part of emergent choice (the value floor) which the private economy cannot provide for itself."

The substantial power and timely relevance of the institutionalist perspective for problem analysis and resolution is well demonstrated by F. Gregory Hayden in a paper on the "Social Fabric Matrix" that concludes this volume. With a unique combination of institutional and systems analyses, he creates conceptual tools with which to understand and guide social change. He demonstrates how, through institutionalist inquiry, a community can determine "which direction is forward." Institutionalists, as "policy scientists, can only operationalize a perspective through tools of analysis, and the tools must exist before analysis can proceed. The tool kit is not as important as the perspective, but it is imperative for giving the perspective meaning in any applied sense." Hayden, therefore, seeks "to extend evaluational analysis" through the development of "a process matrix consistent with institutional intentions," that is, to provide the needed analytical tools. Accordingly, he "integrates the work of leading institutionalists into a transdisciplinary matrix which can be used for nonisomorpohic, nonequilibrium, holistic analysis. The matrix allows for the integration of beliefs and values as well as environmental, social, and technological components." These five categories "are integrated through the processes of reciprocity, redistribution, or exchange." The emphasis is upon what the components deliver to each other, how (by what appropriate rules) they deliver, the location, and the flow level. Techniques "are available in systems theory and computer science for the articulation of institutionalism." Thus, "the social fabric matrix allows for the integration of various techniques in order to allow for data collection, analysis, and social evaluation." The paper concludes with a delineation of inquiry areas for which the social fabric matrix is particularly relevant and important. The productivity (enhanced understanding and policy assessment) of this analytical model has been demonstrated in research undertaken by Hayden and some of his students.

At the outset of this volume, the announced goal was to reopen inquiry to a number of the most basic premises, modes of inquiry, analytical techniques, and policy presumptions reflected in contemporary economic analysis. Through a searching critique of mainstream, orthodox economic analysis, in a context of presenting elements of an alternative perspective—institutional economics—the authors have tried to set inquiry in motion and to sustain it. Whether this goal was reached will be judged differently by individual readers, but what is not assailable is the fact of continuing economic problems and the need for the further development of relevant economic theory. The contributors to this volume believe institutional theory is an alternative to neoclassical, orthodox theory.

If inquiry remains open, the testing and demonstration of this conviction can continue both in academic lecture halls and in the deliberative arenas of policy formulation and implementation. Other volumes in this trilogy explore and buttress this conviction in other subject areas. You are invited to pursue the dialogue begun in these pages in those areas.

26

On the Possibility of a Political Economics

Robert L. Heilbroner

This essay is prompted by a profound sense of dissatisfaction with the state of contemporary economics, a dissatisfaction that finds its expression in the charge, voiced not only by a large number of students but by a growing body of economists, that conventional economic thought lacks "relevance" to the problems of our times. By this I believe most critics mean that conventional economics serves neither to depict accurately the structure or the tendencies of modern economic society, nor to guide reliably efforts to improve it. If this charge is true – and I believe that in large measure it *is* – an examination of the reasons for this lack of relevance would surely seem a matter of some importance. To provide such an examination is one purpose of this paper.

But I have a further end in mind, beyond a critique of conventional economic analysis. With all the risks that such an enterprise entails, I wish to use the occasion to suggest the direction in which I think that analysis must move if economics is to regain a sense of relevance. It should hardly come as a surprise that this direction is political – using the word in the broadest Aristotelian sense – for this is no more than to assert that the missing element in conventional analysis is any systematic consideration of man as the product and the producer of social forces other than those that can be detected by the narrow wave lengths of economic vision. To put it differently, what is required to rescue economics from a condition that I have described as "rigor, but alas, also mortis"[1], is to join the dimensions of political and sociological reality onto the flat-land models through which conventional economics seeks to explicate the nature of the existing social order. Hence my call for a "political economics", the nature of which I shall try to clarify as a second main purpose of this essay.

IRRELEVANCE – A PROBLEM OF SUBJECT MATTER

My aim is clearly an ambitious one, despite the cautious phrasing of my title. Tactically and strategically, then, I think it would be well to begin with the least troublesome aspect of the problem, by examining precisely what we mean when we claim that conventional economics is not "relevant" to the contemporary world. As we shall quickly see, the meaning of that critical word is neither simple nor single-valued, and a study of its definitions will lead us rapidly in the direction of the more difficult issues with which we must finally come to grips.

The first definition of irrelevance is perhaps the one that most closely expresses the impatience of many students with the discipline. It is the failure of the great majority of academic economists (as contrasted with "economics") to interest themselves in any deep criticism of our present social and economic order. A few instances may give substance to that general charge. One of them concerns the absence of professional economic interest in the phenomenon called "imperialism". Between 1950 and 1969, American direct foreign investment increased from less than $12 billions to over $65 billions, and the volume of sales of these foreign branches and subsidiaries ($120 billion in 1966) has mounted until, in Servan-Schreiber's well-known phrase, "Fifteen years from now it is quite possible that the world's third greatest industrial power, just after the United States and Russia, will not be Europe, but *American Industry in Europe.*"[2]

Whatever the accuracy of this prediction, there can be no doubt as to the importance of the American foreign economic expansion. Yet, a student of our times who depended for his knowledge of current economic trends on the main journals or books produced by the economics profession would be almost totally unaware of it. So far as I am aware, no analysis of the "imperial phenomenon" is to be found in the normal range of the professional literature. Until very recently, our knowledge of the extent, nature or consequences of the

American hegemony in foreign trade and investment, both in the underdeveloped and the developed world, has been gained almost entirely from Marxian economists or journalists.

There are other neglected subjects of similar importance. Poverty and environmental decay are probably the most striking. There is today a considerable discussion of poverty and ecology in the economic journals and scholarly books. But I think it is a fair charge to levy against the profession that neither of these critical issues first emerged as a consequence of its own researches, but rather from the inquiries of independent investigators, or from the actual disturbances caused by poverty and pollution themselves.[3]

THE THRALLDOM OF TECHNIQUE

The roster of ignored subjects could be easily expanded. What concerns us here, however, is not to chastize the profession, but to inquire into the reasons for this striking lack of interest in "relevant" issues. There are, I believe, two answers – one subtle, but easy to expound, another obvious, but not so easy to write about.

The first has to do with the current hegemony of the scientific method, or rather, with a particular model of that method that stresses avoidance of explicit value judgments and dependence on relationships capable of rigorous expression, preferrably mathematical notation. This particular paradigm of the scientific method has proved the most powerful intellectual tool that man has so far invented for the control of nature, and it is not surprising that economists should have borrowed it to forge similar tools for the control of society.[4]

The difficulty, however, is that this paradigm, applied to the field of social problems, tends to rule out of bounds those kinds of issues that resist accurate measurement, or that lend themselves only awkwardly or not at all to mathematical representation, or that contain a central and irrepressible value consideration. In a word, it tends to rule out most "political" matters. When confronted with their failure to initiate an examination of problems such as those mentioned above, most economists will reply that they have no "technique" capable of handling such problems, an answer that would imply that the paradigm itself may be a serious limitation to economic understanding. Instead, we find that the paradigm is unquestioningly retained, while those problems that do not yield to it tend to be relegated to the second rank of importance, or better yet, pushed off in the general direction of some other discipline.

So much has been written on the dangers inherent in the

thralldom of technique that I need not rehearse this familiar subject here.[5] Let me only add one remark of a general nature. It is that economists are apt to overlook that the powerful models of physical science, which they seek to imitate, exist for one purpose only – to offer patterns of interdependence or hypothesized relationships that can eventually be put to the test of empirical observation. That is, the main purpose of the model-building method of science is to facilitate the eventual testing of the *premises* on which these models are constructed. In economics, or in social science generally, it is not usually possible to utilize models in this way.[6] The controlled experiment that is the cornerstone of so much of physical science cannot be performed by the social scientist. Thus, models of economic relationships proliferate endlessly because they are not subject to the constraints of application and practice that ultimately winnow the hypotheses of physical science. This is a condition that encourages the exercise of economic imagination for its own sake, with a concommitant indifference as to whether or not the products explain or clarify the underlying social realities.

SOCIOLOGY OF ECONOMIC KNOWLEDGE

These very important questions will require further analysis, but first let me broach a second reason for the lack of interest of professional economists in "political" issues. It is quite simply that economists are mainly of conservative political orientations, and therefore do not *wish* to investigate these questions.

I am not the first to suggest that economists are conservative. In a well-known essay, "The Politics of Political Economists," George Stigler has written, ". . . the professional study of economics makes one politically conservative."[7] The reason for this, in Stigler's words, is "the effect of the scientific training the economist receives. It becomes impossible for the trained economist to believe that a small group of selfish capitalists dictates the main outlines of the allocation of resources. . . He cannot unblushingly repeat slogans such as 'production for use rather than for profit'. He cannot believe that a change in the *form* of social organization will eliminate basic economic problems."[8]

It may be however that there is another reason to which we must look for the prevailing conservatism of economic thought. Stigler refers to it, only to dismiss the thought: "The conservatism of economists cannot be explained by the vulgar argument of venality," he writes. ". . . The current rates of pay for good economists are much below what I would assume to be the going rate for a soul."[9]

I do not know the prevailing rates of pay for economists in 1959 when Stigler's essay was written, but the median going rate in 1967 for full professors was $18,000. In that year an income of $12,000 (just above the median for "superior assistant professors") put one into the top 15 percent of all taxpayers; an income of $14,000 (associate professors) into the top 10 percent; an income of $18,000 into the top 5 percent. "Superior" professors in that year averaged over $21,000 (not counting royalties, lecture or consultation fees), placing them in the top 2 percent.[10] One need not invoke venality to suggest that men who are placed in the upper income echelons of a society tend to share many of its values. What Malthus called "the insensible bias of situation and interest"[11] is a cast of mind that we recognize readily in others, including such august personages as the Justices of the Supreme Court.

In calling attention to the ideological pressures to which economists are consciously or unconsciously subject, I do not seek to impugn their intellectual integrity. The matter goes deeper. For the disturbing characteristic of the kinds of questions from which economists tend to shy away is that they concern problems for which there may be no solutions within the existing socio-political framework. That is, an explicit awareness of the political elements inextricably involved in economic change forces the analyst to the recognition that *powerful noneconomic constraints bound the domain of realistic economic theorizing.* With this recognition comes the unwelcome conclusion that many proposals for change are doomed to futility, and that certain attributes and tendencies of the system are beyond reform.[12]

The very awareness that limits do exist and must be taken into account acts as a powerful depressant on the state of mind of the would-be "value-free" investigator who senses that fatal inconsistencies of a political nature may invalidate the logic of his economic reasoning. A commitment to a political economics does not require that a hostile animus motivate the social analyst, but the questions that it poses serve unquestionably to try the faith of the partisan of the *status quo* or to reveal the disconcerting extent to which his economic conclusions rest on uncertain political assumptions.[13]

IRRELEVANCE AND INADEQUATE CONSTRUCTS

One reason that economics is "irrelevant" is thus that the majority of economists do not wish to make it relevant, partly due to the restrictive effects of the prevailing paradigm and its techniques, partly to an unwillingness to pursue inquiries whose outcome promises an increase in the psychic discomfort of the inquirer, possibly placing him in a position of acute conflict or political jeopardy. Although I cannot prove these assertions, it is my personal conviction that their deterrent effect is both widespread and deep-seated.

But there is a second and perhaps more fundamental meaning of irrelevance. This is a charge leveled not against the omissions of economists, but against those of economics. It is the contention that with the best will in the world, certain problems critical for an understanding of the social order remain irresolvable because the appropriate tools do not seem to be included in that famous tool kit of conventional economics.

The first deficiency is well known to conventional economists who spend a good deal of time trying to overcome it. It is the failure of present-day analytical techniques or conceptual schemes to present a consistent or integrated model of the economic system in the terms in which that system is usually perceived. Primary among these failings is the absence of a unified theoretical framework capable of explaining both macro and micro behavior. A second widely recognized lack is an adequate theory of the major agent of contemporary capitalism – the corporation. What is lacking is a set of premises concerning behavior, technology and organization from which reliable predictions can be made as to corporate behavior. Perhaps at an even more fundamental level are the misgivings expressed by some economists as to the validity of certain prime constructs of economic thought, such as "capital" or "welfare" or even "gross national product."

Certainly the inability of economic theory to cope with such problems lessens its effectiveness. Nonetheless, many of these particular failures of economics appear to be reparable. The gulf between micro and macro economics arises in large part from the different kinds of problems that each isolates, and there seems to be no intrinsic reason, rooted in the nature of economic reality, why a more unitary mode of reasoning should not eventually emerge. Work on the behavior of the corporation has proceeded apace, promising us a new model that seems to account for the observed tendencies toward concentration and oligopoly, and even yielding optimal strategies for growth. The problems of concept and measurement are much more obdurate, but once again, the difficulties do not seem to vitiate the core of economic theory itself, but rather to establish limits on the degree of exactness that can be expected of that theory in use.

I do not wish here to speculate on which areas of economics

will most readily yield to further refinements of conventional theory, but rather to point out a common denominator to be expected in all such advances. It is that *we can anticipate improvements in models that serve as ideal-typical representations of certain aspects of the system, but not in models that are intended to be used for "hard" prediction.*

IRRELEVANCE AND PREDICTIVE LIMITATIONS

The relevance of economic theory as an instrument of prediction depends on two interdependent but separable aspects of the process of theorizing itself. The first consists in the capacity of a theory to filter out from the immense field of our perceptions those attributes deemed significant. The second consists of subsequent efforts to link these mental constructs into a relational system.[14]

The first of these two tasks of theory is in some respects the more fundamental, for it prescribes the terms on which we come to grips with the unmanageable complexity of an unstructured reality. Some of the present lacunae of economic theory – the gap between micro and macro theory, for example – may well be repaired by the design of more "relevant" abstractions with which to handle the economic universe. More to the point, if it is possible to join a political element to the prevailing economic constructs, this would in itself radically alter the ideal-typical model of the economic system itself, perhaps changing very markedly our theoretical understanding of it. That is a matter of which we shall have more to say subsequently. But it is first necessary to examine certain intrinsic limitations within the second aspect of theorizing – to wit, attempts to join the given constructs into the kind of functionally related system that accords with the prevailing scientific paradigm.

These limitations are rooted in two indispensable assumptions that underlie all the functional relationships of conventional economics. One of these is that it is possible to describe in "law-like" terms the behavioral responses to certain critical changes in the economic environment, mainly the responses of buyers and sellers to changes in prices, or of consumers and investors to changes in income and/or interest rates. All models, macro or micro, are built on the bedrock of a presumed behavioral consistency, whether this be pictured as short-run maximizing, long-run satisficing, homeostasis, or whatever.

The second assumption underlying economic theory concerns the nature of the material relationships among the factors of production. Put concisely, economic theory builds its models on the premise that it is possible to describe "engineering" functions to serve as counterparts to the required behavioral functions. These engineering functions serve as necessary constraints on the forces of behavior, specifying the elasticities of substitution among goods or factors in the production process, the economies of scale for all inputs together and so on.

I think there can be no doubt that economic theory cannot build reliable – and in that sense, relevant – models that fit the reigning paradigm unless it can describe, with some degree of confidence, the nature of these essential behavioral and technical functions. Our textbook models of economic society are all grounded in the law of supply and demand, the law of variable proportions and so forth. Moreover, as Adolph Lowe has pointed out, it may well be that from an historical point of view economics was entirely justified in taking the reliability of these functions for granted.[15] In the environment of widespread poverty, small scale enterprise, uninhibited acquisitiveness, and "mechanical" technology characteristic of the middle 19th century, it is likely that both behavior and production displayed the reliable patterns of stimulus-response and change that economic theory attributed to and implicitly required of them.

The problem arises, however, when we ask whether that confidence can be justified in the altered environment of the latter 20th century. As Lowe has pointed out, the structure of a highly industrialized, oligopolistic system is such as to lengthen enormously the time-horizon applicable to "maximizing" decisions, while the concommitant rise of standards of living has greatly increased the importance of "discretionary" expenditure for the consumer. In this relaxed environment, the external pressures that once produced reliable patterns of behavior – short-run maximizing for the firm, negatively sloped demand curves for consumers – have given way to a much looser set of environmentally imposed constraints. As a result, "normal" economic behavior, both for the consumer and for the firm, becomes increasingly unpredictable. In Lowe's words: "[C]onsidering the state of uncertainty in the modern industrial market, opposite actions such as increasing or decreasing output, raising or lowering prices, can be defended in one and the same situation as the most promising step for profit maximization."[16]

Lowe's criticism deals a severe blow to the reliability of economic theorizing in the short run period in which the behavior function is critical. Recently, I have suggested that there is a second and no less substantial obstacle to reliable prediction in the long run, based not on the vagaries of behavior but of technology.[17] For over a long enough period it is possible to regard the perversities of behavior as essentially random departures from a trend line, while expecting the underlying trend to reassert itself persistently after each moment of perversity has passed. To put it differently, profit or utility maximizing may lead to differing actions in the short run, but over a longer period, it is at least plausible that a consistent pattern of behavior will emerge. But when we now examine the possibility of projecting long-run production functions, we find that the unpredictability of short-run individual or institutional behavior has been transferred to the "behavior" of technology. It is simply a fact that we cannot make predictions over a time span of as little as a decade with regard to the proportions of inputs – much less the kinds of inputs – that will be required to produce a unit of given output, or for that matter foresee the mix of outputs themselves. In this long run indeterminacy, changes in taste and motivation play their role, but the prime upsetting factor, including a main reason for changes in taste and motivation, is the unpredictable shape of the production function over time.

As a consequence of this increasing indeterminism of the basic premises on which predictive models are based, economics faces a genuine crisis. The seemingly capricious factor of behavior weakens the relevance of economic prediction in the short run; the unknowable path of technical change undermines it in the long run.

There is, however, a remedy – or at least a partial remedy – for the inadequacies of economics that stem from the erosion of the behavioral or technological determinism on which it was built. This is a reconstruction of economics along the lines that Lowe has described as "instrumental". By this Lowe means the deliberate abandonment of economics as a science that deduces its conclusions or predictions from secure premises of behavior and technology, and its replacement by a conception of economics as a policy-oriented instrument whose major theoretical purpose is to discover what "premises" – what behavioral forces, what technological constraints, what institutions – would be necessary to attain targets or goals. Economics thus overrides the indeterminacy of its behavioral or technological underpinnings by transforming them into the *dependent* variables of the economic model, the appropriate forms of which will be specified by whatever constraints or targets are introduced as parameters.

In this way economics regains relevance by becoming first and foremost a theory of planning, including above all the planning of the appropriate behavioral preconditions for the tasks determined by political choice. In the case of unruly economic behavior, for example, instrumental theorizing would consider what measures might be necessary to restore expectations to a state conducive to "normal" economic activity, while the disturbances inherent in unforeseeable leaps of technology could be minimized within the time spans of economic plans and projects by direct controls, to the extent that they would be necessary or feasible.

IRRELEVANCE OF NON-HOLISTIC THEORY

There are many problems associated with the construction of an instrumental economics, to which I will later revert, but its insistence on a political premise to economic theory brings us naturally to a third, and in some respects most far-reaching definition of the irrelevance of conventional economics. This is the charge that in concentrating on a narrowly defined set of problems, economics no longer asks the questions that are of greatest concern for contemporary society; that it elicits answers that are uninteresting because they do not take into account the political and social attributes of the economic variables on which they concentrate. To put the charge in the language in which it is frequently voiced, this aspect of irrelevance springs from the intellectual mistake of first wrenching the "economy" from the "society", and thereafter treating the abstractions of economics without regard for their inextricably linked noneconomic causes and consequences.

The antithesis to this narrow approach is, of course, the "holistic" approach of Marxian economics, and to a lesser degree the classical economists that preceded Marx. What is it that gives to these earlier doctrines their holistic quality? I believe the answer lies in three characteristics shared by all of them:

1. The holistic models treat as dependent variables (or as constants) aspects of the social process that modern theory treats as independent variables. For instance, a crucial element in Marxian and non Marxian models alike is a subsistence level toward which the wage level constantly tends. *This gives a basic social and political, as well as economic, parameter to the ensuing dynamics.*
2. Class interests are expressly recognized. The main dependent variables of the economic process – wages, rent, profits – are treated not merely as factor returns, but as class returns. *Economics thus emerges as the study of the changing fortunes of social classes under various assumptions concerning behavior, technology, and institutions.*
3. Definite, if sometimes only implicit, notions of welfare form an

> integral part of the model. Benign or otherwise, in every case a clear view of the desired social destination serves to join value judgments and economic analysis. *Economics thus becomes the willing servant of politics.*

Out of these assumptions emerge the "magnificent dynamics" of a great internal struggle within society that can be both clearly divined and unambiguously judged. These dynamics, it need hardly be said, depend on a number of critical assumptions. One of them, as we have already mentioned is the "driven" character of 19th century behavior, both of the worker and the capitalist, whence derives the strict determinism of the schemata. Another is the equally important presence within all these models of flexible wages and "inflexible" technology, which make possible the parameters of a wage level at or tending constantly toward subsistence and an employment level essentially determined by the stock of capital. A third essential premise is the rigid stereotype of class behavior in the political field, to which no modifications of nation or environment are admitted. A fourth is the uncluttered view of "human nature" and of social values in general characteristic of the age.

Alas for the latter day "classicist", none of these assumptions can be accepted today. The driven nature of economic behavior has altered with the shift from atomistic competition to oligopoly and with the appearance of discretionary spending power on the part of the consumer. The convenient relation between wages and population or surplus population no longer operates in the industrialized countries although the classical assumptions still provide important insights in the backward areas. Capital-labor coefficients can no longer be regarded as fixed, so that the employment effects of a changing capital stock cannot be unhesitatingly predicted. And finally, a century of political experience has dealt two severe blows to the political aspects of the holistic model. First, it has uncovered a wide range of variations in class attitudes and behavior among capitalist nations, and has thereby weakened the classical stereotypes of "fixed" economic-political reactions. Second, the experience with socialism has increased uncertainty, not only as to the nature of "human nature", but also as to the relation between economic change and human welfare.

For all these reasons, the goal of a "holistic" analysis is no longer seriously entertained by conventional economists. This carries with it both structural and political consequences for economic thought. On the structural side, the integral connection between economic growth and social change – the very heart of the classical model – has been largely abandoned in favor of models that explore various expansion "paths" for a few variables, with little or no concern for the meaning of whatever changes in the fortunes of the different elements of society are represented by those variables. On the political side, the tacit mutual support of political preferences and economic analysis has now given way to the indeterminate inquiry of "value-free" theory, or to the politically evasive premises of Pareto optima and social welfare functions. Thus, abandonment of the holistic goal has meant the deliberate constriction of economic theory from a discipline that aspired to the towering stature of a truly *social* science to the much more modest status of a science that explicates interactions of the economic elements within the social system, without regard to political or social ramifications.

However reluctantly, we have no choice but to accept much of this deliberate constriction, as more and more elements of the social process have become independent rather than dependent variables. Nonetheless, I am not so quick to acquiesce in the total abandonment of the aims of "holistic" theory, despite this inescapable restriction of its scope. For the loss of its social and political dimensions brings a truly devastating loss to economics as a social science. The difficulty with an "apolitical" economics is that it permits a proliferation of endless models or paths or strategies, all of which are equally plausible, since none have to conform to any requirements of social adaptability or political power, and all equally preferable since social values are rigorously excluded.

Here, I believe, is the crux of the issue of relevance. *It is the recognition, never to be lost to sight, that economic systems cannot be conceived merely as "functional" arrangements for the production and distribution of goods, but must also be seen both as frameworks for the division of social prestige and political power, and as mechanisms for the attainment of some postulated social destination.* In a word, both the "class" and the "welfare" aspects of society can be allowed to disappear from sight only at the cost of expunging the very elements that constitute the vital links between an "economy" and its surrounding social organization. The task for a political economics, then, is to find ways to reintroduce these essential elements into the body of economic analysis.

SHORTCOMINGS OF MARXISM

But are we not merely proposing a return to Marxism? Is not the integration of political and economic attributes the very essence of

Marxian social science? There is no question but that the articulation of a new political economics must use many of the insights of Marxian analysis. The fact remains, however, that a great deal of what passes as Marxian economics today is as irrelevant as neo-classical economics. Despite its political flavor and self-consciously political approach, Marxian economics has so far promised much more than it has delivered. Although it has identified certain problems to which conventional economics has been blind, it has been far from cogent in moving from general forebodings to specific predictions.[18]

In a word, Marxism has the aims but not the accomplishments of a genuine political economics. In particular, it has failed to present an operational model of society because of four major shortcomings:

> 1. Some of the key formulations of Marxian economics – especially the labor theory of value and its related concepts – have proven awkward or useless as a "kit of tools" for analytical purposes.
> 2. The ramifications of technology, which Marxian analysis rightly places at the very center of the historic process, have not been adequately dealt with. In particular the physical and social side-effects of technology, from environmental decay to alienation and affluence, have been described in a doctrinaire fashion that fails to illumine the complex role played by science and technology in all industrial societies.
> 3. The Marxian treatment of social classes and the state has suffered from an excessively rigid aprioristic view. From this inadequate conceptual basis there have followed highly misleading or even outright fallacious conclusions.[19]
> 4. Ultimately, the Marxian model of society has not found a satisfactory paradigm of its own. Its economic core mechanism depends essentially on the same kinds of "mechanical" relationships as does the neo-classical. And whereas the method of dialectics is an effort to relate social and political events to this core in a "non-mechanical" way, the indeterminacy of these dialectical linkages has not permitted the model to serve as a basis for reliable social prediction or guidance.

To point out these serious deficiencies of Marxism serves two purposes. It makes clear that the traditional Marxian analysis must be vastly improved – even transformed – if Marxism is to have a claim to "relevance" that is demonstrably superior to that of orthodox analysis. But the second purpose served by an analysis of Marxian shortcomings is graver. For the most significant failures of Marxian analysis alert us to a more critical issue. *It is that the remedy for some of the faults of Marxian analysis lies beyond our present capabilities as social scientists.* Substitution of some of the more highly refined and flexible tools of conventional economics would add suppleness to Marxian technique. Yet they will not solve the problem of how to treat such semi-independent social variables as ideology, militarism and nationalism. Indeed, to include all these vital elements of the social process within a single model of sufficient particularity to yield reliable foresight seems well beyond our present abilities, at least within a paradigm of a functional model along conventional lines.

TOWARD GREATER RELEVANCE

It follows from my argument that the possibility of increasing the relevance of economics thus hinges on three kinds of changes, each with its own difficulties and likelihood of attainment: (1) the introduction of explicit political considerations into economic research: (2) the widening of the scope of conventional economic theory to include a political dimension; and (3) the supersession of the existing paradigm of "scientific" economics by another, more far-reaching one.

Of the three, the easiest to prescribe is the first. If economics is to become more relevant, economists must direct their energies into areas of the social order that they have heretofore overlooked, particularly areas in which political or sociological elements are intimately intertwined with strictly economic ones. Since I have already suggested some of these areas, I will only add that "institutional" economics would seem preeminently qualified to lead the expedition into this dangerous no-man's land.[20]

The second general remedy is the introduction of a political dimension into economic models to make explicit the tensions in an economic order that is both a functional mechanism and a vehicle for privilege and status. The difficulty is that the simplified class structure by which the classicists combined functional and political analysis seems no longer reliable as a basis for large-scale theorizing.

What can be done in the face of this impasse? First, the construction of models that reveal the political stresses of economic change by linking economic growth with changes in income distribution.[21] These must perforce be much more complicated models than those of the classicists, for the great simplifying triad of workers, capitalists and landlords does not begin to represent the politically active claimants to income under modern capitalism. Moreover the models should not be expected to predict the ultimate outcome of dynamic tendencies, but only to indicate the areas where the tension is likely to be greatest and where, accordingly, we can expect political intervention or collective private action of one kind or another.

An alternative to this "politicizing" of theory lies in the incorporation of *group consciousness* into the constructs whence behavioral functions are derived. An example is a behavioral model of Paolo Leon in which a key determinative factor is the notion of self-conscious class action undertaken by the managers of big corporations. Leon writes:

> Monopolists cannot individually remedy, by altering their investment decisions and wage scales, a disequilibrium in the economy as a whole. In this sense, monopolists and free competition entrepreneurs are not very different. Where they do differ is in the capacity of the former to anticipate events which pertain to the economy as a whole. Therefore if *all* monopolists are aware of a crisis that can damage each of them, it seems reasonable to assume that they will recognize themselves as a class, *or as a group of interests which becomes homogenous at a macroeconomic level.*[22]

It is not my purpose here to defend Leon's concept in particular or to expound the ways in which it affects the development of his model. But his approach – generalized to labor unions and other groups capable of collective action in response to perceived economic stress – opens a second possibility for a reorientation of conventional theory along political lines.

A third avenue of change is more difficult. It is an effort to formulate a theory of the economic behavior of the state. One of the most vitiating assumptions of present-day conventional economics is its tendency to treat government economic activity as either a wholly passive force – for example, the automatic stabilizers – or as a wholly unpredictable independent variable. Yet surely, without descending to the opposite, Marxian view of the state as the creature of a unified capitalist class, it should be possible to indicate the mutual interdependence of the public and private sectors in a more realistic fashion. Such an effort seems within the technical competence of conventional theory and would add immeasureably to the relevance of its models.

TOWARD A NEW PARADIGM

The foregoing suggestions are all intended to enrich the existing paradigm of economic theorizing, and to the extent that they can be implemented, should add a political flavor to the blandness of most present-day economic writing. Yet none of them transcends the paradigm itself. We are left with a representation of social processes that stresses functional relationships and a value-free approach to social problems, even though we know in our bones that society is not, and cannot be, adequately represented by a web of formulae and that value-considerations are clearly at the very heart of the social process itself.

One line of exploration suggests itself at once. It is the search for a new explanatory mode that would arch across the artificial divisions of "economics", "politics" and "sociology" to produce a unified conception of society as a seamless web. It would open up a topography of the social process more ramified than the one to which we are accustomed, thereby enabling us to comprehend the process of social change more thoroughly than is now possible. For example, looking down on society from this new vantage point we should be able to see a cross-linked matrix of activity somewhat like that shown below:

A TOPOGRAPHY OF SOCIAL PROCESSES

	Economics: production and distribution	**Political Science: governance**	**Sociology: social organ-ization**
Role of the individual	*factor of production*	*citizen*	*role-actor*
	consumer	*voter*	
Role of the state	*regulator of economic processes*	*source of force and authority*	*source of bureaucracy*
Role of the firm	*agency of production*	*lobbying and political influence*	*locus of industrial discipline*
Problems of growth	*intersectoral relations*	*planning*	*changes in motivation due to affluence*
Technological change	*effect on profit rates, structure of demand*	*control over externalities*	*changes in work patterns, life-styles*

Such a topographic or taxonomic approach has value because it forces the specialized observer to recognize the multiplicity of ways in which the simplest variable is embedded in society, and because the observation of these juxtapositions may open up new insights into social causality. Yet I do not believe that such an inquiry can take us beyond the limitations of the existing paradigm. For the topographic approach is limited in two ways. On the one hand, because we do not have the insight we seek from this new map of social activity, there is no systematic, ordered way of juxtaposing activities. Hence the taxonomic model yields no more than scattered, *ad hoc* insights, rather than systematic enlightenment.

On the other hand, to the extent that we *can* find behavioral regularities in and among the noneconomic spheres of life, we have not escaped from, but merely enlarged, the existing paradigm. We have then equated the idea of a unified social science with that of the representation of the social process as a system in *n* variables and *n* equations. That such a Laplacean fantasy is an adequate image of the social universe I find hard to believe. For quite aside from the difficulties presented by the vagaries of so many social processes (including, as we have seen, the best behaved of them, economics), such a "deterministic" model of society fails to come to grips with the aspect of the social process that, more than any other, sets it apart from physical processes – namely, the display of *social volition* as an integral part of the behavioral forces by which the system is set into motion.

ECONOMICS AS A GOAL-ORIENTED SCIENCE

This last conclusion points the way, I believe, for a genuine supersession of the existing paradigm. For what is ultimately constricting about the present conception of social "science" is that it plunges us into the free-will *vs* determinism dilemma from which there is no satisfactory exit so long as we conceive of functional relationships in terms of the unconstrained working-out of immutable behavioral forces. Once we drop this Laplacean conception, however, the dilemma disappears. For we can then retain the functional mode of explanation (which is, after all, the only method of causal analysis we possess) while ridding ourselves of its straitjacket implications *by using this mode as a goal-orienting device.* The new paradigm, in other words, consists in an abandonment of the view of social analysis as that of determining the immanent destination of a universe of goalless particles, and substituting a view of social science as the search for the means by which social goals can be attained.

As we have already seen, this instrumental reformulation, applied to economics, departs from the prevailing conception of the discipline by relinquishing the belief in dependable behavioral functions from which future configurations of the system can be deduced. In its place it elevates a desired terminus of the social process – steady growth, ecological balance and so forth – to the status of the initial premise of economic analysis, while relegating behavior, the premise of conventional theory, to the status of an "instrument" by which the terminus is to be attained. From this point of view, a search for the "laws" of behavior – political and social as well as economic – becomes a matter of secondary concern, and the study of modes of influencing behavior rises accordingly in importance.

To this instrumental reorientation of economics, which has been vigorously proposed by Lowe,[23] one can pose two principal objections. The first is that the intrusion of value-laden goals into the economic reasoning process destroys all hope of establishing a genuine science of economics, much less of political economics. To this objection two rejoinders can be made. The first is that so-called "value-free" economic theory in fact represents an acquiescence in the social termini implicit in a laissez-faire universe, and that even the most innocuous assumptions of "value-free" theory are in fact drenched in unrecognized value judgments as to the legitimacy of the institutional order and the starting position of the economic process.

The second rejoinder is that the scientific character of economic reasoning does not rest in its value-free or value-laden assumptions, but in the methods by which it proceeds from its premises to its conclusions. Whether the mode of scientific analysis be taxonomic or mathematical-functional,[24] essentially the claim to being a scientific procedure rests on nothing more than a subscription to orderly, repeatable methods and to the willing submission of hypotheses to empirical testing. These overriding requirements are in no way invalidated by the use of economic reasoning as a means of gaining a previously stated end, rather than as a means of deducing the trajectory of a system from assumed behavioral functions.

To be sure, in the initial selection of these social ends, the economists has no more claim to priority or expertise than any other educated member of the polity; and without question, the ends that will be selected cannot be invested with any more objective validity than the level of current wisdom affords. But this explicit unmasking of the frailty of the goal-chosing process does not worsen the chances that goals will be well-chosen. It merely brings into the open what was often before a *sub rosa* process. One might say that the ultimate political aim of instrumentalism is thus to elevate the process of goal selection to its proper status as the most important of all social activities.

The second major objection to instrumentalism is that it does not in fact offer us an escape from the reigning paradigm at all. If it throws our dependency on unreliable "laws" of behavior out the front door, it smuggles them in by the back. For it is argued, in selecting the appropriate economic or political or social means of influencing behavior to gain a desired end, must we not lean on behavioral regularities after all? Otherwise, how would we know that measure B would produce desired behavior A?

To this two answers can be given. One is that a main task of instrumental inquiry is not behavioral but structural – that is, inquiry into the allocations or technical sequencing needed to achieve a given economic target. Here, of course, instrumental analysis must deal with the unpredictable elements of the long-run production function, but insofar as its aim is to specify the technical preconditions for a postulated target it can legitimately confine itself to the "given" technology, permitting unpredicted technological change to improve on its bill of particulars.

But a second answer can also be given that directs itself specifically to the behaviorial problem. It is that instrumental analysis must depend on generalizations of differing probabilities with respect to behavior. But unlike conventional economics, the scientific application of instrumentalist theory does not collapse if these expectations of regularity prove unfounded. Instead, provided that the target remains the same, it now becomes the task of theory to discover other behavioral routes to the same goal, or to explore specific means of establishing the behavior that is required. Instrumentalism can thus be pragmatic rather than aprioristic with respect to the relevant "laws" of behavior.

Last, it may be objected that an instrumental orientation, by greatly enlarging the importance of controls over behavior, opens the way to a totalitarian drift for a society that practices such a boldly interventionist social science. To this the answer is easy. If a high ranking goal is freedom of behavior itself – that is, a decision not to permit intervention beyond such mild means as fiscal or monetary policy or the normal spectrum of political exhortation – it may then follow that other social goals become impossible to attain. In that case instrumentalism serves the purpose of making clear what opportunity costs must be borne by opting for a given degree of behavioral freedom.

I do not wish to gloss over the difficulties of instrumental analysis or to magnify unduly the possible gains to be had from its application. Our knowledge of social cause and effect is still very crude, and it is possible that an attempt to guide the social body by the rudder of behavioral control may result in wide tacks and little headway. But the purpose of instrumentalism, at this stage in the development of social science, is not so much to achieve an easy mastery over social processes as to free our minds from ways of thinking that prevent us from making our theories "relevant" to the problem of purposeful social change.

Instrumentalism, by placing the welfare of society as the initial premise of all subsequent analysis, opens a perspective from which not only economics but all social science suddenly takes on a new appearance. From this new perspective all the various disciplines fall into place as different ways of examining the means to given ends; "economics", "politics", "sociology" and so forth, each grappling with particular aspects of the overall problem of bringing about desired social change. In time, the refinements in technique needed to fill out this perspective will doubtless be added. In the meanwhile it is important to understand that the rigor of thought and the empirical basis of the conventional paradigm of scientific procedure are not discarded, but placed in the service of the goal-seeking propensities of the community. Since those propensities seem to be the very quintessence of social behavior, this is tantamount to saying that social science is thereby placed in the service of man.

NOTES

1. "Putting Marx to Work," *New York Review of Books,* Dec. 5, 1968, p. 10.

2. Servan-Schreiber, *The American Challenge* (New York: 1968) p. 3. (His italics).

3. A poll of members of the American Economic Association undertaken by Elmo Roper in 1959 revealed that only 52 percent of economists supported Galbraith's contention of a "unbalanced" public-private division of national effort. (*Saturday Review* June 6, 1959, p. 39.)

4. I use the expression "paradigm" in the fashion employed by Thomas Kuhn in his well known *The Structure of Scientific Revolutions.*

5. See, for example, the excoriating remarks by Kenneth Boulding, *Proceedings,* American Economic Association, May, 1966, p. 9.

6. See Joan Robinson, *Exercises in Economic Analysis,* p. xv-xvi.

7. *Quarterly Journal of Economics,* Nov. 1959; reprinted in Stigler's *Essays in the History of Economics* (Chicago, 1965) p. 52.

8. Ibid. (*Essays*), p. 60.

9. *Ibid.* p. 59.

10. Income figures for professors from annual surveys conducted by The American Economic Association; income brackets from *Statistics of Income,* Internal Revenue Service.

11. See *Works of David Ricardo,* (ed. Sraffa) Vol. II, p. 223.

12. Thus Robin Marris writes, in "Towards a Reform of the Big Firm," (*New Society,* Sept. 25, 1969), "We hope by the use of 'hard' disciplines, such as economics, to avoid the clumsiness of revolutionary improvisation. We shall certainly remain bourgeois; but, I believe, our methods may offer some possibility of salvation from present errors *if anyone of power and influence will listen to us and act on what they hear.*" (italics added). But the point is, of course, to ask why schemes for the "reform" of the big firm will in all likelihood not be listened to or acted on. Programs of improvement, calculated to appeal to the "public", or the "enlightened self-interest" of companies are as old as those of Robert Owen. The question for social science, including the "hard" discipline of economics, is not alone to criticize the content of these programs, but to understand and explain why the vast majority of them have come to naught.

13. It may be that my formulation is too mild and that at the very least a receptivity to the possibility of far-reaching structural change is a prerequisite for a willingness to undertake political-economic inquiry. I only mean to imply that such an attitude is by no means identical with a dogmatic or implacable rejection of the existing order – somewhere between the mild measures we call "reform" and the extreme ones we call "revolution" lies the little-explored territory of "radical reform" (A. Hirschman). This raises the difficult question as to what factors determine our position along this political spectrum. No doubt sheerly intellectual judgments play their part in this decision, but an unconscious identification with or rejection of the social order seems to exert an even stronger sway. The passion with which the existing order is defended or attacked suggests that "value-free" inquiry into the merits of society may ultimately be inconsistent with the internalization process by which social reality is apprehended. See Peter Berger and Thos. Luckman, *The Social Construction of Reality,* p. 119f.

14. See, *inter alia,* Fritz Machlup "Operational Concepts and Mental Constructs in Model and Theory Formation" *Giornale degli Economisti e Annali di Economia,* Sept-Oct. 1960.

15. *On Economic Knowledge* (New York, 1965) p. 68f.

16. Ibid, p. 48.

17. "On the Limits of Economic Prediction," *Diogenes,* April, 1970.

18. One of the main troubles in Marxist writing has been that the wish has been all too perceptibly father to the thought. The *Monthly Review,* for example, has predicted outright recession no less than six times between 1954 and 1963. (see issues of December 1954, October 1955, September 1956, November 1958, September 1962 and November 1963) and has failed to predict accurately the economic, political or social course of either the Soviet Union, China or Cuba. On a larger scale, a certain milennial strain continues to infuse socialist theorizing with regard to the long run future. (See my essay on "Socialism and the Future", *Commentary,* December 1969.)

19. One of the most important Marxist works of recent years has been *Monopoly Capital* by Baran and Sweezy. Its main purpose is to present a model of capitalism that will enable us to project the social and political as well as economic tendencies of the system. Two points are of interest in this regard. Although the book was published in 1966, there is no anticipation of inflation as a coming central issue within capitalism; rather, stagnation with its deflationary overtones continues to be the central focus of analytical attention. Second, the book contains statements such as the following: "Such planning and such action [mass low-cost housing], however, will never be undertaken by a government by and for the rich, as every capitalist government is and must be." (p. 300). Even granting the premise of the last clause, does it follow that a government of the rich might not find it politically useful to rid a nation of its slums? The examples of capitalist Switzerland, Netherlands and Scandanavia, are enough to prove that it may indeed. In other words, this

formulation of class interest and its consequences – both empirically and logically – is simply wrong. I should add that not all Marxist analysis is so simplistic, and that many insights of the Baran-Sweezy book are penetrating and powerful. Nevertheless, this kind of mechanical analysis is clearly "irrelevant" – not because it is apolitical, but because it is unpolitical.

20. I cannot refrain from mentioning once again the problem of "imperialism". The multi-national corporation is fast emerging as a major form of enterprise within all industrial capitalisms. Yet we still possess no full-scale study of the transition from national to international enterprise, and of the relationship of such enterprises with their "home" or their "host" governments. Important beginnings, however, may lie in the work of Stephen Hymer and others.

21. A beginning along these lines is to be found in the work of Joan Robinson, Kaldor, and Sraffa.

22. *Structural Change and Growth in Capitalism (1967)* p. 31. Author's italics.

23. Lowe, op cit. See also his essays in *Economic Means and Social Ends,* ed. R. Heilbroner, Prentice Hall, 1970.

24. "There do exist respectable sciences that have essentially no theory at all in the physicists' sense. Mineralogy, and to an even greater extent, taxonomy are primarily concerned with framing assumptions – for in essence a definition is an assumption and the naming of a species is a definition. . . . To say that all of biology [read *economics,*] should have an elegant mathematical framework is as much of an imposition of metaphysics on observation as it was to say that the only suitable astronomic observations must involve cycles and epicycles. . . ." L. S. Slobodkin, "on the Present Incompleteness of Mathematical Ecology," *American Scientist,* Sept. 1965. p. 351. 354.

27

Institutionalist Reflections on the Role of the Public Sector

Philip A. Klein

In 1929, when the U.S. Gross National Product stood at 103.4 billion dollars, government purchase of goods and services constituted 8.8 billion dollars, or 8.5 percent. By 1980 government purchases had risen to 538.4 billion dollars out of a GNP of 2633.1 billion dollars, or 20.4 percent. Thus by this crudest of measures more than one-fifth of total economic activity was located in the public sector. While over the years the share of government spending has shifted somewhat from the federal to the state and local level, total federal spending as a percent of GNP was 7.4 percent in 1980, the year that Ronald Reagan became president. Between 1980 and 1982 federal purchase of non-denfense goods and services rose from 65.8 billion dollars to 78.8 billion dollars.[1] These figures demonstrate that federal non-defense spending rose during Reagan's first two years from 2.5 percent of GNP in 1980 to 3.0 percent by the end of 1982.

Two conclusions seem obvious. (1) The share of GNP devoted to non-defense purposes through direct federal spending is quite modest. But (2) even the president who vowed to *shrink* the size of the federal government and its role in aggregate economic activity has not thus far been able to so much as level off government spending. There must be a reason for this.

Of course, the direct allocation of resources (as in the direct purchase of goods) fails to do justice to what is meant by the public sector. The public sector has two other critical aspects.[2] For one, in addition to direct spending, government upholds a vast amount of regulation. In President Reagan's first *Economic Report* to the Congress, his Council of Economic Advisers provided data on twenty-seven regulatory agencies, which in 1981 spent more than seven billion dollars regulating the sectors they were changed to oversee.[3] These agencies are for the most part well known to the American public and include Agriculture, Commerce, Defense, Energy, and the other major departments of the federal government as well as the special independent regulatory agencies (Civil Aeronautics Board, Federal Communications Commission, Federal Trade Commission), plus the more recently created agencies—the Environmental Protection Agency, Consumer Product Safety Commission, Nuclear Regulatory Commission, etcetera. Surveying the list one is hard put to think of a single price that can be set in the United States today without its setter having to worry whether he or she has complied with the rules set down by a regulatory agency somewhere in the government—mostly federal, but also state and local.

How one perceives the regulatory system that has emerged in the course of our history may, of course, vary. Jimmy Carter, in his last presidential *Economic Report*, commented, "I believe that the government has indeed overregulated and that regulatory reform must continue to be a major objective of the federal government, as it has been during my administration. But I also believe that true reform involves finding better ways to identify and to give proper consideration to gains as well as costs."[4]

This differs only in emphasis from Reagan's stated position: "Regulation is not a substitute for efficient markets but an alternative to unregulated markets which have failed to allocate resources efficiently."[5]

It is instructive to compare this view with that of Alfred Kahn, who concluded a well-known two-volume study of regulation by declaring that the market economy ("a manifestly inefficient system that is better than any of its alternatives") is based on highly imperfect competition, and so one must attempt to reduce the imperfections. However, he adds, "even when imperfect, (competition) can often be a valuable supplement to regulation. Even to the extent that it is intolerably imperfect, the only acceptable alternative is regulation."[6] While Kahn regards competition, however imperfect, as a valuable supplement to regulation, Reagan clearly regards regulation as an unfortunate supplement to mostly perfect competition. A matter of emphasis, perhaps, but one that involves a radically different view of the way in which the economic system performs in actual markets.[7]

Finally, along with direct allocation via taxes and expenditures, and much regulatory action, the public sector is involved in creating public goods for allocation and sets welfare standards.[8]

Economic Theory and the Role of the Public Sector

Whatever else one may say about Keynesian macro-theory, it made a far less clear-cut distinction between normative and positive economic analysis in general and analysis of the role of the public sector in particular than mainstream macro-theory ever did.[9] While J. M. Keynes was at pains to suggest that one of the results that could emerge was what he called underemployment equilibrium, there was no doubt that such a result, when it encompassed 25 percent unemployment rates, as was the case during the depths of the Great Depression, was not an equilibrium that economists need look on benignly. Both under- and, for that matter, over-employment equilibria are results that emerge from economic analysis (which economists produce in the process of doing what they presumably are trained to do), that are directly related to public policy issues, and that can lead to economic policy proposals that become the appropriate focus of a public sector. Today it is fashionable to note that stagflation is a real problem not easily encompassed within a conventional Keynesian framework—a conclusion that Keynes would probably have been the first to agree with. He would have led the attack on this real-world problem and the development of interventionist policy for the public sector to employ against it. In any case, we may note that assessing the character of emergent social value has always loomed large on the institutionalist agenda.

The attitude toward positive versus normative analysis at the macro level is largely a result of the way in which modern Keynesian theory emerged. It emerged in response to clear economic problems—in response to the clear malfunctioning of the macroeconomy of the 1930s—and therefore partially as a quest for appropriate macro policy.

The ultimate result was the passage of the Full Employment Act of 1946, amended by the Humphrey Hawkins Act of 1978. Together they provide explicitly for the macro role of a public sector in a market-oriented economy, and state economic goals. The role is complicated mostly because, as Kahn has said, "entirely apart from the need for comprising economic and noneconomic objectives, there is an inescapable problem of choice and trade-offs even among the economic goals, and no simple blueprint can point the way to maximizing along all fronts simultaneously."[10]

The situation in microeconomics was and is radically different. Mainstream theory did not emerge as a response to perceived problems so much as an effort to describe, in necessarily simplified terms, how markets went about allocating resources. Keynes could brand underemployment equilibrium as "a public scandal,"[11] notwithstanding that it constituted equilibrium. Even though it is easy enough to say that the economic objectives of macroeconomic policy are noninflationary growth, stability, and full employment, policy difficulties arise because more of one of these objectives may well be accompanied by less of another. Nonetheless, narrowly viewed macro theory led to macro policy that can be expressed in reasonably clear terms. Out of macro theory can come a reasonably expressible public policy, and along with it a moderately clear role for the public sector.

None of this is so clear in the case of micro theory and micro policy. In micro theory it is difficult to imagine any equilibrium—even for monopoly—being branded "a public scandal." Nor is the role for the public sector likely to emerge clearly from mainstream analysis in this area. Where growth, stability, and full employment can be posited as goals for macro policy, mainstream micro analysis has little to offer except the quiet assumption that whatever emerges is what ought to emerge subject to *ad hoc* exceptions. Pareto optimality is a very slim reed on which to place much faith.

In short, we are arguing that however ambiguous the normative goals for macro policy, they are less ambiguous than are those for micro policy. Indeed, in macroeconomics a major dilemma for the policy maker is that the explicit objectives may conflict.

This contrasts with the situation in microeconomics. Mainstream economists are hard-pressed to state the policy objectives, because market-clearing equilibrium finesses most of the difficult questions presented by the real world. Thus, in the applied fields micro theory does not easily translate into policy guides.

Kahn recognizes this explicitly, declaring, "There is a long tradition of dissent from the 'conventional wisdom' of normative microeconomic theory and a recognition of its limitations even as a purely economic guide to policy."[12]

Power and the Public Sector

The branch of mainstream economics that attempts to apply microeconomic theory most directly is, of course, industrial organization. If mainstream economists have never been very pleased with either the theory of imperfect competition or oligopoly it is because these theories are neither precise or as formally elegant as either the theory of competition or monopoly theory. Economists accordingly prefer, as Kahn reminds us, to take the well-paved well-lighted highway and go wherever that road goes, than to take the bumpy dirt road going where they might have been expected to wish to go.[13]

In industrial organization, one of the major problems has always been to translate micro theory into something comprehensible as a guide for policy. Was the Sherman Act designed to maintain competition, to preserve competition, or to create competition? The ambiguity arises only because micro theory has consigned so much to the *ceteris paribus* compound on the path to providing a guide for public policy that, in the end, it scarcely provides a guide at all.

Surely many of the historic concerns of institutionalists can be discerned in the literature of industrial organization. From the establishment of the Interstate Commerce Commission in 1887 and the passage of the Sherman Act of 1890 the history of industrial organization in the United States is the historical record of grappling empirically with the inadequate policy guide of mainstream microeconomic theory.

Not only has there been a mainstream effort to analyze the performance of the market economy as it in fact operates in manufacturing, in banking and finance, and in other major sectors of the economy (see J. B. Clark, Joe Bain, George Stigler, et al.), but there is a long heterodox effort stretching from Thorstein Veblen through Rex Tugwell, Adolph Berle and Gardiner Means, and R. A. Brady, to J. K. Galbraith, etcetera.

A recent effort has been the updating of the Berle and Means study conducted for the Twentieth Century Fund by Edward S. Herman and published in 1981.[14] This study essentially reaffirms that the concentration institutionalists have worried about, along with the separation of ownership and control originally delineated in the Berle and Means study, are both still very much a part of the contemporary American economic scene: "In the late 1970s more than 60 percent of the assets of all nonfinancial corporations in the United States were owned by companies with $250 million or greater in assets, and in the important manufacturing sector, the 200 largest firms controlled 60 percent of all assets in 1977, up from 45 percent in 1945."[15]

Not only does Herman argue that corporate strength, influence, and dominance in many areas remain at least as strong as they were in the early days of the century, but that government control even in its role of monitor has often been ineffective and is probably weaker than often supposed. By calling government weak, Herman says he means "unable to plan and implement some coherent and rational vision of domestic economic and social policy."[16] It does not mean necessarily that Herman is advocating planning so much as that the monitoring function of government becomes meaningless if there is no standard of corporate performance against which to measure that which in fact emerges. Without adequate government monitoring of an economy's concentrated private sector, there are dangers in how that economy will function.

We have suggested that two critical roles for government or the public sector are evaluating what emerges in the private sector and making direct public expenditures where that seems necessary or appropriate. The latter involves at least partly the creation of public resources. Neither role can be performed without the standard Herman puts forth. Mainstream economists may be content much of the time to consider that what emerges from the private sector defines itself as coherent and rational. But the society of which the economy is a part has always insisted on imposing, however imperfectly or incompletely, an emergent value system upon the economy. This has been the case from the institution of child labor laws in England in the early eighteenth century on.[17] Institutional economists have always included assessing that system and its implications for emergent social value as a part of their task.

As a guide for public policy, micro theory, therefore, appears less precise than macro theory.[18] We have suggested that this is largely a result of the differences in the origins of the two. But in the final analysis an institutionalist must conclude that neither micro or macro theory provides an adequate guide to public policy if public policy is to play its full role in the system. This will, of course, require that we consider the public sector from an institutionalist perspective.

Institutionalists and the Public Sector

The distinction between mainstream economics and institutionalism is perhaps nowhere as sharp as in the view of the public sector. Mainstream economics regards the competitive model as the "benchmark" against which to judge allocative efficiency in the real world. Exceptions are made in cases where the market performs so inadequately as to require intervention. But the theory gives little guidance. Mainstream economists are prone to claiming that public sector decisions to intervene must be made on non-economic grounds, thereby opting out of the debate about the role of the public sector for the entire discipline. Does "economics *qua* economics" really have nothing to contribute to the debate about the proper role of the public sector?

In recent years mainstream economists have edged into this area, albeit tentatively, by advancing the notion that cost-benefit analysis is indispensable in determining the role of public sector intervention. Presumably national defense passes this test superbly. The costs of publicly providing national defense are clearly no higher than if it were provided privately, and the benefits are presumably enormous (though perhaps "non-economic"). The Reagan administration has gone on record as favoring more extensive use of cost-benefit analysis. While recognizing the difficulties involved in applying it to many areas, it nonetheless concludes in the case of government regulations that "given the increasing concern about the efficiency of federal regulations . . . a more general use of benefit-cost analysis can contribute to a broader consensus on appropriate changes in the nature and degree of federal regulations."[19]

While this may be true as far as it goes, the difficulty is that it does not go nearly far enough. Cost-benefit analysis, to be effective and feasible, must be restricted to those costs and those benefits that are easily quantifiable, that can be captured by emergent market prices, and that, therefore, may well not—almost certainly *will* not—involve the fundamental direction of the economy, the incurring of costs for future generations beyond the ability of current or expected prices to encompass, or the incurring of benefits that (like defense) cannot easily be captured by the valuation mechanisms enshrined in mainstream theory.[20]

A fundamental tenet of institutionalism is that economists *qua* economists (or economics *qua* economics) must be concerned about where the economy is going, how basic economic decisions are made, and about the essential allocative thrust of the economy. Not only would this appear to be an integral part of economics and hence of concern to economists, but it is inescapable because the economy itself plays an integral (if interactive) role in making these decisions. (Along with playing a role in resource allocation, the public sector thus in part creates resources as well.) This is one of the essential truths about how an economy operates customarily ignored by mainstream economic theory. It is ignored despite the fact that in one way or another almost every applied specialty within economics copes with some aspect of this problem, if inadequately and perhaps reluctantly. A major cause of the inadequacy arises, to repeat, from the theory on which the applied field must rest. Mainstream economics remains inadequate by refusing to face up to the inevitability of grappling with questions that "benchmark" theory so conveniently circumvents by means of *ceteris paribus* or other simplifying assumptions.

It is important that we spell out the relationship between theory and policy as it affects the role of the public sector as clearly as possible. Our concern as institutionalists is not whether the values being reflected in public sector resource creation or allocation conform to the specific values possibly espoused by any individual or group. This, one may assume, differentiates institutionalism in one significant way at least from the position of radical economists. Radicals presumably have a notion of, say, what constitutes the best interests of the working class or the proletariat, and judge allocative efficiency according to their notions of what furthers the values they regard as enhancing those interests. Mainstream economists, on the other hand, tend to assume that market allocation is, most of the time, definitionally "ideal" and intervene in the public sector *only* when a clear and explicit case can be made for it (as for example, with national defense).

Institutionalists are neither for nor against intervention *per se*, nor are they necessarily concerned about whether the economy is actively furthering any predefined class or group interests. They most certainly are not ethical relativists. Rather they are concerned with assessing the emergent values of the economy itself and the role of the public sector in partially shaping those values as well as in transmitting them through allocation. Institutionalists are concerned with the relation of the economy to the life process. Allocative efficiency in the institutionalist context must, therefore, be related to economic allocation by the same process that "free elections" or majority voting follow in the pursuit of representative democracy.

Clogged information channels, distorted signals, inability of prices or costs to capture essential parts of the valuation process (and hence the decision process)—these are the things that worry institutionalists because they determine the economy's adequacy to carry out its basic task. That task involves determining and transmitting as well as partially shaping what it is the participants in any economy *choose* to consider in making their overall allocative decisions.

To argue that "the price system" does this, or that what is done by the price system is all that need concern the economist, is clearly inadequate. Consider a primary justification for ridding various sectors of the economy of regulation. Various people often charge that the economy is "overregulated" and substantiate that charge by arguing that regulated industries tend to be corrupted by the regulators, with the result that performance is worse than would be the case in the absence of regulation. This may well be. But performance, in many cases, is critically affected by the concentrated power that produced the demand for regulation in the first place. The result is that concentrated power cannot be controlled in the economy because the concentration is great enough to permit the erstwhile regulated industries to control the would-be regulators. Is this a system in which the allocative implications of conventional economic analysis can be accepted with tranquility? To conclude that regulation as in fact it may occur produces worse results than would be realized in the absence of regulation is scarcely equivalent to concluding that the results produced in the absence of regulation are therefore socially acceptable, let alone desirable.

The Public Sector and the "Collective Ought"

Mainstream economists never tire of pronouncing economics a positive science, a pronouncement never more eloquently stated than in Lionel Robbins's *An Essay On the Nature and Significance of Economic Science.*[21] Beginning students to this day are told that economics is concerned with "what is," not with "what ought to be." A recent principles text, entitled, interestingly enough, *Microeconomics—Private and Public Choice*, tells us that "scientific economics, commonly referred to as positive economics, attempts to determine 'what is.' Positive economic statements postulate a relationship that is potentially verifiable." This is contrasted with "normative economics," which combines the above with ethical judgments. The authors add, "Economics deals with people as they are—not as we would like to remake them. Should people act more charitably? Perhaps so. But this is not the subject of economics."[22] Anyone who has tried to teach conventional elementary economics knows what the authors are trying to say, but is theirs a meaningful view of economics, particularly as they most particularly suggest a role for "public choice"?

Institutionalism appears to reserve for the public sector two critical tasks. The first is to monitor the allocative results flowing from private markets and consider their implications for total allocation. The second is to create some resources for allocation and to directly undertake and direct some part of the allocating. This is true in all market-oriented economies to a significant—if varying—extent. In both of these tasks the public sector contributes to (as indeed it also reflects) the ongoing reshaping of emergent values. These values, indeed, may be thought of at a given time as the current "collective ought."

This "collective ought" involves not only the allocation made and not made directly via the public sector, although this is surely included. Thus, for example, expenditures for national defense may in some sense be regarded as "non-economic decisions" but they surely are economic decisions as well—they involve resource allocation, they provide jobs, they even use prices; they have profound consequences for almost every facet of both the macro and micro economy and to conclude that all this is "non-economic" is to remove from the purview of the economist almost everything of interest to even the most conventional mainstream economist's concept of what economies do and what economists study.

Even more, the "collective ought" is expressed in how we regard the allocation that is in fact left to the private sector. Economies have always monitored the performance of the private sector. We tend, for example, to call infant mortality rates, average nutritional consumption per person, number of doctors per thousand inhabitants, and similar measures "social indicators." They are in fact *economic* indicators as well. They can be, as we shall see, encompassed in a view of efficiency quite as readily as the number of passenger cars produced. Personal charity may or may not be construed as "the subject matter of economics." But surely changing societal views of what is humane are very much a matter of economics. Mainstream economists are quite comfortable adopting what they construe to be a value-free neutrality toward the status quo. But such acceptance of the status quo represents ultimately the most profound intrusion of value judgments into economic analysis.

Surely Marc Tool was profoundly right in suggesting that the economy to be analyzed is a *discretionary economy*—it can choose for itself what it wishes to do, and what it needs most to be concerned with is how well and how completely it permits real choice to emerge.[23] Ultimately, the most critical role for the public sector is in monitoring how well, how efficiently, the economy is reflecting the emergent values—the changing "collective ought." This is why Tool is also on target in suggesting that evolutionary economics must reject both ethical relativism and ethical absolutism.[24] Mainstream economists may be comfortable with the former, radical economists with the latter. When he notes that evolutionary economists have never arrived but "are always en route" he reaffirms the correctness of Clarence Ayres's emphasis on the means-end continuum, which he in turn acquired from John Dewey's instrumental theory of value.[25] Evolutionary economists are indeed "en route"—economic analysis is ultimately a normative as well as a positive process. Ayres put it this way: "To speak of value is to speak of the relation of any single act—choice, preference, decision, or judgment—to the whole life process."[26]

In short, unlike mainstream economists, institutionalists are not ethically neutral—they do not assume that *what is* represents the ideal. They are not radical either, in that they do not have a predetermined notion of "what ought to be" again which they measure "what is." Rather they have a view of efficiency that examines the political economy and asks how well does this economy play its part in shaping and channeling as well as transmitting the ongoing values of its participants?

Here then one finds the important role for the public sector. "The collective ought" is more than the sum of individually expressible wants, and it is impossible to utilize private markets and individual reactions to prices to reflect "the collective ought." Nor is this simply the conventional distinction between public goods and private goods. It is much more, because a major task for the economy is *fully* to inform its participants about alternatives, and fully to transmit the changing values of its participants throughout the system. In the final analysis, then, the economist who attempts a sharp distinction between "what is" and "what ought to be" restricts his view of efficiency to a narrow status-quo-bound mechanistic base and cannot consider the most critical notion of efficiency for any economy: How well does it play its role in accurately reflecting and correctly channeling and reporting emergent values?

Whether one calls it a "reasonable society" (Ayres), a Great Society (Lyndon Johnson), a humane society, or a compassionate society, it must be clearly understood that all these adjectives have no absolute or fixed content—they represent way stations on the road to the future. They do not necessarily represent an unrelieved march to higher and higher material consumption per participant in any one economy (most particularly, perhaps, our own). The economy, like the rest of life, may involve tradeoffs—between one country and another, between one citizen and another, between one generation and another, perhaps between human and nonhuman or environmental aspects to life.

The point is that there are two closely related questions here and economists have a role to play in confronting both. The first is considering what one means by efficiency in this broader sense. It is a fundamental misreading of the task of political economy to argue that "compassion" is a non-economic value, and therefore safely kept out of the economist's back yard. Compassion is a part of social value, as indeed is the economy, and as such it is scarcely immutable. We partly use prices in conveying it at any given time and it is an appropriately defined and definable question to ask, "How well does the economy reflect the values of its participants—all its participants and all the relevant values—in its operation at any given time?"

The second, closely related question, is, "How efficiently does the economic organization facilitate the development and transmission of emergent values?" A critical task for economists in this connection is to develop better means for the economy to perform this task. This is the fundamental task of an economy and this is the basic meaning of the concept of efficiency in connection with economizing.

Clearly, in connection with developing and transmitting emergent values the analogy between the economy and the polity is obvious. Political scientists are not professionally responsible for defining any particular "end" for the system. They are responsible for analyzing how well the polity works in permitting its participants to achieve the evolving ends that they themselves set.[27] That is the real meaning of efficiency for a representative democracy as a political system. Analogously, efficiency for an economy means, how well does that system reflect the emergent values of its participants? That the economy itself plays a role in shaping emergent values makes the task of the economist doubly important.

We see then that economics is indeed a profoundly normative science, because in the final analysis it has the responsibility for judging *what* "the collective ought" is in order to consider how well the economy is reflecting and transmitting it. In the process of reflection and transmission the economy clearly plays an interactive role in the dynamic determination of what "the collective ought" is.

The role of the public sector is central. It is through the public sector that we monitor economic performance and so assess the gap between the ability of the economy to express "the collective ought" through private markets and the need to express it through the public sector. This is the locus of value applied to public expenditures. It leads to the creation publicly of resources to be allocated. But we also utilize the public sector to monitor the operation of the economy as an efficient conveyor of "the collective ought" to the private allocation of resources. Clogged or distorted information channels, concentration of power, huge inequalities in the initial distribution of wealth and income—all these are aspects of the economy that can lead to inefficiency broadly defined—defined to convey notions about the ability of the economy fully to permit its participants to cast informed votes reflecting accurately their values as they are at any given moment.

The Public Sector and Emergent Value

The essential thrust of the preceding argument is beyond dispute in connection, say, with national defense. Beyond that one runs into trouble. Thus Milton Friedman can write that "the market is a system of effective proportional representation," which would no doubt cause any institutionalist to question what he means by "effective." Friedman himself answered almost immediately by noting, "There are clearly some matters with respect to which effective proportional representation is impossible. I cannot get the amount of national defense I want and you, a different amount." This opens the door for him to conclude that the role of government is to act as "rulemaker and umpire."[28]

Institutionalists would not disagree with Friedman's assertion that the public sector involves *partly* the government as rulemaker and umpire. They would, however, add, that if I cannot get a different amount of national defense than you can, neither can I get a different amount of equity, or humaneness or compassion, from the overall economy than you can. An "economy *qua* economy" has *some degree and character of compassion* as a major characteristic at any time. It may (and probably will) change over time, but it exists. For economists to stick to the analysis of "what is" is to accept *de facto* the "isness" of an economy's ability truly to express its humaneness along with its security and all other value characteristics of the economy.

Clearly Friedman accepts the "isness" of the economy. He writes: "The organization of economic activity through voluntary exchange presumes that we have provided, through government, for the maintenance of law and order to prevent coercion of one individual by another, the enforcement of contracts voluntarily entered into, the definition of the meaning of property rights, the interpretation and enforcement of such rights, and the provision of a monetary framework."[29]

The institutionalist objection to this formulation is that Friedman simply presumes too much in one sense and too little in another. He presumes too much because he assumes that our economy truly *does* prevent coercion of one individual by another. In fact the disparities in access to opportunity, training, and education, along with the concentration of both wealth and power, has virtually no relation (proportional or otherwise) to what individuals have achieved or could potentially achieve through market activity alone. Rather than "voluntary exchange" and "voluntary contracts" there is from the outset a very great deal of *de facto* coercion of many in the economy by a relatively few. (Friedman is probably no sympathetic supporter of modern trade unions [they, too, may coerce], but would he have argued that an unorganized worker circa 1900 was "voluntarily" entering into a contract with Henry Ford?) And his argument suffuses extant property rights (what is) with an existential normativeness (they "should be enforced"), though perhaps he leaves himself an out in suggesting that one function of government is to "interpret" them.

Friedman also presumes too little in this acceptance of the status quo. There is no suggestion that the economy we have has largely in fact failed in many significant areas to provide what in fact he presumes the government has provided. In short, the economy that "is" for Friedman presumes an implicit fundamental "ought" that may scarcely be justified by the facts.

Economic Analysis and the Value Floor

It is not hard to imagine the world's reaction to an economist who proclaims, "As an economist I take no position at all on the extermination of six million Jews. However, I would point out that *if* one wanted to exterminate six million Jews, *then* gas chambers represent an extremely efficient way to accomplish the task." Why would the world find it difficult to swallow this? Does it not represent the mainstream economist's customary penchant for separating positive from normative? Does it not represent the necessary application of scientific principles, the effort to separate fact from opinion, the necessity to analyze problems by means requiring clear statements of assumptions, and the carrying out of experiments that can be replicated by anyone? The answer to the first of these questions is no, it does not represent the separation of the normative from the positive. The answer to the second question is that in this context the scientific is relatively meaningless.

Why is this? Because at bottom all scientific analysis, including economic analysis, must be regarded as resting on a value floor without which it makes little sense and cannot be related to human activity. That value floor is the life process itself and more specifically an affirmation of the life process. "There is the life process still in great measure awaiting theoretical formulation."[30] This statement of Veblen's played a central and explicit role in the work not only of Veblen, but of John Dewey and Clarence Ayres. It represents, if you will, the essential—if usually implicit—normative underpinning of the most unremittingly positive theorizing. In sum, there is a value floor to which economic analysis, among other kinds of analysis, must be related and without which it cannot be interpreted.

If we are told that there are six million individuals starving to death (slowly or rapidly) at this moment in this world (or in this country) mainstream economists would indeed say that what we do about it (including nothing) is a matter for normative judgment about which economists *qua* economists have little to say. Nonetheless, all that is being claimed is that what an economy does about starvation—a lot or nothing at all—reflects the operation of that economy *vis-a-vis* a part of its current value floor. Institutionalists would claim that the operation of the economy here can be assessed in light of what is technologically possible, and that such assessment is part of the economist's task.

Therefore, in the institutionalists' view, a major point of difference between mainstream economists and institutionalists is the failure of mainstream economics to see that acceptance of or failure to comment on "what is" is itself a normative pronouncement. The customary sharp distinction between normative and positive economics made by mainstream economics banishes concern for "what economic policies or conditions are good or bad," as one recent text put it, to the realm of the normative—hence to the reals with which economists are to concern themselves (if at all) only *after* they have completed their "scientific" analyses (their contribution to economics as a positive science).[31] We have all read stories of apartment dwellers who heard screams and watched in silence while a rape or murder took place in the street. They remained silent because they "did not want to get involved." Newspaper editorials not infrequently comment on such incidents by noting that "not getting involved" is tantamount to condoning what is occurring.

A social worker or law enforcement official who stated, "I take no position on rape *per se*, but if you want to stop it superior physical force offers a promising possible approach," would not be regarded as a purveyor of very profound analysis. However, a mainstream economist who said, "I take no position on poverty or, indeed, on the distribution of income at all, but if you wish to alter it, here is a promising approach," would be listened to as offering a scholarly dispassionate analysis of economic matters. Is there a difference?

When Clarence Ayres suggested that economics was nothing if not a "science of values," he was not only making a statement that seems profoundly confusing, if not downright wrong, to most mainstream economists, but he was putting his finger on precisely the characteristic of an economy that institutionalists regard as central. Mainstream economists see the point where national defense is concerned; they do not see the point for humanity or compassion, which are characteristics of an economy in precisely the way that security (national defense) is.

This brings us back to Friedman's contention that national defense is "the most basic" of exceptions to reliance on individual action through the market. One cannot banish "humaneness" to a different part of society (outside the economy or the allocation that occurs in the economy) any more than one can banish "security" to some extra-economic compound.[32] Economies are a part of society and as such each economy at any particular point in time has a number of characteristics, among which are both security and humaneness. An economy that provides nothing for defense is obviously insecure and insecurity is a collective stance with respect to national defense just as surely as arming to the teeth. In precisely the same way, an economy that takes no position with respect to questions of poverty, minimal nutritional standards, or minimal provision for clothing, housing, health, and other human needs *has* a position with respect to all of these. Taking no position with respect to these characteristics of an economy *is* to take a position as surely as the passive observer of a rape or murder is taking a position.

In short, institutionalists are telling mainstream economists that an attempt to stick to "what is" *is* to take a position on "what ought" to be, or at the very least on our ability to avoid comment on "oughtness." Because they deny this—or fail to see it—mainstream economists are not as worried as are institutionalists about the disparity between the world in which the real economy functions and the description of it quoted earlier from Friedman.

Like national security, humaneness is indivisible—the national standard is what it is and it cannot be voted by individuals to be other than as it collectively emerges. Two economies with identical resources and the same output of private goods and services could nonetheless differ in the size and quality of their armed might, their infant mortality rates, their death rates, their incidence of disease per thousand inhabitants, etcetera. Were this all we knew of two economies, economists—even mainstream economists—could surely incorporate all these pieces of information into their overall appraisal of "efficiency."

To postulate the existence of a value floor is not to eliminate legitimate disagreement. Presumably "health" or "life" constitute the value floor for both our medical and judicial systems, but to say this is to contribute little to resolving the critical current controversies over abortion, euthanasia, murder in self-defense, and capital punishment—all surely areas where appropriate public policy toward both health and life are constantly being formulated and reformulated. Here, precisely, is the difference. The public sector has a clearly recognized responsibility to play a major role in the ongoing reformulation of social attitudes toward each of these. Can the public sector escape a similar role with respect to the economy and its value floor?

The Public Sector and the Higher Efficiency

We might argue about whether economists have an obligation as economists to comment on the starvation of six million people, particularly when eliminating that starvation lies well within the frontier production possibilities of an economy. But what would appear beyond argument is that there is a *higher efficiency* at work in any economy that economists cannot avoid judging. This is the degree to which the economy structures the choices open to its participants so as to accurately and sensitively reflect their informed judgment about total resource allocation. What would we—collectively—really like to do about, for example, six million starving people? The way in which an economy facilitates the expression of informed opinion, and transmogrifies individual values into social or collective values, is very much a problem in efficiency and one that is perhaps a primary responsibility of economists to analyze.

It is precisely because individual values are not capable of being neatly summed into collective values that, among other things, we need a public sector. If the fallacy of composition means anything it means that individual units cannot fully contribute individually to what we have called here "the collective ought." A useful question, therefore, to be asked about *any* economy is, How fully and how accurately is it expressing and transmitting the current values of its individual participants? Mainstream economists stress narrow efficiency (quantitative outputs per unit of inputs) and recognize certain other characteristics by which economies can be distinguished and judged (although they correctly do not necessarily advance any specific form of these other characteristics). Thus economies are frequently characterized by their stability, growth, income distribution, etcetera.

In addition, a role for the public sector in providing for national defense is seemingly beyond dispute. Here we argue that all economies also reflect at any time some economy-wide attitude toward freedom, equity, and compassion. In precisely the same way in which an economy can be judged with respect to narrow efficiency or security, all economies can be compared with respect to these other qualities, which together form a significant part of emergent value. The "higher efficiency" refers to the extent to which the economy structures choice so as accurately to reflect fully the amount of attention to these other characteristics that the participants in the economy would choose if they were truly and fully free to choose.

Market prices surely have a role to play, but it is a limited role. It always has been. Hence judging the higher efficiency of any economy involves far more than examination of market prices.

Economic Analysis and the Higher Efficiency

It is not that economists do not recognize that the economy reflects extant value only imperfectly in its monitoring of total resource allocation. It is simply that mainstream economists argue that confronting the imperfections is not part of the economist's job, or that the task can be finessed by relying on Pareto optimality, or that it can simply be ignored. Thus a current public finance text, far more sensitive to these matters than many, can nonetheless end a discussion of the political process and economic policy with the comment: "The results will not please everyone, but they will approximate an efficient solution. They will do so more or less perfectly, depending on the efficiency of the voting process and the homogeneity of the community's preferences in the matter."[33]

This is not a promising perspective from which to begin a critical analysis of the role of the public sector in furthering what has here been called the higher efficiency of an economy. Community preferences very probably are *not* easily homogenized, but whether or not this is so the task of an economy is to play a role in transmogrifying individual values into social values—a task that must recognize that some values can be expressed *only* socially; that any given economic mechanism, whether prices, administrative fiat, or any other, is imperfect; and that in playing an interactive role in the dynamic process of transmitting and shaping values the public sector can aspire to no higher purpose than reducing imperfections.

Pollsters have long told us that how the questions they ask are formulated can influence the results they obtain. Political scientists have long told us that one of the difficulties with the operation of the political process in virtually all representative democracies is that voters do not get the choices they might ideally prefer. (And how many times has one read about the American primary system shutting out candidates early who might have ultimately appealed to national voters more than the candidates who in fact survived?)

In light of all this why should economists so single-mindedly stress the allocative marvels of the market-price system as in fact it currently operates to the exclusion of concerns comparable to those of pollsters and political scientists about the kinds of signals prices send, the distortions in real choice that the actual operation of the price system provides, etcetera? Clearly, it does no disservice to the notion so fondly advanced by mainstream economists—that the price system does much allocation in a remarkably efficient way—to suggest that the system as it in fact operates is a far from perfect method of converting emergent values into allocative decisions. Institutionalist concern with clogged information channels, deliberate distortion of information, concentrations of power in the hands of a relatively few participants in the economic process, etcetera, would all seem very much a part of any economist's task.

It is at the interface between the emergent value process and the actual total allocative thrust of a given economy at a given point in time that the role of the public sector stands out most conspicuously. Clearly the public sector represents, among other things, the degree to which the latter has been made to conform to the former. Because the former is in continuous process of changing it is not surprising that the actual economy expresses emergent values only imperfectly. That the economy's valuational reach should exceed its grasp is no more surprising than is the imperfection of any other social institution. That professional analysis of a social institution should claim more for it than it can produce appears to be an occupational failing most conspicuous (in the social sciences certainly) among mainstream economists. To say this is not to push one's individual values onto the comunity. It is to recognize that analyzing "collective oughtness" in an economy is as much the task of the economist as to analyze its "isness."

Conclusion

To summarize, we have argued that among the characteristics that all economies exhibit in some manner, in addition to efficiency—which economists of all persuasions grant—one ought to include equity, freedom, security, and compassion. One must interpret this statement carefully. It is no more necessarily true that all economies choose to produce products by similar efficient means than it is true that all economies choose the same manifestation of any of the other characteristics. Mainstream economists often say that one of the critical choices made is determining where within the production possibility frontier an economy will choose to produce. Thus, despite the critical importance economists attach to efficiency, all economies do not *choose* to be equally, let alone maximally, efficient in producing even reasonably identical products.

In precisely parallel fashion, all economies exhibit *some* attitude toward equity, freedom, security, and compassion. In connection with equity, for example, Friedman accuses some of elevating income equality to a principal objective.[34] This is surely not an objective of institutionalism. Rather institutionalism would view notions of equity as part of the institutional structure, which, therefore, might well change through time. The only question we raise is whether the economy is so structured as to reflect or to hinder and obstruct the changing attitude toward equity that emerges over time. That is one question relevant to showing how well the economy performs its announced task. It is a far different question than is subsumed in a particular distribution of income or any other particular aspect of equity.

Just as all economies have imbedded in them characteristics that reflect that economy's view of efficiency and equity, so too, with freedom, security, and compassion. In simple fact, *all* economies exhibit in some manner each of these characteristics. The manner of exhibiting them is dynamic and therefore subject to more or less constant interpretation and reinterpretation. Rather than embracing a particular manifestation of any of them, the institutionalist position must be that it is a task, among others, of economists to consider whether and to what degree a particular economy in its operation diverges from the kind of adherence to these characteristics that ideally the participants in the economy at any time prefer. This is what has been called earlier *the higher efficiency*—simply, how well does the economy truly reflect the values of its participants? The economy is an aspect of extant social value even as the economy itself contributes to the constant reshaping of that social value.

The institutionalist assesses the character of emergent social value in light of *both* the higher efficiency *and* of the implications for emergent social value of the value implications of dynamic technology. If it is possible to conclude that a given society has deliberately chosen to be less efficient than its technology would permit, it is similarly possible to conclude that a given economy has deliberately chosen to be less humane or free or secure than its technology would permit. Except for defense, mainstream economists would freely grant the argument for efficiency made there but not for humaneness or freedom. *All* these characteristics can be regarded as having a "possibility frontier"—not just production. The higher efficiency governs what society may wish to choose at any time; the institutionalist is concerned as well with what would be possible.

The public sector is, therefore, more than the umpire Friedman permits it to be. It is also part manager and part coach, as well as a sometime player. Even if it never carried the ball, however, the public sector would still play a role greater than mere keeper of the rules, because like all umpires it has a view of the whole that is distinctive and is a crucial complement to the view of the other players. No doubt in football umpires are consulted before critical rules are changed because they have a perspective on the way the game goes that no one else has. They cannot and should not change the rules by fiat or alone, but their view is a valuable input.

As students of the game economists can't be above it. The agent who analyzes the distribution of guns and bullets cannot get away with saying he doesn't care who wins the war. Even if he advocates distribution by random draw, by lottery, or by any other arbitrary system, the fact that he devotes himself to the special problems of how munitions are deployed means *eo ipso* that he is involved in where and what they lead to.

All economies present choice to their participants only imperfectly. Monitoring the choices that emerge and relating them to the dynamic value floor from which they emerge is a critical task for the public sector. In that process the economist has a critical role to play. The other task for the public sector is to provide for the economy that part of emergent choice that the economy cannot provide for itself. Conservatives see the role of the public sector here in providing security against external threats and are generally willing to rely on extant private markets for efficiency, but each of the other characteristics may require direct participation of the public sector. In any other case to argue for no role for the public sector is to tacitly accept the way in which the other characteristics emerge willy-nilly from the economy—and, therefore, is a profoundly normative judgment.

Only a public sector can judge how the economy relates to the value floor—how the economy relates to the life process. For political economy this responsibility is inescapable and is met either well or poorly, tacitly or explicitly. Silence is as normative a statement as any other reaction.

Indeed, there *is* "the life process in large measure still awaiting theoretical formulation." It may be that the dynamism of technological change, which has led us to the thermonuclear age, has at last produced a challenge of adjustment for the institutional structure that is too great—that might therefore end the "means-end continuum," at least insofar as human life is concerned. How well the modern world's economies meet the challenge of the higher efficiency will play no small role in whether this—the greatest crisis for the life process—can be surmounted.

Notes

1. These figures do not include the trust fund expenditures, which are not paid for out of tax revenues.
2. Modern mainstream public finance texts appear to agree that the principal functions of government are to enforce property rights, enforce contracts, and to provide for bankruptcy. (See A. B. Atkinson and Joseph E. Stiglitz, *Lectures in Public Economics* (London and New York: McGraw-Hill, 1981), p. 45. They quote a radical economist, David Gordon, as follows: "It may indeed be argued that the tax and expenditure activities of the government are of minor significance in relation to its primary function of preserving and stabilizing the property relations of the capitalist economy" (p. 51). On this function of government, then, mainstream and radical economists agree. However, Atkinson and Stiglitz suggest that the full listing of governmental economic functions would need to include taxation, public spending, state participation in production, direct controls (rationing, etcetera), regulation, control of firms, and monetary and debt policy (ibid., p. 6).
3. See Table 6-1, p. 136, of the *Economic Report of the President* (Washing-

ton, D.C.: U.S. Government Printing Office, February 1982). In the mid-1960s it was estimated that the formally regulated industries—transportation, communication, public utilities, and finance—accounted for about 11 percent of GNP. (See F. M. Scherer, *Industrial Market Structures and Economic Performance* (Chicago: Rand McNally, 1971), p. 519. (The field of regulation became so complex that Scherer eliminated the regulatory chapter from the 1980 edition, but this estimate could not understate the current figure.)

4. *Economic Report of the President* (Washington, D.C.: U.S. Government Printing Office, January 1981), p. 19.
5. *Economic Report of the President* (Washington, D.C.: U.S. Government Printing Office, February 1982), pp. 165-66.
6. Alfred E. Kahn, *The Economics of Regulation*, vol. 2 (New York: John Wiley and Sons, 1971), pp. 328-29.
7. It is instructive to compare these views of regulation with those early views recalled at the time social security was being debated. Paul H. Douglas comments, "The common attitude of the propertied classes and of their attorneys has been that virtually all regulatory and protective legislation should be declared unconstitutional. If Congress passes such legislation, it is declared to be within the province of the states. If the states take action, then it is said to be a violation of due process. . . . The net result was that for nearly twenty-five years, or roughly between 1884 and 1909, the decisions of the Supreme Court were designed to exalt the theory of laissez faire and to prevent governmental action in the field of economic life." Paul H. Douglas, *Social Security in the United States* (New York: Whittlesey House, McGraw-Hill, 1939), p. 267.
8. It is interesting to note that in the early fight to establish the social security system—advocated in part as "some safeguards against misfortunes which cannot be wholly eliminated in this man-made world"—one of the early institutionalists, Edwin E. Witte, played a critical role. He was selected to head the Commttee on Economic Security as Executive Director. The Committee was established by Franklin Roosevelt and included the Secretaries of Treasury, Agriculture, and Labor as well as the Attorney-General and the Relief Administrator. Douglas, *Social Security*, p. 26.
9. Wrote J. M. Keynes, "In conditions of laissez faire the avoidance of wide fluctuations in employment may prove impossible without fair-reaching change in the psychology of investment markets such as there is no reason to expect. I conclude that the duty of ordering the current volume of investment cannot safely be left in private hands." J. M. Keynes, *The General Theory of Employment, Interest, and Money* (New York: Harcourt, Brace, 1936), p. 320. This passage would appear clearly to establish for Keynes a role for the public sector. As for his views of normative and positive economics, the terms appear nowhere in the *General Theory*, but at one point he does refer to deficient effective demand as producing the "intolerable public scandal of wasted resources" (p. 381).
10. Kahn, *Economics of Regulation*, p. xii.
11. Ibid., footnote 8.
12. Ibid., p. xi. In this connection it is useful as well to recall Wesley Clair

Mitchell's observation that "no class in the community has been satisfied with the workings of private initiative. From capitalists to farmers and workingmen, all of us have tried to use government as an agency for bettering economic organization. The way in which government should be used has been the central issue of our political struggles more often than the question whether government should be used at all." Wesley Clair Mitchell, *The Backward Art of Spending Money and Other Essays* (New York: McGraw Hill, 1939), p. 95.

13. Ibid., p. xi.
14. Edward S. Herman, *Corporate Control, Corporate Power* (Cambridge: Cambridge University Press., 1981).
15. Ibid., p. 1.
16. Ibid., p. 295.
17. In this connection, Wesley Mitchell once wrote, "Even while they were in process of assimilating the doctrine of laissez faire, the English people began using their government as an agency for correcting what they thought to be bad results of private enterprise." Mitchell, "The Social Sciences in National Planning," in *The Backward Art*, p. 86.
18. For an earlier consideration of macroeconomics and institutionalism, see P. A. Klein, "A Reconsideration of Holistic Economics," in *Institutional Economics, Essays in Honor of Allan G. Gruchy*, ed. John Adams (Boston: Martinus Nijhoff, 1980), especially pp. 47-49.
19. *Economic Report of the President*, February 1982, p. 139.
20. Some of this is recognized even in the Reagan *Economic Report*: "Should the loss of a forest . . . be measured only by the value of the timber cut? What of the beauty destroyed?" (Ibid.). The concerns in the text are even more far-reaching.
21. Lionel Robbins, *An Essay on the Nature and Significance of Economic Science* (London: Macmillan, 1946).
22. James D. Gwartney and Richard Stroup, *Microeconomics—Private and Public Choice*, 3rd ed. (New York: Academic Press, 1982), pp. 10-11.
23. See Marc R. Tool, *The Discretionary Economy* (Santa Monica, Calif.: Goodyear, 1979), p. 289.
24. Ibid.
25. C. E. Ayres, *The Theory of Economic Progress* (Chapel Hill: University of North Carolina Press, 1944), p. 224.
26. Ibid., p. 225. After I wrote this, I found that Wendell Gordon also chose to quote this critical comment by Ayres in his *Institutional Economics, The Changing System* (Austin and London: University of Texas Press, 1980), p. 42.
27. I have considered at length the parallels between the goals and methods of political science and political economy in "Confronting Power in Economics: A Pragmatic Evaluation," *Journal of Economic Issues* 14 (December 1980): 871-96.
28. Milton Friedman, *Capitalism and Freedom* (Chicago: University of Chicago Press, Phoenix Books edition, 1962), pp. 23-25.
29. Ibid., p. 27.
30. This famous quotation from Veblen is written on the title page of Ayres, *Economic Progress*.

31. See Edwin G. Dolan, *Basic Economics*, 2d ed. (Hinsdale, Ill.: The Dryden Press, 1980), p. 14.
32. This statement must be interpreted carefully. Not infrequently one reads that a decision to provide for national defense "regardless of cost" is, therefore, non-economic. The argument of the text is that provision for security, because it involves resource allocation, which is the fundamental business of an economy, is, therefore, a critical characteristic of the economy. In precisely the same way, "humanity" is a characteristic of an economy because it too involves resource allocation.
33. Richard A. Musgrave and Peggy B. Musgrave, *Public Finance in Theory and Practice* (New York: McGraw-Hill, 1980), p. 9.
34. "A central element in the development of a collectivist sentiment in this century, at least in Western countries, has been a belief in equality of income as a social goal and a willingness to use the arm of the state to promote it." Friedman, *Capitalism and Freedom*, p. 161.

28

Social Fabric Matrix: From Perspective to Analytical Tool

F. Gregory Hayden

It is our proposition that only the substantive meaning of "economic" is capable of yielding to concepts that are required by the social sciences for an investigation of all the empirical economies of the past and present. . . . This requires a special tool box.

Karl Polanyi

Explanation often consists of substituting complex pictures for simple ones while striving somehow to retain the persuasive clarity that went with simple ones. . . . Seek complexity and order it.

Clifford Geertz

Two principles apply. First, there is the principle of association, *which states that the developer of a model must engage in associating elements of representation systems with those things that are to be modeled. Second, there is the* principle of model exchange, *which states that it is desirable to find ways of transforming a model from one representation system to another to meet the needs of understanding, learning and effective communication.*

John Warfield

The economic system is an evolving process and not a static equilibrium. This process undergoes a cumulative development in which various factors act and react upon one another in a cumulative process of circular causation.

Alan G. Gruchy

As Gunnar Myrdal has said, "There is an inescapable *a priori* element in all scientific work. Questions must be asked before answers can be given."[1] Myrdal also emphasized that "questions are all expressions of our interest in the world. They are at bottom valuations. Valuations are thus necessarily involved already at the stage when we observe facts and carry on theoretical analysis."[2] Since fact gathering and theoretical analysis are basically ideological, it is important to develop analytical techniques consistent with the significant characteristics of the basic ideology.

One of the most significant characteristics of institutionalist thought has been a concern for the "evaluation of matters relating to economic welfare."[3] But before policy scientists can evaluate from the institutionalist perspective, analytical techniques must be developed consistent with it. The consequences of a philosophical perspective can only be understood as it is applied in a social setting. Policy scientists can only operationalize a perspective through tools of analysis, and the tools must exist before analysis can proceed. The tool kit is not as important as the perspective, but it is imperative for giving the perspective meaning in any applied sense. Therefore, in order to extend evaluational analysis, this article will develop a process matrix consistent with institutionalist intentions. The matrix will be developed by tracing the evolution of the institutionalist paradigm, explaining the needs of a process, explaining the social fabric matrix, and suggesting some specific uses of the matrix. (The evaluative aspects of the matrix will not be developed here.)

Thorstein Veblen's Dichotomy

The evolution of the institutionalist evaluation paradigm begins explicitly with Veblen. Despite the complexity of the economic and social model Veblen elaborates, his main tool for evaluation was the technological-ceremonial dichotomy.[4] This mode is reviewed with the aid of Figure 1. The analysis divides the world into two categories—that of social ceremonies and that of technology.[5] Ceremonies are the habitual patterns of behavior based on emotions and social mores; they are therefore past-bound. Technology is the dynamic force which is constantly recombining and providing for new opportunities, thereby constantly disrupting institutional arrangements and ceremonial beliefs. Point 0 in Figure 1 indicates the opposition and contention between these two forces for evaluative dominance. Much of Veblen's analysis was approached in this mode for purposes of policy evaluation. Marc Tool has outlined a series of Veblen's dichotomous categorizations:[6]

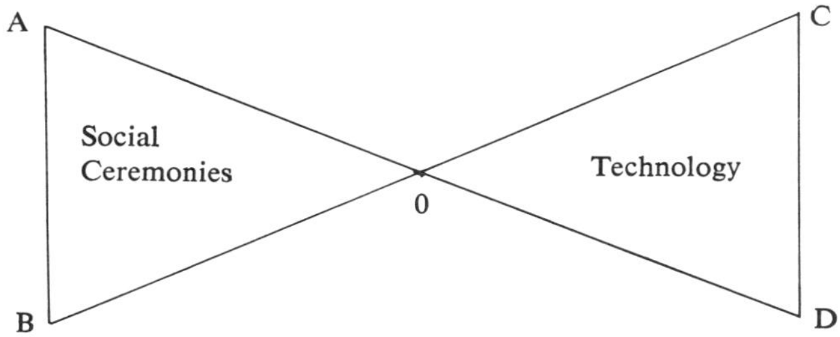

Figure 1. ***Veblen's Dichotomy***

salesmanship	workmanship
business	industry
ceremonial	technological
ownership	production
free income	tangible performance
vested interests	common man
sabotage	community serviceability
pecuniary employment	industrial employment
invidious emulation	technological efficiency
conscientious withdrawal of efficiency	valuable information and guidance
competitive advertising	inordinately productive enterprise
business prosperity	industrial efficiency

The power of this analytical approach has been recognized by institutionalists and systems theorists. An example of the latter is Kenyon De-Greene, who has stated that the unifying theme of systems evaluation is "how the human, that is, behavioral and social, subsystems affect and are affected by the nonhuman, that is, the technological, subsystem."[7] Veblen's hope was to move economic evaluation away from using the world of ceremonial taste and emotion as expressed in the institution of demand. For Veblen, "institutions—the economic structure—may be roughly distinguished into two classes or categories, according as they serve one or the other of two divergent purposes of economic life . . . they are pecuniary or industrial institutions."[8] He wanted to use the technological process and industrial science as an objective standard to provide a reasonable and abundant life for the population in general.

One problem with this dichotomy is that Veblen never developed the criteria for knowing whether a process was ceremonial or technological. To make this point, let us view the transaction of gall bladder surgery for the problem of gall stones. It might be observed that the technological process consists of the knowledge, skills, hygienic procedures, surgical instruments, and equipment in the operating room. The ceremonial aspects might be observed to be the patient's family praying in the waiting room and the insurance forms being processed in the accounting office. However, if enough gall stone cases are observed, it will become clear that the surgery is also usually ceremonial. In most cases it is possible to dissolve or remove gall stones by a combination of the patient drinking some oils and receiving external massages. Like much surgery, cholecystectomies are often for the pecuniary benefit of surgeons and hospitals. This example clarifies the possibility of making the Veblenian distinction without knowing the situational transaction and without establishing criteria. Veblen never developed the evaluative aspects of his paradigm, although "the normative use of this set of distinctions can hardly be in doubt."[9]

Clarence Ayres's Philosophical Guidance

Clarence Ayres explicitly recognized that the purpose of Veblen's dichotomy was evaluation. That is, the purpose is to decide what is bad and deleterious and what is good and efficient. For Ayres, "economics is nothing if it is not a science of value."[10] Thus, Ayres set about the task of developing the philosophical component as reflected in Figure 2. Ayres defines technology to include the tools as well as the skills necessary to operate and organize the tools. This includes intellectual technology and knowledge.[11]

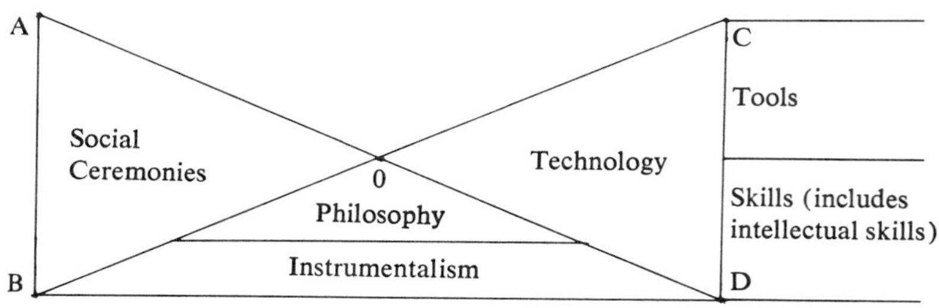

Figure 2. ***Ayres's Institutionalist Economics***

Ayres also said that social institutions, as well as technology, could be reasonable and instrumental in a given social situation.[12] Like Veblen, Ayres recognized that the introduction of new tools would change social relationships and thereby change social institutions and norms. However Ayres did not see the introduction of new technology as automatically good.[13] It must be judged in view of the entire transaction. Ayres's concern for transactional analysis led him to John Dewey's work on instrumentalism. Ayres argued, as Anne Mayhew has stated it,

> that there is a human process—the *process of instrumental valuing*—which allows people to learn by doing and, as they do so, to progress. He also argued that reasoning that this or that must be right because we have been told so by authority was a ceremonialism which inhibited . . . the free inquiry necessary for instrumental valuing. . . . If the source of human progress resides in the *process* of instrumental valuing rather than in technology as artifacts, then it is the *evaluation of the consequences* of any particular use of the tool which is progressive. Ceremonialism is a failure to evaluate by testing consequences.[14]

Ayres thus introduced Dewey's instrumentalism as the philosophical component of the evaluation paradigm. (The numerous subcategories of Dewey's instrumentalism are not displayed in Figures 2, 3, and 4.)

As indicated in Figures 1 and 2, Dewey's instrumentalism as used by Ayres led to a change from Veblen. In Figure 1, social ceremonies and technology are in opposition. Such an opposition is not inherent in Figure 2. Either can be instrumental or either deleterious. For Ayres the legitimacy of an institutional pattern or tool process depends upon instrumental evaluation. There is no point of opposition; rather, instrumentalism should permeate the evaluative judgments about the integrated social and technological patterns. The philosophy category of Figures 2, 3, and 4 differs from the other categories in that the others are categories of reality, while instrumentalism is the selected philosophy to be applied.

Karl Polanyi's Social Evaluation

Karl Polanyi's work had three main effects: (1) it expanded the areas of concern, as indicated in Figure 3; (2) it introduced the concept of sufficiency as an instrumental concern; and (3) it refined the understanding of the instituted process.

Polanyi emphasized the environment, which he defined as the basic flora and fauna upon which we must ultimately base our social structure and from which we must obtain our livelihood.[15] For him the fount of the economy is the "process of interaction between man and his environment."[16] He believed the "elements can be conveniently grouped as ecological, technological, or societal."[17]

For Polanyi, the concern for maximization was a result of the market mentality, which made gain the central motive of human society.[18] Most of Polanyi's work, in one way or another, commented on the illegitimacy of

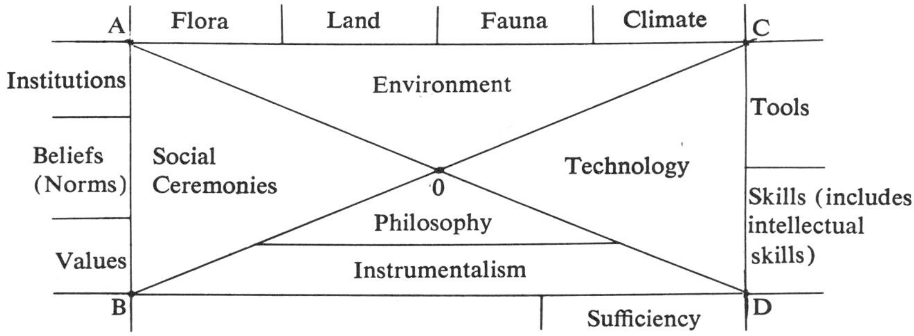

Figure 3. ***Institutionalist Paradigm After Polanyi***

the maximization principle instituted by the exchange system of market society. For him a sufficiency principle was necessary to evaluate and integrate a nonmarket society: "Insuffiency . . . is determined with the help of the simple operation of 'earmarking,' which demonstrates whether there is or is not enough to go around."[19]

As indicated in Figure 3, sufficiency is added to instrumentalism as one evaluative criterion which must be applied. All the subcategories on the perimeter of Figures 3 and 4 do not bear the same relationship to their supra categories. Whereas institutions, values, and beliefs are components which define social ceremonies, such is not the case with the subcategories of instrumentalism. The subcategories of instrumentalism are some of the criteria which must be met in instrumental evaluation.

Karl Polanyi views ceremonies as patterns of behavior that define the relationships among the other elements of society—people, pig iron, pigeons, and prairie hay—are based on rules of prohibition, obligation, and permission. The social process evolves and enforces these rules as norms. At the core of the entire process are the cultural values with which activity-specific norms must agree. This agreement centers interest on values and beliefs.[20]

The social process would not function were it not for the emotional and psychological commitment held by the people in any society to the norms of that society. Therefore, the psychological factors are crucial inputs in any production process. Writes Polanyi:

> In the absence of any indication of societal conditions from which the motives of the individual spring, there would be little, if anything, to sustain the interdependence of the movements and their recurrence on which the unity and the stability of the process depends.[21]

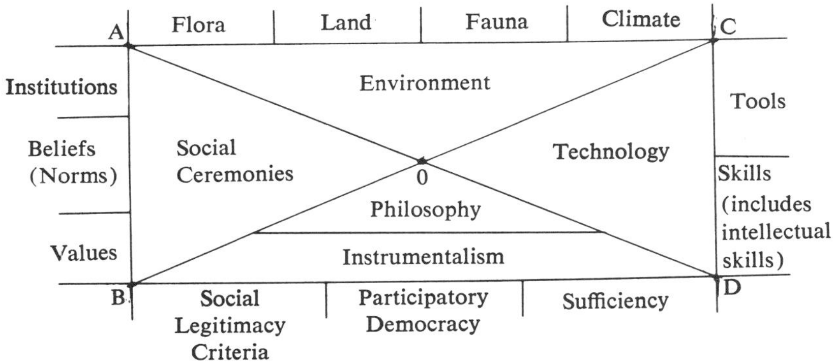

Figure 4. *The Institutionalist Paradigm*

The psychological commitments are provided within and the social institutions structured from patterns of reciprocity, redistribution, and exchange (defined below).

The Instrumental Elements of Walter C. Neale and Marc R. Tool

The work of Walter C. Neale and Marc R. Tool completes the instrumental concerns as presented in Figure 4.[22]

Before making instrumental evaluation and decisions, one must select criteria for judgment. For Neale, social consensus determines the legitimacy of the evaluative and analytical criteria. This is implicit in his many institutional studies and explicit in his policy concerns. Before one can begin policy analysis, one must have criteria to guide the scientific analysis. Before one can take a step in an inquiry, one must make judgments—about which data, about which techniques, about which logic. One must judge the analysis to be using the correct technique in the correct direction. The purpose of policy analysis is to structure social processes. "A requirement for social processes . . . is that they be *legitimate*."[23] Legitimacy requires a social moral consensus on norms with regard to the *consequences* of social policy and with regard to the *procedures* which produce those consequences.[24] Therefore, policy analysis for structuring social processes cannot be fruitful unless the social criteria guiding the policy analysis are fair and just.[25] If there is not a social consensus on these criteria, then the resulting policy will be inconsistent with the social consensus.

For Marc Tool, the legitimate way to obtain social consensus and embed it into social policy is through participatory democracy. Tool's work is consistent with that of Polanyi and Neale, and it extends Ayres's work on the application of Dewey to the economic process. Like Dewey, Tool believes that democracy is consistent with the process of scientific inquiry. Five reasons why Tool selects participatory democracy are: (1) it protects the community welfare and makes the policy analyst accountable; (2) it is an important mode of scientific discovery and social inquiry because the analysis benefits from the contributions of numerous people; (3) it is educational because the experience of participation requires that the participants become knowledgeable about the problem at hand and also that they be in contact with recent analysis. This provides for self-development and closes the gap between technocrats and the public; (4) it builds in information feedback loops and thereby avoids mistakes made when analysis is conducted in isolation from the impact nodes; and (5) it increases the chances that the resulting policy will be successful and lasting.[26]

The Process Matrix

The categories presented in Figure 4, although separated for explanatory purposes, are in fact instituted in many interdependent, transdependent, and recurrent ways to provide for the social process. For example, technology does not exist separately from social institutions, and the societal relations are in turn structured around a tool base. Likewise, the environment does not exist as unmolested nature, that is, there is no natural environment (no natural nature?). Both flora and fauna are embedded—sometimes to extinction—in the social and technical process. "The human economy, then, is embedded and enmeshed in institutions, economic and noneconomic. The inclusion of the noneconomic is vital. For religion or government may be as important for the structure and functioning of the economy as monetary institutions or the availability of tools and machines themselves that lighten the toil of labor."[27] The matrix hereinafter developed exhibits the process characteristics of the institutionalist paradigm.

John Dewey explicated the methodological inadequacies of ends-means thinking. This means, as William Kapp explained,[28] that institutionalist models should not depend on cause-effect (or stimulus-response) representations of reality. Underlying the causality approach is the assumption that a state of affairs (effects) is the result of a state of affairs at a prior time (causes). This defines actors and institutions as passive and memoryless to the extent that we assume that effects are determined wholly by the mapping of the causes onto the effects. However, active social systems are maintained by the goals and rules changing with new situations and at different points in the process. A process is that transaction of transdependent entities; it is a collection of rules that accounts for the history of state transactions. It may include some interdependent or even dependent relationships, but the system process, as Rollo Handy has explained,[29] can be defined as designating the full ongoing process in a field where the connections among the aspects and phases of the field are in common process. The transactional process approach, in contrast to the self-actional or interactional, is one in which "systems of description and naming are employed to deal with aspects and phases of action, without final attribution to 'elements,' or 'realities,' and without isolation of presumptively detachable 'relations' from such detachable 'elements.' "[30] As Handy states, there is nothing mystical about using the holistic frame of reference to view "loans, borrowers, and lenders as aspects of a common transactional framework. Indeed, leaving out the 'system' in which the behavior occurs is surely to make unnecessary problems and difficulties. Separating the borrower from the loaning transaction does not make inquiry more scientific; it tends to obscure some important relations."[31]

The remainder of this article will develop a process matrix consistent with the instituted process paradigm. The matrix is meant to capture the characteristics of the parts, as well as the process of the whole. This is accomplished by a nonequilibrium, noncommon denominator process matrix, as indicated in Figure 5. In this matrix, the ith row and jth column

	j_i	j_2	. . .	j_n
i_1				
i_2				
⋮				
i_n				

Figure 5. ***Noncommon-Denominator Process Matrix***

are the same entry, and cell i = j defines what the ith entity is delivering to the jth entry; or what the jth is receiving. The terms "delivering" and "receiving" are used purposely instead of terms such as "provided" or "required" because basic to this matrix is the idea that there is no final demand, absolute requirement, or end to the process. The participle form is used to denote the process as ongoing. "Process suggests analysis in terms of motion."[32] It is process*ing* or function*ing* as a "going concern," to use John R. Commons's term. Therefore, any event must perforce be traced through the matrix to find additional relationships. For most analysis the concern in the matrix will be divided to correspond to one aspect—let us say a government budget for a tax analysis—and then the relevant sequence can be "laid out" with the aid of digraph theory (Appendix I).

The Social Fabric Matrix

The five categories—values, beliefs, social institutions, technology, and environment—of the social transaction defined in Figure 4 will serve as the basic categories in an expository social fabric matrix. If Figure 4 is rearranged as in Figure 6, the construction of such a matrix can begin.

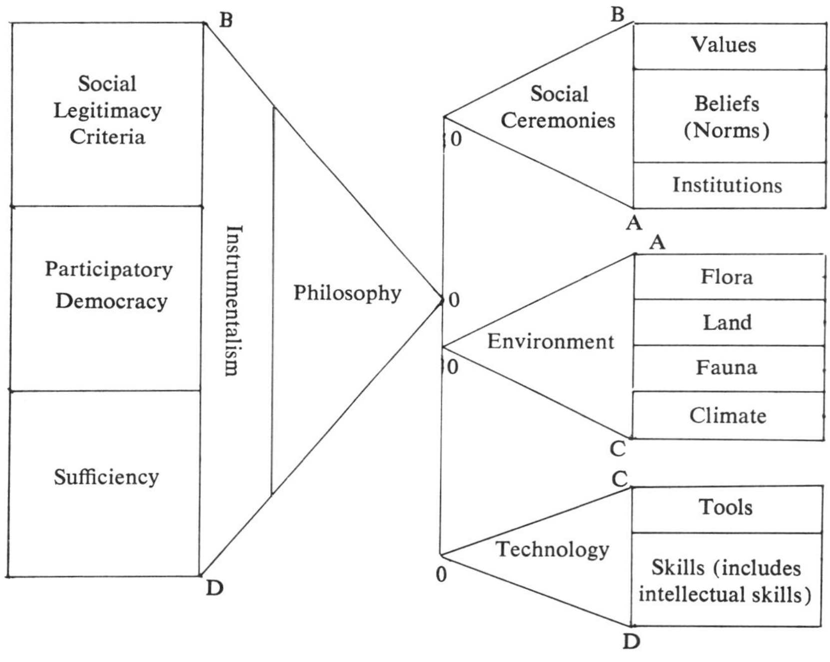

Figure 6. ***Diagrammed Institutionalist Paradigm***

As indicated, the philosophical component (to the left of 0) would provide an overarching guide to the analysis of the system. This would include guidance to both the analytical techniques and the instrumental policy judgments. However, for a matrix of system articulation and description that component is removed. Figure 7 illustrates such a matrix exposition with a limited number of examples within each category. The example entries are taken from Western industrialized society and would be different for other societies. They are also too broadly defined to be of value for anything other than expository purposes.

To understand the matrix, let us begin with familiar terrain. Cells (4,4), (4,5), (5,4) and (5,5) are laid out as the standard industrial input-output matrix. Although the layout is the same, several differences exist. First, it is very apparent that the interindustry transactions are a minor part of the total process. To explain them, other entities outside the I/O table must be delivering. The emotional commitment must be delivered from the belief sector. The correct skills must be nurtured (3,6 and 3,7) and delivered (6,4) before the factories will operate. The government must provide the correct laws (3,4 and 3,5) to structure the industry. The environment must provide the lumber (8,14), and in turn the industry will deliver pollution to the environment (4,8). To look only at interindustry exchanges would provide no information for understanding an industry or for planning for it.

Second, the interindustry relationships do not automatically convert to pecuniary terms. Traditional I/O tables convert to pecuniary terms and lose the important information of substantive flow. The institutionalist's main economic interest is substantive, defined in terms of the quantity and quality of goods and services. For the planning of tool-skill delivery (7,5), it is the level of real flows which is important. The number of lathe operators should correspond to the number of lathes, which should correspond to real substantive output. This does not mean that pecuniary flows are not also of interest.

Third, contrary to the usual I/O tables, there is no "final demand" sector. In a system, no part of the process is final, and there is no simple demand concept which is said to be stimulating (causing) production. Defining the I/O tables in the traditional sense has made them too narrow, the coefficients too rigid, and the matrix too noniterative; this has doomed them to their current low esteem.

The I/O connection is, of course, only one of the characteristics. In addition to their not having a common denominator in the matrix, the relationships cannot be defined in terms of common properties. Some relationships are defined as flows, some as stocks, and some as criteria. To have a *flow* of wheat the environment must provide a *stock* of land, and people must apply a belief *criteria* to judge the appropriateness of the

Receiving Components / Delivering Components	A. Societal Insts. A.1. Kinship 1	A.2. Courts 2	A.3. Govt. 3	A.4. Industry 1 4	A.5. Industry 2 5	B. Technology B.1. Tool & Skill 1 6	B.2. Tool & Skill 2 7	C. Environment C.1. Forest 8	C.2. Land 9
A. Societal Insts. A.1. Kinship 1									
A.2. Courts 2									
A.3. Govt. 3									
A.4. Industry 1 4									
A.5. Industry 2 5									
B. Technology B.1. Tool & Skill 1 6									
B.2. Tool & Skill 2 7									
C. Environment C.1. Forest 8									
C.2. Land 9									
D. Norms (Beliefs) D.1. Work Ethic 10									
D.2. Property Rights 11									
D.3. Egalitarian 12									
E. Values E.1. Dominance over Nature 13									
E.2. Flowing Time 14									
E.3. Dynamic Individualism 15									

Figure 7. ***A Social Fabric Matrix***

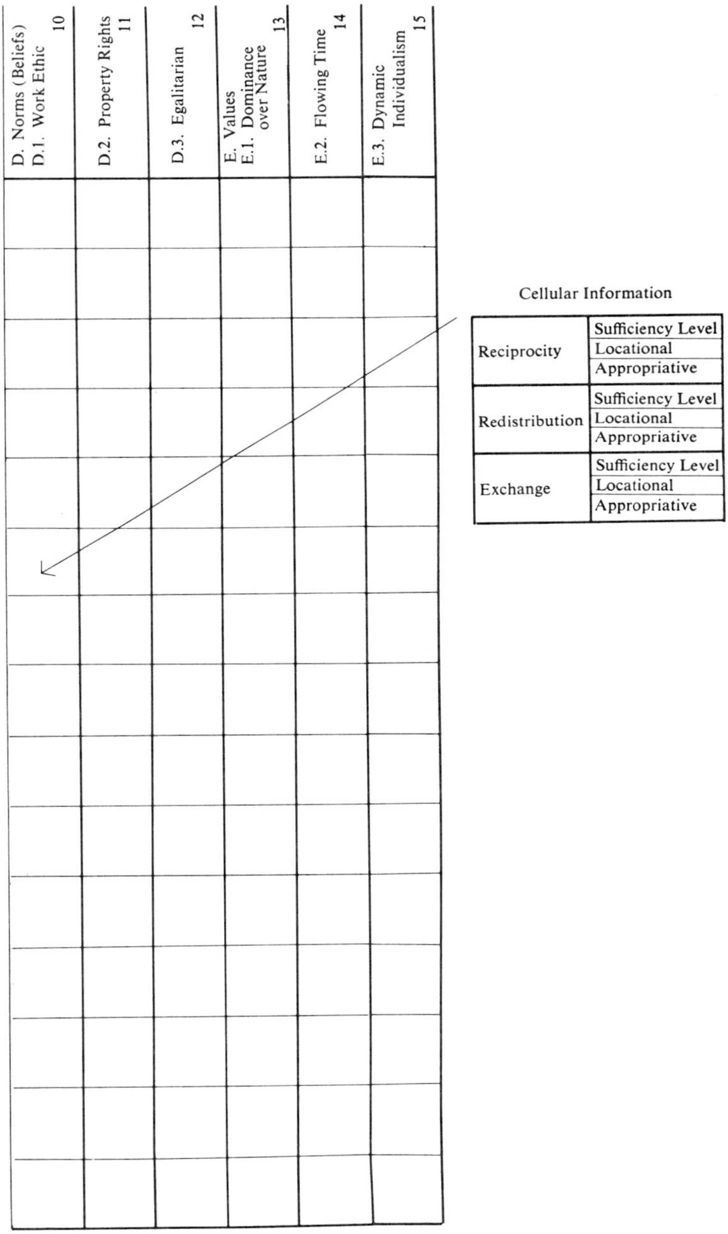
D. Norms (Beliefs)
D.1. Work Ethic
10
D.2. Property Rights
11
D.3. Egalitarian
12
E. Values
E.1. Dominance over Nature
13
E.2. Flowing Time
14
E.3. Dynamic Individualism
15
Cellular Information
Reciprocity
Sufficiency Level
Locational
Appropriative
Redistribution
Sufficiency Level
Locational
Appropriative
Exchange
Sufficiency Level
Locational
Appropriative

procedure. This means that standard algebraic manipulations are not appropriate for this matrix. It also means, consistent with holistic systems, that the rows and columns are not summative.

One characteristic which the matrix is not intending to convey is a system of harmony, or of exclusively want-satisfying delivery. Technology can be delivering cancer to workers (7,5), and the police can be delivering arrests to the family (3,1). Although both are part of the system, neither are wanted by the recipients.

Homeostatic equilibrium is also not implied by the matrix. Social processes are open systems, and open systems are not equilibrium systems. States Kenyon DeGreene, "A much stressed additional property of open systems is that of *equifinality*. This states that a system can reach the same final state from differing initial conditions and along a variety of paths."[33]

Values, although considered transcendental, are only transcendental through norms or beliefs which are activity-specific. Therefore, values serve as criteria only to beliefs, for example, in cells (13,10), (13,11), and (13,12). E.1 would not serve as direct criteria for A.1 through C.2. Values relate only directly with norms, only norms will be delivering to values. Stated differently, D.3 would deliver criteria to A.1 through D.2, but deliver satisfaction indices to E.1 through E.3. (See Appendix II).

There will need to be many different kinds of numerical modalities developed in order to capture the essence of the various relationships and their properties.[34] Institutionalists have never thought it possible to find a single element in the system, such as money, or to design one abstractly that would serve as a common denominator. The social fabric matrix helps articulate the kind of data base that will be needed.

So What's in the Boxes?

In developing the numerical modalities, the cellular data base must be designed to articulate the integrated institutional processes of reciprocity, redistribution, and exchange.[35]

Reciprocity means movements of goods and services among correlative groupings within a society; it is dependent upon a background of instituted groupings, with obligations to respond to common symbols, and with definite institutional enforcement of the expected response through law or custom. Simple reciprocal behavior based on the congeniality of neighbors is not reciprocity because it is not organized, integrated, and enforced by institutional arrangements. It can dissolve and therefore society cannot depend on it. "Reciprocity behavior between individuals integrates the economy only if symmetrically organized structures, such as a symmetrical system of kinship groups, are given. But a kinship group never arises as the result of mere reciprocating behavior on the personal level."[36] Economic integration through reciprocity plays a major role in some complex societies; thus, it is apparent that it is not limited to dual relationships. Numerous groups can be involved, and groups need not reciprocate with one another directly but through corresponding members of a sequence of other groups.

Redistribution means the movements to a center and out again; it is therefore dependent on viable institutions of centricity. "It presupposes the presence of an allocative center in the community, yet the organization and validation of such a center does not come about merely as a consequence of frequent acts of sharing as between individuals."[37] A system is redistributive if goods and services are collected into a center "by virtue of custom, law or *ad hoc* central decision."[38] In some cases it is accomplished by the physical movement of goods to inventory centers for later distribution; at other times it is not physical, especially in the case of intangibles, but an appropriational redistribution with regard to the rights of disposal. Societies at various levels of affluence and technology, including the Tasaday and the Soviet Union, have depended on integration through redistribution.

Exchange means the market *system*, with fluctuating prices determined by the institutions of supply and demand. Exchange as an integrative system need not be explained here.

Not every cell in the matrix exhibits a relationship guided exclusively by these integrative patterns. An example is cell (8,9), which represents a relationship between forest and land. There is environmental delivery without social institutions being involved. That information is still important in the holistic system because that environmental delivery will influence what the patterns of reciprocity, redistribution, and exchange can prescribe for land to deliver to other sectors in other cells.

In most societies, all three patterns of integration exist to some extent. This is especially true in the West, where the strong vestiges of the market system still exist even though the system is being transformed to depend more on reciprocity and redistribution. A simple and incomplete example is outlined in Figure 8.

R_1 is a farmer who, because of a reciprocal inheritance law, must provide part of his yearly income to his brother, R_2, who is a professor and member of the tax-paying middle class. Because of a redistributive tax law, R_2 must pay income tax to the national government, C. R_2 must also, because of a reciprocal custom, provide gifts to his in-laws' daughter, R_3, who is a college student. R_3 is also E_3 because of an exchange relation in

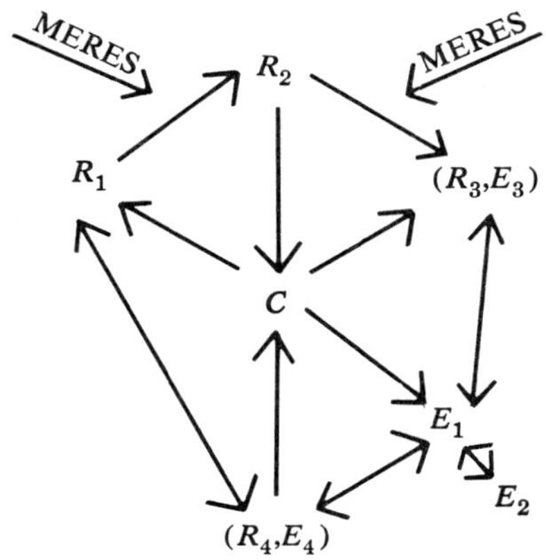

R—those in a reciprocal relationship
C—the center of a redistribution relationship
E—those in an exchange relationship

Figure 8. ***Network Based on Reciprocity, Redistribution, and Exchange***

which she manages an apartment house for E_1, an apartment owner. She is paid in kind with free rent.

E_1 buys apartment furniture from E_2 in an exchange relationship, and buys lawn seed and lawn chemicals from E_4. E_4 is a conglomerate agri-businessman who, in addition to owning the local seed, feed, and chemical store, is also R_4, the step brother of R_1. Therefore, because of reciprocal custom, R_4 and R_1 assist each other in their farming operations.

(R_4, E_4) pays income taxes to the national government on his retailing profits. R_1 pays no income taxes because of C's rules on agriculture cash expensing, and R_3 pays no income taxes because C does not tax gifts and does not pursue small in-kind payments. E_1 does not pay taxes because of C's real estate depreciation laws. R_1, R_3, and E_1 receive farm subsidies, education, and reduced interest rates, respectively. It can also be noted in Figure 8 that supporting each economic relationship is a technological Matrix of Environmental Residuals for Energy Systems (MERES) (see Appendix III).

We can see from this simple example how impossible it would be to attempt to understand the modern economy without a tool such as the social fabric matrix. It also becomes evident that the personal actions are organized and guided by the integrative forms discussed above. Therefore, it is more orderly and more fruitful to organize a study around the five categories contained in the social fabric matrix.

Since the five categories—values, beliefs, institutions, technology, and environment—are integrated through the processes of reciprocity, redistribution, or exchange, data must be collected for each relevant cell with regard to which integrative form is patterning the delivery to the recipient element represented in the cell. For example, Industry 1 may be delivering part of its product to Industry 2 (4,5) through a cartel arrangement (reciprocity), and part of it by selling in the open market (exchange). The data base needed to define each cell is the sufficiency level, the locational aspects, and the appropriative aspects.

The sufficiency level is the amount delivered to meet the needs of the system—for example, the specifications of a contract or agreement. The locational aspects are twofold: the movement of goods as well as the beginning and ending spatial positions. "Locational movements include production alongside of transportation, to which the spatial shifting of objects is equally essential."[39] This is crucial to regional analysis. "The appropriate movement governs both what is usually referred to as the circulation of goods and their administration."[40] The circulation results from transactions as between hands. The administration results from dispositions of a one-sided act of the hand. This data base should allow us to capture the structure of the economic system.

Summary by Way of Hopes and Expectations

This kind of matrix is meant to assist in describing the system and providing the data base for evaluation and planning, especially in a complex technological society. As David Harvey has said, "we must seek to understand the mechanisms of reciprocity, redistribution, and market exchange, as they unfold in an extra-ordinarily complex space economy. This space economy contains hints of previous spatial forms and in some cases is bound down by these previous forms. But the territorial sprawl which contemporary megalopoli characteristically exhibit, means . . . that the process . . . cannot be analyzed in any simple fashion . . . of territorial distinction."[41] The remaining discussion will deal with particular concerns for which the social fabric matrix may have relevance.

First, the expectation is that the institutionalist paradigm, especially with regard to the patterning of reciprocity, redistribution, and exchange, can be applied for policy purposes in a much more complete sense in advanced technological societies.

Second, the author expects that it will serve to close the gap between the institutional perspective and many system techniques now in use, such as cross-impact analysis, MERES, digraph theory, Warfield interaction system, network analysis, and so forth. Future work should determine which of those are consistent with the social fabric matrix.

Third, for policy to be implemented, planning must be completed. The matrix is meant to extend the work of such planning advocates as Rexford Tugwell and Allan Gruchy. Their concern for the land is a case in point. Tugwell said that "intelligent use of the land is the first criterion of any civilization. The fertility of the soil is the ultimate source of wealth. When that is gone, the civilization built upon it soon decays."[42] Gruchy agreed that "a nation which does not bend its efforts toward the preservation of its land and other natural resources cannot hope to preserve its culture for any considerable length of time."[43] With the social fabric matrix, row C.2 can be used to discover the current uses of land and what kinds of appropriative transactions are degrading it. Column C.2 can define the effects that are directing its use. "Land is . . . tied up with the organizations of kinship, neighborhood, craft, and creed."[44] It is also affected by technology and other parts of the environment. This kind of analysis should help overcome Tugwell's criticism of vagueness on the part of institutionalists and provide for the close incisive analysis that he was requesting.[45]

Fourth, the matrix should help with the legitimacy concerns of Walter Neale, George Lodge, and Geoffrey Vickers in directing social psychologists to design new beliefs consistent with the needs of a communitarian society.[46] The matrix can indicate what beliefs are currently used to justify the activities and governing rules of the various columns, and what the results might be if alternative beliefs were substituted.

Fifth, the matrix should be helpful in technological assessment. Institutionalists traditionally have had a great interest in technology and the impact of changing technology. The disruption of institutions and beliefs, as emphasized by Ayres, can be observed if a change in B.1 is traced across the relevant columns. These changes would, in turn, affect their respective rows. The direct and indirect effects can be assessed and evaluated to determine the appropriateness of new technology.

Sixth, J. K. Galbraith's "technostructure" and Louis Junker's "Scientific-Technological Process" contain elements similar to the social fabric matrix and are based on the same ideas. Junker says of his process:

> That process understood in the Technological relations perspective involves, at one and the same time, and as dimensions of each other,

> *Things* (tools, symbols, machines); *Skill* (behavior with things in a productive manner); *Organization* (coherence and integration of relationships in behavior with things); *Administration* (decision-making about coherence and integration of relationships in behavior with things); and Values (evaluational criteria for the overall monitoring and adjusting of decision-making about coherence and integration of relationships in behavior with things).[47]

The social fabric matrix should assist in defining the "integration of relationships" and the "dimensions of each other." Expressing Galbraith's technostructure in this manner should show that it is not a thesis of technological determinism.

Seventh, the matrix should assist historians in providing studies which compare systems at different points. Most historical studies have been just chronological tracking, without justifying the use of Pope Gregory's calendar as the tracking guide. Of course, changes in dates do not change societies. Therefore, historians should be comparing systems and the changes in systems. Generally, historians have offered so little in a system sense that some systems theorists are now claiming that history has no relevance to understanding a system, and that "knowing the past of the system [is] useless information."[48] The author disagrees; a system element can be understood only in the context of a system, and the same element, let us say physicians, may have different functions in different systems. In one a physician may direct preventive measures which reduce environmental niches for diseases; that is, control disease before it reaches the population. In another system, the same element with the same skills may deliver injections, that is, destroy disease after it reaches the population. In one case the physician is an administrator of environmental personnel, in the other the observer of ill bodies and dispenser of drugs.

The only way to know how system elements will behave and react is by knowing the evolution of the system and its elements. Historians can provide that for us in the form of a social fabric lattice for different points in the evolutionary process.

Eighth, an actor table can be identified from the matrix once the relationships have been established. As Polanyi implied, vital for plans is the alternative methods necessary for instituting them.[49] One of those vital methods, according to Robert Keith and David Fischer,[50] is changing actor attitudes and beliefs in order to develop new behavior patterns. The actors and their beliefs can be developed from the matrix.

APPENDIX I

Staged Digraph Map

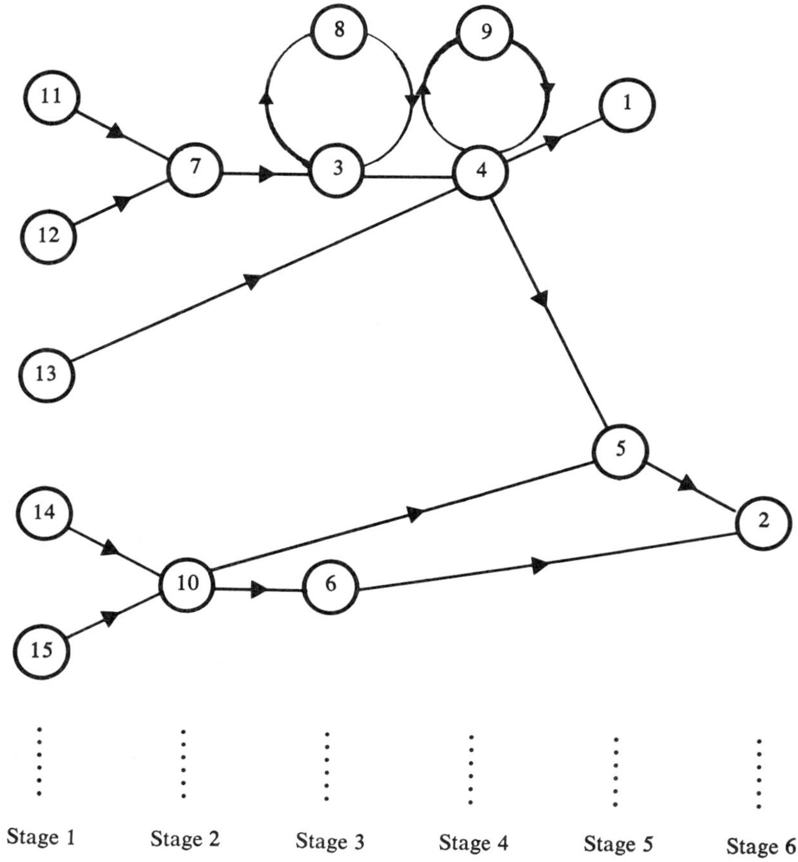

APPENDIX II

Expansion of Bush's Structural Characteristics

Briefly it may be well to note that the value concept here is an expansion of the one presented by Paul D. Bush.* A layer of transcendental values, consistent with the work of Milton Rokeach,** has been added to Bush's behavior-specific values. What Bush terms "values" are here being termed "beliefs." In this paper, behind each belief is a vector of transcendental values—transcendental with respect to all beliefs. These values do not change as the beliefs and the system change.

If we represent each value by V, then the value set can be represented by Nx1 vector as:

$$\begin{bmatrix} V_1 \\ V_2 \\ \vdots \\ V_n \end{bmatrix}$$

and if we represent Bush's values as v instead of V to represent behavior specific beliefs, Bush's axiom #4 can be expanded to encompass transcendental values. This means Bush's general expression of $B\ V\ B$ becomes $B\ v\ B$, which the author will rewrite as $v{:}BB$. Therefore axiom #4 would be expanded to fit this paper as:

$$\begin{bmatrix} V_1 \\ V_2 \\ \vdots \\ V_n \end{bmatrix} \quad : \quad v{:}BB$$

*Paul D. Bush, "An Exploration of the Structural Characteristics of a Veblen-Ayres Defined Institutional Domain," forthcoming in *Journal of Economic Issues.*

**Milton Rokeach, *Beliefs, Values and Attitudes: A Theory of Organization and Change* (San Francisco: Jossey-Bass, 1968).

APPENDIX III

*Technological MERES**

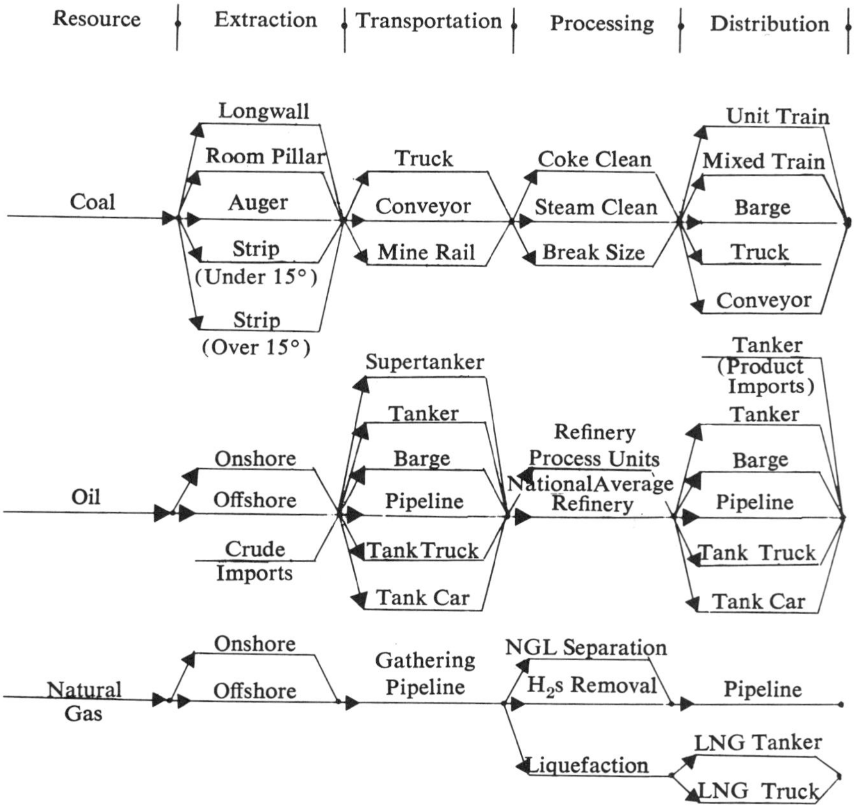

SOURCE: Adapted from Brookhaven National Laboratory, Energy/Environmental Data Group, 1974, "The Reference Energy System and Associated Data Base."

*MERES: Matrix of Environmental Residuals for Energy Systems

Figure 1. *Energy Supply Systems*

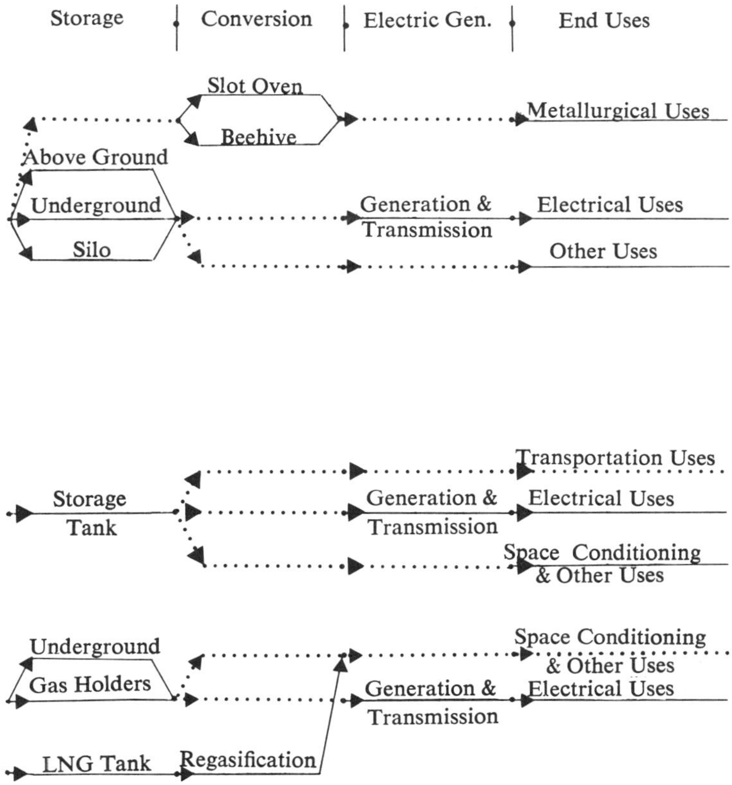

These concepts are illustrated in Figure 1, which shows the coal, oil, and natural gas systems as contained in MERES. Activities are identified across the top of the figure. Processes are indicated by the labeled horizontal lines. A trajectory involves one process from each activity, moving from left to right across the diagram. For example, room and pillar mining, conveyor belt transportation in the mine, breaking and sizing, unit train distribution, above-ground storage, electric generation, and transmission to a specific electrical end-use define one complete trajectory. Sometimes an energy system is also referred to as a subsystem because it is a piece (or "sub-system") of a larger energy supply system.

Notes

1. Gunnar Myrdal, *Objectivity in Social Research* (New York: Random House, Pantheon Books, 1969), p. 9.
2. Ibid.
3. Allan G. Gruchy, "The Concept of National Planning in Institutional Economics," *The Southern Economic Journal* 6 (1939): 121.
4. See Allan G. Gruchy, *Modern Economic Thought: The American Contribution* (New York: Augustus M. Kelley, 1967), pp. 31–132, for an articulation of Veblen's model.
5. This kind of dichotomous approach has been common since Richard T. Ely's work. J. R. Commons used it also; for example, the distinction between use values and exchange values in his *Legal Foundations of Capitalism.* In this tradition, a more recent and elaborate dichotomy is in George Lodge's *New American Ideology.*
6. Marc R. Tool, "A Social Value Theory in Neoinstitutional Economics," *Journal of Economic Issues* 11 (1977): 827.
7. Kenyon B. DeGreene, *Sociotechnical Systems: Factors in Analysis, Design and Management* (Englewood Cliffs: Prentice-Hall, 1973), p. 3.
8. Thorstein Veblen, *The Theory of the Leisure Class* (New York: Modern Library, 1934), p. 34.
9. Tool, "A Social Value Theory."
10. C. E. Ayres, *The Theory of Economic Progress* (New York: Schocken, 1962), p. 208.
11. C. E. Ayres, "The Theory of Institutional Adjustment," in Carey C. Thompson, *Institutional Adjustment* (Austin: University of Texas Press, 1967), p. 5.
12. Anne Mayhew, "Ayresian Technology, Technological Reasoning, and Doomsday," *Journal of Economic Issues* 15 (1981): 514–515.
13. Ibid., pp. 513–514, 517.
14. Ibid., pp. 514, 515–516.
15. By making the environment an integrated part of the transaction, Professor Eric Zimmerman's voluminous and important work can be integrated into the analysis. For example see: Eric Zimmerman, *World Resources and Industries* (New York: Harper & Bros., 1951).
16. Karl Polanyi, "The Economy as Instituted Process," in *Trade and Markets in Early Empires*, edited by Polanyi et al. (Glencoe: The Free Press, 1957), p. 248.
17. Ibid., p. 249.
18. Karl Polanyi, *The Great Transformation* (Boston: Beacon Press, 1944), p. 30.
19. Polanyi, "Instituted Process," p. 246.
20. Ibid., p. 250. The author has substituted the word "beliefs" for "motives" to make it more consistent with modern terminology.
21. Ibid., p. 249.
22. The concerns of John R. Commons are very similar to those in Figure 4 although he did not integrate them in this manner. The difference is that

his transaction would now have to contain more than five persons.
23. Walter C. Neale, "Market Capitalism as Dispute Resolution: The Loss of Legitimacy and the Problems of the Welfare State," *Journal of Economic Issues* 14 (1980): 393.
24. Ibid., pp. 392, 395, 396.
25. Walter C. Neale, "Income Distribution in the Welfare State: Consequences of a Loss of Consensus in Britain," in *Institutional Economics: Contributions to the Development of Holistic Economics*, edited by John Adams (Boston: Martinus Nijhoff, 1980), pp. 144–145.
26. Marc R. Tool, *The Discretionary Economy: A Normative Theory of Political Economy* (Santa Monica: Goodyear, 1979), pp. 148, 173, 199–213.
27. Polanyi, "Instituted Process," p. 250.
28. Allan G. Gruchy, *Contemporary Economic Thought* (Clifron, N.Y.: Augustus Kelley, 1972), pp. 304, 305.
29. Rollo Handy, *The Measurement of Values* (St. Louis: Warren H. Green, 1970), p. 25.
30. John Dewey and Arthur F. Bentley, *Knowing and the Known* (Boston: Beacon Press, 1960), p. 108 as quoted in ibid., p. 24.
31. Ibid., p. 25.
32. Polanyi, "Instituted Process," p. 248.
33. DeGreene, *Sociotechnical Systems*, p. 37.
34. See F. Gregory Hayden, "Toward a Social Welfare Construct for Social Indicators," *The American Journal of Economics and Sociology* 36 (1977).
35. The explanation here of reciprocity, redistribution, and exchange is a summary of Karl Polanyi's explanation in Polanyi, "Instituted Process," pp. 250–256.
36. Ibid., p. 251.
37. Ibid.
38. Ibid., p. 253.
39. Ibid., p. 248.
40. Ibid.
41. David Harvey, *Society, the City, and the Space-Economy of Urbanism*, Resource Paper no. 18 (Washington, D.C.: Association of American Geographers, 1972).
42. Quote taken from Gruchy, *Modern Economic Thought*, p. 448.
43. Ibid., p. 443.
44. Polanyi, *The Great Transformation*, p. 178.
45. Gruchy, *Modern Economic Thought*, p. 425.
46. Walter C. Neale, *op. cit.*, George C. Lodge, *The New American Ideology* (New York: Alfred A. Knopf, 1976), and Geoffrey Vickers, *Making Institutions Work* (New York: Wiley, 1973).
47. Louis J. Junker, "Markings on the Nature, Scope, and Radical Implications of the Ceremonial-Instrumental Dichotomy in Institutional Analysis," paper delivered at the Western Social Science Meeting in Albuquerque, New Mexico (April 1980), p. 20.

48. DeGreene, *Sociotechnical Systems*, p. 19.
49. Polanyi, "Instituted Process," p. 249.
50. David W. Fischer and Robert F. Keith, "Assessing the Development Decision-Making Process: A Holistic Framework," *American Journal of Economics and Sociology* 36 (1977).